ENTREPRENEURSHIP
STARTING AND OPERATING A SMALL BUSINESS

Third Edition

Steve Mariotti • Caroline Glackin

Boston   Columbus   Indianapolis   New York   San Francisco   Upper Saddle River
Amsterdam   Cape Town   Dubai   London   Madrid   Milan   Munich   Paris   Montreal   Toronto
Delhi   Mexico City   Sao Paulo   Sydney   Hong Kong   Seoul   Singapore   Taipei   Tokyo

Editorial Director: Vernon Anthony	**Senior Art Director:** Diane Ernsberger
Executive Acquisitions Editor: Gary Bauer	**Manager, Visual Research:** Mike Lackey
Editorial Assistant: Tanika Henderson	**Photo Researcher:** Sarah Peavey
Director of Marketing: David Gesell	**Cover Art:** Honest Tea
Marketing Manager: Stacey Martinez	**Full-Service Project Management and Composition:**
Marketing Assistant: Les Roberts	Integra
Senior Managing Editor: JoEllen Gohr	**Printer/Binder:** RR Donnelley/Menasha
Project Manager: Christina Taylor	**Cover Printer:** Lehigh Phoenix Color/Hagerstown
Senior Operations Supervisor: Pat Tonneman	**Text Font:** New Aster LT Std

Credits and acknowledgments borrowed from other sources and reproduced, with permission, in this textbook appear on appropriate page within text.

Cover Image Note: Why Honest Tea? The Honest Tea start-up business plan is included in this textbook as a demonstration plan. The story of the company's start-up though their recent sale to Coca-Cola provides an entrepreneurial success story worth studying.

Microsoft® and Windows® are registered trademarks of the Microsoft Corporation in the U.S.A. and other countries. Screen shots and icons reprinted with permission from the Microsoft Corporation. This book is not sponsored or endorsed by or affiliated with the Microsoft Corporation.

Many of the designations by manufacturers and sellers to distinguish their products are claimed as trademarks. Where those designations appear in this book, and the publisher was aware of a trademark claim, the designations have been printed in initial caps or all caps.

Library of Congress Cataloging-in-Publication Data
Mariotti, Steve
  Entrepreneurship: starting and operating a small business / Steve Mariotti, Caroline Glackin. — 3rd ed.
    p. cm.
  ISBN-13: 978-0-13-278408-5
  ISBN-10: 0-13-278408-4
1. New business enterprises—Management.   2. Entrepreneurship.   I. Glackin, Caroline   II. Title.
  HD62.5.M3567 2013
  658.1'1—dc23

                                                                    2011036239

10 9 8 7 6 5

ISBN 10:   0-13-278408-4
ISBN 13: 978-0-13-278408-5

Contents

Chapter 6

Smart Selling and Effective Customer Service   200

Unit 2

Integrated Marketing: Ken Done Studios   225

UNIT 3

Show Me the Money: Finding, Securing, and Managing It   229

Chapter 7

Understanding and Managing Start-Up, Fixed, and Variable Costs   230

Helping Students Own Their Futures

Entrepreneurship: Starting and Operating a Small Business, Third Edition, is the latest in a line of entrepreneurship textbooks written by Steve Mariotti, founder of the Network for Teaching Entrepreneurship (NFTE), and professor and entrepreneur Caroline Glackin.

Business students, as well as those from other disciplines, can benefit from *Entrepreneurship*. For the former, it recasts their prior learning from a typically corporate context and focuses it on small and entrepreneurial enterprises. For students in such fields as hospitality, the arts, engineering, and fashion merchandising, this text introduces key business concepts in the context of a broad range of careers. Cases from hospitality, technology, retail, manufacturing, distribution, real estate, finance, and not-for-profit organizations present a wealth of insights and learning opportunities. Most importantly, *Entrepreneurship* is a balanced mix of the academic and applied components of entrepreneurship education. Students are introduced to the theories, methods, and requisite knowledge and skills required of entrepreneurs, and are then immediately given practical examples and discussion opportunities. Using the Application Exercises and Exploring Online features at the end of each chapter, students are encouraged to take this new knowledge and apply it to their own experiences, so that the course materials are reinforced and internalized.

Combining Street Smarts with Academic Smarts

Entrepreneurship: Starting and Operating a Small Business, Third Edition, is an extension of the programs developed by Steve Mariotti under the auspices of NFTE. Since 1987, NFTE has reached some 450,000 students and professionals and certified more than 6,000 instructors to impart its innovative entrepreneurship curriculum. NFTE is widely viewed as a world leader in promoting entrepreneurial literacy and has a proven track record of helping young people start a great variety of successful business ventures.

This textbook combines Steve Mariotti's experience as an entrepreneur with relevant academic theory and practice, supported by a rich variety of examples and stories that include the experiences of NFTE program graduates who have started their own businesses. Caroline Glackin brings years of experience in the university classroom, as a lender to small and microbusinesses, and as an entrepreneur and former small business owner. Together, they have produced a text that is practical, useful, and academically solid.

The Mariotti/Glackin Learning System

Chapter Openers Set the Stage

Each chapter starts with an inspirational quote, an introduction, and then Performance Objectives that provide a "road map" so readers will know where they are headed. The reader connects with a story of a real business in the opening vignette that sets the stage for the upcoming material.

Chapter **5**

DEVELOPING THE RIGHT MARKETING MIX AND PLAN

"I found that if you give the consumer a snapshot where he could see himself as he really is and the way he wants to be portrayed, people really respond to it."

—Thomas Burrell, founder, the Burrell Communications Group

All of BMW's marketing, from the price of the cars to the advertisements in magazines catering to people who buy expensive things, is designed to remind customers that BMW makes luxury automobiles. If BMW lowered the price of a sedan, would that damage the customer's belief in BMW's market position as a provider of luxury vehicles? This is the question that working through the next step of the marketing process will help answer. BMW illustrates the importance of getting the marketing mix—product, price, place, promotion—right. Without an effective combination of these elements, your business is likely to fail.

Performance Objectives
1. Combine the Four P's—product, price, place, promotion—into a marketing mix.
2. Choose the attributes of your product or service.
3. Price your products for success.
4. Find the best location for maximum efficiency and effectiveness of distribution.
5. Determine the mix of promotion to use for your business.
6. Find a way to add the Fifth P, philanthropy, to your business.
7. Understand the importance of a marketing plan.
8. Identify the critical components of a marketing plan.
9. Use breakeven analysis to evaluate your marketing plan.

BMW positions its products as luxury purchases.

157

"Step into the Shoes" of the Experts

A Step into the Shoes feature appears in each chapter to give insight into the business practices of established entrepreneurs and offers an opportunity to discuss the brief example.

Step into the Shoes . . .
A Sweet Schedule

Andrea Dashiell started Honeecakes Bakery in 2004, when she was a student at Suitland Senior High School in Forestville, Maryland. She took orders and produced homemade pound cakes, pies, and pastries around her school schedule, initially as part of her involvement with the Network for Teaching Entrepreneurship (NFTE). Then, as a full-time college student living two hours away, Andrea continued to operate Honeecakes Bakery through online and telephone ordering, while working around her class schedule. By electing to have a virtual storefront rather than a physical retail site, Andrea, on her terms, maintained her business and furthered her education.
Source: Courtesy of Honeecakes Bakery.

BizFacts

BizFacts impart useful information regarding entrepreneurship statistics, company practices, or particular business applications.

BizFacts

Many salespeople work on *commission*, a percentage paid on each sale. A salesperson making a 10 percent commission selling cars, for example, would earn $1,000 after selling a $10,000 car.

$$.10 \times \$10,000 = \$1,000$$

Entrepreneurs can use commissions to motivate sales staff. When you are starting out and cannot afford to pay sales representatives full-time salaries, you can offer commissions instead—because they get paid as you get paid and earn more as they sell more.

Entrepreneurial Wisdom

Entrepreneurial Wisdom contains insights or advice that will help students in the preparation of a business plan or management of an enterprise.

Entrepreneurial Wisdom . . .

A new business usually will require time before it can turn a profit. Federal Express, in fact, suffered initial losses of a million dollars a month! But if you are not making enough money to stay in business, that is the market speaking. It is telling you that your business is not satisfying consumer needs well enough. Do not take it personally. Many famous entrepreneurs opened and closed a number of businesses during their lifetime.

Henry Ford failed in business twice before the Ford Motor Company was a success. If you want to be a successful entrepreneur, start growing a thick skin and decide right now that you intend to learn from failures and disappointments. Do not let them get you down. Most importantly, learn from them, so that you do not make the same mistakes again.

Global Impact

Global Impact is featured in each chapter, and provides examples of entrepreneurial ventures around the world or information that can be applied in international trade.

Global Impact . . .
Social Gaming Worldwide

Social gaming online has become an international phenomenon, and Zynga Game Network, Inc. has ruled that world with around 65 million daily users, as of the end of 2009. Whereas the popularity of specific games—such as FarmVille, Mafia Wars, and Zynga Poker (Texas Hold'em)—has waxed and waned, CEO Mark Pincus and his team have continued to focus on developing the right marketing mix, and are planning to stay ahead of the curve.

Pincus suggests in an interview, "When we think about next year, we know we have to double down on social, it needs to be more about real user interaction and communication inside of gaming experience. Today, it's very hard to communicate with friends in FarmVille, but people talk about it at the bar, in dorms, on Facebook, and everywhere else."[4] Pincus's focus on social gaming was successful; by 2010 people all over the world were playing Farmville.

New! Honest Tea Business Plan

This is the plan developed by founders Seth Goldman and Barry Nalebuff during Honest Tea's first year of operations. It appears following Chapter 2 and includes a comprehensive market analysis and detailed historical financials. The business raised over $1 million at a time when sales were less than $250,000 and the company had operating losses. The Honest Tea plan is an excellent example for students and one that many of them will understand, to some extent, as customers of bottled tea.

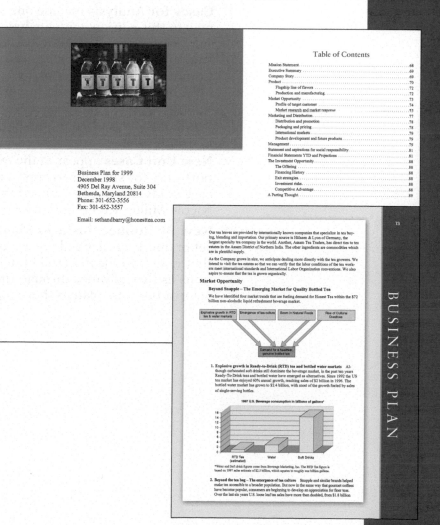

End-of-Chapter Learning Portfolio

End-of-chapter materials help students develop a working understanding of key concepts and develop critical-thinking skills. The chapters include the following:

- **Key Terms** list provides a comprehensive list of important topics in each chapter.

- **Critical Thinking Exercises** require readers to ponder important issues and support a thoughtful response.

- **Key Concept Questions** review core topics.

- **Application Exercises** give readers a structured opportunity to reinforce chapter topics through experience.

- **Exploring Your Community** and **Exploring Online** assignments that invite readers to go into their respective local business communities or search online material for information.

- **Exploring BizBuilder Business Plan Questions** from the business-plan template in Appendix 3 are related to the chapter, so students can build their business plans throughout the course.

- **Cases for Analysis** include one short case and one long one, many new to this edition, with analytical questions drawn from real scenarios. Some of the companies analyzed may be familiar to students, such as Craigslist, Etsy, Honest Tea Company, and Rush Communications. Other organizations may be less familiar, including Dogfish Head, Harold Imports, Luggage Concierge, MIDA Trade Ventures, Conversation on Networking, and Enablemart. These cases reflect a diverse set of entrepreneurs, industries, and geographic locations.

- **New Unit Cases** appear at the end of each unit, providing an opportunity for students to apply concepts to a more comprehensive case study. These cases include real-life scenarios from FASTSIGNS, Nicole Miller, Ken Done Gallery, Mo's Chowder, and Avocent.

- **New BizBuilder Business Plan Questions** Each chapter includes a set of questions derived from the BizBuilder Business Plan Template that relates to the material in that chapter. By answering these questions as they advance through the text, students will gradually develop a business plan as they respond to the content of each chapter.

Highlights of New Content and Changes

Entrepreneurship, Third Edition, contains new content and some changes, including the following:

- **Eight New Chapter Openers.** These feature more small and entrepreneurial enterprises. New cases are: Aravind Eye Care Systems, Bridgecreek Development, Chilly Dilly's, Etsy, iContact, Paula Jagemann, Terracycle, and Zappos.

- **Sixteen New End-of-Chapter Case Studies.** These are: 23andMe, Agritechno Hybrid, Amador Bilingual Voice-Overs, American Electrical, Casino Grande, Chilly Dilly's Ice Cream Company, Craigslist, Conversation on Networking, Enablemart, Holterholm Farms, Honest Tea, Ippy's Islamic Fashions, MooBella, ONLC Training Centers, Sandra Nieto/Accion USA, and Wahoo's Fish Tacos.

- **Five New Unit Cases with Videos.** Prepared by Hattie Bryant with Small Business School video supplements, these are: Nicole Miller, Ken Done Studios, FASTSIGNS, Mo's Chowder, and Avocent.

- **Step into the Shoes, Entrepreneurial Wisdom, BizFacts, and Global Impact Features.** These have been updated and expanded with 31 new featured items, including 12 Step into the Shoes, 6 Entrepreneurial Wisdom, 2 BizFacts, and 11 Global Impact features. These features connect chapter content to business facts and examples to reinforce learning.

- **New Honest Tea Featured Business Plan.** From its early stage funding search, it provides students with an interesting start-up plan for a company that is also featured in the Chapter 14 case study on exiting.

- **BizBuilder Business Plan Questions.** These have been added to chapters to connect the content to student work using the business plan templates.

Additional Changes by Chapter

Chapter 1 Entrepreneurs Recognize Opportunities

- *Establishing Strategies*—Addition of a discussion of strategic approaches using the example of Michael Porter's generic strategies.
- *Many Faces of Entrepreneurship*—Addition of a discussion of gazelles, microenterprises, lifestyle businesses, and mainstream small businesses.

Chapter 2 The Business Plan: Road Map to Success

- *Feasibility Analysis*—Section on feasibility analysis added, including a discussion of financial and market feasibility and Porter's Five Forces model.

Chapter 3 Creating Business from Opportunity

- *Business Valuation*—Section added to illustrate ways of understanding business value.

Chapter 4 Exploring Your Market

- *New Illustration*—Screen shot of a U.S. Census page.

Chapter 5 Developing the Right Marketing Mix and Plan

- *Performance Objectives*—Two additional objectives relating to marketing plans.
- *Location Discussion*—Expanded to include information on location decisions.
- *Promotional Planning Section*—Added to discuss promotional planning and budgeting.
- *Advertising Advantage*—Discusses types of advertising, media planning and budgeting, and marketing materials.
- *Sales Promotion Solutions*—New section covers when to use promotional tools, such as advertising specialties, mall carts or kiosks, and trade show exhibits.
- *Alternative Marketing*—New section includes guerrilla marketing, buzz marketing, product placement and branded entertainment, lifestyle marketing, in-store marketing, and point-of-purchase and shelf placement.
- *E-Active Marketing*—New sections with topics such as e-commerce, interactive marketing, online advertising, brand spiraling, blogs, online social networks, consumer-generated advertising, and viral marketing.
- *Developing a Marketing Plan*—Entire new section.

Chapter 6 Smart Selling and Effective Customer Service

- *Customer Relationship Management (CRM) Systems*—New section on what they are, why they matter, and what the critical components are. Replaces the "Customer Service Is Marketing" segment.

Chapter 7 Understanding and Managing Start-Up, Fixed, and Variable Costs

- *Start-Up Investment*—Worksheet has been expanded to add costs commonly required.
- *Estimate Value*—Brief description of determining investment Net Present Value.
- *Journal Entries*—Journals have been deleted while appendix remains.

Chapter 8 Using Financial Statements to Guide a Business

- *Common-Sized Financial Statements*—Introduced with examples.

Chapter 9 Cash Flow and Taxes

- *Cash Flow Cycles*—Illustrations of possible cash flow cycles for a manufacturer and a residential cleaning service.
- *Cash Flow Budget and Assumptions*—An example of each has been added.
- *Managing Inventory to Manage Cash*—New section highlighting the risks of carrying inventory, and methods to manage it.
- *Managing Receivables to Manage Cash*—New section that includes the development of an A/R aging schedule and the financing of receivables.

■ *Managing Payables to Manage Cash*—New section covering credit, negotiating payables, timing payments, and creating A/P aging schedules.

■ *Capital Budgeting and Cash Flows*—New section introducing the topic of managing capital expenditures.

Chapter 11 Addressing Legal Issues and Managing Risk

■ *The Uniform Commercial Code (UCC)*—New section explaining the fundamentals of the UCC.

■ *The Law of Agency*—New section describing the principles of agency law and its importance to entrepreneurs.

Chapter 12 Operating for Success

■ *Production-Distribution Chain*—Improved graphics for increased clarity.

■ *Facilities Location and Design*—Expanded section includes key factors in deciding on a location, techniques to use, GIS maps, and facilities design and layout.

■ *Special Considerations for Home-Based Businesses*—New section describing location factors and other considerations for home-based businesses.

■ *Special Considerations for Web-Based Businesses*—New section describing location factors and other considerations for Internet enterprises.

Chapter 13 Management, Leadership, and Ethical Practices

■ *Performance Objectives*—Expanded to incorporate organizational culture and structure, as well as human resources.

■ *Chapter reorganized*—Focus on expanded leadership materials, then on management, human resources, and ethics.

■ *Adding Employees to Your Business*—Section expanded to include more details and examples, including tables with suggested interview topics and questions.

■ *Performance Management*—New section regarding performance appraisal and reviews.

■ *Establishing Ethical Standards*—New section that includes information on codes of conduct and ethics, and the Six Pillars of Character.

■ *Balancing the Needs of Owners, Customers, and Employees*—New section dealing with some of the challenges faced by entrepreneurs who try to act ethically.

Appendices

■ *Appendix 1: Business Plan*—The Daily Perc Business Plan is annotated, to provide insights for students as they prepare their own business plans.

■ *Appendix 4: Resources for Entrepreneurs*—Updated and expanded list of books, magazines, Web sites, wholesale sources, award possibilities, and other resources.

■ *Appendix 5: Useful Formulas and Equations*—Expanded for this edition.

MyBizSkillsKit for Entrepreneurship

MyBizSkillsKit for Entrepreneurship, Third Edition, is a resource site containing planning worksheets and templates, access to the Business Plan Pro download, video cases, business-simulation cases, links to helpful Internet resources, and test-prep quizzes. These components of MyBizSkillsKit are detailed as follows.

① BizBuilder Business Plan Worksheets and Templates Online

Downloadable, completely revised business plan and presentation templates that will help students write their plans and present them can be found at www.pearsonhighered.com/mariotti.

- *BizBuilder Business Plan Worksheets* provide step-by-step instructions on building a business plan. The worksheets now include new **Excel Templates** for use in financial sections of the plan.
- *BizBuilder Business Plan Template* provides a professional-looking format for a business plan that ties in with assignments in the text.
- *BizBuilder Business Plan Presentation Template* guides the student through the process of creating a PowerPoint presentation for a business plan.

Students can build their business plans using the BizBuilder worksheets. Appendix 3 will provide them with instructions on how to use the worksheets that mirror the planning process in the book, and contains more questions in some areas than are found in commercially available planning software. Once they have created a plan using the worksheets, students can generate a professional-looking document using the BizBuilder Business Plan Template or Business Plan Pro software.

② Business Plan Pro Software Online

Business Plan Pro is the most widely used professional business-planning software in the nation. Students can download the Business Plan Pro program to a personal computer from within MyBizSkillsKit. Once a student has created a business plan using the BizBuilder worksheet, it will be easy to cut and paste that information into Business Plan Pro. Business Plan Pro includes a number of very useful features:

- Students can study and compare sample business plans with their own, using the Sample Plan Browser to search the library.
- Easy Plan Wizard will guide students through writing a plan.
- Spreadsheet tables with columns, rows, and formulas automatically calculate totals.
- Pie and bar charts can be automatically created from spreadsheets.
- Financial statements can be customized.
- Professional-looking printout of the business plan is available.
- Appendix 7 provides students with an overview of how to get started using Business Plan Pro.

③ Entrepreneurship Videos in MyBizSkillsKit

Included in MyBizSkillsKit are eight video case studies, produced by Hattie Bryant of the Small Business School, that accompany the written cases in the textbook. Some of these are written in the first person by Ms. Bryant, and should not be confused with writing by the authors of the text.

- **Bridgecreek Development** Meet Frank Jao, an immigrant from Vietnam and founder of Bridgecreek Development, who grew a successful land development company in California from virtually nothing. The example of Frank Jao teaches that it is key to envision a new future, invest not spend, combine tangible services and products with good feelings, and learn to speak the language of bankers. This is a story about adapting to a new environment, the power of capital, and the power of an idea and persistence.

- **Nicole Miller** Go to the heart of the fashion industry and behind the scenes at Nicole Miller, a fashion house on Seventh Avenue, to meet the founders, Nicole Miller and Bud Konheim. Starting in 1986, Miller and Konheim built the company's success on the idea that women wanted well-made, fashionable clothing.

- **Texas Jet** Texas Jet is a gas station for airplanes. Owner Reed Pigman doesn't use today's gas station as a model for his business. He knows the tastes and expectations of the owners of private airplanes and uses the upscale-hotel customer-service model as his guide. By copying the strategies of top hospitality service providers, Pigman sells more fuel than his competitors while charging higher prices.

- **Ken Done Gallery** This is the story of an accidental business. Artist Done calls it an accident because he never intended to sell anything but his paintings. When a T-shirt he designed as a marketing gimmick turned out to be a hit, he decided he should listen to the market and do more than paint. Done is now Australia's most recognized contemporary artist and employs more than a hundred employees; he teaches that owners must do what works and then repeat it to achieve profits through scale.

- **Cactus & Tropicals** Cactus & Tropicals is an indoor-outdoor landscaping company based in Salt Lake City, Utah. Founder Lorraine Miller's goal for her company is to deliver to customers more than they pay for through highly motivated, self-guided employees. She demonstrates that you have to be a teacher, leader, and mentor, not "the boss"—*boss* is a four-letter word that is not used at Cactus & Tropicals.

- **FASTSIGNS** This business began on the back of a paper napkin. FASTSIGNS founder Gary Salomon saw how a computer could make high-quality signs in hours instead of days. He jumped at the opportunity to build a business offering this service internationally. FASTSIGNS is America's leading sign company, with more than 550 locations worldwide.

- **Mo's Chowder** Mo's restaurants have been famous for serving clam chowder since 1951. There are three locations on the Oregon coast, and a chowder-base factory. When Mo opened for business, the town of Newport had a lively fishing industry with hundreds of fisherman. Back then, Mo's was a fisherman's hangout. Now it is a key component of local tourism. The evolution of Mo's demonstrates both the principle of adapting to a changing market and the personal business acumen of its present owner.

- *Avocent* Avocent is a manufacturing company that makes an apparatus to remotely control PCs and servers—from a distance of 25 feet to 25,000 miles. This story illustrates what can happen when a founder starts a business to solve a very big problem for customers who have the money to pay for solutions.

Small Business School is the television series created by Hattie Bryant for PBS and Voice of America. Students will discover the largest video library about small business in the world at http://smallbusinessschool.org.

④ Additional Resources in MyBizSkillsKit

- *BizSims illustrated business simulation cases* present students with workplace situations where they have to make the call. These illustrated case applications contain built-in feedback and scoring, and can feed a gradebook, if desired.
- *Test-prep quizzes* are included for each chapter, including true/false, multiple choice, and short essay.
- *PowerPoint Presentations* review each chapter's key topics.
- *Links to Web-based video assignments at the Small Business School* are provided.
- *Web links provide additional resources.*
- *Pearson's MySearchLab: Research, Grammar, and Writing Tips* is a great resource that provides writing assessment and instruction, and gives access to the EBSCO document database and to the Longman Online Handbook for writers.

Value Package

Entrepreneurship: Starting and Operating a Small Business, Third Edition, can be value-packaged with MyBizSkillsKit for Entrepreneurship.

To order *Entrepreneurship: Starting and Operating a Small Business*, Third Edition, with MyBizSkillsKit for Entrepreneurship Access Code, order ISBN: 013295172X.

Instructor Resources

All instructor resources can be downloaded from the Prentice Hall Instructor's Resources Web site at www.pearsonhighered.com. These resources include the following:

1. *TestGen,* a computerized test generator
2. *PowerPoint* lecture presentation package
3. *An Instructor's Manual,* which includes:
   - Answers to all end-of-chapter material, including teaching notes for short and long case studies.
   - Additional instructional material on how to teach students to write a business plan, to supplement end-of-unit business plan sections.
   - Course outlines for 10-week term (short course) and 16-week term (3 hours/week).
   - Additional resources (print and Web sites) for each chapter.
   - Test item file.

CourseConnect Entrepreneurship Online Course: Convenience, Simplicity, Success

CourseConnect courses contain customizable modules of content mapped to major learning outcomes. Each learning object has interactive tutorials, rich media, discussion questions, MP3 downloadable lectures, assessments, and interactive activities that address different learning styles. CourseConnect courses can be delivered in any commercial platform, such as WebCT, BlackBoard, Angel, Moodle, or eCollege. For more information, call 800-635-1579.

About the Authors

STEVE MARIOTTI, founder of the Network for Teaching Entrepreneurship (NFTE), is considered one of today's leading experts in the education of at-risk youth. He has been helping young people develop marketable skills through learning about entrepreneurship for almost 30 years.

Formerly a treasury analyst with Ford Motor Company, Steve changed career paths in 1982 when he moved from operating his own import-export firm to become a special education teacher in the New York City school system. Mariotti's first assignments were in the East New York and Bedford-Stuyvesant neighborhoods of Brooklyn; he also taught in the notorious "Fort Apache" neighborhood of the South Bronx.

While teaching in these demanding environments for five and a half years, Steve gained a breakthrough insight into successfully motivating his economically at-risk students—it was showing them how to start and operate their own small businesses. This perception, combined with his business background, inspired Mariotti to create a program to bring entrepreneurial education to at-risk young people around the world.

In 1987, the Network for Teaching Entrepreneurship was formed, and received nonprofit 501(c)(3) status from the IRS the following year.* Now, almost 25 years later, NFTE continues its mission of bringing entrepreneurship education programs to young people from low-income communities.

NFTE has reached over 450,000 young people since its founding, and at present has programs and licensees in 21 states, as well as in the Netherlands, Germany, Ireland, China, the United Kingdom, India, New Zealand, Bermuda, Canada, Belgium, South Africa, and Israel—including in the West Bank city of Hebron.

Steve Mariotti received a B.B.A. and M.B.A from the University of Michigan, Ann Arbor. He also studied at Harvard University, Stanford University, and Brooklyn College. He has been the subject of many national media profiles, including on *ABC Evening News* and *20/20+*. In addition, he is the co-author of some 20 books and manuals on entrepreneurship that together have sold over one million copies. Mariotti is an active member of the

*As the National Foundation for Teaching Entrepreneurship

Council on Foreign Relations and has presented papers at the World Economic Forum in Davos.

Among the many honors awarded to Steve Mariotti are Best Teacher of the Year, National Federation of Independent Businesses, 1988; Honorary Doctorate in Business and Entrepreneurship, Johnson and Wales University, 1990; Social Entrepreneur of the Year, the Chief Executive Officer's Club; *Inc.* Magazine's Social Entrepreneur of the Year Award; Ernst & Young Entrepreneur of the Year Award, 1992; Award from the Minority Business Development Agency of the U.S. Department of Commerce; University of Michigan Business School Entrepreneur of the Year Award; Association of Educational Publishers Award for Best Math Curriculum, 2010.

CAROLINE GLACKIN, PhD, is a "pracademic" who has successfully worked as a microenterprise and small business owner and manager, as an executive director of a community development financial institution, and as an academic in areas of community development finance, entrepreneurship, and management. She has been assisting entrepreneurs in achieving their dreams for over 25 years.

Glackin earned a doctorate from the University of Delaware, where her research emphasis was on microfinance. She received an M.B.A. from the Wharton School at the University of Pennsylvania and a B.A. from Bryn Mawr College. Her professional career began with the DuPont Company, American Bell, Bell Atlantic, and American Management Systems. She has consulted for businesses and not-for-profit agencies in turnaround and high-growth scenarios. After exiting a family business, she became the executive director of a community development financial institution serving businesses and not-for-profits.

Dr. Glackin has succeeded in leading change in the practical fields of her research, and has received numerous honors and awards. These include the first Gloeckner Business Plan Award at the Wharton School, the Minority Business Advocate of the Year for Delaware from the U.S. Small Business Administration, and the She Knows Where She's Going Award from Girls Inc. Dr. Glackin co-chaired the Delaware Governor's Task Force for Financial Independence and has participated in the Cornell University Emerging Markets Think Tank Series.

Acknowledgments

First, our sincere thanks to the team of reviewers who provided insightful feedback during the development of this book:

Harvey Lon Addams, *Weber State University, Ogden, UT*

John R. Callister, *Cornell University, Ithaca, NY*

Joyce Ezrow, *Anne Arundel Community College, Arnold, MD*

Rita Friberg, *Pueblo Community College, Pueblo, CO*

Vada Grantham, *Des Moines Area Community College, Ankeny, IA*

Linda Ross, *Rowan University, Glassboro, NJ*

William Searle, *Asnuntuck Community College, Enfield, CT*

Dennis R. Williams, *Pennsylvania College of Technology, Penn State, Williamsport, PA*

And thank you to all the consultants and reviewers who assisted in the development of *Entrepreneurship & Small Business Management*, Second Edition:

Elaine Allen, *CPA, Vice Chair, Not-for-Profit Sector, Mitchell & Titus, LLP*

Larry Bennett, *President, Benland Innovations, LLC*

Sunne Brandmeyer, *Retired Lecturer/Advisor, Center for Economic Education, University of South Florida, Tampa, FL*

Stanlee Brimberg, *Teacher, Bank Street School for Children, New York, NY*

Howard W. Buffett, Jr.

John D. Christesen, *SUNY Westchester Community College, Valhalla, NY*

Steve Colyer, *Miami Dade College, Miami, FL*

Laura Portolese-Dias, *Shoreline Community College, Seattle, WA*

Alex Dontoh, *New York University, New York, NY*

Alan J. Dlugash, *CPA, Partner, Marks Paneth & Shron LLP*

Thomas Emrick, Ed.D.

George Gannage, Jr., *West Georgia Technical College, Carrollton, GA*

Thomas Goodrow, *Springfield Technical Community College, Springfield, MA*

Janet P. Graham, *Coastal Carolina University, Conway, SC*

John Harris, *Eastern High School, Bristol, CT*

Deborah Hoffman, *CPA, Director of Finance, Math for America*

Donald Hoy, *Benedictine College, Atchison, KS*

Samira Hussein, *Johnson County Community College, Overland Park, KS*

Eileen M. Kearney, *Montgomery County Community College, Blue Bell, PA*

Sanford Krieger, *Esq., General Counsel and Managing Director, AEA Investors LP*

Jawanza Kunjufu, *D.B.A. President, African American Images*

Corey Kupfer, *Esq., Partner, Hamburger Law Firm, LLC*

Emily H. Martin, *Faulkner State College, Bay Minette, AL*

Alaire Mitchell, *Former Assistant Director of Curriculum Research, New York City Board of Education*

Timothy R. Mittan, *Southeast Community College, Lincoln, NE*

Eric Mulkowsky, *Engagement Manager, McKinsey and Company, Inc.*

Raffiq Nathoo, *Senior Managing Director, The Blackstone Group, LLP*

Ray E. Newton, III, *Senior Managing Director, Evercore Partners Inc.*

Arnold Ng, *Pepperdine University, Rancho Palos Verdes, CA*

William H. Painter, *Retired Professor of Law, George Washington University*

Peter Patch, *Patch and Associates*

Alan Patricof, *Founder, Apax Partners and Greycroft Partners*

Carolyn J. Christensen Perricone, *CPA, SUNY, Westchester Community College, Valhalla, NY*

Robert Plain, *Guilford Technical Community College, Jamestown, NC*

Christopher P. Puto, *University of St. Thomas, Minneapolis, MN*

Richard Relyea, *President, NY Private Equity Network (NYPEN)*

Ira Sacks, *Esq., Partner, Law Offices of Ira S. Sacks LLP*

William Sahlman, *Harvard Business School, Cambridge, MA*

Arnold Scheibel, *MD, Professor of Neurobiology, University of California at Los Angeles*

LaVerne Tilley, *Gwinnett Technical College, Lawrenceville, GA*

Marsha Wender Timmerman, *LaSalle University, Philadelphia, PA*

Liza Vertinsky, *Emory University, Atlanta, GA*

Peter B. Walker, *Managing Director, McKinsey and Company, Inc.*

Walter Lara, *Florida Community College, Jacksonville, FL*

Larry Weaver, *Navarro College, Corsicana, TX*
Donald A. Wells, *University of Arizona, Tucson, AZ*

I would like to thank my co-author, Caroline Glackin, without whose talent and expertise this text would not have been possible, and Tony Towle, who from NFTE's inception has helped me organize my thoughts and experiences. I must single out the help of an outstanding educator, John Harris. I would also like to acknowledge the significant contributions of former and present NFTE executives: Amy Rosen, Michael J. Caslin III, J. David Nelson, Julie Silard Kantor, Leslie Pechman Koch, Dan Delany, Ben Rodriguez, Rick Cruz, Alice Horn, Jane Walsh, Neelam Patel, Daniel Rabuzzi, Tricia Granata, Krista Katsantonis, Laura Maczka, Estelle Reyes, Jennifer Green, Sylvia Watts McKinney, Terry Bowman, Victor Salama, Del Daniels, Deidre Lee, Rupa Mohan, Christine Poorman, Joel Warren, Paul Wisenthal, and Essye Klempner.

Special thanks as well to Gary Bauer and the team at Pearson Education for their professionalism and for their editorial assistance.

Thanks also to Tom Goodrow of the Springfield Enterprise Center and the National Association of Community College Entrepreneurship (NACCE), and to John Christesen of SUNY Westchester Community College.

Also my gratitude to Howard Stevenson, the late Jeffry Timmons, William Bygrave, Bob Pritzker, and NFTE Board Member Stephen Spinelli for imparting their wisdom, and to Richard Fink of Koch Industries, Carl Schramm of the Ewing Marion Kauffman Foundation, and Mike Hennessy and John Hughes of the Coleman Foundation. Special thanks to Eddy Bayardelle and Melanie Mortimer of Merrill Lynch Global Philanthropy, and Kim Davis of the JPMorganChase Foundation.

In addition, I would like to recognize the efforts and contributions of members of NFTE's National Board of Directors, and I would like to acknowledge the inspired guidance provided by our National Executive Committee. I am deeply grateful to the many philanthropists who have supported our work, including the Scaife Family Foundation, the Newark Boys' and Girls' Clubs, the William Zimmerman Foundation, the Goldman Sachs Foundation, the Shelby Cullom Davis Foundation, the Microsoft Corporation, the Nasdaq Educational Foundation, and Ronald McDonald House Children's Charities.

Further, I would like to acknowledge Steve Alcock, Harsh and Aruna Bhargava, Lena Bondue, Dawn Bowlus, Shelly Chenoweth, Janet McKinstry Cort, Erik Dauwen, Clara Del Villar, Christine Chambers Gilfillan, Andrew Hahn, Kathleen Kirkwood,

Michael Simmons, Sheena Lindahl, Cynthia Miree, Henry To, Carol Tully, Dilia Wood, and Elizabeth Wright, as well as Peter Cowie, Joseph Dominic, Paul DeF. Hicks Jr., Ann Mahoney, David Roodberg, Phyllis Ross Schless, and Remi Vermeir, who have all provided countless insights into providing entrepreneurial opportunities to young people.

In addition, I would like to thank my brother, Jack, the best CPA I know, his wife, Beth, and my nieces and nephews Sienna, Nina, Jackson, and Spencer; as well as Vanessa and Nina Beary, and Dan and Julia Schmidt for their continuing love and guidance. And to my father, John, for financing much of NFTE's early work. Thanks are due to all the other teachers, students, experts, and friends who were kind enough to look over this book and help us improve it. Finally, I want to thank my mother, Nancy, a wonderful special education instructor who showed me that one great teacher can affect eternity.

Steve Mariotti

To my co-author, Steve Mariotti, who brought hope, opportunity, and change out of adversity to create the Network for Teaching Entrepreneurship and started this journey—many thanks. Also thanks to Tony Towle, who has provided numerous insights to make this text sing. As Steve noted, the team at Pearson Education has been wonderful to work with again. Faculty reviewers and faculty members who have contacted me directly regarding earlier materials are always a valued source of suggestions.

Most importantly, I appreciate the terrific entrepreneurs who shared their stories with me, including the good, the bad, and the downright ugly! Their interest in communicating their experiences with students and willingness to carve out time to tell their tales demonstrates the kind of generosity and enthusiasm we associate with successful entrepreneurs. They have made this endeavor interesting and engaging.

On a more personal note, I would like to thank my family at Shepherd University for their support and tolerance as I worked on this third edition of *Entrepreneurship: Starting and Operating a Small Business*. Special thanks to Maria Wiedenman, Heidi Golding, Terri Hasson, Carol Ann Weisenfeld, Kimble Byrd, Laura Neal, Ann Marie Legreid, Gordon DeMeritt, Kathleen Corpus, Meg Galligan, William Zimmer, Mindy Walls, Seth Goldman, Kelly Cardamone, and Cheryl Newman. Finally, to Elise and Spencer for being the best cheering section a mother could ever have—thanks and love to you both.

Caroline Glackin

ENTREPRENEURIAL PATHWAYS

Jupiter Images

Chapter 1

ENTREPRENEURS RECOGNIZE OPPORTUNITIES

*Tom Szaky of
TerraCycle, Inc.*
Dario Cantatore/
WireImage

Tom Szaky was a 19-year-old college student in need of inspiration for a business plan competition, when he happened to visit friends who were using red worms to compost waste that they then used as plant fertilizer. The idea captured his imagination, and he created a business plan for an environmentally friendly company that would convert trash into fertilizer. Although he finished in fifth place in the competition, Szaky moved ahead to bring the plan to reality and make the company, TerraCycle, Inc., a viable venture.[1]

TerraCycle has since expanded its product lines to encompass a wide range of recycling and upcycling, including branded products for Target and Kraft Foods. The company is the producer of the world's first product made from and packaged in recycled ones. Szaky sells to some of the world's largest retailers, including Wal-Mart and Home Depot, as well as Target, and has programs that involve entire communities in recycling products. Sales exceed $20 million per year, and the company has collected literally billions of pieces of waste. TerraCycle plant food twice was named the most eco-friendly product carried by Home Depot. Tom Szaky and TerraCycle have turned trash into treasure.

Performance Objectives

1. Explain what entrepreneurs do.
2. Describe how free enterprise economies work and how entrepreneurs fit into them.
3. Find and evaluate opportunities to start your own business.
4. Explain how profit works as a signal to the entrepreneur.

Entrepreneurship Defined

Have you ever eaten a Mrs. Fields cookie? Used an Apple computer? Listened to a Def Jam CD? The entrepreneurs that founded these companies brought those products into your world.

What Is an Entrepreneur?

Most Americans earn money by working in *business*. They are engaged in the buying and selling of products or services in order to make money.

product a tangible item that exists in nature or is made by people.

service intangible work that provides time, skills, or expertise in exchange for money.

- A **product** is something that exists in nature or is made by human beings. It is *tangible*, meaning that it can be physically touched.
- A **service** is labor or expertise (rather than a tangible commodity) exchanged for money. It is *intangible*. You cannot actually touch it.

Someone who earns a living by working for someone else's business is an employee of that business. There are many kinds of employees. At Ford Motor Company, for instance, some employees build the cars, some sell the cars, and some manage the company. But employees all have one thing in common—they do not own the business; they work for others who do. They know how much money they can earn, and that amount is limited to salary plus bonuses and any stock options they may receive.

entrepreneur a person who assumes the risks of organizing and managing a business for the sake of potential rewards.

Some people start their own businesses and work for themselves. They are called **entrepreneurs.** Entrepreneurs are often both owners

---

[1]TerraCycle, Inc., www.terracycle.net, February 4, 2010.

and employees. For an entrepreneur, the sky is the limit as far as earnings are concerned. Unlike an employee, an entrepreneur owns the profit that his or her business earns, and may choose to reinvest it in the company or take it as income.

An entrepreneur is someone who recognizes an opportunity to start a business that fulfills a consumer need other people may not have noticed and jumps on it. As economist Jeffry A. Timmons writes in the preface to his *New Venture Creation: Entrepreneurship for the 21st Century*, "A skillful entrepreneur can shape and create an opportunity where others see little or nothing—or see it too early or too late."

The French word *entrepreneur* began to take on its present-day meaning in the seventeenth century. It was used to describe someone who undertook any project that entailed risk—military, legal, political, as well as economic. Eventually it came to mean someone who started a new business—often a new *kind* of business or a new (and improved) way of doing business. French economist Jean-Baptiste Say wrote at the turn of the nineteenth century, "The entrepreneur shifts economic resources [like wood or coal] out of an area of lower and into an area of higher productivity and greater yield." By doing this, Say argued, entrepreneurs added value to scarce resources. Coal is a resource because it is used as fuel. Wood is a resource because it can be used to build a house or a table or to make paper (as well as be used for fuel). Economists consider *scarce* all resources that have a monetary value.

Debbi Fields took resources—eggs, butter, flour, sugar, and chocolate chips—and turned them into cookies. People liked what she did with those resources so much that they were willing to pay her more for the cookies than it cost her to buy the ingredients to make them. She added value to the resources she purchased by what she did with them, and created a multimillion-dollar business in the process.

Entrepreneurs start and operate their businesses for different reasons, but they share the common focus of creating sustained value for themselves. Entrepreneurs seek opportunities that they envision as generators of incremental income, or wealth. Whether the business is intended to meet short-term household cash needs or to grow into a publicly traded company, *viability* is critical. Each activity of the firm should be considered with this in mind.

The Economic Questions

Since the beginnings of human society, people have had to answer the same basic questions:

- What will be produced?
- When will it be produced?
- How will it be produced?
- Who will produce it?
- Who will get what is produced?

Families and individuals—as well as businesspeople, charitable organizations, corporations, and governments—all have had to answer these questions.[2] The system created by making these decisions is called an *economy*. The study of how different groups answer the questions is called *economics*.

An economy is a region's or nation's financial structure. It is the system that produces and distributes wealth. The United States economy is a **free enterprise system** because anyone is free to start a business. You

free enterprise system
economic system in which
businesses are privately
owned and operate
relatively free of
government interference.

---

[2]Source of definitions throughout chapter: United States Small Business Administration (SBA), http://www.sba.gov, August 3, 2010.

do not have to get permission from the government to start a business, although you will be expected to obey laws and regulations.

The free market system is also called **capitalism,** and is characterized by the following:

- Individuals and companies may compete for their own economic gain,
- private property ownership and wealth are permissible, and
- free-market forces determine prices.

Cash or goods invested to generate income and wealth is called **capital,** and in a free enterprise system anyone who can raise the necessary capital may start a business.

Voluntary Exchange

The free enterprise system is also sometimes referred to as a *free trade* system, because it is based on **voluntary exchange.** Voluntary exchange is a transaction between two parties who agree to trade money for a product or service. Each is eager to take advantage of what the trade offers. The parties agree to the exchange because each will benefit.

Let's say you have a contracting business and your busy neighbors hire you to renovate their kitchen. You need money and are willing to use your skills and time to earn it. They want their kitchen renovated and are willing to give up money to get it done. You each have something the other wants, so you are willing to trade. Trading only takes place when both parties believe they will benefit. Robbery, in contrast, is an *involuntary* trade.

Benefits and Challenges of Free Enterprise

The general public benefits from living in a free enterprise system because it discourages entrepreneurs who waste resources by driving them out of

◀ **Performance Objective 2**

Describe how free enterprise economies work and how entrepreneurs fit into them.

capitalism the free-market system; characterized by individuals and companies competing for economic gains, private property ownership and wealth; free-market forces determine prices.

capital money or property owned or used in business.

voluntary exchange a transaction between two parties who agree to trade money for a product or service.

Global Impact . . .

Free Trade

Buying Ownership in a Business You Understand—Globally and Locally

Theresa Rogers has had a lifelong passion for wine. She has taken that passion, and her extensive knowledge of the industry, and applied it to running Horseneck Wines and Liquors since she purchased the company in 1989. Rogers began studying Hugh Johnson's *Pocket Encyclopedia of Wine* at the age of 19, and then secured a job as a salesperson in the Fine Wine division of Heublein, covering all five boroughs of New York; from working on commission, she rose to managing a sales force. From there, Rogers worked with a small company to build a brand called Bollini Chardonnay, the first Italian chardonnay to be marketed across the United States that sold for less than $10 per bottle. Rogers built the brand to 30,000 cases in the major American markets over a three-year period. She then went to work for the Empson Company, one of the first Italian exporters of the finest Italian wines, such as Gaja from the Piedmont region. Rogers worked with Angelo Gaja to bring his brand to the forefront of the Barbarescos and Barolos.

Rogers bought her first store in 1986 and sold it in 2005. She purchased Horseneck, located in Greenwich, Connecticut, as her second store. Horseneck Wines and Liquors has grown from a $500,000 wine shop into a firm with $5 million in annual sales and one of the largest collections of fine and rare wines in the state.[3] Rogers took an existing business and built upon its potential by plowing her profits back into the company and creating market opportunities. She established her networks and customer base through contributions to charity events, holding wine-tasting parties, and building relationships with local retailers and restaurateurs. As with any wine store, Horseneck sells a range of international wines and spirits, but went one step further—collecting rare wines, and carrying the largest stock of Bordeaux, Burgundies, and Italian wines in Connecticut. Rogers started with an existing business and made it truly her own.

Theresa Rogers, Horseneck Wines and Liquors. (Courtesy of Horseneck Wines and Liquors)

---

business. It encourages entrepreneurs who use resources efficiently to satisfy consumer needs by rewarding them with profit.

The economy as a whole benefits because free enterprise encourages competition between entrepreneurs. Someone who can make cookies that taste as good as Mrs. Fields Original Cookies, and sell them for less, will eventually attract Mrs. Fields' customers. This will force Mrs. Fields to lower prices to stay competitive. Consumers of cookies will benefit because they will get to buy the same-quality product at a lower price.

On the flip side, free enterprise has some disadvantages. If a company fails, the employees lose their source of livelihood. Owners who have invested their financial resources in the business will lose their money. Other companies or individuals may have depended upon the products and services of this failed business and thus may lose customers or suppliers.

What Is a Small Business?

The public often thinks of business only in terms of "big" business—companies such as General Electric, ExxonMobil, Microsoft, McDonald's, and Nike. A small business is defined by the U.S. Small Business Administration's Office of Advocacy as one having fewer than 500 employees and selling less than $5 million worth of products or services in a year (depending upon the industry). So, even a leading local employer could be considered a small business.

Most of the world's businesses are small businesses. A neighborhood restaurant or a clothing boutique is each an example of a small business. Surprisingly, the principles involved in running a large company—like Viacom—and a corner deli are the same. However, the *operation* of a small business is not the same as that of a large one. Most multimillion-dollar businesses in this country started out as small, entrepreneurial ventures. This is why entrepreneurship is often called the engine of our economy. It drives our economic creativity, giving rise to wealth and jobs, and improving our standard of living. It is no coincidence that the United States is both one of the most entrepreneurial countries in the world and the richest.

Why Be an Entrepreneur?

Entrepreneurs put a great deal of time and effort into launching their own businesses. While establishing a business, an entrepreneur may also pour all his or her money into it. He or she may not be able to buy new clothes or a luxury car, go on vacation, or spend much time with family until the business becomes profitable and starts generating cash.

If so much work and sacrifice are involved, why be an entrepreneur? The entrepreneur is working for the following rewards:

1. *Control over time.* Do you work better at midnight than at 8 a.m.? If you start your own business, you will have control over how you spend your time by the type of business it is. Are you the kind of person who likes to work really hard for two weeks nonstop and then take a break? If you are an entrepreneur, you can structure your schedule to make this possible. You can also choose to hire others to perform tasks that you do not like to do or are not good at, so you can stay focused on what you do best. Bill Gates wanted to spend his time designing software. He hired others to manage Microsoft's operations and to market and sell its products. Many eBay entrepreneurs have carved out very flexible schedules for responding to orders. Brick-and-mortar retail stores, on the other hand, do not often afford such flexibility.

BizFacts

- There are 27.3 million businesses in the United States; approximately 99.9 percent of them are small companies with fewer than 500 employees.

- Small businesses in America employed 49.6 percent of the country's private (non-government) workforce, hired 40 percent of high-tech workers, and created 60 to 80 percent of net new jobs annually over the past decade.

- Home-based businesses make up 52 percent and franchises compose 2 percent of small firms.

- Small businesses represent 99.7 percent of all companies with employees.

- Small firms constituted 96.5 percent of all identified exporters and produced 30.2 percent of the country's known export value in fiscal year 2007.

Source: U.S. Small Business Administration, Office of Advocacy, *Small Business Profile: United States,* February 2011, and Office of Advocacy Research and Statistics, http://www.sba.gov, March 11, 2011.

2. ***Fulfillment.*** Successful entrepreneurs are passionate about their businesses. They are excited and fulfilled by their work. Entrepreneurs who are working to reach their full potential are rarely bored because there is always plenty to do. And if one facet of running the business becomes uninteresting to them and they have the income to support it, they can hire someone else for that task.

    Social entrepreneurs who want to contribute to societal improvement find ways to do this while also earning a profit. Founders of not-for-profits create enterprises to address societal needs that are important to them. Other entrepreneurs start lifestyle businesses that allow them to earn money while following their passion. For example, avid pilots may operate aviation-oriented businesses in which they can fly often, such as specialty-delivery companies, or teaching. Art lovers may open galleries, create art-rental companies, or operate special art tours.

3. ***Creation/ownership.*** Entrepreneurship is a creative endeavor. Entrepreneurs put time into establishing enterprises that they expect will survive and become profitable. Entrepreneurs own the businesses they create and the profits that those businesses earn. *Ownership* is the key to wealth. Your goal is to find a business that will generate a continuing stream of earnings. Eventually, you may be able to sell that company for a multiple of those earnings. That is how entrepreneurs build wealth. Many entrepreneurs, such as Bill Gore, the inventor of GORE-TEX fabric, start their own businesses after becoming frustrated or disillusioned in other roles, or having ideas rejected by an employer.

4. ***Control over compensation.*** Entrepreneurs choose how and when they are paid. As owner of your company, when funds permit, you can decide to:

    - Pay yourself a **salary**—a fixed payment made at regular intervals, such as weekly or monthly. Salaries are not payable in sole proprietorships where owners may take a "draw" on revenues or partnerships where they may draw down profits.

    - Pay yourself a **wage**—a fixed rate per hour. This is not a common choice, but it is available.

    - Take a share of the company's profits. As the owner, you can pay yourself a portion of the business's profits. In a corporation this kind of payment is called a **dividend** and must be paid to all shareholders.

salary fixed amount of money paid to an employee at regular intervals.

wage fixed payment per hour for work performed.

dividend each stockholder's portion of the profit-per-share paid out by a corporation.

commission a percentage of a sale paid to a salesperson or employee.

- Take a **commission** on every sale you make. A commission is a percentage of the value of a sale. If you decide to pay yourself 10 percent commission, and sell an item for $120, your commission on the sale would be $12.

If you have a sole proprietorship, the government considers you and the company to be one entity. Earnings of the company are your earnings. Tax and legal rules that govern different types of ownership forms affect what you call and how you account for owners' compensation. For the sake of this discussion, think of your compensation in the form of a salary or a wage. Once you decide on the type of business you are creating, check with an attorney and accountant regarding the appropriate business form and record keeping requirements for the type of business you are starting.

5. ***Control over working conditions.*** As an entrepreneur, you can create a work environment that reflects your values. If you support recycling, you can make sure your company recycles. You will also evaluate your own performance. No one has the power to fire you. If equality is essential, you might have an office with identical working spaces, no special privileges for managers, and few management layers.

Some of the greatest entrepreneurs in the world dealt with problems as they were growing up, such as extreme poverty, abuse, learning disabilities, and other issues. Sir Richard Branson, for example, had such severe dyslexia that he dropped out of high school. He became a successful entrepreneur, however, and has created more than 200 companies—including Virgin Airlines, Virgin Galactic, and Virgin Records. The Virgin Group employs about 50,000 people in 29 countries, and has annual revenues of some $20 billion.[4] Branson has a personal net worth of about $4.2 billion, making him number 254 on the Forbes list of billionaires.[5] As an entrepreneur, he was able to create an environment in which he could succeed.

The Desire to Make Money Is Not the Only Reason to Start a Business

Starting a business is an opportunity and, like any opportunity, it should be evaluated by taking a careful look at the costs and benefits it offers. One thing is for certain, though: *The desire to make money, alone, is not a good enough reason to start one's own business.*

The financial rewards of owning your own business may not kick in until you have put in years of hard work. The desire to make money may not be enough to keep you going through a difficult early period. The typical successful company has been founded by an entrepreneur with a powerful and motivating dream, balanced by dedication and a strong work ethic.

Entrepreneurs have said that they are not in business for the money so often that it has become a cliché, but, like most clichés, it is based on truth.

Definitions of Success—Monetary and Other

Today, the millennial generation (people born between 1977 and 1995) has redefined success. It is more individualized than the traditional concept, and based upon factors beyond those of income and wealth. Business owners may start an enterprise to create a more environmentally friendly approach to a product or process, to provide jobs for a disadvantaged population, or to improve the mental or physical health of themselves or others. For these entrepreneurs, success might be measured by the ability to have

[4]Virgin Group, http://www.virgin.com, March 15, 2009.

[5]"The World's Billionaires," *Forbes*, http://www.forbes.com, July 21, 2011.

an impact on the population they serve. Or, success may mean working to provide a lifestyle that permits a shortened work week or telecommuting. Recognition from peers and others could also be a goal. Financial success may be just one of many measures of achievement for an entrepreneur.

Taking the Long View

Successful entrepreneurs know that it is important to begin with the end in mind—so that they can always maintain the vision of where they want the organization to be at the time of their personal exit point—even before they make the first sale. The daily tactical decisions you make will be affected by what you hope to create in the short *and* long term, so that a clear vision is vital. Some questions to ask yourself include:

- Are you planning to be active in the business until retirement? At what age will you retire? Who will take over then? A family member? A new owner?
- Do you plan to grow the business to a certain size or level of maturity and then sell it? If so, what is the target number? Are you looking at an initial public offering or a small private sale? Would you stay with the business after it was sold?
- Would you want to stay active for a given number of years? Then what would you do?

Taking the long view also means considering personal satisfaction, including conformance with individual values and ethics. Entrepreneurs make hundreds of choices and decisions all the time. When you make these everyday decisions, they can conform with your values and ethics or you can violate them to meet a customer need, provide an expedient or cost-effective solution to an immediate problem, or the like. For your long-term wellbeing and the benefit of those around you, it will be critical to keep your core values in the forefront. Consider the legacy you want to leave for your successors.

Benefits and Costs of Becoming an Entrepreneur

Even if you do have a clear vision that you believe will motivate you through the ups and downs of running a business, look closely at the costs and benefits of being an entrepreneur before you decide whether it is the life for you. Benefits include:

- *Independence.* Business owners do not have to follow orders or observe working hours set by someone else.
- *Satisfaction.* Doing what you love to do, or turning a skill, hobby, or other interest into your own business can be highly satisfying.
- *Financial reward.* Although income potential is generally capped for employees, entrepreneurs are limited only by their own imagination and tenacity. Entrepreneurs built most of our country's great fortunes. At the same time, many people use part-time, seasonal, or occasional entrepreneurship to fund gaps in household income, pay for college, or support extraordinary expenses.
- *Self-esteem.* Knowing you created something valuable can give you a strong sense of accomplishment. It can help you feel good about yourself.
- *Contribution to society.* As a business owner, you decide how you can add value to your community and the wider world. The issues that you care about can be taken into account when you form your company.

Costs include:

- ***Business failure.*** About one in five new businesses fails in the first eight years. Some of this is attributed to entrepreneurs not getting proper training.[6] Perhaps a third of the closures are due to the entrepreneur becoming discouraged and giving up. Entrepreneurs risk losing not only their own money but also the financial investments of others.
- ***Obstacles.*** You will run into problems that you will have to solve by yourself. Your family and friends may actually discourage you, or not support your vision.
- ***Loneliness.*** It can be lonely and even a little scary to be completely responsible for the success or failure of a business.
- ***Financial insecurity.*** You are not guaranteed a set salary or benefits. You may not always have enough money to pay yourself, particularly in the first 18 months or so of a new enterprise. You will have to establish and fund your own retirement fund.
- ***Long hours/hard work.*** You will have to work long hours to get your business off the ground. Many entrepreneurs work six or even seven days a week, often for 12 hours or more per day. While you decide when to work, you may end up working many more hours as an entrepreneur than you would as an employee. Also, do not forget to examine the opportunities you will be giving up to start your own business. What other prospects exist for the investment of your money and time? Some might include going to college or graduate school, or even working for someone else.
- ***Strain on personal relationships.*** Even with the strong support of family and friends, the inherent challenges of a small business can strain relationships to the breaking point.

Not everyone is cut out to be an entrepreneur. Entrepreneurs have to be able to tolerate a higher degree of risk and uncertainty than people who work steady jobs for established employers. With higher risk, however, comes the possibility of higher rewards.

Cost/Benefit Analysis

cost/benefit analysis a decision-making process in which the costs of taking an action are compared to the benefits.

Using a comparison of benefits and costs to make a decision is called **cost/benefit analysis**. It is a helpful tool because people tend to make decisions based upon emotions, not reason, to evaluate pros and cons. Strong emotion may overwhelm you to the point where you see only the benefits and not the costs of an action (or vice versa).

Say you plan to buy a car. You might be overwhelmed by the idea of making such a large purchase, even if the benefits are greater than the cost. On the other hand, you might decide to buy a car at a price that outweighs the benefits it would bring, because you are temporarily blinded by a desire to own a really impressive vehicle. Making a list that includes the dollars and cents of the costs and benefits of your purchase is a concrete way to take the emotion out of a decision.

To turn an opportunity into a business you will have to invest both time and money. Before making this investment, think carefully about:

> ***Costs:*** The money and time you will have to invest—as well as the opportunities you will be giving up—to start and operate the business.
> ***Benefits:*** The money you will earn and the knowledge and experience you will gain.

---

[6]Linda Yu, "Self-Employment on Rise," *Metro*, June 2004.

Opportunity Cost

Cost/benefit analysis is incomplete without considering **opportunity cost**. This is the cost of your "next-best investment." Perhaps your goal is to become a composer who writes scores for movies. You get a full-time job at a local store for $400 a week to support yourself, so you can write and record music in the evenings that you hope to sell to producers, agents, or film companies.

opportunity cost the value of what must be given up in order to obtain something else.

You find, however, that whenever a producer or agent wants to meet with you, you cannot get out of work to go. You realize that, even though you are making $400 a week, you are missing some important opportunities. Perhaps it would be smarter to take a part-time job for $300 a week that would leave your mornings free for meetings. The opportunity cost of the $100 a week you will lose is made up for by the potential income from film-scoring jobs you are missing by not being free to see people in the business. If your first film-scoring job pays $5,000, for example, you definitely would have made the right decision to earn $100 a week less for a few months.

People often make decisions without considering the opportunity cost and then wonder why they are not happy with the outcome. Each time you make a decision about what to do with your time, energy, or money, think about the cost of the opportunities that you are giving up. **Figure 1-1** presents a simple quiz that can help you decide whether you have what it takes to be an entrepreneur.

Avoiding Missteps

While experience is an excellent teacher, using knowledge, skills, and abilities to avoid errors, problems, and delays is much healthier. A savvy entrepreneur learns from the mistakes of others and appreciates the wisdom and experience of trusted advisors and mentors. Of course, it may be difficult to discern which advice is sound and which likely to fuel further missteps.

Preparation and planning are keys to avoiding mistakes. Thoughtful consideration of the entrepreneurship option is an excellent starting point. Thorough research and taking advantage of training and/or technical assistance to bridge gaps in your preparation can make a world of difference.

Two of the best resources for staying on track are mentors and advisors. Finding a committed business mentor with industry-specific knowledge and expertise, broad general business experience, or both, is a worthwhile endeavor. If you can find a successful entrepreneur in your field, perhaps outside of your geographic area, having him or her as a mentor could prove critical. Many successful entrepreneurs will find time to encourage promising newcomers. Unfortunately, becoming a mentor may be more of a commitment than your identified entrepreneur is willing or able to make. Perhaps he or she would consider becoming an advisor instead.

In addition to your paid professional advisors, such as attorneys and accountants, individual advisors or an advisory board can be the difference between success and failure. Even if you are forming a venture with a full slate of experienced technical and managerial professionals, the guidance of a carefully composed advisory board can provide crucial counsel and connections. Such a board might meet only once or twice a year—to listen to your plans, share experiences, and help you avoid mistakes—but its feedback could be decisive. During the times between meetings, advisors may also be willing to offer substantial assistance.

Figure 1-1 *"Do You Have What It Takes?" Quiz*

Take the following quiz to learn more about yourself and whether you have what it takes to be an entrepreneur. Circle the answer that best represents how you feel.

1. You are at a party and a friend tells you that the guy in the expensive-looking suit recently invested in another friend's business. What do you do?
   a. Race over to him, introduce yourself, and tell him every detail of your business idea while asking if he would be interested in investing in it.
   b. Ask your friend to introduce you. Once introduced, you hand the potential investor your business card and politely ask whether you might be able to call on him sometime to present your business plan.
   c. Decide that it is probably not a good idea to bother the man at a party. After all, he is here to relax. Maybe you will run into him again somewhere else.
2. Your boss asks you to take charge of researching office supply stores and choosing the one that you think would be best for the company to use. What is your response?
   a. Yes! Finally, a chance to show the boss what you are made of—plus, you will be able to spirit a few of the supplies away for your own business.
   b. You are terrified; this is more responsibility than you really want. What if you make a mistake and cost the company money? You do not want to look bad.
   c. You are excited. This is a good opportunity to impress your boss and also learn how to compare and negotiate with suppliers — something you will need to do for your own business.
3. You are already going to school full time when you are offered a part-time job that is in the same field as the business you want to start when you graduate next year. What do you do?
   a. Take the job, after talking with your student advisor about how to juggle your schedule so it will fit, because you believe the experience and the contacts you will develop will be invaluable when you start your business.
   b. Take the job. In fact, you ask for extra hours so you can finally start making some real money. Who needs sleep?
   c. Turn down the job. School is hard enough without working, too. You do not want your grades to suffer.
4. You are offered a job as a survey taker for a marketing firm. The job pays really well but will require you to talk to a great many people. What do you do?
   a. Take the job. You like people and this job will be a good way to practice getting to know what consumers want.
   b. Turn down the job. Just the thought of approaching strangers makes you queasy.
   c. Take the job so you can conduct some market research of your own by also asking the people you survey what they think about your business idea.
5. Your last job paid well and was interesting, but it required you to put in long hours and sometimes work on the weekends. What was your response?
   a. You put in the extra hours without complaint, but mainly because you felt that the rewards were worth it.
   b. You went a little overboard and worked yourself into a state of exhaustion; moderation is not your strong suit.
   c. You quit. You are strictly a nine-to-five person. Work is definitely not your life!
6. You are such a good guitar player that friends keep offering to pay for you to give them lessons. What is your response?
   a. You spend some money to run a six-week advertisement in the local paper, announcing that you are now available to teach at the same rate that established teachers in the area charge.
   b. You start teaching a few friends to see how it goes. You ask them what they are willing to pay and what they want to learn.
   c. You give a few friends some lessons but refuse to take any money.
7. Your best friend has started a business designing Web sites. He needs help because the business is really growing. He offers to make you a partner in the business even though you are computer-illiterate. What is your response?
   a. You jump in, figuring that you will learn the ropes soon enough.
   b. You ask your friend to keep the partnership offer open but first to recommend a class you can take to get your skills up to speed.
   c. You pass. You do not see how you can work in a business you know nothing about.

Analysis of the "Do You Have What It Takes?" Quiz

Scoring

1. a = 2	b = 1	c = 0
2. a = 2	b = 0	c = 1
3. a = 1	b = 2	c = 0
4. a = 1	b = 0	c = 2
5. a = 1	b = 2	c = 0
6. a = 2	b = 1	c = 0
7. a = 2	b = 1	c = 0

Figure 1-1 *"Do You Have What It Takes?" Quiz*

12 points or more: You are a natural risk-taker and can handle a lot of stress. These are important characteristics for an entrepreneur to have to be successful. You are willing to work hard but have a tendency to throw caution to the wind a little too easily. Save yourself from that tendency by using cost/benefit analysis to carefully evaluate your business (and personal!) decisions. In your enthusiasm, do not forget to look at the opportunity costs of any decision you make.

6 to 11 points: You strike an excellent balance between being a risk-taker and someone who carefully evaluates decisions. An entrepreneur needs to be both. You are also not overly motivated by the desire to make money. You understand that a successful business requires hard work and sacrifice before you can reap the rewards. To make sure that you are applying your natural drive and discipline to the best possible business opportunity, use the cost/benefit analysis to evaluate the different businesses you are interested in starting.

5 points or fewer: You are a little too cautious for an entrepreneur, but that will probably change as you learn more about how to run a business. You are concerned with financial security and may not be eager to put in the long hours required to get a business off the ground. This does not mean that you cannot succeed as an entrepreneur; just make sure that whatever business you decide to start is the business of your dreams, so that you will be motivated to make it a success. Use cost/benefit analysis to evaluate your business opportunities. Choose a business that you believe has the best shot at providing you with both the financial security and the motivation you require.

Of course, taking advantage of courses in entrepreneurship, whether single workshops, individual college courses, a certificate program, or a degree program, can give you considerable advantages. The opportunity to learn from the experience of others—to systematically explore entrepreneurial options and build skills—is invaluable.

A well-prepared entrepreneur is more likely to stay on the path to success.

Entrepreneurial Options

Entrepreneurship can extend beyond the traditional views of for-profit enterprises that are most commonly associated with it. There are many variations on entrepreneurship, and the opportunities are virtually limitless. Entrepreneurship may include for-profit enterprises that support the missions of not-for-profit organizations, businesses designed for social impact, and ventures that are environmentally oriented.

Social entrepreneurship has multiple definitions and forms, but in general it is commonly thought of as a for-profit enterprise that has the dual goals of achieving profitability and attaining beneficial social returns. Another view is that of taking an entrepreneurial perspective toward social problems. Duke University Professor J. Gregory Dees created the following definition:

social entrepreneurship a for-profit enterprise that has the dual goals of achieving profitability and attaining social returns.

Social entrepreneurs play the role of change agents in the social sector by:

- adopting a mission to create and sustain social value (not just private value),
- recognizing and relentlessly pursuing new opportunities to serve that mission,
- engaging in a process of continuous innovation, adaptation, and learning,
- acting boldly without being limited by resources currently in hand, and
- exhibiting heightened accountability to the constituencies served and for the outcomes created.[7]

---

[7]Gregory Dees, "The Meaning of 'Social Entrepreneurship'," http://www.fuqua.duke.edu/centers/case/documents/dees_SE.pdf. May 30, 2001. Used by permission.

venture philanthropy
a subset or segment of social entrepreneurship wherein financial and human capital are invested in not-for-profits by individuals and for-profit enterprises with the intention of generating social rather than financial returns on their investments.

green entrepreneurship
enterprise activities that avoid harm to the environment or help to protect it in some way.

In this view, social entrepreneurship is less about profit than it is about social impact.

In addition, **venture philanthropy** is a subset—segment—of social entrepreneurship. Financial and human capital is invested in not-for-profits by individuals and for-profit enterprises with the intention of generating social rather than financial returns. In some cases, venture philanthropy may involve the investment of capital in the for-profit, commercial part of a not-for-profit. In others, it may mean investing in not-for-profits directly, to encourage entrepreneurial approaches to achieve social impact.

Green entrepreneurship is another form of social entrepreneurship, and can be defined as: "Enterprise activities that avoid harm to the environment or help to protect the environment in some way."[8] TerraCycle is an excellent example of green entrepreneurship. According to the Corporation for Enterprise Development (CFED), green entrepreneurship can:

- create jobs and offer entrepreneurship opportunities;
- increase energy efficiency, thus conserving natural resources and saving money;
- decrease harm to workers' health;
- enable businesses to tap into new sources of local, state, and federal funding;
- take advantage of consumer preference for environmentally friendly goods, and
- preserve limited natural assets on which businesses and communities depend for business and quality of life.

Each of these alternative approaches offers opportunities for innovation and growth for the right entrepreneur.

How Do Entrepreneurs Find Opportunities to Start New Businesses?

In the twentieth century, Joseph Schumpeter expanded on Jean-Baptiste Say's definition of entrepreneurship, adding that entrepreneurs create value "by exploiting an invention or, more generally, an untried technological possibility for producing a new commodity or producing an old one in a new way, by opening up a new source of supply of materials or a new outlet for products, by reorganizing an industry and so on."[9] This view emphasizes innovation as the key to entrepreneurship. Management expert Peter Drucker simplified this view to the essential core of creating a new business, taking on risk, and persevering in light of uncertainty.[10]

Schumpeter's definition describes five basic ways that entrepreneurs find opportunities to create new businesses:

1. Use a new technology to produce a new product.
2. Use an existing technology to produce a new product.
3. Use an existing technology to produce an old product in a new way.
4. Find a new source of resources (that might enable the entrepreneur to produce a product more cheaply).
5. Develop a new market for an existing product.

[8]Corporation for Enterprise Development, "Green Entrepreneurship," *Effective State Policy and Practice*, vol. 5, no. 2, http://www.cfed.org, April 2004.

[9]Joseph A. Schumpeter, *Capitalism, Socialism and Democracy* (New York: Harper & Row, 1942).

[10]Peter Drucker, *Innovation and Entrepreneurship: Practice and Principles* (New York: Harper Collins, 1985).

Entrepreneurs Creatively Exploit Changes in Our World

Today's economists and business experts have defined entrepreneurship even more sharply. Drucker pointed out that, for a business to be considered entrepreneurial, it should exploit changes in the world. This is in alignment with Schumpeter's definition of entrepreneurship but explicitly goes a step further—to take advantage of circumstances. These changes can be technological, like the explosion in computer technology that led Bill Gates and Paul Allen to start Microsoft, or cultural, like the collapse of communism, which led to a great many new business opportunities in Eastern Europe.

Nothing changes faster than technology—which is defined as science that has been applied to industry or commerce. Not so many years ago, there were no bar codes, no electronic scanners, and hardly anyone used e-mail or mobile phones. Today, even the smallest of organizations needs to use current technologies to be competitive. Smart entrepreneurs multiply their efficiency by taking advantage of the latest breakthroughs in business technology. To learn about what's new in technology, read current business and trade magazines and visit Web sites, such as:

- The Business Technology Network, http://www.techweb.com.
- BusinessWeek Technology News, http://www.businessweek.com/technology.

Peter Drucker defined an entrepreneur as someone who "always searches for change, responds to it, and exploits it as an opportunity." Entrepreneurs are always on the lookout for ways to create opportunities from change.

Where Others See Problems, Entrepreneurs Recognize Opportunities

Here is a simple definition of an entrepreneur that captures the essentials: An entrepreneur recognizes opportunities where others see only problems.

Many famous companies were started because an entrepreneur turned a problem into a successful business. An entrepreneur recognized that the problem was actually an opportunity. Where there are dissatisfied consumers, there are definitely opportunities for entrepreneurs.

Anita Roddick was an excellent example of an entrepreneur who started off as a dissatisfied consumer. She founded the Body Shop International because she was tired of paying for unnecessary perfume and fancy packaging when she bought makeup, and she thought many other women might feel the same way. Harlan Beverly is another

---

How Do Entrepreneurs Create Business Ideas?

1. *They listen.* By listening to others, entrepreneurs can get ideas about improving a business or starting a new one. Create a business idea by listening. Describe how you got the idea.
2. *They observe.* By constantly keeping their eyes open, entrepreneurs get ideas about how to help society, about businesses they could start, and about what consumers need. Create a business idea by observing. Describe how you got the idea.
3. *They think.* When entrepreneurs analyze a problem, they think about solutions. What product or service could solve that problem? Create a business idea by thinking about a problem. Describe how you got the idea.

problem solver. He realized that online gamers were frustrated by the lag time on response while playing their favorite online games, and created products to address the problem. His BigFoot Networks has become an industry leader.

Train Your Mind to Recognize Business Opportunities

The first step in becoming an entrepreneur is to train your mind to recognize business opportunities. The next step is to let your creativity fly. Roddick suggested developing entrepreneurial instincts by asking yourself such questions as:

- What frustrates me the most when I go to buy something?
- What product or service would really make my life better?
- What annoys or makes me angry?
- What product or service would take away my aggravation?

Entrepreneurs Use Their Imaginations

Businesses are also formed when entrepreneurs not only fume about products or services that annoy them but fantasize about products or services they would love to have in their lives. Jump-start your imagination by asking yourself such questions as:

- What is the one thing I would love to have more than anything else?
- What would it look like? What would it taste like?
- What would it do?
- What innovative product or service idea have I been mulling over in my mind?
- What problem have I encountered in everyday life and thought, "There has to be a better way to do this"?

Consider posing these questions to friends and family members as well. You might hear about an opportunity you had not, or at least not yet, recognized.

An Idea Is Not Necessarily an Opportunity

Not every business idea you may have or prospective invention you may explore is an actual *opportunity*. In fact, most ideas are not viable business possibilities. An opportunity has a unique characteristic that distinguishes it from an ordinary idea. An opportunity is an idea that is based on what consumers need or want and are willing to buy sufficiently often at a high

---

BizFacts

Entrepreneurship has proven to be an effective way for minorities and women to enter the business world.

- Approximately 5.8 million businesses were minority-owned in 2007, and in 2002 they employed 4.8 million people and generated $694 billion in revenues.
- There were more than 12.4 million nonfarm businesses owned by women (or co-owned equally with men), accounting for 45.7 percent of all U.S. companies.

Source: U.S. Small Business Administration, Office of Advocacy, *Small Business Profile: United States,* February 2011, and Office of Advocacy Research and Statistics, http://www.sba.gov, March 11, 2011.

Entrepreneurial Wisdom . . .

A useful way to evaluate a business idea is to look at its Strengths, Weaknesses, Opportunities, and Threats (SWOT). This is called SWOT Analysis.

- **Strengths**—All the capabilities and positive points that the entrepreneur has, from experience to contacts. These are internal to the organization.

- **Weaknesses**—All of the negatives that the entrepreneur faces, such as lack of capital or training, or inability to set up a workable accounting system. These are internal to the organization.

- **Opportunities**—Any positive external event or circumstance (including lucky breaks) that can help the entrepreneur get ahead of the competition.

- **Threats**—Any external factor, event, or circumstance that can harm the business, such as competitors, legal issues, or a declining economy.

---

enough price to sustain a business. A successful business sells products or services that customers need, at prices they are willing to pay. Many a small business has failed because the entrepreneur did not understand this. It is critical that the idea "has legs" for it to go on to success.

In addition, according to Jeffry Timmons, "An opportunity has the qualities of being attractive, durable, and timely and is anchored in a product or service which creates or adds value for its buyer or end user."[11]

Timmons defines a business opportunity as an idea, plus these four characteristics:

1. It is attractive to customers.
2. It will work in your business environment.
3. It can be executed in the window of opportunity that exists.
4. You have the resources and skills to create the business, or you know someone who does and who might want to form the business with you.

The window of opportunity is the length of time you have to get your business idea to your market. You might have a great idea, but if several other competitors have it, too, and have already brought it to the marketplace, that window of opportunity has been closed.

Remember, not every idea is an opportunity. For an idea to be an opportunity, it must lead to the development of a product or service that is of value to the customer.

Opportunity Is Situational

A problem is one example of an opportunity that entrepreneurs need to be able to recognize. A changing situation or trend is another. Opportunity is *situational*, meaning it is dependent on variable circumstances. There are no rules about when or where an opportunity might appear. Change and flux create opportunities.

Think about recent changes in computer technology. In the early 1990s, the conventional wisdom was that only the biggest telecommunications companies were going to be in a position to exploit the Internet and all the opportunities it had to offer. How could entrepreneurs compete with established, resource-loaded companies? The opposite has been true, however. Entrepreneurs have penetrated and, indeed, dominated the market for Internet-based services. Think of AOL, Google, and Yahoo!. Each one is an entrepreneurial venture that left the telecom giants scrambling to catch up.

---

[11]Jeffry Timmons, *New Venture Creation: Entrepreneurship for the 21st Century*, 5th ed. (New York: Irwin/McGraw-Hill, 1999), p. 7.

Step into the Shoes . . .

Russell Simmons Makes Rap Happen

(Matthew Simmons/Getty Images)

In the late 1980s, Russell Simmons was promoting rap concerts at the City University of New York. At the time, rap was considered a passing fad, but Simmons really loved it. Even though most record executives thought rap would be over in a year or two, Simmons truly believed it was a business opportunity. He formed Def Jam Records with fellow student Rick Rubin for $5,000. Within a year, they produced hit records by Run DMC and LL Cool J, and Simmons became a multimedia mogul.

Simmons took a chance on this opportunity because he believed that, if you personally know 10 people who are eager to buy your product or service, 10 *million* would be willing to buy it if they knew about it. Luckily, he was right about rap's popular potential, but he could have been wrong. That can be a problem with perceived opportunities—you may be passionate about something but there may not be enough consumer interest to sustain an actual business venture.

Simmons loved rap and hoped that other people would, too. That was the internal factor—he had the passion to sustain himself as he worked 24/7 to make his dream come true. As it turned out, music fans were a little bored with rock at that time and were looking for a fresh sound. Rap filled the bill. This was an external opportunity that happened to coincide with Simmons's internal commitment.

As Timmons has pointed out, it can take a huge corporation (think dinosaur) over six years to develop and implement a new business strategy. Entrepreneurs, in contrast, can dart in and out of the market like roadrunners. Successful entrepreneurs can, as the saying goes, "turn on a dime rather than a dollar bill."

Performance Objective 3

Find and evaluate opportunities to start your own business.

The Five Roots of Opportunity in the Marketplace

There are "five roots of opportunity" that entrepreneurs can exploit.[12] Notice how similar these are to Schumpeter's definition of entrepreneurship.

1. **Problems** that your business can solve.
2. **Changes** in laws, situations, or trends.
3. **Inventions** of totally new products or services.
4. **Competition.** If you can find a way to beat the competition on price, location, quality, reputation, reliability, or speed, you can create a very successful business with an existing product or service.
5. **Technological Advances.** Scientists may invent new technology, but entrepreneurs figure out how to use and sell it.

Integrating Internal and External Opportunities

It is helpful not only to be aware of the five roots of opportunity in the marketplace, but to think also about how we perceive opportunities ourselves. Opportunities fall into two classes: internal and external. An internal opportunity is one that comes from inside you—from a personal hobby, interest, or even a passion—or your organization. It could present itself in the form of the resolution of a problem, such as creating a viable product from scrap material, or the potential for a new product line.

An external opportunity, in contrast, is generated by a noticeable outside circumstance. External opportunities are conditions you notice that make you say to yourself, "Hey, I could start a great business from that!"

---

[12]Adapted from John Clow (ed.), *Master Curriculum Guide: Economics and Entrepreneurship* (New York: Joint Council on Economic Education, 1991).

For example, you see that people in your neighborhood are complaining about the lack of available day care, so you start a day care center. But what if you find out very quickly that two-year-olds get on your nerves? That can be a major drawback for an external opportunity. Your idea may fill a market need, but you may not have the skills or interest to make it a successful business.

The best business opportunities often combine both internal and external factors. Ideally, a business that you are passionate about will fill a huge need in the marketplace.

Establishing Strategies

Business success hinges upon the creation and application of profitable strategies to the work at hand. A **strategy** is a plan for how a business intends to go about its own performance and outdo that of its competitors. Michael Porter created a "strategy framework" in his book, *Competitive Advantage*, which has remained valid. This framework delineates "cost leadership" and "differentiation" as low-cost and product-uniqueness strategies. It also layers in the concept of focus strategies, which work in narrow market segments rather than broad ones. The illustration in **Figure 1-2** shows how each of Porter's generic strategies relates to the other.

A firm using a product-uniqueness strategy bases its competitive advantage on its ability to differentiate the firm's products and/or services from others in its competitive market space. Such factors as quality, availability, customer service, and the like are critical to differentiation, as will be discussed in greater detail in the marketing chapters of this text.

If you choose to emphasize a low-cost approach, you will be using a cost-leadership strategy. This means that you are finding ways to reduce the costs of operations and management sufficiently to be able to undercut the prices of your competition and sustain a price advantage.

Porter's focus strategy suggests a narrow line of attack, a laserlike focus on a particular market segment. Rather than strategically targeting an entire industry, you are finding a particular niche or subset of the customer base and focusing your marketing efforts on that niche. If you are able to find a sufficiently large niche to sustain your business, you can set the company apart from the competition, and then maintain the advantage. A focus strategy can work with differentiation or cost leadership.

strategy a plan for how an organization or individual plans to perform and outdo competitors.

Figure **1-2** *Porter's Generic Strategies*		
Scope of Target	**Strategic Advantage**	
Market	**Product Uniqueness**	**Low Cost**
Industry-Wide (Broad)	Differentiation Strategy	Cost Leadership Strategy
Market Segment (Narrow)	Focus Strategy (Differentiation)	Focus Strategy (Low Cost)

Adapted from Michael Porter, *Competitive Strategy: Techniques for Analyzing Industries and Competitors* (New York: The Free Press, 1998).

Paths to Small Business Ownership

Not all business owners start their ventures from the ground up. Although the emphasis of this book is on starting and growing your own enterprise, the paths to business ownership are varied. You could buy an existing company, secure franchise rights, license or purchase critical technology or methods, inherit a company, or be hired as a manager.[13] There are pros and cons to each approach, and it is worthwhile to give thought to every option. Note the list of possibilities in **Exhibit 1-1**.

Securing Franchise Rights

franchise a business that markets a product or service developed by a franchisor, typically in the manner specified by that franchisor.

According to the U.S. Small Business Administration, "A **franchise** is a legal and commercial relationship between the owner of a trademark, service mark, trade name, or advertising symbol and an individual or group seeking to use that identification in a business."[14] The two primary forms of franchising are product/trade name franchising and business format franchising. Franchisors can provide assistance in marketing, site selection, securing financing, training, product supply, and business systems. McDonald's is an example of a business format franchise. Each company's franchise agreement is different and, while franchises fail less often than fully independent businesses, they cannot guarantee success. For many people who want to own and operate a business, it is worthwhile to consider franchising as a path to business ownership. Some factors to consider before selecting this option are shown in **Exhibit 1-2**.

Buying an Existing Business

acquisition the purchase of a business.

A business purchase, or **acquisition,** might be a good way to jump-start your entry into small business ownership. If you are purchasing a company,

Exhibit 1-1 Selected Business Entry Options

	Start a Business	Buy an Existing Business	Secure a Franchise or License	Licensing Technology
Customers	None	Established	None—but may have name recognition	None
Location	Needed	In place	Assistance possible	Needed
Management Control	Owner	Owner	Owner within terms of license	Owner within terms of license
Operational Control	Owner	Owner	Owner within terms of license	Owner
Marketing	Needed	In place (+/−)	Assistance possible. Rules absolutely.	Needed
Reputation	None	In place (+/−)	Should exist. If not, why license?	Possible
Royalties/Fees	Not usual	Maybe	Ongoing	Likely
Financing	Needed	Prior owner may provide	Assistance possible	Needed
Disclosures	None	Buyer beware	UFOC and contracts	Agreement

[13]Jerome A. Katz and Richard P. Green, *Entrepreneurial Small Business* (New York: McGraw-Hill/Irwin, 2008).

[14]U.S. Small Business Administration Workshop, "Is Franchising for Me?" http://www.sba.gov/idc/groups/public/documents/sba_homepage/serv_sbp_isfforme.pdf, December 2007.

Exhibit 1-2 *Factors to Consider before Becoming a Franchisee*

1. **Franchisor success**—How many similar franchises are nearby? In total? How are they performing? What name recognition exists? What's its reputation? Ask franchisees and consumer protection agencies.
2. **Franchisor durability**—Determine the length of experience. Is this a long-term opportunity or a fad? Does the franchisor own any intellectual property?
3. **Franchisor financial health**—How healthy is the company? Financial statements should be in the disclosure documents. Be certain you understand them.
4. **Start-up investment**—What is the amount and what does it buy? Ask about all potential franchise costs. Be certain that ongoing costs and start-up costs are clear.
5. **Financing support**—Does the franchisor offer competitive financing? How much do you need until you reach positive cash flow? Do the financial projections under various conditions and know your options.
6. **Purchasing requirements**—Do you have to buy from the franchisor or its list of suppliers? Are there minimum purchases? Can you purchase from others? How does the pricing from the required suppliers compare?
7. **Term of the agreement**—What is it? What, if any, are the terms for selling the franchise rights to another operator? What are your renewal rights?
8. **Competition**—Are there any restrictions on how you can compete within your territory? Is there assistance to help you compete? What kind? What is the level of competition?
9. **Management fit**—Does the management style and level of control exerted by the franchisor fit for you? Is the loss of independence worth the potential gains?

you should perform **due diligence,** which is the process used to learn about its true financial condition (the current owners may have incentives to provide incomplete, misleading, or inaccurate information), its reputation, and its continuing viability. There is both an art and a science to buying an existing business.

due diligence the exercise of reasonable care in the evaluation of a business opportunity.

The challenge is to perform a complete, in-depth analysis of the opportunity, just as you would for a startup, with the added dimension of having an existing history, whether for better or worse. Be wary of owners whose business seems to be too good to be true or who are overly eager to sell. Be thorough, whether you are buying an entire firm, a customer list, some or all of its assets, or taking on some or all of its debts. Done well, buying a business can be the starting point for success. Done poorly, buying a business can be more challenging and problematic than starting a new venture.

Licensing Technology

One way to potentially shorten the product-development cycle and to access innovative technology is to identify and *license* technology—that is, to enter into a contract to use it without purchasing the rights to own it. Whether you acquire such rights through a university, state economic development office, federal agency such as NASA, or an individual scientist/inventor, you can create a business based on technology transfer. Or, you may find that it makes more sense to purchase it outright or over time.

Entrepreneurial Wisdom . . .

Franchising Worldwide

Want to be an international mogul? Check out these Web sites:

- International Franchising Opportunities at http://www. franchise-international.net/.
- World Franchising at http://www.worldfranchising.com.

International Franchising's directory lists more than 1,000 North American franchises that train and support franchisees overseas. It also provides contact information for consultants and attorneys specializing in international franchising. World Franchising lists the top 100 franchises worldwide, as well as the top 50 franchises that have fewer than 50 operating units.

Step into the Shoes . . .

Putting Spring into a Third-Generation Business

T.J., Tom, and David Walker of Oregon Mattress.
(Oregon Mattress Company)

Brothers Tom and David Walker grew up at Oregon Mattress Company, in Newburg. Their grandfather founded the company in 1932 and their father operated it into the 1990s. Tom and David worked with their father for a number of years to expand the business and enhance its overall viability. They moved from producing under the Lady Americana label to Restonic, a well-respected national brand, and Sleep E-Z, their own brand.

Late in 2009, Oregon Mattress opened two retail stores featuring mattresses produced in its Portland-area factory. The BedCo Mattress Superstores are located in Lake Oswego and Beaverton.[15] The Walkers saw an opportunity to increase their share of the local market through direct retail sales of locally produced mattresses, including hard-to-find custom sizes and shapes and their signature round beds. Now, as the fourth generation of Walkers joins Oregon Mattress Company, the firm is bouncing back in a weak economy.

The MBA team of Bruce Black and Matt Ferris, from the University of Georgia, developed a business plan that garnered numerous competitive awards for the KidSmart Vocal Smoke Detector, which was created by an inventor and brought to market by them. The product is now available in major retail stores and on the Internet through the successor company, Signal One.

Before securing franchise rights, purchasing a business, or licensing technology, be certain to do your research thoroughly to understand what you are and are not buying and what your ongoing obligations (financial, operational, legal, and reporting) will be. Because these transactions are complex and can have significant financial and personal implications for you, it is important to invest in qualified legal and financial counsel before signing any agreements of this kind.

Do Not Take Unfair Advantage of Someone Else's Creativity

You would be upset if someone made money from your invention or artistic creation, so resist the urge to base your business on someone else's creative work. Not only is it unethical, it is against the law. Be sure that any business you start respects the intellectual property of others.

- Do not sell counterfeit knockoffs of popular brands.
- Do not take graphics, music, or content from the Web without permission and/or payment.
- Always know the source of the goods you buy from suppliers to avoid the risk of receiving stolen property.

The Many Faces of Entrepreneurship

Entrepreneurs are as diverse as the composition of the economy. They are of all ethnicities, races, religions, and from every socioeconomic level. They enter into self-employment for a wide range of reasons and as many choose to continue as entrepreneurs as return to outside employment. Record numbers of women, minorities, and young people have become

---

[15]Nick Peterson, "Oregon Mattress Co. Goes Retail," *The Times*, December 11, 2009.

entrepreneurs. Continuing an American tradition, there are also refugee and immigrant entrepreneurs.

This diverse and ever-changing pool of entrepreneurs does not reflect a single view of entrepreneurial success. Rather, the types of businesses formed are many. In addition to full-time enterprises founded to maximize growth and wealth, there are firms that are started as small, part-time enterprises, such as "gazelles," microenterprises, and mainstream small firms.

Gazelles

The classic entrepreneurial story is that of a single inventor—or pair of inventors—who develops a new, innovative technology or product in a garage, basement, or dormitory, lifts him/herself up by the bootstraps into a wildly successful business venture in virtually no time, takes it public, and becomes incredibly wealthy in the process. This entrepreneurial stereotype is a description of a high-potential venture and its founder. **Gazelles** are companies that achieve an annual growth rate of 20 percent or greater, typically measured in the growth of sales revenue.

> **gazelle** a company that achieves an annual growth rate of 20 percent or greater, typically measured by the increase of sales revenue.

They tend to be the exception rather than the rule for entrepreneurial ventures, but are a significant type of firm. Gazelles are financed by a combination of found resources plus significant outside assistance. They rely heavily upon external financial support and counsel.

Microenterprises

Most businesses are founded as **microenterprises,** which are defined as firms with five or fewer employees, initial capitalization requirements of under $35,000, and have the regular operational involvement of the owner. In fact, over 60 percent of all U.S. firms have four or fewer employees, according to the U.S. Small Business Administration.[16] The Association for Enterprise Opportunity (AEO) estimates that the more than 24 million microenterprises in the United States account for 87 percent of all businesses and 18 percent of all private employment.[17]

> **microenterprise** a firm with five or fewer employees, initial capitalization requirements of under $35,000, and the consistent operational involvement of the owner.

Microenterprises are founded for a variety of reasons and often are more fluid than other types of businesses. These firms may be started to provide full-time or part-time employment for their owners. They may be intended as long-term enterprises and may or may not have the goal of growing larger. Or, they may be planned as only temporary ventures to provide income during periods of unemployment, or to supplement household finances for a particular purpose. **Lifestyle businesses** are microenterprises that permit their owners to follow a desired pattern of living, such as supporting college costs, or taking vacations. On the other hand, a microenterprise could make the difference between a family living in poverty and achieving economic stability.

> **lifestyle business** a microenterprise that permits its owners to follow a desired pattern of living, such as supporting college costs or taking vacations.

Mainstream Small Firms

These constitute the bulk of the small businesses in the public perception, in the press, and in community visibility. They are those that provide, or have the potential to provide, substantial profits for their owners. Mainstream small firms can be operated by founder-entrepreneurs, subsequent generations of family members, successor owners, or franchisees. They create many of the jobs noted by the U.S. Small Business Administration and employ the majority of American workers. Unlike

---

[16]U.S. Small Business Administration, Office of Advocacy, 2006.

[17]Association for Enterprise Opportunity, http://www.microenterpriseworks.org, March 16, 2009.

many microenterprises, they are established with continuity and permanent wealth building in mind, and are more often registered with local, state, and federal agencies.

Making the Business Work Personally and Professionally

What makes a business work is not solely profitability and cash flow, although these are of course necessary. Each entrepreneur has his or her own goals and objectives for the business. As an entrepreneur, it will be up to you to determine how you want your business to be, and to make it happen.

A Business Must Make a Profit to Stay in Business

profit amount of money remaining from the revenue of a business after all costs are deducted.

No matter how big or small, a business must make a **profit,** a positive monetary gain from operations after all expenses are subtracted. Most businesses do lose money initially, because entrepreneurs have to spend money to set up operations and advertise to attract customers. If the business cannot make a profit and generate cash, eventually the entrepreneur will be unable to pay the bills and will have to close.

Closing a business is nothing to be ashamed of, if you operate ethically and learn from the experience. In fact, most successful entrepreneurs open and close more than one business during their lives. If your venture is not making a profit after you have gotten it up and running, that is a signal that you may be in the wrong business. Closing it may be the smartest decision.

An entrepreneur may change businesses many times over a lifetime, in response to changing competition and consumer needs.

Profit Is the Sign That the Entrepreneur Is Adding Value

Performance Objective 4 ▷

Explain how profit works as a signal to the entrepreneur.

Profit is the sign that an entrepreneur has added value to the scarce resources he or she is using. Debbi Fields added value to resources by creating something that people were willing to buy for a price that gave her a profit. In contrast, not making a profit is a sign that the entrepreneur is not using resources very well and is not adding value to them.

Profit Results from the Entrepreneur's Choices

An entrepreneur's choices directly affect how much profit the business makes. For example, suppose, like Debbi Fields, you have a business selling homemade cookies. You might decide one week to buy margarine instead of butter because it is cheaper, even though the cookies may not taste as good made with margarine. This type of choice is called a **trade-off.** You are giving up one thing (taste) for another (lower costs).

trade-off the act of giving up one thing for another.

If your customers do not notice the change and continue to buy your cookies, you have made a good decision. You have conserved a resource (money) and increased your profit by lowering your costs. The increase in profit confirms that you have made the right choice.

If your customers notice the change and stop buying your cookies, your profit will decrease. The decrease in profit signals that you have made a bad choice. The following week you should probably go back to butter. The profit signal taught you that your customers were dissatisfied and the trade-off was not worth it. Every choice an entrepreneur makes is a trade-off.

Seven Rules for Building a Successful Business

Russell Simmons and Rick Rubin were successful in creating Def Jam because they instinctively applied the seven basic rules of building a flourishing business:

1. *Recognize an opportunity.* Simmons believed that rap music was an untapped business opportunity.
2. *Evaluate it with critical thinking.* He tested his idea by promoting concerts and observing consumer reaction.
3. *Build a team.* Simmons formed a partnership with Rubin.
4. *Write.* Simmons and Rubin created a realistic business plan.
5. *Gather resources.* Simmons and Rubin pooled their $5,000.
6. *Decide ownership.* Simmons and Rubin formed a legal partnership.
7. *Create wealth.*

The Team Approach

Let's take a closer look at step 3: Build a Team. Alone, neither Simmons nor Rubin had enough money to launch a record label, but together they were able to do it. Their business was also helped by the fact that each knew different artists and had different contacts in the recording industry.

Everyone you know is a potential business-formation opportunity. Your friends or family members may have skills, equipment, or contacts that would make them valuable business partners. Perhaps you very much want to start a Web site design business because you know of companies in your community that want to put up Web sites. You are a graphic artist but you do not know how to use Web site development programs. If you have a friend who has that knowledge, you might start a business together. Or maybe you would like to start a DJ business, but you only have one turntable or laptop computer. If you form the business with a friend, you can pool equipment. (When forming a business team, organize the venture so that everyone involved shares in the ownership and profits. People work much better when they are working for themselves.) Just be careful of jumping into business relationships with undue haste.

Entrepreneurial Wisdom . . .

Build Your Brain

Becoming a successful entrepreneur is all about making connections, those *Aha!* moments when you realize what your business opportunity is, or when you figure out how to do something better than the competition. Research indicates that mental exercise will help your brain become better at making such connections. Many cutting-edge scientists recognize the value of activities that encourage brain cells to make new connections. Robotics engineer Hugo de Garis, who has worked on such projects as building an artificial brain for an artificial cat, plays classical piano every day before he sits down at the computer. "This helps to build my own brain," he told the *New York Times.*[18] Arnold Scheibel, head of the University of California–Los Angeles Brain Research Institute, suggests the following brain-builders:

- Solve puzzles.
- Play a musical instrument.
- Fix something; learn to repair cars or electrical equipment.
- Create art; write poetry, paint, or sculpt.
- Dance.
- Make friends with people who like to have interesting conversations.

[18]Nicholas D. Kristof, "Robokitty," *New York Times*, August 1, 1999.

Now carry this idea a step further. Every person you meet is a potential contact for your business, just as you may be a valuable contact for theirs. Thinking this way will encourage you to *network*, or exchange valuable information and contacts with other businesspeople. Keep your business cards on you at all times and truly view every individual you meet as an opportunity for your business. Remember, though, that networking is a two-way street. See how you can help the people you meet rather than focusing only on how they can help you. The results can be nothing short of amazing.

Chapter Summary

Now that you have studied this chapter, you can do the following:

1. Explain what entrepreneurs do.
   - Entrepreneurs start their own businesses and work for themselves.
   - Entrepreneurs recognize opportunities to start businesses that other people may not have noticed.
   - Entrepreneurs shift economic resources from an area of lower productivity into an area of higher productivity and greater yield. By doing this, they add value to scarce resources.
2. Describe how free enterprise economies work and how entrepreneurs fit into them.
   - The free enterprise system is based on voluntary exchange. Voluntary exchange is a trade between two parties who agree to exchange money for a product or service. Both parties agree to the trade because each benefits from it.
   - The free enterprise system encourages entrepreneurs who use resources efficiently to satisfy consumer needs by rewarding them with profit.
3. Find and evaluate opportunities to start your own business.
   - The five roots of opportunity are:
     1. Problems that your business can solve.
     2. Changes in laws, situations, or trends.
     3. Inventions of totally new products or services.
     4. Competition. (If you can find a way to beat the competition on price, location, quality, reputation, reliability, or speed, you can create a very successful business with an existing product or service.)
     5. Technological advances. (Scientists may invent new technology, but entrepreneurs figure out how to sell it.)
4. Explain how profit works as a signal to the entrepreneur.
   - Profit is the sign that an entrepreneur has added value to the scarce resources he or she is using.
   - Not making a profit is a sign that the entrepreneur is not using resources well and is not adding value to them.
5. A business opportunity is an idea plus these three characteristics:
   - It is attractive to customers.
   - It will work in your business environment.
   - It can be executed in the window of opportunity that exists.

6. Use cost/benefit analysis to make decisions.
   * Cost/benefit analysis is the process of comparing costs and benefits in order to make a good decision.
   * Cost/benefit analysis can be inaccurate unless you take into account opportunity cost. This is the cost of missing your next-best investment.
7. Use SWOT analysis to evaluate a business opportunity.
   * Strengths: All of the capabilities and positive points that the entrepreneur has, from experience to contacts. These are internal to the organization.
   * Weaknesses: All of the negatives that the entrepreneur faces, such as lack of capital or training, or failure to set up a workable accounting system. These are internal to the organization.
   * Opportunities: Any positive external event or circumstance (including lucky breaks) that can help the entrepreneur get ahead of the competition.
   * Threats: Any external factor, event, or circumstance that can harm the business—such as competitors, legal issues, or a declining economy.

Key Terms

acquisition	microenterprise
capital	opportunity cost
capitalism	product
commission	profit
cost/benefit analysis	salary
dividend	service
due diligence	social entrepreneurship
entrepreneur	strategy
franchise	trade-off
free enterprise system	venture philanthropy
gazelle	voluntary exchange
green entrepreneurship	wage
lifestyle business	

Entrepreneurship Portfolio

Critical Thinking Exercises

1. What would be the best thing about owning your own business? What would be the worst?
2. Identify three nonfinancial benefits of entrepreneurship that might be important to you. Write a paragraph about each.
3. If you were to start a business, what would be your opportunity cost? In other words, what is the next-best use of your time? How much money could you make working at a job instead? The answer to this question will give you a rough idea of how to value your time when you start a business and have to figure out how much to pay yourself.
4. Describe an idea that you have for a business. Explain how it could satisfy a consumer need.
5. Explain how a business opportunity differs from a business idea.
6. Give an example of a change that has occurred or is about to occur in your area/neighborhood. Discuss any business opportunities this change might create.
7. List five business opportunities in your area/neighborhood and the need(s) each would satisfy. Note whether the opportunity you describe is internal, external, or a mix.

Key Concept Questions

1. Define small business.
2. Explain how profit works as a signal to the entrepreneur.
3. Do you agree that it will probably take about three months for your business to start earning a profit? Why or why not? If not, how long do you expect it to take, and why?
4. Describe three things you have learned about capitalism.
5. Visit the U.S. Small Business Administration for brochures and other material. Find an office in your area or go to http://ww.sba.gov.

Application Exercises

Have a conversation with a friend or relative. Ask this person to tell you about the things he or she finds frustrating in the area/neighborhood. Write down the complaints.

Step 1:   Generate at least three business opportunities from the conversation.

Step 2:   Use the checklists below to evaluate your three business ideas as opportunities.

Step 3:   Choose the best of the business opportunities and write a SWOT analysis for it.

Step 4:   Create a cost/benefit analysis for starting this business. Use the analysis to explain why you would or would not actually start it.

Business Idea 1 _____	Critical Evaluation	
Would it be attractive to potential customers?	Yes _____	No _____
Would it work in your business environment?	Yes _____	No _____
Is there a window of opportunity?	Yes _____	No _____
Do you have the skills and resources to create this business?	Yes _____	No _____
If you do not have the skills and resources to create this business, do you know someone who does and might want to create the business with you?	Yes _____	No _____
Business Idea 2 _____	**Critical Evaluation**	
Would it be attractive to potential customers?	Yes _____	No _____
Would it work in your business environment?	Yes _____	No _____
Is there a window of opportunity?	Yes _____	No _____
Do you have the skills and resources to create this business?	Yes _____	No _____
If you do not have the skills and resources to create this business, do you know someone who does and might want to create the business with you?	Yes _____	No _____
Business Idea 3 _____	**Critical Evaluation**	
Would it be attractive to potential customers?	Yes _____	No _____
Would it work in your business environment?	Yes _____	No _____
Is there a window of opportunity?	Yes _____	No _____
Do you have the skills and resources to create this business?	Yes _____	No _____
If you do not have the skills and resources to create this business, do you know someone who does and might want to create the business with you?	Yes _____	No _____

Exploring Your Community

Interview an entrepreneur in your community. Entrepreneurs are busy people, but most are willing to spend time talking with someone who is interested in what they are doing. Meeting over a meal might be the most efficient use of the entrepreneur's time. Before the interview, brainstorm 10 questions in the following four categories. If you can, tape the interview with the entrepreneur's permission. After the interview, be sure to write a thank-you note.

1. *Information gathering.* Open the interview with questions about the entrepreneur's family (any other entrepreneurs in it?) and educational and work background.
2. *About the business.* Next, ask questions about how the business was started. How did the entrepreneur recognize an opportunity and develop it?
3. *Running the business.* Ask about the problems that came up as the business got underway and how they were solved.
4. *Reflection.* Ask the entrepreneur to reflect. What advice would he or she give to an aspiring entrepreneur? Has running a business been rewarding?

Exploring Online

Visit an Internet search engine, such as http://www.google.com, http://www.yahoo.com, http://www.dogpile.com, http://www.AltaVista.com, http://www.BING.com, or http://www.MSN.com. Search for one of the following sets of terms: business ideas, businesses for sale, or franchise opportunities. For the search that you selected, answer (1) which search engine and term was used, and (2) the number of matches ("hits"). Next, find a site that looks promising and answer these questions:

1. What is the Web site (URL and name)?
2. Who is sponsoring the Web site?
3. Is the Web site selling a product or information (as a primary function, not through banner ads)? If so, what?
4. Identify three businesses or ideas from the site, and state why they might, or might not, be viable opportunities.

| # Craigslist: Organic Entrepreneurial Opportunity

Craig Newmark's e-mail blasts to friends and co-workers morphed into one of the most popular sites on the Internet. Newmark was not planning to start a business at all when he began sending out e-mail blasts about San Francisco-area events. In 1995, Newmark was a software engineer at Schwab and sent the e-mails for fun. The number of people on the list continued to grow until e-mail blasts were no longer viable, due to the number of recipients.

In 1999, Newmark moved into the full-time role of operating a start-up venture based on sending out lists by e-mail. Even the name was user-driven. Newmark had another name in mind, but people had been calling the blasts Craig's List, and the name stuck. Over time, Newmark developed a Web-based site that connected people looking for apartments, jobs, relationships, and more.

Craigslist generated an estimated $122 million in revenues in 2010 with profits of $88 to $99 million, according to an AIM Group report. It generates in excess of 20 billion page views and has approximately 50 million unique visitors monthly. Driven by user demand, Craigslist has over 700 local sites in 70 countries. Yet, the company continues to operate out of a previously residential building in the Inner Sunset neighborhood of San Francisco.

Craig Newmark defies the rules of online business. Craigslist only charges fees for brokered apartment listings in New York City, job advertisements in 18 cities, and ads in its adult services category. The company relies upon word-of-mouth for advertising and trust for content. The site itself is relatively simple from a user perspective, consciously avoiding many of the present-day Web-design dictates.

Newmark himself continues to serve as the company's customer service representative. There is a team of about 30 that handles the rest of the company roles. In today's world, Craigslist could command considerably greater revenues

(NetPhotos/Alamy)

and have even greater visibility, but Newmark set his own goals early on, and is sticking by them.

Case Study Analysis

1. What unmet needs of the customer, or conditions in the apartment hunting and job search processes, contributed to the success of Craigslist?

2. Do you think Craig Newmark thought through the Craigslist idea well enough before he launched the business?

3. How is Newmark's personality reflected in his company?

4. Is there a future for Craigslist? What might that future look like?

Case Sources

Craigslist, http://www.craigslist.org, March 11, 2011.

Craigslist.org site profile on *Compete*, http://site-analytics.compete.com/craigslist.org, March 11, 2011.

Peter Zollman, "Craigslist Revenue, Profits Soar," AIM Group blog, http://aimgroup.com/blog/2010/04/30/craigslist-revenue-profits-soar/, April 30, 2010.

Case Study | Extreme Entrepreneurship

Extreme Entrepreneurship Education LLC

Michael Simmons and Sheena Lindahl are 2005 New York University graduates who found their calling in entrepreneurship education. Michael, a management and marketing major, and Sheena, who majored in communication studies, formed Extreme Entrepreneurship Education (EEE) as a limited liability company in 2003, headquartered in New York City. However, the story really began a number of years earlier, when Michael was 16.

Michael Simmons and Sheena Lindahl.
(Extreme Entrepreneurship Education Corporation)

Using the Internet to Start a Business

While attending high school, Michael and his friend, Calvin Newport, decided to start their own Web development company, Princeton Web Solutions (PWS). For $80, they created their own Web site and submitted it to the online search engines. Only a few weeks later, they were hired to do their first project, for $1,000.

With each new commission, the young men's confidence grew. They were able to make a profit and still stay competitive in the market by charging $75 per hour, about half the price of other Web developers. The success of PWS led to public recognition in 2000, when *YoungBiz Magazine* rated the business as the number one youth-run Web development company in the United States.

After the dot-com market collapsed, many of PWS's potential clients disappeared. Michael used an online class scholarship, which he had won from the National Foundation for Teaching Entrepreneurship (NFTE)—now the Network for Teaching Entrepreneurship—to learn more about running a business. The course was not only extremely valuable, it helped him overcome his fear of public speaking.

Sharing a Vision for Success

In college, Michael was inspired to write a book that he called *The Student Success Manifesto*. It was intended to help students think in a whole new way, while taking action toward reaching their goals. He explains, "I decided to write the book at the end of my freshman year when I realized, after my experience as an entrepreneur, that I had knowledge which could help my peers find passion, purpose, and prosperity in their own lives,"[19]

Through the Liberty Partnerships Program, established by the New York State Education Department to help prevent young people from dropping out of high school, Michael also got involved in teaching inner-city high school students about entrepreneurship. Michael remembers, "I had certain perceptions going in, that were changed after I really experienced the influence [of the program] in an environment that was very different from the one I was raised in."[20]

Attending NYU at the same time as Michael, Sheena shared his entrepreneurial mindset. Sheena became financially independent from her parents at the age of 17, and paid her own way through college. Sheena honed her entrepreneurial and educational skills while working at GreenHills Ventures, a venture capital firm, and teaching at Project R.E.A.D., a nonprofit organization that seeks to raise the reading skills of inner-city elementary school children.

Together, Michael and Sheena founded the EEE, which was dedicated to helping college students realize their dreams through entrepreneurship. They also formed a life partnership as husband and wife and as parents.

Making a Strategic Shift

At first, Michael and Sheena had intended to be publishers of entrepreneurial content. After publishing *The Student Success Manifesto*, they believed they were moving in the right direction. The profit per book unit was good, but they

[19]Kate Tobin, "NYU Student Writes Book For Entrepreneur Hopefuls," http://www.extremetour.org/press/youngmoney.html, April 2009.

[20]Ibid.

needed to sell a lot of units in order to make publishing profitable enough to support them full time.

To sell more books, Michael and Sheena began seeking bulk purchases from schools and other youth organizations. One marketing strategy included talking to groups of students when the schools purchased books. This tactic helped Michael and Sheena to realize that people would pay them to speak, whether books were purchased or not. So, they started charging for their speaking appearances.

One thing led to another. As more and more students expressed appreciation for the message Michael and Sheena shared, the two of them explored ways to also include the stories of other young, successful entrepreneurs. Many ideas were discussed and rejected, but eventually the Extreme Entrepreneurship Tour (EET) was launched in 2006.

The EET was the first national collegiate entrepreneur tour in which students from all academic disciplines participated in half-day events, held on campus. A tour event can also be customized for a high school audience or local community members. A tour will focus on one of two themes: entrepreneurship or "dream action" (the entrepreneurial mindset). The content for a particular tour event can be customized to fit either theme.

Each tour event includes exhibits, a successful young entrepreneur as the keynote speaker, a workshop, speed networking, and a panel discussion with local entrepreneurs. An example of a typical event's program can be seen on the EET Web site.[21]

Operating the Tour

Running the tour involves a considerable investment of financial resources. For example, a customized 31-foot Winnebago transports the speakers and tour manager, EET banners, technical equipment, and registration setup equipment. For each event, there are at least three speakers—two of which are not EET employees—for whom there are expenses, including travel. EET provides pre-event support to local organizers, including conference calls and a point person to answer any questions.

Event organizers can visit the Web site to find templates for promotional posters and flyers, best practice information for participation, and information for pre-event setup. The

Extreme Entrepreneurship tour bus.
(Extreme Entrepreneurship Education Corporation)

Type	Who	Content	Time
Event Introduction	EET & School Representative	Intro to event and entrepreneurship, speakers, and corporate partners.	3:00 – 3:15 p.m.
Inspirational Keynote 1	Successful Young Entrepreneur	"How they did it" story with lessons.	3:15 – 3:45 p.m.
Workshop	EET Workshop, Facilitator, and Entrepreneur	Dream/idea creation with action plan and accountability.	3:45 – 4:45 p.m.
Networking Break / Exhibits			4:45 – 5:00 p.m.
Inspirational Keynote 2	Successful Young Entrepreneur	"How they did it" story with lessons learned.	5:00 – 5:30 p.m.
Speed Networking		Attendees share their ideas with each other and partner up.	5:30 – 5:45 p.m.
Networking Break / Exhibits			5:45 – 6:00 p.m.
Extreme Entrepreneurship Panel	EET Moderator, Students & Alumni, and Entrepreneurs	Panelists choose one to two questions to discuss and open up for other questions.	6:00 – 7:00 p.m.

schools are responsible for the promotion, the event's venue, refreshments, and the like. EET develops and prints an event program/workbook with speaker biographies, one semester at a time.

[21]http://www.extremetour.org/about/event-format.php, April 2009.

A tour event is made financially possible through one or more sponsors, which may include local companies and economic/workforce development organizations. In turn, student body participation and media coverage benefit the event sponsors by allowing them to connect with hundreds or even thousands of students in a positive way. Opportunities to create company awareness, foster brand or product loyalty, and promote employee recruiting are some of the benefits sponsors can reap from a tour event.

Since the EET was started in 2006, over 200 events have been held, and that number keeps growing. Aside from Michael and Sheena and two other full-time employees, the staff has been mostly contractual. Revenues are based on fees charged to the host institution or organization and event sponsorship.

The tour has won recognition for its excellence by receiving Northern Michigan University's 2007–2008 Program of the Year Award, and the 2008 Innovation Award from the National Association of Development Organizations. In addition, Michael and Sheena were listed in *BusinessWeek's* 25 Under 25 list in 2006 and *Inc. Magazine's* 30 Under 30 list in 2011.

Following Up Events with Action

After an EET event, students are able to continue benefiting from the experience by subscribing to the Extreme Entrepreneurship Virtual Speaker Series and using JourneyPage, a virtual incubator for launching a business.

The Virtual Speaker Series provides monthly interactive, live, virtual broadcasts, making it possible for organizations to bring dry topics to life, bring top-notch, hard-to-get national speakers into their region, offer an easily organized speaker series, and provide co-curricular programming for distance-learning students. Each broadcast is archived with notes and teaching materials. Every month, one young entrepreneur speaker is interviewed live and in-depth for one and a half hours on a topic relevant to starting a business or using the entrepreneurial mindset.

JourneyPage is made up of tools and information that encourage personal accountability, allow students to continue relationships formed at a tour event, and provide access to entrepreneurial mentors. For example, JourneyPage has a Web-based accountability tool that helps students reduce procrastination and maintain motivation and momentum. This is facilitated by goal tracking, and partnering with other students who have similar aspirations. The accountability tool works in the following ways:

- Each member has an accountability partner.
- Every day, members enter their three most important business-related goals for that day.
- At the end of a day, a goal may be marked as completed or it can be reset or delayed.
- Weekly scores are computed, based on goal completion. This data is tracked, so that accountability partners and other friends using JourneyPage can see a member's progress.
- Accountability partners and friends can offer feedback, encouragement, and coaching to their fellow members.

In addition to the accountability tool, JourneyPage provides content such as articles, audio, and video segments from tour keynote speakers, business and legal templates, resource lists, and a searchable database. Although JourneyPage is available for personal use, it can also be licensed by schools and development centers/agencies.

Keeping the Business on Track

In order to stay on course and be successful, Michael and Sheena evaluate key performance indicators on a regular basis. Weekly measures center on budget versus actual performance. Calculations are primarily the number of students who attend the event, the student and host ratings of the event, and the budget performance. On a semester basis, the repeat customer percentage, the referral rate, the number of events, and the level of revenues are critical. Sheena explains, "We measure what is meaningful to our growth and what we can measure given our time and financial resource capacity."

Michael and Sheena also formed a high-powered advisory board in 2007 that meets to review financial performance and work on specific issues. Sheena and Michael continue to keep their eyes on the key performance indicators, so that they can continue to bring the EET to colleges and universities nationwide.

Looking Back at the Planning Process

Some ideas that were considered but rejected included creating young entrepreneur book lines and applying the entrepreneurial mindset to various career book lines. However, looking back on how the EET evolved, Sheena points out that it was the gradual accumulation of small actions that put them in the position to create the tour, not long sessions of brainstorming. The building of relationships with people in their market enabled Sheena and Michael to understand their customers' needs and wants. The tour business model best met those needs.

To gauge potential costs of running the tour, Michael and Sheena used the "economics of one unit," and they tested their idea in the marketplace to find out whether they could sell it. In other words, they started slowly, with a scaled-down version of the program. For example, in the EET's first year, they did not use a tour bus. Based on her experience, Sheena suggests, "If you can try the business at some level without a huge investment, essentially doing mini-tests, you can see if things are working without taking a sizeable risk."

Over the years, Michael and Sheena have created many formal business plans and executive summaries for competitions to raise money. Now, they mostly use PowerPoint presentation slides to help them build their internal business strategies. This less formal approach is simpler, makes it easy to adjust their plans, but still helps ensure that all the angles are considered.

Balancing Business and Family

Michael and Sheena find working together enjoyable. However, they do set limits and expectations to help minimize the stress of the business on their relationship. Specific times are set aside for work, family, and personal time. They also believe in the importance of communication. For example, if they are going out to dinner, they agree beforehand whether it will be a dinner to discuss business or just time to be together and have fun.

Investing in Yourself

When asked about the best way for college students to make more money, Michael replies, "I would definitely recommend that students invest their money in themselves and not in nearsighted whimsical things that they won't have around, won't help them succeed, tomorrow or ten years from now. When you invest the money you make in yourself, you receive compound interest and incredible returns."[22]

Case Study Analysis

1. Prior to starting the EET, what types of things did Michael and Sheena do to help themselves build entrepreneurial knowledge/skills?
2. What motivated Michael and Sheena to start the EET?
3. How did Michael and Sheena determine that the EET was a sound idea? Did they use a feasibility analysis? What ideas did they discard before deciding on the EET?
4. What are the key messages that the EET delivers to prospective entrepreneurs?
5. Is the EET a business model that would be conducive to franchising? Why or why not?
6. EET is a family business. How do Michael and Sheena address the issues of balancing the demands of the business with those of the family?

Case Sources

Extreme Entrepreneurship Education Corporation, http://www.extremee.org, August 4, 2010.

Extreme Entrepreneurship Tour, http://www.extremetour.org, August 4, 2010.

Extreme Entrepreneurship Virtual Speaker Series, http://virtualspeakerseries.org/

JourneyPage, http://journeypage.com/.

Liberty Partnerships Program, http://www.highered.nysed.gov/kiap/precoll/lpp/, August 4, 2010. Used by permission of Extreme Entrepreneurship Education LLC.

---

[22]Kate Tobin, "NYU Student Writes Book for Entrepreneur Hopefuls," http://www.extremetour.org/press/youngmoney.html, April 2009.

THE BUSINESS PLAN: ROAD MAP TO SUCCESS

G reat business ideas can grow into great businesses, or they can wither away from neglect or unfavorable circumstances. One thing that successful businesses have in common is a sound idea and an entrepreneur who has a plan for turning the idea into reality.

Frank Jao worked as a translator for the American military during the war in Vietnam, and when Saigon fell in 1975, he and his wife, Kathy, were flown out of the country to Camp Pendleton, California.[1] They had the clothes on their backs and about 20 dollars.

Frank got a job selling vacuum cleaners door to door within 48 hours of arriving in California. He also met with a community college counselor who discovered that Frank had sold heavy equipment in Vietnam. The counselor suggested that, because such equipment was a big-ticket item with a long sales cycle, perhaps Frank should try real estate—which was also a big-ticket item with a long sales cycle.

He joined a firm that had commercial and residential divisions and was assigned to work in residential sales. Frank observed that the agents working on the commercial side were making more money than those in his group, so he set a goal to earn the right to move to the commercial division. In 1979, he made a sale that brought a commission of $350,000 that he and Kathy used to purchase a parcel of raw land in Westminster, California.

Frank dreamed of building and operating a shopping area that would provide a place for the Vietnamese community to buy and sell the types of products and services they enjoyed in their native land. This dream was realized as the Asian Garden Mall. It is a modern indoor mall that stands at the center of what is known in Orange County as Little Saigon. Frank has done so much for this community that the city leaders gave him his own exit on the busy Interstate 405 freeway.

Was it easy to parlay the $350,000 into Asian Garden? No. Remember that Frank put all his cash into the raw land. Next, he had to convince a banker to loan him the $3 million he needed to build on the land. The banker told Frank that to get a loan he must bring back a feasibility study and a loan package. In 1979, there was no Internet on which to find free business-plan and feasibility-analysis templates—and he did not have enough money to pay for a professionally prepared loan package with a business plan.

That night after Frank met with the loan officer, when the bank was closed and the parking lot dark, he climbed into the bank dumpster, in which he found several loan packages (privacy rules were different in 1979). He figured that, because they were in the trash, no one would miss them. Using these as guides, he and Kathy created a loan package. Three weeks after his first meeting with a commercial lender, Frank was back with a complete loan package, and that same banker made the $3-million loan.

Because of Frank and Kathy's creativity, courage, and persistence over the years, their company, Bridgecreek, has developed more than 2 million square feet of retail, condo, and apartment space. It owns and manages 1.5 million square feet of space in Southern California and employs 18 people.

Performance Objectives

1. Know what a feasibility analysis is and when to create one.
2. Know what a business plan is and how to describe it.
3. Explain the various purposes of a business plan and the audience for each.
4. Understand the components of a business plan.
5. Be able to demonstrate proper development and formatting of a business plan.

---

[1]Original case prepared by Hattie Bryant, creator of *Small Business School*, a television series made for PBS and Voice of America, http://SmallBusinessSchool.org.

Feasibility Analysis: Will My Idea Work?

The time and energy involved in generating and exploring business ideas can be extensive, with the SBA reporting that, for many entrepreneurs, the process can take years. With that sort of extensive investment, it is an advantage to filter out the ideas that are viable from those that are not. A **feasibility analysis** will assist in making the go/no go decision based upon a close examination of product/service, market, industry, and financial data in a sufficient degree of detail to ensure confidence in the results. This is an excellent precursor to committing the time and resources to planning the implementation of the business and then presenting it for financing after the creation of a comprehensive business plan. The feasibility analysis essentially tests a business concept for viability in three areas:

1. product and/or service feasibility,
2. market and industry feasibility, and
3. financial feasibility.

This study presupposes the business's desirability and that you are interested in this segment of the industry.

Analyzing Product and/or Service Feasibility

Entrepreneurs are often described as committed to their business idea. They take on an almost religious zeal and essentially fall in love with the concept of the product or service, creating a fantasy of what the business will be. Conducting a product or service feasibility analysis serves the dual purpose of determining whether realization of the product or delivery of the service is possible at a profit, and whether customer demand is sufficient. Without affirmative answers to both these queries, success will be elusive at best.

A product or service is only worthwhile pursuing if it can be produced and delivered at a profit in an ongoing manner. For example, scientists develop innovative technologies in their laboratories that can significantly outperform any technology that is commercially available. Some entrepreneurs may want to introduce products that embody the next big technology, and then move down the path toward securing financing and establishing marketing strategies, only to find that the production cost would lead to an unreasonable retail price or the volume of production would be too low to serve the target market. In order to avoid such unwelcome surprises, you can create the production design for your product and create a working model, called a *prototype*, fabricated for testing by laboratories and prospective customers. Services can also be tested for timeliness and cost of delivery.

Determining whether a product appeals to prospective customers, and whether the appeal will translate into

Prototype.
(Patrick Breig/Shutterstock.com)

sales, will be vital to assessing feasibility. Subsequent chapters of this text will address specific sources of information that you can use to determine feasibility. These sources can be direct from the targeted customer base (primary), or through already existing research (secondary).

It is important to perform this feasibility study in order to avoid wasting valuable resources. An amazing product or innovative service would not necessarily translate into enough sales to sustain your business.

If the results of the feasibility analysis are negative, it is time to seriously rethink the product or service and its potential fit in the marketplace. Inconclusive or positive results on the product or service itself can be considered with the balance of the analysis to decide whether or not to proceed to the business-plan stage.

Analyzing Market and Industry Feasibility

Evaluating the targeted market and industry is essential to determining the viability of a business idea. Just as a seed will grow in fertile soil and wither away in barren earth, business ideas will take hold or fail based largely upon the market and industry in which they are launched. This segment of a feasibility analysis examines the attractiveness of the proposed industry and the opportunity to find strategic, defensible niches. Later chapters will provide good resources for conducting such analysis in greater detail.

One tool that is particularly valuable for industry feasibility analysis is the "five forces" model created by Michael Porter of Harvard University, which focuses on the competitive intensity of a market.[2] The model is designed to assess the overall industry competitiveness level in which closely related or similar products and/or services are sold. You would create a separate model for each proposed line of business. **Figure 2-1** provides a visual summary of the model.

Figure 2-1 *Porter's Five Forces Analysis*

Bargaining Power of Suppliers
(Supplier Power)

Threat of New Entrants
(Barriers to Entry)

Competitive Rivalry
among
Existing Firms

Threat of Substitute
Products

Bargaining Power of Customers
(Buyer Power)

---

[2]Adapted from Michael Porter, "How Competitive Forces Shape Strategy," *Harvard Business Review*, March/April 1979, pp. 137–145.

It is the interaction of the forces that creates the industry environment, and the attractiveness of participating in it, for a given business. The five industry forces identified by Porter are essentially:

1. competitor rivalry,
2. barriers to entry,
3. threat of substitutes,
4. supplier power, and
5. buyer power.[3]

Competitor Rivalry

The degree of rivalry among existing competitors is generally the strongest force in an industry. Some industries are more aggressive and competitive than others and you will want to know how your business would perform in the existing environment. For example, look at the number of Chinese restaurants in a large city or the competitive environment for power companies. Key aspects include the following.

Competitor Rivalry Factor	More Attractive to Entrant
Number of firms	More or fewer than five
Size of firms	Varied
Industry size/trend	Growing rapidly
Differentiation	Differentiation matters

Barriers to Entry

The threat of new entrants into an industry will be greater the larger the number of new entrants. As an entrant, you want the barriers to be low. As an established firm, you will want them to be high. Once you enter, you want the barriers to be high enough so that others cannot easily do the same. For example, it is relatively simple to start a landscaping company, so competitors will range from the neighborhood teenager with the family mower to larger companies with more expensive equipment and many employees.

Barriers to Entry Factor	More Attractive to Entrant
Capital requirements	Low for entry
Cost advantage	Not based upon company size
Economies of scale and/or scope	Minimal or absent
Switching costs	Low cost for changing suppliers
Brand loyalty	Customer resistance to change is low
Distribution channels	Established, but open
Public policies	Do not impede entry; may facilitate entry

Threat of Substitutes

The level of threat posed by alternative products and services that may provide benefits to industry customers matters to a potential entrant.

---

[3]Ibid.

For example, newspapers are closing because people increasingly receive their news and other information via electronic media. The retail movie-rental business had been seen as a threat to movie theaters; now those retail rental stores are vanishing with the advent of Netflix and pay-per-view movies.

Threat of Substitutes Factor	More Attractive to Entrant
Convenience	Not readily available
Substitute pricing	Prices not significantly lower
Supply of substitutes	Supply is uneven or limited
Switching costs	High cost for changing suppliers
Public policies	Substitution difficult or illegal

Supplier Power

The less power and control the suppliers of raw materials, components, and labor have over competitors, the more attractive the industry. Where there are a few powerful suppliers, new entrants will have little flexibility and control, both of which they need.

Supplier Power Factor	More Attractive to Entrant
Brand reputation	Not critical
Substitutes for supplies	Commodities, easy substitution
Switching costs	Relatively low
Impact of individual supplier on costs	Small portion of overall cost of finished product

Buyer Power

This force is similar to that of suppliers, but on the demand side. The larger and more diverse the customer base, the less dependent competitors in an industry will be on particular customers. Where customers are many, they can exert control to force prices downward, quality upward, and profit margins to the floor. Generally, the more a company is recognized for being the low-price leader in its industry, the more it applies pressure on its suppliers—with the power to get what it wants.

Buyer Power Factor	More Attractive to Entrant
Buyer size	Variable
Number of buyers	Large number of buyers
Product importance	Not a large part of the cost of finished goods
Delivery demands	Restricted geographic area
Switching costs	Relatively high
Product differentiation	More differentiation, fewer commodities
Information availability	Hard for customers to compare features and prices

As you examine the industry in relation to each business idea, it will become easier to determine the attractiveness of the industry. To further analyze the information, you can create a table listing each factor and assign a weight to each to come up with a quantitative analysis of the competitiveness in each industry.

Once you have selected the industry, it is time to find a defensible target or set of targets that you can claim and protect. You can design a successful focus strategy to foster business success if you have identified a niche of sufficient size to permit profitability. Identifying this niche and the potential growth of the segment is an excellent precursor to completing financial feasibility analysis.

Analyzing Financial Feasibility

Having completed the product or service feasibility analysis, and also one for the market and industry, you can complete the process by assessing the financial viability of your business idea. This analysis does not need to be detailed. At this point, addressing capital requirements, revenues, costs, and earnings should suffice.

The amount of start-up capital required will be a function of the size and type of organization you are starting. For example, a business that is bringing a patented technology to market by assembling components manufactured by other companies will have lower capital costs than one that manufactures and assembles the parts. Some businesses require very little start-up capital (less than $35,000), whereas others might require millions of dollars before making a single sale. A complete financial feasibility analysis will forecast and incorporate such factors.

An entrepreneur can assess feasibility better with a reasonable projection of revenues, based upon anticipated pricing and volume. Using industry-comparable data, particularly any growth statistics for similar firms, can help to make such estimates valid. There is often a temptation to be either overly optimistic or overly pessimistic at this stage, so tempering these extremes with solid data can be significant.

Finally, cost factors should be calculated and returns on investment projected. The earlier analysis of the product or service viability feeds directly into this calculation. By understanding projected costs and offsetting them against revenues, profit projections are possible. With these estimates in hand, you can evaluate the return on the capital invested to make a go/no go decision.

The outcome of the feasibility analysis will show whether the business idea can be a profitable venture with a sufficiently large return on investment. This is a step in the filtering and selection process that narrows and focuses the business idea so that it can be further developed in a business plan or set aside for a stronger concept.

What Is a Business Plan?

business plan a document that thoroughly explains a business idea and how it will be carried out.

By the time you complete this book, you will have written a **business plan** that you can use to design, start, and operate your own venture. A business plan is a document that thoroughly explains a business idea and how it will be carried out. The plan should include the following:

- the story of what the business is and will be,
- all costs and a marketing plan,
- description of how the business will be financed, and
- an estimate of projected earnings.

The foremost reason to write a business plan is to organize your thoughts *before* starting a business. Many of the entrepreneurs mentioned in this book wrote a business plan before they made a single sale. However, many, if not most, businesses are started based upon a concept in the founder's head. Writing a business plan is a daunting and time-consuming process. Even though creating a plan is a best practice, many entrepreneurs do not elect to do so, often to their detriment. In fact, a well-written plan will guide you every step of the way as you develop your business.

Why Do You Need a Business Plan?

Whether you are planning a microenterprise with virtually no start-up costs, or a multimillion-dollar venture, you will find a business plan an essential tool. No serious professional investor will agree even to see you unless you have put together a comprehensive, convincing business plan. A plan can also help you determine on paper whether your business is viable before you make mistakes in the real world, allowing you to adjust accordingly. It will force you to analyze markets and opportunities in realistic terms before you attempt to secure financing. The business plan is vital to current and proposed businesses as a guide to operations and direction, which can be modified as the organization evolves.

◀ **Performance Objective 2**
Know what a business plan is and how to describe it.

Writing a Business Plan Early Will Save You Time and Money

While you work on your plan, you will also be figuring out how to make your business successful. Before you serve your first customer, you will have answered every question you can think of. How much should you charge for your product or service? What exactly *is* your product or service? What is one unit of sale? What will your costs be? How are you going to market your product or service? How and where will you sell it? Figuring all this out in advance will save you time and money.

◀ **Performance Objective 3**
Explain the various purposes of a business plan and the audience for each

The business plan can be a front line of defense against a poor idea. In fact, according to entrepreneurial expert Joseph Mancuso, "If your proposed venture is marginal at best, the business plan will show you why and may help you avoid paying the high tuition of business failure. It is far cheaper not to begin an ill-fated business than to learn by experience what your business plan could have taught you at a cost of several hours of concentrated work."[4]

If you start your business without a plan, these kinds of questions can overwhelm you. By the time you have completed the exercises in this book, though, you will have answers, and you will be able to chart a road map for your own business! You can use the BIZ Builder online tools to create a professional plan, and a Microsoft PowerPoint presentation that will emphasize the highlights of your strategy.

Writing a business plan will allow you to address all angles of your business idea.
(George Doyle/Stockbyte)

[4]Joseph R. Mancuso, *How to Write a Winning Business Plan* (Englewood Cliffs, NJ: Prentice-Hall, 1985), p. 44.

There are several software packages on the market designed to help you write a business plan, including:

- Tim Berry's Business Plan Pro® (Palo Alto Software, http://www.BusinessPlanPro.com). There is also a Social Enterprise Edition available.
- Linda Pinson's Automate Your Business Plan for Windows (Out of Your Mind and into the Marketplace, http://business-plan.com/automate.html).
- Biz Plan Builder (JIAN, http://www.BizPlanBuilder.com).
- Business PlanMaker Professional (Individual Software, Inc., http://www.individualsoftware.com).

These software packages and their sample business plans will provide guidance in developing your own unique design. Be wary of creating a cookie-cutter plan and falling into the trap of using the data and financial projections of sample plans. In the end, a business plan must be the creation of the individual who will operate the business.

In addition, by using the Web, you can save some time and money by presenting your business plan to several investors at a time, no matter where they are located. With a presentation program like PowerPoint, you can broadcast your presentation in real time over the Web or send it electronically to interested parties. With proper technology, you can also include audio to accompany the presentation. Whereas it is always preferable to make a presentation in person, this can be an effective way to present your business plan to investors at their convenience. Remember, though, that proper nondisclosure agreements are an absolute necessity because business plans are the valued property of their developers.

Your Business Plan Is the Key to Raising Capital

As mentioned, bankers and other potential investors will refuse to see an entrepreneur who does not have a business plan. You may have a brilliant idea, but if it is not written out, people will be extremely unlikely to invest in your business or loan you money.

A well-written plan will show investors that you have carefully thought through how you intend to make your business profitable. The more detail you offer investors about how their money will be used, the more willing they will be to invest. The financial projections should be realistic and attainable. Your plan should be so thoughtful and well written that the only question it raises in an investor's mind is, "How much can I invest?"

The Business Plan Is an Operations Guide

Whether or not you need to raise capital, a business plan can be a vital tool for guiding the internal operations of your business. Business owners and managers increase the probability of success by taking the business plans formed in their heads and committing them to paper. The transition may be bumpy, because the process of writing a coherent plan will require answering difficult questions. However, the process of developing the plan will generate an increased clarity of vision, mission, and goals for the entire team. With your business plan as your benchmarking tool, you can compare your company's progress to your stated plan. You can also use the business plan as a point of reference when it seems you are going off track or becoming distracted from your goals.

The presence of financial and operational goals and measures, as well as mission and vision statements, can feed a drive for success and motivate a team to excellence.

Business Plan Components

As you begin a new enterprise, you can find a seemingly endless variety of problems to address and questions to answer. Such a situation could quickly overwhelm you if you don't have a plan. However, by the time you have worked through all of the steps of a business plan, you will have answers. You will develop a love for the business, rather than being in love with the *idea* of the business and having unrealistic expectations. The order of the components of a plan can vary somewhat, but there are elements common to all. An outline of one kind of business plan is illustrated in **Exhibit 2-1.**

◄ **Performance Objective 4**
Understand the components of a business plan.

Exhibit 2-1 *Business Plan Outline*
Cover Page
Table of Contents
1.0 Executive Summary
2.0 Mission, Vision, and Culture
3.0 Company Description
4.0 Opportunity Analysis and Research
4.1 Industry Analysis
4.2 Environmental Analysis
4.3 Competitive Analysis
5.0 Marketing Strategy and Plan
5.1 Products/Services
5.2 Pricing
5.3 Promotion
5.4 Place
6.0 Management and Operations
6.1 Management Team
6.2 Research and Development
6.3 Physical Location
6.4 Facilities
6.5 Inventory, Production, and Quality Assurance
7.0 Financial Analysis and Projections
7.1 Sources and Uses of Capital
7.2 Cash Flow Projections
7.3 Balance Sheet Projections
7.4 Income Statement Projections
7.5 Breakeven Analysis
7.6 Ratio Analysis
7.7 Risks and Assumptions
8.0 Funding Request and Exit Strategy
8.1 Amount and Type of Funds Requested
8.2 Exit Plan
8.3 Milestones
Appendices
Résumés
Sample Promotional Materials
Product Illustrations/Diagrams
Detailed Financial Projections

Cover Page and Table of Contents

Begin the plan as you intend to continue it. The cover page should be professional, neat, and attractive. It should provide the name of the business and the principals, the date, contact information, and any confidentiality statement. The table of contents should be sufficiently detailed so an investor or manager can easily find a section, but not so detailed that it takes up pages of the plan.

Executive Summary: A Snapshot of Your Business

The executive summary has to be compelling and comprehensive. It may be the only part that many people will read. It is the hook that either reels in potential investors or loses their attention. If a reader doesn't fully understand the business concept and the purpose of the plan from the executive summary, the rest of the plan is likely to remain unread. Thus, the executive summary must encapsulate the story of the business clearly and concisely, propose the funding request, and inspire enthusiasm for the possibility of success.

This section should be written last and be limited to one or two pages. It should answer the who, what, when, why, and how questions for the business. Who will manage the business? What will it do and what is the owner asking for in the plan? When will the proposed plan be implemented? Why are you starting this business? How will the business succeed? Done well, the reader will have a light bulb moment and be eager to read the rest of the plan.

Mission and Culture: Your Dreams for the Organization

Each company has the opportunity to create its own unique mission, vision, and culture. The founding team can determine how to strategically use the company's competitive advantage to satisfy customers. Culture can be shaped according to the environment and the manner of treating employees, customers, and other stakeholders that the owner(s) model and support. The **mission** of your business, expressed in a mission statement, is a concise communication of strategy, including your *business definition* and *competitive advantage*. The function of a **mission statement** is to clarify what you are trying to do; it also can provide direction and motivation to those who are involved in the business.

A clearly stated mission statement not only tells your customers and employees what your business is about, but can also be a guide for every decision you make. It should capture your passion for the business and your commitment to satisfying your customers. To encourage clarity and conciseness, the mission statement should be limited to 40 or 50 words.

The **vision** for your business should be broader and more comprehensive, painting the big picture of what you want your organization to become. It is built on the core values and belief system of the founders of the organization. It is typically shorter than the mission statement, with a loftier perspective.

The **culture** of an organization, whether intentionally or unintentionally created, is largely defined by its leadership. You can build a culture for your company by making the beliefs, values, and behavioral norms explicit and intentional. A business's culture has many components, including norms for risk tolerance and innovation; orientation with respect to people, team formation and outcomes; attention to detail, and communication. Whether you want a free-thinking, aggressive company

mission a concise communication of strategy, including a business definition and explanation of competitive advantage.

mission statement a brief, written statement that informs customers and employees what an organization's goal is, and describes the strategy and tactics to meet it.

vision a broader and more comprehensive perspective on an organization than its mission; built on the core values and belief system of the organization.

culture the beliefs, values, and behavioral norms of an organization.

Global Impact...

Upcycling Waste Internationally—TerraCycle, Inc.

In 2003, John Szaky's TerraCycle[5] won a business plan contest from Carrot Capital for $1 million in seed funding. But the venture capital firm wanted TerraCycle to drop its environmental focus and Szaky turned down the offer. It was a critical decision that later helped the business achieve its competitive advantage.

One innovation was implemented when TerraCycle ran out of money to buy bottles in which to sell fertilizer. They decided to use recycled soda bottles to package the converted worm waste. This concept grew into the production of other green products. TerraCycle converts unrecyclable packaging waste to upcycled products. Pencil holders made from Kool-Aid packets, tote bags made from Capri Sun drink pouches,

and backpacks made from Clif Bar wrappers are just a few examples. TerraCycle calls this process turning branded waste into sponsored waste.

Today, more than 100 TerraCycle products are sold in large retail chains, including Home Depot, Whole Foods, Wal-Mart, and Target. The concept has spread to the United Kingdom, Brazil, Mexico, and Canada, with the greatest impact in the United Kingdom. By working with groups in each country, TerraCycle has the potential of becoming an icon that represents upcycled waste.

Sources: TerraCycle, Inc., http://www.terracycle.net, January 20, 2010, and Tom Szaky, *Revolution in a Bottle* (New York: Penguin Group, Inc., 2009).

---

with informal communications or a structured organization with formal communications, it is you who will set the standards and be the role model for your company's culture.

Company Description: Background and Track Record

If the company is already established, is a franchise, or is the reincarnation of a previous business, there will be a history to share with the reader of the plan. The business description does not need to be long. It should simply provide the background for understanding the rest of the plan. It should include summary information about the company's founding, its progress, and its financial success.

If this is a start-up venture, this section should describe briefly the background story of the company, explaining what you have done thus far and why you have done it. The legal form of the business (i.e., sole proprietorship, corporation, LLC, partnership) should also be noted.

Opportunity Analysis and Research: Testing Ideas

The opportunity analysis and research section will provide the credible data and reasoning to determine and demonstrate the market viability of your proposed business on paper, and perhaps in the field, before you start. It should be a clear description, based on sound research and logic, of why the business presents an excellent opportunity. Entrepreneurs often either put little time and attention into this section, or they ignore any data that do not agree with their view of the opportunity. This can prove to be a fatal flaw in business planning. A well-researched opportunity analysis can help to move your business to the head of the line for financing.

The **industry analysis** will provide the broad context for your business plan. It will deal with such factors as industry definition, industry size and growth (or decline), product and industry life cycle, and any current or anticipated legal or regulatory concerns. Determining industry structure, including geographic distribution, business size of member firms, concentration of power, and rates of failure, is also important.

industry analysis a critical view of industry definition, industry size, and growth (or decline), product and industry life cycle, and any current or anticipated legal or regulatory concerns.

---

[5]See Chapter 1.

For example, the failure rate of restaurants is notoriously high and should be addressed in a business plan for a restaurant concept. This is also the place to discuss how you will track industry developments on an ongoing basis.

The **environmental analysis** addresses the roles of the community, region, nation, and the rest of the world as they relate to your business. Whether or not demographic and family changes are working in your favor could mean adjustments for the business. Changes in technologies and economic conditions might radically alter your plans. Examples of this could include the aging of the baby boomer generation or the prevalence of computer technology.

The opportunity analysis should include a **proof of market** investigation that will provide evidence of a market opportunity for your organization. This should identify market size, both in terms of dollars and units. There have to be enough customers who will purchase your products or services in sufficient quantity at a high enough price, and often enough, for your business to be sustainable.

Next, this analysis should describe your **target market** segments, which are groups that are defined by common factors such as demographics, psychographics, age, or geography. For example, your target market segment for a gospel club might be African American Christians between 18 and 25 years of age living in the Detroit metropolitan area. Discuss the size of your target market and the market share that would be attainable. This is also where you can describe your "10 identified customers" (remember Russell Simmons's comment).

A **competitive analysis** is the next important component of the opportunity analysis. This should compare your organization with several direct and indirect competitors by name, and include comparisons that would be meaningful to potential customers. The format of a competitive analysis can vary significantly, but it must make clear where your competitive strengths and weaknesses are and where there are holes in the competitors' businesses. Factors to compare may include—but would not be limited to—location, product selection, market share, product or service quality, experience, advertising, pricing, finances, capacity, hours, size and skill of workforce, and reputation. It is often most effective to create a chart or table to illustrate this.

Marketing Strategy and Plan: Reaching Customers

A description of how you will reach your customers and your anticipated sales volume brings the opportunity and research discussion to the bottom line of sales. Your **marketing mix** will be the combination of the four factors ("the Four P's") —product, price, promotion, and place — that form your competitive advantage, also known as *core competency*. As you choose the elements of your **marketing plan**, always keep your vision in mind. What is the benefit your product or service is providing to customers?

- *Products/services.* The product or service should meet or create a customer need. The distinctive features and benefits of the product or service must be clearly stated. Remember, the packaging is also part of the product. Your customer may throw away your packaging but that does not mean it is unimportant. If you are introducing an innovative technology, the value of the innovation to customers warrants explanation here.

environmental analysis a review that addresses the roles of the community, region, nation, and the rest of the world, as they relate to a business.

proof of market an investigation that provides evidence of a market opportunity.

target market the groups of interest to a business that are defined by common factors such as demographics, psychographics, age, or geography.

competitive analysis research that compares an organization with several direct and indirect competitors by name in a manner that is meaningful to targeted customers.

marketing mix the combination of the four factors—product, price, place, promotion—that communicates a marketing vision.

marketing plan a statement of the marketing goals and objectives for a business and the intended strategies and tactics to attain them.

- *Pricing.* The product or service has to be priced such that target customers will buy it and the business will make a profit. Price should reflect your vision, strategy, and policy. It has to be right. For example, if you are marketing a luxury item, a relatively low price might not send the right message to your target customer. Highlight competitive advantages such as quality, credit terms, warranty type and length, service, and innovativeness that support the pricing.

- *Promotion.* Promotion consists of advertising, publicity, and other marketing devices, such as discount coupons or giveaways. By definition, publicity is free, advertising is purchased. The description of your promotional plans should be specific with respect to the methods used, the time line for implementation, and the budget. Often this section is further divided into advertising, public relations and publicity, and direct marketing. **Advertising** consists of paid promotion through media outlets, such as broadcast or cable television, the Internet, radio, magazines, and newspapers. **Public relations** consists of community activities that are designed to enhance your organization's image. **Publicity** is free notice presented as news in the media. **Direct marketing** includes telemarketing, direct mail, in-person selling, and other personalized targeting. Remember to include samples of your promotional materials in the appendices of your plan, if possible.

- *Place.* This is the venue from which you will sell and distribute your product. Your selling location should be where consumers in your target market do their shopping. Where should you go to bring your product or service to the attention of your market? If you are selling a luxury item, you will need to place it in stores or on Web sites that are visited by customers who can afford it. Included in *place* is your selection of a type of sales force (i.e., independent, company, single line, or multiline), any geographic definition of your market, and all channels of distribution. Are you going to sell directly to consumers, work through wholesale distributors, be Web-based, or sell at retail?

advertising paid promotion through media outlets.

public relations community activities that are designed to enhance an organization's image.

publicity free promotion.

direct marketing a promotional method that includes telemarketing, direct mail, in-person selling, and other personalized marketing tools.

Management and Operations: Making the Plan Happen

The people you hire and the processes that you plan to implement will be an essential part of your business plan. This is where the rubber meets the road in the planning process.

The management team is often the deciding factor for financial support of a business. Moreover, with all other factors being equal, a strong management team will succeed in making a business a success, whereas a weak one will fail. The team must be composed of an effective balance of members with technical expertise (e.g., engineering, marketing, accounting, operations), experience in the field, and life experience. Briefly discuss the current and proposed management team and reference their resumes in the appendices.

It can also be worthwhile to add an organizational chart representing the company as proposed for the near term and with growth. In addition, descriptions of key roles and responsibilities, and the compensation rates and structures for each, will need to be included.

If your business will be involved in **research and development (R&D)**, this section should describe it. Include the current state of the development, such as prototype, testing, or commercialization. Any patents,

research and development (R&D) investigation and experimentation that a business authorizes with a view to finding new products or ways to make operations more efficient.

Step into the Shoes...

From Paper to Reality

(Caro/Alamy)

Frederick W. Smith wrote a paper about air-freight shipping in the coming computer age while an undergraduate at Yale in 1965.[6] Just a few years later (1971), after four years in the Marine Corps, Smith purchased controlling interest in an Arkansas-based aviation company. Though incorporated as Federal Express in 1971, Smith's company began actual operations in Memphis, Tennessee (rather than in Arkansas), in 1973.

Since then, FedEx has continued to expand its operation globally and is the largest airline in the world—based upon number of aircraft and tons of freight flown. The 658 planes in today's FedEx fleet fly to over 375 destinations. FedEx continues to have its headquarters and super hub at Memphis, but now also has eight other domestic hubs: Anchorage, Forth Worth, Greensboro (North Carolina), Indianapolis, Miami (Florida), Newark (New Jersey), and Oakland. International hubs are located in Paris, Toronto, and Gaungzhou Baiyun International Airport in Southern China. A solar-powered hub, at Cologne-Bonn Airport in Germany, opened in 2010.[7]

patents pending, or other intellectual property should be discussed within the limits of law (not losing proprietary protection) and the stage of commercial readiness.

The description of the physical location is similar to the discussion of *place* in the marketing mix, but with the emphasis on logistics and work force readiness. Describe the desired physical location(s) of the organization and the rationale. For example, if you require a concentration of highly skilled scientists, you might want to locate near a university with a strong science orientation or near other firms with similar labor-pool requirements. Local wage rates and community support are other factors to discuss. In addition, geographic proximity to customers and/or suppliers or distributors may be a critical site factor. Other aspects to consider are business-friendly laws and courts, tax rates and structures, school systems, overall quality of life, andenvironment.

The facilities required for the success of your enterprise should be discussed in detail. You should describe the building according to its type and size, and equipment should be specified and "costed out" (details can be included in the appendices). If you know that you require production, warehousing, showroom, and office space, you can describe each. This is where you can discuss your plans to lease or purchase property and equipment and any tipping points for going from lease to purchase. Remember that it isn't financially prudent to buy a building when you could just rent a small incubator space to get started. Nascent entrepreneurs often immediately want to buy their own facilities and brand new equipment. In reality, leasing space and equipment reduces required start-up capital and can provide greater flexibility.

The production methods and inventory control systems that you plan to use will be critical to your success. Even if you are in a service enterprise, you will have supply issues to address in terms of staffing, logistics, and materials. The business plan is an opportunity to set inventory control systems, production processes, and quality assurance methods. You can highlight any technological innovations that will enhance the company's competitive position. What to include will vary considerably, but the identification of your choices and methods of measurement is essential.

[6]FedEx Web site at http://about.fedex.com/our_company/, November 19, 2009.
[7]"Fed Ex Opens Solar-Powered Hub at Cologne Bonn Airport," *Environmental Leader*, http://www.environmentalleader.com/2010/10/28/fedex-opens-solar-powered-hub-at-cologne-bonn-airport/, October 28, 2010.

Financial Analysis and Projections: Translating Action into Money

The financial section of the business plan will be the numerical representation of all that you wrote previously. This section should demonstrate organizational viability in financial terms. Commercial lenders in particular will often go directly from the executive summary to the financials before reading further. If the numbers make sense, they may look at the rest of the plan. If not, it may well land in the trash basket. Your financial estimates should be as realistic as you can make them. Don't pad the numbers; it is not in your best interest to create unrealistic expectations, to delude yourself and your business associates, or to have potential investors or lenders reject your projections as pie-in-the-sky. You are likely to show initial losses, and you should be up front about this. The financials should match both the general market and the other information you provided throughout the business plan. Investors can sense overblown numbers and will react accordingly. The following should be included in the financial section of your business plan.

The facilities and equipment for your business should be discussed in detail with the entire management team. (Getty Images/Digital Vision)

- *Sources and uses of capital.* This section is the numeric representation of the start-up costs, plus a verbal description of capital requirements. It states where you expect to obtain your financial support and how you will use the funds. When securing bank or community-development financing, your lender may require you to *draw down* (take in incremental amounts) funds in accordance with your list of costs. It is essential to make the list as complete and accurate as possible. It is a sad day for everyone when an entrepreneur's credit and cash are completely exhausted just short of the start-up point. A sample start-up cost list is shown in **Exhibit 2-2**.

- *Cash flow projections.* The **cash flow statement** shows cash receipts minus cash disbursements over a period of time. Creating your cash flow projections for three years will bring financial potential and risks into clear focus for you and your stakeholders. Don't be alarmed to see negative numbers on your first couple of efforts at this. However, if the numbers truly do not work, it might be time to reconsider your business approach or the basic concept, rather than simply manipulating the numbers to achieve satisfactory results on paper.

    In a start-up business, cash flow is likely to be negative at various points, such as the early months or in certain seasons. A business cannot survive long with negative cash flow, so it must increase cash coming in (revenues, loans, equity investments, and the like) and/or reduce the amount of cash going out (expenses, equipment purchases, debt repayment, and so forth). Remember, be realistic about these projections. Be careful of significantly increasing your revenue projections solely to improve the numbers. If you add debt, account for its interest and principal repayment in future periods. When you have finished your business plan, it should never show a negative cash balance at the end of a period, because negative cash means you are overdrawn in your accounts, and projecting overdrawn accounts in a business plan, or operating

cash flow statement
a financial document that shows cash receipts less cash disbursements for a business over a period of time.

Exhibit 2-2 *Start-up Costs*

Item	Cost	Estimate/Actual
Start-Up Expenses		
Accountant Fees	$300	Estimate
Expensed Equipment	900	Actual
Financial Institution Fees	350	Estimate
Identity Set/Stationery	750	Estimate
Insurance	2,200	Estimate
Legal Fees	3,000	Estimate
Licenses/Certificates/Permits	550	Actual
Marketing Materials	4,400	Estimate
Payroll (with Taxes)	5,500	Estimate
Professional Fees—Other	300	Estimate
Rent	1,200	Actual
Research and Development	200	Estimate
Travel	3,200	Estimate
Utilities	200	Estimate
Web Fees	8,000	Estimate
Other	1,500	Estimate
Total Start-Up Expenses	**$32,550**	
Start-Up Assets		
Cash Balance for Starting Date	$10,000	Actual
Equipment	41,800	Actual
Furniture and Fixtures	21,975	Actual
Leasehold Improvements	5,200	Estimate
Machinery	3,700	Actual
Rent Deposit	1,200	Actual
Signage	6,000	Estimate
Utility Deposit	400	Actual
Other	1,500	Estimate
Total Start-Up Assets	**$91,775**	
Total Start-Up Requirements	**$124,325**	

balance sheet a financial document that summarizes the assets, liabilities, and net worth of a business.

that way, is hardly a best practice. You may very well have suffered losses that will be reflected on your income statement, but the ending cash balance cannot be negative. **Exhibit 2-3** shows how cash balances are calculated.

- *Balance sheet projections.* Your three years of projected **balance sheets** will provide snapshots of your business at specific points

Exhibit 2-3 *Cash Flow Calculations*

Starting Cash	(+)
Cash In from Operations [Sales]	(+)
Cash Out from Operations [Cost of Goods Sold, Expenses, Taxes]	(−)
Cash In from Investing [Equity Infusions, Earnings on Investments]	(+)
Cash Out from Investing [Equipment Purchases, Repaying Investors]	(−)
Cash In from Financing [Loans]	(+)
Cash Out for Financing [Repayment of Debt]	(−)
Ending Cash Balance [Starting Balance for Next Period]	(=)

Exhibit 2-4 *Balance Sheet Summary Format*

Balance Sheet for XYZ Company
As of (Month) (Day), Year

Assets	Year 1	Year 2	Year 3
Cash	$_____	$_____	$_____
Accounts Receivable	_____	_____	_____
Inventory	_____	_____	_____
Capital Equipment	_____	_____	_____
Other Assets	_____	_____	_____
Total Assets	**$xxxxx**	**$yyyyy**	**$yyyyy**
Liabilities			
Short-Term Liabilities	$_____	$_____	$_____
Long-Term Liabilities	_____	_____	_____
Owner's Equity	$_____	$_____	$_____
Total Liabilities & Owner's Equity	**$xxxxx**	**$yyyyy**	**$yyyyy**

in time, such as the last day of a month, quarter, or year. Balance sheets show the business's **assets** (what you own), **liabilities** (what you owe), and **net worth** (**owner's equity**). These statements provide insights into your financing strategy and overall business health. **Exhibit 2-4** shows a rudimentary balance sheet format.

$$\text{Assets} = \text{Liabilities} + \text{Owner's Equity}$$

- *Income statements for three years.* An **income statement**—or **profit and loss statement (P&L)**—summarizes income and expense activity over a specified period, such as a month, quarter, or year, and shows *net profit* or *loss*. Generally, start-up enterprises suffer losses for several months or even a few years, depending on the type of business. You can show initial losses in your statements, but they must be comparable to industry norms, and you must have cash to cover any shortfalls. The projections that you provide should clearly be your best estimate and based on the detailed breakdown of sales, pricing, cost, and other data contained in your plan. It is helpful to show best case, worst case, and expected scenarios for income. Be careful to avoid "ski-slope" projections, which add projections linearly, with profitability occurring suddenly in either year three or five. A simple example of an income statement is shown in **Exhibit 2-5**.

- *Breakeven analysis.* This calculation will determine your organization's **breakeven point**, that is, when the volume of sales exactly covers the fixed costs. Calculating the breakeven point will help demonstrate whether there is a viable market for your business. For example, if there are 1,500 students in a school and you must sell 2,500 yearbooks to reach breakeven, you know that it is time to reconsider your plan. Breakeven is calculated as

$$\frac{\text{Fixed Cost (\$)}}{\text{Gross Profit per Unit (\$)}} = \text{Breakeven Units}$$

asset any item of value.

liability a business debt.

net worth the difference between assets and liabilities.

owner's equity net worth.

income statement a financial document that summarizes income and expense activity over a specified period and shows net profit or loss.

profit and loss statement (P&L) an income statement.

breakeven point the moment when the volume of sales in a business exactly covers the fixed costs.

Exhibit 2-5 *Income Statement Summary Format*

Income Statement for XYZ Company
For the Year Ending December 31

	Year 1	Year 2	Year 3
Net Sales Revenue (+)	$_____	$_____	$_____
Cost of Goods Sold (−)	_____	_____	_____
Gross Profit (=)	$_____	$_____	$_____
Operating Expenses (−)	$_____	$_____	$_____
General Expenses (−)	_____	_____	_____
Other Expenses (−)	_____	_____	_____
Net Income before Taxes	$_____	$_____	$_____
Taxes	$_____	$_____	$_____
Net Income	$_____	$_____	$_____

- *Ratio analysis.* In order to understand your business performance relative to your industry peers, you can use ratio analysis. A business plan should include standard ratios: gross profit, quick, current, debt, collection period, receivable turnover, inventory turnover, net profit on sales, net profit to assets, and net profit to equity. One of the best ways to interpret your calculated ratios is to compare them with others in your industry via the Risk Management Association (RMA) Annual Statement Studies, which you may access at a library or purchase online for specific industries (http://www.rmahq.org). If you use Business Plan Pro, industry ratios will be available when you calculate them for your business plan. By comparing your business from one period to another and looking at the industry norms, you can adjust the way you will operate, or you can explain why you are outperforming your industry through your competitive advantages or underperforming due to specific circumstances.

- *Risks and assumptions.* All businesses take risks and make their projections based on assumptions. In order for your plan to be realistic, you will need to state your assumptions and known risks explicitly. You will have done some of this in your SWOT analysis; this section pertains to the financial projections. For example, you can include the per-unit costs and volume projections, anticipated tax and benefits rates, and other calculated and projected values. You can also articulate the risks of implementation delays, cost overruns, lower-than-expected sales, industry price wars, and so forth. As with the other sections in your plan, this should be balanced and realistic, not overstated or underplayed.

Funding Request and Exit Strategy: The Ask and the Return

Your business plan should explicitly state the amount of funds you need in accordance with the financial projections you provide. Whether the need is $500 or $50 million, the reasoning for the request will have to be clear and compelling. You then should identify the type of financing you require or are requesting and include your own financial contribution and that of any partners or co-owners, the amount of debt (loans) you will need to take on, and the percentage of equity (ownership) you want to retain. This is where you state the financing terms that you want, including rates, repayment periods, and the like. Recognize that this is part of a negotiation process and that the request should be very carefully structured. If you intend to sell shares of stock in a corporation or are forming a business partnership, legal counsel will be essential so that you do not violate federal laws and regulations or create an improper agreement. The importance of your "ask" cannot be overemphasized. Business plan readers need to know what you want.

The exit strategy is the manner in which you and/or your investors expect to leave the company someday in a planned and orderly way. For investors, this might mean a buyout plan for their equity, or an **initial public offering (IPO)** when the company goes public, that is, puts itself on the stock exchange. It could mean the sale of the business when certain benchmarks are met, or at a predetermined point in time. It could mean having you give up day-to-day operations according to a succession plan. Lenders and investors will want to know how they will recoup their investment and earn enough profit to warrant the risk they are taking.

initial public offering (IPO) first presentation of corporate stock to investors on the open (public) market.

Any business plan is only as strong as its implementation schedule. Therefore, the schedule or timetable of *milestones* (goals) that you include will be important to your business and your stakeholders. By establishing realistic deadlines for the completion of activities, you demonstrate knowledge and understanding of the necessary tasks. You can use PERT or GANTT charts, techniques that will be described in the final unit of this book, or any structured method that details the starting and ending dates of tasks and enumerates the resources needed and the responsibilities of personnel. Using a software tool such as Microsoft Project or Excel can make this process easier to manage.

Appendices: Making the Case in Greater Detail

The appendices will provide you with an opportunity to strengthen your business plan with examples and details that are not critical for inclusion in the main portions. This is the place to add management resumes, sample promotional materials, and illustrations or diagrams of products and packaging. In some cases, the detailed financial projections will appear in the appendices. Each appendix should be numbered and placed in the plan according to the order of reference in the text. The appendices should be listed in your table of contents.

Business Plan Suggestions

As you put together your business plan, there are a number of guidelines and suggestions that can help you get the most value for your time and effort. These will make the plan look more professional, easier to read, and more likely to be thoughtfully considered. In fact, you will find it easier to refer back to your business plan if it is clear, concise, visually appealing, and well organized. In your plan, you should:

◄ **Performance Objective 5**
Be able to demonstrate proper development and formatting of a business plan.

- **Write for your audience.** Whether the plan is for an internal (you and your team) or an external (lenders and investors) audience, it will need to address issues and concerns in language the readers will understand. They will need to see that this business is something they want to be on board with (if company personnel) or that it satisfies a market need (if potential investors).

- *Show that you have skin in the game.* No matter who the audience is, they will want to know that you are emotionally, intellectually, and financially invested in the business.

- *Be clear and concise.* Simple, direct language written without too many adjectives or unnecessarily complex terminology is best. Even for highly technical sections, the business plan should avoid jargon and repeated references made through acronyms and initials. This includes writing in a pompous way. Keep it simple. Readers know that explaining a complex subject in a clear, concise manner requires a thorough understanding of the subject. Depending on your audience and the type of business, your plan should be from 15 to 40 pages long, including appendices.

- *Use current data and reports for your industry.* This will demonstrate that you are being realistic and have truly done your research. If you are out of step with current and anticipated conditions, the assumptions that you make for your financial and market performance are likely to be inaccurate and unrealistic.

- *Choose a voice and stick with it.* It is best to write your business plan in the third person (not the first-person "I" or "we") to give it an objective tone. Be careful not to switch back and forth between voices.

- *Use a consistent, easy-to-read format.* Choose a format and use it consistently throughout the plan. For example, using 1-inch margins, double spacing, and a serif font (such as Times New Roman) will make the document easy to read.

- *Number and label.* Number pages, figures (drawings, illustrations, photos), and tables, and refer to each in the text by number and title to make it easy for the reader to understand and find sections of the plan. Each figure or table should be numbered sequentially and given a heading.

- *Present it professionally.* A professional business plan on high-quality paper with a neat, attractive cover, cover page, and professional binding will go a long way in impressing the reader. A dirty, dog-eared, or unbound business plan will probably not even be read; alternately, an overly fancy, elaborate plan with four-color glossy illustrations bound like a book may cause the reader to wonder why you have gone to such unnecessary expense and suspect that you either are wasteful or are perhaps camouflaging an unsound plan with bells and whistles.

It is a good idea to have others look at your business plan before you circulate it to potential investors. If you can get relatively objective friends, colleagues, or family members to read the plan as early as the first draft, you can probably get valuable feedback and ideas for improvement. If you need assistance with spelling and grammar, or any other aspect of the format, this is the time to get it. It is also a good opportunity for utilizing community resources that may be available to you, such as a Small Business Development Center (SBDC) or Rural Entrepreneurship Center.

Presenting Your Business Plan

A written business plan is only one component of the business-planning process. It may open the door for a presentation to potential investors (stakeholders) or it may be the leave-behind document that will remind them of your pitch. In either case, the presentation of the road map for your venture, whether live, Web-based, or in some other form, is your opportunity to convey your business concept to a particular audience and then to have an interactive discussion regarding the proposal.

Business plan presentations may be formal or informal, and you may have anywhere from only a few minutes to a couple of hours for the complete proposal and discussion. Presentations to venture capitalists may be limited to 5 to 20 minutes. Regardless of the setting or audience, your presentation should be articulate, well thought out, organized, rehearsed, polished, and professional. As you work on plans for your enterprise, it is a good idea to include an **elevator pitch** that immediately conveys to the listener in an engaging way what you are proposing and why he or she should be interested. This lightning-fast spiel should take 15 to 30 seconds (the duration of an elevator ride). It is often more challenging to boil the business plan down to its essentials than to make a full exposition. For a formal presentation, an attractive multimedia presentation—free from errors, excessive animation or other distractions—is advisable. Some venture presentation tips are given in **Exhibit 2-6**.

elevator pitch a 15-to-30-second presentation that conveys in an engaging way what an entrepreneur is proposing and why the listener should be interested.

Exhibit 2-6 *Venture Presentation Tips*	
Timing	• Be prompt and ready to start on time. • Use the entire time allocated and use it productively.
Audience	• Know your audience and tailor the presentation accordingly. • Establish rapport with the audience.
Presentation Style	• Dress appropriately and maintain a professional demeanor. • Be enthusiastic, but not artificial or arrogant. • Use proper pronunciation and language.
Presentation Contents	• Create a "hook" to capture the audience quickly. • Hit the highlights without going into excessive detail. • Keep it simple by emphasizing key points and avoiding technical jargon and acronyms that will lose your audience's interest. • Use visual aids, such as slides and sample or prototype products, to reinforce your message without distracting from it. • Emphasize the benefits of the opportunity so that they are absolutely clear to the audience. • Conclude with a "Thank You."
Follow-Up	• Expect and prepare for questions. Be thoughtful and positive in your responses. • Contact each audience member to move toward your goals.

Source: Adapted from Thomas W. Zimmerer and Norman M. Scarborough, *Essentials of Entrepreneurship and Small Business Management,* 5th ed. (Upper Saddle River, NJ: Prentice Hall, 2007).

Business Plan and Venture Competitions

Numerous business plan and venture-funding competitions are held each year for high-school students, undergraduate college students, graduate students (primarily MBAs), and nonstudent professionals. Many business schools hold internal competitions and then advance winners to regional, national, and even international levels. Prizes may range from $500 to financing and professional services packages worth millions. A list of regional, national, and international competitions for undergraduate and graduate students can be found in **Exhibit 2-7**.

Business plan and pitch competitions have advantages and disadvantages. Certainly, the preparation for a competition is an excellent opportunity to put a deadline on the creation of a plan, and the presentations are opportunities to hone public-speaking skills and strengthen the concept. Also, competitions may provide significant cash prizes and access to venture capital. However, business plan competitions

Exhibit 2-7 *Business Plan and Venture Competitions for Undergraduate and Graduate Students*

Competition	Host/Sponsor	Web Site
Asia Venture Challenge Competition	Tammasat University, Thailand	www.asiamootcorp.org
Camino Real Venture Competition	University of Texas at El Paso	caminorealcompetition.org
Cardinal Challenge Business Plan Competition	University of Louisville	business.louisville.edu
CEO Best Elevator Pitch Competition	Collegiate Entrepreneurs' Organization	www.c-e-o.org
Emerging Business Leaders Summit (EBLS) Business Plan Competition	Minority Business Development Agency	www.medweek.gov
Global Social Venture Competition	University of California at Berkeley, London Business School, Columbia University, Indian School of Business, Thammasat University	www.gsvc.org
IBK Capital-Ivey Business Plan Competition	University of Western Ontario	www.iveybpc.com
Idea to Product Competition (I2P)	University of Texas at Austin	www.ideatoproduct.org
McGinnis Venture Competition	Carnegie Mellon University	www.mcginnisventurecompetition.com
New Venture Championship	University of Oregon	www.oregonnvc.com
OFC Venture Challenge	Clark Atlanta University	www.ofcvc.org
Rice Business Plan Competition	Rice University	www.alliance.rice.edu/alliance/RBPC.asp
Spirit of Enterprise Graduate Business Plan Competition	University of Cincinnati	www.uc.edu/ecenter/
Utah Entrepreneur Challenge	University of Utah	www.uec.utah.edu
Venture Challenge	San Diego State University	www.emc.sdsu.edu
Venture Labs Investment Competition	University of Texas at Austin	www.mootcorp.org
West Virginia Statewide Collegiate Business Plan Competition	West Virginia University	www.be.wvu.edu/bpc/

Sources: Compiled and updated March 2011 from www.Mootcorp.org and Mark Cannice, "Getting in on the University Business Plan Competition Circuit," *Entrepreneur,* October 19, 2009.

are time consuming and can prove a distraction from making progress on the business itself. A competition's guidelines might not match the structure of your business team, so members of the team could have varying levels of interest and commitment, which could create tension or inefficiency. Even if you win a competition, your time might have been better spent elsewhere. Weigh the pros and cons before investing the time and effort.

Chapter Summary

Now that you have studied this chapter, you can do the following:

1. Know what a business plan is and describe it.
   - It is a road map to success.
   - It is a history and a plan for an organization.
   - It must meet the needs of various audiences.
2. Explain the various purposes of a business plan and the audiences for it.
   - A business plan is used by entrepreneurs to organize their thoughts before starting a business, and to determine business viability.
   - It can be used to raise money from investors and lenders. Almost always, bankers and other potential investors will refuse to consider funding an entrepreneur who does not have a business plan.
   - It can help guide the operation of the business.
3. Understand the components of a business plan.

   The parts of a business plan include a cover page; table of contents; executive summary; mission, vision, and culture; company description; opportunity analysis; marketing strategy and plan; management and operations; financial analysis and projections; funding request; exit strategy.
4. Be able to demonstrate proper development and formatting.

   A solid, viable business plan that is sloppy and filled with errors may be rejected on that basis alone. The business plan should be well organized, neatly presented, and written in correct English.

Key Terms

advertising	liability
asset	marketing mix
balance sheet	marketing plan
breakeven point	mission
business plan	mission statement
cash flow statement	net worth
competitive analysis	owner's equity
culture	profit and loss statement (P&L)
direct marketing	proof of market
elevator pitch	public relations
environmental analysis	publicity
feasibility analysis	research and development (R&D)
income statement	target market
industry analysis	vision
initial public offering (IPO)	

Entrepreneurship Portfolio

Critical Thinking Exercises

1. Shawn is creating a business that provides advertising on public restroom stall doors. He is funding the project from his personal savings of $5,000 and does not expect to use any outside financing. Should he create a business plan? Why or why not?

2. Charity and Devon are planning to license technology from NASA that would make it impossible to accidentally lock a child in a car. The technology is complex, and the market analysis and financial assumptions take up a lot of pages. The two women have written an 80-page business plan. Explain your concerns about the length of the plan in light of the chapter text.

3. What factors make the difference between a good business plan and an excellent one? (*Hint:* Use the chapter data and rules from competitions.)

4. Visit an Internet shopping site such as the Home Shopping Network (http://www.HSN.com) or QVC (http://www.QVC.com). Select five products that are being sold that you find interesting or unusual. Make a list of the products and your explanation of the market opportunities they reflect.

5. "Errors of omission can sometimes be greater than errors of commission." How does this statement apply to business plans?

Key Concept Questions

1. Explain why the executive summary is the most important section of any business plan.

2. One mistake entrepreneurs make in their business plans is that of including only an income statement. What other financial statements should be incorporated and why?

3. Print an assignment or any body of text with 1-inch margins, double spaced, using 12-point Times New Roman. Then, print the same document with 0.8-inch margins, single spaced, using the 10-point Arial typeface. Which is easier to read? Why? How would this relate to a business plan?

4. Name three categories of investors/lenders that might have an interest in your business plan.

5. How can spending time researching and writing a business plan save an entrepreneur time and money in the short and long term?

6. Why is it important to identify a business's culture from the beginning?

Application Exercises

Call and visit an entrepreneur in your community to discuss business plans.

1. Ask whether he or she wrote a business plan before starting the business. Since then?

2. If he or she did write a plan, for what has it been used?

3. If he or she did not write a plan, why not?

4. Did the owner have any assistance in writing or reviewing the plan?

5. If so, what was the source of assistance?

Exploring Online

Find a business plan on the Internet (not on the Business Plan Pro disk). Examine it to see whether it follows the guidelines provided in this text. Use a highlighter to mark the sections of the plan that are present. Then, make a list of missing or incomplete sections. Indicate how it does/does not follow the rules for formatting and content. Is the plan viable? Why or why not? Would you invest in it? Why or why not?

In Your Opinion

If an entrepreneur presents a business plan that an investor believes is deliberately vague and has provided inflated financial statements, what should that investor do?

Honest Tea
Business Plan

Business Plan for 1999
December 1998
4905 Del Ray Avenue, Suite 304
Bethesda, Maryland 20814
Phone: 301-652-3556
Fax: 301-652-3557

E-mail: sethandbarry@honesttea.com

Table of Contents

BUSINESS PLAN

Mission Statement

Honest Tea seeks to provide bottled tea that tastes like tea—a world of flavor freshly brewed and barely sweetened. We seek to provide better-tasting, healthier teas the way nature and their cultures of origin intended them to be. We strive for relationships with our customers, employees, suppliers and stakeholders which are as healthy and honest as the tea we brew.

Executive Summary

Honest Tea, a bottled iced tea company, has completed a strong summer of sales in the mid-Atlantic region and is now raising capital to fund the brand's expansion across the United States as well as overseas. Since the all-natural tea first hit the mid-Atlantic market in June of 1998, Honest Tea has developed a loyal following of customers who have made the product the best-selling tea in its largest account, Fresh Fields/Whole Food Markets, significantly outselling Snapple and the Whole Foods 365 brand. In addition to success in retail channels, Honest Tea has also been warmly received in food service channels.

Unlike the sweetened tea drinks made from concentrate or powder which currently dominate the $2 billion bottled tea market, Honest Tea is brewed with loose leaf tea and then barely sweetened with pure cane sugar or honey. The product is poised to take advantage of the rapid growth in the bottled tea, bottled water, and natural food markets, as well as the developing "tea culture" in the United States. It also has potential to tap into the large market of health-conscious diet soda drinkers. The target audience is an emerging subset of the population, which seeks out authentic products and is attuned to global and environmental issues.

Toward the end of the summer and through the fall the company continued to penetrate large supermarket chains and is in the process of finalizing a national network of brokers and distributors for 1999. In September 1998 the company hired two sales managers, each of whom brings more than 15 years of experience and contacts to the business.

Although there was an often painful and occasionally costly product development phase, the company has now perfected the brewing and production process to the point where it can produce several thousand cases in one shift with the desired consistency. In early 1999 the company will add a West Coast site to its current East Coast production site. In addition, the company will be implementing steps to consolidate its packaging operation which will widen the per case profit margin.

The company has demonstrated an ability to gain free media coverage, including stories in the *Washington Post*, the *Wall Street Journal*, and *Fitness Magazine*. It has also cultivated a loyal customer base among some of the country's most influential celebrities which it intends to publicize at the appropriate time. It has just entered into a contract with a well-recognized public relations firm, which has demonstrated its success with several early-stage companies. Finally, the company has finalized a partnership with a Native American tribe that will position Honest Tea to emerge as a leader in the socially responsible business movement.

Honest Tea is looking to raise up to $1.2 million in equity capital to finance the national distribution of the product as well as the introduction of two new flavors and international sales.

Company Story

Honest Tea is a company brewed in the classic entrepreneurial tradition. After a parching run through Central Park in 1997, Seth Goldman teamed up with his Yale School of Management professor, Barry Nalebuff, to reignite their three-year old conversation on the beverage industry. While at Yale Goldman and Nalebuff had converged on the opportunity in the beverage market between the supersweet drinks and the flavorless waters. The energy they share around the idea of a less-sweet beverage leads to several marathon tea-brewing sessions. Their conversation is fueled in part by their extensive travels through tea-drinking cultures such as India, China and Russia. As ideas and investors for the company gather critical mass, Seth takes the dive. He leaves his marketing and sales post at Calvert Group, the nation's largest family of socially and environmentally responsible mutual funds, and launches Honest Tea out of the guest room in his house. Using five large thermoses and label mock-ups, he sells the product to the eighteen Fresh Fields stores of the Whole Foods Market chain. Once the tea has been manufactured, the company moves into a small office and distributes tea out of U-Hauls until other distributors start carrying the product. By the end of the summer, Honest Tea has become the best-selling tea throughout the Fresh Fields chain and has been accepted by several national supermarket chains and distributors.

The Product

The Taste:

Bottled tea that tastes like tea, freshly brewed and barely sweetened.

Somewhere between the pumped-up, sugar-saturated drinks and the tasteless waters, there is a need for a healthier beverage which provides genuine natural taste without the artificially concocted sweeteners and preservatives designed to compensate for lack of taste.

Honest Tea allows people to enjoy the world's second most popular drink the way hundreds of civilizations and nature intended it to be. Tea that tastes like tea -- A world of flavor freshly brewed and barely sweetened. The concept of Honest Tea is as direct and clear as the tea we brew – we start with select tea leaves from around the world, then we brew the tea in spring water and add a hint of honey or pure cane sugar. Finally, we filter the tea to produce a pure genuine taste that doesn't need a disguise.

Unlike most of the bottled teas in the marketplace, Honest Tea is not made with bricks of tea dust, tea concentrate, or other artificial sweeteners or acids. The tea has no bitter aftertaste or sugar kick, and does not leave a syrupy film on the drinker's teeth. To make a comparison with wine, today's leading iced teas are like jug wine and Honest Tea is like Robert Mondavi Opus One. But unlike fine wine, premium bottled tea is quite affordable, usually priced under $1.50 for 16 ounces.

Although taste is the primary benefit of drinking Honest Tea, the product has three other benefits which enhance its acceptance and marketability:

Low in calories:

A 12-ounce serving of Honest Tea has 17 calories, dramatically less than other bottled teas or comparable beverages. We have found that the low-calorie profile of Honest Tea makes the drink attractive to three key audiences – 1) Disenchanted bottled tea drinkers who think the drinks are too sweet, 2) Bottled water drinkers who long for taste and variety and 3) diet soda drinkers who are interested in a low-calorie beverage that doesn't contain artificial sweeteners such as Nutrasweet. The following table illustrates the difference between Honest Tea and the rest of the beverage market:

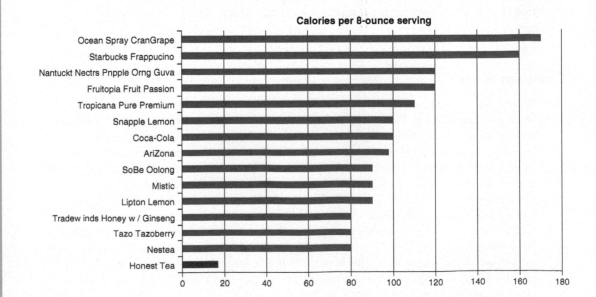

Calories per 8-ounce serving

There are three other players in the less-sweetened bottled tea market that can be considered among the competition for Honest Tea: TeJava, Malibu Teaz and The Republic of Tea. All three brands are currently based and primarily focused on the West Coast. We are heartened by their existence because it confirms our belief that there are untapped opportunities in the beverage market, particularly on the East Coast, where none of the new entrants has any significant presence. TeJava, which is enjoying a warm reception in California, is a mild-tasting, zero-calorie unsweetened tea produced by Crystal Geyser that comes in only one flavor. We believe this product, which has been described by a beverage consultant as "water with a tea aftertaste," would be more flavorful if it were barely sweetened. While TeJava clearly competes with our product, we believe there is room for more than one product in the low-calorie tea marketplace. We also believe that Honest Tea has an edge over TeJava because our drinks are more flavorful and come in a wider variety of flavors.

Malibu Teaz is a company focused on lightly sweetened herbal tea, 35 calories for an 8 ounce serving. The products seem to have limited distribution and the label, which features a topless mermaid, seems designed to cater to a different clientele than Honest Tea.

The Republic of Tea is a well-established producer of loose leaf teas which has recently begun selling unsweetened bottled tea exclusively through its catalogue and premium restaurants. The cost of a four-pack in the catalogue is $15.00, or $3.75 for a 17 ounce bottle. We believe that this price is not viable in retail channels and have spoken with several disillusioned distributors whose experience confirms that assumption. Even if the Republic of Tea changed its sales strategy, we still see room for more than one player in the low-calorie tea market. We also think the modest amount of natural sweetener in Honest Tea helps create a superior flavor.

One other brand that can be considered competition is Tazo, which presents itself as "The reincarnation of Tea." While Tazo is enjoying some success in natural foods channels, we feel that Honest Tea is different from Tazo in three important ways: first Honest Tea is genuine tea whereas Tazo is usually tea mixed with juice or other sweeteners, (usually 80 calories for an 8-ounce serving). Secondly, Tazo's packaging, with its mysterious symbols and discussion of "the mumbled chantings of a certified tea shaman" is designed to reach a New Age audience. In contrast, the colorful art on the Honest Tea labels are accessible to a wider audience, offering a more genuine tea experience. Finally, Tazo's price point is significantly higher than Honest Tea in supermarket channels, selling for $1.69 versus Honest Tea's price of $1.19. Where the two brands have competed head-to-head, Honest Tea has significantly outsold, and in many cases, eliminated Tazo from the shelf. Our response to Tazo's "reincarnation of tea" is that tea doesn't need to be reincarnated if it is made right the first time.

Health benefits of brewed tea:

The curative properties of tea have been known for thousands of years. Because Honest Tea is brewed from genuine tea leaves it imparts many health benefits not found in tea-flavored drinks. In addition to serving as a digestive aid, tea has powerful antioxidants, which impair the development of free radicals which contribute to cancer and heart disease. The antioxidants in green tea are believed to be at least 100 times more effective than Vitamin C and twenty-five times better than Vitamin E at protecting cells and DNA from damage believed to be linked to cancer, heart disease and other potentially life-threatening illnesses.

Cultural experience of tea:

Each Honest Tea flavor is brewed based on a recipe perfected over generations in a specific region of the world. As a result, drinking Honest Tea becomes a cultural experience, from the genuine tastes to the distinctive international art and information on the label. While some bottled teas seek to cloak themselves in a cosmopolitan mantle by including exotic-looking drawings on the label, the front of each Honest Tea label features authentic art from the culture of origin.

Flagship line of flavors

Our flagship line of teas come from four different continents:

Kashmiri Chai – The people of Kashmir have mixed spices into their chai for generations. Our recipe is made with spring water, premium tea leaves, crushed cardamom, cinnamon, orange peel, cloves, pepper, ginger, malic acid and a touch of sucanat evaporated sugar cane juice. Approximately one third the caffeine of coffee.

Black Forest Berry – Our Black Forest Berry tea is a fruit infusion made with spring water, hibiscus, currants, strawberries, raspberries, brambleberries, elderberries, and a touch of unrefined organic cane sugar. Caffeine-free.

Moroccan Mint – Our Moroccan Mint is a tightly rolled green tea from China blended with a generous amount of peppermint, brewed in spring water with citric acid and a touch of white clover honey. Approximately one fourth the caffeine of coffee.

Gold Rush – Our Gold Rush tea is an herbal infusion made with spring water, rooibush, rose-hips, chamomile, cinnamon, peppermint, ginger, orange peel, malic acid, and a touch of raw cane sugar, and natural flavors. Caffeine-free.

Assam – These golden-tipped flowery leaves from the Sonarie Estate gain their distinctive taste from being picked as tender leaf buds at the height of the season. Brewed in spring water with Vitamin C, malic acid, unrefined organic cane sugar, and a hint of maple syrup. Approximately one half the caffeine of coffee.

In early 1999 we will be introducing two new teas:

Decaf Ceylon – In response to feedback from more than 500 sampling events where we continually heard requests for a decaffeinated black tea, we will be introducing a Decaf Ceylon with lemon grass. The label for this tea features original art which captures the cultural and relaxing attributes of the tea.

First Nation's Peppermint – After months of negotiation and a consultation with the tribal elders, we have developed an organic herbal tea in conjunction with a woman-owned company based on the Crow Reservation in Montana. This tea is exciting not only for its flavor but also for the partnership we have developed with the tribe. In addition to licensing the flavor and artwork from the tribe, we are also buying the tea from our partner on the reservation with the understanding that over time the community will develop the capacity to grow all the ingredients on the reservation. This unprecedented relationship should prove to be a valuable public relations tool.

Production and Manufacturing

Though we had our share of "learning experiences" along the way, we have developed several proprietary brewing tools and techniques which enable us to manufacture several thousand cases of tea a day on both coasts with the desired consistency. In addition, since we have a full-time brewmaster on staff, the company retains the knowledge of manufacturing the product, instead of relying on a co-packer for that information.

The tea is brewed at a brewing and bottling facility located within driving range of the target market. The site was selected based on numerous criteria including capacity, reputation, quality control, production efficiency and willingness to invest in a long-term partnership with Honest Tea. All partners involved in the production process meet United States Department of Agriculture Hazard Analysis Critical Control Plant (HACCP) standards. We are in the process of obtaining Kosher certification from the Orthodox Union ("Circle U").

In early 1999 we will be making a change in our manufacturing process that will not affect the quality of the product but will have important ramifications for our profitability. Instead of a two-step packaging process, we will consolidate the brewing and labeling under one roof. This consolidation will save Honest Tea more than two dollars a case.

Our tea leaves are provided by internationally known companies that specialize in tea buying, blending and importation. Our primary source is Hälssen & Lyon of Germany, the largest specialty tea company in the world. Another, Assam Tea Traders, has direct ties to tea estates in the Assam District of Northern India. The other ingredients are commodities which are in plentiful supply.

As the Company grows in size, we anticipate dealing more directly with the tea growers. We intend to visit the tea estates so that we can verify that the labor conditions of the tea workers meet international standards and International Labor Organization conventions. We also aspire to ensure that the tea is grown organically.

Market Opportunity

Beyond Snapple–The Emerging Market for Quality Bottled Tea

We have identified four market trends that are fueling demand for Honest Tea within the $72 billion non-alcoholic liquid refreshment beverage market.

1. **Explosive growth in Ready-to-Drink (RTD) tea and bottled water markets** – Although carbonated soft drinks still dominate the beverage market, in the past ten years Ready-To-Drink teas and bottled water have emerged as alternatives. Since 1992 the US tea market has enjoyed 60% annual growth, reaching sales of $2 billion in 1996. The bottled water market has grown to $2.4 billion, with most of the growth fueled by sales of single-serving bottles.

1997 U.S. Beverage consumption in billions of gallons*

*Water and Soft drink figures come from Beverage Marketing, Inc. The RTD Tea figure is based on 1997 sales estimate of $2.5 billion, which equates to roughly one billion gallons.

2. **Beyond the tea bag – The emergence of tea culture** – Snapple and similar brands helped make tea accessible to a broader population. But now in the same way that gourmet coffees have become popular, consumers are beginning to develop an appreciation for finer teas. Over the last six years U.S. loose leaf tea sales have more than doubled, from $1.8 billion

in 1990 to $4.2 billion in 1996[1] According to the Tea Council, there are over a thousand tea houses or tea parlors in the country, mostly opened within the last two or three years. These parlors focus almost exclusively on tea, products that go with tea as well as tea hardware. They carry names such as Teaism, TeaLuxe, Elixir Tonics and Teas, and Tea & Company. Even Lipton is opening a flagship tea bar in Pasadena, California. In addition to the burgeoning of tea cafes, tea culture is spreading in the form of tea magazines, tea-flavored ice cream, frozen tea ice bars, tea-scented perfume and bubble bath, tea jelly, tea calendars and even books about tea. The paperback Loving Tea was recently spotted as a "cash register book" at the bookstore, commanding prime space next to Dilbert and Chicken Soup for the Soul.

3. **The natural foods boom** – The natural product category has also exploded in the past 6 years. Fueled by an increase in health consciousness and rising environmental awareness, demand has grown for foods and products which are best when eaten or used as close to their original state in nature. According to Natural Foods Merchandiser, the natural products industry has nearly tripled in size since 1990 from $4.2 billion to $11.5 billion in 1996. And the boom is expected to continue well into the next decade. Analysts, such as Mark Hanratty of Paine Webber, are forecasting 15–20 percent annual growth over the next three to five years, reaching $50 billion by 2003.

4. **Rise of Cultural Creatives** – Market research in the past three years has identified a consumer mindset which would seem to be particularly receptive to Honest Tea. A 1996 study by the market research firm American LIVES identified a subset of the population, roughly 44 million Americans, which they labeled "Cultural Creatives."[2] Among the key characteristics and values identified for this group, the following seem to make them ideal customers for Honest Tea:

- Experiential consumers – they want to know where a product came from, how it was made, and who made it

- Holistic – they view nature as sacred; they form the core market for alternative health care and natural foods

- Aggressive consumers of cultural products, love of things foreign and exotic

- Desire for authenticity – favoring high integrity over high fashion

- Disdainful of mainstream media and consumerist culture which, in their view, is too superficial, not enough attention to the full story

- Attuned to global issues and whole systems, have a sense of belonging to a global village

Profile of Target Customer

When we combine these four trends and compare them with the demographics of the Cultural Creatives study as well as other market demographic information[3], we are able to develop a profile of our target customers:

- 60% women, 40% men

- Median age 42, with a range from 30–65

- Likely to live near a concentrated urban area

- Likely to have graduated college or have an advanced degree

- Likely to currently be bottled water or RTD tea drinkers, occasionally drink iced cappuccino

- Interested in running, hiking and outdoor healthy activities

- Average family income $52,000

---

[1] Investor's Business Daily, "Tea: Are you Prepared to Join the Party?", January 30, 1998, p1.

[2] American Demographics, February 1997, Dr. Paul H. Ray

[3] 1997 MRI Spring data, population weighted

Market Research

To test the receptivity of this audience to Honest Tea, we held two focus groups in New York. The sessions, facilitated by an independent market research firm, provided encouraging results and helpful guidance in terms of product line and label presentation. The first focus group consisted of health-conscious women between the ages of 30 and 60, all of whom occasionally drink bottled tea or bottled water. The second group was a mix of men and women who were selected based on their responses to questions which identified them as fitting the Cultural Creatives profile. The sessions began with a discussion of what was missing in the beverage market. Within 5 minutes, unprompted by the moderator, both groups agreed that they wanted something that was not as boring as water but didn't have all the "junk" in commercial bottled tea.

One important lesson from the focus groups was that most consumers have a limited understanding about the differences between tea varieties. The situation may be comparable to the way many consumers thought about wine several decades ago. At first people distinguished wines in terms of red and white wine, then in terms of rose and chablis, then in terms of California wines versus French wines, later by the kind of grape, and today some people select wines based on the estate. The focus groups suggested that the American tea market is still in the red versus white stage. One implication of this finding was that our labels and other communications needed to include some educational information about each tea, including health benefits, history and country of origin.

Market Response

More important than our pre-market focus group is the market response to Honest Tea, i.e. sales. In the eighteen Fresh Fields/Whole Foods Markets of the mid-Atlantic region Honest Tea has become the best-selling bottled tea, outselling Snapple and the house brand. During the month of August, when Honest Tea was promotionally priced at 99 cents, 22,417 bottles of teas were sold, with several stores averaging more than 100 bottles per day.

Perhaps more important than the numbers from one region are the thousands of responses we have gotten from our customers via unsolicited emails, letters, phone calls, and conversations at hundreds of sampling events. The feedback we have received make it clear that we have created something that was missing in the marketplace. Every week we receive several unsolicited emails and letters from customers. Typical comments include the following (see Exhibit A for more tea-mail – Excluded in the interest of space):

```
Subject: BEST TEA EVER!

Dear Honest Tea,

I have never bought a product that I thought was so fantastic that I felt
the need to write about it. I love tea, but I always would brew it myself
and cart it around because I can't stand the syrupy-sweet "tea" that is
sold most places.

I saw your tea at Fresh Fields in Annapolis, MD. At first I was hesitant
because I have it in my mind that all bottled iced teas = yucky sweet.
But I was intrigued by the flavor choices and yes, the pretty bottles
and bought one of each. Well, I went to my car and proceeded to drink all
of them right then and there. The first one was so good and so different
that I couldn't help myself and had to try the rest. It actually tasted
like tea! THEN... when I turned the bottle over and saw how few calories
were in it I flipped! There is no reason not to drink this tea! You guys
have truly done it, this is quality stuff! So keep it up and get this tea
out there! I wish you success and happy brewing!

-Cindy W., Annapolis, MD
```

RE: Help! I need Honest Tea!

I just returned from a trip to Wash, DC (I live in Pittsburgh) and found
that your tea is not available here. I love it and must have more. Can
you ship it to me? Price is no object (to some degree).

If you cannot ship it to me please advise me of any support groups or
counseling that I may seek in order to recover from this lack of Honest
Tea. I must warn you that I may get desperate, causing me to highjack an
Honest Tea truck in the Washington area and bring it back to Pittsburgh.
I am becoming a heartless, Honest Tea junkie. I hope that you can help.

Thanks, EEOber

Subject: Chai tea was great!

I just came from my local Fresh Fields Market in Reston, VA after trying a bottle of your Kashmiri Chai tea. Fantastic! Imagine my surprise
to learn the entire bottle was only 34 calories and 1/3 the caffeine of
coffee!

This is great stuff folks - my only complaint is that I can't seem to
find anywhere that sells it by the case. I don't mind buying a couple
bottles at a time for occasional consumption, but I would appreciate being able to purchase a case to bring to work and a case to keep at home.
It would be a great way to replace soda and other sugary, high calorie
drinks in my diet. Unfortunately, I cannot spare the time to stop at the
store everyday to pick up a couple bottles. Any plans to sell by the case
(hopefully at a slight discount)??

Colin C. Reston, VA

Re: Honest Tea!

Your tea is fabulous! I have never written a letter in support of a food
product before, but ever since I stumbled across your Honest Tea last
week at Fairway, I've been raving about it! At last, someone intelli-
gent enough to realize that not all people like that syrupy junk that is
on the market, and that nutri-sweet and artificial sweeteners taste like
crap. I've grown so tired of "well, it's what the consumers are demanding." Not. The rest of us have spent the last decade or so brewing tea at
home and keeping it in our refrigerators since traditional marketing researchers have been incapable of using their research to produce anything
innovative. Bravo, bravo, bravo. Nice labels, too.

Lisa P., New York City

The response from grocery buyers at the corporate level has been equally as exciting.

The new products buyer for Wild Oats/Alfalfa Community Market approved Honest Tea for sale in all of the chain's 60+ stores. Here is her comment to the grocery buyers which she sent out on the Product Approval Form (see Exhibit B – Excluded in the interest of space):

> Mark My Words: Honest Tea will be a success. The *only* bottled tea that is not loaded with sugars and tastes great. This is what people (like me) have been seeking for years. Too good to be true? No! I mean it now – BRING THESE IN!

The natural foods buyer for Harris Teeter chose to carry the product in all 140 stores. Her buying committee told her this was the first innovation in the iced tea market they'd seen in about five years. Some even said that Honest Tea represents a new beverage category.

In addition to this feedback, Honest Tea has been presented with several promising opportunities to be plugged into several large supermarket chains. The status of these opportunities is as follows:

Store	# of outlets	Region	Status	Penetration
Albertson's	96	Florida	December decision	
Food Emporium	40	NY/NJ	December decision	
Genuardi's	32	NJ/PA/DE	Approved for all stores	Will go on sale in December '98
Giant	179	C/MD/VA/DENJ/PA	Approved	On sale in flagship store
Harris Teeter	140	NC/SC/GA/VA/ KY/TN	Approved for all stores	On sale in all stores
Shaw's	127	New England	Approved	On sale in test market store
Superfresh	78	NJ/PA	Approved for all stores	On sale in some stores
Ukrop's	40	VA	Approved for all stores	On sale in some stores
Whole Foods	117	Nationwide	Approved for mid-Atlantic and SE	On sale in 20 stores
Wild Oats/Alfalfa's	60	Nationwide	Approved for all stores	On sale in 12 stores

In addition to success in the supermarket channel, Honest Tea is also being warmly received in food service and retail accounts. We have experienced strong repeat sales in cafeterias such as Bear Stearns, Lazard Freres and have just been approved for sale in the NFL corporate cafeteria. Honest Tea is the best-selling beverage at the Mangia gourmet eatery in Manhattan where it is priced at $2.50 a bottle. Honest Tea is also sold in well-known restaurants such as Legal Sea Foods. Finally, we have also had strong repeat sales from food outlets on the campuses of Boston University, Harvard University, Yale University and Wellesley College.

As with Snapple and other bottled iced teas, there does seem to be a seasonality affect to the sales of Honest Tea, particularly in the supermarket channel. However, as we expand our distribution to the Southern states and to more upscale cafeterias, we expect to see less of a dip in sales during the winter months.

Marketing & Distribution

Given the above market trends, target customer profile and record of success in the mid-Atlantic natural and specialty foods market, Honest Tea's marketing and distribution strategy for 1999 is as follows:

1. National natural/specialty foods channels, working with brokers and distributors to achieve full distribution throughout the Whole Foods and Wild Oats chains as well as natural foods buyers in mainstream supermarkets.

2. Higher end food service – working with large national food distributors such as Sysco, Aramark and Marriott to penetrate restaurants and institutional eateries.

3. Opportunistic public relations and extensive sampling in health and natural food settings to build the brand name as well as facilitate trial.

National natural/specialty foods channels

We are in the process of finalizing national distribution and brokerage arrangements. We are currently working with Haddon House, the largest retail distributor of gourmet foods on the East Coast. In addition, we have recently contracted with numerous natural food brokers to represent our product for the East Coast, Midwest, West Coast and the South.

Higher end food service

We are working food management companies to expand our presence in business and institutional cafeterias. and has been approved for sale in Restaurant Associates and Marriott International. We are currently in discussions with Aramark and Sysco. We are also in conversation with several large restaurant chains and sports arenas.

Promotion

We recognize that because we are not as well-financed or as well-established as much of our competition, whenever we play by their marketing rules, we are at a disadvantage. Therefore, instead of spending a lot of money on advertising, Honest Tea relies instead on opportunistic ways to gain public attention and promote trial of the product.

We have proven our ability to gain positive free media coverage in *The Washington Post, The Wall Street Journal, Christian Science Monitor* and *Fortune* magazine. (See Exhibit C). In addition to what has already been printed, several articles are in the pipeline, including upcoming articles in magazines such as *Shape, Self, Fitness, Start-Ups,* and *Seventeen*. We are currently finalizing a contract with a highly-regarded public relations firm, which has a proven track record of gaining extensive exposure for early-stage companies. Just as we have paid a portion of our label designer's expenses in the form of equity, we intend to pay a portion of the PR firm's retainer in stock to encourage their investment in our business. We also have developed a web page at www.honesttea.com which has regularly attracts 50 visitors a day and has helped attract several new accounts.

In addition we have been very aggressive with sampling. Because Honest Tea started the summer as an unknown product and is unlike any product currently on the market, we took great pains to introduce as many people to the product as we could. During the month of August we organized demos as often as eight times a month per Fresh Fields/Whole Foods Market (See Exhibit D – Excluded in the interest of space).

Finally, we have developed a loyal following among several nationally-known celebrities which we hope to use to our advantage this coming Spring. For example, we recently rushed the delivery of ten cases to Oprah Winfrey's studios at her personal request.

Packaging and Pricing

Honest Tea's flagship line of products is sold in 16 ounce glass bottles. All of our labels feature culturally authentic artwork from the tea's country of origin. All of our caps have a distinctive black matte finish which complements the black border on the front of the label. In 1999 our caps will have the "pop-button" seal. Our packaging communicates the attributes of the tea inside in four ways:

1. High quality – By using colorful and artistically sophisticated artwork presented with spot labels, (i.e,. front and back instead of wraparound) our bottles evoke comparisons with a bottle of fine wine or other gourmet food.

2. Culturally authentic – By using artwork directly from the culture where the tea comes from, we are presenting the tea as is, without any "spin" or Westernized interpretation of what an Indian painting might look like.

3. Honest – By using the spot labels, there is more space for the consumer to see the tea. Since we use real tea leaves, we have nothing to hide inside.

4. Simplicity – The essence of this millenia-old drink of water and leaves is its simplicity. Our packaging has no flashy slogans, advertising call-outs or marketing hype. The package helps condition the consumer for what they are about to experience, an honest taste of tea.

In 1999 we plan to introduce a "Varietea" pack which will contain a selection of flavors, and will help introduce consumers to our product. The Varietea pack will be sold at a modest discount to encourage first-time trial.

The retail price for a 16 ounce Honest Tea varies between $1.19 and $2.00, slightly more expensive than Snapple, which usually sells for $.99. In food service accounts we have seen the price range from $1.29 to $2.50.

International Markets

Since tea is the world's second most popular beverage, there is an intrinsic international appeal for Honest Tea's world of flavor freshly brewed and barely sweetened. Although our primary energies are directed toward the US market, we have recently entered into a contract with a firm that has extensive international marketing expertise. They will be showing our product in the UK early next year with the intent to sell the bottled tea in the Spring of 1999.

Product Development and Future Products

In 1999 we will be introducing at least two new flavors in direct response to feedback from our customers. Our Decaf Ceylon will be the only decaffeinated black tea served in a Ready-to-Drink bottle. The decaf tea has a great taste and a captivating label.

In addition to being our first organic tea, our First Nation Peppermint has a smooth taste and a compelling label featuring an intense photo of a Crow warrior. This product should also attract free media coverage for the innovative partnership we have forged with the Crow Nation.

Despite the thousands of tea flavors that exist, we have taken a relatively conservative approach by identifying accessible flavors from different continents. In addition to Decaf Ceylon and First Nation's Peppermint, several more flavors have been identified which will be introduced within the next twelve months. Some are as accessible as the flagship products, others may be more appealing to certain segments of the population. For example, Japanese green tea has a strong taste which can repel untrained Western tastebuds, but we believe this product has commercial viability provided it is strategically marketed and distributed.

In addition to other bottled tea flavors, we are exploring related products such as "Tea"-shirts featuring art from our labels, tea bags sold under the Honest Tea name and other tea-related products such as tea marinade and even "tea bags" for the bathtub.

Management

The management team of Honest Tea has a proven record of entrepreneurial success and innovative business strategy and has recently added two senior sales managers with extensive experience in the specialty foods and beverage industries. They are, in order of seniority:

President & TeaEO

Seth Goldman launched Honest Tea after leaving the Calvert Group where he was Vice President of Calvert Social Investment Fund, the nation's largest family of mutual funds that invest in socially and environmentally responsible companies. In this role, Seth managed the marketing and sales efforts, including a ground-breaking public awareness campaign that increased website traffic eightfold and doubled sales in the company's flagship equity fund. His other work at Calvert Group includes active involvement in the company's private equity portfolio and managing a corporate child labor initiative for the Calvert Foundation.

His previous work includes directing a nationally-recognized demonstration project for Americorps, the president's national service program, and serving as Senator Lloyd Bentsen's Deputy Press Secretary for two and a half years. Before that he worked for a year in China (1987-1988) and a year and a half in the former Soviet Union (1989-1990), where he developed, among other things, an appreciation for the role tea plays in bringing people together.

Seth graduated from the Yale School of Management in 1995. While at Yale, he and a classmate were winners of the inaugural Connecticut Future Fund New Enterprise Competition for a business plan they developed based on a diagnostic invented at the Yale School of Medicine. Seth is a graduate of Harvard College, where he was elected Class Marshal and was a member of the Varsity Track team. He serves as Chair of the Yale School of Management Annual Fund and the Montgomery Public Schools Educational Foundation. He is a former board member of Students for Responsible Business.

Seth's experience at Calvert Group has enhanced his contribution to Honest Tea in two important ways. As Calvert's most visible presence within the community of socially responsible businesses, Seth's contacts and connections help give Honest Tea a mark of credibility which is essential for the brand identity the Company is trying to create. In addition, the target customer for Calvert's equity funds is very much in line with the Cultural Creative profile discussed earlier. Seth's record of success in communicating with this audience while at Calvert Group has conveyed well to Honest Tea.

Chairman of the Board

Barry Nalebuff is the Milton Steinbach Professor of Economics and Management at Yale School of Management. He taught at Harvard and Princeton before coming to Yale. He teaches competitive strategy, mergers and acquisition, political marketing, and decision-making and game theory at the management school negotiation at Yale law school, and social choice, political theory, and welfare economics to undergraduates. An expert on Game Theory, he has written extensively on its applications for managers. Barry is co-author of *Thinking Strategically: The Competitive Edge in Business, Politics, and Everyday Life*. His new book on business strategy, *Co-opetition*, co-authored with Adam Brandenburger, was a *Business Week* bestseller. He has applied the use of game theory in consulting to companies in banking, consumer products, healthcare, high-tech manufacturing, insurance, oil, pharmaceuticals software, and telecommunications. A graduate of M.I.T. and a Rhodes Scholar, he earned his doctorate in economics at Oxford University.

Brewmaster

George Scalf joined Honest Tea in March of 1998 to manage the production of the tea. As the founder of numerous natural beverage enterprises including Blue Range Natural Foods and New Dawn Natural Foods, George brings more than 20 years of expertise and contacts in beverage manufacturing. He also has numerous contacts in the natural foods marketplace.

National Sales Director

Jim Lambert joined Honest Tea in September from Stanley Foods where he was the Vice President of Sales for the DC/ Baltimore area's premier specialty food distributor. Jim is a 15 year veteran of the food industry. His previous positions include Chain Accounts Manager at US Foodservice Baltimore and with Atlantic Foodservices. In his role as National Sales Director, Jim is responsible for overseeing all sales and distribution relationships, with particular focus on food service and mainstream supermarket accounts.

Retail Sales Manager

Melanie Knitzer came to Honest Tea in October from her post as Director of Corporate Sales with Gourm-E-Co Imports, a mid-Atlantic specialty food distributor. Melanie also brings 15 years of experience to Honest Tea, including roles as General Manager with Dolce Europa and Gourmand. In her role as Retail Sales Manager, Melanie is responsible for managing all natural foods and gourmet foods retail accounts.

Consultants and Advisors:

Throughout the development of the Honest Tea business planning process, we have been fortunate to tap into a wealth of tea, beverage, natural foods, and entrepreneurial expertise. The people listed below have served as resources for us. Several of them may continue to play a role in the company in the future.

Joe Dobrow – Director of Marketing Programs, Fresh Fields/Whole Foods Markets

John May – Managing director, New Century Partners, social venture capital investment advisor

Lawrence Omene – Quality Assurance Manager, Mid-Atlantic Coca-Cola Bottling Company

Karin Schryver – Natural foods buyer for Harris Teeter, chain of l40 upscale supermarkets in the Southeastern United States

Statement and Aspirations for Social Responsibility

Although a statement of social and environmental responsibility is not usually found in most business plans, these issues are central to Honest Tea's identity and purpose. Not only is the value of our brand based on authenticity, integrity and purity, but our management team is committed to these values as well. We will never claim to be a perfect company, but we will address difficult issues and strive to be honest about our ability or inability to resolve them. For example, we recognize that the labor and environmental conditions on many tea estates are below internationally accepted standards. We will strive to work with our suppliers to promote higher standards while recognizing the limited influence we have as a small company. We value diversity in the workplace and we intend to become a visible presence in the communities where our products are sold. When presented with a purchasing decision between two financially comparable alternatives, we will attempt to choose the option which better addresses the needs of economically disadvantaged communities.

We have taken our first substantive step in that direction with the development of our newest tea flavor, First Nation's Peppermint. After much negotiation with Itchik, a woman-owned company based on the Crow reservation, we have created a partnership that allows the Crow community to be economically involved in the production and sale of the tea. Itchik is serving as Honest Tea's buyer for the ingredients, charging a modest administrative fee per kilo of tea with the understanding that over time Itchik will develop the capacity to harvest the tea on the reservation. In addition Itchik is licensing the recipe and artwork to Honest Tea in a royalty arrangement. A portion of the royalties will be directed to the Pretty Shield Foundation, a non-profit created to address the needs of foster Native American children.

Financial Statements–Year-to-Date and Projections

Exhibit E presents the monthly income statement and balance sheet for Honest Tea from January 1998 through November 30, 1998. Exhibit F presents the 1999 projected income and cash flow statement, with assumptions included at the bottom.

BUSINESS PLAN

Exhibit E
Honest Tea Balance Sheet 1998

	February 28	March 31	April 30	May 31	June 30	July 31	August 31	September 30	October 31	November 30
ASSETS										
Current Assets										
Checking/Savings										
Chevy Chase Bank Checking	$ 16,875	$264,699	$364,259	90,394	$ 48,470	13,740	$ -	$ -	$ -	$ -
FCNB Checking Account	$ -	$ -	$ 1,000	19,759	$ 11,281	(2,616)	(27,575)	13,063	(7,896)	23,493
FCNB Repo Account	$ -	$ -	$ -	228,029	$ 230,028	252,031	232,084	135,015	67,006	17,187
Total Checking/Savings	$ 16,875	$264,699	$365,259	338,181	$ 289,779	263,155	204,509	148,078	59,110	40,680
Accounts Receivable	$ -	$ -	$ -	12,866	$ 21,047	23,512	67,252	78,081	64,774	59,201
Other Current Assets										
Cert. of Deposit/Capital Bank			$ 24,000	24,000	$ 24,000	24,300	24,300	24,300	24,300	24,300
Inventory										
Raw Materials	$ -	$ -				2,976	2,976	2,976	2,976	2,976
Total Inventory	$ -	$ -				2,976	2,976	2,976	2,976	2,976
Total Other Current Assets	$ -	$ -	$ 24,000	24,000	$ 24,000	27,276	27,276	27,276	27,276	27,276
Total Current Assets	$ 16,875	$264,699	$389,259	375,047	$ 334,826	313,943	299,038	253,436	151,160	127,157
Fixed Assets										
Computer Equipment		635	635	635	2,687	2,687	2,687	2,687	6,277	6,277
Office Furniture & Equipment				3,500	3,709	3,709	3,709	3,709	3,709	3,709
Coolers/Glide Racks						352	352	9,582	9,582	9,582
Tea Brewing Equipment						-	-	-	3,000	3,000
Total Fixed Assets	$ -	$ 635	635	4,135	6,396	6,748	6,748	15,978	22,568	22,568
TOTAL ASSETS	$ 16,875	$265,334	$389,893	$379,182	$341,222	$320,691	$305,786	$269,413	$173,728	$149,725

LIABILITIES & EQUITY	February 28	March 31	April 30	May 31	June 30	July 31	August 31	September 30	October 31	November 30
Liabilities										
Current Liabilities										
Accounts Payable	$ -	$ -	-	-	-	-	$ (16)	$ -	$ -	$ -
Total Accounts Payable	$ -	$ -	-	-	-	-	$ (16)	$ -	$ -	$ -
Credit Cards										
First USA		$ 231	$ 826	968	$ 604	2,694	$ 188	$ 1,679	5,239	1,471
Halssen and Lyon		$ (5,000)	(2,560)	(2,560)	(2,438)	538	$ -	-	-	$ -
Mayer Bros.		$ (5,000)	(5,000)	(500)	7,585	7,295	6,298	-	-	-
Slate Packaging			(30,800)	(12,914)	436	7,295	14,000	-	-	$ -
Staples					170	181	$ -	66	219	$ -
Strasburger and Siegel, Inc.		$ (1,000)	356	$356	356	-	$ -	-	-	$ -
Total Credit Cards	$ -	$ (10,770)	$ (37,179)	$ (14,651)	$ 6,713	18,003	$ 20,486	$ 1,745	$ 5,458	1,471
Total Current Liabilities	$ -	$ (10,770)	$ (37,179)	$ (14,651)	$ 6,713	18,003	$ 20,471	$ 1,745	$ 5,458	1,471
Total Liabilities	$ -	$ (10,770)	$ (37,179)	$ (14,651)	$ 6,713	18,003	$ 20,471	$ 1,745	$ 5,458	1,471
Equity										
Capital Investment @ 0.01 PAR	$ 20,000	$ 300,001	$ 505,001	507,501	$ 517,501	$ 517,501	517,501	$ 517,501	$ 517,501	$ 517,501
Net Income	$ (3,125)	$ (23,898)	$ (77,929)	$ (113,668)	$ (182,992)	$ (214,813)	$ (232,186)	$ (249,833)	$ (349,231)	$ (369,248)
Total Equity	$ 16,875	$ 276,103	$ 427,072	393,833	$ 334,509	$ 302,688	285,315	$ 267,668	168,270	148,253
TOTAL LIABILITIES & EQUITY	$ 16,875	$ 265,334	$ 389,893	$ 379,182	$ 341,222	$ 320,691	$ 305,786	$ 269,413	$ 173,728	$ 149,725

BUSINESS PLAN

BUSINESS PLAN

Exhibit E Honest Tea Income Statement 1998

	Feb	Mar	Apr	May	June	Jul	Aug	Sep	Oct	Nov
Ordinary Income/Expense										
Income										
Sales - Glass Bottles	$ -			14,035	9,396	26,806	55,988	49,221	31,633	31,003
Sales Discounts Off Invoice Glass Bottles				(21)	(22)	(101)	(2,878)	(1,985)	-	(181)
Total Income	$ -	$ -	$ -	14,014	9,374	26,705	53,109	47,236	31,633	30,822
Cost of Goods Sold										
Contract Labeling		$ 5,000	23,831	5,461	3,169	6,859	6,277	-	12,901	8,420
Bottles & Caps			(5,000)	-	19,656	8,017	6,552	15,121	17,633	-
Label Printing			33	12,425	10,182	-	-	-	6,485	-
Spring Water				1,250	2,025	675	1,660	1,350	1,104	675
Sweeteners				2,694	-	2,784	-	3,346	-	-
Tea			7,480	2,700	445	1,877	2,520	5,155	3,180	3,594
Freight - Glass Bottles				1,891	2,833	1,480	3,033	6,741	5,953	2,400
Brewmaster Fees - Glass				4,500	10,962	4,710	6,775	5,214	15,146	2,415
Broker Fees					144	-	-	-	-	-
Tea Supplies	-	381	112	13	-	-				23
Total Cost of Goods Sold	$ -	$ 5,381	26,456	30,934	49,415	26,402	26,817	36,927	62,403	17,527
Gross Profit	$ -	$(5,381)	(26,456)	(16,920)	(40,041)	302	26,293	10,308	(30,769)	13,295
Expense										
Broker Commissions								100	1,638	-
Consultants & Interns										
Consultants	1,323	$13,000	3,000	7,244	6,000	6,600	3,915	7,290	11,337	6,390
Total Consultants & Interns	1,323	$13,000	3,000	7,244	6,000	6,600	3,915	7,290	11,337	6,390
G & A Expenses										
Bank Fee		15	10	120			44		9	60
Payroll Fee			86	46	49	47	91	49	137	94
Other Licensing		20	-						-	-
Legal						490	-	-	18,991	-
Miscellaneous	50	236	486	-	110	400			(10)	(178)
Computer Supplies/Software					30	241				45
G & A Expenses - Other							-	-	-	(5)
Insurance - Business						1,751	-	-	-	-
Memberships		300	-	-	-	290	300	-	30	-
Office Supplies		252	106	3	642	513	971	73	367	-
Photocopies			30	3			61	1,185		-
Recruitment						26	362	292		-
Rent				1,833	-	-	3,666	917	917	917
Postage and Delivery		65	330	263	234	1,377	687	552	813	943
Telephone	90	149	166	161	505	756	665	623	626	520
Total G & A Expenses	140	$ 1,036	1,214	2,428	1,568	5,891	6,848	3,691	21,880	2,395

	Feb	Mar	Apr	May	June	Jul	Aug	Sep	Oct	Nov
Marketing Expenses										
Marketing & Promotions					14	2,544	-	4,640	4,096	84
Wearables				1,550	1,394	675	3,257		7,571	2,126
Corp. Samplers, Demos						831	1,641	344	486	-
Independent Samplers, Demos						164			140	-
Packaging Supplies for Samples				105						213
Public Relations					-	115	10,000	377	5,586	-
Donations				30						-
Sampling Wages							521			-
Trade Show Fees & Other Exp.					45	64		555	500	300
Website Fees		-	35	35	35	135	35	35	35	35
Total Marketing Expenses	$ -	$ -	$ 35	$ 1,720	$ 1,488	$ 4,528	$ 15,454	$ 5,950	$ 18,414	$ 2,758
Payroll Taxes & Benefits										
Medical Insurance										796
Payroll Taxes			1,208	493	1,188	1,184	1,405	843	1,251	1,532
Total Payroll Taxes & Benefits	$ -	$ -	$ 1,208	$ 493	$ 1,188	$ 1,184	$ 1,405	$ 843	$ 1,251	$ 2,328
R&D										
Product Development			4,461	1,161	-	410	-	-	146	-
Market Research					6,398					-
Graphic Development	100	112	5,000	-		-	-	-	-	-
Total R&D	$ 100	$ 112	$ 9,461	$ 1,161	$ 6,398	$ 410	$ -	$ -	$ 146	$ -
Payroll Wages										
Salaries and Wages		-	12,500	5,792	12,250	12,250	14,917	10,040	11,566	17,066
Total Payroll Wages	$ -	$ -	$ 12,500	$ 5,792	$ 12,250	$ 12,250	$ 14,917	$ 10,040	$ 11,566	$ 17,066
State/Federal Taxes										
State Franchise Tax	50		-	-	-	-	-	-	-	-
Licenses & Fees		970	79						245	250
Total State/Federal Taxes	$ 50	$ 970	$ 79	$ -	$ -	$ -	$ -	$ -	$ 245	$ 250
Travel & Entertainment										
Travel and Lodging			55	375	446	918	1,336	642	2,127	214
Mileage		252	-	62	724	1,462	330	30	164	1,925
Meals		22	23	63	134	73	370	12	195	102
Total Travel & Entertainment	$ -	$ 274	$ 78	$ 500	$ 1,303	$ 2,453	$ 2,036	$ 683	$ 2,485	$ 2,241
Total Expense	$ 1,612	$ 15,392	$ 27,575	$ 19,340	$ 30,196	$ 33,316	$ 44,574	$ 28,598	$ 68,960	$ 33,427
Net Ordinary Income	$ (1,612)	$ (20,773)	$ (54,032)	$ (36,259)	$ (70,237)	$ (33,014)	$ (18,282)	$ (18,289)	$ (99,729)	$ (20,133)
Other Income/Expense										
Other Expense										
Interest/Dividend Income										
Interest Income	$ -	$ -	$ -	$ (520)	$ (914)	$ (1,193)	$ (909)	$ (642)	$ (331)	$ (116)
Total Interest/Dividend Income	$ -	$ -	$ -	$ (520)	$ (914)	$ (1,193)	$ (909)	$ (642)	$ (331)	$ (116)
Total Other Expense	$ -	$ -	$ -	$ (520)	$ (914)	$ (1,193)	$ (909)	$ (642)	$ (331)	$ (116)
Net Other Income	$ -	$ -	$ -	$ 520	$ 914	$ 1,193	$ 909	$ 642	$ 331	$ 116
Net Income	$ (1,612)	$(20,773)	$ (54,032)	$ (35,739)	$ (69,324)	$ (31,821)	$ (17,373)	$ (17,647)	$ (99,398)	$ (20,017)

BUSINESS PLAN

BUSINESS PLAN

Exhibit F
Honest Tea Cash Flow Projections 1999

	Jan	Feb	Mar	Apr	May	Jun	Jul	Aug	Sep	Oct	Nov	Dec	1999
Starting Cash	$ 100,000	$ 1,046,136	$ 941,078	$ 863,133	$ 848,706	$ 908,967	$ 971,072	$ 1,047,802	$ 1,346,907	$ 1,488,037	$ 1,635,398	$ 1,776,446	$ 100,000
Cash in from Operations (Sales)	$ 80,219	$ 96,525	$ 162,338	$ 266,906	$ 347,344	$ 363,188	$ 377,813	$ 402,188	$ 377,813	$ 337,594	$ 281,531	$ 201,094	$ 3,294,553
Cash out from Operations (COGS, Expenses, Taxes)	$ 134,083	$ 201,583	$ 240,283	$ 281,333	$ 287,083	$ 301,083	$ 301,083	$ 303,083	$ 236,683	$ 190,233	$ 140,483	$ 137,233	$ 2,754,246
Cash in from Investing (equity infusions, earnings on investments)	$ 1,000,000	$ -	$ -	$ -	$ -	$ -	$ -	$ 200,000	$ -	$ -	$ -	$ -	$ 1,200,000
Cash out from Investing (equipment purchases, repaying investors)	$ -	$ -	$ -	$ -	$ -	$ -	$ -	$ -	$ -	$ -	$ -	$ -	$ -
Cash in from Financing (loans)	$ -	$ -	$ -	$ -	$ -	$ -	$ -	$ -	$ -	$ -	$ -	$ -	$ -
Cash out for Financing (repayment of debt)	$ -	$ -	$ -	$ -	$ -	$ -	$ -	$ -	$ -	$ -	$ -	$ -	$ -
Ending Cash Balance (= starting balance for next period)	$ 1,046,136	$ 941,078	$ 863,133	$ 848,706	$ 908,967	$ 971,072	$ 1,047,802	$ 1,346,907	$ 1,488,037	$ 1,635,398	$ 1,776,446	$ 1,840,307	$ 1,840,307

ASSUMPTIONS

Collections = Net 45 day

Purchases = Prepaid 30 days

Equity raised in January and August totaling $1.2 million

Debt not required for financing

Other assumptions per Profit and Loss Projection for 1999

Exhibit F Honest Tea Income Statement Projections 1999

	Jan	Feb	Mar	Apr	May	Jun	Jul	Aug	Sep	Oct	Nov	Dec	Total
Ordinary Income/Expense													
Income													
Sales	$ 80,000	$ 112,000	$ 240,000	$ 320,000	$ 400,000	$ 400,000	$ 400,000	$ 400,000	$ 400,000	$ 320,000	$ 240,000	$ 160,000	$ 3,472,000
Sales Discounts and Damage	$ 800	$ 1,120	$ 31,200	$ 3,200	$ 4,000	$ 52,000	$ 4,000	$ 4,000	$ 52,000	$ 3,200	$ 2,400	$ 1,600	$159,520
Total Income	$ 79,200	$ 110,880	$ 208,800	$ 316,800	$ 396,000	$ 348,000	$ 396,000	$ 396,000	$ 348,000	$ 316,800	$ 237,600	$ 158,400	$ 3,312,480
Cost of Goods Sold													
Total Cost of Goods Sold	$ 72,800	$ 156,000	$ 160,000	$ 200,000	$ 200,000	$ 200,000	$ 200,000	$ 200,000	$ 160,000	$ 120,000	$ 125,000	$ 80,000	$ 1,873,800
Gross Profit	$ 6,400	$ (45,120)	$ 48,800	$ 116,800	$ 196,000	$ 148,000	$ 196,000	$ 196,000	$ 188,000	$ 196,800	$ 112,600	$ 78,400	$ 1,438,680
Expense													
Broker Commissions	$ 3,200	$ 4,480	$ 9,600	$ 12,800	$ 16,000	$ 16,000	$ 16,000	$ 16,000	$ 16,000	$ 12,800	$ 9,600	$ 6,400	$ 138,880
Consultants & Interns	$ -	$ -	$ -	$ -	$ 4,500	$ 4,500	$ 4,500	$ 7,500	$ -	$ -	$ -	$ -	$ 21,000
G & A Expenses	$ 31,420	$ 31,420	$ 31,420	$ 31,420	$ 31,420	$ 31,420	$ 31,420	$ 31,420	$ 31,420	$ 31,420	$ 31,420	$ 31,420	$ 377,040
International					875	875	875	875	875	875	875	875	7,000
Marketing & Promotion	$ 7,000	$ 8,000	$ 12,500	$ 15,300	$ 16,300	$ 30,300	$ 30,300	$ 29,300	$ 15,400	$ 12,200	$ 5,700	$ 5,700	188,000
Miscellaneous	1,736	1,736	1,736	1,736	1,736	1,736	1,736	1,736	1,736	1,736	1,736	1,736	20,832
Research & Development	15,000	3,000	2,000	2,000	-	-	-	-	-	-	-	-	22,000
Sales Support	8,750	8,750	8,750	8,750	8,750	8,750	8,750	8,750	8,750	8,750	8,750	8,750	105,000
Total Expense	$ 67,106	$ 57,386	$ 66,006	$ 72,006	$ 79,581	$ 93,581	$ 93,581	$ 95,581	$ 74,181	$ 67,781	$ 58,081	$ 54,881	879,752
Net Ordinary Income	$ (60,706)	$ (102,506)	$ (17,206)	$ 44,794	$ 116,419	$ 54,419	$ 102,419	$ 100,419	$ 113,819	$ 129,019	$ 54,519	$ 23,519	558,928
Other Income/Expense													
Other Expense													
Interest/Dividend Income													
Interest Income	$ 200	941	863	848	908	971	1,047	1,146	1,288	1,435	1,576	1,640	12,863
Total Interest/Div. Inc.	$ 200	941	863	848	908	971	1,047	1,146	1,288	1,435	1,576	1,640	12,863
Total Other Expense													
Net Other Income	200	941	863	848	908	971	1,047	1,146	1,288	1,435	1,576	1,640	12,863
Net Income	$ (60,506)	$ (101,565)	$ (16,343)	$ 45,642	$ 117,327	$ 55,390	$ 103,466	$ 101,565	$ 115,107	$ 130,454	$ 56,095	$ 25,159	571,791

ASSUMPTIONS

Effective invoice price (case)	$ 16.00
Cost per case on 4/99	$ 8.00
Cost per case until 4/99	$ 10.40
Percent of brokered sales	80%

International Marketing

R&D	$ 7,000
Total	$ 7,000

Overhead & GNA Monthly

Salaries	$ 24,000
Insurance	$ 220
Office rent	$ 2,300
Legal expenses	$ 1,000
Accounting	$ 400
Benefits/staff support	$ 1,500
Phone/computer	$ 1,000
Travel	$ 1,000
Total	$ 31,420

Marketing & Promotion

Trade shows	$ 10,000
PR agency & ex	$ 50,000
Sales sheets &	$ 8,000
Sampling	$ 70,000
Shirts & promo	$ 12,000
Postage/shipping	$ 6,000
Reg. radio ads	$ 30,000
Website	$ 2,000
Total	$ 188,000

Sales Support

Slotting/intros	$ 80,000
Coolers	$ 25,000
Total	$ 105,000

Finished Inventory

12/31/98 inventory	$ 120,000
12/31/99 inventory	$ 125,000

1999 Totals

Gross income	$ 3,312,480
Total COGS	$ 1,873,800
Gross profit	$ 1,438,680
Gross Profit Margin	43.4%
Expenses	$ 879,752
Pretax net	$ 571,791
Profit Margin	17.3%

The Investment Opportunity[4]

Honest Tea is seeking equity investments totaling $1.2 million in equity capital to finance the national distribution of the product as well as the introduction of two new flavors and international sales.

The Offering

(Excluded from the Plan)

Financing History

Initial financing for Honest Tea came from the founders, Seth Goldman and Barry Nalebuff, and their friends and family. This equity funding of approximately $500,000 was used to start the business and to generate the first production run.

Exit Strategies

Investors in Honest Tea would be able to realize a return on the appreciation of their investments under any of the following scenarios:

Investment by a strategic partner – As Ocean Spray's recent purchase of a significant share of Nantucket Nectars demonstrates, there may be opportunities for investors to realize their gains through the sale of their Honest Tea shares to a strategic investor who can help the company expand its production and distribution.

Acquisition – There are numerous precedents of companies that might be interested in leveraging the integrity and purity of Honest Tea's brand. Some recent examples are the acquisition of Mistic and Snapple by Triarc. Honest Tea has already been approached by some well-known beverage companies to discuss possible acquisition opportunities.

Initial Public Offering – If Honest Tea meets our expectations for growth, the Company might consider some form of public offering to raise capital for expansion in the future.

Investment Risks

In addition to the economic and business factors which pose risks for most early-stage companies, an investment in Honest Tea carries several other risks:

Product Risk – Although we are insured for product liability, a health-related incident such as the one Odwalla experienced several years ago could do significant damage to the Honest Tea brand name. Of course, since our product is pasteurized twice, there is less of a risk that the same types of bacteria could emerge.

Competitive Risk – Republic of Tea, a company that has a well-established brand name among tea lovers, might decide to enter the retail market with a more competitively priced product. Such a move could dampen the uniqueness of our message. Crystal Geyser, a company which has deep pockets and preexisting distribution relationships, might decide to introduce additional products beyond TeJava and spread its distribution more aggressively beyond the West Coast.

Management Risk – At this point, the development of the company has been concentrated largely in the hands of Seth Goldman and Barry Nalebuff. If either of them were unable to continue to play a role in the Company's progress, the growth of Honest Tea might be impaired.

Competitive Advantage

The results of this past summer clearly indicate that Honest Tea has tapped into a market opportunity. When we were planning the company's strategy last year we entertained the idea

[4]The Investment Opportunity section, including the offering and financing history is not included in the business plan as available on the Honest Tea Web site. The comments included here are based upon multiple sources and are meant to be a fair representation of the original information.

of spending several years building up a strong presence in a local market before expanding nationally. We have chosen to grow in a more aggressive manner for several reasons:

Market Niche – We have created a new beverage category and are currently the only company filling that category. If we hesitate, other companies are likely to move in.

Compelling brand image and story – The packaging, presentation and profile of the Honest Tea brand fit together extremely well with the product. Although we may improve on the bottle design in the future, this is a package that comes close to selling itself. It is also a brand and a story, which has successfully gained free media coverage, and should continue to do so.

Management Team – We have developed a team with the right combination of sales experience and market creativity that is capable of growing the company on a national, and even international, scale.

A Parting Thought

Prospective investors in Honest Tea are advised to keep in mind the words of Sung Dynasty poet Li Chi Lai who cited the three great evils that might beset the land:

> the spoiling of gallant youths through bad education; the degradation of good art through incompetent criticism; and the waste of fine tea through careless making.

While we may not be able to have much direct influence over education and the arts, Honest Tea stands poised to restore integrity to a beverage that has brought people together for hundreds of generations and throughout dozens of civilizations. There has never been a time when consumers have been so overwhelmed with choices. And yet there has never been a time when integrity and authenticity are as cherished as they are scarce. There has never been a better time for Honest Tea.

Chapter 3

CREATING BUSINESS FROM OPPORTUNITY

Tony Hsieh
Bloomberg/Getty
Images

Entrepreneurs find and take advantage of opportunities that others don't recognize or cannot access the resources to exploit. When Zappos.com founder Nick Swinmurn became frustrated by looking for shoes, both in stores and online, he saw an opportunity to create an online megastore that carried a multitude of sizes, styles, and colors. Swinmurn was three years out of college when he launched Shoesite.com in 1999 with $150,000. Within a month, he relaunched as Zappos.com. In 2000, Tony Hsieh of Venture Frog Incubators saw the opportunity in Zappos, investing $1.1 million and joining Swinmurn. The company thrives on providing the best selection and service, with a focus on the "wow" factor. Zappos.com carries more than 1100 brands, stocks more than 3 million shoes, employs more than 1,300 people, and had annual revenues in excess of $1 billion in 2009. In November 2009, Amazon.com acquired Zappos.com, Inc. in a deal valued at $1.2 billion on the initial closing day. Zappos.com has expanded its product offerings to include handbags, clothing, and other items and was restructured into 10 separate companies.[1]

Performance Objectives

1. Define your business.
2. Articulate your core beliefs, mission, and vision.
3. Analyze your competitive advantage.
4. Perform viability testing using the economics of one unit.
5. Understand how to value a business.

Apple and the Personal Computer

market a group of people or organizations that may be interested in buying a given product or service, has the resources to purchase it, and is permitted by law and regulation to do so.

In 1943, IBM's founder Thomas Watson said, "I think there is a world market for about five computers." A **market** is a group of people or organizations that may be interested in buying a given product or service, has the resources to purchase it, and is permitted by law and regulation to do so. When Watson made his statement, computers were forbiddingly large and expensive machines that only the government, universities, and a few giant corporations could afford. That was the *market* for computers at the time.

By the 1970s, however, a few people were talking about creating personal computers. These enthusiasts were outside of mainstream thinking. One such visionary was Stephen Wozniak, who had landed his first job at Hewlett-Packard, then as now, a major company. He was also attending meetings of the Homebrew Club, a Palo Alto–based group of electronics hobbyists. Wozniak was determined to build a small personal computer to show the club members, using existing technology. He believed that there was a much larger market for hobbyist computers than IBM and Hewlett-Packard thought. Tandy, Hewlett-Packard, and IBM all had personal computers on the market, but not of the sort Wozniak envisioned.

Wozniak offered Hewlett-Packard a chance to co-develop his small computer. The company was not focused on desktop computing, and the technology did not fit into its computer or calculator strategies, so it turned him down. Wozniak's friend Steve Jobs also was interested in the technology and set out to sell some hobbyist computers. After some time and considerable effort, Jobs sold 100 circuit boards to a local start-up

---

[1]Zappos.com, Inc., http://www.zappos.com, March 13, 2011.

Apple cofounder Stephen Wozniak.
(Tony Avelar/Bloomberg via Getty Images)

computer shop, and then Wozniak, Jobs, and three helpers soldered together components in the garage of Jobs's home in Cupertino, California.

Wozniak worked on his design concepts until he created the Apple II, which could display pictures and text and is now considered one of the great achievements in the computer industry. Jobs, meanwhile, searched for an investor. Finally, after being turned down by friends and family, he found Mike Markkula, who also saw the possibilities of Apple. Markkula agreed to invest $80,000 in the company in return for a significant share of equity. He also put together Apple's business plan and worked to secure additional investors. This is a classic demonstration of entrepreneurs recognizing opportunities that others do not see.

By 1984, Apple had sales of $1.5 billion, and over $65.2 billion in fiscal year 2010. Wozniak and Jobs recognized an opportunity that led to a product that satisfied the needs of an enormous market that the giants of the industry did not recognize.

Business Definition

Performance Objective 1 ▶
Define your business.

In order to operate a successful enterprise, you will need to be able to provide a complete company description. This description should include the need for your product or service that is either unsatisfied by the current players in the market or is something you can provide better, differently, or more economically.

Before you can start a business, you must define it in several dimensions. The *business definition* answers three questions: who, what, and how?

1. **Who** will the business serve? In other words, who are the potential qualified customers in the market for your product or service? They may not currently recognize a need for *your* product or service, but they are in the market for the products or services of your competition.

2. **What** will the business offer the customer? What is the complete bundle of products or services your enterprise will provide? This should address not only the tangible product or intangible service but the benefits it will bring. For example, a mattress store sells "restful sleep" rather than just mattresses.

3. **How** will the business provide the products or services it offers? What are the primary actions and activities required to conduct this business? All businesses must produce a product or service, sell it to customers, deliver it, and receive payment. This part of the business definition includes the primary activities of:

   - buying or developing or manufacturing the product;
   - identifying its potential qualified customers and selling the product to them;
   - producing and delivering the product, and
   - receiving payment.

A solid business definition has three elements:

1. *The offer.* What will you sell to your customers? That is called the *offer* and includes exactly which products and services you will bring to the market and how you will price them. For example: You will provide an online and telephone fitness-consulting service for an initial four-week period at $25 per week, or eight weeks at $20 per week.

2. ***Target market.*** Which segment of the consumer market are you aiming to serve? As discussed in Chapter 4, this is your *target market*. Defining your target market in a way that will help you identify potential customers is an important factor in achieving success. This definition must be precise enough so that you can identify a viable market for the business and focus your marketing efforts. A target market of every adult in the United States is clearly too broad and unfocused. A market of every member of Congress from the state of Rhode Island (three individuals) would be too narrow.

3. ***Production and delivery capability.*** How will you provide your offer to your targeted customers? This includes how to perform the key activities required to produce the product or service, deliver it to your customers, and ensure that they are satisfied.

Apple began as a manufacturing business, making a product. There are four basic types of businesses:

1. **Manufacturing** produces a tangible product and sells it, either through distributors or directly to end customers.
2. **Wholesale** buys in bulk from manufacturers and sells smaller quantities to retailers.
3. **Retail** sells individual items to consumers.
4. **Service** sells an intangible product to businesses or consumers.

manufacturing the making or producing of a tangible product.

wholesale the buying in bulk from manufacturers and selling smaller quantities to retailers.

retail the selling of individual items to consumers.

service the selling of an intangible product to businesses or consumers

What Sort of Organization Do You Want?

Each organization has the opportunity to create a unique mission, vision, and culture that are supported by core values. The management team can determine how to use the company's competitive advantage to satisfy customers. The organization's culture can be shaped according to the business environment, and by the way employees, customers, and other stakeholders are to be treated—an example that is set by the founding entrepreneur (owner).

Your Company's Core Values

When you start your own company, what beliefs will you use to guide it? These are the **core values** of your business. Core values include the fundamental ethical and moral philosophy and beliefs that form the foundation of the organization and provide broad guidance for all decision making. Examples of the core values of a business might be:

◀ **Performance Objective 2**
Articulate your core beliefs, mission, and vision.

core values the fundamental ethical and moral philosophy and beliefs that form the foundation of an organization, and provide broad guidance for all decision making.

- "At Superior Printing, we engage in business practices that affect the environment as little as possible."
- "At Sheila's Restaurant, we believe in supporting local organic farmers."

Exercise

Imagine you are Nick Swinmurn of Zappos.com. On a separate sheet of paper, define your business:

1. Who will the business serve?
2. What will the business offer? What are the products (or services) the business will sell?
3. How will the business provide the products or services it offers? What are the primary actions and activities required to conduct this business?

Core values will affect business decisions. The owner of Superior Printing, for example, will choose ink that is less harmful to the environment over a cheaper ink that is more harmful. Superior Printing may also have a paper-recycling program to minimize its paper consumption. The owner of Sheila's Restaurant will buy fruits and vegetables from local organic farmers. Your core beliefs will affect everything, from the cost of materials to the prices you charge to how you treat customers. For additional examples of core values, see **Exhibit 3-1**.

Your Company's Mission Is to Satisfy Customers

The mission of your business, expressed in a *mission statement*, is a concise communication of your purpose, business definition, and values. The function of a mission statement is to clarify what the business is trying to do in the present, but it can provide direction and motivation for future action through a clear and compelling message.

As noted in Chapter 2, a well-crafted mission statement will not only tell your customers and employees what your business is about but can (and should) be a guide for every decision you make. It should capture your passion for the business and your commitment to satisfying your customers. A mission statement should be limited to 40 or 50 words, to induce clarity in concept and expression. The mission statement should address the following topics: target customers; products and services;

Exhibit 3-1 *Core Values*

Tyson Foods Inc.

Based on our heritage of more than 65 years, these are the core values that we strongly believe in (listed in alphabetical order):

- *Brand Excellence*
- *Commitment, Fun, and Opportunity*
- *Environmental, Food Safety, and Team Member Safety Responsibility*
- *Family and Social Responsibility*
- *Innovation*
- *Integrity*
- *Market and Customer Focus*
- *Self-leadership and Learning*
- *Teamwork*

Dow AgroSciences

To ensure the prosperity and well-being of Dow AgroSciences employees, customers, and shareholders, cumulative long-term profit growth is essential. How we achieve this objective is as important as the objective itself. Fundamental to our success are the core values we believe in and practice.

- *Employees are the source of Dow AgroSciences' success. We communicate openly, treat each other with respect, promote teamwork, and encourage personal initiative and growth. Excellence in performance is rewarded.*
- *Customers receive our strongest commitment to meet their needs with high-quality products and superior service.*
- *Products are based on innovative technology, continuous improvement, and added value for our customers and end users.*
- *Our conduct demonstrates a deep concern for human safety and environmental stewardship, while embracing the highest standards of ethics and citizenship.*

DuPont Company

Safety, concern and care for people, protection of the environment, and personal and corporate integrity are this company's highest values, and we will not compromise them.

Exhibit 3-2 *Mission Statements*

Nike—*Crush Reebok.*

Walt Disney—*To make people happy.*

W. L. Gore & Associates—*Our products are designed to be the highest quality in their class and revolutionary in their effect.*

Slumber Parties, Inc.—*We seek to empower women at every stage of life through our products, demonstrations, and careers. To achieve this goal, we offer women the opportunity to become more confident and satisfied in all aspects of their lives.*

DuPont Company—*Sustainable Growth: Increasing shareholder and societal value while reducing our environmental footprint.*

Dell Computers—*With the power of direct and Dell's team of talented people, we are able to provide customers with superb value; high quality; relevant technology; customized systems; superior service and support; and products and services that are easy to buy and use.*

markets served; use of technology; importance of public issues and employees; and focus on survival, profitability, and growth.

Here is an example of a mission statement for the Most Chocolate Cake Company:

> *The Most Chocolate Cake Company will create the richest, tastiest, most chocolaty cakes in our area. They will be made from the finest and freshest ingredients with our own extraordinary frostings and fillings. Baked to order and individually decorated for that special occasion, they will make any event as special as our cakes!*

The Most Chocolate Cake Company's mission statement defines the business and its competitive advantage, the core of its strategy. Examples of mission statements from a range of organizations appear in **Exhibit 3-2**.

Your Company's Vision Is the Broader Perspective

The *vision* for your business will be broader and more comprehensive than its mission, painting a picture of the overall view of what you want your organization to become in the future, not what it is at the moment. It is built upon the core values and belief systems of the organization. It should energize your people, and they should embrace it with enthusiasm and passion. This means that the vision must be compelling across the organization. It has to matter. Employees need to be empowered in order to fulfill the vision. Examples of vision statements appear in **Exhibit 3-3**.

Your Company's Culture Defines the Work Environment

The culture of an organization is largely shaped by its leadership. *Culture* is composed of the core values of the organization in action. Leaders of a company build a particular culture by making the beliefs, values, and behavioral norms explicit and intentional. Culture includes factors such as risk tolerance and innovation; orientation with respect to people, teams, and outcomes; attention to detail; and communications norms. Organizational culture is learned by members of the team in a number of ways, including anecdotes, ceremonies and events, material symbols, and particular use of language. For example, at General Electric, stories of Jack Welch are legendary. At Hewlett-Packard there was the "Hewlett-Packard Way," based on anecdotes passed down from one generation of employees to the next. Those who work in small enterprises often see the top management daily and take their cues directly because there are very few or no layers between them. As enterprises become larger, leaders may not often be on view to most employees and frequently take on larger-than-life roles through stories.

Exhibit 3-3 *Vision Statements*

Caterpillar—Be a global leader in customer value.

McDonald's—Our vision is to be the world's best quick-service restaurant experience. Being the best means providing outstanding quality, service, cleanliness, and value, so that we make every customer in every restaurant smile.

General Motors—GM's vision is to be the world leader in transportation products and related services. We will earn our customers' enthusiasm through continuous improvement driven by the integrity, teamwork, and innovation of GM people.

Bimbo Bakeries USA—To be the baking leader in the United States through quality, freshness, service, and the building of our brands.

DuPont Company—Our vision is to be the world's most dynamic science company, creating sustainable solutions essential to a better, safer, healthier life for people everywhere.

Cargill—Our purpose is to be the global leader in nourishing people. We will harness our knowledge and energy to provide goods and services that are necessary for life, health, and growth.

Ceremonies can make a significant difference in a company's culture. Are there periodic recognition events for innovation? Does the company invite family members to appropriate occasions throughout the year? Is there a birthday celebration for each employee? Are years of service recognized? Material symbols come in many shapes and forms. At the Wilmington, Delaware, headquarters of Legacy MBNA America, the values of the company appear on every archway, and handprints of the employees make colorful wall art in some buildings. At any business, reserved parking spots and special privileges for certain employees send a message to everyone. Are these spaces for top executives, or expectant mothers? Are office sizes determined by pay grade? Finally, language tells a lot about the culture. Is everyone on a first-name basis with everyone else? Are some people addressed informally and others not? Is the language around the company in general formal or informal? Is communication respectful?

These and many other factors are all part of the culture of an organization. Culture should be crafted to follow the core beliefs of the founding entrepreneur and support the mission and vision of the business.

The Decision Process

Translating opportunity into success can and has happened in literally millions of ways. Each business has a different story. However, there are three primary routes in the deliberate search process to identify opportunities:

- The entrepreneur looks for business opportunities through a process of identification and selection, beginning with self-developed (or group-developed) ideas.
- The entrepreneur uses essentially the same process but starts with research on hot businesses or growth areas.
- The entrepreneur has an idea for a product or service and searches for a market.

These processes are illustrated in **Figure 3-1.**

In each case, a decision is made based on personal values and thinking. Whereas each ultimately funnels the procedure down to a business concept, the processes are repeated—often with many ideas being considered—before a viable picture emerges. The first two options are market driven; the third is product driven. Entrepreneurs do better looking to the market(s) of interest, rather than creating a product and then trying to find a customer base. You can do this all alone, but it is best to work with others who will provide honest, constructive feedback.

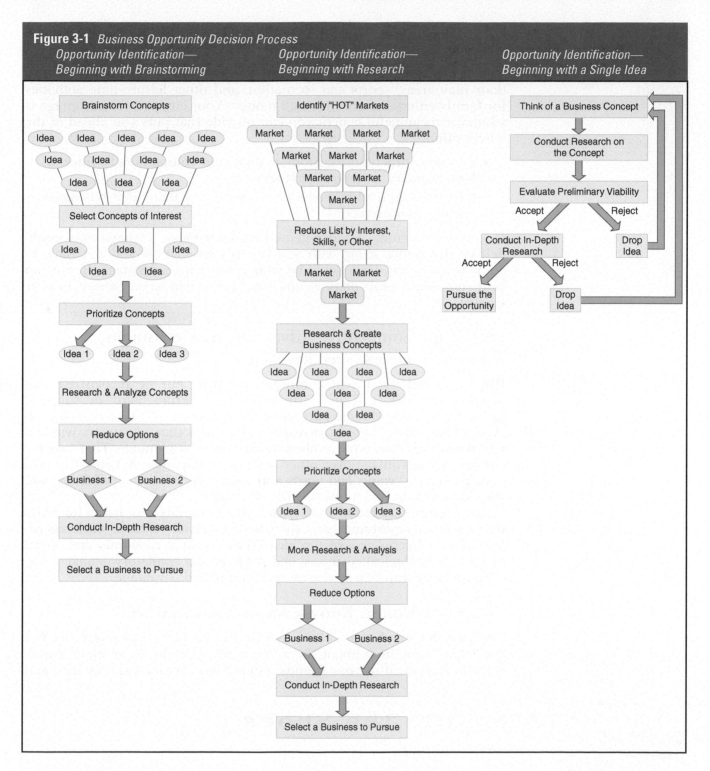

Figure 3-1 *Business Opportunity Decision Process*

Your Competitive Advantage

For your business to be successful and to fulfill your mission and vision, you will need a strategy for beating the competition. This is your *competitive advantage,* or core competency. It is whatever you can do better than the competition that will attract a sufficient number of customers to your business so it can succeed. The competitive advantage must be *sustainable* in order to create long-term viability. Your competition is defined by your

> **Performance Objective 3**
> Analyze your competitive advantage.

target market and can be *direct* (selling the same or similar products to the same market) or *indirect* (selling different products that compete for the same share of customer spending). For example, a children's museum will indirectly compete with rental movies/movie theaters, indoor/outdoor play areas, sports and recreation, and other leisure-time activities for family entertainment time and money. Your competitive advantage is whatever meaningful benefit you can provide that puts you ahead of the competition.

- Can you attract more customers than your competitors by offering better quality or some special service?
- Can you supply your product at a lower price than other businesses serving your market?

If you are running a video-game-rental business, perhaps you could deliver the games along with snacks, so customers would not have to come to the store. That would be your competitive advantage. If you can beat your competitors on price *and* service, you will be very strong in your market.

Find Your Competitive Advantage by Determining What Consumers Need and Want

Bill Gates did not invent computer software, but he recognized that people were frustrated and intimidated by it. From there, he supplied operating systems that he purchased from another software company to IBM, created user-friendly software applications that consumers wanted, and packaged them attractively with easy-to-read manuals. That was his competitive advantage over other software companies. When you know your customers' wants and needs and your competitors' capabilities, you should be able to find a competitive advantage.

Remember, as you identify environmental trends and search for product or service opportunity gaps, there will be outside forces at work regardless of the effectiveness of the idea. These include economic and social factors, technological advances, and political and regulatory changes. Any of these forces can be a source of opportunity and advantage.

You Have Unique Knowledge of Your Market

You may be wondering, "How do I figure out what customers need? I don't know anything about them." Actually, you do. Your market may well be composed of your friends, neighbors, classmates, relatives, and

(Courtesy of Honeecakes Bakery)

Step into the Shoes . . .

A Sweet Schedule

Andrea Dashiell started Honeecakes Bakery in 2004, when she was a student at Suitland Senior High School in Forestville, Maryland. She took orders and produced homemade pound cakes, pies, and pastries around her school schedule, initially as part of her involvement with the Network for Teaching Entrepreneurship (NFTE). Then, as a full-time college student living two hours away, Andrea continued to operate Honeecakes Bakery through online and telephone ordering, while working around her class schedule. By electing to have a virtual storefront rather than a physical retail site, Andrea, on her terms, maintained her business and furthered her education.

Source: Courtesy of Honeecakes Bakery.

Global Impact . . .

SoftTribe Founders See That Tropical Tolerance Is Needed for Software in Ghana

Hermann Chinery-Hesse and Joe Jackson saw an opportunity in the need for adapting software for tropical climates when they founded SoftTribe in 1991. Their company develops software, taking into consideration the unique requirements of the West African social and business environment. According to their partner, Microsoft, "The SoftTribe software is practical and resilient, functional under conditions of intermittent connectivity, power fluctuations, low bandwidth, and operators who, as a rule, are less familiar with computing than in some other parts of the world."[2]

Chinery-Hesse has been called the Bill Gates of Ghana for his success in building SoftTribe, and for his desire to "spark an entrepreneurial revolution in Africa by bringing e-commerce to the most remote corners of the continent."[3] SoftTribe is the largest software company in sub-Saharan Africa, using its partnership with Microsoft as a means of expansion.

(Benedicte Desrus/ Sipa/Newscom)

colleagues. You already have the most important knowledge that you need to succeed. Or, if you are starting a business to address a problem that you have encountered, chances also are that you know your market very well.

Sir Richard Branson, the CEO of Virgin Corporation, chose "Virgin" because it reflected his total inexperience in business. His empire, which includes Virgin Megastores, Virgin Atlantic Airways, and Virgin Mobile, began as a tiny discount mail-order record company, which he started at age 19 after he had dropped out of high school. "I realized I'd be hopeless at studying," Branson told *Woman's Journal* magazine in 1985. "So I quit to do something I knew I could do and which interested me." Branson knew his market—other young people who were into music—very well. Then, he learned about the other markets before he entered them.

How will you know if a business idea is going to be successful? You cannot have a guarantee, but your market will tell you a lot about your chances. The answer will come in the form of the signal called *profit*. You can learn a lot about the potential for success well ahead of starting your enterprise through customer and market research, in addition to competitive analysis.

The Six Factors of Competitive Advantage

Competitive advantage comes from one or a combination of six factors:

1. *Quality.* Can you provide higher quality than competing businesses?
2. *Price.* Can you offer a lower price on a sustained basis than your competition?
3. *Location.* Can you find a more convenient location for customers?
4. *Selection.* Can you provide a wider range of choices than your competitors can?
5. *Service.* Can you provide better, more personalized customer service?
6. *Speed/turnaround.* Can you deliver your product/service more quickly than the competition?

[2]"Taking African Business Global," Microsoft Unlimited Potential, http://www.microsoft.com/unlimitedpotential/, January 13, 2010.

[3]Max Chafkin, "Meet the Bill Gates of Ghana," *Inc.*, http://www.inc.com/magazine/20081001/, October 1, 2008.

Is Your Competitive Advantage Strong Enough?

When deciding whether or not your business concept is viable, it will be essential to determine your competitive advantage and whether it is strong enough. According to Jeffry Timmons, a successful company needs to do one of the following.[4]

- *Sell to a market that is large and growing.* The market for digital cameras is a good example of this. New products are being marketed to meet the demand, such as printers that turn digital photos into prints with digital photo frames.

- *Sell to a market where the competition is able to make a profit.* It will be interesting to observe what happens in the market for hybrid cars. Right now the jury is out as to whether the companies manufacturing them can make a profit, so most automakers are not yet entering the field. There may not be a sufficiently large market at present to make entry worthwhile.

- *Sell to a market where the competition is succeeding but is not so powerful as to make it impossible for a new entrepreneur to enter.* Microsoft has been taken to court several times by competitors who argue that it is so big that new software companies cannot enter the market. **Barriers to entry** are the factors that contribute to the ease or difficulty of a new competitor joining an established market, and they cannot be so high that market entry and success are not possible.

barriers to entry the factors that contribute to the ease or difficulty of a new competitor joining an established market.

- *Sell a product or service that solves problems consumers may have with the competition.* Problems can include poor quality or slow delivery. FedEx beat its competition—the Flying Tigers, the U.S. Postal Service, and United Parcel Service (UPS)—when it entered the package-delivery market with its guaranteed overnight service.

- *Sell a product or service at a competitive price that will attract customers.* UPS fought back by offering a less-expensive overnight delivery service than FedEx's.

In addition to the above, it is also necessary to:

- understand the needs of your customers,
- have a sustainable competitive advantage or multiple advantages, and
- deliver a product or service that meets your customers' needs at the right price.

Entrepreneurial Wisdom . . .

A new business usually will require time before it can turn a profit. Federal Express, in fact, suffered initial losses of a million dollars a month! But if you are not making enough money to stay in business, that is the market speaking. It is telling you that your business is not satisfying consumer needs well enough. Do not take it personally. Many famous entrepreneurs opened and closed a number of businesses during their lifetime.

Henry Ford failed in business twice before the Ford Motor Company was a success. If you want to be a successful entrepreneur, start growing a thick skin and decide right now that you intend to learn from failures and disappointments. Do not let them get you down. Most importantly, learn from them, so that you do not make the same mistakes again.

---

[4]Jeffry A. Timmons, *New Venture Creation*, 6th ed. (New York: McGraw-Hill/Irwin, 2003).

Step into the Shoes . . .

What's in a Name? Just Ask Lexicon Branding, Inc.

(Peter Chadwick/Alamy)

What do Proctor & Gamble's Swiffer® and Febreze® brands, Verizon's FiOS®, Research in Motion's Blackberry®, and Colgate's Wisp® have in common? The brand names all were developed by the team of linguists and creatives at Lexicon Branding.

According to Lexicon, a new brand name must:

- work across multiple media platforms and across the Internet;
- be easy to search—yet distinctive within the context of blogs, YouTube and Twitter environments;
- have the potential to be registered in key countries;
- have the capability of being used around the world.[5]

When CEO David Placek founded Sausalito, California-based Lexicon in 1982, he recognized an opportunity and created a business that now engages 70 linguists in 50 nations.[6] Placek's creatives use marketing and advertising principles with structural linguistics expertise to create strong, memorable brand names. By following the four seemingly simple principles for naming a brand, they offer companies a service that cannot be matched internally.

The mission of Lexicon Branding has always been "To create extraordinary brand names. Names that get attention, names that generate interest, and names that tell the relevant consumer something new."[7]

Having completed over 2,500 projects around the globe, Lexicon uses research in a variety of areas to keep it in a leading position.[8] Investigations include consumer trends and technologies, as one might expect, but additional areas include linguistics, sound symbolism, and the potential for words to convey encoded messages.

Checking Out the Competition

One useful exercise is to learn everything you can about particular competitors, especially those that have earned the respect of the marketplace. Try to identify the sources of their competitive advantage. Look at their Web sites. Conduct Internet searches. Track their advertising and promotion, including print, broadcast, Internet, and sponsorships. If they are retailers, shop their stores or have your friends and family do so. Get to know them (but do not do anything unethical or illegal to obtain information). You will also need to keep an eye on your competition after you have started your business, because new factors might undermine your competitive advantage.

Today's entrepreneurs, even those starting very small ventures, may face competition from far beyond their neighborhoods because customers can go shopping on the Web. Optimism is a trait that goes with entrepreneurship, so entrepreneurs tend to get excited about the Web's potential customer base. What they often do not consider is that, "The world already is selling to their customers—aggressively and seamlessly."[9] Therefore, get online yourself and conduct a thorough search of your industry. You may find that there is literally a world of opportunity or, conversely, that the world is full of competitors.

To determine whether you have a competitive advantage that will enable you to outperform your closest and strongest competition, consider the following.

- ***Competitive offers.*** How does your offer compare with those of your leading competitors? What are the key features of each?

[5]Lexicon Branding, "Our Brand Naming Process," http://www.lexiconbranding.com, January 23, 2011.

[6]Dan Heath and Chip Heath, "How to Pick the Perfect Brand Name," *FastCompany*, January 3, 2011.

[7]Lexicon Branding, "About Lexicon," http://www.lexiconbranding.com, January 23, 2011.

[8]Ibid.

[9]Fred Hapgood, "Foreign Exchange," *Inc.*, June 1997.

unique selling proposition (USP) the distinctive feature and benefit that sets a company apart from its competition.

- *Unique selling proposition.* Based on that comparison, what is your **unique selling proposition (USP),** the distinctive feature and benefit that sets you apart from your competition? This will require a comparison of offers and identifying what is unique about yours. What is it about your offer that your competitors cannot or will not match?
- *Cost structure.* What is different about your business activities and the cost of doing business, compared to the competition? Overall, are you at a cost advantage or disadvantage?

To be successful, you must have a USP that will attract customers to buy from you. Second, you must have a cost structure that is sufficiently advantageous so that, when all of your costs are deducted from your revenue, you will have sufficient profit left over. If you can achieve a cost advantage or at least minimize any cost disadvantage, this will help you achieve a profit. This profit is your reward for operating a successful business.

The Most Chocolate Cake Company

There are a number of ways to highlight your competitive advantage and identify opportunities. In this example, Amy makes and sells chocolate cakes. She chose this product because she loves chocolate and she enjoys baking cakes. She decided to make the *most chocolate* cakes possible. From this decision, she came up with the concept for her product and the name of her business, the Most Chocolate Cake Company.

Amy's target market was the segment of the public that loved chocolate cakes but did not have the time or interest in baking them. Because cakes are usually purchased for special occasions, our entrepreneur believed she could charge a good price, at least as much as a bakery store cake. She decided she would make the cakes special by:

- using the finest ingredients (quality);
- personalizing each cake through expert custom-decorating (selection), and
- baking the cakes to order, so they would be fresh for the event (quality).

Amy bakes her cakes at home in her specially designed commercial kitchen, which makes them literally homemade and thus reduces the cost of producing them—she is not renting commercial space or paying a staff. Of course, the flip side of baking at home is that her production is limited. Also, she may have to take time to deliver each cake, depending on local zoning regulations regarding retail trade.

Business Definition Question	The Most Chocolate Cake Company
1. *The Offer:* What products and services will be sold?	Chocolate cakes for special events at a price competitive with neighborhood stores.
2. *Target Market:* Which consumer segment will the business focus on?	People who love chocolate and those who want a special cake for a special event.
3. *Production Capability:* How will that offer be produced and delivered to those customers?	Homemade and baked to order to ensure freshness, using high-quality ingredients.
4. *Problem Solving:* What problem does the business solve for its customers?	Specialty made-to-order cakes of top quality.

The chart below shows how Amy answered the key questions about competitive advantage for the Most Chocolate Cake Company.

Competitive Advantage Question	Competitive Advantage
1. *The Offer:* What will be better and different about the products and services that will be sold?	Most Chocolate will use more and higher-grade chocolate and better ingredients in general, especially in frostings and fillings; will have personalized decorations; will be freshly baked to order.
2. *Target Market:* Which consumers should be the focus of the business to make it as successful as possible?	People who love chocolate and those who want a special cake for a special event.
3. *Production and Delivery Capability:* What will be better or different about the way that the offer is produced and delivered to the customers?	Homemade and baked to order to ensure freshness, using highest-quality ingredients.

Our entrepreneur is betting that her more chocolaty cake with its special frosting and decoration, as well as its freshly homemade quality, will be successful in the marketplace. This is her USP. She hopes it will be a source of competitive advantage, along with the cost advantage of baking the cakes at home. Based on this analysis, she has determined how she wants to make her offering better and different from those of her competitors.

Another approach to the analysis is to compare your business concept with the competitors that you have identified through your research. A simple comparative table is a good way to display this. The table should include each of the six factors of competitive advantage. Plus, if there are particular features that you want to highlight, or specific aspects of the six factors, adding them to the table will make them more prominent. These ratings can be done solely by you or your team through market-research techniques, or however you think you can get the most unbiased responses.

There are many ways to construct this type of competitive analysis table. **Exhibit 3-4** shows ratings of excellent, good, moderate, fair, and poor for each factor with each competitor. This makes competitive advantages and weaknesses readily apparent. However, it does not yield an overall rating.

The chart in **Exhibit 3-5** is an example of a more quantitative approach to competitive analysis. First, based upon industry data or quality customer research, each factor is assigned a weight according to its importance to the company's target customers, with the total of all factors equaling 1.00. For example, *quality* could be weighted 0.20, *location* weighted 0.10, with other factors adding up to 0.70, if customers are very concerned about the quality of the product and whether they can buy it on the Internet. Second, each competitor should be rated on an odd-numbered scale, such as 1 to 5—with 1 being lowest and 5 the highest—on each factor. For example, the Most Chocolate Cake Company could rate a 5 on quality and 2 on selection, whereas the supermarket could rate 2 on quality and 5 on location. Third, to calculate a weighted score, each rating should be multiplied by the associated weight to obtain a total. For example, if quality is rated 0.20 and Most Chocolate's quality is rated 5, the weighted value is 1.00. Looking across the competitors at scores on individual factors can yield insights into areas of strength or vulnerability. Finally, all the weighted values for each company should be totaled and an overall rating calculated. By looking at the ratings, it becomes apparent which are the strongest and weakest competitors, and a company can address the results of the analysis.

Exhibit 3-4 *Comparative Analysis—Qualitative—The Most Chocolate Cake Factory*

	Most Chocolate Cake Company	Mega Super Market, Inc.	Average Bakery Co.	Fancy Bakery, LLC
Quality	Excellent	Fair	Fair	Excellent
Price	Fair	Good	Moderate	Poor
Location	Moderate	Excellent	Moderate	Good
Selection	Fair	Moderate	Good	Moderate
Service	Excellent	Fair	Moderate	Fair
Speed/Turnaround	Good	Excellent	Moderate	Fair
Specialization	Excellent	Poor	Fair	Moderate
Personalization	Excellent	Moderate	Good	Excellent

Exhibit 3-5 *Comparative Analysis—Quantitative—The Most Chocolate Cake Company*

		Most Chocolate Cake Company		Mega Super Market, Inc.		Average Bakery Co.		Fancy Bakery, LLC	
	Wt.	Rating	Wtd. Rating	Rating	Wtd. Rating	Rating	Wtd. Rating	Rating	Wtd. Rating
Quality	0.20	5	1.00	2	0.40	2	0.40	5	1.00
Price	0.10	2	0.20	4	0.40	3	0.30	1	0.10
Location	0.10	3	0.30	5	0.50	3	0.30	4	0.40
Selection	0.15	2	0.30	3	0.45	4	0.60	3	0.45
Service	0.10	5	0.50	2	0.20	3	0.30	2	0.20
Speed/Turnaround	0.05	4	0.20	5	0.25	3	0.15	2	0.10
Specialization	0.20	5	1.00	1	0.20	2	0.40	3	0.60
Personalization	0.10	5	0.50	3	0.30	4	0.40	5	0.50
Total	1.00	xxxxx	**4.00**	xxxxx	**2.70**	xxxxx	**2.85**	xxxxx	**3.35**

Competitive Strategy: Business Definition and Competitive Advantage

Your business will only succeed if you can offer the customers in your market something more, better, and/or different from what the competition is doing. Your competitive advantage (core competency) is essential and, once you establish it, your business decisions will start to fall into place. Every advertisement, every promotion—even the price of your product and the location of your business—should be designed to get customers excited about your competitive advantage.

competitive strategy the combination of a company's business definition with its competitive advantage.

Your **competitive strategy** combines your business definition with your competitive advantage. A competitive advantage must be *sustainable*, meaning that you can keep it going. If you decide to beat the competition by selling your product at a lower price, your advantage will not last long if you cannot afford to continue at that price. Small business owners should realize that price alone is not likely to work as an advantage in the long run. A larger business can almost always beat you on price because it can buy larger quantities than you can and thus probably receives a greater discount from suppliers.

Being able to temporarily undercut the competition's prices is not a competitive advantage. Being able to *permanently* sell at a lower price because you have discovered a cheaper supplier *is* a competitive advantage. Being able to develop and maintain proprietary product or service features and benefits is another approach to finding a sustainable advantage.

Strategy versus Tactics

Your **strategy** is the plan for outperforming the competition. Your **tactics** are the ways in which you will carry out your strategy.

strategy a plan for how an organization or individual intends to outdo competitors.

tactics the specific ways in which a business carries out its strategy.

If you plan to open a bookstore, how will you compete with the chain outlet in the neighborhood? This competitor buys more books and will receive higher discounts from wholesalers, so you probably will not be able to compete on price. How else could you attract customers? Perhaps you could make your bookstore a kind of community center, so people would want to gather there. What tactics could you use to carry out this strategy?

- Hold poetry readings and one-performer concerts to promote local poets and musicians.
- Create special-interest book-discussion groups.
- Offer free tea and coffee.
- Provide comfortable seating areas for conversation and reading to encourage customers to spend time in your store.
- Set up a binder of personal ads as a dating service.

If your tactics attract enough customers to make a profit, you will have found a strategy for achieving a competitive advantage.

To discover a competitive advantage, think about everything your business will offer. Examine your location, product, design, and price. What can you do to be different, and better in some way, than the competition?

Feasibility Revisited: The Economics of One Unit as a Litmus Test

Once you have chosen a business idea and determined your competitive advantage, you should make a preliminary analysis to determine whether the business can be financially viable. In other words, can you provide your product or service at a price that will cover your costs and provide you with a profit? Wozniak and Jobs were able to set up business in an office once they secured Markkula's investment in Apple. This gave them a better environment to develop and introduce the Apple II, which provided operating profits. Before investing considerable time, effort, and money on your business concept, you can use what you learned from your competitive analysis to make a preliminary assessment of the financial opportunity. There is considerably more financial analysis to be done before opening your doors, but this is a good point at which to do a preliminary evaluation.

Entrepreneurs use profits to pay themselves, to expand their businesses, and to start or invest in other businesses. Therefore, every

◀ **Performance Objective 4**
Perform viability testing using the economics of one unit.

gross profit total sales revenue minus total cost of goods sold.

economics of one unit of sale (EOU) the amount of gross profit that is earned on each unit of a product or service a business sells.

unit of sale the basic unit of a product or service sold by the business.

entrepreneur needs to know how much **gross profit** (price minus cost of goods sold) the business will earn on each item it sells. To do this, entrepreneurs calculate the **economics of one unit of sale (EOU),** which will reveal how much gross profit is being earned on each unit of the product or service that is sold.

Defining the Unit of Sale

Begin with the **unit of sale,** which is the basic unit of the product or service sold by the business. Entrepreneurs usually define their unit of sale according to the type of business. For example:

> *Manufacturing.* One order (any quantity; e.g., 100 watches).
> *Wholesale.* A dozen of an item (e.g., 12 watches).
> *Retail.* One item (e.g., 1 watch).
> *Service.* One hour of service time (e.g., one hour of lawn mowing) or a standard block of time devoted to a task (e.g., one mowed lawn).

If the business sells a combination of differently priced items (such as in a restaurant), the unit of sale is more complicated. The entrepreneur can use the average sale per customer minus the average cost of goods sold per customer to find the economics of one unit of sale. The formula would be as follows:

> Average Sale per Customer – Average Cost of Sale per Customer = Average Gross Profit per Customer

A business that sells a variety of items may choose to express one unit of sale as an average sale per customer (see **Exhibit 3-6**).

Cost of Goods Sold and Gross Profit

cost of goods sold (COGS) the cost of selling one additional unit of a tangible product.

To get a closer look at one unit of sale, entrepreneurs analyze the **cost of goods sold (COGS)** of one unit. These are:

- the cost of materials used to make the product (or deliver the service), and
- the cost of labor directly used to make the product (or deliver the service).

For a product, the cost of direct labor used to make the product plus the cost of materials used are the COGS. The equivalent for a service

Exhibit 3-6 *Unit of Sale as a Combination of Different Items*

Unit of Sale and Economics of One Unit of Sale			
Type of Business	**Unit of Sale**	**Economics of One Unit of Sale**	**Gross Profit per Unit**
1. Retail & Manufacturing	One item (e.g., one tie)	$7 – $3 = $4	$4
2. Service	One hour (e.g., one hour of mowing a lawn)	$20 – $10 = $10	$10
3. Wholesale	Multiple of same item (e.g., one dozen roses)	$240 – $120 = $120	$120
4. Combination	Average sale per customer minus average cost of goods sold per customer (e.g., restaurant meals)	$20 – $10 = $10	$10 average gross profit

business, the **cost of services sold (COSS),** are the cost of the direct labor used to produce the service plus the cost of the delivery of the service.

The cost of goods sold can be thought of as the cost of selling "one additional unit." If you buy watches and then resell them, your COGS per unit is the price you paid for one watch. Once you know your COGS, you can calculate gross profit by subtracting COGS from revenue (see **Exhibit 3-7**).

> **cost of services sold (COSS)** the cost of selling one additional unit of an intangible service.

Your Business and the Economics of One Unit

The economics of one unit of sale is a method for seeing whether your business idea could be profitable. If one unit of sale is profitable, the whole business is likely to be. On the other hand, if one unit of sale is *not* profitable, then no matter how many units you sell, the business will never be successful. Let's use **Exhibit 3-7** as an example.

Say you have a simple business selling decorative hand-blown wineglasses that you buy from a local artist wholesale for $12 each and resell to friends for $20 each. The cost of goods sold for each wineglass is the wholesale price of $12 (gross profit = $8).

You buy a dozen glasses for $12 each wholesale. Your unit of sale is one glass. Your cost of goods sold is $12 per unit, assuming you have no direct labor cost.

You sell all the glasses at $20 each. Here is how you would calculate your gross profit:

Total revenue = 12 glasses × $20 selling price = $240

Total cost of goods sold = 12 glasses × $12 purchase price = $144

Total gross profit (contribution margin) = $96

$240 revenue – $144 COGS = $96

Total Revenue – Total Cost of Goods Sold = Total Gross Profit

You made a gross profit of $96.

For a manufacturing business, one unit might be one pair of sneakers. The costs would include **direct labor,** the money paid to the people who make the product (sneakers, in this example), and the supplies, such as fabric, rubber, and leather (see **Exhibit 3-8**).

The manufacturer makes a gross profit of $3 for every pair of sneakers sold. That may not seem like much, but manufacturers sell in *bulk*. In other words, a manufacturer might sell several million pairs of sneakers per year.

The economics of one unit also applies to wholesale, retail, and service businesses. Assume the wholesaler buys a set of one dozen pairs of sneakers from the manufacturer for $180 and sells them to a retailer for $240 (see **Exhibit 3-9**).

The retailer pays the wholesaler $240 for one dozen pairs of sneakers. The retailer's COGS, therefore, is $20 ($240/12 for the shoes only; the

> **direct labor** the wages of employees that can be figured into the cost of a product or service.

Exhibit 3-7 *Economics of One Unit of Sale versus Total Gross Profit*

	Economics of One Unit (EOU)	Total Gross Profit for 12 Units (@ $10 per Unit Sold)
Price Sold/Revenue	$20	$240 (12 × $20)
– Cost of Goods Sold	– $12	$144 (12 × 12)
Gross Profit	$8	$96 (12 × 8)

retailer does not add direct labor). The store sells one pair at a time to its customers for $35 (see **Exhibit 3-10**).

The economics of one unit for a service can be shown by a hair stylist who charges $50 per cut (see **Exhibit 3-11**).

Exhibit 3-8 *Economics of One Unit, Manufacturing*

ECONOMICS OF ONE UNIT (EOU)		
Manufacturing Business: Unit = 1 Pair of Sneakers		
Selling Price per Unit:		**$15.00**
Labor Cost per Hour:	$4.00	
No. of Hours per Unit:	2 hours	$ 8.00
Materials per Unit:		4.00
Cost of Goods Sold per Unit:	$12.00	12.00
Gross Profit per Unit:		$ 3.00

Exhibit 3-9 *Economics of One Unit, Wholesale*

ECONOMICS OF ONE UNIT (EOU)	
Wholesale Business: Unit = 1 Dozen Pairs of Sneakers	
Selling Price per Unit:	**$240.00**
Cost of Goods Sold per Unit:	180.00
Gross Profit per Unit:	$ 60.00

Exhibit 3-10 *Economics of One Unit, Retail*

ECONOMICS OF ONE UNIT (EOU)	
Retail Business: Unit = 1 Pair of Sneakers	
Selling Price per Unit:	**$35.00**
Cost of Goods Sold per Unit:	20.00
Gross Profit per Unit:	**$15.00**

Exhibit 3-11 *Economics of One Unit, Service*

ECONOMICS OF ONE UNIT (EOU)		
Service Business: Unit = 1 Hour		
Selling Price per Unit:		**$50.00**
Supplies per Unit (hair gel, etc.):	$ 2.00	
Labor Costs per Hour:	25.00	
Cost of Goods Sold per Unit:	$27.00	27.00
Gross Profit per Unit:		**$23.00**

The Cost of Direct Labor in the EOU

Janet has a business designing handmade bookmarkers. Her unit of sale is one bookmarker. Below is additional information about Janet's business:

- She sells 40 bookmarkers per week to a bookstore in her neighborhood.
- Her selling price is $4.50 each, including an envelope.
- Her costs per marker are 80 cents for materials (construction paper, glue, and paint) and 20 cents for an envelope, for a total of $1.00.
- On average, it takes her one hour to make six bookmarkers.
- Janet pays herself $9 an hour.

The direct labor for each bookmarker is $1.50 ($9/6). Janet wisely realizes that she must include the cost of her labor in the EOU. **Exhibit 3-12** shows how she does this.

Janet's gross profit is $2 per bookmarker sold. Assuming no other expenses, she will keep this as owner of the business. She also earns $1.50 per bookmarker by supplying the labor, thus ending up with a profit of $3.50 per bookmarker.

Now, think back to Amy of the Most Chocolate Cake Company and perform a similar analysis.

- Amy takes an average of two hours to bake a cake.
- It costs $5 for the ingredients for an average cake.
- Amy pays herself $15 an hour.
- The average price of a cake is $40.

This yields a gross profit of $5 per cake. With the gross profit of $5 and the $30 she paid herself, Amy ends up with $35 per cake. Assuming she does not have to deliver the cakes, this may be sufficient for her. If she needs to earn more, she will have to charge more, work faster, work more hours, or decrease the costs. These may or may not be realistic options.

Hiring Others to Make the Unit of Sale

Janet realizes that if the bookstore wants to order more bookmarkers or if she can sell them to additional bookstores, she will not have enough time to make them all herself. To solve this issue, she hires a friend to make the bookmarkers for $9 per hour. Although the EOU will stay the same, Janet will have more time to look for new opportunities for her business. Her income from the business will now come solely from the gross profit, which is currently $2 per unit.

Amy can produce about 20 cakes during a 40-hour workweek and 30 cakes in 60 hours. That means she can earn $600 to $750 per week, or between

Exhibit 3-12 *EOU Example, Janet's Company*

ECONOMICS OF ONE UNIT (EOU)		
Manufacturing Business: Unit = 1 Bookmarker		
Selling Price per Unit:		$4.50
Materials:	$1.00	
Labor:	1.50	
Cost of Goods Sold per Unit:	$2.50	2.50
Gross Profit per Unit:		$2.00

$31,200 and $39,000 per year before taxes, without allowing for vacation or sick days. There would be an additional $100 to $150 in gross profit per week before other expenses are figured. Assuming Amy can sell 20 to 30 cakes per week at $40 each, she will have a maximum income of about $46,800.

Amy knows that she will have other expenses, so $40,000 is more realistic. Amy wants to earn more than that per year so, like Janet, she, too, could add employees if the market would support greater volume. If she paid her employees $15 per hour (assumed for this example as the minimum living wage), she would need to sell 8,000 cakes per year to make her $40,000. That is 154 cakes per week, requiring perhaps seven full-time bakers. This would not be possible in her home kitchen.

However, we have to be sure that Amy is not comparing apples to oranges when making the analysis. With more workers, the tasks could be delegated so that it would take only one hour per cake, bringing the gross profit to $20. If Amy could also get better pricing on ingredients because of increased volume, the gross profit would be even higher. At $20 per unit gross profit, Amy would need to sell only 2,000 cakes per year, or 39 per week. That could be accomplished with two full-time bakers. As a home-based business, that would be more realistic.

Amy, like any entrepreneur, has to decide what is achievable and what her goals are.

Going for Volume

Janet meets a bookstore supply wholesaler. He offers to buy 2,000 book-markers if Janet can deliver them in one month and sell them for $3.50 each, $1 less than she has been getting. This would reduce her gross profit but offer higher revenue. Three questions immediately come to mind:

1. *Can I produce the 2,000-unit order in the required time frame?*
2. After doing some calculations, Janet realized that if she hired 10 people, each to work 35 hours a month, she could deliver the order in time. Janet convinces 10 people to take on the one-month commitment by offering $12 per hour.
3. *If I lower the price from $4.50 to $3.50 for each bookmarker, will I still make an acceptable gross profit per unit?*
4. To answer this question, Janet created a chart (see **Exhibit 3-13**) and realized that her new gross profit per unit would be $1. Let us look at the EOU if she factors in labor at $12 per hour, or $2 per bookmarker.
5. *How much in total gross profit will I make from the order?*
6. To answer this question, Janet created another chart (see **Exhibit 3-14**) and realized that her total gross profit would be $1,000.

Exhibit 3-13 *EOU Example, Janet's Company with Employees*

ECONOMICS OF ONE UNIT (EOU)		
Manufacturing Business: Unit = 1 Bookmarker		
Selling Price per Unit:		$3.50
Materials:	$1.00	
Labor:	1.50	
Cost of Goods Sold per Unit:	$2.50	2.50
Gross Profit per Unit:		$1.00

Exhibit 3-14 *Gross Profit Projection, Janet's Company with Employees*

GROSS PROFIT PROJECTION (BASED ON EOU)		
Janet's Total Gross Profit		
Revenue ($3.50 × 2,000 bookmarkers):		$7,000.00
Materials ($1 × 2,000):	$2,000.00	
Labor ($2.00 × 2,000) :	4,000.00	
Cost of Goods Sold:	**$6,000.00**	6,000.00
Gross Profit:		**$1,000.00**

Janet concluded that $1,000 in gross profit was much better than earning $80 a week in gross profit, plus $60 a week for her labor (what she earned making the bookmarkers herself each week at a selling price of $4.50). Even though the wholesaler was asking for a lower selling price, her total revenue, and therefore her total gross profit, would be much higher. When Janet realized that she could deliver the order in the required time and earn $1,000, she accepted the offer. Five breakthrough steps entrepreneurs can take are:

1. calculating the unit of sale,
2. determining the economics of one unit of sale,
3. substituting someone else's labor,
4. selling in volume, and
5. creating jobs and operating at a profit.

currency a term for money when it is exchanged internationally.

At first, an entrepreneur can be part of his or her own economics of one unit. If you start making (manufacturing) computers in your garage, like Steve Jobs and Stephen Wozniak did when they started Apple, you should include your labor on the EOU worksheet.

Over time, though, Jobs and Wozniak made enough profit to hire others to manufacture the computers. Jobs and Wozniak took themselves out of the economics of one unit so they could be the creative leaders of the company. And, by lowering prices, they were able to sell millions of units.

foreign exchange (FX) rate the relative value of one currency to another.

Global Impact . . .

Selling Your Product around the World

Through the Internet, even a very small business run by one person can reach customers internationally. What if a customer from Germany contacts you through your Web site and wants to buy your product in euros, the currency of much of Europe? **Currency** is a term for money when it is exchanged internationally. In the United States, the currency is the dollar. In Japan, it is the yen. In Mexico, it is the peso.

The **foreign exchange (FX) rate** is the relative value of one currency to another. It describes the buying power of a currency. The FX rate is expressed as a ratio. If one dollar is worth 1.25 euros, to calculate how many euros a certain number of dollars is worth, multiply that number by €1.25.

$$\$5 = 5 \times €1.25 = €6.25$$

How would you figure out how many dollars €6.25 is worth? Simply divide €6.25 by 1.25 to get $5.

Tip: There are currency converters available online, such as at http://finance.yahoo.com/currency?u.

Performance Objective 5 ➤
Learn how to determine the value of a business.

Determining the Value of a Business

The valuation of a business is reached through a combination of art and science, and is ultimately a matter of arriving at a price and set of terms that both the buyer and seller find acceptable. For a public company, valuation is the worth of the stockholders' equity. For a going concern with audited financials, the determination can be based upon projected earnings and cash flows. For other going concerns, the process is more complex because the quality and reliability of the financial information is less certain. The primary methods of valuation are *asset*, *earnings*, and *cash flow*.

Asset Valuation Method

asset valuation a method that analyzes the underlying value of a business's assets as a basis for negotiating a price.

Asset valuation analyzes the underlying value of a business's assets as a basis for negotiating the price. The four most common techniques are:

1. *Book value.* Starting with the value of assets reported in the books and records of the firm as a reference point, the actual value will depend upon its accounting practices—such as allowances for losses and depreciation.

2. *Adjusted book value.* This takes into account any of the discrepancies identified in the calculation of book value, and looks at the actual market value versus the stated book value. Intangible assets are often excluded in this method.

3. *Liquidation value.* This is a determination of the net cash that could be obtained through disposing of assets via a quick sale, with liabilities either paid off or negotiated away. It also includes the cost of liquidating. Neither buyers nor sellers are particularly interested in establishing a price based upon liquidation, but it does establish a floor, or minimum value, for the firm.

4. *Replacement value.* This is the determination of the cost of newly purchasing the assets, as would be required to start up the firm. This is also used more as a point of reference than as a pricing option.

Earnings Valuation Method

earnings valuation a method that assesses the value of a business based upon a stream of earnings that is multiplied either by an agreed-upon factor (the capitalization factor) or by the price/earnings ratio (for a publicly traded company).

Earnings valuation assesses the worth of a business based upon a stream of earnings that is multiplied, either by an agreed-upon factor (the capitalization factor) or by the price/earnings ratio (for a publicly traded company). As with any methodology of this nature, the challenge is how to determine the variables. Three ways of looking at earnings are:

1. *Historical earnings.* Start with the value of earnings reported in the books and records of the firm over multiple years. This can then be adjusted for items that would distort earnings, such as salaries of family members or depreciation. Historical earnings can be valid if future earnings can be reasonably projected as a result.

2. *Future earnings under current ownership.* This considers additional information that is available above and beyond historical earnings, such as economic changes, the competitive environment, and new products and services that have been introduced.

3. *Future earnings under new ownership.* This is a determination of the projections that you make vis-à-vis the changes you plan to implement. This may be the upper limit of what you would be willing to consider.

In addition to determining which type of earnings to use, valuation will depend upon which measure of earnings is selected. Will it be before or after taxes? Will it be earnings before interest and taxes (EBIT), or operating income? The measure selected may make a significant difference in the valuation. It is traditional to use the after-tax earnings value without extraordinary items. However, if the new owner will be putting a different financing structure in place, using EBIT may be best. Ultimately, a price must be negotiated to the satisfaction of both the buyer and seller.

Cash Flow Valuation Method

Cash flow valuation calculates the worth of a business using projected future cash flows and the time value of money to arrive at a figure. This requires assessing the future expectations of cash flows from the business and applying financial calculations to arrive at the current value. It is less likely to be used for an entrepreneurial venture, but may be considered as an option.

cash flow valuation a method of calculating the worth of a business by using projected future cash flows and the time value of money.

Whatever value is calculated through the quantitative methods above, the final price should also reflect nonfinancial variables. While performing due diligence, you gathered information regarding the market space, the competitive environment, the legal and regulatory status of the firm—and any pending changes in the physical environment or labor situation or need for investment in plant, property, or equipment. The value of customer goodwill must also be factored into the price, and the competitive and legal environments will also play a role in the pricing. The offer price and the maximum amount you are willing to pay should take into account all the factors you have identified. This price may have to be tempered by what you can afford.

Chapter Summary

Now that you have studied this chapter, you can do the following:

1. Define your business.
   - Identify the four basic types of business.
     - Manufacturing makes a tangible product.
     - Wholesale buys in quantity from the manufacturer and sells to the retailer.
     - Retail sells to the consumer.
     - Service sells an intangible product to the consumer.
2. Articulate your core beliefs, your mission, and your vision.
3. Analyze your competitive advantage.
   - Your competitive advantage is whatever you can do better than the competition that will attract customers to your business.
   - Find your competitive advantage by thinking about what consumers in your market need. You have unique knowledge of your market.
4. Perform feasibility analysis by calculating the economics of one unit of sale.
   - The EOU is the basis of business profit.
   - Entrepreneurs use profits to pay themselves, expand the business, or start or invest in new businesses.
   - The entrepreneur chooses how the unit is defined:
     - One item (unit).
     - One hour of service time (if the business is a service business).
     - If the business sells differently priced items (such as in a restaurant), use the average sale per customer as the unit. The average would be total sales divided by the number of customers:

Total Sales/Number of Customers = Average Unit of Sale

- To get a closer look at the costs involved in figuring one unit, entrepreneurs analyze the cost of goods or services sold (COGS or COSS) of a unit.
  - The cost of materials used to make the product (or deliver the service).
  - The cost of labor used to make the product (or deliver the service).
- Once you know your cost of goods sold, you can calculate gross profit. Subtract total COGS from your total revenue to arrive at gross profit.

5. Learn how to determine the value of a business.
   - Use asset, earnings, and/or cash flow valuation methodologies to arrive at a range of potential prices.
   - Consider the spectrum of nonfinancial factors in the price.
   - Arrive at offer and maximum price before entering the negotiations.

$$\text{Revenue} - \text{COGS} = \text{Gross Profit}$$

Key Terms

asset valuation	foreign exchange (FX) rate
barriers to entry	gross profit
cash flow valuation	manufacturing
competitive strategy	market
core values	retail
cost of goods sold (COGS)	service
cost of services sold (COSS)	strategy
currency	tactics
direct labor	unique selling proposition (USP)
earnings valuation	unit of sale
economics of one unit of sale (EOU)	wholesale

Entrepreneurship Portfolio

Critical Thinking Exercises

1. Use the following charts to define a business you would like to start or can envision, and analyze your competitive advantage.

Business Definition Question	Response
The Offer: What products and services will be sold by the business?	
Target Market: Which consumer segments will the business focus on?	
Production Capability: How will that offer be produced and delivered to those customers?	
Problem Solving: What problem does the business solve for its customers?	
Competitive Advantage Question	**Competitive Difference (USP)**
The Offer: What will be better and different about the products or services that will be sold?	
Target Market: Which segments of consumers should be the focus of the business to make it as successful as possible?	
Production and Delivery Capability: What will be better or different about the way the offer is produced and delivered?	

	Weight	Your Company		Competitor Number 1		Competitor Number 2		Competitor Number 3	
		Rating	Weighted Rating	Rating	Weighted Rating	Rating	Weighted Rating	Rating	Weighted Rating
Quality									
Price									
Location									
Selection									
Service									
Speed/Turnaround									
Specialization									
Personalization			_____		_____		_____		_____
Total	1.00	xxxxx		xxxxx		xxxxx		xxxxx	

2. Are there customers for this business in other countries? How would you plan to reach them?
3. Describe any international competitors you have found who may be able to access the same customers. How would you compete?
4. Describe three core values you would use to run your own company.
5. What are three of the concepts that a mission statement should contain and why?
6. Write a mission statement for your planned or envisioned business.

Key Concept Questions

1. Gross profit is the money earned by a business before which other costs are subtracted?
2. What is the average unit of sale for the following businesses?
   - Business 1: A restaurant that serves $2,100 in meals to 115 customers per day.
   - Business 2: A record store that sells $1,500 worth of CDs to 75 customers per day.
3. Sue, of Sue's Sandwiches, sells sandwiches and soda from a sidewalk cart in a popular park near her house. She sets up her cart in the summers to earn money for college tuition. Last month she sold $1,240 worth of product (sandwiches and sodas) to 100 customers. She spent $210 on the sandwich ingredients and buying the sodas wholesale. Her unit is one sandwich ($4) plus one soda ($1). Define the unit of sale and calculate the economics of one unit for Sue's Sandwiches.
4. When Stephen Wozniak and Steve Jobs envisioned a computer in every home, computers were large, expensive machines available only to the government, universities, scientists, and very large companies. What technology currently available today to only a few people can you envision meeting a need for many consumers in the future?
5. Is there a service presently available to only a few consumers? Or one that is not available yet? Write about a service that you can imagine eventually becoming very popular and the need(s) it will meet.

6. If the FX rate between the U.S. dollar and the Japanese yen is 1:119, how many yen will it take to equal $20?
7. If the FX rate between the Japanese yen and the euro is 189.35:1, how many yen will equal 10 euros?
8. Explain three ways that businesses can be valued.

Application Exercises

You own a small record label. You sell CDs through your Web site for $15, including shipping and handling. You get an offer from someone who owns a record store in Germany who wants to buy your CDs at $10 each and sell them for €30. He says his profit from each sale would be €12 and he will split it with you. Assuming the exchange rate between the dollar and the euro is $1 = €2:

1. How much profit would you get from the sale of each CD in the German store?
2. How much would that profit be in dollars?
3. Is this a good business opportunity for you? Why or why not?
4. If the FX rate between the dollar and the euro falls to $1 = €1, would this still be a good business idea for you? Why or why not?

Exploring Online

1. Use the Internet to research suppliers for a business you would like to start or can envision. Describe the business and list the URL, e-mail, phone and fax, and street address for five suppliers you located via the Internet.
2. Visit http://www.download.cnet.com/windows and find three share-ware programs that would be of value to you as an entrepreneur.

BizBuilder Business Plan Questions

1.0 Executive Summary
A. What is the name of your organization?
B. What products or services will you offer?

2.0 Mission, Vision, and Culture
A. Write a mission statement for your organization in 21 or fewer words that clearly states your competitive advantage, strategy, and tactics.
D. Create a vision statement for your organization.
C. Describe the core beliefs you will use to run your organization and how they will be reflected in its culture.
D. Identify the ways you plan to run a socially responsible organization.

Case Study | Ibtihaj "Ippy" Amatul-Wadud— Ippy's Islamic Fashions

Although she didn't know it at the time, Ippy Amatul-Wadud laid the foundation for a future business when she began learning how to sew at age 10. Using the sewing machine her mother bought for her, Ippy eventually became a good seamstress. Ippy began using her skills to make her own clothes because there were no local stores that sold apparel for Muslim women. If she, her mother, and four sisters wanted to buy appropriate Islamic clothing, they had to travel from Springfield, Massachusetts—where they lived—to New York or New Jersey.

As a teenager, Ippy began participating in an after-school Excellence in Youth Entrepreneurship (E.Y.E.) class sponsored by the Springfield Technical College's Entrepreneurial Institute. As its name implies, the E.Y.E. program teaches entrepreneurial knowledge and skills to young people. The program uses the nationally acclaimed Network for Teaching Entrepreneurship (NFTE) curriculum. High school and college-aged students in the Greater Springfield area who are interested in learning how to create a business plan or start a business are invited by outreach workers from local high schools to contact the Entrepreneurial Institute.

Ippy realized that she could create a business that would solve a resource problem for Muslim girls such as herself. She wrote a business plan that won second place in the Entrepreneurial Institute's regional YES! Business Plan Competition and also placed third in NFTE's New England Regional Business Plan Competition. And that wasn't all. Ippy later became a finalist in *BusinessWeek*'s 2008 "America's Best Young Entrepreneurs" annual contest.

Working from home, Ippy sews custom-made clothing, primarily for American Muslim women and girls. For apparel worn outside the home, she sews long, loose dresses and scarves for covering the head, neck, and ears. She also makes a traditional outfit, called a *salwar kameese*, which is often worn at parties inside the home.

In the beginning, Ippy did not spend money to advertise her business. Customer interest spread by word of mouth, and networking became a means for generating more sales. From there, she began making plans for expansion via a Web

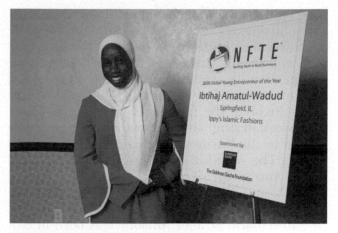

(Courtesy of Ippy's Islamic Fashions)

site, and eventually a storefront. Ippy believes that it's important for entrepreneurs to dream big, and she hopes someday to be able to sell worldwide.

Case Study Analysis

1. How did Ippy identify her market?
2. What knowledge, skills, and abilities did Ippy have before starting her company? What start-up costs did she have?
3. Why might *BusinessWeek* have named Ippy as an America's Best Young Entrepreneurs finalist?
4. Ippy participated in a program that helped her turn her sewing talent into a business. What type of assistance was it? Who provided it?

Case Sources

AllBusiness.com, Inc., "Area Dressmaker Fills Need," http://www.allbusiness.com/company-activities-management/company-structures/11876739-1.html.

Bloomberg Businessweek, "America's Best Young Entrepreneurs: Class of 2008," http://images.businessweek.com/ss/09/10/1009_alums_roundup/14.htm.

Springfield Technical Community College's Entrepreneurial Institute Web site, http://www.stcc.edu/ei/.

Case Study | Translating Talent in Three Businesses

Rosi and Brian Amador apply their talents to three businesses. Sol y Canto (Sun and Song) is a six-member Latin-roots musical group led by Rosi and Brian. MusicAmador Productions is an independently owned record label producing Sol y Canto's recordings. Amador Bilingual Voice-Overs involves the family in professional voice-over work in English and Spanish. The common thread in the businesses is voice and communication. The Amadors have leveraged their finely honed professional musical talents and native English and Spanish-speaking skills to create business opportunities.

Rosemarie Straijer Amador was born in San Juan, Puerto Rico, to an Argentine father and Puerto Rican mother. Rosi was raised by performer parents, who passed on to her their love of Latin American rhythms and musical styles. Her mother, Josefina (Josephine) Del Mar (stage name) was a dancer, singer, and actress, who appeared in the United States and Europe with Bob Hope, Dean Martin, and Jerry Lewis, among others, and in Mexico with comic actor Cantínflas (Mario Moreno). Her father, Jaime Andrada (stage name) (Straijer), began in radio in Buenos Aires and later became an actor, touring all over Latin America. When they settled down to have a family, Rosi's parents opened their own publishing company in San Juan to service the horse-racing community.

Rosi moved to the United States for the last two years of high school and then graduated with a degree in Spanish and French from Bryn Mawr College. She briefly worked in retail and administrative roles and served as the manager of the socially conscious Underground Railway Theater for five years, where she learned how to manage, fundraise, and book performing arts ensembles nationally. With her husband Brian, she co-founded their first Latin band, Flor de Caña (1984–1994) which she also managed and booked. In 1992 she founded MusicAmador, initially a Latin music booking agency representing eight Latin music and dance ensembles. In 2005 she merged her agency with two other booking agencies to become the Vice President of the Roots Agency and its Latin Division Direct until 2007. In 1994 Rosi and Brian founded Sol y Canto, once again taking on managing and booking duties.

Brian Amador is a self-described Chicano-gringo mongrel from Albuquerque, New Mexico.

(MusicAmador)

He graduated from the New England Conservatory of Music, having studied classical guitar, composition, and improvisation. He also studied flamenco guitar in Albuquerque and Madrid. In 1995, he received a highly competitive grant for musical composition awarded to "exceptional artists" by the Massachusetts Cultural Council. For five years, he was principal guitarist for the Ramón de los Reyes Spanish Dance Theater.

As musical director and guitarist for Sol y Canto, he has produced several CD's, arranged and composed in styles from all over Latin America and the Caribbean, and developed a unique guitar style that incorporates Latin American, flamenco, and African elements. He has written and arranged music for different permutations of Sol y Canto as well as for that ensemble with string quartet and orchestra. In 2009, the nation's oldest and most prestigious artists' colony, the MacDowell Artist Colony, granted Brian a fellowship, where he composed the bulk of his latest major work, "Sabor y Memoria: A Musical Feast in Seven Courses" for Sol y Canto and string quartet.

Sol y Canto

Rosi explains, "Sol y Canto was founded as a result of an experience. In 1984 my husband and I met through a three-week cultural exchange tour to Nicaragua. We created our first band, Flor de Caña, out of that life-changing event, committed to singing about the reality in Central America and opening the eyes of the North American people as to the role of our government in Nicaragua's war in the mid-1980s. We never intended to create a band; it happened organically." The band has been deeply influenced by popular Latin music, flamenco, jazz, North American folk, blues, and contemporary African vocal styles. Rosi is the lead vocalist and percussionist (bongo drums). Brian is the group's guitarist, composer of original songs, and musical director.

Sol y Canto's mission is "to create music and performances that move, delight, excite, and connect—connect the audience to the richness of Latin American culture; connect individuals, Hispanic and non-Hispanic, to each other through shared experience of music, poetry, humor and a joyful, playful vibe; and connect us all to our hopes and visions of a better world."[11] This three-time Boston Music Award-winning band has performed nationally—including at the Kennedy Center, the White House, Boston's Symphony Hall, the California World Music Festival, the Philadelphia Art Museum, and the Museum of Art in San Juan, Puerto Rico—offering a wide variety of Latin American musical performances of traditional, contemporary, and original repertory with a socially conscious message to audiences of all ages. The group features rich vocals and lush instrumentation that includes Spanish guitar, saxophone, flute, acoustic bass, piano, and Latin percussion. The group performs in varying sizes from a duo to a sextet with special guest string quartet or symphony orchestra.

Sol y Canto markets concerts and workshops as educational services that celebrate Latin American culture through its musical manifestations, addressing themes of positive social change, love, and personal observations of day-to-day realities in a changing world, as well as promoting cultural bridge-building. The audiences range from preschoolers to senior adults in a wide variety of settings. The events last between 45 minutes and two hours and are priced according to the number of musicians and length of the concert/workshop, location and size of venue, capacity to bring in ticket income, whether the organization is nonprofit or for-profit, and other factors, including how far from the Amadors' home base it is located. Typically, they work with nonprofit arts presenters and receive a guarantee. Sol y Canto often does residencies, in which a variety of performances and educational services are contracted by one arts presenter. For the past few years the band has been averaging 30 to 40 shows annually. Recently, Rosi and Brian decided to focus on the voice-over business and reduce their time away from home and their twin teenage daughters.

The band performs their educational and entertaining concerts and workshops primarily in the United States and Puerto Rico. Sol y Canto performs in theaters or concert halls (and outdoor concert venues), and also in school settings or senior centers, as part of a nonprofit's mission to serve its community. They know that concert attendees are satisfied when they respond by clapping enthusiastically, signing up on their e-mail list and Facebook pages, and send positive comments. The band also knows it's done well when the arts presenters say how happy they were with the services and the audience response. The arts presenters include performing arts centers that have subscription series, schools, summer concert series, festivals, clubs, museums, arts councils, cultural concert series, coffeehouses, benefits for nonprofit organizations, and (accepted in a limited number) private parties. In addition, the Amadors have received three Boston Music Awards as "Outstanding Latin Act," were named "Best of Boston by *Boston* magazine, and have received critical acclaim from publications such as the *Boston Globe*, the *Washington Post*, and *People en Español*.

MusicAmador

The Amadors initially created MusicAmador as a Latin booking agency. Rosi grew it over 12 years into representing a dozen touring music and dance ensembles from around Latin America. After considerable reflection, and recognition that this was not a sustainable path, MusicAmador ceased serving as a booking agency and became an independently owned record label in 2008 for Sol y Canto—releasing the band's fifth CD.

---

[11]Sol y Canto, http://www.solycanto.com, March 13, 2011.

(MusicAmador)

Amador Bilingual Voice-Overs

Amador Bilingual Voice-Overs began organically in 1994. Fans of Sol y Canto asked the Amadors to narrate children's audio books, or e-learning modules, which led to occasional voice-over requests. In 2008, Rosi made a decision to put more effort into pursuing voice-over work for herself (she was noticing a decline in the bookings business) and began to realize that there was a big market for bilingual voice-overs. As she explains, "I began researching, taking courses and seeking out mentors in the field, all of which confirmed that this was a viable business and one I could do out of a home studio and in local studios in the Boston area, without moving to Los Angeles or New York."

Through Amador Bilingual Voice-Overs, Rosi and Brian provide accent-free (unless an accent is desired) voice-overs in English and Spanish from their own broadcast-quality professional studio. Their twin daughters, Alisa and Sonia, are also involved in the business by providing voice-overs. Clients include the U.S. Department of Health and Human Services, National Geographic, Comcast, Verizon Wireless, and PBS/WGBH Boston, among many others. You can hear Rosi's voice in Spanish on most Motorola and Blackberry phones if you select "Latin American Spanish"!

Rosi explains her interest in this business, "Ever since my childhood my parents always encouraged me to be a good communicator in both Spanish and English. Little did I know just how much I would appreciate the love they passed on for both speaking and singing bilingually. My love for communication is the heart of my work and I'm honored to be able to put my skills at the service of my voice-over clients."

The target market for the company is North American media producers, Hispanic media producers, and producers specializing in creating media, including e-learning, documentaries, children's audio books, audio tours for cities and museums, medical/health media, Latino media projects, bilingual tutorials, Spanish or bilingual telephony/IVR, and "industrials" (instructional guides and motivational employee media). The Amadors market bilingual voice-overs with no accent in either language (unless an accent is required), in neutral North American English or neutral Latin American Spanish, to a wide variety of buyers who want to communicate a message to a targeted consumer group. The voice-overs range from 20 seconds to up to 20 hours, depending on their use (podcast, TV or radio spot, Web narration). Prices vary depending on client—local, regional, national—and by the type of client—small company, major television network, or other.

Rosi and Brian record bilingual voice-overs primarily from their home studio or from local professional studios in the Boston area using broadcast-quality sound equipment, and they deliver sound files electronically via the Internet. They check after a job is done to make sure the customer is satisfied. They also know because they receive referrals and testimonials from happy customers, many of whom become regular clients. In addition, the Amadors work with three agents and online voice casting Web sites, which have given them high ratings/evaluations, leading to more prospective clients. In 2010 they narrated an audio book that received the American Literacy Association's "Notable Children's Recording" award. Industry magazines praised the quality of their narration and the creativity of their original music.

The Amadors have several competitive advantages in the voice-over business. They can provide accent-free (or slightly accented) English and Spanish voice-overs and have the acting experience to convey emotions in a pleasing, flexible tone of voice, representing characters of different ages. The company's pricing is competitive; their onsite facilities eliminate the cost of studio rental fees. They guarantee their service and have dozens of testimonials from satisfied clients documenting the quality of service. They offer 24-hour turnaround for smaller projects and one week on larger ones. In addition, they are native speakers of Spanish, offering clients translation or script supervision services when needed. When narrating translated texts, they easily catch script errors. For audio book projects, they offer original music in authentic Latin styles as well as sound effects and can deliver finished masters.

The Amadors expect the business to grow dramatically in the next few years, so that it will replace and considerably exceed the music income they had been receiving. Rosi's goal is to acquire contracts for ongoing work in a variety of mediums to large clients who need bilingual or Spanish voice-overs, and then become the signature voices for those companies. According to Rosi, "We have exceeded our goals thus far. Since focusing on increasing our voice-over business, it has quintupled in gross sales. I see this trend continuing given the projected explosion of the Hispanic population in the United States."

Organization and Culture

The Amadors' businesses employ a small, combined staff of one part-time administrative assistant/engineer and frequent college-age interns (up to three at a time) in addition to Brian (composer/guitarist/technical director) and Rosi (company director/lead singer). Twice a month they bring in a bookkeeper. The office culture is informal, warm, supportive, cheerful, and fosters open, regular communication. Sol y Canto's musical personnel consist primarily of Rosi, Brian and the four other seasoned Latin musicians who make up the sextet. An atmosphere of camaraderie exists within the group, and the musicians have developed a close friendship over the years.

The culture of the organizations is one of respect, consideration, and open communication, to ensure that all independent contractors are happy. If problems emerge, they are brought into the open and resolved. Weekly staff meetings ensure that this happens in the office. Meetings, and discussions—by e-mail, in person or on the road—address concerns with musicians. With this in place, the Amadors are able to offer customers reliable and professional service, always prioritizing the needs of the customer and guaranteeing their work.

Rosi Amador sums up her favorite aspects of the businesses: "I love to sing and communicate positive ideas for social change surrounded and supported by wonderful musicians. I also love to sing my husband's compositions and songs by other of my favorite Latin songwriters. In addition, it's a delight to be able to perform with our teenage twin daughters. I truly enjoy most of my voice-over work, especially educational works with positive social messages, e-learning work and bilingual audio books for children, and projects that promote better health and lives for people of all ages."

Case Study Analysis

1. How does Sol y Canto define its business? Identify the offer, the target market, and the product and delivery capability.
2. Describe the culture of the Amadors' businesses.
3. Which methods of deciding upon business opportunities did Rosi and Brian Amador pursue?
4. What competitive advantages does Amador Bilingual Voice-Overs have in the voice-over field? List them and indicate whether each is based upon quality, price, location, selection, service, or speed/turnaround—or a combination of these.
5. If you were consulting to the Amadors, what advice would you give them?

Case Sources

A. J. Alfaro, "Sol y Canto at Satalla," http://www.bboogie.com/Sol_y_Canto_Satalla.htm, March 19, 2004.

Bryn Mawr College, "Latin Roots Musicians Sol y Canto Bring Multimedia Musical Feast to Bryn Mawr," http://news.brynmawr.edu/?p=8162, March 11, 2011.

Rosi Amador Profile. Voices.com, "Rosi Amador," http://www.voices.com/people/Rosi_Amador, February 27, 2011.

Sol y Canto, http://www.solycanto.com, March 13, 2011.

University of Delaware, "Up Coming: Sol y Canto Trio to Perform July 13 in Bacchus Theatre," *UpDate*, July 7, 1994, http://www.udel.edu/PR/UpDate/94/37/14.html.

Nicole Miller Company

Small Business School **video clip titles are in red**
Case prepared by Hattie Bryant, creator of Small Business School, *the television series made for PBS and Voice of America, http://SmallBusinessSchool.org.*

BE WILLING TO BUCK THE SYSTEM

In 1982, Nicole Miller and Bud Konheim noticed that in department stores the trendy dresses were found in the junior department while the well-made dresses were in the missy department. Nicole and Bud were working together at a large clothing manufacturer and they began discussing the need for dresses that were trendy and well made. With the blessing of their employer, Nicole and Bud started a new company to fill what proved to be an enormous niche in women's fashion. Every product has started on Nicole's sketch pad, and as of 2010 the company had generated $650 million in revenue.[12]

Create a Win/Win

The startup was smooth because Nicole and Bud essentially took one division of a large manufacturer and spun it out into what is now Nicole Miller. Bud kept his role as manager and Nicole maintained her role as designer. At the request of their former employer, they sold off the inventory owned by the old company, then launched their new line selling to the same customers.

According to Bud, "Day one was a change of name as far as the customers went. We had a three-week period that my employer was paying the salaries and wishing me well, we had our salespeople informing all of the customers that everything they had on order was going to be shipped as of June 1, 1982—they were going to get their shipments on time, just the way they ordered them—but the name on the label was going to be Nicole Miller. And they were going to get an invoice from Nicole Miller and they were going to pay Nicole Miller. We were just switching the names. Everybody went along with it because all they wanted was the merchandise—it was fine. In our first month we shipped $600,000. It was lucky in a way, but we had prepared for the luck. It was like—we gave luck a chance to happen."

When Bud started selling the new Nicole Miller label, the buyers were uncertain about the placement of these hybrid dresses. The combination of trendy and well-made did not fit neatly into their existing merchandising. The dresses were too trendy for the missy department and too expensive for the junior department. As a veteran dress salesperson, Bud knew how to ease their concerns and, even more importantly, he had a relationship with the buyers that had developed over the years when he was with the old company. They trusted him. What appeared to be success right out of the chute actually happened because Nicole and Bud started a business that grew out of their extensive experience, plus recognition of a market opportunity.

---

[12]Julia Chaplin, "Our Lady of Fiestas," *Elle*, November 2010.

SELL HAPPINESS

Nicole told me that her goal is to create timeless designs and her customers tell me that Nicole has succeeded. I wear Nicole Miller designs and have had some of them for 10 years. Customers I met in the Nicole Miller shop in La Jolla, California, told me they were anxious to find something they loved from Nicole Miller because they knew they would be wearing it for years. Yet, the designs are fresh enough to fulfill the initial mission of creating trendy, well-made clothes.

In addition to creating stylish yet timeless clothing, Nicole and Bud committed to making the price affordable. Designer labels at one time were out of reach for the average American woman, but Nicole Miller changed this by finding just the right mix of design, fabrication, and cost of manufacturing.

As clichéd as it may sound, Bud says, "We sell happiness. The dress has to be hip, well made, and priced so the woman has a smile on her face when she leaves the store." The style, the craftsmanship, and the price all combine to make the customer feel as if she is wearing more than she paid for. Nicole spends her time looking for new fabrics and creating new designs while Bud is monitoring the competition and keeping a sharp eye on costs.

Keep Manufacturing at Home

According to the Fashion Center Web site, New York City's Garment District is composed of 18.4 million square feet, extending from Fifth to Ninth Avenues and from 35th to 41st Streets, in zip code 10018.[13] More than 100,000 people work in the industry there and the Nicole Miller Company is proud to say that their clothing is made, from idea to finished product, in New York City. Nicole and Bud enjoy doing business close to home because they are veteran New Yorkers. They know its fashion district and the people who run the businesses that support the making of clothing in New York. On top of that, they know their customers.

Having the garments sewn a few blocks from their office makes quality assurance more manageable for the general product lines. Also, about one-third of Nicole Miller's clothing revenues come from its bridal collections; quality assurance is particularly critical for bridal gowns. When a woman selects a Nicole Miller gown and/or bridesmaid dress, it is custom sewn. Bridal salons take measurements and send them to New York, where the gowns are made when the orders are received. This type of business would be considerably more difficult to manage if the sewing were done elsewhere. By keeping the entire process in New York, the turn-around time can be less than one week.

Also, Nicole Miller does not mass-produce any one item. Its strategy depends upon fresh designs every month, with those items produced in small lots and sent to the stores. Once those garments are sold, there is no reordering. Nicole Miller is already producing the next new thing.

This company is not interested in competing head-to-head with the mass-market chains and large manufacturers. Its goal is to serve a niche of loyal repeat customers, as well as any new ones attracted by the designs. Those customers do not want to see what they are wearing on someone else. By controlling quantity and quality, Nicole Miller keeps their customer base happy. And, as Bud says, Nicole Miller's core product is happiness.

---

[13]Fashion Center Business Improvement District (BID), http://www.fashioncenter.com, August 23, 2010.

STUMBLE INTO MILLIONS BY TAKING ADVANTAGE OF OPPORTUNITIES

There is an old saying about making lemonade when life gives you lemons, and this is what Nicole did when she thought she had selected a dress fabric that flopped. She told me, "We just made ties as a joke out of a fabric that was not selling when we put it out there as a dress. Sometimes the best things that happen are flukes." The tie collection led to her handbags, eyeglass cases, socks, and other items. Today, the licensing of her designs for these specialty products generates half of the company's revenue. This is another example of finding and exploiting an opportunity.

Break with Tradition

In a cost-cutting effort, Bud decided Nicole Miller would stop participating in the major New York fashion shows. His rationale was that the expense of participation and the effort in getting the press to write about the Nicole Miller lines in the shows was more about name recognition than closing sales. To get the attention of the press, the company would have to design outrageous garments, which their customers would never buy. He calculated that they never got a strong return on their investment when they participated.

Because no one store ordered her entire collection every month, Nicole debated with Bud, opining that, without the fashion shows, no one would ever see her entire collection. To address that concern, she suggested that they open their own shop, which would be the place for everyone in New York to see every piece in every collection. It worked. The store even made money.

When this first boutique was running smoothly, Bud and Nicole realized that they could continue to grow with department store orders and with their own chain of boutiques simultaneously. There are presently 15 company-owned shops and 15 licensed locations. Taking on the task of operating retail stores on top of creating, manufacturing, and marketing Nicole Miller clothing has been satisfying for both Bud and Nicole. The small shops present the right image to customers. The image they strive for is that they are unique and they provide warm service, fashion-savvy salespeople, and custom gowns for brides. The shops say to the customer, "We are small and you are very important to us."

See the Work as a Circle

Bud thinks of the business process as a circle. He put his thoughts on a chart that everyone in the company can see. The chart makes it clear that he views each individual as adding an equally valuable part to the whole. He does not see himself or Nicole at the top, sending down instructions. He envisions the work flowing through the creation to the sewing to the shipping to the selling teams, and he does not step in unless there is a problem.

Bud is the CEO, and he is ultimately responsible for the success of the business. He is the one who takes on all of the headaches. He has even said, "I get paid for taking Excedrin. I tell everybody that I want to hear the bad news. The good news will take care of itself. Give me the bad news because that is what I am here for." However, his quick smile and warm personal communication style telegraph to everyone in the organization that he is a team player, not a lone wolf.

He says, "I don't tell it, I sell it." This means that he works hard to get the employees to move along in his direction, but he takes the time to engage them in the process and gain their agreement. That's what he means by selling. Bud is continually selling ideas to his team. If they refuse to buy what he is selling, he will adapt when it makes business sense.

Growing Is Harder Than Anticipated

Nicole told me, "I have to say about this business, that it only gets harder. When you start out a business it is all so simple—there is one person that does this and one person that does that and one person that does that. And then before you know it, there are like a hundred people and five of them are doing this and you don't know what people are doing anymore. And you are saying, 'How did we manage when we just had one person in this position?'" Growth has not been a painless process for Nicole Miller. The entire team has had to learn to adapt and grow with the company.

Nicole Miller and Bud Konheim consider themselves fortunate to have found each other and lucky that they have been able to stay partners. Nicole is a sensitive artist, whereas Bud is a bundle of energy and optimism. They respect each other's differences, and have made the division of labor so clear, that no matter how great the challenge, together they have always found a way to work through it and ultimately profit. When I asked Bud what he thought about the future, I laughed when he said, "The end game is, come to my funeral."

Case Analysis

1. What was the opportunity that Nicole Miller and Bud Konheim noticed?
2. How did the founders manage to launch a company and see $600,000 in sales the very first month?
3. Can a company's pricing strategy really be about selling happiness?
4. Why did this dress design and manufacturing company open its own store?
5. Why does the company sew their clothes in New York City when they could get them sewn cheaper in Asia?
6. Would you like to work for Bud Konheim? Why or why not?

INTEGRATED MARKETING

Comstock Images

Chapter **4**

EXPLORING YOUR MARKET

© Comstock/Thinkstock

The original McDonald's was a modest burger restaurant in San Bernardino, California, owned by brothers Maurice and Richard McDonald. Ray Kroc was a 52-year-old salesman of Multimixer milkshake machines; the McDonald brothers' restaurant was his best customer. When Kroc received an order from the McDonald brothers for eight Multimixers, enough to make 40 milkshakes at once, he had to learn more about the operation and its market.

What Kroc found was that the McDonald brothers had hit upon a unique value proposition that drew customers from miles around. The restaurant combined three features:

1. fast, friendly service;
2. consistent quality in its burgers, shakes, and fries; and
3. low prices.

The McDonalds had found the magic formula for fast-food success. They knew they could expand their business beyond the several outlets that they had, but they both hated to fly and wanted to stay locally focused. In 1955, Kroc offered to form a partnership to create identical McDonald's restaurants around the country. In 1961, Kroc bought out the brothers for $2.7 million, but he strictly adhered to their original recipes and value proposition. Kroc wanted every McDonald's customer, from Anchorage to Miami, to eat an identical product. According to Bill Bryson's history of McDonald's, *Made in America,* Kroc "…dictated that McDonald's burgers must be exactly 3.875 inches across, weigh 1.6 ounces, and contain precisely 19 percent fat. Big Mac buns should have an average of 178 sesame seeds." Today, there are more than 31,000 McDonald's outlets in more than 100 countries.

Performance Objectives

1. Explain how marketing differs from selling.
2. Understand how market research prepares you for success.
3. Choose your market segment and research it.
4. Position your product or service within your market.

McDonald's has a formula for success.
(© Doug Steley A/Alamy)

Performance Objective 1 ➤

Explain how marketing differs from selling.

marketing the development and use of strategies for getting a product or service to customers and generating interest in it.

Markets and Marketing Defined

A *market*, as you will see in Chapter 5, is defined as a group of people or organizations that may be interested in buying a given product or service, can afford it, and can do so legally. A market is identified by attitudinal, behavioral, demographic, and other characteristics.

Marketing is satisfying the customer at a profit.[1] Marketing is the business function that identifies your potential customers and their needs and wants. Through marketing, the name of your business will come to mean something clear and concrete in the customer's mind. As an entrepreneur, your current and future customers should always be your top priority.[2] Above all, marketing is the way a business tells its customers that it is committed to meeting their needs. Marketing should constantly reinforce your competitive advantage.

Nike sells athletic shoes. It puts them in stores where consumers can buy them. But Nike also *markets* athletic shoes. Nike creates advertisements and promotions designed to convince customers that Nike sneakers will inspire them to *Just Do It*. You can choose sneakers from many companies, but Nike hopes you will feel inspired enough by its marketing to seek out and buy its brand.

A Business That Markets versus a Market-Driven Business

Do not make the mistake of treating marketing as an isolated business function rather than the engine that drives all business decisions. Most experts agree that, to be successful, a business must develop its marketing vision first and then use it as the basis for subsequent judgments.

Performance Objective 2 ➤

Understand how market research prepares you for success.

Market Research Prepares You for Success

Whether you have a product or service that you want to market, or are searching for a market opportunity and are creating a product or service to fill that need, research can help you succeed. Your research can be conducted at the level of the industry, the market segment, or the individual consumer. Whereas the questions you ask will be very different at each level, the methods for answering them are similar.

The Nike "swoosh"—a logo recognized worldwide. (Sandy Feisenthal/Corbis Images)

Research Your Market *before* You Open Your Business

Large corporations spend a great deal of money on market research before they introduce a product or service. They need to get it just right. Take a lesson from the big companies—do not begin until you have researched your market thoroughly. Be open to criticism. It is not always pleasant to hear, but it will be valuable. Criticism can help you fine-tune your business.

---

[1]Adapted from Philip Kotler and Gary Armstrong, *Principles of Marketing*, 9th ed. (Upper Saddle River, N.J.: Prentice-Hall, 2001).
[2]Ibid.

Exercise

On a separate piece of paper,

1. Give an example of a company that you believe operates as a market-driven organization, and why you think so.
2. Give an example of a company that functions as an organization that markets.

Types and Methods of Research

How you conduct your research will be very important in determining whether it is reliable and valid. Clearly, you do not want to make business decisions based upon partial or incorrect information. The quality of your research will define the value of the answers to your research questions. If you do not already know how to perform research, be certain to learn how to generate reliable and valid data before embarking upon a research project. Using incorrect or invalid methods can lead to dangerously wrong answers to research questions, resulting in wasted resources, poor performance, and even business failure.

You or a market research firm (or a group of students) can carry out two types of research. **Primary research** is conducted directly on a subject or subjects. **Secondary research** is carried out indirectly, through existing resources. For example, if you conducted 100 interviews with students on a campus, it would be primary research. If you examined a study on those students conducted by someone else, it would be secondary. Often, primary research is expensive and time-consuming to conduct. However, if you want to test a product or idea, it can be your best option.

Bear in mind that, when you design a market research survey, the method you use will affect the answers you get. A combination of primary and secondary research will generally be best, and for each type there is a set of methods that you can select to fit your needs. These are tools that can aid you in determining the viability of your business concept and/or product. The number of options is seemingly endless; which methods to use will depend upon your level of analysis (individual, market, industry, and so forth), your research questions, and the time and money you can devote to them. Remember, it is better to do your research and discover that you should revamp your plans rather than skip this step, or ignore the results, and then suffer an expensive failure in the marketplace.

primary research a type of investigation performed directly on a subject or subjects.

secondary research a type of investigation carried out indirectly, through existing resources.

Getting Information Directly from the Source: Primary Research

When you need to ask questions specific to your product or service or need to observe how people act or react, it is best to conduct primary research. Primary research methods include:

- **Personal interviews.** Interview individuals in person, using either question guides that have flexibility, or structured, step-by-step surveys. For example, you could interview students in your school or consumers in a shopping area.
- **Telephone surveys.** These are personal interviews conducted via telephone. When your customer base will not be strictly local or readily accessible in person, you can reach more people this way. However,

in the United States, telephone surveys are regulated, so you have to be careful to comply with the law. Also, with the increasing usage of cellular telephones, land lines are decreasing in popularity, and samples may be skewed because older populations have the majority of the existing land lines.

- *Written surveys.* These can be administered via the postal service or by e-mail. There are numerous survey programs available on the Internet that can simplify this process. One is Survey Monkey (http://www.surveymonkey.com), which creates efficient, written surveys online. The survey questions should be clearly stated, easy to understand, and relatively short.

- *Focus groups.* If you want to get information that is generated through guided group discussion, you can use focus groups. There are facilities designed specifically for conducting focus groups, or you can simply find a quiet space with adequate facilities.

- *Observation.* By watching, you can observe patterns of interaction, traffic patterns, and volumes of purchase that will help you understand your prospective customers and your competition. Secret shoppers (people who are hired to shop a store) fall in this category. Also, attending an event, such as a trade show or professional meeting, is an opportunity to observe and learn. Make certain you do this ethically and legally.

- *Tracking.* It can be useful to track advertisements, prices, and other information through the media. You can compile this data to see pricing and promotion patterns, as well as the marketing strategies, of your competitors.

Getting Information Indirectly: Secondary Research

When you want to learn about your industry, competition, or markets, secondary research may be your best option. Some of these methods are:

- *Online searches.* By using search engines such as Google, Yahoo!, Search, Dogpile, Ask.com, Live Search, and Excite, you can find stories, historical records, biographical information, and statistics. Be wary of sources when using Internet data, as the facts may not always be accurate. Many of them use information contributed by users; this data may not be verified or reliable.

- *Database searches.* Public databases such as the U.S. Census (www.census.gov) are available to you via the Internet. Such sources can provide you with extensive consumer and business information, and some industry reports. **Exhibit 4-1** is a screen shot of a Census page. You can visit the U.S. Securities and Exchange Commission's **EDGAR** Database to find publicly traded companies in your industry.

    You can use proprietary databases at a university or public library to find articles and books about your market. Interestingly, much of the information available on businesses, populations, markets, and the like is not available through Internet search engines. Libraries sign up for databases that are available only through (relatively costly) paid subscriptions. They also have services to provide certain journal and magazine articles for downloading or printing. For example, you can secure financial data through Hoover's subscription information services, articles from **JSTOR** or **ABI/INFORM**

Exhibit 4-1 *Census Data*

United States and states - Home health care services, Table 1. Selected Industry Statistics for th...   Page 1 of 1

U.S. Census Bureau
American FactFinder

Home health care services
NAICS: 621610
Table 1. Selected Industry Statistics for the U.S. and States: 2007

[NOTE. Data based on the 2007 Economic Census and the 2007 Nonemployer Statistics. For information on confidentiality protection, sampling error, nonsampling error, and definitions, see Survey Methodology. Data in this table represent those available when this report was created; employer and nonemployer data may not be available for all NAICS industries or geographies. Data in this table are subject to employment- and/or sales-size minimums that vary by industry.]

Geography	Number of establishments	Number of employees	Annual payroll ($1,000)	Sales, shipments, receipts, or revenue ($1,000)	Nonemployer Number of establishments	Nonemployer Sales, shipments, receipts, or revenue ($1,000)	2007 population estimate
United States	(r)22,975	(r)972,791	(r)23,373,475	(r)46,174,331	N	N	301,621,157
Alabama	423	13,011	355,117	756,080	N	N	4,627,851
Alaska	41	1,732	35,606	50,138	N	N	683,478
California	2,341	56,251	1,724,312	3,575,223	N	N	36,553,215
Colorado	282	13,530	321,077	594,989	N	N	4,861,515
Connecticut	235	15,305	451,262	807,103	N	N	3,502,309
Delaware	44	2,126	68,047	137,058	N	N	864,764
District of Columbia	27	1,835	39,559	67,455	N	N	588,292
Georgia	543	16,554	454,692	960,141	N	N	9,544,750
Hawaii	65	2,872	68,463	120,117	N	N	1,283,388
Idaho	131	3,155	70,309	136,468	N	N	1,499,402
Kentucky	224	6,755	232,449	569,028	N	N	4,241,474
Louisiana	575	15,995	418,448	870,415	N	N	4,293,204
Maine	126	5,308	125,346	239,455	N	N	1,317,207
Maryland	292	8,548	260,959	516,607	N	N	5,618,344
Massachusetts	477	21,321	659,614	1,283,325	N	N	6,449,755
Mississippi	256	7,196	208,528	497,109	N	N	2,918,785
Montana	70	2,019	36,258	73,299	N	N	957,861
Nevada	170	4,646	124,500	247,911	N	N	2,565,382
New Hampshire	96	4,206	106,488	198,819	N	N	1,315,828
New Jersey	537	34,883	848,764	1,494,002	N	N	8,685,920
New Mexico	138	6,466	135,201	243,558	N	N	1,969,915
New York	944	144,246	3,444,280	6,432,091	N	N	19,297,729
North Carolina	1,067	43,154	808,238	1,559,896	N	N	9,061,032
Ohio	993	46,744	1,051,297	2,065,541	N	N	11,466,917
Oregon	178	4,574	143,902	377,065	N	N	3,747,455
Pennsylvania	774	33,622	963,647	1,875,883	N	N	12,432,792
Rhode Island	67	4,571	114,136	209,787	N	N	1,057,832
South Carolina	237	10,025	226,321	478,973	N	N	4,407,709
Tennessee	465	14,404	435,930	1,031,242	N	N	6,156,719
Utah	153	5,110	155,271	376,066	N	N	2,645,330
Vermont	42	2,345	57,662	99,920	N	N	621,254
Virginia	523	18,633	441,868	825,367	N	N	7,712,091
Washington	300	11,136	294,518	566,998	N	N	6,468,424
West Virginia	104	3,061	80,304	163,178	N	N	1,812,035
Wyoming	42	442	10,933	26,197	N	N	522,830

Source: U.S. Bureau of the Census, 2007 Economic Census

D: Withheld to avoid disclosing data for individual companies; data are included in higher level totals.
N: Not available or not comparable.
Q: Revenue not collected at this level.
r: Revised.
S: Withheld because estimate did not meet publication standards.
s: Sampling error exceeds 40 percent.
X: Not applicable.
Z: Less than half the unit shown.
Additional symbols

http://factfinder.census.gov/servlet/IQRTable?_bm=y&-ds_name=EC0700A1&-NAICS2007=62...   7/12/2010 databases, and industry comparables from Risk Management Associates on a fee basis. Even viewing articles from the *Wall Street Journal* can require a paid subscription.

Also, reference librarians can assist you in your research, which will help you use your research time more effectively.

- *Industry associations, chambers of commerce, and public agencies.* These types of organizations frequently collect demographic and statistical data on and for their members or constituents. They issue publications that contain valuable data in such areas as pricing trends, productivity, cost structures, legal matters, economic and environmental topics, and statistics. This kind of information is sometimes extremely expensive to gather but can be of great value to a start-up enterprise.
- *Review of books and records.* Although you may not get access to other companies' records or those of a company you want to buy, if you can examine records (or even journals or research notes) that are pertinent to your business, you could gain valuable insights. This is particularly true if you are practicing due diligence with a view to buying a business.
- *Competitor Web sites.* Look for annual reports, which are available to the public and reveal marketing and other information about a company. Annual reports provide information for benchmarking and include industry insights. In addition, check out company blogs and newsletters. It is amazing what you can find if you just look.

Market Research Helps You Know Your Customer

Before you can put a marketing plan in place and deliver a competitive advantage to your customers, you will need to find out who your customers *are* or *can be.* **Market research** is the process of finding out:

- who your potential customers are,
- where you can reach them,

market research is the collection and analysis of data regarding target markets, industries, and competitors.

Entrepreneurial Wisdom

Finding Foreign Partners

Large corporations often maintain foreign operations, or have relocated because of lower costs or other market advantages. Changes in technology have made it easier than ever for small companies to benefit from such cost savings, too. UPS, FedEx, and other international shipping companies are all competing for your business. You can also ship larger items by boat. Ocean freight is slower but much less expensive. The World Wide Web, electronic mail, and teleconferencing have made the world smaller, so that it is easier for entrepreneurs to find opportunities globally. For example, locating an overseas manufacturing partner could turn your idea into a profitable business. Knowing where and how to look for such partners can make a huge difference in your success.

The following resources can help you find foreign partners:

- The CIA's World Factbook at http://www.cia.gov/cia/publications/factbook includes such country-by-country information as how much the average worker earns per year, how much education the citizens have, and which languages are spoken.
- Locate foreign companies through foreign search engines. Find "International Search Engines," or "[your country of interest] Search Engines," to get connected.
- Foreign countries have embassies in Washington, DC, and consulates in the larger cities. They can be good starting points for making international business connections.

- what they want and need,
- how they behave, and
- what the size of your potential market is.

Through market research, business owners ask prospective customers questions. President Woodrow Wilson once stated, "I not only use all the brains that I have, but all that I can borrow."

You can learn a lot if you actively listen to what your customers are telling you and engage them in discussion. Whether your customers are private consumers or other businesses, you will want to get into their minds and find out what they really think about such subjects as:

- your product or service,
- the name of your business,
- your location,
- your logo and branding materials,
- your proposed prices, and
- your promotional efforts.

If you listen to your customers and talk to them, your business can only benefit.

Market research helps you get a fix on who your customers are by answering such questions as:

- How old are they?
- What kind of income do they earn?
- What are their hobbies and interests?
- What is their family structure?
- What is their occupation?
- What is the benefit your product or service offers that would best attract them?

The ideal customer should be at the center of your marketing plan. This profile will guide every marketing decision you make. If your target customer is affluent, for example, you might decide to price your product fairly high to reflect its quality. If your target market is more middle income, you might choose a strategy of lower prices to beat the competition.

Do You Know 10 People Who Love Your Product? You May Have a Winner!

Not everybody has to like your product. What's important is that some people love it—a lot. As we have seen, Russell Simmons started one of the first rap record labels, Def Jam Records, and became a multimillionaire. His perception was that if you personally know 10 people who love your product, you could have a winner.

What if you conduct your market research and learn that you do not have a winner? Is your business concept dead? Only the one you thought of first! Think positively; this is an opportunity to develop an even better idea.

Customer Research

You will want to find out everything you can about your ideal customers. What do those individuals eat, drink, listen to, and watch on TV? How

Woman conducting a market survey about banking habits with pedestrians at the Lincoln Road Mall in Miami Beach. (© Jeffrey Greenburg/Photo Researchers, Inc.)

much do they sleep? Where do they shop? What movies do they like? How much do they earn? How much do they spend?

A large corporation might hire a consulting firm or advertising agency to conduct market research or may have its own marketing division. Small business owners can and should conduct market research, too. This can vary from a simple survey of friends and neighbors or target customers that can be carried out in a day to detailed statistical studies of a large population.

Several of the methods described above are well suited to learning about your prospective customers. If you already have a customer base, you should be learning from them, too. A few examples follow:

- *Surveys.* Well-designed marketing surveys ask people directly, in interviews or through questionnaires, what they would think about a product or service if it were available. Your survey should ask about:

  - product or service use and frequency of purchase,
  - places where the product is purchased (the competition!) and why consumers like to purchase from these businesses, and
  - business names, logos, letterheads—everything that will represent your business in a customer's or potential customer's mind.

  Make sure your marketing survey also gathers specific information about consumers that will help you understand them better:

  - interests and hobbies,
  - reading and television-watching habits,
  - educational background,
  - age,
  - occupation,
  - annual household income,
  - gender, and
  - family size and structure.

- *Focus Groups.* Another way to survey people about a product or service in development is to hold focus-group discussions. A focus group is composed of perhaps 10 to 12 people who meet screening criteria, such as being users or prospective users of a particular product. The group is typically led by a facilitator, trained in market research, who asks questions about the product or service. The resulting discussion is usually videotaped or audiotaped for later analysis. Competing communications companies, such as AT&T and Verizon, regularly hold focus groups to stay current with how consumers feel about their respective services or to determine how they will react to new calling plans or promotions.

- *Research Reports.* Market research firms are paid by businesses looking to gather information. Academic researchers study consumers and their purchasing and consumption patterns. The federal government also collects statistics on consumers, such as from the U.S. census. These sources can provide statistics on the following:

  - age;
  - annual income;
  - ethnic or religious background;
  - gender;

- geographic location (zip code, census tract, electoral district);
- interests;
- occupation;
- type of dwelling—single-family home, condominium, townhouse, or apartment (rental or owned), and
- spending and savings patterns.

Market research companies keep records of the typical consumer in a given area. They can then provide statistics based on age, occupation, geographic location, income, or ethnic/religious background. Market researchers also delve into consumers' hobbies and interests and whether they own or rent their homes. Statistics dealing with the behavior of groups of people are called **demographics.**

demographics population statistics.

Many kinds of statistics are available from the U.S. Government Printing Office. The latest edition of *The Statistical Abstract of the United States* is available online and provides 1,400 statistical tables.

Industry Research: The 50,000-Foot Perspective

Industry research focuses not on individual consumers, but on a segment of business as a whole. It provides a broader perspective and shows trends, new and emerging opportunities, and industry norms. If you want to start a record label, you will need to know how the recording industry is doing. Is it growing? Are people buying more or fewer CDs this year? Who are the major consumers of CDs? Which age group buys the most recordings? What kind of music is selling?

To make the best use of industry data, you will have to correctly identify your industry and examine it. The codes of the North American Industry Classification System (NAICS) or Standard Industrial Classification (SIC) are generally used as industry identifiers. Once you have the NAICS code (six digits), you can readily search many sources of data. You can find NAICS and SIC codes at the library in the *North American Industrial Classification System: United States, 2007* (NTIS, 2007) and the *Standard Industrial Classification Manual, 1987* (NTIS, 1987), respectively. You can also find your NAICS code online at the U.S. Census Web site (http://www.census.gov/epcd/naics02/), in which you will enter a keyword and then narrow your selections until you find the best fit for your organization.

Once you have identified your industry, you can perform data searches to find relevant statistics and reports. Some additional places to look include the Standard and Poor's *Industry Surveys*, Wetfeet.com (http://www.wetfeet.com/asp/industries_atoz.asp), and BizMiner (http://www.bizminer.com). A local college or university may subscribe to services such as IBISWorld or Dun and Bradstreet. The census data will include the number of firms, revenues, number of paid employees, and more. In many cases, there are industry reports available on the census site. There are numerous other sources as well. Once you identify them, you can answer such questions as:

- What is the scale (size) of the industry, in units and dollars?
- What is the scope (geographic range) of the industry? Is it local (city or neighborhood only), regional (covering a metropolitan area or state), national, international (present in two or more countries), or global (everywhere)?
- Is it a niche industry or does it reach a mass market?

- What does industry and individual company profitability look like?
- What trends are occurring in the industry? Is it growing? Declining? Stagnating?
- What is the structure of the industry? Is it highly concentrated, with a few companies in control? Is it highly fragmented, with a lot of competition?
- What competition is in the market space and what are they doing? Perform an industry SWOT analysis to visualize this.

The methods to use for industry research overlap with those for customer research to some extent, but they reach further. Some methods to try include:

- *Interviews.* Perhaps you can find people in the industry (staff) or who study the industry (stock analysts, professors, economic development professionals) who will share insights and data.
- *Observation.* This might include taking public tours of industry facilities, visiting trade meetings, and so forth.
- *Tracking.* Keeping track of industry advertisements and reports could help. For example, you may want to start a financial services company, so tracking interest rates is vital.
- *Written sources for statistical data.* There are a variety of written sources, including those mentioned earlier. Check out the Internet Public Library at http://www.ipl.org/div/subject/browse/bus82.00.00/. For industry and individual company profitability, try online services for a fee, such as Risk Management Association (RMA) or BizMiner. Or use free library resources, such as *RMA Annual Statement Studies: Financial Ratio Benchmarks.*
- *Books and articles.* There are books and articles about almost any business topic that you can imagine. If your library doesn't have what you need, you might be able to acquire it through interlibrary loan.
- *Competitor Web sites.* As noted previously, annual reports often include excellent descriptions of companies within an industry and their respective operating environments.
- *Trade associations and chambers of commerce.* Virtually every industry has at least one professional or trade association. You can search online by industry plus the word *association* to find them. Or, you can look in Gale Publishing's *Directory of Associations* at a library. The American Society of Association Executives gateway (http://www.asaecenter.org) has an online list of members, and you can find association magazines and journals at http://www.mediafinder.com.

By taking the time to research and understand your industry, you can be more successful in your own business. Plus, you will learn a lot more about your field!

Ford and Chrysler each spent millions on market research before producing, respectively, the Mustang and the minivan. It was worth millions of dollars to determine if the public wanted these automobiles, because it was going to cost the companies tens of millions to produce them.

Make Market Research an Integral Part of Your Business

Market research is not something you do only once. Make it an ongoing part of your operations. Just as your tastes and desires change as you learn about new ideas and products, so do those of your customers. By continuing to survey your customers as your business develops, you will stay current with their needs and how they feel about your product. You can provide customers with prepaid response cards, conduct in-store surveys, or carry out telephone surveys, depending upon your business. By carefully reviewing your customer purchasing and contact history, you can target your surveys for maximum effectiveness.

How Customers Decide to Buy

How will you figure out who the potential customers are for *your* business? It is critical to understand not only which consumers are in your target market, but how they will purchase your product (or service).

    Step 1 If you have developed a product or service, ask yourself what consumer need it will serve. Arm & Hammer turned this marketing question into a gold mine by developing its simple baking-soda powder into toothpaste, air and carpet fresheners, and deodorants.

    Step 2 Think about who might actually buy your product. Remember that the people who use a good or service are not always the purchasers. Mothers generally buy children's clothes; if you are making children's playsuits, they should offer features/benefits that appeal to mothers. They could be marketed as very easy to clean, for example.

    Step 3 Analyze the buying process that will lead customers to your product.

- **Awareness.** The customer realizes a need. Advertising is designed to make consumers and business customers aware of potential needs for everything from dandruff shampoo to office supplies to automobiles.

Global Impact . . .

Naked Communications

The last notable British Invasion may have been the arrival of the Beatles in 1964, but the latest seems to have come in the form of a global communications firm, Naked Communications, which arrived in the United States in 2006 with considerable attention and interest. Naked Communications is a global organization with offices in London and New York. Clients include Honda, Minute Maid, Nokia, Boots (the U.K.'s largest pharmacy chain), and ad agencies such as BBDO, Lowe, and Leo Burnett. Naked Communications is neither an advertising agency nor a traditional media planning firm, and it chose a name that conveyed the company's approach to integrated marketing—stripping the concept bare and then working to find the best promotional path.

    The team at Naked believes that the right approach to advertising is to gather all the people who have brand responsibility together and work toward an answer to the question, "What's the right message communicated in the right way through the right channel in order to effectively reach the right consumer?"[3] Global businesses require global communications and organizations to support them. Naked Communications does just that.[4]

[3]Danielle Sacks, "Is Mad. Ave. Ready to Go Naked?" *Fast Company*, http://www.fastcompany.com/magazine/99/naked.html, December 19, 2007.
[4]www.nakedcomms.com, July 2009.

- **Information search.** The customer seeks information about products that could fulfill the need. Someone looking for a multivitamin might pick up a brochure on the counter of the local health food store, or simply look on the shelves of a supermarket. A retailer might search a business-to-business phone directory for sign companies.
- **Evaluate alternatives.** Once information is gathered on a single product, the customer may want to examine alternatives before making a purchasing decision. The individual looking for a multivitamin might check out what's available in the health food store and compare the price and content with the more commercial brands found in the local supermarket or drug store. The store owner might get several quotations on the needed business signs.
- **Decide to purchase.** The first purchase is really a test; the customer is trying your product to see how well it performs (or testing the quality of your service).
- **Evaluation of purchase.** If your product or service is satisfactory, the customer may begin to develop loyalty to your business and also tell others about it. Now, how can you keep that customer for life?

Owning a Perception in the Customer's Mind

More valuable to McDonald's than all the Big Macs it sells every year is the perception it owns in the minds of its customers—that every time they patronize a McDonald's, they will eat food that tastes exactly the same as at every other McDonald's, that the prices will be reasonable, and that the service will be friendly and fast.

For Burger King to compete with McDonald's, it had to fight for a mind share of the fast-food customer. Burger King opened its attack with "Have It Your Way," which targeted McDonald's mass-manufacturing approach to making hamburgers. It followed up with "Broiled, not Fried" and "The Whopper Beats the Big Mac."

It is almost impossible to topple an established leading brand in a market. Burger King's executives wisely decided that their goal was to be a strong number two. As number two, you try to create a new category (broiled instead of fried hamburgers, for instance) rather than attempting to take over the competitive advantage of the number one company in the market. Avis lost money for 15 years because it tried to overtake Hertz. The company finally accepted its number two position and turned it into a competitive and very profitable advantage through its advertising campaign: "We Try Harder!"

You do not have to be number one to be successful; discover a competitive advantage and attack the market by creating a new category in the customer's mind. Domino's Pizza found a competitive advantage by delivering orders in less than 30 minutes. That one marketing insight created a hugely successful company.

Features Create Benefits

There is a subtle, but important, difference between the benefits and the features of a product. The features are facts. The features of a drill might include its hardness and sharpness, but the benefit is that it makes a hole. The feature of a Teflon coating on a pan creates the benefit of easy cleaning. The essence of selling is showing how and

Step into the Shoes . . .

Robin Sydney: A Line of Products Worn by A-List Stars

Robin Sydney.
(Zorbits)

Could a 19-year-old take $100 in cash and a $5 pile of rocks and create a multimillion-dollar business? Robin Sydney and her mother, Marian, did just that when they created Sun-Rocks—which later became Zorbitz, Inc. Sydney sought out a mentor. She found the marketing genius behind VISA and Reebok. The women also learned about retail and wholesale from the owner of one of the largest gift stores in Los Angeles. For Sydney, stumbling upon Chinese feng shui jade good-luck charms while conducting research on another idea, led to selling bead bracelets to Whole Foods Markets and becoming the top-selling gift product in that company's southern Pacific region. Zorbitz has grown with the addition of Karmology Bead Bracelets—which combine lucky karma beads with powerful gemstones to help bring good luck and good karma.

Zorbitz emphasizes the "healing" qualities of its products (e.g., love, health, wealth, and miracles), the A-list stars that wear them (e.g., Ashlee Simpson, Halle Berry, Paris Hilton, Freddie Prinze, Jr.), and the charitable contributions it makes worldwide. So in this case, $100 in cash and $5 in rocks, considerable creativity, and promotional savvy added up to more than $2 million in annual sales.

Source: Zorbitz Web site at http://www.zorbitz.net and "California Teen Creates Million Dollar Idea And Zorbitz Takes Off," *Los Angeles Cityzine*, December 20, 2007, http://www.la.cityzine.com/2007/12/20 (May 20, 2009). Courtesy of Zorbitz, Inc.

why the outstanding features of a product or service are *benefits* to the customer. Smart marketers always emphasize benefits, not features, because consumers will buy what solves their problems or makes their lives more pleasant.

Home Depot: Teaching Customers So They Will Return

Home Depot's marketing vision is not just to sell tools and materials but to teach people how to use them to improve their homes and lives. The company's marketing vision focuses on what its customers need Home Depot products to do.

Successful companies are not built on one-time sales but on repeat business. The owners of Home Depot have calculated that a satisfied customer is worth more than $25,000 in sales over the customer's lifetime. Bernie Marcus, one of Home Depot's founders, has said, "All of our people understand what the Holy Grail is. It is not the bottom line. It is an almost blind, passionate commitment to taking care of customers."

Home Depot's multimillion-dollar insight was that its customers not only needed the products it sold but they also needed help in using them.

BizFacts

Minority business owners (often defined to include women) should contact local corporate offices and ask about minority purchasing programs, find the local office of the National Minority Supplier Development Council (http://www.nmsdcus.org), or a government diversity agency. Many companies and most government agencies are committed to buying up to 25 percent of their supplies and services from minority-owned businesses.

Needs, Wants, and Demands

Home Depot is meeting its customers' needs for help and guidance with home improvement, not just tools. What are needs, really, and how do they differ from desires (wants) or demands?

- ***Needs.*** Northwestern University Professor Philip Kotler's classic marketing textbook defines human *needs* as "states of felt deprivations."[5] Meeting a customer need is solving a problem or helping someone achieve comfort.
- ***Wants.*** Kotler defines *wants* as "the form taken by human needs as they are shaped by culture and individual personality."[6] Wants are objects that will satisfy a need. "I'm hungry; I want a hamburger," a New Yorker might say. "I'm hungry; I want jerk chicken," a Jamaican might say. Essentially, wants are needs with individual preferences.
- ***Demands.*** Demands, according to Kotler, are wants backed by buying power. A poor student might translate hunger into a demand for a Big Mac, whereas a successful lawyer might transform his hunger into a demand for a steak dinner. People demand the products and services that best satisfy their wants within the limitations of their resources.

The most successful companies pay close attention to consumer demands. They constantly observe their customers, survey them, and analyze their wants, needs, and demands. They hire people to look for customer needs that might be going unfulfilled. This is all part of customer analysis, one step in developing a marketing plan.

Performance Objective 3 ➤
Choose your market segment and research it.

Which Segment of the Market Will You Target?

Marketing strategies are focused on the customer, and a business has to choose which customers to target. Almost certainly, your product will not be needed by everyone. You will have to figure out which segments of the market to go after.

There is a huge market for home repair, including professional carpenters and builders. Home Depot's competitive advantage would not be strong in the market segment composed of professionals, in which the distribution channels are select and well established. A **market segment** is composed of customers who have a similar response to a certain type of marketing. Home Depot chose to market primarily to the nonprofessional, private individual.

market segment a group of consumers or businesses that have a similar response to a particular type of product or service.

In the cosmetics industry, one segment reacts positively to luxuriously packaged, expensive brands. Another is most responsive to products that claim to reduce signs of aging. Another's primary concern is (reasonable) price. A company that recognizes these market segments and chooses one to concentrate on will do better than a business that tries to sell its cosmetics to every adult female in the country.

It is difficult to target diverse segments of a market simultaneously. Volvo, for example, has established a reputation as a safe, family car. It targets parents with young children. Volvo would have a difficult time also trying to market a two-seat convertible sports car to young adults concerned more with style and speed than safety.

---

[5]Philip Kotler and Gary Armstrong, *Marketing: An Introduction* (Upper Saddle River, N.J.: Prentice Hall, 1997), p. 6.
[6]See Kotler and Armstrong, *Marketing*, p. 7.

Successful Segmenting: The Body Shop

The Body Shop is a good example of the success that can result from choosing the right market segment. Founder Anita Roddick disliked paying for expensive packaging and perfuming when she bought cosmetics. She was also annoyed by the extravagant claims made by many cosmetics companies and the high prices of their perfumes and lotions. Price became an integral part of the image for many products. A brand called Joy, for example, was marketed as the most expensive perfume in the world.

Roddick saw an opportunity to create a different line of cosmetics. She would use natural products that would be packaged inexpensively and marketed without extravagant claims. As she said in her book, "It is immoral to deceive a customer by making miracle claims for a product. It is immoral to use a photograph of a glowing sixteen-year-old to sell a cream aimed at preventing wrinkles in a forty-year-old."[7]

Roddick tapped into a segment of the cosmetics market that had been neglected, and her business grew explosively as a result. Her success proves that selling an honest product straightforwardly can be the best marketing strategy of all.

But what if Roddick had found that there were very few women interested in natural cosmetics? If she had determined this before starting, then she could have changed her segmentation strategy. If not, her business would not have survived, because even though the cosmetics market is large, her segment would have been too small to support the venture. As *The Ten-Day MBA* author Steven Silbiger points out, "The easiest mistake to make is to believe that your *relevant* market includes the total sales of your product category."[8]

It is possible to go after a small, niche segment, but then your price would have to be high enough to make a profit, and the customers would have to buy often enough to keep your business going. Jaguar and Rolls-Royce each sell far fewer cars than Honda or Ford, but at much higher prices. Jaguar and Rolls target the luxury segment of the car market.

Applying Market Segmentation Methods

Marketers have developed four basic ways to segment:

- *Geographic.* Dividing a population by location.
- *Demographic.* Dividing a population based on a variable such as age, gender, income, or education. For business customers, variables such as sales volume and number of employees would matter.
- *Psychographic.* Dividing a population by psychological differences, such as opinion (conservative versus liberal) or lifestyle (sedentary versus active).
- *Behavioral.* Dividing the market by purchase behaviors that have been observed, such as brand loyalty or responsiveness to price.

Say you want to make and sell hacky sacks on your college campus. Twenty thousand students attend the college. If 50 of 200 surveyed express interest in buying your hacky sack, you could expect that approximately 5,000 of the 20,000 students would represent your total potential market. Which segments of that market should you target?

---

[7]Anita Roddick, *Body & Soul, Anita Roddick Tells the Story of the Body Shop, Inc.* (New York: Crown Publishers, 1991).
[8]Steven Silbiger, *The Ten-Day MBA* (New York: William Morrow, 1993), p. 31.

Step into the Shoes . . .

How Thomas Burrell Became a Leader in Marketing to African Americans

Thomas Burrell, Burrell Advertising.
(Michael L. Abramson//Time Life Pictures/Getty Images)

To market a product or service to a specific market segment, you must research what the people who comprise it want. In the late 1960s, major corporations became more conscious of the potential clout of African American consumers but were unsure how to market to them.

In 1971, Thomas Burrell opened one of the first black-owned advertising agencies in the United States. By 1972, Burrell had convinced McDonald's that Burrell Advertising could help the huge company expand into the African American market. Burrell came to be the fastest-growing and largest black-owned advertising agency in the United States.

Burrell Advertising has created more than 100 commercials for McDonald's. Other Burrell clients have included Coca-Cola, Ford Motor, Johnson Products, Schlitz Brewing, Blockbuster Entertainment, Procter & Gamble, Jack Daniel Distillery, Polaroid, Stroh Brewing, and First National Bank of Chicago.

Burrell himself could probably quote the demographics of the African American market off the top of his head. He has combined his company's thorough market research with his own personal experience as an African American male to create powerful appeals to the targeted market. Burrell describes his marketing philosophy as "positive realism." He adds, "We wanted to make sure the consumer understood the advertiser was inviting that consumer—that black consumer—to participate as a consumer of their product. Black consumers have not felt they were being extended an invitation."

If your company has very limited resources, you might choose to target only one segment. A large company might decide to appeal to the entire market by designing a product tailored for each segment. Gap Inc., for example, has three product lines—Old Navy, Gap, and Banana Republic—each priced for and tailored to a segment of the sportswear market.

For your hacky sack venture, you could use any of the four segmentation methods listed below:

- *Geographic.* You could decide that your market is everyone who lives within two miles of the campus.
- *Demographic.* You could decide to focus on health-minded students.
- *Psychographic.* You could decide to market to individuals who like rock music.
- *Behavioral.* You could decide to market to individuals who buy Frisbees or play soccer.

One way to gauge your market would be to interview a sample of 200 students with a structured survey, showing them the product and asking such questions as:

- Do you play Frisbee?
- If so, how often do you play?
- Do you own a hacky sack?
- Would you be interested in purchasing this hacky sack, if it were available?
- How much would you pay for this hacky sack?
- How many of these hacky sacks would you buy per year?
- What suggestions do you have to improve this hacky sack?

Once you have chosen your market segment, you can fine-tune your market research because you now have to focus only on these individuals—not on every potential customer in your market. Collecting data from the people in your market segment can be fun as well as financially rewarding. Here are questions you can adapt to your own product or service:

- Do you currently use this type of product?
- What brand(s) of this product do you currently use?
- Where do you buy it? Please be specific about the source, such as the name and location of the store, a direct marketing representative, or a Web site.
- How much do you pay for it? (Probe for size and price, if appropriate.)
- How often do you buy it?
- Would you buy our product/service?
- How much would you be willing to pay for it?
- Where would you shop for it?
- How would you improve it?
- Now that you have seen/tasted/felt/smelled this product, who do you consider to be its closest competitor?
- Is our product/service worse or better than those of our competitors? Please explain.

The Product Life Cycle

You will also need to analyze where your market is in its **product life cycle (PLC).** The PLC is the sequence of the four stages that a product or market goes through. **Figure 4-1** illustrates two product life cycles.

1. ***Introduction.*** Your product or service is in the invention and initial-development stages. It is new to the market and is essentially unknown, so you will need to introduce it to potential customers, who may be curious about your product but not familiar with it. Marketing at this stage will require education and testing with price and presentation. Some tinkering with the design or technology may also be required. When the personal home computer was first introduced,

product life cycle (PLC)
the four stages that a product or service goes through as it matures in the market—introduction, growth, maturity, and decline.

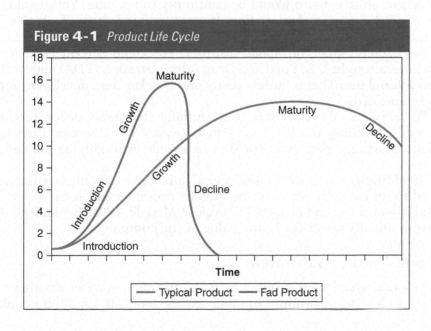

Figure 4-1 *Product Life Cycle*

Apple's marketing was focused on convincing consumers how easy it would be to use. Apple used the same strategy in the introduction of the iMac.

2. *Growth.* Once you achieve success in introducing your product or service to the marketplace, your organization will grow and inevitably invite attention from the competition and perhaps attract new entrants to the field. Perceiving your growth in sales, competitors now start entering your market, or perhaps more strongly defend their own market spaces—efforts at this stage will have to focus on communicating your competitive advantage to consumers. Customer purchases increase dramatically; you have reached the limits of your market.

3. *Maturity.* At this stage, consumers have become knowledgeable about both you and your competitors. The market has become relatively crowded, and there is no more growth as your product or service is currently offered. Advertising will need to focus on promoting brand loyalty. Stability of profits now depends more on cost strategies as demand has become relatively flat.

4. *Decline.* At this point, your competitive advantage has eroded, and sales and profits are declining. New developments will be necessary to revive the market's interest.

Product life cycles are applicable in different ways. For example, the Pet Rock, essentially a small stone that people were to pretend was a pet, had a very short life cycle. Such fad items attain popularity quickly and mature and decline equally rapidly. Other products, such as prescription drugs, will have longer life cycles because of patent protection, high market-entry costs, and their medical necessity for certain population groups. Ideally, you will look at the overall life cycle of a market to determine where your product or service will fit.

It is important for you to understand where each product or service is in the PLC. See **Figure 4-1** for an illustration of the PLC of a normal product and for a fad item. It is important to have a continuous flow of new products, so that your organization as a whole is not on the decline. For example, if you owned a pharmaceutical company, you would want to introduce new medicines well before the existing ones reached maturity/decline, so that there would be continuity in revenue. You would also want to find new uses for existing drugs, to extend their life cycles. For example, AstraZeneca's Seroquel was initially approved for schizrenia and was used off-label for bipolar disorder. To extend Seroquel's life cycle, AstraZeneca sought U.S. Food and Drug Administration (FDA) approval for the additional use. This is far less costly and quicker than developing a new brand-name drug.

For services, the life cycle is essentially the same as for products. However, extending the life cycle can be easier for a service than for a product. Starting a new cycle could be as simple as modifying the delivery process.

In addition, if you are considering acquiring an existing business, it is critical to understand where in the PLC its products and services are. Are they all toward the end of their life cycles? Mixed? At the beginning? This will dramatically affect the future value of the company.

Is Your Market Saturated?

Figuring out where your product is in the PLC will tell you whether your market is close to saturation. In other words, have all 3 million people in your market already bought a competitor's product? Nokia, for example, has a 39 percent share of the global market of $1.1 billion in mobile phones.[9] But that market is nowhere near saturation. Meanwhile, Nokia introduced its Short Message Service (SMS), which allows e-mail messages to be sent between mobile phones in Finland. SMS quickly became Finnish teenagers' favorite way to communicate. Observing how quickly the technology spread among Finnish teenagers gave the Nokia management ideas about how they would market SMS in the 140 countries where they sold cell phones.

Market Positioning: Drive Home Your Competitive Advantage

After deciding which market segments to target, an entrepreneur will need to figure out what position the company should try to occupy in those segments. *Position* is defined by Philip Kotler as, "the place that the product occupies relative to competitors in consumers' minds."[10] The goal of market **positioning,** therefore, is to distinguish your product or service from others being offered to the market segments you have targeted. You can do that by focusing on your competitive advantage. "Have It Your Way," Burger King promised, driving home its competitive advantage—that at Burger King you can specify exactly how you want your hamburger prepared and garnished.

◀ **Performance Objective 4**
Position your product or service within your market.

positioning distinguishing a product or service from similar products or services being offered to the same market.

As you can see from the Burger King example, positioning involves clearly communicating your competitive advantage to the consumer and demonstrating how your product/service is different. Your goal is to position your product/service clearly in the mind of your target market as the brand that provides that difference. Try using the following format to develop a positioning statement for your business:

> (Your business name/brand) is the (competitive industry/category) that (provides these benefits, or points of difference) to (audience/ target market).

Here is an example: (Microsoft) is the (U.S. software producer) that (provides affordable computer solutions) to (American businesses).

By the time you have completed the four steps of your marketing plan, you will know your potential customers, your competitors, and your market intimately. It is a lot of work but well worth it. Make a commitment to let marketing drive your business decisions, and you will greatly increase the odds that your business will be successful.

Developing a Marketing Plan

After you understand how marketing should permeate your business, you will be ready to develop a plan for introducing your product to your market. The marketing plan, as discussed in Chapter 5, can serve as a stand-alone document or be part of an overall business plan. Either way, it should reflect a functioning, evolving part of the business. We began with customer analysis because before you can develop a marketing vision, you will need to know who your customers are and what they want.

---

[9]Mark Landler, "Nokia Pushes to Regain U.S. Sales in Spite of Apple and Google," *The New York Times*, December 10, 2007.
[10]Adapted from Kotler and Armstrong, *Principles of Marketing*, 9th ed. (Upper Saddle River, N.J.: Prentice-Hall, 2001).

Q: Why does a customer go to a hardware store to buy a drill?

A: Because she needs to make a hole.

The *hole* is what the customer needs, not the drill. If the hole could be bought at the hardware store, the customer would not bother with the drill.[11] If you are marketing drills, therefore, you should explain to the customer what good holes they make! If someone invents a better hole-maker, drill manufacturers will soon be out of business.

Your marketing plan must include an understanding of prospective customers and their wants, needs, and demands. It should also identify and analyze market segments. The plan should incorporate industry research and trend analysis and will describe your market-positioning approach. In short, a marketing plan examines all aspects of the potential market space for your enterprise, from the broadest perspective to the narrowest.

Chapter Summary

Now that you have studied this chapter, you can do the following:

1. Explain how marketing differs from selling.
   - Marketing is the business function that identifies your customers and their needs and wants.
   - Through marketing, the name of your business comes to mean something clear and concrete in the customer's mind. Above all, marketing is the way a business communicates its competitive advantage to its market.

2. Understand how market research prepares you for success. Market research is the process of finding out who your potential customers are, where you can reach them, and what they want and need.
   - Getting the information directly from the subject: primary research.
     - Personal interviews
     - Telephone surveys
     - Written surveys
     - Focus groups
     - Observation
     - Tracking
   - Getting information indirectly: secondary research.
     - Online searches
     - Books and articles
     - Trade associations, chambers of commerce, public agencies
     - Review of books and records
     - Researching customers and industries

3. Choose your market segment and research it.
   - Before you can develop a marketing vision for your business, you will need to know who your customers are and what they want.
     - I. A market segment is composed of consumers who have a similar response to a certain type of marketing.

---

[11]Special thanks to Joe Mancuso for this concept.

II. Segmentation methods:
   a) Geographic. Dividing a population by location.
   b) Demographic. Dividing a population based on a variable like age, gender, income, or education.
   c) Psychographic. Dividing a population by psychological differences such as opinion (e.g., conservative versus liberal) or lifestyle.
   d) Behavioral. Dividing the market by observable purchase behaviors such as brand loyalty or responsiveness to price.
4. Position your product or service within your market.

   • The goal of market positioning is to distinguish your product or service from others being offered to the same market segments. You can do that by focusing on your competitive advantage.

   • Use the following format to develop a positioning statement for your business: (Your business name/brand) is the (competitive industry/category) that (provides these benefits, or points of difference) to (audience/target market).

Key Terms

demographics	positioning
market research	primary research
market segment	product life cycle (PLC)
marketing	secondary research

Entrepreneurship Portfolio

Critical Thinking Exercises

1. Step One: Consumer Analysis
   Describe the typical consumer for your business or for one that you can envision.

Attribute	My Customer
Age	
Income	
Education	
Hobbies	
Other	

What need do you plan to satisfy for this consumer?

2. Step Two: Market Analysis

   • How large is the total market for this product or service? How did you arrive at this figure?

- Which segment of this market would you target? Why? How large is the segment?
- Describe your segmentation method. Why did you choose this method?

3. Choose five people from your identified market segment to research with a survey. Write 10 questions in a yes-or-no format, and ask the survey participants to frame their responses on a scale of one to five—or design your own range. Also ask five open-ended questions (questions that cannot be answered with a yes or no).

Key Concept Questions

1. Which four factors should market research include and why?
2. Write a positioning statement for your business or one that you can envision.
3. Describe where you think your product or service is in the product life cycle.
4. Read and interpret the chart in Figure 4-2.
   - Which single provider has the largest market share? What is the percentage?
   - What share do the two largest suppliers enjoy together?
   - How much bigger is IBM's share than Apple's?
   - If there are approximately 100 other smaller makers of personal computers, about how much market share would each, on average, have?

5. Research can give you a great deal of information, but you will have to use your arithmetical skills to make it more useful. For example, imagine you are interested in opening a dog care service, and you have gathered the following facts:

- In 2000, the U.S. Census Bureau estimated that there were 2.67 people per household.
- According to your city's public records, the population of your community is 80,000.
- The *U.S. Pet Ownership & Demographics Sourcebook*[12] estimates that the number of dog-owning households in a community equals 0.361 multiplied by the total number of households.
- The *Sourcebook*[13] also estimates that the number of dogs in a community equals 0.578 multiplied by the total number of households—or 1.6 multiplied by the number of dog-owning households.

Determine:
   a. The number of dog-owning households in your community.
   b. The number of dogs in your community. Round your answers off to the nearest whole number.

Figure 4-2 *Global PC Market Share*

18.60% = Dell
= HP
15.60% = IBM
52.70% = Fujitsu
5.50% = Apple
4.60% = Others
3%

---

[12] 2007 American Veterinary Medical Association, Schaumburg, Illinois.
[13] Ibid.

Application Exercises

Order food at three different fast-food restaurants and then answer the following:

1. Did you observe any differences in how the employees handled your order? Describe them.
2. Describe what you believe to be the marketing vision of each restaurant based on what you observed. Write a positioning statement for each restaurant.
3. Analyze the market for each restaurant, using the four methods of market-segmentation analysis: geographic, demographic, psychographic, and behavioral.
4. Where do you think each restaurant is in the product life cycle?

Exploring Online

Go online and conduct an industry-wide search for competition for your own business or for one that interests you. Create a profile of the competition (this may be written using a word processing program or shown as a table using Excel). It should include minimum and maximum prices, minimum and maximum ordering times, and any other information you feel is pertinent.

BizBuilder Business Plan Questions

4.0 Opportunity Analysis and Research

A. Describe your research methods (surveys, focus groups, general research, and statistical research).
B. Describe your target customer along as many dimensions as you have defined (demographic, geographic, needs, trends, and decision-making process).

4.1 Industry Analysis

A. What is the industry or set of industries in which your organization operates? Include the NAICS codes.
B. What factors influence the demand for your product or service?
C. What factors influence the supply for your product or service?
D. How large is your industry (historic, current, projected size)?
E. What are the current and anticipated characteristics and trends in the industry?
F. What are the major customer groups for the industry (consumers, governments, businesses)?
G. How large is your target market (number of customers, size of purchases, frequency of purchases, trends)?

4.2 Environmental Analysis

A. Perform a SWOT analysis of your organization.
B. What external/environmental factors are likely to impact your business?
C. Are there customers for your business in other countries? How do you plan to reach them?

4.3 Competitive Analysis

A. How do you define/describe your competition, both direct and indirect?

B. Describe your competitive advantage.

C. Find three competitors and describe them.

D. Describe any international competitors you have found who may be able to access your customers. How do you intend to compete?

E. Describe your strategy for outperforming the competition.

F. What tactics will you use to carry out this strategy?

G. What barriers to entry can you create to block out competitors?

American Electrical: Understanding the Market Sparks a New Venture

Entrepreneur Tom McCormick was the vice president of sales for an $800-million global manufacturer of electrical components when he proposed an idea for expansion to his boss. By creating another company to sell accessory items to the 50 percent of the market not being supplied through the existing company because of distribution restrictions, the manufacturer could generate considerable profits. McCormick led the skunk works project that created a business plan and proposals. The projections were extremely favorable, but due to other pressing issues within the organization, it was ultimately decided that the concept did not fit the company's strategy.

McCormick always wanted to have his own business: "I talked about it constantly to the point where some close friends made fun of me!" In college, he sold T-shirts, met with business brokers, and networked. When his employer rejected his business proposal, McCormick decided that it was time to take the business plan and run with it. He says, "I knew where my first 100 sales were going to be and I had already researched who and how." He found suppliers, starting with one in Germany, and hired a graphic designer to produce two short product catalogs. In July of 1997, he took $60,000 from his retirement fund and founded American Electrical, Inc. (AEI).

Today, McCormick's company generates approximately $3 million per year in sales and has three full-time employees. It operates from a 5,000-square-foot office/warehouse in Richmond, Virginia. American Electrical imports electrical and electronic controls from 10 companies, primarily in Europe, for the industrial

Tom McCormick, American Electrical, Inc.
(American Electrical, Inc.)

controls marketplace in the United States. Tom McCormick took his business plan and turned it into a successful venture.

Case Study Analysis

1. In what areas of the market did McCormick do research before starting his business?
2. What research methods would you recommend for AEI today? Name three specific sources of information.
3. How did McCormick identify AEI's market? Name the segmentation method and the segment they chose.
4. What is the role of marketing in McCormick's business?

Case Study | Russell Simmons, Hip-Hop Entrepreneur

Russell Simmons turned off his cell phone and took a rare moment to admire the view from his fourteenth-floor office in midtown Manhattan. At 47, Simmons knew he had a lot going for him. As the president of Rush Communications, he sat at the helm of a constellation of successful enterprises, including a record label, a clothing line, a philanthropic arts foundation, and a multimedia production company. Lately, he had been thinking about how to leverage his influence as a hip-hop mogul to inspire young people to get involved in social issues such as voter registration and education reform. Yet, when he was growing up in Hollis, Queens, in the 1960s and 1970s, Simmons never could have imagined that his life would have turned out as it had.

Window of Opportunity

Early on, Simmons decided that he wanted to make his own way in the world. His father had been a teacher and his mother worked as a recreation coordinator. Both enjoyed stable jobs, but Simmons was not driven by a need for security. He wanted to live a fast-paced life and call his own shots. In 1977, Simmons, who never liked school very much, enrolled at the City College of New York as a sociology major. That year, something happened that permanently changed the course of his life. He went to hear a rap artist named Eddie Cheeba perform and was amazed to see how the rapper had cast a spell over the audience with his freestyle rhymes. In Simmons's own words,"Just like that, I saw how I could turn my life in another, better way.... All the street entrepreneurship I'd learned, I decided to put into promoting music."[14]

At that time, rap and hip-hop were underground music styles, but Simmons set out to change that. He believed that rap music had the potential to reach a larger audience and so he teamed up with another aspiring rap producer, Rick Rubin. Rubin had built a recording studio for rap artists in his New York University dorm room. Together, they decided to transform Rick's studio into a viable record label. By 1985, Def Jam Records was officially underway.

Def Jam experienced its first surge of success when it scored a hit with Run DMC's remake of the Aerosmith classic, "Walk This

Russell Simmons, media mogul.
(Getty Images, Inc.)

Way." Bridging the worlds of rock and rap music turned out to be a stroke of genius. Simmons and Rubin single-handedly introduced a whole new market of mostly white, suburban, heavy-metal music fans to hip-hop. Suddenly, Run DMC was being featured on MTV, and rap was no longer an underground fad.

Marketing Insight: Authenticity Matters

Simmons learned an important lesson from Run DMC's success. He realized that these artists had gone to the top of the charts because they had remained true to their street style and musical origins. Whereas Run DMC may have popularized wearing gold chains, branded sneakers, and name-plate belts among suburban teenagers, these were the fashions that its core audience of urban youth had already embraced. Simmons understood that being perceived as authentic was key to making it in his segment of the music industry: "You have to tell the truth. It endears you to the community. The [people] can smell the truth, and they're a lot smarter than the people who put the records out."[15]

[14]Russell Simmons, *Life and Def: Sex, Drugs, Money + God* (New York: Crown Publishing, 2002).

[15]Jennifer Reingold, "Rush Hour," *Fast Company*, no. 76, November 2003.

Simmons knew how to market his product, and his ability to promote rap music and the hip-hop lifestyle was influenced by how close he was to it.

Simmons has maintained the philosophy of "keeping it real" throughout his business career. It permeates everything he does and is even reflected in his preference for wearing Phat Farm sweatshirts instead of Brooks Brothers suits. Since those early days, Simmons has gone on to launch many other business ventures, which are all geared toward the same target market: urban teens and young adults. This market has the power to influence the tastes and preferences of other consumers.

Simmons's Empire Grows

In 1999, Simmons sold his stake in Def Jam records to Polygram Records for over $100 million. He has since focused his energies on developing the various entertainment, fashion, and multimedia companies that make up Rush Communications. Simmons's business goals have evolved from promoting hip-hop music to developing new products and services for the urban youth market.

Simmons also began using his status as a tastemaker and hip-hop entrepreneur to influence public debate about political issues. In 2002, he organized a youth summit in New York, featuring hip-hop artists such as Jay-Z and Alicia Keyes. When Simmons put out a call to action over the airwaves, over 20,000 students showed up at New York's City Hall to protest the mayor's proposed cuts to the education budget. Simmons has demonstrated that he has the skill and sophistication to market ideas as well as products and services. He continues to sit at the helm of Rush Communications, where he keeps his radar attuned to new opportunities in the marketplace.

Case Study Analysis

1. Why do you think Russell Simmons has been successful?
2. Describe the target market that Simmons is trying to appeal to in all of his business ventures. What does this target market value?
3. Simmons grew up surrounded by hip-hop music and culture. In what ways did this give him an advantage in the marketplace? How might his insider's knowledge also function as a limitation?
4. Brainstorm a business idea that you could pitch to Russell Simmons that would be appropriate for Rush Communications. What market research would you need to conduct in advance to assess whether or not your idea had the potential to be successful?
5. Russell Simmons invested $5,000 to start Def Jam and then later sold his business to Polygram Records for $100 million. Calculate Simmons's return on investment (ROI).

Case Sources

Jennifer Reingold, "Rush Hour," *Fast Company*, no. 76, November 2003.

Russell Simmons, *Life and Def: Sex, Drugs, Money + God* (New York: Crown Publishing, 2002).

DEVELOPING THE RIGHT MARKETING MIX AND PLAN

All of BMW's marketing, from the price of the cars to the advertisements in magazines catering to people who buy expensive things, is designed to remind customers that BMW makes luxury automobiles. If BMW lowered the price of a sedan, would that damage the customer's belief in BMW's market position as a provider of luxury vehicles? This is the question that working through the next step of the marketing process will help answer. BMW illustrates the importance of getting the marketing mix—product, price, place, promotion—right. Without an effective combination of these elements, your business is likely to fail.

Performance Objectives

1. Combine the Four P's—product, price, place, promotion—into a marketing mix.
2. Choose the attributes of your product or service.
3. Price your products for success.
4. Find the best location for maximum efficiency and effectiveness of distribution.
5. Determine the mix of promotion to use for your business.
6. Find a way to add the Fifth P, philanthropy, to your business.
7. Understand the importance of a marketing plan.
8. Identify the critical components of a marketing plan.
9. Use breakeven analysis to evaluate your marketing plan.

BMW positions its products as luxury purchases.
(Niall McDiarmid/Alamy)

The Four Marketing Factors

The Four P's—product, price, place, and promotion—together will communicate your marketing vision and competitive advantage to your customer. If you tweak one P, you will have to pay attention to how it affects the others. If you raise your price, for example, are you now still selling the product in the right place? Or will you need to move to a location that will put you in contact with consumers willing to pay the new price? Where will you promote your product at the higher price? Will you have to take out ads in different magazines or newspapers to reach these other consumers?

As you choose the elements of your marketing plan, always keep your vision in mind. What is the benefit your product or service is providing to consumers?

Performance Objective 1

Combine the Four P's—product, price, place, promotion—into a marketing mix.

- **Product.** The product (or service) should meet or create a customer need. The product is the entire bundle, such that the packaging is also part of the product. Your customer might not be consciously aware of your packaging, but that does not mean it is unimportant. Starbucks revolutionized the American coffee shop partially by introducing Italian names for the different serving sizes.

- **Price.** Generally, a product has to be priced low enough so the public will buy it and high enough for the business to make a profit. Price should also reflect your marketing vision. If you are marketing a luxury item, a relatively low price might confuse the consumer, who will be led to wonder about its quality.

- **Place.** The location where you choose to market your product—whether a retail store, in a customer's home, on an online storefront, or from a cart on the street—must be where customers who will want or need it shop. Selling bathing suits on a beach in Alaska in February is not going to fill a customer need. Where should you go to bring your product or service to the attention of your market? If you are selling a luxury item, you will need to place it in stores that are visited by consumers who can afford it.

- **Promotion.** Promotion is the development of the popularity and sales of a product or service through advertising, publicity, or other promotional devices such as discount coupons or giveaways. As we have said: Publicity is notice that is free; advertising is purchased. If a newspaper writes an article about your business, it is publicity. If you buy an ad in that newspaper, you are advertising.

Product: What Are You Selling?

Steve Jobs and Stephen Wozniak were in their early twenties in California when Jobs sold his Volkswagen minibus and Wozniak sold his Hewlett-Packard calculator to raise the $1,300 that started Apple. They soldered together the circuit boards with three friends to fill their first substantial order.

Jobs made sales calls to every computer store in the area with their one sample machine and finally convinced a small start-up store in Mountain View to order 50 circuit boards. The owner agreed to pay Apple $548 for each (and would then have to add the remaining components).

Jobs and Wozniak had one month to build the 50 circuit boards, but they did not have the money to buy the necessary parts. Using the order, though, the partners found a supplier that was willing to give them $25,000 worth of parts on 30-day credit. They started building the circuit boards. By the end of the month, they had built 100 and delivered 50 to the store in Mountain View. They paid the supplier on the twenty-ninth day. Apple has come a long way since then.

Your business, no matter how humble its beginnings, may have the potential to grow into a multimillion-dollar company, so it is important that you think through every step of its development. How you define and refine your product or service will have a tremendous impact on your ability to grow.

Create Your Total Product or Service Concept

A *product* is something that exists in nature or is made by human industry, usually to be sold, whereas a service is *intangible*—work, skills, or expertise provided in exchange for a fee. Your product will be defined by its physical attributes (e.g., size, color, weight, shape), its performance characteristics (e.g., speed, strength, efficiency, durability), as well as its pricing, branding, and delivery. It is the total package that people are buying. A dirty stone glued onto a piece of cardboard with a scrawled, handwritten price and sold by a kid on the street would be a much different product from a Pet Rock (a real fad product in 1975) that has been cleaned, polished, placed in a nest of attractive packing material in a box, and displayed in an upscale retail store.

A parallel exists for services. Think about a one-person cleaning business in which the individual arrives in an old, battered van, is unkempt and appears to be tired. Compare that image with neatly dressed, uniformed personnel that arrive in a new vehicle (with the name of the company on the side of the truck) to work as a team. Retail service businesses sell directly to the end consumer, but there are also service companies that have only wholesalers or manufacturers as customers.

The selection of your product or service and its branding will be a critical part of your marketing mix.

Focus Your Brand

The key to building a successful brand is to focus tightly on the primary benefit you want customers to associate with your business. Marketing expert Al Ries explains that the most successful businesses *focus* their marketing, so that they come to own a category in the customer's mind.[1] You want to own a benefit the way Volvo owns safety or Federal Express owns guaranteed overnight delivery.

Even entertainers can become a brand. Oprah Winfrey is among the most recognized and wealthiest celebrities in the world today. She is the head of a global media empire and is a philanthropist.[2] From her roots in Nashville radio, Winfrey has become a media mogul, with such well-recognized names as *The Oprah Winfrey Show; O, The Oprah Magazine; O at Home; Oprah & Friends Radio*; Harpo Films, and Oprah.com.[3]

Ford's Costly Failure: The Edsel

One of the most notorious examples of a product whose failure was caused by lack of focus is the car the Ford Motor Company introduced in 1958, the Edsel.

Ford tried to include every kind of gadget and design element the company thought consumers might possibly want in a car. They also

[1]Al Ries, *Focus: The Future of Your Company Depends on It* (New York: HarperCollins, 2005).
[2]Information available at http://www.oprah.com, July 9, 2009.
[3]*The Oprah Winfrey Show* went off the air in 2011 after 25 years. *Oprah & Friends* is a registered trademarks of Harpo, Inc. *O, The Oprah Magazine* and *O at Home* are registered trademarks of Harpo Print LLC.

Oprah Winfrey, philanthropist and media mogul.
(AP Photo/Mark J. Terrill)

manufactured multiple models at varying prices that overlapped some Mercury models, thus confusing the public as to which brand was a step up from which. The goal seemed to be to try to appeal to everyone, but Ford soon learned that trying to appeal to everyone resulted in appealing to almost no one. The Edsel had no outstanding benefit that could be clearly marketed. In addition, consumers didn't really like the way the car looked. In the first year, some 63,000 Edsels were produced when sales had been estimated at 200,000.

Even millions of dollars of promotion will not make consumers buy a product they do not want. Ford spent more money on advertising the Edsel than had ever been spent on one line of cars. Three years and $350 million later, Ford pulled the plug on the Edsel.

Ford's Focus on Success: The Mustang

Ford learned from the Edsel mistake, however. When it introduced the Mustang in 1964, it focused very clearly on a target market of individuals from 20 to 30 years old who wanted a powerful car. Everything about the Mustang, from its design to the colors it came in, was focused on appealing to young drivers. The marketing described the Mustang as "for the young at heart." Only one model was offered. The Mustang was a huge success.

Interestingly, Ford tried to offer some luxury and four-door versions of the Mustang a few years later. Sales dropped, probably because the brand had started to lose focus. The Mustang remains one of Ford's stronger sellers.

How to Build Your Brand

You can build your own brand by following these steps:

- *Choose a business name that is easy to remember, describes your business, and helps establish mindshare.* This is the degree to which *your* business will come to mind when a consumer needs something that your product or service could provide.

logo a company trademark or sign (short for logotype).

- *Create a logo that symbolizes your business to the customer.* A logo (short for *logotype*) is an identifying symbol for a product or

Global Impact . . .
Social Gaming Worldwide

Social gaming online has become an international phenomenon, and Zynga Game Network, Inc. has ruled that world with around 65 million daily users, as of the end of 2009. Whereas the popularity of specific games—such as FarmVille, Mafia Wars, and Zynga Poker (Texas Hold'em)—has waxed and waned, CEO Mark Pincus and his team have continued to focus on developing the right marketing mix, and are planning to stay ahead of the curve.

Pincus suggests in an interview, "When we think about next year, we know we have to double down on social, it needs to be more about real user interaction and communication inside of gaming experience. Today, it's very hard to communicate with friends in FarmVille, but people talk about it at the bar, in dorms, on Facebook, and everywhere else."[4] Pincus's focus on social gaming was successful; by 2010 people all over the world were playing Farmville.

[4]Eric Eldon, "Interview with Zynga CEO Mark Pincus on Social Gaming in 2010," *Inside Social Games*, http://www.insidesocialgames.com/2009/12/29/, December 29, 2009.

business. A logo is printed on the business's stationery, business cards, and flyers. When a logo has been registered with the U.S. Patent and Trademark Office to protect it from being used by others, it is called a **trademark**, which is any word, name, symbol, or device used by a manufacturer or merchant to distinguish a product. The Nike swoosh is an example of a logo. So are McDonald's golden arches.

A company uses a trademark so that people will recognize its product instantly, without having to read the company name, or even having to think about it. Rights to a trademark are reserved exclusively for its owner. To infringe on a trademark is illegal.

- *Develop a good reputation.* Make sure your product or service is of the quality you promise. Always treat your customers well. You want people to feel good when they think of your brand or hear it mentioned.
- *Create a brand personality.* Is your brand's personality youthful and casual, like the Gap's? Safe and serious, like Volvo's? Customers will respond to brand personality and develop a relationship with it. Personality will reinforce your name and logo.
- *Communicate your brand personality to your target market.* What type of advertising will best reach your target market? Where should you put flyers? Which newspapers or magazines does your target market read?

Always present yourself and your business in such a way that people will have confidence in your product or service. Anything that harms your reputation will damage your sales and profits. Anything that boosts your reputation will have a positive impact on your business. There are seven things you can do to build and maintain your brand and its reputation:

1. provide a high-quality product or service;
2. maintain the highest ethical standards;
3. define your product or service clearly—*focus*;
4. treat your employees well;
5. make all your advertisements positive and informative;
6. associate your company with a charity, and
7. become actively involved in your community.

trademark any word, name, symbol, or device used by an organization to distinguish its product.

The world's best-known trademark, McDonald's golden arches.
(© James Leynse/CORBIS)

Step into the Shoes . . .

Texas Jet—Premium Pricing for Premium Service

(Small Business School)

Texas Jet is a gas station for airplanes. However, owner Reed Pigman uses the Ritz Carlton Hotel chain as his guide rather than gas stations. Reed says, "The people who fly and ride in private planes are the same people who stay at a Ritz Carlton or other luxury hotel. That means they don't compare us to the corner gas station, they compare us to the luxury service they get when they travel."

Reed's business operates 13 hangars and supplies two-thirds of the fuel at Meacham Field in Fort Worth, Texas. Private aircraft depend upon a network of fueling stations, called fixed-base operations (FBO), and Texas Jet is one of the best in the world, according to *Professional Pilot* magazine and *Aviation International News*. In 2009 and 2010, Texas Jet was named the number one FBO by the pilots surveyed. *Professional Pilot* named Texas Jet number one because it is a place the pilots enjoy while they are waiting for their customers. More significantly, the pilot's customer is given the red-carpet treatment.

Texas Jet arranges for the ground transportation to pick passengers up right at plane side and, if they need food on the airplane, that is handled too. While the passengers are taking care of obligations in Fort Worth, the pilots have a place at Texas Jet to sleep, work out, eat, relax, visit with other pilots, watch TV, send e-mails, check the weather, and work on flight plans. Reed understands that pilots have to spend a lot of time away from their families and his goal is to make Texas Jet an extended family for every pilot who buys fuel from him.

Excellence pays. Reed charges more for fuel than his competitors, but he sells two-thirds of all the fuel purchased in his market. Reed says, "It took me a while to realize that I've got to charge a fair price for the fuel I sell....I've got to make a margin so I can keep the best people here and so I can reinvest in the business."

The facilities and services offered increase the costs for Texas Jet, justify the higher cost of fuel, and provide reasons for the customers to return. They provide competitive advantages that increase the value of Texas Jet's products and services.

Note: Original case prepared by Hattie Bryant, creator of *Small Business School,* the television series made for PBS and Voice of America, http://SmallBusinessSchool.org.

Price: What It Says about Your Product

Performance Objective 3 ▶

Price your product for success.

As reported by author Jay Conrad Levinson, a study of consumers in the furniture industry found that price came ninth when they were asked to list factors affecting their decision to make a purchase.[5] Confidence in the product was number one and quality was the number two influence on buying patterns. Service was third.

Although your customers may not think exactly like those who buy furniture, the lesson here is that simply undercutting your competitors' prices will not necessarily win you the largest market share. For one thing, consumers tend to infer things about the quality or specialness of a product or service based on its price. It is important, therefore, for entrepreneurs to consider not only the economics but also the psychology of pricing. Studying the pricing strategies of your competitors will tell you a lot about the importance of psychological pricing in your market.

Strategies and Tactics for Effective Pricing

Pricing strategy is not a one-size-fits-all proposition. As you define the marketing strategy for your company, including your target market(s), competitive advantages, and overall marketing mix, a range of appropriate pricing strategies will emerge. For example, an exclusive, highly specialized product targeted toward upscale consumers would logically be priced at a premium. However, at its point of introduction, it may have to be priced in line with the competition until it is established as the market leader. At the same time, mass-market products may be priced at a lower

---

[5]Jay Conrad Levinson, *Guerrilla Marketing Attack* (Boston: Houghton Mifflin, 1989).

Exhibit 5-1 *Eight Steps to Better Pricing*
1. Assess what value your customers place on the product or service.
2. Look for variations in the way customers value the product.
3. Assess customers' price sensitivity.
4. Identify an optimal pricing structure.
5. Consider competitors' reactions.
6. Monitor prices realized at the transaction level.
7. Assess customers' emotional response.
8. Analyze whether the returns are worth the cost to serve.

Source: Robert J. Dolan, "How Do You Know When the Price Is Right?" *Harvard Business Review,* September–October 1995.

level. There are multiple factors to be considered when creating your pricing strategy, as illustrated in **Exhibit 5-1**. The particular pricing strategies that are commonly used are described below.

Value Pricing Strategy

A popular strategy is **value pricing,** which offers "more for less" by underscoring a product's quality while at the same time featuring its price. Value pricing is not just price cutting. It means finding the balance between quality and price that will give your target customers the value they seek. Value pricing began in the 1990s as a reaction to the glamorous 1980s, when marketers used high prices to pitch luxury and extravagance. Companies such as Wal-Mart and Procter & Gamble have effectively shifted to value pricing. This strategy requires a delicate balance to avoid customer confusion and mixed marketing signals.

value pricing a strategy in which the quality of a product is emphasized in relation to its price.

Prestige Pricing Strategy

When a firm sets high prices on its products or services to send a message of uniqueness or premium quality, it is using a **prestige pricing** strategy. For this to be effective in the long run, the product must fulfill the image and sustain it.

prestige pricing a strategy in which a firm sets high prices on its products or services to send a message of uniqueness or premium quality.

Cost-Plus Pricing Strategy

The **cost-plus pricing** method is one of the most commonly used pricing strategies; you take your cost and add a desired profit margin. It is the simplest cost to calculate, once your complete costs are known and your desired rate of return is established. However, it fails to take marketing vision and market conditions into consideration. For example, the competitive environment is neglected, as is the value of the product or service to your targeted customers.

cost-plus pricing a strategy that takes the organization's product cost and adds a desired markup.

Markup Pricing Strategy

Markup pricing is a cost-plus pricing strategy in which you apply a predetermined percentage to a product's cost to obtain its selling price. Markup pricing is described in greater detail later in this chapter.

markup pricing a cost-plus strategy in which a predetermined percentage is applied to a product's cost to obtain its selling price.

Penetration Pricing Strategy

Penetration pricing offers a low price during the early stages of a product's life cycle to gain market share. Japanese companies employed this method

penetration pricing a strategy that uses a low price during the early stages of a product's life cycle to gain market share.

to dominate consumer electronics markets. In the emerging market for hybrid automobiles in the United States, Toyota priced the Prius at about $3,000 below cost to secure a leadership position. The risk with penetration pricing is that, once you start at a low price point, it is often difficult to raise it, or to depend upon cost savings to increase profitability.

Skimming Price Strategy

The **skimming price strategy** is the opposite of penetration strategy because it seeks to charge high prices during the introductory stage—when the product is novel and has few competitors—to take early profits, and then reduces prices to more competitive levels. This strategy recognizes that competition and product maturity may erode the firm's capacity to maintain the pricing later. RCA used this strategy when it introduced color television in the 1960s.

Meet-or-Beat-the-Competition Pricing Strategy

It is common for service businesses to use a **meet-or-beat-the-competition pricing** strategy, which entails constantly matching or undercutting the prices of your competition. Airlines tend to compete intensely by lowering their ticket prices. The more you can show that your business is different from your competition, however, the less you will have to compete with your price. When Sir Richard Branson started Virgin Atlantic Airways, he offered massages and individual videos at each seat. His marketing emphasized how much fun it was to fly on Virgin. This strategy was successful, even though Virgin did not always offer the lowest fares.

Follow-the-Leader Pricing Strategy

A **follow-the-leader pricing** strategy is similar to meet-or-beat-the-competition but with a particular competitor as the model for pricing. Typically, the leader is a dominant firm in the industry and controls a substantial portion of market share.

Personalized Pricing Strategy

The **personalized (dynamic) pricing** strategy is one in which a company charges a premium above the standard price for a product or service to certain customers, who will pay the extra cost. Personalized pricing is particularly applicable when the product or service is highly valued by certain customers, perhaps for its performance, importance to the production process, or for outstanding delivery or service aspects. Such pricing works only when products are not easily compared and customers are not likely to communicate with one another.

Variable Pricing Strategy

Businesses often use **variable pricing strategy** without conscious recognition of it. So that they can offer discounts, easier credit terms, and price concessions to certain customers, firms set different prices for a single product or service.

Price Lining Strategy

In addition to selecting from among the specific pricing strategies described above, you may want to create distinctive price levels for your merchandise. **Price lining** is the process of creating graded pricing levels. For example, Sears carries "good, better, best" product lines in its paint products, and prices them accordingly.

---

skimming price strategy an approach that seeks to charge high prices during the introductory stage of a product, when it is novel and has few competitors, to take early profits, and then to reduce prices to more competitive levels.

meet-or-beat-the-competition pricing a strategy that entails constantly matching or undercutting the prices of the competition.

follow-the-leader pricing a strategy that is similar to a meet-or-beat-the-competition method, but uses a particular competitor as a benchmark.

personalized (dynamic) pricing a strategy in which a company charges a premium above the standard price for a product or service to those customers who are willing to pay it.

variable pricing strategy an approach that provides different prices for a single product or service.

price lining the process of creating distinctive pricing levels.

Step into the Shoes . . .

The Laub Family—Harold Import Company

(Harold Import Company)

If you like to cook, have ever purchased a gourmet cooking item, or ever shopped in a gourmet kitchen store, chances are you have a Harold Import Company (HIC) product in your kitchen. Since its start in 1957, HIC has sold over 20 million pieces of porcelain dinnerware worldwide. Today, HIC distributes over 3,500 houseware, gourmet, and kitchen products from 25 different countries. HIC is still run by members of founder Harold Laub's family, who continue to diversify the product lines while maintaining high quality.

As a standard procedure, HIC asks each new business customer to fill out a form containing basic company information. Items on this form include mailing, shipping, and e-mail addresses; contact names and telephone numbers; the type of business and its resale tax identification number; and the customer's desired method of payment. If the customer wants to establish an account with terms of net 30 days, a credit application must also be completed. This form requires the contact information for three vendors from whom the customer has previously purchased goods.

Harold Import Company calls each of the trade references to find out the customer's payment history. If responses are positive, an HIC account with credit is set up. HIC staff looks at the amount of credit that the customer is requesting and the amount of credit their references currently provide to determine their level of comfort. If feedback indicates late payments, HIC asks the customer to provide banking information. In these questionable cases, the customer may pay with a credit card or send a prepayment, which is almost always a company check. By using this process, HIC is able to provide multiple payment options to potential buyers while keeping risk at a minimum.

Place: Location, Location, Location!

◀ **Performance Objective 4**
Locate and distribute for maximum efficiency and effectiveness.

Regarding place, the type of business you are running will influence your choice of location and your distribution system for reaching out from that place to your customers. For a retail business, site location is the key to attracting clientele. Ideally, you will want your store or business to be where your market is. This is why you did the work of consumer and market analysis—to figure out who your customers were. You should know where they shop. Your goal is to find a location you can afford that is also convenient for your potential customers.

Wal-Mart has done an efficient job of choosing locations that were ideal for attracting its potential customers, yet underserved by similar retailers. Wal-Mart was the first mass-merchandise store to choose locations in rural and semi-rural markets. This strategy has been so successful that other stores now seek to be located near a Wal-Mart.

Of course, the Internet has made it possible for an entrepreneur to start a retail business out of his or her home and reach customers all over the world. This has led to the belief that online stores can forego the expense of renting a location that caters to foot traffic. As the old saying goes, however, you can lead a horse to water but you can't make it drink. How do you get your customers to your site and then induce them to buy? If you are going to start a retail business online, you must figure out how you will attract customers to your Web site, that is, how you will *market* the site.

For nonretail businesses, the key to location might be cost or convenience rather than proximity to the market. Wholesale businesses that require a great deal of storage space do best in areas where rent or property costs are low, where there is space for large commercial buildings, and where their trucks and vans have easy access to roads and highways.

The Internet is making it easier for people who provide services—such as graphic or Web site design, writing/editing, or accounting—to start businesses at home. Communication with clients is easy via e-mail,

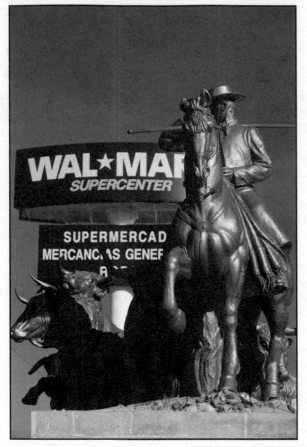

Wal-Mart location.
(Planetpix/Alamy)

and the overhead costs are certainly minimal. On the other hand, working at home requires discipline and a tolerance for isolation. If you are the sort of person who would not be happy spending your workdays by yourself, it is probably not for you.

Key Factors in Deciding upon a Location

The key factors in deciding upon a location are dependent upon the nature of the business and its customers. Considerations include the following:

- access for customers;
- access to suppliers;
- climate and geography;
- convenience;
- cost of facilities (rent, construction, and the like);
- demographics;
- economic conditions and business incentives;
- governmental regulations and laws, including environmental impact;
- labor pool;
- proximity to competitors, and
- visibility.

Figure 5-1 shows the factors affecting location decisions at the country, regional/community, and site levels.

Promotion: Advertising + Publicity

Promotion is the use of advertising and publicity to get your marketing message out to your customers. Advertising, as discussed in Chapters 2 and 4 and above, is paid promotion that is intended to generate increased sales of your product or service. Examples of advertising include television commercials, billboards, and magazine ads. Publicity is free mention of a company, person, event, product, or service in media outlets, such as newspapers and magazines or on radio or television.

Entrepreneurial Wisdom . . .

Raw Material Prices Challenge Manufacturers

When the price of crude oil rises, much of the world feels the pain. Manufacturers using crude oil in their production are affected. When copper prices rise, the effects are also felt worldwide. Volatile raw material costs in one place can have huge ripple effects upon costs and prices globally. Whereas labor costs frequently are perceived to be a primary driver of manufacturing costs, the impact of changing raw material costs may also be quite significant, particularly when they are unpredictable. Manufacturers must control raw material costs to create sustainable profits.

Manufacturers have to buy smarter, explore alternate materials, and evaluate their ability to increase prices to their customers. Manufacturers purchase materials sourced globally to attain the most favorable pricing, making any changes in pricing a global issue. Thus, a price increase in crude oil in Saudi Arabia has ripple effects on Main Street U.S.A.

Source: Jill Jusko, "Rethinking Raw Materials," *IndustryWeek.com*, August 1, 2006.

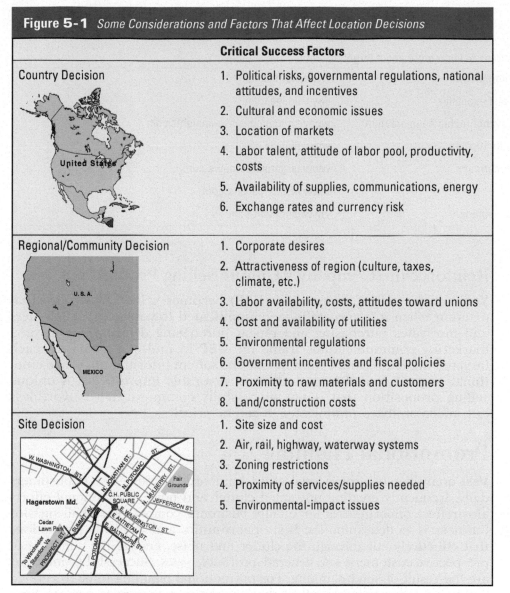

Figure 5-1 *Some Considerations and Factors That Affect Location Decisions*

	Critical Success Factors
Country Decision	1. Political risks, governmental regulations, national attitudes, and incentives
	2. Cultural and economic issues
	3. Location of markets
	4. Labor talent, attitude of labor pool, productivity, costs
	5. Availability of supplies, communications, energy
	6. Exchange rates and currency risk
Regional/Community Decision	1. Corporate desires
	2. Attractiveness of region (culture, taxes, climate, etc.)
	3. Labor availability, costs, attitudes toward unions
	4. Cost and availability of utilities
	5. Environmental regulations
	6. Government incentives and fiscal policies
	7. Proximity to raw materials and customers
	8. Land/construction costs
Site Decision	1. Site size and cost
	2. Air, rail, highway, waterway systems
	3. Zoning restrictions
	4. Proximity of services/supplies needed
	5. Environmental-impact issues

Source: Jay Heizer and Barry Render, *Operations Management*, 8e (Upper Saddle River, N. J.: Pearson Prentice Hall, 2007), p. 249.

Use Integrated Marketing Communications for Success

Marketing communications promotes your business to your current and prospective customers and to those who influence the purchasing and sales decisions. All communications include an originator or source, a specific message (overt and/or subliminal), a channel for dissemination, and a target or receiver. By integrating your communications, you can maximize the impact of your communications resources, primarily as expended for promotion.

Promotion has expanded beyond advertising, sales promotions, and personal selling to include database marketing, sponsorships, direct marketing, alternative marketing, e-active marketing, and public relations. Promotion should be based upon an organization's strategic marketing plan and is meant to create a unified communications program. Promotional tools, applied well, get the marketing message out to your customers.

Entrepreneurial Wisdom . . .

Take advantage of these resources to learn more about target markets.

Consumer geodemographic information	www.claritas.com
Advertising statistics, trends, and examples	www.adage.com
Values and lifestyles (VALS) psychographic segmentation	www.strategicbusinessinsights.com
Target information—Web site for women	www.iVillage.com
Target information—African Americans	www.targetmarketnews.com
Target information—Hispanics	www.hispaniconline.com
Target information—gays and lesbians	www.planetout.com

Reinforce the Company's Unique Selling Proposition

Your unique selling proposition (USP) becomes valuable to your organization when it is successfully communicated to your target customers and motivates purchasing and repeat purchasing decisions. Integrated marketing communications frame the USP in multiple media to reach targeted audiences and communicate the salient information, evoke emotional responses, and create effective, favorable impressions. A unique selling proposition that is not successfully communicated is worthless but, successfully communicated, it can be priceless.

Promotional Planning

Vast quantities of promotional effort bombard businesses and consumers daily, frequently creating unwanted clutter and noise. Promotional efforts also reflect opportunities for quality customer contact. The challenge for business is to determine the best opportunities and to create promotions that effectively cut through the clutter and noise, engage the attention of prospective customers, and generate profitable sales. Successful promotions are the result of solid planning. For promotional planning to be integrated within your organization, all of the company's components need to have meaningful roles in the planning process.

Determine a Promotional Budget

The creation and careful control of a promotional budget is essential to marketing success. A well-structured budget based upon the promotions-opportunity analysis, promotional objectives, and an effective strategy will support measurement and control. These in turn will foster improved performance. There is no single correct way to determine your promotional budget. However, there are several methods that can be used in combination, including percentage of sales method, competitive spending method, excess funds approach, and objective and task method.

Percentage of Sales

Percentage of sales is a common way for calculating the aggregate budget amount. It is the simplest to use because the budget is derived either from the prior year's sales or the current year's anticipated sales. The percentage to be used is best taken from a comparable industry, but may be whatever you want to employ.

The percentage-of-sales method of budgeting is preferable to not establishing a promotional budget, but suffers from several drawbacks. This approach seems counterintuitive to the promotional needs of an organization, because you spend less when you most need promotion—when sales are low. You spend more when you are selling more. Also, this technique may not take competitive spending into account and does not consider your overall strategy.

Competitive Spending

Competitive spending is another way to set a promotional budget. It entails researching your competition to determine their level of spending. This may be as simple as investigating financial-statement studies or as complex as attempting to track and cost out all of their promotional activities. This meet-the-competition method is often used in highly competitive markets, in which the objective is to prevent market-share loss.

Although knowing what your competitors are doing and spending is good practice in general, setting your budget based upon theirs is not optimal. This benchmarking implies that you can make a complete assessment, that competitors are spending the right amount of money, and that this would also be the correct amount for you to spend. The competition may be spending based upon a percentage-of-sales method or according to their excess funds, or even based upon which media and advertising salespeople they are comfortable with. In other words, competitors may not be using the best methods to create their promotional budgets, so copying what they do could easily be ineffective.

Excess Funds

The excess funds approach to promotional budgeting means determining what is left over, or what you can afford after other expenses are calculated, and allocating funds based upon the results. This is among the least strategically based of the budgeting methods because it is completely internally driven. While better than having no budget at all, simply using excess funds is not recommended. This is a particularly poor option for start-up companies and businesses in periods of rapid growth, because there are rarely excess funds to spend at the very times when promotional efforts are most needed.

Objective and Task

The objective-and-task method is to budget expenditures according to the specific strategies and tactics developed to reach promotional objectives. This entails building a budget based upon what you have determined is needed to be successful. In order to create this type of budget, management enumerates the objectives for the year and the budget required to reach them. The more specific you can be about measurable objectives, and the specific media and methods to be used, the stronger the focus of your efforts will be and the more effective your budget can be as a guide and control.

There is no single, perfect method of establishing a promotional budget because there is both art and science involved. As an entrepreneur, using the best aspects of each method is your best bet. Rather than determining what you can easily afford, estimate what you would ideally spend and decide how much you could actually invest to accomplish your goals and objectives. Know where you plan to spend the funds and how you will monitor and control them. This budget should support your strategy and tactics, but not control them so tightly that you cannot take advantage of opportunities if they arise.

The Advertising Advantage

The topic of advertising and advertising management has a certain glamour about it. The popular media have portrayed advertising as a fast-paced, highly creative, fun, and lucrative career choice. At the same time, advertising itself has often been shown to be false, manipulative, deceitful, and coercive. For some, it is something to be avoided whenever possible. Others embrace it and enjoy wearing branded clothing, promotional T-shirts, caps, and the like, and watch the annual NFL Super Bowl as much or more for the newly unveiled television ads than for the football. It does not matter where you fall personally in this spectrum. It is important to determine the best, most effective method of advertising for your business to reach your prospective and current customers—to run a successful company. This is where advertising management becomes critical.

As with any aspect of your business, advertising has specific objectives that make it an integral component of the marketing mix. Advertising aids the marketing effort by creating brand awareness and reinforcing the purchasing decision. The aims of advertising and its management reflect those of promotion; successful advertising will achieve these objectives:

- building brand and image,
- providing information,
- persuading,
- stimulating action, and
- reinforcing the purchasing decision.

Advertising builds brand recognition and creates a positive image. For example, General Mills's Lucky Charms cereal and Malt-O-Meal's Marshmallow Mateys are essentially the same products, with slightly better nutritional value in Marshmallow Mateys—but Lucky Charms has significantly greater advertising and brand recognition and commands a higher average price per pound ($3.17 versus $2.20).[6] Advertising can work for your company, too.

Types of Advertising

institutional advertising promotion that provides information about an organization as a whole, rather than a specific product, and intended to create awareness about the firm and enhance its image.

product advertising a strategy to create awareness and interest, influence purchasing behavior, and supply post-purchase satisfaction for specific products and services.

Advertising is not a one-size-fits-all proposition; rather, it comes in so many forms and options that the types of advertising seem to be limitless. However, there continue to be two primary kinds: institutional advertising and product advertising. **Institutional advertising** provides information about an organization rather than a specific product, and is intended to create awareness of the firm and enhance its image. This advertising is exemplified by the Bank of America ads that focus on the company as the "bank of opportunity" rather than promoting particular financial products. Such advertising is designed to build general credibility and recognition for specific products or services. **Product advertising** is designed to create awareness, interest, purchasing behavior, and post-purchase satisfaction for specific products and services. Typically, small, entrepreneurial companies expend their advertising resources on product advertising. For example, they may want to promote a particular item, or a storewide sale.

Institutional and product advertising are not mutually exclusive. For example, all advertisements placed by an organization might include a tag line or feature that extols a virtue of the firm—such as local ownership,

---

[6]Pricing and nutritional information from Malt-O-Meal, http://www.malt-o-meal.com, May 13, 2009.

length of time in business, quality of workmanship—while simultaneously promoting a particular product or service. Ads that are more "evergreen" (of longer duration)—as in directories or on promotional items—may be more institutional, whereas those that are less "durable" (e.g., daily or weekly newspaper ads) can focus on products. How you decide to promote your organization and products should be defined by your strategy, your industry, available options, and your budget.

Media Planning and Buying: Focus on Your Customer

An effective advertisement for a business typically concentrates on the benefit the product or service provides the customer. This is why it is important that you carry through your consumer analysis. You will need to know who your customers are and what their lifestyle is in order to know how to effectively reach them. It is valuable to know and understand the media habits of people in your target market. What are their reading, viewing, and listening patterns? What appeals to them? What doesn't? If you are advertising a snowboarding trip, it would be a waste of money to take out an ad in a magazine featuring tropical vacations. By visualizing and knowing your customer, you will avoid wasting money in outlets in which the audience won't be interested in your product or service. Combine this common-sense approach with solid research to maximize advertising effectiveness. **Exhibit 5-2** shows the pros and cons of select media options.

Marketing Materials Should Reinforce Your Competitive Advantage

All promotional items for your business should reflect and reinforce your marketing vision, which in turn will reinforce your competitive advantage. They should include the name of your business, your logo, and a slogan, if you have one. All your business materials, in fact—order forms, invoices, receipts—should also reflect and reinforce your business's competitive advantage.

You will have a much stronger impact if all your business materials are tied together with a strong, coordinated image. This should extend beyond your logo into the format, font style, colors, and look of your materials. As you create your stationery and business cards (identity set), advertisements, publicity pieces, and brochures, the consistency of your image will help to convey your competitive advantage. If it is done well, your image will be in alignment with your strengths and you will be positioned for success. If this is done poorly, you will lack credibility, which can then harm, if not destroy, your chances of success.

Sales Promotion Solutions

Sales promotions provide another set of tools to add to the mix. Various efforts to increase sales volume by specified levels, which either reward purchases or provide discounts, can be effective for both consumer and business-to-business marketing. Sales promotion solutions do not have to be complex or sophisticated in order to work. In fact, it is best if they are simple and easily understood. If an incentive program is difficult to figure out, customers may simply not bother to participate, because it isn't worth the trouble. **Exhibit 5-3** identifies some common types of sales promotion methods.

Exhibit 5-2 *Pros and Cons of Selected Advertising Media*

	Pros (Advantages)	Cons (Disadvantages)
Television	Low Cost per Thousand	High cost for ad campaign
	Highly targeted with cable	Clutter
	High intrusion value	Short life of advertising message
	High reach and frequency potential	High production costs
	Message is immediate	Long lead time
Radio	Relatively low cost	Auditory only
	Short-term commitment	Clutter—information overload
	Short lead time	Short life of advertising message
	Message is immediate	Low attention
	Promotes recall	Local nature
	Mobility (radios travel with people)	
Newspapers	Geographic targeting	Expense may be high
	Short lead time	Demographic targeting is limited
	Flexibility and credibility	Short shelf life
	More copy potential	Declining readership
	Direct response possible	Waste
		Poor-quality production
Magazines	Targeted reader interest	Lack of immediacy
	High color/production quality	Exposure dispersed over time
	Direct response possible	Longer lead times
	Long shelf life	High cost
Internet	Targeting potential	Not ubiquitous
	Moderate cost	Banner ads feed-click through to full ads
	Global reach	
	Relatively short lead time	
Outdoor Media	Repeat exposures	Limited message size
	Geographic selectivity	Limited demographic selectivity
	Moderate Cost per Thousand	Initial design and production costs
	High-impact, dramatic ads possible	Short exposure time

When to Use Promotional Tools

Promotional tools are best used when the strategy calls for a highly targeted, time-limited boost in response. They can be excellent tools for encouraging new product trials or for raising seasonal performance. They should always be part of the overall marketing strategy and budget. Contests and sweepstakes are a way of securing product engagement and, potentially, repeat sales (e.g., for a game that requires collecting game pieces). Coupons require the customer to actively seek out your product on the shelves or to contact you for the product or service. *Sampling* brings the product or service message to life for the customer through experience. Bonus packs and tie-ins lead to a trial of additional products.

Exhibit 5-3 *Sales Promotional Tools*	
Consumer	**Business-to-Business**
Coupons	Incentives
Contests and Sweepstakes	Contests
Refunds and Rebates	Refunds and Rebates
Sampling	Sampling
Premiums	Allowances
Tie-ins	Trade Shows
Bonus Packs	

Advertising Specialties

The strategic inclusion of advertising specialty items can be an effective sales promotion tool. Freebies are always a draw with customers, but do not disappoint them with objects that look and feel cheap. The best giveaways are those that are useful, such as pens, on which prospective customers will see your business name and contact information. Visit wholesalers or search online to investigate discount prices on quantities of calculators, watches, pens, or other appropriate items.

Trade Show Exhibits

The use of trade show exhibits is a proven promotional strategy for business-to-business companies and can also succeed for certain types of consumer marketing. This is one of the best forms of experiential marketing, because it lends itself to having prospective customers engage in trying out your products (or having your services demonstrated). Whereas the cost of trade show space, a professionally designed booth, transportation, and other related expenses can be relatively high, the opportunity to have impact can make it worthwhile. This is particularly true for business-to-business marketing that can be accomplished at targeted professional conferences. There is often no better way to reach so many potential customers so efficiently with a consistent message. Tsnn.com reports that there are 15,000 trade shows, exhibitions, public events, and conferences each year. The keys to successful trade show promotion include preparation, booth training for staff, quality exhibits, careful goal setting, and concerted efforts to reap the benefits of the investment.

Business cards carry your message and image.
(Don Farrall/Photodisc/Getty Images)

Mall Carts or Kiosks

For many seasonal businesses, or businesses that are working to create full-scale retail operations, mall carts or kiosks may prove effective. Signing a multiyear lease for a retail store is not likely to make sense for a seasonal business, such as one based on Christmas or Halloween. Sometimes such operations can find vacant retail space to rent for just their critical season, or they can partner with others to rotate in and out of a store. In other scenarios, they can create a business model of changing seasonal inventory and focus. However, for many business owners, these options are not practical or desirable, and having a temporary retail location is preferable. Also, if you are working on a retail concept and want to try out an idea, products, prices, and so forth, a temporary location is a good opportunity to test-drive your business before investing in longer-term, more costly retail space. Such a trial run may also provide you with sales and marketing data that will assist you in attracting financing. For an investment of $1,500 to $10,000, plus inventory and rental fees, you could be up and running.

Alternative Marketing

The marketing approaches described above have been practiced for many years and are considered to be tried-and-true methods to successful promotion. However, marketing has evolved with changing times and technology to include more recent concepts. The following is a discussion of some of the alternative forms of marketing in use today.

Guerilla Marketing

guerilla marketing original, unconventional, and inexpensive small-business strategies.

Jay Conrad Levinson coined this term in 1984 in his book of the same title. It means original, unconventional, and inexpensive small-business strategies. Since then, **guerilla marketing** has expanded to encompass viral marketing, buzz marketing, word-of-mouth advertising, and grass-roots marketing. The notion is to find creative, surprising ways to get your message to your target market without spending a fortune.

Buzz Marketing

buzz marketing another term for word-of-mouth marketing.

This is another name for word-of-mouth advertising. **Buzz marketing** can occur naturally (*organic buzz marketing*) or can be jump-started by the organization (*amplified buzz marketing*). It is one of the most effective forms of promotion available because people are sharing their excitement and enthusiasm about a product or service with others who trust and value the advice. By giving your customers an outstanding experience, you are encouraging organic buzz marketing. If you can create *amplified* buzz marketing, it will boost recognition still further.

Product Placement/Branded Entertainment

The use of product placement in television, movies, and other scenarios is another excellent promotional tool. Such placements reach consumers on a more subconscious level and do not contain an overt sales pitch. When the movie *E.T.* hit the theaters, Reese's Pieces were included as a product placement, and they continue to be associated with the movie decades later. The quantity of in-show brand appearances during an average hour of prime-time network television programming was just short of eight minutes during the fourth quarter of 2008, with an average of almost fourteen minutes during unscripted reality programming and just about six minutes per hour during scripted programs.[7] Today, there are firms that focus on locating and negotiating product placements, including Creative Entertainment Services (acreativegroup.com) and GameShowPlacements. com (for game and cable shows). Depending upon your product, it may be worthwhile to pursue placement possibilities.

---

[7]TNS Media Intelligence press release, May 4, 2009.

Lifestyle Marketing

In order to successfully market their brands, companies are striving to align them with consumer needs, interests, desires, and values, and to apply lifestyle marketing with knowledge of consumer behavior. This form of marketing reaches beyond the traditional demographic approaches to engage customers based upon how they live.

In-Store Marketing

There are numerous options for carrying out in-store marketing, whether in your own space or in stores where your product is sold. For example, signage, shelf placement, sampling, and "edutainment" can all play roles. Which ones are best will depend upon your marketing strategy.

- ***Samples or demonstrations.*** Offer samples of your product to potential customers who pass by your business. Or take samples to a high-density location, such as a park or town square. If you are selling a service, consider demonstrating it outdoors or in a mall (get permission first). When you open your business, you can give away samples of your product to encourage customers to tell their friends about it. Many large businesses, such as BJ's Wholesale Club and Sam's Club, make extensive use of sampling and edutainment to encourage purchases. **Edutainment** combines education and entertainment to make a more lasting impression upon an audience. You might use this method to show the originality of your product and engage prospective customers to learn about it.

- ***Point-of purchase and shelf placement.*** These opportunities include the complete visual component of your in-store placement, such as packaging, any coupons connected with shelf placement, and special display units. By putting products where prospective customers will be drawn to them visually, you are increasing the chances of purchase. Well-designed point-of-purchase materials can make a huge difference in sales.

edutainment a combination of education and entertainment used in promotion to make a more lasting impression on an audience.

Other Media Venues

There are a number of other possibilities worth noting. These options should also be considered in your media planning. See **Exhibit 5-4** for examples.

E-Active Marketing

Internet advertising has grown with the expansion and adoption of Internet technology. Not only have entrepreneurs and major corporations come to include online advertising and promotion as a regular part of the media

Exhibit 5-4 *Other Media Venues*

Ambient Advertising	Indoor Advertising	Other Advertising
Parking Lots	Movie Theaters	Carry-Out Menus
Tunnels	Video Games	Shopping Bags
Escalators	Bathroom Stalls	Advertising on Clothing
Benches (Bus Stops)	Commercial Trucks	Brochure Racks
	Airline In-Flight	

mix, entire industry segments have evolved to serve the interactive media field. The number of advertising opportunities is seemingly infinite, ranging from Google to little-known sites. Businesses can elect to use display advertising in the form of banner ads, pay to raise their visibility within search engines, or partner with other online companies to obtain mention and have customers directed to them. They can use social media, blogs, and e-mail. These options continue to expand and evolve at a rapid pace. When the two major components of Internet marketing—e-commerce and interactive marketing—combine, **e-active marketing** results. You can make the best use of e-active marketing styles by marrying them with your offline efforts to create a unified approach to marketing. **Figure 5-2** shows the level of interest in various types of information from businesses.

e-active marketing a combination of the two major components of Internet marketing—e-commerce and interactive marketing.

E-Commerce

The provision of an electronic storefront and/or other forms of electronic commerce is one way of implementing your marketing strategy, as will be discussed in Chapter 6.

Interactive Marketing

According to John Deighton of Harvard University, interactive marketing is the ability to address the customer, remember what he or she says, and address that same customer again in a way that illustrates that the personal information has been remembered.[8] Whereas interactive marketing is not necessarily online marketing, the collecting of customers' information and communicating with them is facilitated by the Internet. An excellent example of the use of interactive marketing is Amazon.com, which collects user information to make purchase recommendations.

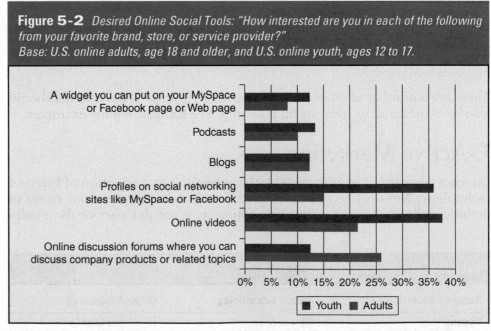

Figure 5-2 *Desired Online Social Tools: "How interested are you in each of the following from your favorite brand, store, or service provider?"*
Base: U.S. online adults, age 18 and older, and U.S. online youth, ages 12 to 17.

Sources: North American Technographics Media and Marketing Online Survey, Q2 2008; North American Technographics Youth Online Survey, Q2 2008; Forrester Research, Inc., "The Social Tools Consumers Want from Their Favorite Brands," report prepared by Josh Bernoff, http://blogs.forrester.com/a/6a00d8341c50bf53ef01156f8 27e11970c-pi, April 16, 2009.

---

[8]John A. Deighton, "The Future of Interactive Marketing," *Harvard Business Review* 7, no. 6 (November–December 1996) pp. 151–160.

Online Advertising

This typically takes the form of banner ads on Web sites. These can be highly targeted, based upon the online habits and interests of consumers. Such ads can be purchased directly from the owners of the Web sites on which you want to advertise, or through brokers who purchase online advertising for specific target markets. For small, local businesses with a Web site, it might be possible to work in partnership with other companies that sell complementary products to create click-through opportunities for their customers to visit your site and vice versa. This type of advertising includes pay-per-click (PPC), wherein firms bid on keywords that they expect their potential customers to use to search for their goods and services so that they can appear in the search-return results as "sponsored ads," and thus become considerably more visible. With this type of advertising, you only pay when someone clicks on your advertisement.

Brand Spiraling

Integrating a company's conventional offline branding strategy with its Internet strategy can be accomplished through **brand spiraling**— companies using conventional approaches through print and broadcast media to drive traffic to their online sites. Once customers are guided to their sites, the companies take advantage of Internet interactivity and learn more about them. The companies then use this knowledge to further refine their products and sales and marketing tactics. They also can use e-mail addresses and other information to reach customers in additional ways. The brand spiral is a continuous learning and changing process for a company—it assists in reaching and influencing customers through both online and offline tactics.

brand spiraling the integration of a company's conventional offline branding strategy with its Internet strategy, which uses conventional approaches to drive traffic to its online sites.

Blogs

A **blog** (short for Web log) is a journal that appears on the Internet periodically (perhaps daily) and is intended for the public. **Blogosphere** is the term used for all the blogs on the Internet. Businesses provide blogs, often written by their owners, to create a personal connection with the customers. These are only effective if the information is kept interesting and timely and customers are led to the sites by other promotions. Some blog-hosting services include:

blog a journal that appears on the Internet periodically (often daily) and is intended for the public (short for Web log).

blogosphere the aggregate term for all the blogs on the Internet.

Blogger	www.blogger.com
LiveJournal	www.livejournal.com
Twitter	www.twitter.com (microblogging)
TypePad	www.typepad.com
Vox	www.vox.com
WordPress	www.wordpress.com
Xanga	www.xanga.com

Online Social Networks

The number and variety of online social networks has grown phenomenally in recent years and is expected to continue to do so for the near future. Social networks such as Facebook, MySpace, and LinkedIn, as well as those for interest-specific niches (e.g., Flickr, imeem, BlackPlanet,

Classmates.com, Goodreads, and MyHeritage), continue to evolve as new and different uses emerge. Advertising opportunities on these networks are more complex than those on Web sites with banner ads. For many social networks, advertising and promotion are either banned or taboo. Some users create subtle promotion through what are essentially scripted conversations on these sites. These "undercover"—deceptive—marketing efforts are intended to appear as if they happened naturally, and are referred to as **stealth marketing.**

stealth marketing
undercover or deceptive marketing efforts that are intended to appear as if they happened naturally.

Recent research by the Internet Advertising Bureau in the United Kingdom addressed the methods for maximizing results from social networking: "The IAB research found that exclusive content, which appeals to 28% of social networkers, and genuine interest in the message, which attracts 37%, are the keys to a positive response from consumers on social networks. And because only 5% say they actively dislike messages from brands, there are big opportunities for marketers who can hit the right notes."[9] In addition to online social networking, the option of **mobile social networking**—the updating of social network sites via mobile handsets—is increasing. This means that users are accessing the information at all times and at any location.

mobile social networking
the updating of social network sites via mobile handsets.

Consumer-Generated Advertising

This can include campaigns in which the company solicits advertisements from customers. You can ask your customers to create videos, stories, print advertisements, and the like—generally through a contest or promotion—to fuel your advertising programs. Such advertising creates authenticity and credibility in a way that company-generated advertising cannot. Consumer-generated media (CGM) also come in a variety of forms that are not specifically solicited by companies, such as message-board posts, blogs, forum commentary, and the like. Consumer-generated advertising can create enthusiasm and engagement as well as increased loyalty.

Viral Marketing

viral marketing the process of promoting a brand, product, or service though an existing social network, in which a message is passed from one individual to another.

Interactive marketing options have been expanded through technology to include **viral marketing,** a term coined by Tim Draper, of Draper Fisher Jurvetson. Viral marketing is defined as the process of promoting a brand, product, or service though an existing social network, typically an online network such as MySpace or Facebook, in which a message is passed from one individual to another—much as a virus spreads. A viral campaign can be an e-mail or a video that could include hyperlinked promotions, advertisements, games, online newsletters, and so forth. There has to be a reason for people to tell others about the message or pass it along, such as entertainment value, uniqueness, or potential financial reward.

In August 2007, with a budget of $150,000, TuitionBids.com's agency, Fanscape, created a viral marketing campaign targeted at 16-to-24-year-old high school and college students and their parents, with the intention of creating buzz and awareness of the company, and to drive sales leads.[10] The strategy used was to "surround and deliver [the] target audience with valuable information." They used a multifaceted approach that "fused online Content and Promotional Integration programs, Social Media techniques, dedicated e-mails from Fanscape's proprietary database, a pay-per-click (PPC) campaign, and display ad buys to create as

---

[9]Emma Hall, "How to Get the Most Out of Social Networks and Not Annoy Users," *Advertising Age*, April 27, 2009, p. 30.
[10]WOMMA [Word of Mouth Marketing Association] Web site, http://www.womma.org. Case study accessed May 18, 2009, at http://www2.fanscape.com/tuitionbids/omma0808.html.

many relevant touch points with the target audience as possible." This included an e-mail to 100,000 members of the Fanscape database. The results included "32 million branding impressions with over 40,000 clicks, 150 WOM [word of mouth] placements, 26 editorial placements for over 2 million unique views, 8 contests, adding another 3 million unique views, a 25% open rate on the Fanscape email (well above industry averages)." Tuitionbids.com had a 6.4% conversion rate, which is about three times the industry average.

By creatively generating interest in and excitement about your story or an aspect of your business, you can work to create a viral campaign. Kristen Smith, Executive Director of WOMMA, suggests the following six ways to keep people talking about your company and your products:[11]

1. Listen, speak, listen some more.
2. Be transparent and disclose.
3. Evaluate ROI (return on investment) continually.
4. Spread the word, not the manure.
5. Encourage an enterprisewide WOMM (word of mouth marketing).
6. Employ online and offline WOMM (see footnote 11).

Publicity Potential

Generating Publicity

Publicity is defined by the Institute of Public Relations as: "[T]he planned and sustained effort to establish and maintain goodwill and mutual understanding between an organization and its public." Always save any publicity you receive. Frame and display articles prominently in your place of business and make copies to send or hand out when it is appropriate. Each item of publicity has enormous value. Consumers give publicity credibility because it is not paid for.

Publicity is very important for a small business, which often has a negligible advertising budget. To get publicity, you will need to mail or fax a pitch letter and a press release to the magazine, newspaper, TV station, or radio station you hope to interest.

A **pitch letter** sells the story. It tells the person reading it why he or she should be interested in your business. A **press release** is an announcement sent to the media to generate publicity, and states the "who, what, when, where, and why" of a story. A pitch letter allows you to explain the story behind the press release, and why it would be interesting and relevant to the media outlet's readers, listeners, or viewers.

Before mailing or faxing a pitch letter and press release, call or e-mail the outlet and ask to whom you should direct the material. Say something like, "My name is Jason Hurley, and I'm a young entrepreneur with a delivery/messenger service downtown. I'd like to send WKTU a press release about the commitment we have just made to donate 10 hours of free delivery service per month to Meals on Wheels for seniors. To whom should I direct the press release?" Sometimes you can find this information on the Internet.

Get to know the print, radio, and television journalists pertinent to your business, so you can get publicity. The most effective way to get notice for your business is to contact the reporters yourself. You might be tempted to hire a professional publicist, but many reporters are bombarded by requests from these people and would rather hear directly from you.

pitch letter correspondence designed to explain the story behind a press release and why it would be interesting and relevant to the media outlet's readers, listeners, or viewers.

press release an announcement sent to the media to generate publicity.

---

[11]Kristen Smith, "Six Ways to Leverage Word-of-Mouth," http://www.womma.org, March 1, 2009.

Dedicate a block of time to send e-mails and make phone calls pitching your business and explaining why your story is worth covering. Be totally honest and build positive relationships. The type of reporting you want will develop most often because the writer comes to care about your story and sees it as interesting and important. Once you establish rapport and credibility with reporters, they are likely to call you for stories, insights, and information.

Press releases can generate positive reports and stories about your business in newspapers, magazines, and on radio stations. For newspapers, make sure you send the release about a month before the event you are promoting. Follow up with a phone call two weeks later, and then one week after that (a week before the occasion). The precise timing will depend on the media outlet and its publication or broadcast schedule.

Telling the Story

Younger entrepreneurs can have an advantage here because relatively few young people start their own businesses. The print, radio, and television journalists in your area may want to hear about you.

Bear in mind, however, that reporters are looking for stories that will interest their readers. It is fine to send out a press release announcing the opening of your business, but be aware that it will not be a story until it is up and running. There is no point in sending out a pitch letter and press release until you are actually in business and have a story to tell. The fact that your business is open, however, doesn't necessarily translate into a story of interest to reporters. You have to make the connection:

- Who are you and what has happened to you or what have you done that would make you and your business an interesting story?
- Did you have to overcome any obstacles in order to start your business?
- What about your product or service is unique? Is it something your community really needs?
- When is a specific event taking place that is *newsworthy*—of interest—for a story?
- Where are you locating the business, or where is the event or activity occurring?
- How has your business changed you and/or helped members of the community?

Always answer the basic questions of who, what, when, where, why, and how. Answers to these questions will help them determine whether your story might be of interest to their readers or viewers. Reporters are very busy people, so keep your answers to these questions tight and concise. Try to find one focus or angle for your story: What's the "hook"?

Sample Press Release

A press release must provide contact information (name, phone, e-mail, and Web site) and answer the who, what, when, where, why, and how questions (see **Figure 5-3**).

Entrepreneurial Wisdom . . .

Be sure to obtain videotapes of any mention you receive on television. There is no more powerful sales tool than a video that includes a story, however brief, on your business.

Figure 5-3 *Sample Press Release*

DOGFISH HEAD COLLABORATES With 3 BREWERS, BATALI & BASTIANICH ON NYC BREWPUB

Fri, 02/19/2010 - 11:54 am — mariah

The International Craft Brewing Renaissance Taken to New Heights

FOR IMMEDIATE RELEASE

February 20, 2010

Four well-known brewers are joining forces with Mario Batali, Joe Bastianich, and Italian food emporium Eataly to open a brewery-pub on a New York City rooftop with breathtaking views of the Flatiron and Empire State Buildings.

Four Brewers.
(Four Brewers)

The four breweries collaborating on this project include two Italian craft brewers—Teo Musso, Brewmaster of Birrificio Le Baladin and Leonardo Di Vincenzo of Birra del Borgo, and two Italian-American craft brewers—Sam Calagione of Dogfish Head Craft Brewery and Vinnie Cilurzo of the Russian River Brewing Company.

The first floor of the building at 200 5th Avenue will house Eataly, an epic Italian specialty foods market, and multiple restaurants that pair gourmet foods with artisanal beers and wines. Additionally, there will be an 8,000-square-foot rooftop brewery and restaurant operated by B&B Hospitality's Mario Batali and Joe Bastianich.

The rooftop bar and restaurant will house a copper-clad brewing system. The idea is to create an artisanal, old-world Italian craft brewery that just happens to be located on a rooftop in Manhattan, says Dogfish Head's Sam Calagione. The four brewers are working together on recipes for Eataly's house beers. Those beers will feature Italian and American ingredients. The beers will be unpasteurized, unfiltered, naturally carbonated, and hand-pulled through traditional beer engines for the most authentic and pure presentation. The four individual brewers will also occasionally brew beers under their own names on site. The rooftop restaurant project will pair artisanal, rustic, homemade beers with the artisanal, rustic cooking of Chef Mario Batali. Additional Italian and American regional craft beers will be served both at the rooftop bar and in the downstairs restaurants.

Craft beer sales continue to gain traction in America and around the world. With all the diversity, complexity, and food-compatibility of world-class wine at a fraction of the price, the craft-beer segment enjoys continued growth in a challenging economy.

The four consulting brewers met in Boston this week to brew the first test batch of Eataly beer, an English Mild fermented with Italian chestnut powder (photos above). Plans call for Eataly New York to open in late summer 2010.

More from the brewers…

"Eataly is the representation of the earth, its products and an example of real Italian taste. The brewery will surely be a fusion of Italian and Italian/American styles and I am very happy to make this journey with this fantastic group!"—Teo Musso, Brewmaster, Birrificio Le Baladin.

"In 2006 I went to the Slow Food Salone del Gusto in Italy. Upon meeting many Italian craft brewers, I was not only impressed by the quality of their beer, but their passion for brewing as well. It was at that time I learned how great Italian craft beer was! To now collaborate with two of the most dynamic Italian craft brewers, along with my friend Sam Calagione, at Eataly New York will not only be a lot of fun, but very educational as well."—Vinnie Cilurzo, Brewer/Owner, Russian River Brewing Company.

"Eataly Brewery will be a great fusion of the well-known Italian gastronomic culture and our rising beer culture with the taste and the creativity of the American craft beer movement. This may well be the craziest and most amazing brewery in the world."—Leonardo Di Vincenzo, Brewmaster, Birra del Borgo.

"While the Italian craft brewing renaissance started later than ours here in the states, they have quickly made up for lost time with world-class artisanal beers. Both Dogfish Head and Russian River have pushed the boundaries of beer, particularly those that pair well with food, for many years. We are looking forward to working with our Italian Brewing Brethren, Mario Batali, Joe Bastianich, and the folks at Eataly to further strengthen the bond between world-class beer and world-class food in the most beautiful setting for a brewery I have ever seen."—Sam Calagione, President/Founder, Dogfish Head Craft Brewery.

Follow Up a Press Release

Follow up your press releases with phone calls and e-mail. Try to reach the journalists directly. Be polite but persistent. Do not wait for a newspaper or radio station to return your call; call again (but do not make a pest of yourself)—they receive many press releases every day.

As we have said, save all publicity you receive to show potential customers. Publicity has enormous value because it can attract more publicity and more customers. Remember, it has greater credibility for consumers than advertising, which you will have paid for.

Public Relations

In addition to publicity, you can build positive public relations for your company through involvement in the local community and in local, national, and international professional organizations that pertain to your business. Some ways of doing this are with special events, sponsorship, networking, and public speaking.

Special Events

Hold contests, throw parties, or put together unusual events to attract attention and customers. Contests and sweepstakes can gather valuable names for your mailing list. Or, participate in special events yourself to gain publicity for your business through effective networking with other participants.

Sponsorships

Sponsoring a local sports team is a great way to involve your business in the community and meet potential customers. Sponsorships are a way of advertising. Just be certain that the audience for the event fits into your target market.

Networking

Networking, as discussed in Chapter 1 with respect to effective selling, is the exchange of information and contacts. When done efficiently and courteously, networking can serve as an excellent promotional vehicle.

Public Speaking

philanthropy a concern for human and social welfare that is expressed by giving money through charities and foundations.

not-for-profit organization an entity formed with the intention of addressing social or other issues, with any profits going back into the organization to support its mission.

foundation a not-for-profit organization that manages donated funds, which it distributes through grants to individuals or to other nonprofit organizations that help people and social causes.

Taking advantage of opportunities to address members of your target audience as a guest speaker or paid professional can build your credibility and attract recognition and customers. When you are a guest speaker, you have the added weight of the sponsoring organization behind you.

The Fifth P: Philanthropy

There is a long, proud connection in the United States between entrepreneurs and **philanthropy,** a concern for human and social welfare that is expressed by giving money through charities and foundations. A **foundation** is a **not-for-profit organization** that manages donated funds, which it distributes through grants to individuals or to other nonprofit organizations that help people and social causes.

Many philanthropic organizations in the United States were established by entrepreneurs. As a business owner, you have a responsibility to help the communities you serve. The people and causes you choose to support should be those that matter to you. Your philanthropy may also generate positive publicity because you can choose to promote your giving.

For this reason, marketing experts sometimes consider philanthropy as the fifth marketing P.

◀ **Performance Objective 6**
Find a way to add the Fifth P, philanthropy, to your business.

The Bill and Melinda Gates Foundation is one of the world's largest charitable organizations, with over $33 billion in capital. This money comes from the personal wealth they earn from Microsoft. As a private foundation, it is required by the federal government to give away 5 percent of the fair market value of its assets every year (this is usually less than the earnings on the fund's investments). The Gates Foundation provides a great deal of money annually (about $1.65 billion, based on a $33-billion fund) to other charities. These in turn use the money for social and community programs that the Gates Foundation supports, such as those relating to education and health care.

You can be philanthropic even if you have very little money to donate. You can give your time in volunteer work for an organization you believe in. If you know how to paint a house, for example, or if you have some carpentry skills, you could contribute your efforts to help build homes for an organization such as Habitat for Humanity, which provides affordable housing for low-income families. If you love animals, volunteer at your local animal shelter.

Cause-Related Marketing

Cause-related marketing—marketing inspired by a commitment to a social, environmental, or political cause—is an easy way to work philanthropy into your business. You could donate a fixed percentage of your profits (perhaps 1 or 2 percent) to a particular charity and then publicize that in your marketing materials. Or you could contribute something from your business. If you own a sporting goods store, you could donate uniforms to the local Little League team.

cause-related marketing promotion inspired by a commitment to a social, environmental, or political cause.

Encourage your employees to participate in charitable work, too. Volunteerism is a great way to improve morale and make a difference. AT&T pays its employees to devote one day a month to community service.

Gaining Goodwill

Many entrepreneurs try to make a difference in their communities by giving money and time to organizations that help people. Microsoft, for example, made it possible for the National Foundation for Teaching Entrepreneurship (NFTE—now the Network for Teaching Entrepreneurship) to develop an Internet-based entrepreneurial curriculum, BizTech. Microsoft has donated both money and computer-programming expertise to this project. Why would Microsoft do this?

- First, Bill Gates and other Microsoft executives believed in NFTE's mission and wanted to help young people learn about business. The Internet-based program has made it easier to teach entrepreneurship to youth around the world.

- Second, Microsoft has gained publicity and **goodwill**—which is composed of intangible assets such as reputation, name recognition, and customer relations. Goodwill can give a company an advantage over its competitors.

goodwill an intangible asset generated when a company does something positive that has value.

Not-for-Profit Organizations

Not-for-profit organizations are those whose purpose is to serve a public or mutual benefit rather than to accrue profits for investors. The Internal Revenue Service classifies nonprofits under section 501(c)(3) in the tax code. These corporations are tax-exempt, which means they do not have to pay federal or state taxes and that they are neither privately nor publicly owned. Essentially, a board of directors controls the operations of a 501(c)(3) nonprofit.

Such well-known institutions as the Boys and Girls Clubs of America, the YMCA, the Girl Scouts, the Red Cross, and Big Brothers/Big Sisters are examples of nonprofits. Their founders were social entrepreneurs and, although they did not earn large sums of money personally and could not have sold their organizations at a profit, they received great satisfaction and made a difference. Wendy Kopp of Teach for America, and Michael Bronner of Upromise, described in the following section, are two examples of social entrepreneurs who founded innovative and successful nonprofit organizations.

Teach for America and Upromise

Founded in 1990 by Wendy Kopp, Teach for America recruits recent college graduates to become public school teachers. The organization has trained some 28,000 young teachers and placed them in two-year teaching positions in under-resourced schools, where they impact approximately 500,000 students annually.

Upromise was founded in 2001 by Michael Bronner, a former marketing executive who became a social entrepreneur. Bronner felt strongly that the cost of sending a child to college had become much too expensive for most families and that there needed to be a better way of helping families save money for higher education.

Bronner developed the idea that a portion of the money that families already spent on popular goods and services, such as groceries and toys, could go into a college savings account for their children. Upromise works with thousands of organizations, such as Sprint, Dell, Century 21, and Expedia.com. Every time one of the over 10 million members makes a purchase from one of these companies, a percentage of the sale automatically goes into a special college savings account.

What Entrepreneurs Have Built

Many philanthropic organizations in this country were created by entrepreneurs who wanted to do good works with some of the wealth they had earned. Entrepreneurs have financed great museums, libraries, universities, and other important institutions. Some foundations created by famous entrepreneurs, in addition to the Gates Foundation, include the Rockefeller Foundation, the Coleman Foundation, the Charles G. Koch Foundation, the Ford Foundation, and the Goldman Sachs Foundation.

Some of the most aggressive entrepreneurs in American history, such as Andrew Carnegie, have also been the most generous. In 1901, after a long and sometimes ruthless business career, Carnegie sold his steel company to J. P. Morgan for $420 million. Overnight, Carnegie became one of the richest men in the world. On retiring, he spent most of his time giving away his wealth to libraries, colleges, museums, and other worthwhile institutions that still benefit people today. By the time he died in 1919, Carnegie had given away over $350 million to philanthropic causes.

You Have Something to Contribute

You may not have millions of dollars to give to your community—yet. But there are many ways you can be philanthropic that will help others, get your employees excited, and create goodwill in your community:

- Pledge a percentage of your profits to a nonprofit organization you have researched, believe in, and respect. Send out press releases announcing your pledge.
- Become a mentor to a younger entrepreneur. Help that individual by sharing your contacts and expertise.
- Volunteer for an organization that helps your community. Find out how you can serve on its board of directors or fill another vital role.
- Sell your product to a charity that you support at a discount. The charity can then resell it at full price to raise money.
- When you give it some thought, you will realize that you have a lot to give. Remember, making a contribution does not necessarily mean giving money. You can donate time, advice, and moral support.

These days, customers have access to a lot of information about what companies do with their money. Make sure you are always proud of your business. Choose to support causes that are important to you and that make business sense, too. Philanthropy will strengthen your relationship with your customers because it goes beyond the sale and into what is truly important in everybody's life.

Developing a Marketing Plan

‹ Performance Objective 7
Understand the importance of a marketing plan.

The marketing plan can be a stand-alone document or the section of a business plan that identifies the organization's marketing strategy and tactics and presents a comprehensive statement of how it will secure and retain its customers. The plan will include a clear discussion of the product (or service), price, promotion, and channels of distribution for the company, and a detailed description of the competition and target market. The marketing plan clarifies how you will sell your products or services and where you fit into the competitive landscape. According to entrepreneurial expert Donald Kuratko and management expert Richard Hodgetts, the roles of the marketing plan include:[12]

- convincing skeptical investors that your plan has merit,
- using and disclosing market studies,
- identifying the target market for the organization,
- evaluating the competition,
- demonstrating the pricing strategy, and
- detailing the advertising plan.

‹ Performance Objective 8
Identify the critical components of a marketing plan.

Either a stand-alone marketing plan or one incorporated into a business plan will include the same market-analysis information. The stand-alone plan should also include a *situation analysis*; financial projections and information; an implementation time line or outline; and methods for evaluating success and assuring it, as well as any supplemental supporting materials. **Exhibit 5-5** shows the components of each type of plan. As with business plans as a whole, marketing plans should be organic documents that are reviewed and revised on a regular basis, to keep them timely and useful.

Marketing Analysis

An analysis of the market is the heart of the marketing plan that brings the various strategic and tactical components of the promotional efforts

---

[12]Donald F. Kuratko and Richard Hodgetts, *Entrepreneurship: A Contemporary Approach*, 5th ed. (Mason, Ohio: Southwestern Publishing, 2000).

Exhibit 5-5 *Marketing Plan Components*		
Component	Stand-Alone Plan	Business Plan Section
OPPORTUNITY ANALYSIS	√	
Industry Analysis	√	
SWOT Analysis	√	
Environmental Analysis	√	
Competitive Analysis	√	
MARKETING ANALYSIS	√	√
Overall Market and Target	√	√
Goals and Objectives	√	√
Marketing Strategy	√	√
Product/Service	√	√
Pricing Strategy	√	√
Promotion Strategy/Plan	√	√
Place/Distribution	√	√
Philanthropic Plan	√	√
Future and Contingency Plans	√	√
FINANCIAL PROJECTIONS	√	
IMPLEMENTATION TIME LINE	√	
MEASUREMENT	√	
SUPPLEMENTAL MATERIALS	√	

together into a single comprehensive section. It is essential that the template for the sales plan includes the Five P's of marketing—the product, price, promotion, place, and philanthropy—that are detailed here. Wrapped around the core marketing strategy and selling plan are the descriptions of the overall market and the specific target market for the company, the marketing goals and objectives, and any future and contingency plans. Future plans could include a discussion of planned research and development, as well as any growth designs, whether through product-line expansion, additional channels of distribution, or by other means. Contingency plans show how your organization will react to moves by your competitors or to other changes in the marketplace. Contingency plans will diagram strategies and options that you will use to address these changes and demonstrate your understanding of the need to be prepared for change in a competitive landscape.

Performance Objective 9

Use breakeven analysis to evaluate your marketing plan.

Marketing as a Fixed Cost

Let's say you want to launch a new software program. You have researched the consumer environment, pinpointed your market segment, and determined your marketing mix. You are now ready to implement a marketing plan that will get your vision out there. There is one more question: Can you afford to carry out your plan?

Marketing is part of your business's fixed costs. Marketing should not be budgeted as a percentage of sales but rather as money that is needed to drive sales. As you remember, fixed costs are those that do not vary with sales; they can be remembered as USAIIRD (utilities, salaries, advertising, insurance, interest, rent, and depreciation). There are also variable costs, such as commissions, that fluctuate with sales. For a business to survive, though, it must be able to cover its fixed costs. Most fixed costs, such as rent, insurance, and utilities, are hard to cut back if your sales are slow.

Marketing costs are more flexible. They fall into the category of "advertising" but may also show up under "salaries" if you hire a marketing consultant or full-time marketing staff. They will be a critical component in determining your company's breakeven point and its viability.

Calculate Your Breakeven Point

The question is this: Can you sell enough units to pay for your marketing plan? The breakeven point, as discussed in Chapter 2, is the moment at which a business has sold enough units to equal its fixed costs. If you estimate that your market is approximately 3 million people, but you have to sell 5 million units just to cover the cost of your marketing, the plan is not viable.

This is why calculating the breakeven point will tell you if your marketing plan will work. It shows whether or not you can cover your fixed costs with the number of units you plan to sell. If not, the one place you can cut costs is in your marketing plan. However, you should do this with care.

Breakeven Analysis for an Artist

David is an artist who supports his painting career by creating unique tank tops with airbrushed designs. The shirts are very popular with the young women in Manhattan's East Village, and David sells the shirts each weekend at a flea market on East 4th Street. Let's say he buys eight dozen (96) tank tops for $576. He airbrushes them and sells them all at the weekend flea market for $1,152. David considers one tank top his unit of sale. The cost of goods sold (COGS)—without labor—would be calculated as $576/96 = $6, with a selling price per unit of $1,152/96 = $12.

- How much did each tank top cost David? This is his cost of goods sold (COGS).
- How much did he charge for each tank top? This is his selling price per unit.
- David's unit of sale is one tank top.
- David's cost of goods sold is $6.
- David's selling price is $12.

$12 (Selling Price per Unit) − $6 (Cost of Goods Sold per Unit)
= $6 (Gross Profit per Unit)

- David's gross profit per unit is $6 per tank top.

Next, David needs to take a look at his fixed costs. Let's say he spends $150 a month on renting his space at the flea market and $30 monthly on flyers (advertising). His monthly fixed costs are $150 + $30 = $180. How many tank tops does he have to sell to cover his fixed costs? Use the following formula:

$$\frac{\text{Fixed Cost}}{\text{Gross Profit per Unit}} = \text{Breakeven Units}$$

$$\frac{\text{Fixed Cost: } \$180}{\text{Gross Profit per Unit: } \$6} = 30 \text{ Breakeven Units}$$

David needs to sell 30 tank tops to cover his fixed costs. David typically sells about 20 tank tops each weekend, so in one month he can expect to sell

$$20 \text{ Units} \times 4 \text{ Weekends} = 80 \text{ Units}$$

David can definitely afford to spend $30 per month on flyers. He could even afford to add another expense to his marketing plan, such as getting business cards printed or setting up a Web site from which customers could order shirts and find out where he will be selling each weekend, since his specific location varies.

We do need to recognize that David did not include any labor cost, because he paid himself from the profits. If David were to add in $3-per-shirt of labor costs, his COGS would rise to $9, and his gross profit per unit would drop to $3. His new breakeven point would be 60 units. Additionally, any payment for the time it took to sell the shirts would come out of the profits.

Breakeven Analysis of a Restaurant

Here is a breakeven analysis from a chicken restaurant in Florida called Mary Ann's.

Typically, a customer at Mary Ann's buys a bucket of chicken for $8 and a drink for $2, so the average sale per customer is $10. Therefore, a business unit is defined as a $10 sale. The cost of goods sold for each unit is $3.50 for the chicken and $0.50 for the drink, so the cost of goods sold is $4.00 per unit.

Mary Ann's fixed costs for a month are

Utilities	$1,000
Salaries (indirect labor)	$3,000
Ads	$1,000
Interest	0
Insurance	$1,000
Rent	$2,000
Total	$8,000

The restaurant is open, on average, 30 days per month.

To figure out how many units Mary Ann's has to sell each month to break even, divide the gross profit per unit into the monthly fixed costs.

$$\text{Gross Profit per Unit} = \text{Unit Price } (\$10) - \text{COGS } (\$4) = \$6$$

$$\text{Breakeven Units} = \frac{\text{Monthly Fixed Costs (\$8,000)}}{\text{Gross Profit per Unit (\$6)}} = 1{,}333 \text{ Units}$$

Because the store is open 30 days per month, to break even Mary Ann's has to make 45 average sales per day:

$$\frac{1{,}333 \text{ Units}}{30 \text{ Days}} = 44.43 \text{ (45 Units per Day)}$$

Breakeven is the point at which fixed costs are recovered by sales, but no profit has yet been made. Once you have determined your breakeven point, the next question in the analysis is, "Can my business reach breakeven in its relevant market?" In the previous example, can Mary Ann's reasonably expect to break even and sell 45 buckets of chicken with drinks a day? The answer to this question for your business venture will be in the market research you have conducted to get to this, the last step in creating a marketing plan. You should know the answer. If not, you must conduct further research until you can confidently gauge whether or not you can afford your marketing plan. Of course, revising your plan is another option.

Breakeven analysis is a good tool for examining all your costs and should be performed frequently. It is especially important after you have completed your marketing plan and before you open your business, to see if your plan is realistic.

Chapter Summary

Now that you have studied this chapter, you can:

1. Combine the Four P's—product, price, place, and promotion—into a marketing mix.
2. Determine the attributes of your product or service.
3. Price your products for success. Implement strategies and tactics to reach your goals.
   - Value pricing
   - Prestige pricing
   - Cost-plus pricing
   - Markup pricing
   - Penetration pricing
   - Skimming price strategy
   - Meet-or-beat-the-competition pricing
   - Follow-the-leader pricing
   - Personalized (dynamic) pricing
   - Variable pricing
   - Price lining strategies
4. Locate and distribute for maximum efficiency and effectiveness.
   - Know and use the key factors for site selection.
5. Choose where and how to advertise your business.
   - Promotion is the use of advertising and publicity to get your marketing message out to your potential customers.
   - Publicity is free mention of your business—in newspapers or magazines or on radio or television.

- An advertisement is a paid announcement that a product or service is for sale. Examples of advertising include television commercials, billboards, and magazine ads.

6. Decide how your business will help your community philanthropically.

   - Philanthropy is the giving of money, time, or advice to charities in an effort to help solve a social or environmental problem, such as homelessness, pollution, or cruelty to animals.

   - You can be philanthropic even if you have very little or no money to offer. You can donate your time by volunteering for an organization that has aims you want to support.

7. Understand the importance of a marketing plan:

   - convincing skeptical investors that your plan has merit;
   - using and disclosing market studies;
   - identifying the target market for the organization;
   - evaluating the competition;
   - demonstrating the pricing strategy;
   - detailing the advertising plan.

8. Identify the critical components of a marketing plan:

   - opportunity analysis,
   - marketing analysis,
   - financial projections,
   - implementation time line,
   - measurement, and
   - supplemental information.

9. Use breakeven analysis to evaluate your marketing plan.

   - Breakeven is the point at which a business sells enough units to cover its costs.

   - Breakeven analysis tells you if your marketing plan is viable. It shows whether or not you can cover your fixed costs with the number of units you expect to sell. If not, the one place you can cut costs is in your marketing plan.

Key Terms

blog	mobile social networking
blogosphere	not-for-profit organization
brand spiraling	penetration pricing
buzz marketing	personalized pricing
cause-related marketing	philanthropy
cost-plus pricing	pitch letter
e-active marketing	press release
edutainment	prestige pricing
follow-the-leader pricing	price lining
foundation	product advertising
goodwill	stealth marketing
guerilla marketing	trademark
institutional advertising	skimming prices strategy
logo	value pricing
markup pricing	variable pricing strategy
meet-or-beat-the-competition pricing	viral marketing

Entrepreneurship Portfolio

Critical Thinking Exercises

1. Describe how a product or service will fit into and complement your marketing mix.
2. Explain how pricing tells a story about your product.
3. Where do you plan to locate your business? Explain.
4. How do you plan to include philanthropy in your marketing mix?
5. Use the following chart to describe your marketing mix.

	Your Business
Product	
Place	
Price	
Promotion	
Philanthropy	

6. Use computer software to create a logo for your business. Do you intend to trademark your logo? Explain.
7. Where would you locate your business, and why?
8. If you were to start a home-based business, what would it be? Why? What key factors would you consider before startup?
9. Why is physical location critical for a distribution business?
10. What is the role of demographic information in the selection of a retail-location option?
11. Identify a well-known public figure and discuss his or her brand. How has this individual enhanced this brand? How has he or she damaged it?
12. Why does viral marketing have such success potential? How can a viral marketing campaign work against a company?
13. What role should the unique selling proposition play in a company's advertising strategy?

Key Concept Questions

1. Define cost-plus pricing. Why is it used so frequently? What are the drawbacks associated with using it?
2. What is penetration pricing? Can you think of an example of a company that has used penetration pricing to introduce a new product? Which firm was it and what was the product?
3. Brainstorm five creative ways for a small business with a very low budget to advertise and promote its products or services using the latest developments in communications and Internet technology.
4. Visit Yahoo! Small Business or another provider of online storefronts. List three advantages and three disadvantages of opening a Web site for your business through such a service.
5. Explain why breakeven is such a critical concept for any organization.

6. Name four common marketing objectives. Explain why each is important.
7. What are the types of communications budgets? What is the best method of budgeting?

Application Exercises

1. Visit a library (public or college) and locate its reference section. Which resources could help you to open a business like Honest Tea? Identify at least six such resources.

2. Use the following chart to describe the basics of your marketing plan section.

Component	What Will You Include?
OPPORTUNITY ANALYSIS	
Industry Analysis	
SWOT Analysis	
Environmental Analysis	
Competitive Analysis	
MARKETING ANALYSIS	
Overall Market and Target	
Goals and Objectives	
Marketing Strategy	
Product/Service	
Pricing Strategy	
Promotion Strategy/Plan	
Place/Distribution	
Philanthropic Plan	
Future and Contingency Plans	
FINANCIAL PROJECTIONS	
IMPLEMENTATION TIME LINE	
MEASUREMENT	
SUPPLEMENTAL MATERIALS	

3. Visit three independently owned businesses in person that are in the same industry. Identify the target market for each (demographic, lifestyle, and the like). Note the various advertising and promotional methods in use at each location. Search online for a company Web site. Ask the store owner or manager where the business advertises and whether it creates press releases. Report back on the results.

4. Meet with a partner and discuss the pros and cons of the basic pricing strategies—value pricing, cost-plus, penetration strategy, skimming strategy, and meet-or-beat-the-competition—for your respective businesses. Present your recommendations to the class.

5. What is the relationship between price and image? Why is it important?

6. Answer the questions below and use them to write a press release for your business.

- What was your life like before you began the study of entrepreneurship?
- Were you having any problems in school or at home?
- What have you learned about business that you did not know before?
- What is the best thing about running your own business? What obstacles have you had to overcome to get your business going?
- Has running your own business changed how you are doing in school? Has it changed how you get along with your family?
- Are you more involved in your community since you started your business?
- How has your business changed your life? What would you be doing if you were not an entrepreneur?
- If you could give one piece of advice to students who were thinking about starting a business, what would it be?
- What are your goals for the future?

7. Use your press release to write a pitch letter for the opening of your business.
8. Create a chart like the one below to outline your marketing plan in detail. If you do not have a business concept, create a plan for a religious bookstore in a location that you specify. Include each media supplier (listed in the box below) and draw a line through the types that you are not expecting to use.

Company Name: _____

Media Type or Promotional Method	Name of Outlet(s) (list each separately)	Target Market	Budget ($)	Objective(s)
Newspapers				
Magazines				
Directories				
Television				
Radio				
Outdoor				
Internet				
Brochures				
Flyers				
Newsletters				
Business Cards				
Signs				
Sales Promotions				
Advertising Specialties				
Trade Shows				
Carts/Kiosks				

Media Type or Promotional Method	Name of Outlet(s) (list each separately)	Target Market	Budget ($)	Objective(s)
Alternative Marketing				
Other Media				
Direct Response				

Exploring Online

1. Visit the U.S. Census Bureau Web site at http://www.census.gov. Pull up the census tract data both for your home address and for your campus address. If the tracts are the same, pick another college or university. Compare and contrast the two locations as potential sites for each of the following. Use a street map, too, if it will help.

   - A bookstore
   - A store specializing in golfing-related goods
   - A children's day care center
   - A distribution center for cleaning supplies

2. Select either your own company or an entrepreneurial venture that interests you. Find three similar businesses on the Internet and select the two best sites. What features make them attractive? Why did you think they were better than the third site? How would you distinguish your own site?

3. Obtain ad rates from two local radio stations, a local newspaper, and a cable television channel and complete the table below.

Media	Advertising Rates	Reach
Radio		
Radio		
Newspaper		
Cable		

4. Perform an Internet search on either a product or service comparable to what you plan to market, or one that you personally own or use. Attempt to find at least three sites that sell it.

   - List the applicable price point, including all discounts, allowances, and promotions, plus any shipping and handling required.
   - Are there more or fewer than three prices available? Why do you suppose this is?
   - Explain any challenges you had in performing the steps in this exercise. What do they tell you about the product or service? The companies selling them?

BizBuilder Business Plan Questions

5.0 Marketing Strategy and Plan

A. Explain how your marketing plan targets your market segment.

B. What percentage of the market do you feel you need to capture for your business to be profitable?

C. Write a positioning statement for your business.

D. How do you plan to grow the organization (self-generated, franchising, acquisition)?

5.1 Products/Services

A. What products/services do you intend to sell?

B. Explain how your product will meet a customer need.

C. Where is your product/service in the product life cycle?

D. Describe the features and benefits of the product/service your business will focus on selling.

E. What existing copyrights or patents do you own or expect to own?

F. How will your organization help others? List all the organizations to which you plan to contribute. (Your contribution may be time, money, your product, or something else.)

G. Do you intend to publicize your philanthropy? Why, or why not? If you do, explain how you will work your philanthropy into your marketing.

5.2 Pricing

A. Describe your pricing strategy and structure and the gross margins you expect to generate.

B. What will your discount structure, if any, be?

C. Will you accept personal checks from customers? Credit cards? Will you offer charge accounts or customer credit?

5.3 Promotion

A. Identify the ways you plan to promote your product or service, including the message, the media, and the distribution channels. Describe why you have chosen these methods and why you think they will work.

B. Show examples of the marketing materials you intend to use for selling.

C. What is your business slogan?

D. Do you have a logo for your business? How do you intend to protect it?

E. Where do you intend to advertise? Be specific, including identifying reach and frequency.

F. How do you plan to get publicity for your organization?

G. List ways in which you will provide superior customer service.

H. Write a one-minute sales pitch for your product/service and describe five sales prospects you intend to pitch.

I. How will you keep your customer database? What essential questions will you ask every customer in order to build your database?

5.4 Place

A. Where do you intend to sell your product? Describe the advantages and disadvantages of your location(s).

B. What are the surrounding businesses? Access routes?

C. If vehicular traffic is important to your business, what is the traffic density for this location?

D. What is the workforce availability in the area, as it pertains to your needs?

Recent years have seen an explosion in genetic research and the use of DNA technology. 23and Me, founded in 2006 by Linda Avey and Anne Wojcicki, helps each customer understand his or her unique genome, made up of 23 pairs of chromosomes. 23andMe's Personal Genome Service—winner of *Time* magazine's 2008 Invention of the Year award—gives people data about their ancestry, including possible predispositions for dozens of diseases and health conditions. Individuals are also given the chance to help advance genetic research. According to Avey, "We're generating information that not only gives you an idea of what your risks are, but it's prognostic information, too."[13]

The basic service may be purchased on the company's Web site for a one-time fee of $399 plus shipping costs. A collection kit is shipped to the customer, who sends a saliva sample to 23andMe. Several weeks later, the customer can view the results online. By participating in this service, 23andMe's customers can provide data for a genetic research initiative with the Parkinson's Institute in Sunnyvale, California.

In the fall of 2008, 23andMe dropped its basic price from $999 to $399, to help increase customer demand. Avey indicated that lower costs for mechanisms used to scan genomes helped to make the price reduction feasible. 23andMe's primary competition, Navigenics, and deCODE genetics, charged about $2,500 and $1,000, respectively, for similar services. Avey explained: "It's really more about getting the price down to a point that is more affordable. If that was what was holding [customers] back, this will be a better price for them to get involved."[14]

When 23andMe reduced its price, the chief executive of Navigenics, Mari Baker, commented that cheaper does not always mean better. Baker admitted that her company's costs were much greater than 23andMe's new price. Avey pointed out that the lower price not only makes genetic information accessible to more individuals, it simultaneously helps to find more answers to genetic-risk problems. Referring to the research database 23andMe is building, Avey said, "It's all

Anne Wojcicki and Linda Avey of 23andMe.
(Donald Bowers/Getty Images for The Weinstein Company)

about numbers and having as many people enrolled as possible."[15]

23andMe is located in the Silicon Valley, a region in the San Francisco Bay area known for its technological firms. 23andMe now stands alongside many other high-tech businesses such as Microsoft, Apple, and Intel, as part of Silicon Valley's history of entrepreneurial innovation. 23andMe is funded in part through prominent health-science and technology companies, angel investors, and venture capital firms—listing Google, Inc.; Genentech, Inc.; and New Enterprise Associates on its promotional information. In short, 23andMe brings medical technology to individual consumers at a price designed to encourage purchase, and thereby increase genetic data.

Case Study Analysis

1. What is the product/service offered by 23andMe?

2. What could 23andMe's new pricing structure suggest about its brand? In other words, what risk(s) did 23andMe take when it cut its basic price by more than half?

---

[13]Dennis Romero, *DNA: The Next Dotcom?* http://www.entrepreneur.com/magazine/entrepreneur/2009/february/199580.html.

[14]Andrew Pollack, *DNA Profile Provider Is Cutting Its Prices*, http://www.nytimes.com/2008/09/09/business/09gene.html, June 2009.

[15]Ibid.

3. What role does company location likely play in 23andMe's marketing strategy?

4. List factors to include in a breakeven analysis for 23andMe. Suggest the company's strategy for achieving a breakeven point.

5. How has 23andMe woven philanthropic attitudes into its business? Name some specific ways in which the company could incorporate philanthropy further into its marketing mix.

Case Sources

23andMe, Inc., http://www.23andme.com.

"DNA: The Next Dotcom?" *Entrepreneur,* http://www.entrepreneur.com/magazine/entrepreneur/2009/february/199580.html.

"DNA Profile Provider Is Cutting Its Prices," *New York Times,* http://www.nytimes.com/2008/09/09/business/09gene.html.

Silicon Valley Web site, http://www.siliconvalleyonline.org.

Malia Mills Swimwear

When 38-year-old Malia Mills decided to launch her own swimwear company, she set out to do much more than just sell high-end bathing suits. Mills wanted to inspire a beauty revolution that would fundamentally change the way that women felt about themselves. Before she became an entrepreneur, Mills had worked in the fashion world as a designer for established apparel companies. Mills, a native of Hawaii, saved the money for her start-up investment by working for many years as a waitress in New York City. She started Malia Mills Swimwear in 1991.

The motto of Mills's business is "Love Thy Differences," and Mills is passionate about encouraging all women, regardless of age, weight, or body type, to feel good about themselves and to celebrate their uniqueness. In Mills's world, if a woman does not like the way she looks in a swimsuit, it is the suit that has to change, not the woman. As she explains, "We are passionate about inspiring women to look in the mirror and see what is right instead of what is wrong."

The Polaroid Project

If you walk past the Malia Mills Swimwear flagship store in New York's SoHo, the first things you will notice are the photographs in the window. Instead of showcasing fashion models, the window display features a collage of Polaroid pictures of customers wearing the company's signature swimwear. According to Mills's sister, Carol, who manages the store, "We've had so many customers walk in off the street because of those photographs. People are thrilled to see actual women in all colors, shapes, and sizes wearing our suits." The Polaroid project actually began as an offbeat idea thought up by a summer intern on a particularly slow sales day. Mills liked the idea of using photographs of her customers because it resonated with the core mission of her business.

Place Matters: Setting the Right Tone

To create a comfortable environment for her customers, Mills has constructed her stores to look and feel like cozy lounges. She herself always hated trying on bathing suits in department stores under the glare of unflattering fluorescent lights. In her boutiques, the lighting is soft and dressing rooms are located in the back

Malia Mills has apparel for all body types.
(Andre Perlstein/Image Bank/Getty Images)

so that the customers will not feel exposed to other shoppers. She provides free bottled water so that they can feel relaxed and at home. Sales associates are always on hand to assist with finding the appropriate suits. Mills does not believe in a one-size-fits-all design philosophy. People's bodies do not come in packages of small, medium, or large. Accordingly, her tops are sized like lingerie, and bottoms come in sizes 2 to 16. All pieces are sold as separates, which allows customers to mix and match across different style and fabric options, as well as size.

The Price/Production Connection

Malia Mills's suits are priced at the high end of the swimwear market. A bikini top or bottom will cost somewhere between $130 and $165, and one-piece suits run an average of $325. This pricing scheme reflects some of the choices Mills has made as an entrepreneur about how her suits are produced. For example, she chooses to manufacture in New York City instead of outsourcing production to Asia or elsewhere, where labor costs are lower. According to Mills, "It costs us much more per unit to sew our suits locally but supporting our community is worth it. The women (mostly) who sew our suits do so with extra care—we visit them often and they know how important quality is to us."

Mills chooses to import the fabrics she uses from Europe and she typically buys them in small quantities, which is more costly, so that her designs stay fresh. Mills also pays a premium to the fabric mills that custom-dye her materials in unique colors and this also contributes to the bottom line of her manufacturing costs. Her suits are so well made that she sometimes worries about undercutting herself in the marketplace. If the average woman owns two or three bathing suits and a Malia Mills suit can last several years, it could take a long time for a customer to seek a replacement.

Smart Selling Requires Trial and Error

Early on, Mills sold her suits wholesale to department stores, but she found that this strategy did not fit well with her core mission. Mills's suits got lost on the racks next to other brand-name apparel, and the salespeople did not understand how to answer customers' questions about the unique features of her product, such as how they are sized differently from other swimsuits. Eventually, Mills decided to sell directly to the consumer. Maintaining control over the sales process has allowed Mills to stay true to her mission of providing women with an enjoyable and empowering experience, purchasing swimwear that fits in a relaxed environment.

Promotions: Getting the Word Out

Over the years, Mills has been successful in generating PR. Her company has been profiled in major publications such as the *New York Times*, *Sports Illustrated*, and *Harper's Bazaar*. It has helped to have celebrities such as Madonna wearing her suits, especially when they are photographed in public. Recently, Mills began purchasing advertising for the first time in local print media. She is doing this as an experiment to see if it has a noticeable impact on generating new customers. In the meantime, the growth of Malia Mills Swimwear continues to be propelled by word of mouth and customer loyalty. Each day, the business connects with passersby who are lured into the store by the Polaroid photographs of ordinary women wearing her bathing suits. Once these women walk in off the street, there is a pretty good chance that they will walk out as customers.

Case Study Analysis

1. Describe the unique features of Malia Mills's product.
2. Malia Mills Swimwear is not inexpensive. Why do you think customers are willing to pay a premium for her suits?
3. The case mentions that Malia Mills Swimwear is currently experimenting with paid advertising. If you were in charge of marketing for the company, how would you assess whether or not it was cost effective to continue purchasing advertising?
4. What kind of environment is Malia Mills trying to create in her stores? Why is this important?
5. Besides her own boutiques, specialty stores, and through the Internet, what might be some additional sales venues for Malia Mills Swimwear to consider exploring?
6. Why was the "Polaroid project" a successful promotional venture?
7. Imagine a scenario in which Malia Mills Swimwear hired you as a media consultant. Answer the following:
   - Come up with a cause-related marketing strategy for the company.
   - Describe three strategies for the company to pursue in obtaining media coverage.

Case Sources

Malia Mills Web site, *http://www.maliamills.com*.

Pamela Rohland, "Chic to Chic—Turn Style into Sales with a Clothing-Design Company," *Business Start-Ups* magazine, December 1999, *http://Entrepreneur.com/article/0,4621,231846,00.html*.

Chapter 6

SMART SELLING AND EFFECTIVE CUSTOMER SERVICE

Barry Austin
Photography/
Photodisc/Getty
Images

Smart selling is a process that is complex and challenging. Ryan Allis, and the company that he co-founded in July 2003, iContact, seeks to support the communication between businesses and their customers to increase sales success. iContact is the "leading provider of e-mail marketing tools for small business," according to its Web site.

Allis, the son of an Episcopal priest and a social worker, is a young, serial entrepreneur who is no stranger to selling. Allis started his first business at the age of 11, when he sold his time and expertise to older residents of Anna Maria Island, Florida, teaching them how to use personal computers. As a student at the University of North Carolina at Chapel Hill, Allis worked with Aaron Houghton to create iContact. They raised $18.3 million in seed investment funds from several sources, and another $40 million in second round strategic growth investment in 2010.[1] In 2011, iContact reached a capitalization of $53 million, and had 270 employees. It is headquartered in Morrisville, North Carolina.

iContact products provide small- and medium-sized companies relatively low-cost options to create and measure their e-mail marketing efforts. When communications are effective, better sales relationships, loyalty, and customer relations result.

Performance Objectives

1. Explain the importance of selling based upon benefits.
2. Use the principles of selling to make effective sales calls.
3. Know how to make a successful sales call.
4. Analyze and improve your sales calls.
5. Provide superior customer service.
6. Define customer relationship management and understand its value.

Selling Skills Are Essential to Business Success

Personal selling is dealing with a potential customer face to face and trying to convince him or her to make a purchase. Salespeople often become successful entrepreneurs because they learn to listen to what the customer needs and wants on a daily and personal basis. Some great American entrepreneurs who started out in sales are:

- Ray Kroc, founder of McDonald's who, as we saw in Chapter 1, was selling milkshake machines when he was inspired to turn the McDonald brothers' hamburger restaurant into a national operation.
- Aristotle Onassis was a wholesale tobacco importer and salesman before becoming a multimillionaire in the shipping business.
- King C. Gillette was a traveling sales representative when he invented the safety razor.
- W. Clement Stone started out selling newspapers at the age of six before going on to build a great fortune in the insurance industry.
- Mary Kay Ash was in direct sales for 25 years before she co-founded Mary Kay Cosmetics with her son.

---

[1]iContact Web site, "iContact Receives $40 Million Strategic Growth Investment from JMI Equity," http://www.icontact.com/static/pdf/2010-08-30-iContactReceives-40Million-Investment.pdf, February 20, 2011.

Selling Is a Great Source of Market Research

If a customer is dissatisfied, it is often the salesperson who hears the complaint. In that sense, selling is a constant source of valuable market research. Depending upon the business you start, in the early days you will probably not be able to hire a sales staff. You will most likely be the sales staff.

Even if you have never sold anything in your life, you can develop into an excellent salesperson. In fact, you already have a lot of practice selling. Everyone tries to persuade ("sell") others to agree to something or to act in a certain way. Being face to face with customers and trying to sell your product may make you uncomfortable, but if you think of rejections as learning experiences and opportunities for continuous market analysis, you will look forward to sales encounters throughout your entrepreneurial career.

The Essence of Selling Is Teaching

Performance Objective 1 >

Explain the importance of selling based upon benefits.

The creative art of selling is teaching the customer how features are benefits. Inexperienced salespeople make a common mistake: They think telling the customer about the features of a product will sell it. But remember our marketing example: A customer who buys a drill does not need a drill; the customer needs to make a hole.

The essence of selling is teaching how and why the outstanding features of your product or service will benefit your customers.

The Principles of Selling

Performance Objective 2 >

Use the principles of selling to make effective sales calls.

Every entrepreneur has to be able to identify the benefits his or her product can provide and utilize them in making an effective sales call. Entrepreneurs sell constantly, not just to customers but to potential investors, bankers, and potential employees. Commit the following selling principles to memory and you will be on your way to becoming a successful salesperson. These principles apply to any product or service.

Make a Good Personal Impression

When selling your product or service, prepare yourself physically. A salesperson must be clean and well dressed, and it is important to dress appropriately for your customer base. If you are selling oil to gas station owners, do not wear expensive suits—but dress professionally. Some suggest that, for sales calls, your business card should not identify you as president or owner, so your prospects can talk with you more easily. This would depend upon who you are meeting, so use common sense.

BizFacts

Many salespeople work on *commission*, a percentage paid on each sale. A salesperson making a 10 percent commission selling cars, for example, would earn $1,000 after selling a $10,000 car.

$$.10 \times \$10,000 = \$1,000$$

Entrepreneurs can use commissions to motivate sales staff. When you are starting out and cannot afford to pay sales representatives full-time salaries, you can offer commissions instead—because they get paid as you get paid and earn more as they sell more.

Know Your Product or Service

Understand its features and the benefits they can create. It is your chance to teach the customer about the product or service. Explain the benefits without overselling. Do not try to share everything you know, however, as that is likely to be too much information. You don't want to alienate or bore the customer.

Believe in Your Product or Service

Good salespeople believe in what they are selling and feel good about selling it. If, during this stage, you begin to feel that your product or service does not measure up to your personal standards, reconsider selling it. Your business will fail if you do not believe it is of the quality and value that you promise. Always be on the lookout for ways to improve your product or develop a better one.

Know Your Field

Invest in understanding the industry and your competition. Read the trade literature. Learn about your competitors. Buy their products or try their services and compare them to yours. If possible, experience a call from one of your competitors' salespeople. This could be a gold mine of information. Study the strengths and weaknesses of your competitor's product or service; your sales prospects may inquire about them during your own calls and you should be prepared.

Know Your Customers

Be thorough in analyzing your customers. What are their needs? How does your product or service address them? Understand what makes them tick. Use resources such as the Internet to get publicly available background information, and access any other resources that you can.

Prepare Your Sales Presentation

Know ahead of time how you want to present your product or service. Identify the key points you believe are important to this particular customer. Jot them down on a note card. Study it. Put it away. Practice the sales call. Role play. Know how to overcome objections.

Think Positively

This will help you deal with rejections you may experience—before you make your first sale. Many people do not realize how mentally strong you have to be to conduct sales calls. One entrepreneur went on 400 calls for his import-export firm before he closed a sale of more than $1,000, but the experience made him a much better salesperson.

Keep Good Records

Have your record-keeping system, including invoices and receipts, set up before you go on your first sales call. Use a database system to keep records of your sales calls and to remind you of appropriate follow-up actions. This will be the start of your customer-relationship management process.

Make No Truly Cold Calls

Unless you are selling door to door or from a retail outlet, your prospect meetings should be "warm" calls. You can send an introductory letter, e-mail, or postcard so that the customer will know why you want to make the call. Or, better yet, try to get a personal introduction, or referral, so that the prospect feels more comfortable with you from the start.

Make an Appointment

People will be more likely to listen when they have set aside time to speak with you, whether by phone or in person. They will be less than receptive if you interrupt their day unannounced.

Treat Everyone You Sell to Like Gold

Joe Girard sells cars and has been dubbed "The World's Greatest Salesman" 12 times by *The Guinness Book of Records*. In his book, *How to Sell Anything to Anybody*, Girard explains his Law of 250 as follows: "Everyone knows 250 people in his or her life important enough to invite to the wedding and to the funeral." He goes on to explain, "This means that if I see 50 people in a week, and only two of them are unhappy with the way I treat them, at the end of the year there will be about 5,000 people influenced by just those two a week."[2] Obviously, if each person you sell to influences 250 others, you cannot afford to alienate even one sales prospect! (However, this does not mean that you keep trying to sell beyond rejection.)

The Sales Call

A sales call is an appointment with a potential customer to explain or demonstrate your product or service. During the sales call, you will want to do the following:

- make the customer aware of your product or service,
- make the customer want to buy that product or service, and
- make the customer want to buy it from *you*.

Electronic Mail, Blogs, and Newsgroups

In today's technology-savvy environment, there are multiple methods for communicating with sales prospects. Among these options are electronic mail, newsgroups, and blogs. Which, if any, is best suited to your business will require careful consideration on your part. Electronic mail (e-mail) is defined as correspondence sent via the Internet. **Newsgroups** are online discussion groups focused on specific subjects. In addition, social networking services such as Facebook, MySpace, and Twitter afford means of frequent communication.

Sending e-mail or posting messages on newsgroups or blogs can help contact sales prospects and keep in touch with customers you already have, but you must use these methods carefully. In the physical world, you can look for sales prospects by distributing flyers or by calling people from a list. Using e-mail or newsgroups in a similar fashion can result in your e-mail box being jammed with "flames"—hate mail. Most newsgroups do not appreciate receiving unwanted advertisements, called **spam**, and members may respond angrily.

If done correctly, becoming involved in a newsgroup or social network can lead to qualified prospects. Let's say you sell photographic supplies and you hear about an interesting newsgroup for photographers. Do not blitz it with ads. Instead, before posting any messages, **lurk** for awhile, meaning that you just read messages and get a feel for the discussions taking place without participating. Once you are comfortable, try posting a message. For example, see the text in **Exhibit 6-1**. Because this is not a sales pitch, no one in the newsgroup should take offense, and your message may attract potential sales prospects to your Web site.

newsgroup an online discussion group focused on specific topics or interests.

spam unwanted Internet advertisements or e-mails.

lurk to read messages and get a feel for discussions on a Web site, newsgroup, or the like without participating in the online conversation.

---

[2]Joe Girard, *How to Sell Anything to Anybody* (New York: Warner Books, 1986), p. 48.

Exhibit 6-1 *Message to a Newsgroup*

This week's discussion on the advantages of the new Nikon mini-camera was very interesting. I'm in the photography-supply business and am looking for interesting items to add to my Web site. I have already posted articles from Advanced Photography magazine and tips from some of my clients. Does anyone have any other ideas for useful information that I could post? Thanks!

Sandra Bowling
PhotoSupply Online
http://www.photosupply.com
E-mail: photosupply@AOL.com
The Photographer's Source for Supplies and Advice

Prequalify Your Sales Calls

Before calling to make an appointment for any sales call, identify and list your **prospects**, the people and organizations that may be receptive to your sales pitch. Include everyone you can imagine, but then go through it carefully and ask:

prospect a person or organization that may be receptive to a sales pitch.

- Is this individual in my market?
- Does he or she need my product?
- Will my product or service remove a problem or source of "pain," or improve the individual's life?
- Can he or she afford it?

If the answer to any of these questions is no, making a sales call on that individual will probably be a waste of time for both of you. People spend money to buy things they want or need. If your product or service helps, that's great. If not, do not hesitate to move on to consider the next prospect (sometimes called a *suspect* until the call is qualified). Asking such questions is called *prequalifying* a sales call. Invest the time it takes to get your prospect list organized and analyzed. Abe Lincoln's famous saying applies here: "If I had ten hours to chop down a tree, I'd spend nine sharpening my axe." Remember, you can purchase or develop lists of potential customers and conduct research.

Focus on the Customer

During each call, focus on one thought: What does the customer need? Visualize your product or service fulfilling that need. If you believe in your product or service, and there is a good fit, you will be able to see this without any problem. In general, focusing on listening to the potential customer will help you overcome self-consciousness. If you actively listen and probe, the customer will tell you what is personally important, either directly or indirectly. A feature that creates a benefit in your mind may be meaningless to one prospect but extremely important to another. Pay attention.

Mental visualization will help you perform better when you are in the actual situation. Practice the sales call in your mind, visualizing how you want it to go, but be prepared to deviate from that vision. Visualization will enlist your subconscious mind in the sales process, instinctively providing you with subtle verbal and body language cues that can convince a customer to buy from you. You will be better prepared and more comfortable in your role.

Step into the Shoes . . .

Luggage Concierge

(Creatas)

Every year, millions of bags are mishandled by U.S. airlines. Luggage Concierge alleviates this problem by shipping luggage to or from customers' travel destinations. The travelers benefit from faster and easier airport check-ins, fewer worries about late or lost luggage, and the freedom from hauling their bags around.

Luggage Concierge's shipping service is initiated by visiting its Web site or calling its toll-free telephone number. The customer provides the addresses for where the luggage is to be picked up and where it is going. The number of pieces, as well as their sizes and shapes, are also given. This information, the type of service (one-way or round trip), and the required delivery time determines the price.

Luggage Concierge has many strategic business partners, including credit card companies, resorts and hotels, cruise and travel businesses, shipping companies, and more. For example, as part of the alliance with Crystal Cruises, Luggage Concierge provides a dedicated 24/7 telephone line for passengers. Crystal's repeat customers also get a 20 percent discount on luggage shipments to and from the cruise ships.

When it made an alliance with UPS International in 2009, Luggage Concierge was able to expand its shipping services to 220 destinations worldwide, more than any of its competitors. The "Wheels Up Customs Clearance" that this partnership provides allows Luggage Concierge's customers to have their luggage delivered to most countries within eight business days. Customers can also know where their luggage is at all times, thanks to real-time tracking capability and superior customer service.

The Eight-Step Sales Call

Performance Objective 3

Know how to make a successful sales call.

Whereas sales calls will be as different as the individuals involved, there are eight steps to follow that will make them more successful.

1. ***Preparation.*** Prepare yourself mentally and through organization. Think about how the product or service will benefit this specific customer. Have the price, discounts, all technical information, and any other details on the tip of your tongue or at your fingertips. Be willing to obtain further information if your customer requests it. Visualize the sales call in your mind until it goes smoothly and successfully. Jot down a few key probing questions and points you think will help. Bring the appropriate materials, samples, and data with you.

2. ***Greeting.*** Greet the customer politely and graciously. Do not plunge immediately into business talk, unless you know from prior experience or your network of contacts that your prospect prefers to do so. Take the time to know the person's style and be sensitive to it. The first few words you say may be the most important. Keep a two-way conversation going. Maintain eye contact and keep the customer's attention. Remember that the prospect is first and foremost a human being with whom you can make a connection. The more you can learn about his or her family, hobbies, interests—anything to help develop a genuine relationship—the better your chances of eventually securing a sale. You can avoid being perceived as nosy or overly personal by remaining honest and genuine. The best salespeople keep records on their customers with all sorts of information, to remind them of details for future conversations and to follow up over time. Sales may depend upon the characteristics and benefits of the product or service, but individuals buy from salespeople they know and like when they have a choice. They usually have a choice.

3. ***Showing the Product or Service.*** Personalize your product or service by pointing out its benefits for this particular customer. If possible, demonstrate the product or service to showcase its unique

selling proposition. Use props and models (or the real thing) where appropriate.

4. *Listen to the Customer.* Begin with the customer's needs in mind and be wary of making assumptions about those needs. If you listen actively and probe carefully, you can learn the challenges he or she is facing and tailor your sales pitch accordingly. After you pitch your product or service once, sit back and let the customer talk. This is how you will get your most valuable information. Neil Rackham, the author of *SPIN Selling*, had his consulting firm, Huthwaite, analyze more than 35,000 sales. He discovered that in successful calls it was the buyer who did most of the talking.[3]

5. *Dealing with Objections.* The best, most effective way to deal with objections is to prevent them from being raised. Address the known objections in a positive light before the customer raises them. During the listening phase, you will hear other objections to your product or service. Always acknowledge objections and handle them. Do not pretend you did not hear, or overreact, or be afraid to listen. A famous real estate entrepreneur, William Zeckendorf, said, "I never lost money on a sales pitch when I listened to the customer." Do not hesitate to tell the absolute truth about any negative aspect of your product or service. Each time you admit a negative, you gain credibility in the customer's mind. However, be careful not to overemphasize a flaw or complain about the product or service.

6. *Closing the Sale.* Review the benefits of your product or service. If negatives have come up, point out that, at this price, the product or service is still an excellent buy. Narrow the choices the customer has to make. Close the sale, if it is time to do so. Do not overstay your welcome. Stop while you are ahead. Here's an important rule of thumb: If a customer says no three times, you still have a chance. If he or she says it the fourth time, it really means no. If the answer *is* no, take it gracefully. Remember that the sales cycle for your product or service is a critical factor here. Some sales take months or even years to close. A no today is not necessarily a no forever. You will learn to tell the difference.

7. *Follow up.* Make regular follow-up calls to find out how the customer liked the product or service. Ask if you can be of any further help. If the customer has a complaint, do not ignore it. Keeping the customer's trust after the sale is the most important part of the whole process.

    A successful business is built on repeat customers. Plus, every time you talk to a customer you are deepening your friendship. Your best sales prospects in the future are people who have already bought something from you. Keep them posted on the progress of your business by sending postcards or flyers.

8. *Ask for Referrals.* Ask your customers to refer you to other potential customers. Try to set up a system that encourages others to send sales prospects your way. Offer discounts, gift certificates, or other incentives to those who refer people to you, for example. Give customers a few business cards to pass on to their friends.

---

[3]Neil Rackham, *SPIN Selling* (New York: McGraw-Hill, 1996).

Three Call Behaviors of Successful Salespeople

Neil Rackham, during his research, discovered that successful salespeople exhibit certain sales-call behaviors.[4] He concluded that there are three actions that lead to more sales:

1. ***Let the customer talk more than you do.*** According to *SPIN Selling,* "The more your customer talks, the more you will learn about their needs, which puts you in a better position to offer them the most customized and most helpful solutions." Encourage your customers to tell you about their situations and problems. As they talk, they will begin to understand their own needs better and realize the importance of solving the problem.

2. ***Ask the right questions.*** How do you get customers to talk to you? Rackham notes that you have to ask the right questions. If your sales calls are leaving you with little information and few sales, you are not asking the questions that uncover your customers' needs. Again, instead of focusing on selling your product, focus on listening to your customer. Try to draw him or her out. Be an active listener. You need to correctly understand the problem *before* suggesting that your product or service provides a solution.

3. ***Wait to offer products and solutions until later in the call.*** First, let your customer talk. Second, once you have the customer talking, ask the right questions to help uncover the problem. Now you are ready to offer your product or service as a solution. As Rackham writes, "You cannot know what solution to offer if you do not uncover customer needs and decision criteria first. For example, if you spend your time with the customer talking about how quiet your machine is, and noise is not a factor your customer cares about, you've wasted your time (and theirs)."[5] You cannot offer a valuable solution until you know what problem the customer needs to solve.

Analyze Your Sales Calls to Become a Star Salesperson

Performance Objective 4

Analyze and improve your sales calls.

Every sales call is an opportunity to improve your selling skills—even if you did not make a sale. The star salesperson analyzes each call by asking:

- Was I able to get the customer to open up to me? Why, or why not?
- Did I do or say anything that turned the customer off, or was offensive, or caused him or her to disbelieve me?
- Which of my questions did the best job of helping the customer focus on his or her challenges? How can I ask better questions?
- Was I able to make an honest case for my product or service being the one that could solve the customer's problem?
- Did I improve my relationship with this individual during the call?

Rackham's research shows that, unless you analyze your selling at this level of detail, you will miss important opportunities for learning and improving your selling skills.

---

[4]Rackham, *SPIN Selling,* p. 110.
[5]Rackham, *SPIN Selling,* p. 84.

Turning Objections into Advantages

Getting the customer to open up may lead to being told things that you may not want to hear about your product or service. These objections, however, can be valuable sources of marketing data. Sales expert Brian Tracy recommends writing down the objections and comments that customers make about your product. He believes that all objections fall into one of six categories and suggests making a list of every objection you have ever heard, and then grouping them under the following headings:

1. price,
2. performance,
3. follow-up service,
4. competition,
5. support, and
6. warranties and assurances.[6]

Direct-selling experience can be a great foundation for an entrepreneur.
(Digital Vision)

Once you have listed the objections under these headings, take a close look at them. Try to rephrase each set of objections in a single question of 25 words or less.

Work on developing objection-proof answers to each of these questions, answers that are backed by proof, testimonials from customers, research, and data comparing your product with the competition's. If you make the effort to do this, you will learn to appreciate hearing objections. More importantly, you may be able to head off objections before they arise. You will have well-prepared responses, backed by written documentation, and if you do hear a new objection for which you have not developed a response, you will be excited about the opportunity to address it.

Use Technology to Sell

Where appropriate and applicable, use the latest advances in technology to sell your product, help your customers understand and use it, and stay in touch with them. Some examples include:

- a multimedia demonstration or presentation of your product;
- a Web site that customers can visit for updates and product facts, to share ideas, and to find technical data;
- using e-mail, blogs, and social networking to stay in touch with customers;
- webinars (seminars or conferences held on the Internet) and audio conferences to educate and introduce;
- digital planners and calendars and sales-and-contact-management software to keep prospect lists organized and log sales calls and customer information;
- personal digital assistants (PDAs) and other technology to place orders and secure immediate responses to customer inquiries.

All the technological concepts used to identify customers through market research can be instrumental in selling to your segment of the market.

---

[6]Brian Tracy, *Be a Sales Superstar: 21 Great Ways to Sell More, Faster, Easier in Tough Markets* (San Francisco: Berrett-Koehler Publishers, 2003), p. 84.

Global Impact . . .

Lourdes "Chingling" Tanco, MIDA Trade Ventures, Inc.

(Jaimie Duplass/
Shutterstock.com)

Chingling Tanco has traveled the world to bring success to her companies, MIDA Trade Ventures, Inc. and MIDA Food Distributors, Inc. Started in the Philippines, these sister companies are in the seafood trade business. MIDA Trade acts as the buying agent and MIDA Food focuses on the distribution of frozen seafood at home and abroad.

MIDA Trade was the first company to export seafood from Indonesia to the United States. The strong, international business network that Chingling and her team have built over the past 20 years helps to keep MIDA at the top of its industry. MIDA has offices across Southeast Asia in the Philippines, Indonesia, Vietnam, and Singapore. As many as 200 different kinds of seafood are stocked by MIDA Food, including a wide variety of fish, mollusks, crustaceans, and cephalopods. MIDA also distributes products in which the seafood has been prepared in some manner. For example, some items include portioned entrees and appetizers and MIDA has a division for canned seafood.

MIDA recognizes that knowing its clients means understanding their laws and cultures, as well as their product needs and expectations. MIDA's staff members travel extensively to develop and maintain customer relationships. This includes attending international trade shows and conferences to stay on top of market trends. MIDA is also a member of multiple professional seafood associations, and it subscribes to many seafood-related publications.

MIDA regularly inspects processing plants to assess how well its suppliers are complying with environmental and social responsibilities. Environmental issues include proper water disposal, mangrove destruction/replanting, and practicing sustainable aquaculture practices. Social responsibilities include preventing child labor and meeting minimum-wage standards. In addition, Chingling serves on the Fisheries and Aquaculture Board of the Philippines.

BizFacts

Kay Keenan and Steve Smolinsky are the consummate networkers. They have written a book on the topic, *Conversation on Networking.* Following are some tips from their book:

- It's a lot more fun to be with upbeat people. Negative stories push people away; positive stories bring them closer.

- If you go to an event or meeting with someone, split up. It improves your chances of meeting interesting people.

- Only if you're dead is it okay to answer "Nothing" when asked, "What's new?"

- Go early (to an event) and study the name tags on the registration table.

- Strong relationships are a two-way street.

- Learn to appreciate silence in a conversation. You can often see people thinking, but you rarely can hear their brain working.

- If you don't ask, you don't get. That means referrals, as well as most other things.

- Being comfortable with yourself leads to being comfortable with others.

- Carry your own name tag with you. Wearing a name tag is a great conversation starter, and your name will always be spelled correctly!

- A wonderful meeting not followed up is like having a winning lottery ticket and not cashing it in.

Source: Kay Keenan and Steven Smolinsky, *Conversation on Networking: Finding, Developing, and Maintaining Relationships for Business and Life* (Birchrunville, PA: Forever Talking Press, 2006).

The One-Minute Sales Call

Believe it or not, it is a challenge for most people to pay attention to someone for more than a minute. You will do best if you keep the core of your sales calls under a minute. Write down your sales pitch, and practice delivering it to friends or relatives. Time yourself. You will be surprised at how fast a minute can go by. You cannot practice your sales pitches enough. Spending time planning a call is better than agonizing over why a call failed.

Here is an example to get you started. Let's say you make baby food from organic fruits and vegetables. You are trying to convince the owner of Johnson's General Store to buy your products. Remember, you need to leave open spaces to engage the customer in the conversation, and this should be tailored to the specific challenges disclosed previously.

> *Hello, Mr. Johnson. Thank you for agreeing to see me today. I'm excited about this product and think you and your customers will be, too.*
>
> *I brought you a jar of our baby applesauce. It is nicely packaged, don't you think? (pause) We hand-decorate each jar. It makes a nice gift for new or expectant parents.*
>
> *We use only organic fruits and vegetables, no sugar, and very little salt. Our label explains that some babies are sensitive to the additives and dyes found in certain commercial baby foods. Our food is very gentle on the baby's stomach, and that makes the parents' lives much easier!*
>
> *I understand your concern that our product costs 25 cents more than your current brands. Recent industry research shows that customers will pay up to 50 percent more for products like ours. Also, because we add very little water to our product, customers actually get more food for the money than some of the less-expensive brands.*
>
> *You could start a local trend by stocking our baby food, Mr. Johnson. There has been a shift in the market toward healthy food for adults, and those adults are also looking for healthy baby food. Our product combines an eye-catching look with healthy ingredients that customers will find irresistible. How many jars would you like to order to start with?*

Successful Businesses Need Customers Who Return

Making a sale to a customer is actually only the first step in your relationship with this individual. Your real goal is not the first sale, but to develop repeat business—customers who will buy from you over and over again. Successful companies are built on repeat business. As noted earlier, the co-founder of Home Depot has calculated that one satisfied customer is worth more than $25,000 in sales over a lifetime.

Customer Service Is Keeping Customers Happy

Customer service is everything you do to keep your customers happy, especially *after* they've bought something. It includes maintaining and repairing the product or service once it has been sold and dealing with customer complaints. Many businesses do not take the time or effort to provide superior customer service. Smart entrepreneurs understand, however, that investing in customer service is likely to have a high return, because it retains customers and minimizes their dissatisfaction. Here are some suggestions that may work for your business:

customer service
everything a business does to keep the customer happy.

- Know your customers by name.
- Deliver the product or service on time, every time.
- Help customers carry their purchases to their vehicles.

- Suggest a less expensive product, if it will meet the customer's need, or recommend a product that, even if you do not sell it, is what they need and you cannot offer a substitute.
- Provide a full refund to any customer who is dissatisfied.
- Take time to listen politely and with empathy to complaints.
- Provide a toll-free customer-assistance phone line that is easy to use.
- Offer product or service information of interest to customers in a nonthreatening manner.

Smart entrepreneurs pay close attention to their customers. They constantly ask questions and analyze their needs. They train their employees to look for customer needs that might be going unfulfilled. The most successful entrepreneurs become customer-service experts. Superior customer service, combined with smart selling and a product that offers a unique competitive advantage, will lead to success.

Step into the Shoes . . .

Positively Outrageous Service

T. Scott Gross.
(Courtesy of T. Scott Gross, author Positively Outrageous Services)

T. Scott Gross is a motivational speaker and management training consultant who has operated in both the entrepreneurial and corporate worlds. He was the national director of training for the Church's Chicken chain, and became a Church's franchisee in 1985.[7] Gross was fortunate to be able to use his earnings from speaking and consulting to keep the restaurant in business. He and his staff quickly learned that running a restaurant by the book simply was not sufficient. That led to the concept of Positively Outrageous Service (POS).

How much service is enough? How good does it need to be? For Gross and his team, it was not enough just to satisfy customers. Businesses should delight and astound them.[8] He describes POS as, "[T]he story you can't wait to tell... unexpected service delivered at random.... It is a memorable event and is so unusual that the customer is compelled to tell others."[9]

Gross tells the following story:

In the borderline bizarre category is our now-famous drive-through windshield-washing service. It was my response to a suggestion by my brother, Steve, our manager, that we should do "something outrageous." Now, while a Church's employee wielding a spray bottle

attacks their windshields, I handle the microphone and the other half of the fun: "Good afternoon. Thanks for choosing Church's. As soon as that tubby guy gets out from in front of your car, pull up to the window for the best lunch you've had all day. No, on second thought, when he gets in front of your car, pull on up!" If a woman customer jokes that we should clean the car's interior, too, I might say: "Oh, madam, we aren't going to do insides. But if you come through tomorrow, we're going to try our hand at hair styling, and on Saturday, we're going to take a shot at dentistry!" The result is almost always a customer who is laughing when he or she reaches the pickup window. Doing the unexpected for our customers has earned us a reputation as a fun place to do business, where you can count on getting treated well.[10]

Positively Outrageous Service

- is random and unexpected: the element of surprise is part of its power;
- is out of proportion: it's an extravagant gesture that catches attention;
- involves the customer personally: it's an invitation to play that personalizes the service;
- creates positive word of mouth: more powerful than advertising, POS generates its own buzz.[11]

Could providing Positively Outrageous Service fit into your business?

[7] T. Scott Gross, "Outrageous Service Keeps Them Laughing—Getting the Customer Involved in Surprise Services Brings Satisfaction and Sales Increases," *Nation's Business*, 1992. Gale Group, 2004, http://findarticles.com/p/articles/mi_m1154/is_n3_v80/ai_11921694/print, August 31, 2010.
[8] T. Scott Gross, *Positively Outrageous Service: How to Delight and Astound Your Customers and Win Them for Life*, 2nd ed. (Chicago: Dearborn Trade Publishing, 2004).
[9] Ibid.
[10] Gross, *Positively Outrageous Service*.
[11] Available at http://www.tscottgross.com.

The Costs of Losing a Customer

Have you heard the expression, "The customer is always right?" There will be times when a customer may get angry at you, complain, or make demands that you believe are unreasonable. In *Customer Service: A Practical Approach*, Elaine Harris describes four costs of losing a customer.[12]

1. *Loss of current dollars.* These are the funds the customer was spending at your business.
2. *Loss of jobs.* Harris describes an advertising agency that lost one client because of a lack of courtesy and follow-through by the agency. Losing that client forced the owner of the business to close the office, putting 50 people out of work.
3. *Loss of reputation.* Remember Joe Girard's Law of 250. Do you really want to send a person away unhappy? One unhappy customer can keep many people away from your business.
4. *Loss of future business.* Once the customer is gone, so is the hope of any future purchases by that customer.

Use your self-control to stay polite, even when a customer is getting angry. Do your best to find a solution that will send him or her away satisfied, and diffuse any lingering ill will. Your effort will protect your business and may even earn you a customer for life. Often, if you simply ask, "What will it take to make you a satisfied customer?" you will find that the customer will pause and suggest a reasonable solution.

Customer Complaints Are Valuable

You may not enjoy hearing a customer complain about your product or service, but a complaint is full of valuable information that probably no one else will tell you—and you will not have to pay for it! Listen closely to learn what your customers need and want:

- Always acknowledge and deal with complaints and criticism. Never pretend that you did not hear a negative comment. If the customer *perceives* a problem, it *is* a problem.
- Do not overreact to negative comments and, above all, do not take them personally.
- Always tell the truth about any negative aspect of your product or service. When you admit a negative, you gain the customer's trust. However, this is different from complaining about your own product, a vendor, or your customers. You need not emphasize weaknesses but should acknowledge them when asked and offset them with benefits.

Remember, a successful business is built on repeat customers. When you listen to a customer, you are building a relationship. You are encouraging loyalty to your business.

The Better Business Bureau

If you have a business and treat a customer poorly, he or she may report you to the local Better Business Bureau (BBB). The BBB is a nonprofit, composed of for-profit and nonprofit organizations, which publishes reports about the reliability, trustworthiness, and performance of businesses and charities. You may want to consider the value of becoming a

◀ **Performance Objective 5**
Provide superior customer service.

---

[12]Elaine Harris, *Customer Service: A Practical Approach* (Upper Saddle River, NJ: Pearson Education, Inc., 2003).

Exhibit 6-2 *Words Matter; Smart Customer Service*

Words to Use	Words to Avoid
Please	Cannot
Yes	Never
May I	Do not
Consider this	You have to
Do	Do not tell me no
Let's negotiate	Will not
Will	Not our policy
Thank you	Not my job
You	Profanity
Us	Vulgarity
Appreciate	Problem
Can	Sorry
Use customer's name	Endearments (honey, sweetie, etc.)
Would you like	We'll try
Opportunity	Haven't had time
Challenge	Hang on for a second
Regret	

BBB-accredited company. The BBB bases much of its reporting on complaints submitted by customers. Think about that when you are tempted to ignore a customer's request or lose your temper. Even if you believe you are in the right, you could damage your business's reputation.

An angry customer can make you feel angry, too. It is crucial that you and your team members stay calm when dealing with a customer who is upset. Ask the person to explain the situation and do not interrupt. This will provide time for him or her to vent and then calm down. If you show that you are willing to listen, you will probably defuse much of the irritation.

If the customer is using profanity, however, say something like, "I understand your frustration, but I'm not comfortable with the way you are expressing it. Let's find a solution for you."

Exhibit 6-2 shows Elaine Harris's list of words to use and words to avoid when dealing with customers.[13]

Customer Relationship Management Systems

customer relationship management (CRM) companywide policies, practices, and processes that a business uses with its customers to generate maximum customer satisfaction and optimal profitability.

One approach to securing and sustaining customers is to implement a **customer relationship management (CRM)** system, which is made up of the companywide policies, practices, and processes that a business uses to manage its interactions with customers to generate maximum customer satisfaction and optimal profitability. CRM is a deliberate implementation of guidelines for excellence in customer service and relationship management, and is designed to ensure positive interactions and encourage repeat purchases and referrals. The sales and customer-service skills and the best practices introduced in this chapter can be components of a customer relationship management system. CRM can be very simple—such as techniques for greeting and treating customers—to very sophisticated, such

---
[13]Harris, *Customer Service.*

as using state-of-the-art technology to provide highly targeted customer information and analytics.

CRM affirms that customer service is an aspect of marketing. Marketing brings a customer to your business, but it does not stop there. Once the customer is inside your door or on the phone, his or her treatment should be consistent with your marketing. If your competitive advantage is speedy service, make sure your employees move quickly. If your advantage is a cozy, easygoing environment, make sure each customer is warmly welcomed and made to feel at home. Your customer service must reinforce your overall marketing plan. Through a well-designed and executed CRM system, you are reinforcing and building marketing effectiveness.

Why Does CRM Matter?

Customer relationship management can be the component of your business that makes it a sustainable entity. The cost of securing a new customer is invariably much higher than that of keeping a repeat customer. According to the Customer Service Institute, 65 percent of a company's business comes from existing customers, and it costs five times as much to attract a new customer as it does to keep an existing one satisfied.[14] *Losing* a customer is even more expensive. According to TARP Worldwide's recent word-of-mouth (WOM) survey, "42% of consumers who hear about a positive product experience will buy that product for the first time and another 21% of those consumers will increase their purchasing. The effects of positive WOM mirror those of negative WOM, as 42% of consumers who hear a negative WOM stop buying that product and 14% will buy less of it. However, consumers with negative experiences provide more detailed explanations through more channels than those who have positive experiences."[15]

When you know the purchasing patterns and interests of a customer, you can make informed decisions about the products, services, and promotional offers that will be of interest and result in additional sales. With CRM, you can focus on optimal interactions with customers during all types of transactions (i.e., purchases, returns, ordering, inquiries, and complaints), as well as using and building on data about customer behavior to foster positive transactions.

Because customer service is also a valuable source of market research, CRM supports market research for companies that employ it. Market research should not end once you open your business. Each customer can be a valuable source of information. Some easy ways to collect market research as part of your customer service for retail businesses include:

- Providing a short survey on a stamped postcard with every item purchased or including a survey link and reward with every receipt from sales. Or include a survey that can be redeemed for a discount on the next item purchased.
- Asking selected customers to fill out a longer survey—again, offering a discount or prize drawing as an incentive.

[14]Customer Service Institute of America Web site, http://www.serviceinstitute.com/CCSM.htm, June 23, 2009.
[15]TARP Worldwide press release, "Consumer Word of Mouth Changes Buying Habits 60% of the Time, TARP Worldwide Poll Finds: Men and Senior Citizens Most Likely to Complain," February 12, 2008, http://www.tarp.com/news_wom_poll.html,, June 23, 2009.

- Always asking—and having your employees ask—standard questions when completing a sale, such as "Do you have any suggestions on how we could improve our product?" or "Were you satisfied with the service you received today?" or "Were you able to find everything that you wanted?"

Components of CRM for the Small Business

CRM has consistent components that may be incorporated across business types and sizes. It reaches across the marketing, sales, and service functions of a business to create positive customer experiences. **Exhibit 6-3** shows the solution map of CRM as described by SAP, the top seller of CRM systems. In the case of businesses that purchase highly sophisticated software, these components are part of the software solution, but for companies with less complex operations and fewer resources, many of the functions can be carried out without software applications beyond basic record keeping and with simple databases, contact management software, and industry-specific systems.

The U.S. Small Business Administration Web site (http://www.sba.gov) offers a perspective on customer service and CRM in general—relating it to the axiom of the Golden Rule, "Do unto others as you would have them do unto you"—stating: "Companies of all sizes are realizing that their strongest selling point can sometimes boil down to treating customers as they would like to be treated—or better."[16] The message is getting through. According to John Goodman, president of TARP Worldwide, "In the past few years, companies began to realize that service was really a competitive factor, and began to view it as an integral part of their product."[17] It is often in the area of service and CRM that a small business can outclass its larger competitors, so that customers may spend more to buy

Exhibit 6-3 *SAP Solution Map for CRM*

Marketing	Sales	Service
Marketing Resource Management	Sales Planning and Forecasting	Service Sales and Marketing
Segmentation and List Management	Sales Performance Management	Service Contracts and Agreements
Campaign Management	Territory Management	Installations and Management
Real-Time Offer Management	Accounts and Contacts	Customer Service Support
Lead Management	Opportunity Management	Field Service Management
Loyalty Management	Quotation and Order Management	Returns and Depot Repair
Communication Promotion	Pricing and Contracts	Warranty and Claims Management
	Incentive and Commission Management	Service Logistics and Finance
	Time and Travel	Service Collaboration, Analytics, Optimization

Source: SAP Web site, http://www.sap.com/solutions/business-suite/CRM/businessmaps.epx, June 20, 2009. SAP Solution Map for CRM courtesy of SAP AG.

---

[16]U.S. Small Business Administration Web site, http://www.sba.gov, June 20, 2009.
[17]Ibid.

from them because of the service differential. The SBA offers three golden rules for small businesses with respect to CRM:

- Golden Rule 1: Put the customer first.
- Golden Rule 2: Stay close to your customers.
- Golden Rule 3: Pay attention to details.

The SBA offers further advice on the components of customer care in the form of five rules. These principles are part of the essential components of successful CRM.

1. ***Conduct your own survey.*** Profit from the ideas, suggestions, and complaints of your present and former customers. Talk and meet with your customers. Ask questions. Learn their attitudes, what they want, and what they dislike.
2. ***Check employees' telephone manners periodically.*** This link is particularly important for small businesses because bad telephone handling can undermine other constructive efforts to build a profitable enterprise.
3. ***Rules such as prompt answering and a cheerful attitude of helpfulness are of critical importance.*** Have someone whose voice is unfamiliar play the role of a customer or prospective customer, preferably a difficult one.
4. ***Make customer service a team effort.*** Use group meetings, memos, posters, and in-house publications to build customer consciousness throughout the organization. Continually drive home the crucial rule that getting and holding customers requires team play; invite employees' ideas.
5. ***Extend your efforts after hours.*** It's the friendly feelings people have that draw them to you and your business. Take advantage of the relaxed atmosphere of social occasions, or a neighborly chat over the back fence, to turn friends into customers or to reinforce the loyalty of existing ones.[18]

How Technology Supports CRM

The general conception of CRM is that it is technology used to build and maintain customer relationships. Certainly, as noted, the use of computer technology can have a significant role in CRM, but the system should be inclusive of all forms of relationship management, from the use of sophisticated software systems to greeting a customer on the phone, in person, or on the home page of your Web site. With CRM, customer interactions with all parts of the company are unified and customer information is tracked, analyzed, and used to improve customer satisfaction and business profitability. Specialized CRM software is available to companies large and small. **Exhibit 6-4** shows the top vendors of CRM software. The total expenditures for CRM in 2007 were $8.1 billion.[19]

It truly is not necessary to invest in a sophisticated CRM software system to use technology to benefit your customer relationships. You can purchase a database package to create significant gains. A **database**

database a collection of information that is generally stored on a computer and organized for sorting and searching.

[18]Ibid.
[19]Gartner, Inc. press release, "Gartner Says Worldwide Customer Relationship Management Market Grew 23 Percent in 2007," July 7, 2008, http://www.gartner.com/us/crm, June 20, 2009. Research represents Gartner's historical perspective and may not represent the current market.

Exhibit 6-4 *Worldwide Vendor Revenue Estimates for Total CRM Software (millions of U.S. dollars)*

Company	2007 Revenue	2007 Market Share (%)
SAP	$2,050.80	25.4
Oracle	$1,319.80	16.3
SalesForce.com	$676.50	8.4
Amdocs	$421.00	5.2
Microsoft	$332.10	4.1
Others	$3,289.10	40.6
Total	$8,089.30	100.0

Source: Gartner, Inc., *Dataquest Insight: Customer Relationship Management, Worldwide, 2007,* http://www.gartner.com, June 19, 2009. Data updated periodically by Gartner.

is a collection of information that is generally stored on a computer and organized for sorting and searching. Create a database on your computer to collect any information you obtain from customers, either by using a package such as Microsoft Access or via a specialized customer software system for your industry. Your database should include every customer you have ever had, as well as potential customers: friends, family, and other connections. The database should include contact information (i.e., name, e-mail address, phone and fax numbers, and mailing address); any preferences or pertinent personal information (e.g., sizes, birthdays, family, hobbies, memberships); and purchase and payment history. Also, include such notes as when the connection was made, who was involved, what type of exchange it was (e.g., in person, telephone, text, social network, e-mail), and a note about the topics of discussion and any appropriate follow-up. Design the database and start collecting this information from the beginning and you will be ahead of the game when you are ready to make sales calls or send out marketing material.

As your database grows, you can make it more sophisticated by organizing it by region, customer interest, or any number of other variables, and send out targeted e-mails. If you sell gourmet sauces, for example, your notes could tell you whether a customer is interested in hot sauces or dessert sauces. When you add a new hot sauce to your product line, you will know whom to target with an e-mail announcement introducing it, possibly with a special offer. Use the resources available to you to maximize your culture of focus on the customer, and maintain a strong customer-relationship management.

Exercise

Contact your telephone company—either by phone or through Internet research—to find out how to set up an 800 number for your business, so customers can call toll free. Some long-distance providers offer special discounts to small-business owners. AT&T has a program called Small Business Advantage.

How much will an 800 number for your business cost?
Did you find any special discounts?

Chapter Summary

Now that you have studied this chapter, you can do the following:

1. Explain the importance of selling based upon benefits.
   - Features are the qualities of a product or service.
   - Benefits are what the product or service can do to fill customer needs.
   - Customers purchase based upon perceived benefits.
2. Use the principles of selling to make effective sales calls.
   - Make a good personal impression.
   - Know your product or service.
   - Believe in your product or service.
   - Know your field.
   - Know your customers.
   - Prepare your sales presentation.
   - Think positively.
   - Keep good records.
   - Make an appointment.
   - Treat your customers like gold.
3. Know how to make a successful sales call.
   - Use technology to assist you.
   - Prequalify your leads, so that you are making the best use of your time and theirs.
   - Focus on the customer, not on the product or service.
   - Incorporate the eight-step sales call.
4. Analyze and improve your sales calls.
   - Was I able to get the customer to open up to me? Why, or why not? Did I do or say anything that turned the customer off?
   - Which of my questions did the best job of helping the customer zero in on his or her problem?
   - Was I able to make an honest case for my product or service being the one that could solve the customer's problem?
   - Did I improve my relationship with this individual during the call?
5. Provide superior customer service.
   - Customer service is everything you do to keep your customers happy, especially after the sale. It includes maintaining and repairing the product or service once it has been sold, and dealing with customer complaints.
   - A successful business is built on repeat customers.
6. Define customer relationship management and understand its value.
   - Identify the key components of CRM.
   - Recognize that CRM can vary from simple to complex and that you can incorporate technology into it to obtain higher value.
   - Use CRM to tailor your products, services, and promotions to yield increased profitability.

Key Terms

customer relationship management (CRM)	lurk
	newsgroup
customer service	prospect
database	spam

Entrepreneurship Portfolio

Critical Thinking Exercises

1. Describe the features of each product listed below and then create a benefit statement for each that you would use as selling points.
   Product
   - wristwatch with daily-events calendar
   - milk-free chocolate
   - vegetarian dog food
   - personal lie detector

2. Create a customer profile database for your own business or a home and office delivery-and-pickup dry cleaning service containing at least 20 data fields. Which five questions would you ask every customer?

3. Describe a business that you deal with as a customer. Describe the customer service at this business. What do you like or dislike about it? How could it be improved?

4. List five things you intend to do in your business or in the home and office delivery-and-pickup dry cleaning company to offer superior customer service.

5. Identify five specific sales call prospects for your business. Prequalify them using these questions: (1) Is the prospect in my market? (2) Does he or she need my product or service? (3) Will my product or service remove a problem or source of "pain," or improve the individual's life? (4) Can he or she afford it?

6. Have you created any marketing materials for your business? If so, have three friends and a mentor (someone older whom you respect and who can give you good business advice) look at your materials and give you feedback. Write a memo listing their suggestions and what you plan to do to improve your marketing materials.

7. Write a one-minute sales call for the product or service your business will be selling. Try your pitch out on a partner and write down his or her objections. Rewrite your pitch to incorporate those criticisms. Try your pitch again. Repeat this process until you think you have a strong sales call.

Key Concept Questions

1. Explain Joe Girard's Law of 250 in your own words, and give examples of it from your own life.
2. Why is customer service an extension of marketing?
3. Give three reasons why it is important to keep collecting market research even after you have opened your business.
4. What do you expect your personal look to be when you start selling your product or service, and why?
5. What sources of information can you use to develop a customer profile?
6. List three ways you intend to provide superior customer service.
7. Create a company signature for your business e-mail. Keep it under eight words.

Application Exercises

1. Develop a one-minute sales pitch for three items that you are wearing. Try out the pitch for each on a partner. Have your partner help you time the pitches to one minute. Do the same for your partner.

2. Write a memo to your partner discussing his or her sales calls and how they could be improved. Use the eight steps of a sales call in the text as your guide when analyzing your partner's efforts.

3. Arrange to receive a sales pitch from a competitor in the business field that you intend to enter. After the presentation, write down your objections to purchasing the product or service. Use Brian Tracy's method to categorize your objections and then phrase them in a single question composed of 25 words or less. Be conscious of doing this ethically.

Exploring Your Community

1. Visit three businesses in your community and take notes on your experience as a shopper. Write a memo comparing the customer service at each. Include such information as the following: Were you greeted when you came in? Did anyone offer to help you? If you bought something, were you given a survey? What differentiates the best firm from the worst in terms of customer service?

2. Interview an entrepreneur about the type of CRM he or she uses. Discuss customer service and complaint handling in particular. Summarize the interview in a short paper.

BizBuilder Business Plan Questions

5.0 Marketing Strategy and Plan

5.3 Promotion

G. List ways you intend to provide superior customer service.

H. Write a one-minute sales pitch for your product/service and describe five sales prospects you intend to pitch.

I. How will you keep your customer database? What essential questions will you ask every customer for your database?

Kay Keenan and Steve Smolinsky—Conversation on Networking

In late 2004, Howard Weisz had a problem. As a long-time member of the Mid-Atlantic Consultants (MAC) Network, he had agreed to organize a program for the group on networking. As the date approached, Howard realized that he really didn't want to moderate this event. His solution was to ask Kay Keenan, founder of Growth Consulting, to present the program. Kay had previously worked for Howard before she became a well-known speaker and consultant on networking.

Kay felt there should be more than one presenter, because the topic was networking. So, she created a panel of volunteers from the MAC members. Steven Smolinsky, founder of Benari LTD, volunteered even though he did not know Kay. Later, Steve received a call from Kay telling him that all the other panelists had cancelled, so it was just going to be the two of them. They decided to use a conversational approach that involved the audience. Thus, Conversation on Networking was born.

During the program, the audience reacted with incredible enthusiasm, interest, and participation. Afterwards, testimonials flowed in as attendees discovered rapid results from using the skills they had learned. Word spread fast, and many requests were made for a repeat session. Kay and Steve responded by taking the show on the road. Since that time, numerous public and private events have been held around the country.

As the name implies, Conversation on Networking is a fully interactive program about how to effectively meet people and develop those contacts into long-term relationships. Kay and Steve recognize that there is no single, correct answer to a networking issue, because appropriate advice is dependent on a particular situation. As a result, the discussions that occur between the presenters and the attendees focus on real, everyday issues that people have experienced.

To further customize their advice, Kay and Steve provide forms that an attendee may complete before or after an event. This information is used to create a report with individualized feedback. The goal of the program is to help participants obtain immediate results after leaving a Conversation on Networking event.

In addition to events, Kay and Steve use many other ways to share their experiences and ideas. The Conversation on Networking Web site includes basic information about services and

Steve Smolinsky and Kay Keenan of Conversation on Networking.
(Conversation on Networking)

events, networking tips, short video clips, links for e-mailing Kay and Steve, and a link to Steve's blog. You can sign up to receive a newsletter as well as purchase their book and/or a DVD, via the Web site. Customer testimonials are also posted online. The newsletter and blog often mention readers and clients, giving an extra boost to the networking information that is shared.

Case Study Analysis
1. How does Conversation on Networking reinforce the importance of selling based upon benefits?
2. List three things that Kay and Steve have done that you could adopt to help build business relationships.
3. What principles of selling do Kay and Steve employ to sell Conversation on Networking?
4. How do Kay and Steve support their customers and colleagues, and utilize customer referrals?

Case Sources
Conversation on Networking Web site, http://www.conversationonnetworking.com.

Kay Keenan and Steven Smolinsky, *Conversation on Networking: Finding, Maintaining, and Developing Relationships for Business and Life* (Birchrunville, PA: Forever Talking Press, 2006).

Off-Centered Ales—On Target Sales: Dogfish Head Craft Brewery

One look at Dogfish Head Brewery's Web site (http://www.dogfish.com) or a few minutes in the presence of the business's founder, Sam Calagione, and it is apparent that sales and customer service are key components of this company's success. Sam and Mariah Calagione opened Dogfish Head Brewings and Eats (DFH) at Rehoboth Beach, Delaware, in 1995. Since then, Dogfish Head has expanded to include a 103,000-square-foot brewery and a small distillery, with 50 distributors in 25 states. There are also DFH Alehouses in Gaithersburg, Maryland, and Falls Church and Chantilly, Virginia. DFH has been on the *Inc.* 500 list of fastest-growing companies in the United States, and is the fastest-growing small brewery.

Sam became fascinated with craft brews when he worked in a New York City restaurant that featured microbrews. In *Brewing Up a Business*, he writes, "I first decided to open my brewery when I was 24 years old…I worked as a brewer's assistant as I wrote my business plan.…I made pilot batches of beer and developed recipes and brand names." Sam and Mariah wanted to create a successful brewpub, rather than a stand-alone beer-production facility, so that they would have direct interaction with customers. As the Web site reports, "We quickly got bored brewing the same things over and over—that's when we started adding all sorts of weird ingredients and getting kind of crazy with the beers!" By serving the results in the brewpub, DFH could modify and improve them based on customer response. This customer focus has been central to DFH from its inception.

Dogfish Head offers "off-centered ales for off-centered people," creating brews for hard-core "beer geeks, wine people, and foodies." They market brews with creative names and ingredients and interesting back stories, whereas the objective continues to be designing unique and enticing beers. For example, Midas Touch is "an ancient Turkish recipe using the original ingredients from the 2,700-year-old drinking vessels discovered in the tomb of King Midas himself." Raison D'être, which was voted American Beer of the Year in 2000 by *Malt Advocate*, is a deep-mahogany ale brewed with beet sugar, green raisins, and Belgian yeast. The DFH flagship beverage is 60 Minute IPA, a heavily hopped India Pale Ale (IPA). DFH's 90 Minute Imperial IPA has been described by *Esquire* as "perhaps the best I.P.A. in America."

Dogfish Head's Seasonal Punkin Ale label art.
(Dogfish Head Brewing)

DFH sells its 30-plus styles of ale and a half-dozen types of spirits. They are known for their quality, distinctive, extreme brews using nontraditional ingredients with stronger flavor and higher alcohol content than average American beers. They also are priced significantly higher than those of the larger brewing companies.

The DFH way of doing business is to understand that selling is all about finding out your customers' needs and delivering products and services to meet those needs—exceeding customer expectations. Sam learned about the market by making a point of spending time to "get out and meet your brand through the eyes of the world.…In the case of the beer business that means I spend time with my distributors, retailers, and my customers."[20] He and the DFH team continue to do so. All DFH team members are passionate and knowledgeable about the company and its products, and this passion attracts and retains customers. Sam writes, "If you take the time to roam constructively, you will learn a tremendous amount about your company and its place in the competitive environment. You will be able to gauge your company's successes and failure through the eyes of your customer."[21]

Sam articulates his view of customer service and selling: "Always remember that you are your customers and your customers are you. To treat them any differently than you would expect to be treated just because you are the seller and they are the buyer would be a mistake.…In business large and small, loyal customers are earned from trust, respect, and the consistent quality of products and services based on personal values." A dedication to people, and respect for them, is a priority for DFH.

[20]Sam Calagione, *Brewing Up a Business* (Hoboken, NJ: John Wiley and Sons, Inc., 2005).
[21]Mariah Calagione of DFH.

Dogfish Head focuses on education as the pathway to sales, eschewing advertising campaigns. Sam writes, "Knowledge gives the customer the power to make a decision; the quality of the experience gives them the power to decide if the experience was worth the price." The company spends approximately 20 percent of its advertising budget on samples and tastings for customers and prospective customers. DFH only advertises in beer publications, and in local Delaware publications for the brewpub. They focus their funds on ingredients and innovative equipment and let respected third parties speak for them. The accolades continue to accumulate. International beer expert Michael Jackson has dubbed Dogfish Head "America's most interesting and adventurous small brewery."

The sales force is actively involved in the establishment of revenue goals and the creation of the budget. The sales managers work with the 50 distributors to establish the forecast for the coming year's sales volume and mix. This information helps create the budget. The sales team is informed of and agrees to the final budget, so that they are clearly attuned to the relationship between the budget and their commissions and bonuses. The goals are clear and exceptional performance is rewarded.

Every team member is a salesperson at DFH. Everyone must know the difference between DFH products and those of competitors and needs to understand why DFH's are better. They have to have basic knowledge of the company, its philosophy, and its products. Team members are given opportunities to walk in the shoes of their colleagues by experiencing different roles within the company. They can build a more robust picture of the entire organization and become more passionate and knowledgeable about DFH. Sam encourages creating a "sales-centric" mentality.

In 2010, the popularity of DFH grew substantially when Sam was the host of *Brew Masters* on the Discovery Channel. Inventory shortages, which already were somewhat of a challenge, became routine and exponential and DFH could not meet the demand, nor did they want to move toward becoming a mass-production brewery. Even with a 303-percent expansion in production over the past five years, they simply could not keep up with the demand; shortages even resulted in hoarding. DFH created an allocation system to ease customer service issues, particularly with respect to service in its local area. Having ended certain discounts and still seeing increases in demand, in March of 2011, DFH announced its withdrawal from Indiana, Rhode Island, Tennessee, and Wisconsin.[22]

Sam Calagione of Dogfish Head.
(Dogfish Head Brewing)

The company has strategically decided to control its growth and remain focused on its core customers. It is easy to understand why DFH has been so successful.

Case Study Analysis

1. Through which channels does Dogfish Head sell its products?
2. According to Sam Calagione, what does education have to do with sales?
3. What are the roles of the customers of DFH?
4. How do members of the sales force participate in goal setting?
5. Why is sampling an important part of the sales process for DFH?
6. What is the relationship between the sales strategy for DFH and its pricing strategy?
7. How can growth cause issues in customer service? How did DFH address this?

Case Sources

Dogfish Head Brewery Web site at http://www.dogfish.com.

Sam Calagione, *Brewing Up a Business: Adventures in Entrepreneurship from the Founder of Dogfish Head Craft Brewery* (Hoboken, NJ: John Wiley and Sons, Inc., 2005).

Nitasha Tiku, "The Way I Work: Dogfish Head's Sam Calagione," *Inc.*, July 1, 2009.

Eric Ruth, "Delaware Business: Dogfish Reins in Distribution," Delawareonline.com, March 12, 2011, http://www.delawareonline.com/fdcp/?1300028917015, March 14, 2011.

---

[22]Eric Ruth, "Delaware Business: Dogfish Reins in Distribution," Delawareonline.com, March 12, 2011, http://www.delawareonline.com/fdcp/?1300028917015, March 14, 2011.

Ken Done Studios

Small Business School **video clip titles are in red**
Case prepared by Hattie Bryant, creator of Small Business School, *the television series made for PBS and Voice of America and available on its Web site at http://SmallBusinessSchool.org.*

DO WHAT WORKS

Ken Done is Australia's most recognized modern artist. Since 1975, he has painted nearly every day. From his massive body of work has sprung an enterprise that employs more than 100 people. He has galleries in London, New York, and other locations, where his paintings are sold. Customers may purchase swimwear, sportswear, and accessories—all designed by the Ken Done studios—at boutiques and online. At its peak, sales were in excess of 100 million AUD—with most revenue coming from licensed products.

Done spent 16 years in the advertising industry in London, New York, and Sydney. This uniquely prepared him to be a working artist who would avoid the starving stage that so many painters struggle through. Like most successful entrepreneurs, Done paid his dues by working for others. Then he had a gut feeling that he could make his own idea work financially. When he left his secure job in New York City at the advertising agency giant J. Walter Thompson and returned to his country to make his way as a fine artist, he did not expect to attain the success he has today.

While sitting with Ken in one of his galleries in Sydney, he told me, "This is an accidental business. To get into the businesses that we're in at the moment, it was surprising in the sense that from my first exhibition, even though I'd been painting all my life—for my first exhibition when I was 40, I made 12 T-shirts to give to the press to remind them of that particular show. And, look, they liked them so much that people wanted more."

"It's a very straightforward exercise, isn't it? If you make something and it's well priced and people like it, almost inevitably you realize you can make some more. And in this sense—I mean, I'm a painter. That's how I spend all my time. But the concept of repeating the singular effort or taking one part of a piece of design and multiplying it is essentially, you know, what business, I suppose, is about."

Done's paintings can be translated into multiple media, ranging from the original art that is sold in galleries, to prints sold online, and tote bags, watches, swimwear, cover-ups, and T-shirts sold in retail stores and online.

Done didn't intend to sell T-shirts; he intended to sell paintings. The T-shirts were a marketing stunt that changed his life. Fortunately, his wife, Judy, had worked as a fashion designer. Combining their backgrounds and talents, the two have built a company that started with Ken's paintings and grew as Judy applied the art to clothing and accessories.

Since the art press liked his T-shirts so much, the demand exceeded his supply; he printed more, and he didn't give them away. He sold them for $12 each. Even though his profits were slim on this first item, he knew he was on to something that he never would have thought of on his own.

By being open to what his potential customers might buy, he launched a solid business.

Giving away the T-shirts to people who could talk up his paintings was a perfect integrated marketing idea. This is called viral marketing. Done wanted the art press to say good things about his exhibition, so that customers with the resources to buy would find their way to his gallery and buy his paintings. Regardless of what the art press wrote about that first exhibition, they talked about the T-shirt, creating that word-of-mouth marketing—*buzz*—that every business craves. The press reaction and subsequent buzz about Done's work is an excellent example of viral marketing. He has relied heavily upon viral marketing and direct sales, as well as his Web site, to keep his brand successful. Just as the use of the T-shirts to capture the attention of the press was creative and innovative, Done's marketing of his art in its various forms uses creativity and innovation to reinforce the brand and extend its markets.

If he had spent his exhibition marketing budget on champagne and hors d'oeuvres, some might think, "This is the right kind of marketing. He is serving high-end refreshments to sell his expensive paintings." With the benefit of time, we can see that there was probably nothing he could have done better than making those T-shirts from his own designs that captured the spirit of his paintings.

Ken told me, "I made 12 T-shirts. People liked them so much, I made 12 more. Those 12 sold very quickly, so suddenly I thought—because that original T-shirt—it was a blue drawing on white—I think made this giant mental leap of thinking, 'Let's do one white on blue.' Suddenly, there are two. It's a choice. It's a product range. So from having a choice of two to a number of shops and licensing arrangements, that's just, you know, like a game. But you have to make something that people want."

Over time, Done and his team have developed an approach to their markets that relies heavily upon physical locations and word-of-mouth for its promotion, with less than 5 percent of revenues devoted to advertising. The product mix is divided between T-shirts and seasonal apparel (40 percent), women's fashion (20 percent), swimwear (15 percent), children's products (10 percent), accessories (10 percent), and artwork (5 percent). Ken Done products are priced for the midmarket, with different products playing different roles. For example, the bread-and-butter items are priced competitively, while maintaining solid margins. Other products are sold to set the pitch of the retail environments, and priced accordingly.

SELL BEAUTY

Beauty is the brand, and plenty of art critics snub Ken Done, but he sticks to his core belief. He told me that photographers and film makers are so good at showing us the sad, dark side of the world that he does not want to compete on that level. Done's world is color. The stunning sea, sand, sky, flora and fauna of his country never bore him.

In addition to painting, over the years he has taken on projects that align with his brand. From 1988 to 1999, Done created the cover art for a Japanese fashion and lifestyle magazine, and I had a chance to see for myself that this work made him a star in Japan. While I was in the gallery with Ken, a couple of Japanese women came in and they could not believe their eyes. They had no idea that he would be in the gallery and, to them, he was bigger than Elvis. Well, maybe they had never heard of Elvis, but I could tell that they were overwhelmed. I offered to take their picture with the artist, and they were most grateful.

Done is one of just 13 artists who have created a BMW Art Car, he redesigned the restaurant at Sydney's Powerhouse Museum, and he created the official logo for the Sydney 2000 Olympic Games. According to the publishers of, *Ken Done: The Art of Design*, Done has not only built his own successful business, he has helped define the image of Australia.

SIGN CONTRACTS ONLY WITH THOSE WHO DON'T NEED ONE

To protect his brand, Done pulled out of lucrative contracts with large American department stores. He had licensed his art to handbag, shoe, and clothing manufacturers, but he was not happy with how the final products had been executed in the hands of others. And they made a request that he simply refused to grant.

He told me, "We had to work in Neiman Marcus, in Bloomingdale's, in Macy's. And that arrangement was good. It was fine. But we started to lose control in a sense that because it was often going into colder parts of America and they wanted more winter clothes. They want brown. They said, 'Brown's very important in Chicago.' I said, 'I'm playing golf. I don't care whether brown's in Chicago.' I'm not putting it down, it's just that America's like this huge ball; it's really, really, really hard to get it rolling. And once it starts to roll, it's incredible—and it was just too much for us. And the clothing wasn't looking exactly like our stuff. So we decided at that point in time we would cut out all wholesaling and all licensing, and we cut our business by fifty percent in one hit, because we couldn't control it."

He got out of the contract by picking up the phone and telling the person who handled the American business: "I'm not going to do it anymore." Fortunately, Ken understands that you should not sign a contract with a person who won't let you out of it. Business owners enter into a lot of agreements with customers, suppliers, and employees. Contracts are a way of documenting these agreements. They ensure that the understanding of the parties regarding performance and compensation is the same on both sides. The contracts are signed to protect businesses and to manage business risk. Done had a good relationship with his American partner, and there were no hard feelings or lawsuits when Ken needed to rein in his product line and quit the American market.

CHANGING CHANNELS TO MAINTAIN BRAND INTEGRITY

Done has changed his channels of distribution several times, to maintain brand integrity and to take advantage of opportunities—or address threats. Oscar Done, Ken's son and managing director of the company, reports that the firm gained international recognition through licensing agreements in Australia, the United States, and Japan. The upside was the wide distribution and increased brand recognition. The downside was the loss of control and the receipt of licensing fees rather than the usual profit margins. The company was unhappy with the licensing arrangements and changed its course. Later in the 1990s, Done-branded products were sold only in company retail stores, with no distributors or licenses.

The focus on company-owned retail stores in Australia worked well leading up to the 2000 Sydney Olympics. Done was an official Olympic supplier, and benefited greatly from tourism. However, the tourism was severely impacted the following year, after the September 11, 2001, terrorist attacks and the SARS virus. Revenues declined and fixed costs escalated.

Ken Done once again entered into a licensing agreement in the early 2000s, this time focusing on swimwear and resort wear. The company created a network of sales agents across the United States to promote the premium Done products. Distribution reached approximately 200 stores, including a number of high-end retailers. Oscar explains, "While this did deliver new channels of distribution, it was very laborious, and we faced the unpredictable challenges of currency values, market regulation, and logistics that virtually made it a profitless exercise at the end of the day, if we were to remain price competitive. We needed to develop a more robust infrastructure in the U.S. which meant further investments of time and money." Ultimately, management decided that they did not want to pursue that route and retrenched.

In order to focus on the company's strengths in design, Done has downsized to two boutique retail shops in Sydney, and a comparatively narrow product range.

Done's paintings sell for $30,000 to $50,000 (USD), and you can buy a T-shirt from his Web site for $20. I don't think he will ever retire; the last thing he said to me was, "I wanted to work this morning. I want to work every day."

Case Analysis

1. How does Ken Done incorporate the Four P's into a creative, effective, integrated marketing effort?
2. What is the product mix that Ken Done's enterprises have developed?
3. How are his products distributed (through what channels)?
4. Take a look at Done's retail stores on the Internet. Set the pricing to USD and browse through the Web site. What pricing strategy is employed by the company?
5. Discuss the company's global marketing.
6. What was Done's first marketing effort?
7. What was the result of this effort?
8. How does Done extend his brand?

Case Sources

http://www.done.com.au/

http://www.kendone.com/

SHOW ME THE MONEY: FINDING, SECURING, AND MANAGING IT

Blend Images/Alamy

Chapter **7**

UNDERSTANDING AND MANAGING START-UP, FIXED, AND VARIABLE COSTS

Jupiter Images

Medical services have become global—with advances in technology, ease of travel, and variety of cost structures. Aravind Eye Care System (AECS), a social enterprise, is based in Maduri, India, and claims it is "the largest and most productive eye care facility in the world." Aravind provides eye surgery and outpatient care at each of its five hospitals. AECS was founded in 1976 by Dr. Govindappa Venkataswamy with the goal of eliminating blindness. In 2008, Dr. P. Namperumalsamy, chairman of AECS, was awarded the Ernst & Young Entrepreneur of the Year for Health Care in Mumbai.

In addition to the facilities at its hospitals, AECS provides award-winning telemedicine services in rural areas of the country. It has become an international training center (Lions Aravind Institute of Community Ophthalmology), and AECS treats patients from around the globe. The program has focused on creating cost efficiencies in the delivery of care to enable outreach to a broader base of patients. In addition, AECS manufactures optical products (specifically, intraocular lenses for cataract patients) through its Aurolab division for use in their hospitals and for outside sale to raise funds to serve more patients in poverty. Funding for AECS comes from organizations around the world, and among the ophthalmology interns are many from the United States.

The efficiencies achieved by AECS allow it to provide well over half of its surgical care at reduced fees or no cost. By creating what is essentially an assembly-line process and layout for cataract surgeries, and working in small, specialized teams, the time necessary for each surgery is minimized—and the surgeons complete a maximal number of operations per day. Also, because Indian laws differ from those in the United States, more than one patient can be in an operating room at a time, so that surgeons can rapidly move from one patient to the next with minimal down time.

Between April 2008 and March 2009, in excess of 300,000 people underwent surgeries at one of the Aravind Eye Hospitals, and more than 2.7 million obtained care on an outpatient basis. More than half of the surgeries were under its free-care programs for the poor.

(© Picture Partners/Alamy)

Performance Objectives

1. Identify the investment required for business startup.
2. Describe the variable costs of starting a business.
3. Analyze your fixed operating costs and calculate gross profit.
4. Set up financial record keeping for your business.

What Does It Cost to Operate a Business?

To run a successful business, you will need to keep track of your costs and have more cash coming in than is going out. The bedrock principle of business is that it should earn a profit, by selling products or services for more than they cost.

Because everything sold has related costs, a business can make a profit only if the selling price per unit is greater than the cost per unit. A litmus test for profitability is the *economics of one unit* (EOU), discussed in prior chapters. It tells an entrepreneur if the business is earning a

Performance Objective 1 ▷

Identify the investment
required for business startup.

profit on each individual unit of sale. Knowing your EOU will be helpful as you determine your venture's viability.

Many costs are associated with the establishment and growth of a small business. These include start-up purchases, fixed and variable costs, and cash reserves. All are components of your accounting records, the documents that are used to classify, analyze, and interpret the financial transactions of an organization.

Start-Up Investment

Performance Objective 2 ▷

Describe the variable costs
of starting a business.

There is another critical cost to discuss before you can establish good accounting records for your business. We have talked about the costs of producing one unit and the costs of operating a business, but what about the money required to *start* the business? Start-up investment, or **seed capital,** is the one-time expense of opening a business. In the case of a restaurant, for example, start-up expenses would include stoves, food processors, tables, chairs, silverware, and other items that would not be replaced very often. Also included might be the one-time cost of buying land and constructing a building. Some entrepreneurs also choose to consider the amount of time they put into getting their businesses off the ground as part of the start-up investment. To do so, place a value on your time per hour and multiply by the number of hours you think you will be spending to get your business going. You might be shocked at how big that number is.

seed capital (start-up investment) the one-time expense of opening a business.

For a hot dog stand, the start-up investment list might look like this:

Hot dog cart	$2,500
Business licenses (city and state)	200
Business cards and flyers	150
Beginning inventory (hot dogs, mustard, buns, etc.)	50
Cash box and other	100
Total start-up investment without contingency	$3,000
Contingency: 10% of start-up investment	300
Total start-up investment with contingency	$3,300

For a more complex business, such as a 24-hour franchise fitness center being opened in an existing leased space, the summary start-up sheet might be as shown in **Exhibit 7-1**. The items would be broken down into greater detail in order to secure quotations. For example, each piece of equipment would be identified and a quote secured, assuming the franchisor does not have a specific package of equipment for purchase.

For a manufacturing business, developing a prototype for the item being manufactured could be a major start-up cost, perhaps totaling in the millions. A **prototype** is a model or pattern that serves as an example of how a product would look and operate if it were manufactured. Companies that specialize in creating prototypes can be found in the *Thomas Register of American Manufacturers.*

prototype a model or pattern that serves as an example of how a product would look and operate if it were produced.

Brainstorm to Avoid Start-Up Surprises

Before starting your business, try to anticipate every possible cost by thinking of all components of the investment. Talk to other business owners in your industry and ask them what start-up costs they failed to anticipate. Use **Exhibit 7-2** to estimate your start-up investment.

Exhibit 7-1 Seed Capital Estimate for a 24-Hour Fitness Center		
Item/Category	**Cost**	**Estimate or Quote**
Equipment, furniture, and fixtures	$105,000	Quote
Leasehold improvements	$3,200	Quote
Installation of equipment and fixtures	$2,800	Quote
Computers and other technology	$5,000	Quote
Employee wages, salaries, and benefits	$3,100	Estimate
Owner time (valued at $25 per hour)*	$5,000	Estimate
Professional services (attorney, accountant, architect, engineers, and the like)	$3,000	Estimate
Promotion and advertising	$1,800	Mixed
Licenses and permits	$300	Quote
Deposits on rent and utilities	$5,600	Quote
Rent on location identified	$2,000	Quote
Utilities	$400	Estimate
Insurance	$1,000	Quote
Debt service (interest on $130,000 at 10%)	$2,167	Estimate
Taxes (wage and other)	$500	Estimate
Memberships (trade associations, chamber of commerce, and the like)	$900	Mixed
Training, conventions, seminars	$1,000	Quote
Franchise fees	$40,000	Quote
Financing costs and fees (2% of $130,000)	$2,600	Estimate
Supplies	$400	Estimate
Inventory	$200	Estimate
Petty cash	$300	Quote
Total pre-opening investment	$186,267	
Allowance for contingencies/ emergencies (10%)	$18,626	
Initial Investment†	**$204,893**	

*If no wage or salary is being paid to the owners, this is a "soft" cost and can be considered an optional item on the list. However, including it makes the list more comprehensive and more reflective of the total cost.

†This figure does not include cash reserves, or cash requirements for cash shortfall during initial operations. Both should be added to reflect total financing needed.

Once you have brainstormed a list, take it to your advisors or mentors and have them look it over. They will probably find start-up costs you have overlooked. You might not have realized that the electric company would require a $1,000 deposit to turn on its service, for example. Or you may need licenses and insurance you did not expect. To cover contingencies and emergencies, tack on an additional 10 percent to your total estimate.

Exhibit 7-2 *Start-Up Investment Checklist*		
Item	**Cost**	**Assumptions**
Start-Up Expenses		
Certificates		
Certifications		
Expensed Equipment		
Financial Institution Fees		
Identity Set/Stationery		
Insurance		
Licenses		
Marketing Materials		
Payroll (with taxes)—pre-opening		
Payroll Owner (in-kind)*		
Permits		
Professional Fees—Accounting		
Professional Fees—Legal		
Professional Fees—Other		
Rent		
Research and Development		
Supplies—Office		
Travel		
Utilities		
Web Fees		
Other		
Total Start-Up Expenses		
Start-Up Assets		
Cash on Hand		
Building (if purchased)		
Equipment (including installation)		
Furniture and Fixtures		
Inventory—Raw Materials		
Inventory—Semi-Finished Goods		
Inventory—Finished Goods		
Land (if purchased)		
Leasehold Improvements		
Machinery		

Exhibit 7-2 *Start-up Investment Checklist*

Item	Cost	Assumptions
Rent Deposit		
Signage		
Utility Deposits		
Vehicle(s)		
Other 1		
Other 2		
Total Start-Up Assets		
Total Start-Up Requirements		
Contingency Funds (10%)		
Start-Up with Contingency†		

*If no wage or salary is paid to the owners, this is a "soft" cost and can be considered an optional item on the list. However, including it is more comprehensive and more reflective of total costs.
†This figure does not include cash reserves or cash requirements for initial cash shortfall during operations. Both should be added to reflect total financing needed.

Research the Costs

In addition to brainstorming and consulting with your advisors, you can do some research to accurately assess your start-up costs. Look at business plan models in your industry, if possible. Adapt the cost data to fit your business and obtain quotations on pricing from potential suppliers. Look at available industry data. Do not be caught by surprise on costs that you could have predicted.

Keep a Reserve Equal to One-Half of Start-Up Investment

Start-up investment should include one more thing: a **cash reserve,** an emergency fund of cash resources that equal at least half your start-up costs. For the previously mentioned hot dog cart example, therefore, the reserve would be half of $3,300, or $1,650, raising to $4,950 the total start-up sum required.

cash reserve emergency funds and a pool of cash resources.

Entrepreneurs must be prepared for the unexpected; the only good surprise is no surprise. The reserve will provide a moderate cushion of protection when you need it. If your computer goes down or your biggest supplier raises prices, you will be glad you had this money on hand.

Having a cash reserve will also allow you to take advantage of opportunities. Say you own a vintage clothing store and you hear from a friend whose great-aunt died and left him a great deal of authentic vintage clothing and jewelry. He is willing to sell you the whole lot for $500, which you figure you can resell in your shop for at least $2,000. If you did not have the extra cash on hand, you would have lost this profitable opportunity.

Predict the Payback Period

When compiling and analyzing start-up costs, one consideration will be how long it will take for you to earn back your start-up investment. The **payback period** is an estimate, for you and your investors, of how long it will take your business to bring in enough cash to cover the start-up investment. It is measured in months.

$$\text{Payback} = \frac{\text{Start–Up Investment}}{\text{Net Cash Flow per Month}}$$

Example

Ashley's business requires a start-up investment of $1,000. The business is projecting a net cash flow per month of $400. How many months will it take to make back the start-up investment?

$$\text{Payback} = \frac{\$1000}{\$400} = 2.5 \text{ Months}$$

Knowing the payback period is important for a start-up (or an existing firm), so that the time horizon is known and timing of funds availability is clear. However, the payback period does not take into consideration future earnings, opportunities for alternative investments, or the overall value of the company. It is based upon net cash and is a good indicator of the time needed to earn back initial funding.

Estimate Value

Financial managers use several tools to determine the current value of proposed investments, of which net present value (NPV) is widely accepted as the most theoretically sound. Entrepreneurs can use such a technique to consider the financial returns on their initial investment. If the NPV calculation yields a positive value, the investment will result in a positive return based upon the owner's (and investors') required rate of return.

There are multiple methods of calculating NPV, including using a formula, tables, a spreadsheet program, or a financial calculator. You can calculate NPV with the following information: required rate of return (%), annual net cash flows (see Chapter 14), initial investment, and number of years of cash flows. **Exhibit 7-3** shows an NPV calculation for a business with an initial investment of $1.5 million.

Variable and Fixed Costs: Essential Building Blocks

Small business owners divide their costs into two categories. **Variable costs** change based on the volume of units sold or produced. **Fixed costs** are expenses that must be paid regardless of whether or not sales are being generated.

Variable costs change with production and sales. They fall into two subcategories:

1. *Cost of goods sold (COGS) or cost of services sold (COSS).* Each is associated specifically with a single unit of sale, including:
   - The cost of materials used to make the product (or deliver the service).
   - The cost of labor used to make the product (or deliver the service).

Exhibit 7-3 *Calculating Net Present Value with Excel*

Description	Data	Notes
Initial investment	$1,500,000	Seed capital needed to start the business
Required rate of return	0.12	Return required by investors (owners)
Net Cash Year 1	$0	First year of operations, yielding no net cash
Net Cash Year 2	$100,000	Second year of operations with earnings
Net Cash Year 3	$200,000	Subsequent year
Net Cash Year 4	$500,000	Subsequent year
Net Cash Year 5	$850,000	Subsequent year
Net Cash Year 6	$1,200,000	Subsequent year
Net Cash Year 7	$600,000	Results show declining market
Net Cash Year 8	$400,000	Further decline
Net Cash Year 9	$0	Company closed
Calculated Present Value	$2,063,067	Use NPV formula
Net Present Value	**$563,067**	**Value above initial investment**
NPV > $0?	Yes	NPV is positive, so it is a go

2. ***Other variable costs.*** These include:
   - Commissions or other compensation based on sales volume.
   - Shipping and handling charges.

Fixed costs stay constant whether you sell many units or very few. Examples of fixed costs include rent, salaries, insurance, equipment, and manufacturing facilities.

Henry Ford spent money on efficient manufacturing equipment (a fixed cost) but saved a fortune on labor (**COGS**) by doing so. This reduced his total costs because labor was used in each of the millions of cars Ford produced, but he only had to pay for the plant and equipment once.

For any product, you can study its economics of one unit to figure out what it cost to make that sale. **Exhibit 7-4** shows an example from a business that sells hand-painted T-shirts.

Calculating Critical Costs

To determine the most important factors with respect to costs in your business, you can calculate *critical* costs. This will help you to determine profitability and the factors that can and cannot be easily changed to impact your profits and cash flow.

> **Performance Objective 3**
> Analyze your fixed operating costs and calculate gross profit.

Calculating Total Gross Profit (Contribution Margin)

You can use EOU to calculate whether and by how much you will come out ahead on your per-unit costs for each sale. By using the EOU, you can figure the gross profit per unit (**contribution margin** per unit sold, which is the selling price minus total variable costs plus other variable costs).

> **contribution margin** gross profit per unit—the selling price minus total variable costs plus other variable costs.

Exhibit 7-4 *Manufacturing Business*

Economics of One Unit (EOU) Analysis				
Unit = 1 Hand-Painted T-Shirt				
Selling Price (per Unit)				$35.00
COGS (Cost of Goods Sold)				
Materials per Unit		$7.00		
Labor per hour	$10.00			
# of Hours per Unit	0.75			
Total Labor per Unit	7.50	7.50		
Total COGS (per Unit)		$14.50	$14.50	14.50
Gross Profit (per Unit)				$20.50
Other Variable Costs				
Commission (10% of selling price)		3.50		
Packaging		0.50		
Total Other Variable Costs		$4.00	4.00	4.00
Total Variable Costs (per Unit)			$18.50	
Contribution Margin				$16.50

Calculating EOU When You Sell Multiple Products

Most businesses sell more than a single product and they can also use EOU as a value measure of product profitability. A business selling a variety of products has to create a separate EOU for each item to determine whether each is profitable. When there are many similar products with comparable prices and cost structures, a "typical" EOU can be used.

Example

Jamaal sells four kinds of candy bars at school. He sells each bar for $1, but he pays a different wholesale price for each:

Snickers	$0.36 each
Almond Joy	$0.38 each
Butterfinger	$0.42 each
Baby Ruth	$0.44 each

Rather than make separate EOUs, Jamaal uses the average cost of his four candy bars (see **Exhibit 7-5**).

Exhibit 7-5 *Retail Business*

Economics of One Unit (EOU) Analysis		
Unit = 1 Candy Bar		
Selling Price		$1.00
COGS (direct cost of the product or service)		
Average Cost of Candy Bars (COGS)	$0.40	
Average Shipping Cost per Unit	0.06	
Total COGS	$0.46	0.46
Gross Profit		$0.54
Other Variable Costs (none)	—	—
Contribution Margin		$0.54

Costs of the four candy bars = ($0.36 + $0.38 + $0.42 + $0.44) ÷ 4

Average cost of the four candy bars = $1.60 ÷ 4

Average cost of each bar = $0.40

Using an average works if the costs are close, and as long as Jamaal sells roughly the same number of each brand of bar. If he can no longer get Snickers and Almond Joy at some point, for example, he should then change his EOU to reflect the higher price of the other two bars.

What if each unit of sale is made up of a complex mix of materials and labor? The EOU can still help you figure the COGS, other variable costs, and gross profit for the product, although the process will be more complex.

Many small businesses have inventory costs.
(Jose Luis Pelaez Inc/Blend Images/Alamy)

inventory costs expenses associated with materials and direct labor for production until the product is sold.

Example

Denise sells sandwiches from her deli cart downtown on Saturdays. She sells each for $5. The materials and labor that go directly into making each sandwich are the COGS. The costs of the materials and direct labor for production are called **inventory costs** until the product is sold. There will also be some other variable costs, such as napkins, a paper wrapping for each sandwich, and plastic bags.

First, make a list of the COGS and any other variable costs. The variable costs will include the supplies that are used every time a sandwich is sold, but are not strictly part of the sandwich's production.

COGS

- Turkey costs $2.60 per pound. Each sandwich uses 4 ounces of turkey meat (1/4 of a pound).
- Large rolls cost $1.92 per dozen. One roll is used per sandwich.
- A 32-ounce jar of mayonnaise costs $1.60. One ounce of mayonnaise is used per sandwich.
- Lettuce costs 80 cents per pound. One ounce (1/16 of a pound) is used on each sandwich.
- Tomatoes cost $1.16 each. Each sandwich uses one-fourth of a tomato.
- Pickles cost 5 cents each. Each sandwich comes with two pickles.
- Employees are paid $7 per hour and each can make 10 sandwiches per hour (we are assuming no down time and no payroll expenses).

Other Variable Costs

- Napkins cost $3 per pack of 100. One napkin is included with each sale.
- Paper wrapping costs 20 cents per foot (on a roll). Each sandwich uses two feet of paper.
- Plastic carryout bags cost $7 per roll of 100. Each sandwich sold uses one plastic carryout bag. (In practice, more than one sandwich might go into a bag.)

The EOU for the turkey sandwich is shown in **Exhibit 7-6**.

Exhibit 7-6 *Retail Business*

Economics of One Unit Analysis					
Unit = 1 Turkey Sandwich					
Selling Price per Unit:					**$5.00**
Cost of Goods Sold	**Price**	**Units**	**Quantity Used**	**Cost Each**	
Turkey (4 oz.):	$2.60	Per lb.	¼ lb.	$0.65	
Bread (roll):	$1.92	Per dozen	½ dozen	$0.16	
Mayonnaise (1 oz.):	$1.60	Per 32-oz. jar	½ jar	$0.05	
Lettuce (1 oz.):	$0.80	Per lb.	⅙ lb.	$0.05	
Tomato	$1.16	Each	¼ each	$0.29	
Pickles (2):	$0.05	Each	2 each	$0.10	
Direct Labor (6 min.):	$7.00	Per hr.	⅒ hr.	$0.70	
Total Cost of Goods Sold per Unit:				**$2.00**	**2.00**
Gross Profit					**$3.00**
Other Variable Costs					
Napkin:	$3.00	Per 100-pack	⅟₁₀₀ pack	$0.03	
Paper Wrapping:	$0.20	Per foot	2 feet	$0.40	
Plastic Bag:	$7.00	Per roll (100)	⅟₁₀₀ roll	$0.07	
Total Other Variable Costs per Unit:				**$0.50**	
Total Variable Costs per Unit:					**0.50**
Contribution Margin per Unit:					**$2.50**

Fixed Operating Costs

fixed operating costs
expenses that do not vary with changes in the volume of production or sales.

Costs, such as rent or the Internet bill, which do not vary per unit of production or service, are called **fixed operating costs.** Fixed operating costs are not included in COGS (or COSS) because they are not directly related to the creation of the product (or service).[1] Fixed operating costs are not included in other variable costs because they do not vary directly with the number of sales made.

Fixed operating costs do not change based on sales; therefore, they are not included in the EOU. A sandwich shop has to pay the same rent each month whether it sells one turkey sandwich or a hundred. However, the owner of the shop can change the cost of the rent by moving, or can increase or decrease the advertising budget—and the like. These changes are not calculated on a per-unit basis.

An easy way to remember the seven common fixed operating costs is with the acronym USAIIRD:

Utilities (gas, electric, telephone, Internet service)
Salaries (indirect labor)
Advertising
Insurance
Interest
Rent
Depreciation

depreciation the percentage of value of an asset subtracted periodically to reflect the declining value.

Most of these categories are self-explanatory, but *depreciation* may need clarification. **Depreciation** is the percentage of value of an asset

---

[1]Cost of goods sold is used for businesses that sell products. Service businesses use the term cost of services sold.

subtracted each year until the value becomes zero, to reflect wear and tear on the asset. It is a method used to *expense* (listed as an expense on the income statement) costly pieces of equipment. Fixed costs are expensed during the year the money is spent. When a company pays for advertising, it subtracts that cost from the gross profit for that year. Some items, however, such as a computer, are expected to last for a number of years. A business could choose to expense a computer during the year it was bought, but that would not be accurate. A computer that will be used for four years will have been only 25 percent "used up" during the year it was purchased. Expensing the entire cost of the computer during that year would make the accounting records and financial statements inaccurate. If more than 25 percent of the computer's cost is expensed in the first year, the income statement will show a lower profit than it should. Meanwhile, profits in subsequent years will appear to be higher than they should.

This problem is addressed by depreciation, which spreads the cost of an item purchased by a business over the period of time during which it will actually be in use. If the computer will not be replaced for four years, then the full price should be shown as an asset, and then expensed 25 percent each year for four years. In this way, the cost of the computer and its value to the company will be reflected more accurately.

Fixed Operating Costs Do Change over Time

If you pay your restaurant manager $3,600 per month in salary, you will have to pay that amount whether the restaurant sells one meal or a thousand. The cost is fixed.

Fixed operating costs do change over time; at some point you may give your restaurant manager a raise. Or, you might hire a new manager at a lower salary. The word *fixed* does not mean the cost *never* changes, just that it does not change in response to units of production or sales. For instance:

- Advertising. The cost of advertising will change based on decisions the entrepreneur makes about how much to spend to reach the consumer, not because of current sales (although low sales may provoke an increase in advertising).
- Heating and cooling costs. The price of heating or cooling goes up or down based on the weather and utility prices, not on the amount of revenue the business earns.

Global Impact . . .

Direct Foreign Investment

Global companies experience opportunities and challenges when determining initial investments in foreign countries. Opportunities arise from such sources as incentives for direct foreign investment (DFI) and lower facilities construction or fit-out costs. In addition, start-up inventory costs may be lower. At the same time, there could be barriers to DFI, such as legal and permit costs, standards, and other requirements that would increase initial investment. Clearly, having a full understanding of the initial start-up investment is crucial and is potentially more complex.

Monetary exchange rates and the economic and political environment in a foreign country will have a significant impact on start-up investment. As is true with domestic start-ups, the estimate of the initial investment is a vital consideration in the investment decision.

Allocate Fixed Operating Costs Where Possible

Business owners like to know, whenever they make a sale, how much of that revenue will have to be used to cover the cost of goods sold and other variable costs.

Whatever is left over after you pay the COGS and other variable costs is your *contribution margin* (gross profit). You will pay your fixed operating costs from the contribution margin. Whatever is left over after you pay your fixed operating costs (and taxes) is your **net profit.**

net profit the remainder of revenues minus fixed and variable costs and taxes.

Fixed operating costs can be dangerous because they have to be paid whether or not the business *has* a gross profit. The entrepreneur should be careful about taking on fixed costs, but does not have to worry so much about variable ones because, if sales are low, variable costs will be low as well. Wherever possible, the entrepreneur should seek to allocate (distribute) as many costs as possible into the variable category.

Here is an example of how to fully allocate your costs, so that you will know, each time you sell a unit, how much of your fixed and variable costs the sale is covering:

Example

If you sell 300 watches per month at $15 per watch (see **Exhibit 7-7**), your COGS is $2 per watch and your other variable costs are commissions of $2 per watch and shipping charges of $1 per watch.

Gross profit per unit is $13 ($3,900 in gross profit divided by 300 watches sold). Contribution margin per unit is $10 ($3,000 ÷ 300). Some of this gross profit will have to be used to cover the business's fixed operating costs. It is helpful to determine how much profit will be left over after paying the fixed operating costs, assuming your sales are stable. (**Exhibit 7-8** shows the calculation of the total cost per unit.)

For every watch you sell, your total cost, fixed and variable, is $6.50. If you receive $15 for each watch, therefore, your profit before taxes is:

$15.00 Selling Price – $6.50 Total Cost per Unit = $8.50 Profit before Taxes

The Dangers of Fixed Costs

If a business does not have enough sales to cover its fixed costs, it will lose money. If losses continue, the business will have to close. As we have discussed, fixed costs are dangerous because they must be paid whether or not the business is making enough sales to cover them. Variable costs, on the other hand, do not threaten a business's survival because they are proportional to sales.

Exhibit 7-7 *Retail Business: Unit = 1 Watch*

Analysis—300 Watches Sold			
Sales (300 watches × $15 per watch):			$4,500
COGS ($2 per watch × 300 watches):		$600	600
Gross Profit (on 300 watches sold)			$3,900
Other Variable Costs			
Commission ($2 per watch)	$600		
Shipping ($1 per watch)	300		
Total Other Variable Costs	$900	900	900
Total Variable Costs (per Unit)		$1,500	
Contribution Margin			$3,000

Exhibit 7-8 *Retail Business: Total Cost per Unit*

Total Variable Costs (COGS + Other Variable Costs):		$1,500
Fixed Operating Costs (per month):		
Utilities	$50	
Salaries	100	
Advertising	50	
Insurance	50	
Interest	50	
Rent	50	
Depreciation	100	
Total Fixed Operating Costs:	$450	450
Total Costs (Fixed + Variable) =		$1,950
Total Cost per Unit ($1,950 ÷ 300 watches) =		$6.50 per watch

How Inflation Can Hurt Small Business Owners

Inflation is the gradual, continuous increase in the prices of products and services, usually resulting from a rise in the amount of money in circulation in an economy. It can be the enemy of the small business owner. If you save $600 per year to buy new tables and chairs (which cost $3,000 the last time you bought them) for your restaurant, but find at the end of five years that the cost of replacing them has risen to $5,000 because of inflation, your business could be in trouble if you cannot get the additional $2,000. Savvy entrepreneurs keep up with economic trends by reading the financial section in the newspapers, as well as financial magazines and Web sites. By staying up to date on what is happening, you can invest wisely and plan effectively for the future.

inflation the gradual, continuous increase in the prices of products and services.

Step into the Shoes . . .

Bob's Discount Furniture[2]

As of November 2011, Bob's Discount Furniture own 43 furniture stores in the Northeast and mid-Atlantic area.[3] Bob's Discount Furniture, the 2008 Furniture Retailer of the Year, is one of the largest TV advertisers in Connecticut. When Bob was starting out in the furniture business in 1982, though, he needed to find creative ways to minimize his costs.

Bob found a store to rent for his furniture business, but the landlord wanted him to sign a one-year lease. Bob knew that rent was a fixed cost. This meant he would have to pay rent every month, whether he could afford to or not, for a full 12 months. He realized that if sales were low he would get into trouble quickly because he would not have cash in reserve.

What Bob needed was to change his rent from a fixed to a variable cost. He negotiated with the landlord to pay the rent as a percentage of the monthly sales. That way, if sales were low, Bob's rent would also be low. If sales were high, his rent would be more, but he would be able to pay it. Rent was Bob's largest fixed cost. By changing it to a variable, he cut out a lot of risk from his new business venture.

Bob's Discount Furniture became extremely successful. That rental arrangement helped Bob out when his business was small. Today, the company owns many of its locations and pays fixed rent on the rest.

Bob Kaufman of Bob's Discount Furniture.
(Bob Kaufman)

[2]Thanks to John Harris for the original case.
[3]Bob's Discount Furniture Web site, http://www.mybobs.com, March 20, 2011.

Using Accounting Records to Track Fixed and Variable Costs

Now you are ready to set up your financial records. Nothing that you learn as an entrepreneur will be more important than keeping accurate records f the money flowing in and out of your business. The systematic record- g, reporting, and analysis of the financial transactions of a business ≥eping statistical records of inflows and outflows) is called *accounting*. It is the primary language businesspeople use to communicate. When you talk to an investor or a supplier about your business, you will need to use accounting terms. He or she will want to see the financial statements for your business that describe its performance at a glance.

Before you can create financial statements, however, you must be able to keep track of your daily business transactions. If you develop record keeping into a habit, you will be well ahead of the many businesspeople that tend to get careless when it comes to keeping good records consistently.

Three Reasons to Keep Good Records Every Day

1. ***Keeping good records will show you how to make your business more profitable.*** Perhaps your profits are down this month over last. Did your expenses go up? Maybe you need to try lowering your costs. Did your sales drop? Maybe you are not spending enough on advertising. Use accurate records as a base to constantly improve your business.

2. ***Keeping good records will document your business profitability and cash position.*** If you want people to invest in your business, show them that it is profitable. Keep accurate records to create financial statements and ratios that prove your business is doing well. Remember, you will *always* need to maintain your business's financial statements so that you will be up to date on your company's performance.

3. ***Keeping good records proves that payments have been made.*** Accurate, up-to-date records help prevent arguments because they prove you have paid a bill or that a customer has paid you. Records can also prove that you have paid your taxes—the fee charged (*levied*) by a government on an income, product, or activity that is imposed on an individual or legal entity (corporation). Sometimes the Internal Revenue Service, the federal agency that collects taxes, will visit a business and check its financial records in a process called an **audit**. If you keep good records and pay your taxes in a timely fashion, you will have nothing to fear from audits.

audit a review of financial and business records to ascertain integrity and compliance with standards and laws, particularly by the U.S. Internal Revenue Service.

Suggestions for Keeping Good Records

U.S. tax law allows business owners to deduct many expenses from their taxes. These deductions, or write-offs, are reductions in the gross amount on which taxes are calculated, and they will save you money. But you must keep receipts and record check payments to show that you actually had the expenses. A good practice is to write the purpose of an expense on the receipt.

Accounting Software

There are many excellent computer software programs on the market to help the small business owner keep good records and generate financial statements and analytical reports. These include Intuit QuickBooks, Microsoft Office Accounting, and Peachtree Accounting. In addition, companies such as Net Suite offer Web-based accounting for a monthly access fee. There are also programs to help you manage your money. You can use them to write checks, balance your bank account, and track your income. Some software creates project quotes and invoices. There is specialized software for particular types of businesses and for nonprofit organizations. It may save you time and money to purchase industry-specific software from the start. The URLs for some of the accounting software companies are:

> Microsoft, http://www.microsoft.com
> QuickBooks, http://www.quickbooks.com
> Peachtree Software, http://www.peachtree.com

Many software companies offer free products that you can try for a limited period of time, or that are free but do not have as many features as the versions for sale. This is a great way for you to try out different accounting and other business software before you buy. The costs of these packages have dropped considerably over time, making them a better value for even the smallest companies. For example, if your business provides services, and potential customers expect estimates, they can be generated and tracked by professional-services software. Take the time to find the software best suited to your needs.

Receipts and Invoices

For a very small business, it is possible to work with a manual system, including a journal and files for storing records of your transactions. As your business grows, you can add organizational tools. However, if you are intending to grow the business beyond a handful of transactions per week, you should use a good computer-based system from the start. Whatever system you elect to use, there are certain records that should be kept.

- A *receipt* is a slip of paper with the date and amount of the purchase on it. *Always get a receipt for every purchase you make.* Issue a receipt for all sales if you have a retail business, whether you create it manually or from your point-of-sales system.

- An *invoice*, or bill or statement, shows the product or service sold and the amount the customer is to pay. Your invoice becomes the customer's receipt. Keep a copy of each invoice in an organized fashion (i.e., numerically, alphabetically, or in order by date), and record all payments promptly.

Keep at Least Two Copies of Your Records

Always keep a copy of your financial records in a location away from your business, preferably in a fire-retardant safe or concrete-lined file cabinet. If you are using software, back up your data and keep the media (CD, jump

Entrepreneurial Wisdom . . .
Rockefeller's Record Keeping

John D. Rockefeller, who founded Standard Oil (now ExxonMobil) and built one of the most famous family fortunes in history, reportedly kept track of every penny he spent from age 16 until his death in 1937 at the age of 98. His children said that he never paid a bill without examining it and being certain that he understood it.

Being up to date with your financial records will give you control over your business and a sense of security.

John D. Rockefeller.
(Hulton Archive/Getty Images)

drive, etc.) in a different location. At the end of each day, week, or month, move your new receipts and invoices to this location. How often you do this will depend upon your transaction volume and how much data you are willing to risk losing. By having regular off-site backups, if anything happens to your journal or your business site, you will still have your financial records. Follow federal records-retention rules with these documents.

Use Business Checks for Business Expenses

Get a checking account to use only for your business. It is inadvisable to commingle your personal and business funds, regardless of your business type. Financial institutions routinely require business checks to be deposited into business accounts rather than personal ones, so any customer check payments made out to your business name will have to be deposited into a business account.

- *Avoid using cash for business.* If you must pay in cash, get an itemized receipt, record the expenditure, and file the receipt promptly. It is easy to lose track of cash receipts and miss out on tax deductions for business expenses.
- *Deposit money from sales right away.* When you make a sale, the transaction will not be complete until the cash is deposited or the check has cleared. Again, recording every sale is critical to documenting profitability and cash flow. It will also ensure that business receipts and sales match in transaction records.

Cash versus Accrual Accounting Methods

Financial accounting for business is divided between the *cash* and *accrual* methods, and each company selects which one it will use. Small businesses use either procedure, whereas large firms almost invariably use accrual accounting. It is best to seek professional advice on this issue when starting your business. With the **cash accounting method,** the only time an accounting entry is made is when cash is paid out or received. With the **accrual method,** entries are made according to the occurrence of the transactions, without regard to the date of payment (e.g., for a manufacturer, purchases would be billed when the product is shipped).

> **cash accounting method** the procedure wherein transactions are recorded as cash as paid out or received.

> **accrual method** accounting process wherein transactions are recorded at the time of occurrence, regardless of the transfer of cash.

Recognizing Categories of Costs

Even if you are using accounting software to record your business transactions, it will be helpful to understand the key categories of accounting data. These are briefly described below. A more detailed list appears in the Appendices, and will be particularly useful if you elect to use a manual record-keeping system.

- *Variable costs (VC).* Any cost that changes based on the number of units sold. Includes cost of goods sold (COGS). Multiply COGS by the number of units sold to get total COGS.
- *Fixed costs (FC).* Business expenses that must be paid whether or not sales are made. Remember USAIIRD: utilities, salaries, advertising, insurance, interest, rent, and depreciation.
- *Capital equipment.* Money spent on business equipment that is expected to last a year or more.
- *Investment.* Start-up capital plus any money you or others have invested in the business, but not loans. This is only for money invested in exchange for part ownership (equity).

- *Loans.* Any funds you have borrowed to start or operate the business.
- *Revenue.* Money received from sales.
- *Inventory.* Anything purchased for resale is *inventory*. Includes shipping costs from the supplier.
- *Other costs.* Anything that does not fit into the other expense categories.

Chapter Summary

Now that you have studied this chapter, you can do the following:

1. Identify the investment required for a business start-up.
   - Brainstorming, consulting advisors, and research can be combined to create a comprehensive set of investment requirements.
   - Contingency funds and cash reserves should be added to minimize the impact of unanticipated costs, and to permit flexibility to take advantage of opportunities.
   - Payback period is the estimation of time required to bring in enough cash to cover the seed funding.
   - Net present value shows the viability of an investment opportunity that considers investment-return criteria.
2. Describe the variable costs of starting a business.
   - Start-up investment is the one-time expense of starting a business.
   - Cost of goods sold is the direct cost of producing the product or service.
   - Operating costs comprise the funds necessary to run the business, not including the cost of goods sold. Operating costs can almost always be divided into seven categories. An easy way to remember these is through the acronym USAIIRD:
     - Utilities (gas, electric, telephone, Internet)
     - Salaries
     - Advertising
     - Insurance
     - Interest
     - Rent
     - Depreciation
3. Divide your costs into two categories: variable and fixed.
   - Variable costs change (*vary*) with sales. They are divided into two subcategories:
     a. Cost of goods sold, which are the costs associated specifically with each unit of sale, including the cost of materials used to make the product (or deliver the service), and the cost of labor used to make the product (or deliver the service).
     b. Other variable costs, including commissions, shipping and handling charges, and so forth.
   - Fixed costs stay constant whether you sell many units or very few. Examples of fixed costs include rent, salaries, and insurance.
   - Set up a financial record-keeping system for your business.
   - Recognize the importance of keeping complete, accurate, and timely records.
   - Determine whether to use the cash or accrual accounting method.
   - Categorize the accounting entries properly, whether using a manual or computer-based system.

Key Terms

accrual method	inflation
audit	inventory costs
cash accounting method	net profit
cash reserve	payback period
contribution margin	prototype
depreciation	seed capital
fixed costs	variable costs
fixed operating costs	

Entrepreneurship Portfolio

Critical Thinking Exercises

1. Give an example of a business that you have observed lowering the price of a product. How do you think the business was able to reduce the price?
2. Describe the record-keeping system you intend to set up for your business.
3. What bank accounts do you intend to open for your business? Which bank will you use? Why?
4. Imagine that you have invented a guitar strap that goes over both shoulders, thereby reducing shoulder strain for the guitarist. This item could be a big seller, but, before you can apply for a patent or convince investors to back your producing it, you will need a prototype. Find at least three manufacturers that could create such a prototype for you.
5. For a business you would like to start, estimate what you think the fixed and variable costs would be. Choose a category for each cost from **USAIIRD**: utilities, salaries, advertising, insurance, interest, rent, and depreciation.

Key Concept Questions

1. What is the reason to calculate the payback period and the net present value for a business investment? What distinguishes the two?
2. Calculate total revenue for the items below.

Units Sold	Selling Price	Total Revenue
a. 25	$4.64	$116.00
b. 30	$10.99	
c. 12	$1,233.00	
d. 75	$545.75	
e. 20	$45.03	

3. Calculate Total Variable Costs for the same items.

Units Sold	Total Variable Costs per Unit	Total Variable Costs
a. 25	$2.00	$50.00
b. 30	$5.50	
c. 12	$620.00	

Units Sold	Total Variable Costs per Unit	Total Variable Costs
d. 75	$280.00	
e. 20	$20.00	

4. Calculate Total Contribution Margin for the same items.

Total Revenue	Total Variable Costs	Total Contribution Margin
a. $116.00	$50.00	$66.00
b.		
c.		
d.		
e.		

5. Calculate total profit for the same items.

Total Contribution Margin	Total Fixed Operating Costs	Total Profit
a. $66.00	$25.00	$41.00
b.	$60.00	
c.	$425.00	
d.	$12,000.00	
e.	$200.00	

6. Calculate profit per unit for the same items.

Units Sold	Total Profit	Profit per Unit
a. 25	$41.00	$1.64
b. 30		
c. 12		
d. 75		
e. 20		

7. The business concepts below have been developed by your colleagues and they have asked you to provide feedback on each as a potential investment. Using the data provided, calculate the payback period and NPV of each. Remember that you may use Excel for this problem.

Project	Seed Capital	Rate of Return	Net Cash Flow Year 1	Net Cash Flow Year 2	Net Cash Flow Year 3	Net Cash Flow Year 4	Net Cash Flow Year 5	Other Net Cash Flow	Payback Period	NPV
A	$1,000	5%	$200	$300	$400	$500	$0	$0		
B	$250,000	8%	$2,000	$25,000	$25,000	$1,000,000	$148,000	$200,000 per year for 5 years		
C	$8,000,000	17%	$0	$0	$0	$1,000,000	$5,000,000	$6,000,000 for 3 years		

Project	Seed Capital	Rate of Return	Net Cash Flow Year 1	Net Cash Flow Year 2	Net Cash Flow Year 3	Net Cash Flow Year 4	Net Cash Flow Year 5	Other Net Cash Flow	Payback Period	NPV
D	$50,000	25%	$0	$1,000	$29,000	$35,0000	$70,000	$0		
E	$120,000,000	6%	$0	$0	$20,000,0000	$80,000,000	$40,000,000	$20 million in Year 6, $5 million in Year 7		

Application Exercise

Last month, Sue, of Sue's Sandwiches, sold $3,000 worth of product (sandwiches and sodas) from her sidewalk cart to 300 customers. She spent $600 on the sandwich ingredients and buying the sodas wholesale. Her monthly costs are the following: Utilities = $60, Salary = $1,500, Advertising = $0, Insurance = $50, Interest = $0, Rent (for the cart) = $300, Depreciation = $0.

   a. What are Sue's variable costs? Explain.

   b. What is Sue's COGS? Explain.

   c. What are her other variable costs? Explain.

   d. What are her fixed costs? Explain.

   e. What is Sue's EOU?

   f. How much cash reserve should she keep in the bank?

Exploring Your Community

Ask an entrepreneur in your neighborhood to discuss his or her accounting system. Write a one-page essay about the pros and cons of the system and use it to make an oral report to the class.

Exploring Online

Research different accounting software programs online. Choose a program (or programs) for your business and explain your choice(s) in a brief essay.

In Your Opinion

Would you rather keep your financial records in an accounting ledger or on your computer? Why? In each case, how would you protect your records from being lost in a disaster, such as a fire, or, in the case of the computer, a hard-drive crash?

BizBuilder Business Plan Questions

7.0 Financial Analysis and Projections

   A. Describe your record-keeping system.

   B. List the types of bank accounts you will open for your organization.

7.1 Sources and Uses of Capital

   A. How much capital do you need? When? What type and on what terms?

   B. How will you use the money that you raise? Be specific.

   C. List the items you will need to buy to start your business and add up their respective costs to get your total needed start-up capital. Then, add a cash reserve of one-half this total.

Case Study | A Cool Business— MooBella, Inc.

Freshly made hard-packed ice cream from a vending-machine-sized dispenser—dream or reality? For thousands of customers in New England, this is a reality. MooBella, Inc., founded as Turbo Dynamix in 1992 and based in Taunton, Massachusetts, introduced these innovative machines on a trial basis in 2006, and commercially to universities and medical facilities in 2010.

MooBella's founder and CEO, Bruce Ginsberg, literally grew up in the ice cream business. He took over International Ice Cream from his ailing father in 1985 and revived it from operating at $1 million in the red on $8.5 million in revenues to earning $50 million in revenues in 1993. Ginsberg recognized that ice cream can be up to one year old by the time of consumer purchase and that the crystals that develop detract from the taste and texture. He became fascinated by an ice cream-dispensing machine which he saw in 1999 that was being developed by Turbo Dynamix. He wanted to create made-to-order hard-pack ice cream that would have an excellent flavor and texture because of its freshness. Turbo Dynamix became MooBella, Inc., and Ginsberg continued his quest.

This seemingly simple concept is technically complex and took 18 years and nearly $85 million to bring to market. The research and development and start-up processes were riddled with challenges. One observer notes, "For all their promise, MooBella's early machines were hideously complex and cost roughly $1 million to make."[4] Ultimately, the MooBella team ended up working with Project Genesis at MIT to bring the dream to reality. The machines include "... seven modular mechanical units, including pneumatics, base refrigeration, flavor, primary refrigeration, foodzone, and mixing modules. A Linux-based computer operates each module through a distributed control system based on a CANopen bus."[5] It took five years to complete the computer portion of the project, and improvements are an ongoing process. Today, it is possible to select any of 96 available flavor combinations for a fresh-made ice cream cup priced at about $3 per 4.5 ounce serving, and have it ready in about 40 seconds. Customers choose from any combination of 2 base mixes, 3 mix-ins (dry ingredients), and 12 flavor mixes. The production process is as follows: "A quantity of base mix is precisely measured and pumped,

(Aaron Amat/Shutterstock)

aerated, flavored, and sprayed onto a flat rotating surface, where it is flash frozen. The product is then scraped up by a tiny snowplow, formed into a cylinder and dispensed into a paper cup."[6] The specially formulated ingredients require no refrigeration until opened, making them more convenient to store.

In addition to the research and development costs required to create viable technology, MooBella has encountered significant marketing expenditures to create the brand and to gain trial and acceptance opportunities. At approximately $40,000 per machine (or $400 per month on a lease), the investment is considerably higher than traditional vending machines and is targeted differently. MooBella's Web site stated a goal of placing 1,000 machines by the end of 2011.

The start-up investment for MooBella has reached nearly $85 million in investment capital since 2000. Investments were critical to keeping the company afloat while Ginsberg and his team pursued the opportunity. Some of the start-up funding included:

- Saturn Asset Management—$25 million in equity (2000–2005)
- Inventages (Swiss venture firm)—$15 million in 2007 and $18 million in 2009
- Bruce Ginsberg—$1 million[7]
- W Health LP—$9 million (November 2010)
- Debt—$17.5 million in high-interest loans and convertible notes

[4]Maureen Farrell, "Big Scoop," *Forbes*, November 22, 2010, p. 122.
[5]"Device Profile: MooBella on-demand ice cream maker," LinuxDevices.com, February 8, 2006, http://www.linuxfordevices.com/c/a/Linux-for-Devices-Articles/, January 23, 2011.
[6]Ibid.
[7]Maureen Farrell, "Big Scoop."

Bruce Ginsberg owns almost 5 percent of the company after all the outside investments. Inventages controls the majority of MooBella.

MooBella has demonstrated that it has developed a technology that works. Will the investment pay off?

Case Analysis

1. What categories of costs would you expect to see in a list of MooBella start-up costs?
2. It took nearly 20 years from idea to market for MooBella. Clearly, it had a long development and start-up period. Reflect on the emotional and other nonmonetary factors that were likely involved for Bruce Ginsberg.
3. What was the mix of funds used by MooBella to get started?

4. What are the start-up costs that you would expect to encounter if you were a company that purchased a MooBella machine?

Case Sources

"Device Profile: MooBella on-demand ice cream maker," LinuxDevices.com, February 8, 2006, http://www.linuxfordevices.com/c/a/Linux-for-Devices-Articles/, January 23, 2011.

Maureen Farrell, "Big Scoop," *Forbes*, November 22, 2010, p. 122.

MooBella, Inc., http://www.moobella.com, January 23, 2011.

Sandi Goldfarb, "MooBella, Inc. Closes $9 Million Funding," MooBella, Inc. press release, November 16, 2010.

Case Study | Richard's Party Promotions

The Problem

The telephone rang. Richard Futrell put on his headset and answered, "Good evening, Boston Teen Hotline. My name is Richard. How can I help you?" The year was 1999. Richard had been working as a hotline counselor at the mayor's Youth Committee for three years. Every night, from 6 to 11 p.m., he took calls from teenagers in the Boston area, advising them on many different issues: relationships, family problems, school, and more. Richard had a natural talent for being a good listener. In fact, he listened so well that over time he started noticing similarities in the types of problems that young people were discussing on the hotline. Specifically, Richard observed that younger teens in the Dorchester and Roxbury communities did not feel safe going out on the weekends in their own neighborhoods. Parents were also worried about the safety of their children, and sometimes called to ask whether the Youth Committee ever sponsored teen parties or other gatherings. Richard always felt bad telling parents that the committee did not have the funds to organize these types of events. Richard liked helping people, but this was the kind of problem he did not feel he could solve.[8]

Problems Can Lead to Opportunities

But then, one day in October, Richard came up with an idea: "Everybody was asking, 'Is there going to be a Halloween party?' But there was not anyone who was throwing a party, so I said, I'll throw my own party. I did not know how to DJ, but I had friends who worked as professional DJs. I just contacted everyone I knew who could help out and then made it happen."

Richard decided to use all $700 of his own personal savings to purchase services and supplies for the party. His intention was to earn this money back and also generate a profit by charging a $10 admission fee. He thought that $10 was a reasonable price because it was about the same amount that teens would typically spend on a weekend night to go out to a movie or play video games at the arcade. Richard knew that he had to be careful about how he allocated his resources, because a $700 start-up investment was not going to get him very far.

(Comstock)

Getting Organized

Richard's first step in planning his party was to brainstorm a list of all the things he would need to purchase and arrange. The list he created was as follows:

Item	Cost
Space Rental	
DJ	
Security	
Insurance	
Flyers	
Food	
Party Decorations	

He thought this was a pretty good list; the only problem was that he did not know how much each item would cost. Could he pay for these goods and services with his limited funds? He was not certain. First, he needed to do some research.

Richard Investigates His Costs

Richard called his friend James, who worked as a professional DJ, to find out how much he would charge to spin records at the party. James normally got $200 as a DJ at Boston's hottest clubs, but he agreed to reduce his fee to $100 because he saw that Richard was trying to do something positive for the community.

[8]This case is based on a real-life example, but selected details have been fictionalized. Thanks to Stephen Spinelli and Alex Hardy, of Babson College, for granting permission to adapt this case from its original version.

Richard then spoke with another friend, who worked as a security guard, to ask if he could organize a security squad for the event. The friend agreed to find four co-workers who could staff the party for $50 each.

Richard needed a large, centrally located venue where he could host the party. He remembered that his friend Janelle had once rented a dance studio in an old, converted factory. The studio would be perfect because it was located in the heart of downtown Boston, near the highway and directly across the street from a subway station. He contacted the studio's owner and negotiated a deal to rent the space for $200 for four hours. This rental fee included insurance, in case there was an accident.

Throughout the planning process, Richard leveraged his personal network to assemble the necessary components for the party. He explained: "If I had to go out and hire professionals, I wouldn't know them. And the fact that I did not have the money right then to pay full market prices for people's services—but these people trusted me and said, 'We believe in what you're doing, so we'll provide our services at a discount.'"

Richard's final step was to get the word out about the party to teens and parents. He called his friend Zeke, who freelanced as a graphic designer, and offered to pay him $50 to design and print 300 flyers. By this point, Richard had already committed $600 of his savings toward entertainment, space rental, security, and promotional costs. With his remaining $100, he decided to purchase chips, soda, cups, and napkins. He figured that he could recoup his investment by selling these snacks at a modest profit.

After making these arrangements, Richard filled in the actual cost of each item on the list.

Item	Cost
Space Rental and Insurance	$200
DJ	100
Security	250
Graphic Design and Flyer Production	50
Food, Decorations, and Misc. Supplies	100
Total	$700

Richard felt satisfied that he had managed his limited resources effectively. He was finally ready for the party. All he had left to do was decide on a Halloween costume to wear.

The Party

On the night of the party, Richard arrived early to set up. Despite weeks of planning, he still felt nervous. He had never done anything like this before. What if no one showed up and he lost all his money? The doors opened at 9 p.m., and by 10 only 20 people had arrived. Richard realized that, at $10 apiece, that was only $200. The room looked empty, no one was on the dance floor, and Richard's nerves were on overdrive. Suddenly, at 10:30, the party filled up quickly and, by 11, Richard was amazed to see that a line of kids had formed outside the door. The studio had a fire-hazard limit of 300, and by 11:30 the party was filled to capacity.

Keeping Good Records

In the end, Richard's party was a great personal and financial success. When he sat down to calculate his revenue, he discovered that the party had generated $3,750. Richard tabulated his receipts and created the chart below, so that he could see how he had accomplished this.

Item	Selling Price per Unit	Number of Units Sold	Revenue Generated
Admission Tickets	$10.00	300	$3,000.00
Chips	$0.50	300	150.00
Soda	$1.00	600	600.00
Total Sales Revenue			$3,750.00

It had taken Richard three long years of careful saving to put away $700 from his part-time job at the hotline, so he was amazed that so much money could be generated in a single evening. As he reflected on the experience, Richard realized: "Even if not many people had come to the Halloween party, it would have been a success because I put something together, and I profited from it. Not only profited financially, but profited as an individual. It was something deeper than just the money. You've got to go into business because it is something you love to do and you want to create that independence. If you do something that you love, you always do your best."

Future Possibilities

As he drove home after the party, Richard's mind was reeling. He was thinking about the future and what he wanted to accomplish. Maybe he would use some of the profit he earned to throw an even bigger party, or perhaps start a party-planning business. He was not sure. After all, organizing the party had caused him a lot of stress. Or maybe he would put the money in his bank account so that he could save up for graduate school. He had several possibilities to consider. Richard parked his car, got ready for bed, and resolved to think further about his future plans in the morning.

Case Study Analysis

1. Assume that Richard decides to start a party-planning business:

   - Identify two ways he could assess the cost of goods or services sold for this business.

   - Which costs, described in the case, would become part of Richard's operating-cost structure?

   - Make a list of additional items Richard would need to purchase to get his business off the ground. Research the cost of these items.

2. One of the reasons why Richard earned a substantial profit is because he convinced his personal contacts to provide their services at a discounted rate. If Richard decides to grow his party-planning business, do you think that he could continue to use this strategy? Why or why not?

3. Brainstorm three things Richard might have done differently in planning his party to increase his sales revenue.

4. At the end of the case, Richard describes how he profited as an individual from the experience of throwing the Halloween party. What do you think he meant by this? Is it possible to profit from something on a personal level, even if you do not necessarily earn a financial profit? Can you think of an example from your own life where this happened? Explain.

Chapter 8

USING FINANCIAL STATEMENTS TO GUIDE A BUSINESS

> **"The propensity to truck, barter, and exchange one thing for another is common to all men."**
>
> —Adam Smith,
> Scottish economist

The allure of an ice cream truck is undeniable as it travels through a neighborhood where children and adults eagerly gather for frozen treats. For Dylan Bauer, a recent Temple University entrepreneurship graduate and founder of Chilly Dilly's Ice Cream Company, in York, Pennsylvania, the allure was far greater.[1] However, Dylan learned early that it was not enough to have a "cool" business. This young entrepreneur learned the importance of detailed and accurate financial statements early, so he knows the financial condition of Chilly Dilly's at all times. "I love playing with Excel, conducting analysis using different margins scenarios."

Each year, Dylan creates the next season's cash budget in order to plan major expenditures. The majority of his sales occur between June and September, so "Each October I am sitting on a ton of cash, but it gets used up over the winter months paying bills and planning for the next season." After five years of operations, he experienced a 105.7 percent increase in profits, and the fifth year saw a rise of more than 250 percent in revenues over the fourth year. However, as he evaluated his future options, Dylan recognized that such growth would likely be unsustainable, and financing would be a challenge. Having reached the maximum use of his line of credit with the only possible local lender, he looked to fund growth internally.

Fortunately, Dylan understood his financial circumstances and saved cash for investing, rather than repaying his debt early. Still, it was not sufficient to fund his desired growth. In order to grow his dream, Dylan relied on his financial savvy, marketing expertise, and the input of trusted advisors. During the slow winter months of 2011, he used a combination of his cash reserve and the sale of several assets to finance his latest business idea: Chilly Dilly's Sun Sno. His "sno huts" are completely solar powered and his products organic. He predicts that this extension of his business will provide him with the financial success he seeks.

Dylan Bauer of Chilly Dilly's Ice Cream Company.
(Dr. Jay Azriel & Dr. Andrew Sumutka/New York College of Pennsylvania)

Performance Objectives

1. Understand an income statement.
2. Examine a balance sheet to determine a business's financing strategy.
3. Use the balance sheet equation for analysis.
4. Perform a financial ratio analysis of an income statement.
5. Calculate return on investment.
6. Perform same-size (common-sized) analysis of an income statement.
7. Use quick, current, and debt ratios to analyze a balance sheet.

Scorecards for the Entrepreneur: What Do Financial Statements Show?

In this chapter you will learn how to prepare and use the income statement and balance sheet to guide your business and keep it strong. Entrepreneurs use three basic financial statements to track their businesses:

- an income statement,
- a balance sheet, and
- a cash flow statement.

---

[1]Based on a case prepared by Dr. Jay Azriel and Dr. Andrew Sumutka of York College of Pennsylvania.

Together, they will show the health of a business at a glance.

Best practice for entrepreneurs is to use their financial records to prepare monthly income statements and balance sheets, and then finalize these at the end of the fiscal year. Cash flow statements (as will be discussed in Chapter 9) should be prepared at least monthly. These statements will provide concise, easily read and understood company financial pictures. Whereas transaction records—such as those kept in a journal or check register—will show the cash balance on hand, the income statement and balance sheet give an overview of the organization. By performing financial-statement analysis, you can gain a comprehensive understanding of how any enterprise is doing.

Income Statements: Showing Profit and Loss over Time

The income statement shows whether the difference between revenue (sales) and expenses (costs) is a profit or a loss over a given time period. If revenues are greater than expenses, the income-statement balance will be positive, showing that the business is profitable. If costs are greater than sales, the income-statement balance will show that the business has incurred losses (is unprofitable).

The income statement is a scorecard for the entrepreneur. If the business is not making a profit, examining the statement can reveal what may be causing the problem. Steps can then be taken to correct it and prevent insolvency. *Profit* is the reward for making the right business choices. The income statement will enable you to determine whether your decisions have kept you on the right track.

Parts of an Income Statement

The income statement is composed of the following:

Performance Objective 1 ▶

Understand an income statement.

1. ***Revenue.*** Income from sales of the company's products or services. For companies using the cash method of accounting, sales are recorded when payment is received.
2. ***COGS (cost of goods sold)/COSS (cost of services sold).*** These are the costs of the materials used to make the product (or deliver the service) plus the costs of the direct labor used to make the product (or deliver the service). An income statement reports total COGS for a period.
3. ***Gross profit.*** The result of revenues minus COGS.
4. ***Other variable costs (VC).*** Costs that vary with sales.
5. ***Contribution margin.*** The result of revenues minus COGS and other variable costs, or gross profit minus other variable costs.
6. ***Fixed operating costs.*** Costs of operating a business that do not vary with sales. The most common fixed operating costs are utilities, salaries, advertising, insurance, interest, rent, and depreciation (USAIIRD).
7. ***Earnings before interest and taxes (EBIT).*** The result of gross profit minus other variable costs minus fixed costs, except interest and taxes.
8. ***Pre-tax profit.*** EBIT minus interest costs. This is a business's profit after all costs have been deducted, but before taxes have been paid. Pre-tax profit is used to calculate how much tax the business owes.

Entrepreneurial Wisdom . . .

Whenever a number in a financial statement is enclosed in parentheses, it is negative. If you see ($142,938) at the bottom of an income statement, it means the business had a net loss of $142,938.

9. ***Taxes.*** A business must pay taxes on the income it earns as a separate entity from the owners' personal taxes, depending upon its legal form (e.g., a corporation). It may have to make monthly or quarterly estimated tax payments.

10. ***Net profit/(loss).*** This is the business's profit or loss after taxes have been paid.

A Basic Income Statement

The power of the income statement is that it will tell you whether you are fulfilling the formula of buying low, selling high, and meeting customer needs. See **Exhibit 8-1** for an example of an income statement for a relatively simple business. It illustrates how the income statement functions.

Example

David buys 100 handbags at $10 each and sells them all at $25 each at a flea market, for revenue of $2500. He gives each customer a little charm (at a cost of 50 cents) to attach to the handbag. He also spends $25 on flyers to advertise that he will be selling on Saturday at the flea market and $500 to rent the booth. The income statement in **Exhibit 8-2** quickly shows whether or not he made a profit. The income statement not only shows that David's business is profitable but also illustrates exactly *how* profitable.

The Double Bottom Line

The expression, "What's the bottom line?" refers to the last line on an income statement, which shows whether a business has made a profit or not.

Another bottom line can be considered, though, aside from whether the organization (either for-profit or not-for-profit) is making money. Is your business achieving its mission? If your dream was to have your venture fill a need in the community, is this goal being realized? Are you able to make a profit and operate the business in a way that makes you feel satisfied and fulfilled? Goals that go beyond profit might include:

- being a good citizen by doing business in a way that respects the environment: recycling, minimizing waste, looking for energy sources that do not pollute;
- encouraging local people to invest in the business and become equity owners;
- always dealing honestly with customers and suppliers, and treating everyone you do business with the way you would like to be treated;

Working on an income statement with colleagues.
(© Yuri Arcurs/Shutterstock.com)

Exhibit 8-1 *Basic Income Statement*

A Basic Company, Inc.
Income Statement
for the Month Ended June 30, 2011

Sales/Revenue			$ 24,681
COGS (Cost of Goods Sold)			
Total Materials	$ 2,468		
Total Labor	3,579		
Total COGS	$ 6,047	$ 6,047	6,047
Gross Profit			$ 18,634
Other Variable Costs			
Commissions	$ 1,234		
Packaging	236		
Total Other Variable Costs	$ 1,470	$ 1,470	1,470
Contribution Margin			$ 17,164
Fixed Operating Costs (USAIIRDO)			
Utilities	$ 200		
Salaries	3,000		
Advertising	600		
Insurance	300		
Interest	300		
Rent	1,000		
Depreciation	50		
Other	50		
Total Fixed Operating Costs:	$ 5,500		5,500
Pre-Tax Profit			$ 11,164
Taxes (0.34%)			3,796
Net Profit			$ 7,368

Total Sales/Revenue = Units Sold × Unit Selling Price

Total Cost of Goods or Services Sold = Units Sold × Cost of Goods or Services
Sold per Unit

Gross Profit = Sales − COGS

Total Other Variable Costs = Units Sold × Other Variable Costs per Unit

Total Variable Costs = Total Cost of Goods or Services Sold + Total Other Variable
Costs

Contribution Margin = Total Sales − Total Variable Costs

Total Fixed Costs = Total of USAIIRDO

Pre-Tax Profit/(Loss) = Contribution Margin − Total Fixed Costs

Taxes = Profit × .34 (Estimated)

Net Profit = Pre-Tax Profit − Taxes

- treating employees with respect regarding their health and safety, and
- setting up profit-sharing plans, especially so that they will share in the success they help create.

Ideally, you want to have a positive *double* bottom line; you are making a profit so you can stay in business *and* achieve your mission. Not-for-profit organizations all have a double bottom line to measure. They must achieve successful financial results in order to continue operations and work toward their mission. Not-for-profits explicitly strive to attain successful double bottom lines.

Exhibit 8-2 *Flea Market Seller Income Statement*

David's Income Statement
Handbag Sales at Flea Market (one time), for One Month

Sales:	100 handbags × $25/bag		$2,500
Less COGS	100 handbags × $10/bag	$1,000	1,000
Gross Profit			$1,500
Other Variable Costs	100 charms × $0.50/charm	50	50
Total Variable Costs		$1,050	
Contribution Margin			$1,450
Fixed Costs			
Rent ($500 to rent booth)		$500	
Advertising ($25 for flyers)		25	
Total Fixed Costs		$525	525
Pre-Tax Profit			$925
Taxes (25%)			231
Net Profit			$694

An Income Statement for a More Complex Business

The income statement in **Exhibit 8-3** follows the same format as the previous one and its goal is still the same—to show how profitable the business is. However, this statement includes the category of *depreciation*.

Exhibit 8-3 *Income Statement for Lola's Custom Draperies, Inc., for the Month of March 2011*

Sales:		$85,456
Cost of Goods Sold:		
Materials	$11,550	
Labor	17,810	
Total COGS:		29,360
Gross Profit:		$56,096
Other Variable Costs:		
Sales Commissions	8,000	8,000
Contribution Margin:		$48,096
Fixed Operating Costs:		
Factory Rent and Utilities	$8,000	
Salaries and Administrative	12,000	
Depreciation	2,000	
Total Fixed Operating Costs:		22,000
Profit Before Taxes:		$26,096
Taxes (25%):		6,524
Net Profit/(Loss):		$19,572

Publicly traded companies have the same essential format as shown in Exhibit 8-3. Their statements are available to shareholders and other members of the public through their quarterly and annual filings with the U.S. Securities and Exchange Commission (10Q and 10K reports), and annual reports to shareholders. If you are not familiar with financial statements, it may help to look at the annual report of a large public company in a peer industry. The reports are generally available in the investor- or shareholder-relations section of company Web sites.

Performance Objective 2 ➤

Examine a balance sheet to determine a business's financing strategy.

net worth (owner's equity) the difference between assets and liabilities.

owner's equity (net worth) the difference between assets and liabilities.

The Balance Sheet: A Snapshot of Assets, Liabilities, and Equity at a Point in Time

You can quickly see a company's financing strategy by looking at its *balance sheet* (see **Exhibits 8-4** and **8-5**). A balance sheet is a financial statement that shows the assets (what the business owns), liabilities (debts), and the **net worth** of a business. The net worth is the difference between assets and liabilities and is also called **owner's equity**.

1. *Assets.* Items a company owns that have monetary value.
2. *Liabilities.* Debts a company has that must be paid, including unpaid bills.

Exhibit 8-4 *Balance Sheet (horizontal)*

A Basic Company, Inc.
Balance Sheet
As of December 31, 2011

Assets			Liabilities		
Current Assets			**Current Liabilities**		
Cash		$75,000	Accounts payable		$475,000
Accounts receivable		250,000	Notes payable		175,000
Inventory		500,000	Accrued wages payable		75,000
Supplies		80,000	Accrued taxes payable		20,000
Prepaid expenses		15,000	Accrued interest payable		25,000
Total Current Assets		**$920,000**	**Total Current Liabilities**		**$770,000**
Long-Term (Fixed) Assets			**Long-Term Liabilities**		
Land		$500,000	Mortgage		$900,000
Buildings	$700,000		Notes payable		500,000
Less accum. depreciation	70,000	630,000	**Total Long-Term Liabilities**		**$1,400,000**
Vehicles	$200,000				
Less accum. depreciation	60,000	140,000	**Owner's Equity**		
Equipment	$250,000		Prime Owner, paid in capital		$197,500
Less accum. depreciation	12,500	237,500	Common stock		100,000
Furniture and fixtures	$50,000		**Total Owner's Equity**		**$297,500**
Less accum. depreciation	10,000	40,000			
Total Fixed Assets		**$1,547,500**			
Intangibles (goodwill)		$0			
Total Assets		**$2,467,500**	**Total Liabilities and Owner's Equity**		**$2,467,500**

Exhibit 8-5 *Balance Sheet (vertical)*

A Basic Company, Inc.
Balance Sheet
As of December 31, 2011

Assets

Current Assets

Cash		$75,000
Accounts receivable		250,000
Inventory		500,000
Supplies		80,000
Prepaid expenses		15,000
Total Current Assets		**$920,000**

Long-Term (Fixed) Assets

Land		$500,000
Buildings	$700,000	
Less accum. depreciation	70,000	630,000
Vehicles	$200,000	
Less accum. depreciation	60,000	140,000
Equipment	$250,000	
Less accum. depreciation	12,500	237,500
Furniture and fixtures	$50,000	
Less accum. depreciation	10,000	40,000
Total Fixed Assets		**$1,547,500**

Intangibles (goodwill)		**$0**
Total Assets		**$2,467,500**

Liabilities

Current Liabilities

Accounts payable		$475,000
Notes payable		175,000
Accrued wages payable		75,000
Accrued taxes payable		20,000
Accrued interest payable		25,000
Total Current Liabilities		**$770,000**

Long-Term Liabilities

Mortgage		$900,000
Notes payable		500,000
Total Long-Term Liabilities		**$1,400,000**

Owner's Equity

Prime Owner, paid in capital		$197,500
Common stock		100,000
Total Owner's Equity		**$297,500**

Total Liabilities and Owner's Equity		**$2,467,500**

Global Impact

By the Numbers—Quintiles Transnational Corporation

As the leader in the $20 billion industry of outsourcing clinical trials, with 23,000 employees in 60 countries, Quintiles Transnational relies on data collection and analysis as its core business. Dennis Gillings, a British statistician and former professor at the University of North Carolina at Chapel Hill, is the founder and 24 percent owner of the company that provides clinical, commercial, capital, and consulting solutions in bio and pharmaceutical services.

However, clinical data is not all that Quintiles tracks. Financial information is essential to guiding company performance. Although privately held, the company does report annual sales of $3 billion. Quintiles also reported, "$500 million in earnings before interest, taxes, depreciation, and amortization, and $400 million in free cash flow."[2]

In 2011, Quintiles recognized the opportunity to improve its financial performance by restructuring its debt financing.

On a press release dated March 8, it announced the beginning of the refinancing of $2.425 billion in credit facilities to take advantage of better debt terms. Then, on March 10, Quintiles Transnational Holdings, Inc. (parent of Quintiles Transnational Corporation) announced a cash tender offer for outstanding debt up to $525 million (9.5% senior notes due in 2014).

Understanding and using financial data is critical for this global leader. This financial savvy helped Dennis Gillings grow his entrepreneurial venture from humble beginnings in a trailer on the UNC Campus.

Sources: Matthew Herper, "Money, Math and Medicine," *Forbes,* November 22, 2010, pp. 140, 142–43.

Quintiles Transnational Corporation. http://www.quintiles.com, March 15, 2011.

---

3. ***Owner's Equity (OE).*** Also called net worth; this is the difference between assets and liabilities. It shows the amount of capital in the business. It consists of common equity, preferred equity, paid-in capital, and retained earnings.

The balance sheet for a large business is typically prepared quarterly and at the end of the fiscal year—unlike cash flow and income statements, which are prepared monthly. The **fiscal year** is the 12-month accounting period chosen by the business. A fiscal year may differ from the calendar year (January 1 through December 31). A business that uses the calendar year as its fiscal year would prepare its balance sheet for the annual time frame ending December 31.

fiscal year the 12-month financial reporting period for a company.

Many entrepreneurs, however, also prepare a monthly balance sheet. To keep the business on track, business owners use three financial tools: the balance sheet, the income statement, and the cash flow statement (to be discussed in Chapter 9).

Short- and Long-Term Assets

Assets are all items of worth owned by a business—such as cash, inventory, buildings, vehicles, furniture, machinery, and the like. Assets are divided into short-term (current) and long-term (fixed).

current assets cash or items that can be quickly converted to cash or will be used within one year.

- **Current assets** are cash itself and items that could be quickly turned into cash *(liquidated)*, or that will be used by the business within one year. Current assets include accounts receivable, inventory, and supplies.

long-term assets those that will take more than one year to use.

- **Long-term assets** are those that would take more than one year for the business to use. Equipment, furniture, machinery, and real estate are examples of long-term assets.

---

[2]Matthew Herper, "Money, Math and Medicine," *Forbes,* November 22, 2010, p. 142.

Current and Long-Term Liabilities

Liabilities are all debts owed by the business, such as bank loans, mortgages, lines of credit, and loans from family or friends.

- **Current liabilities** are debts that are scheduled for payment within one year. These include the portion of long-term debt due within that year.
- **Long-term liabilities** are debts to be paid over a period of more than one year.

current liabilities debts that are scheduled for payment within one year.

long-term liabilities debts that are due in over one year.

The Balance Sheet Equation

The terms *owner's equity*, *capital*, and *net worth* all mean the same thing: what's left over after liabilities are subtracted from assets. Owner's equity is the value of the business on the balance sheet to the owner. The equation for calculating owner's equity is the *balance sheet equation*. As the name suggests, the balance sheet must always be in balance, with assets equal to the sum of liabilities plus equity. A sure sign of a calculation or record-keeping error is to have an imbalance.

◀ **Performance Objective 3**
Use the balance sheet equation for analysis.

Assets − Liabilities = Net Worth (or Owner's Equity or Capital) or

Assets = Liabilities + Owner's Equity or

Liabilities = Assets − Owner's Equity

- If assets are greater than liabilities, net worth is positive.
- If liabilities are greater than assets, net worth is negative.

For example, if Dos Compadres Restaurant has $10,000 in cash on hand, owns $8,000 in equipment, and owes $5,000 in long-term liabilities, what is the restaurant's net worth?

$18,000 (Assets) − $5000 (Liabilities) = $13,000 (Net Worth)

The Balance Sheet Shows Assets and Liabilities Obtained through Financing

Every item a business owns was obtained through either debt or equity. That is why the total of all assets must equal the total of all liabilities and owner's equity.

- If an item was financed with *debt*, the loan is a liability.
- If an item was purchased with the owner's own money (including that of shareholders), it was financed with *equity*.

Example

If a restaurant owns its tables and chairs (worth $3,000), its stoves (worth $5,000), has $10,000 in cash, and $4,000 in inventory, the business has a total capital equipment investment of $3,000 + $5,000 = $8,000, and $4,000 in inventory plus the $10,000 in cash. The restaurant also has a $5,000 long-term loan, which was used to buy the stove. Its total assets are $22,000. It has $5,000 in liabilities (the loan for the stove), which leaves $17,000 of owner's equity (OE).

Assuming the restaurant has no other assets and liabilities, **Exhibit 8-6** shows how its balance sheet would look.

Exhibit 8-6 *Balance Sheet*			
Restaurant Balance Sheet as of Dec. 31, 2008			
Assets		**Liabilities**	
Cash	$10,000	Short-Term Liabilities	$ 0
Inventory	4,000	Long-Term Liabilities	5,000
Capital Equipment	8,000		
Other Assets	0	Owner's Equity	17,000
Total Assets	**$22,000**	**Total Liabilities + OE**	**$22,000**

Again, on a balance sheet, assets must equal the total of liabilities and owner's equity.

Total Assets = Total Liabilities + Owner's Equity (OE)

The OE is $17,000. It is equal to the total of the cash ($10,000), the stove, tables, and chairs ($8,000), plus $4,000 in inventory, minus the $5,000 in liabilities.

The $5,000 stove was acquired with a loan (debt financing). This is a long-term liability. Together, the liabilities and the owner's equity have paid for the assets of the business. When reviewing a side-by-side balance sheet, remember that the assets (what you own) on the left are funded by the liabilities (what you owe), plus equity (the owners' stake), on the right.

The Balance Sheet Shows How a Business Is Financed

The balance sheet is an especially effective tool for examining how a business is financed. It clearly shows the relationship between debt and equity financing. Sometimes businesses make the mistake of relying too heavily on either debt or equity. The appropriate mix depends upon the industry and the individual firm.

- An entrepreneur that relies too much on equity financing from outside investors (who have thus become owners) can lose control of the company. If the other owners control enough of the business, they may insist on making the decisions, or may impede decision-making and create inefficiency and confusion.
- An entrepreneur who takes on too much debt and is unable to make loan payments can lose the business, and possibly personal assets as well, to banks or other creditors.

All the information you need to analyze a company's financing strategy—total debt, equity, and assets—is in its balance sheet. People who invest in businesses use *ratios* to grasp a company's financial situation quickly. As an entrepreneur, you will want to understand these ratios so you will be able to talk intelligently with investors and to analyze costs (vendors) and sales (customers).

Analyzing a Balance Sheet

Comparing balance sheets from two points in time is an excellent way to see whether or not a business has been financially successful. If it is, the OE will have increased. The ending balance sheets for two consecutive years may be compared to analyze annual progress.

Exhibit 8-7 *Comparative Balance Sheet*

Restaurant Balance Sheet

	As of Dec. 31, 2011	As of Dec. 31, 2010
Assets		
Current Assets		
Cash	$8,000	$10,000
Inventory	5,000	4,000
Less accum. depreciation	9,000	8,000
Total Assets	**$22,000**	**$22,000**
Liabilities		
Total Current Liabilities	$1,000	$0
Long-Term Liabilities	4,000	5,000
Owner's Equity	17,000	17,000
Total Liabilities and Owner's Equity	**$22,000**	**$22,000**

Example

Let's look at the restaurant example again. This time, several other assets and liabilities have been included (see **Exhibit 8-7**).

The first balance sheet was prepared as of December 31, 2010. The ending balance sheet was compiled a year later, on December 31, 2011. Compare the two documents (Exhibit 8-7) to see how the numbers have changed over the course of a year.

Assets

- *Cash* has decreased from $10,000 to $8,000. Businesses have cash coming in and going out all the time, so this is not necessarily a bad thing, as long as the bills are being paid, but it should be monitored carefully.

- *Inventory* has increased from $4,000 to $5,000. If greater inventory will allow the restaurant to put more items on the menu, it could help increase business. If inventory is accumulating without adding value, however, it can be problematic, because it is effectively cash sitting on a shelf. In any case, inventory is an *asset* because it has monetary value.

- *Capital equipment* has increased from $8,000 to $9,000. The restaurant must have bought more equipment during the year. This is another increase in assets.

- *Other assets* have remained constant.

- *Total assets* have not changed. The business is keeping less cash but now has more inventory and capital equipment with which to operate.

There are no more assets at the end of the year than there were at the beginning. Does this mean it did not have a successful year? (The rest of this analysis will help you figure that out.)

Liabilities

- *Short-term liabilities* have increased from $0 to $1,000. On the surface, this seems to be a negative because it means the restaurant owes more money than it did. However, it may mean that suppliers have extended trade credit to the company, so that it can add inventory without tying up as much cash.

- *Long-term liabilities* have declined from $5,000 to $4,000 because the restaurant paid off 20 percent of the loan principal. When you make monthly payments on a loan, it is usual for part of the payment to go for interest and the rest to reducing the principal. So, part of the payment is an expense and part is reducing a liability.
- *Owner's equity* has stayed the same. The restaurant has no more value than it had at the beginning of the year, even though its assets and liabilities are distributed differently.

The restaurant does not have more total assets than it had at the beginning of the year, and it has less cash. On the other hand, the business has less debt than it did. The balance sheet equation shows that the owner's equity in the business has not changed because, although the owner paid down some long-term debt, short-term debt was added.

Exhibit 8-8 shows another look at the balance sheet, with a Percentage Change column added. This represents how much change took place over the year. (Remember, any value set in parentheses is negative.)

Total assets are unchanged, and the restaurant's liabilities (debts) are the same, which is an unusual set of circumstances. Short-term liabilities are $1,000 greater, and long-term liabilities are less than they had been at the start of the year. Owner's equity is the same.

The restaurant used its cash to increase its inventory and capital equipment, keeping its debt and equity the same. Reallocating your asset mix in such a way can be a smart strategy.

The growth of owner's equity is one good way to measure company success. **Exhibit 8-9** shows how investors might view different rates of owner's equity growth.

Depreciation

As we have learned, depreciation is a certain portion of an asset that is subtracted each year until the asset's value reaches zero. Depreciation reflects the wear and tear on an asset over time, or other loss of value, through obsolescence. Depreciation reflects this reduction in the asset's value. A used car or computer, for instance, is almost always worth less money than a new one.

Balance sheets with significant long-term assets show depreciation as a subtraction from those assets. Because different types of assets depreciate at

---

Exhibit 8-8 *Balance Sheet Variance Analysis*

Restaurant Balance Sheet

	As of Dec. 31, 2011	As of Dec. 31, 2010	% Change
Assets			
Current Assets			
Cash	$8,000	$10,000	(20)%
Inventory	5,000	4,000	25%
Capital Equipment	9,000	8,000	13%
Total Assets	**$22,000**	**$22,000**	**0%**
Liabilities			
Short-Term Liabilities	$1,000	$0	N.A.
Long-Term Liabilities	4,000	5,000	(20)%
Owner's Equity	17,000	17,000	0%
Total Liabilities and Owner's Equity	**$22,000**	**$22,000**	**0%**

Exhibit 8-9 *Annual Rates of Growth in Owner's Equity of Major U.S. Corporations*

Annual Growth	Assessment of Annual Growth Rate
3%	Very slow, and unsatisfactory in most cases
6%	Slow, but acceptable in some cases
10–11%	Average growth rate
16%	High growth rate
24%	Extremely high growth—not many companies can achieve this, much less keep it up

different rates, and because assets are purchased at various points in time, businesses keep *depreciation schedules* to track the valuation of each asset that is being depreciated. There are multiple methods of depreciation, and it is best to consult with an accounting/tax professional on this topic.

Financial Ratio Analysis: What Is It and What Does It Mean to You?

So far, we have only looked at how an income statement or balance sheet can tell you whether or not your business is making a profit, and whether owner's equity is increasing or decreasing. This is only the tip of the iceberg with respect to what you can learn about a business through financial-statement analysis. You can also create financial ratios from your income statement and balance sheet that will help you analyze your business in greater depth. By making comparisons of your company's performance from period to period and against industry norms, you can adapt your operations and strategies to improve results.

Income Statement Ratios

To create income statement ratios, analysts simply divide sales into each line item and multiply by a hundred. In this way, line items are expressed as a percentage of sales. Expressing an item on the income statement as a percentage of sales makes it easier to see the relationship between items than when dollar values are used. In the example shown in **Exhibit 8-10**, for every dollar of sales, 40 cents went to the cost of goods sold. The contribution margin per dollar was 60 cents. The net profit was 20 cents— after 30 cents was spent on operating costs and 10 cents on taxes.

Analyzing the common-sized (or "same size") income statement makes clear how each item is affecting the business's profit. Examining the income statement makes it easy to experiment with ways to improve your business, by changing values to test different financial scenarios.

◄ Performance Objective 4
Perform a financial ratio analysis of an income statement.

To increase contribution margin, you could try cutting the cost of goods sold by 10 percent. The next time you analyze your monthly income statement, you will be able to see if this cost cutting increased the contribution margin and by how much.

Return on Investment

An **investment** is something you put time, energy, or money into because you expect to gain profit or satisfaction in return. When you start your own business, you are investing time and energy in the venture, as well as

investment something that a person or entity devotes resources to in hopes of future profits or satisfaction.

Exhibit 8-10 *Common-Sized Income Statement*

Excellence, Inc. Income Statement for the Month Ending June 30, 2011			
	Amount (in millions)	Calculation	% of Sales
Sales	$ 10	$10/$10 × 100	100%
Less Total COGS	$ 4	$4/$10 × 100	40%
Less Other Variable Costs	0		
Contribution Margin	$ 6	$6/$10 × 100	60%
Less Fixed Operating Costs	$ 3	$3/$10 × 100	30%
Profit	$ 3	$3/$10 × 100	30%
Taxes	$ 1	$1/$10 × 100	10%
Net Profit/(Loss)	$ 2	$2/$10 × 100	20%

Performance Objective 5 ➤

Calculate return on investment.

return on investment (ROI) the net profit of a business divided by its start-up investment (percentage).

wealth the value of assets owned minus the value of liabilities owed.

money. You do this because you believe that someday your business will return more than the value of the time, energy, and money you put into it. One way to express this idea mathematically is to calculate a **return on investment (ROI)**, the net profit of a business divided by the start-up investment, expressed as a percentage of that investment.

Investors think in terms of **wealth**—the value of assets owned minus the value of liabilities owed at a particular point in time, rather than money, per se, because a business may own assets (such as equipment or real estate) that have value but are not actual cash. Return on investment measures how wealth changes over time. To measure ROI, you have to know these three things:

1. *Net profit.* The amount the business has earned beyond what it has spent to cover its costs.
2. *Total investment in the business.* This includes start-up investment (the amount of money that was required to open the business plus all later additional funding).
3. *The period of time for which you are calculating ROI.* This is typically one month or one year.

$$ROI = \frac{\text{Net Profit}}{\text{Investment}} \times 100 = ROI$$

Entrepreneurial Wisdom...

Accounting Differences between Countries

Businesses in different countries prepare and present the income statement differently, and even have different names for it. In the United Kingdom, for example, the income statement is called a group profit and loss account. Categories where global practices can differ widely include inventory measurement methods and ways in which property and equipment are valued. Countries also have varying laws regarding when a sale can be recognized as income and be included on an income statement.

In the United States, United Kingdom, Denmark, Norway, Belgium, Brazil, and Japan, for instance, income from a long-term contract can only be included on the income statement as each percentage of the contract is completed. If you have done 10 percent of the work, you can show 10 percent of the income on your statement. In Germany, on the other hand, you cannot include any of the income on your statement until the contract has been 100 percent completed.

There is an easy way to remember the ROI formula: *What you made over what you paid, times one hundred.* Normally, ROI is calculated on an annual basis, although it can be calculated for shorter time periods, such as days, months, or quarters.

Example

If David wants to figure out what his ROI was for the day at the flea market, he must know the following:

1. *Net profit.* His income statement shows this to be $694.
2. *Investment.* David invested $1,000 in handbags, $25 in flyers, $50 for charms, plus $500 to rent a booth, for a total of $1,575.
3. *Time period.* In this case David is calculating his ROI for one day.

He divides his investment into the net profit.

$$\frac{\text{Net Profit (\$694)}}{\text{Investment (\$1000 + \$25 + \$50 + \$500)}} \times 100 = \frac{\$694}{\$1,575} \times 100$$

$$= .4406 \times 100 = 44\%$$

David's ROI was 44 percent for the day. ROI will tell you what the rate of return was on your investment.

Return on Sales

Return on sales (ROS) is the percentage created when sales are divided into net income. This is an important measure of the profitability of a business.

$$\text{Return on Sales (ROS)} = \frac{\text{Net Income}}{\text{Sales}}$$

ROS is also called the **profit margin.** To express this ratio as a percentage, multiply it by 100 (as you would to express any ratio as a percentage).

A high ROS ratio can help a company make more money; however, the amount of revenue will make a difference. The size of the sale will also make a difference. Hardware stores sell inexpensive items, so they have to have a higher profit margin on each to make a profit. Auto dealers sell expensive items, so they can afford a smaller ROS on each car they sell.

Common-Sized Statement Analysis

Financial ratio analysis will also allow you to compare the income statements from different months or years more easily, even if the sales are different amounts. The percentages let you compare statements as if they were the "same size." For this reason, financial ratio analysis is sometimes called same-size analysis, as well as common-sized analysis.

When the ratio of expenses/sales is used to express expenses as a percentage of sales, it is called an **operating ratio.** The operating ratio expresses what percentage of sales dollars the expense is using up. You can use operating ratios to compare your expenses with those incurred by other businesses in your industry, or for your own company at different times. If your rent is $2,000 per month, and your sales in a given month are $10,000, your operating ratio for rent is 20 percent. Is that high or low for your industry? Check trade association data or statement studies to find comparative values. If it is high, you might want to consider moving

---

return on sales (ROS) net income divided by sales for a particular time period (percentage).

profit margin (return on sales) net income divided by sales (percentage).

◀ **Performance Objective 6**

Perform same-size (common-sized) analysis of an income statement.

operating ratio an expression of a value versus sales.

to another location. Remember that industry norms may not be industry ideals; the whole industry may be operating inefficiently, and you can bring individual efficiency to it. Also, look at whether a ratio is higher or lower than it was a year earlier. This can be particularly helpful for analyzing variable costs within a company, as company performance versus industry performance.

Relating each element of the income statement to sales in this fashion will help you notice changes in your costs from month to month or year to year.

Balance-Sheet Analysis

Taking the time to perform a similar analysis on the balance sheet can also yield valuable historic information, and provide perspectives on opportunities for improvement.

Current and Quick Ratios

Performance Objective 7 ▶
Use quick, current, and debt ratios to analyze a balance sheet.

liquidity the ability to convert assets into cash.

current ratio liquidity ratio consisting of the total sum of cash plus marketable securities divided by current liabilities.

marketable securities investments that can be converted into cash within 24 hours.

quick ratio the calculation of cash in relation to covering current debt.

In addition to what you can learn from an income statement, a balance sheet will tell you about a business's **liquidity**, that is, its ability to convert assets into cash. Businesspeople use **current ratios** to immediately understand what is going on with a business's liquidity. Many entrepreneurs prepare a balance sheet monthly, and at the end of the fiscal year, to keep an eye on liquidity.

$$\text{Quick Ratio} = \frac{\text{Cash + Marketable Securities}}{\text{Current Liabilities}}$$

Some entrepreneurs create fortunes by establishing successful businesses, selling them, and using the resulting wealth to create new enterprises and more wealth. Entrepreneurs also use their wealth to support political, environmental, and social causes. The major philanthropic thrust of the Estée Lauder Company is to provide support to the Breast Cancer Research Foundation, which addresses a major health concern of its customer base. What will you do with *your* entrepreneurial wealth?

Marketable securities are investments, such as certificates of deposit or Treasury bills, which can be converted to cash within 24 hours. The **quick ratio** tells you whether you have enough cash to cover your current debt. The quick ratio should always be greater than 1. This means that you would have enough cash at your disposal to cover all current short-term debt. In other words, if you had to pay all your bills tomorrow (not loans, just bills), you would have enough cash to do so.

$$\text{Quick Ratio} = \frac{\text{Current Liabilities} - (\text{Inventory} + \text{Prepayments})}{\text{Current Liabilities}}$$

Exercise

Compare the common-sized income statements shown in **Exhibit 8-11**. Rocket Rollerskate did not have as much revenue and did not make as much profit in February as it did in January. The company was able to lower both its COGS and its other variable costs in February, though. Which month was better for Rocket? Can you explain your thinking?

Exhibit 8-11 *Common-Sized Income Statements*

Rocket Rollerskate Co. Income Statement		For the Month of January 2008	
Revenue	**100%**		**$250,000**
COGS	24%	$60,000	60,000
Gross Profit	**76%**		**$190,000**
Other Variable Costs	14%	35,000	35,000
Total Variable Costs	38%	$95,000	
Contribution Margin	**62%**		**$155,000**
Fixed Costs	34%		85,000
Pre-Tax Profit	**28%**		**$70,000**
Taxes (20%)	5.6%		14,000
Net Profit	**22.4%**		**$56,000**

Rocket Rollerskate Co. Income Statement		For the Month of February 2008	
Revenue	**100%**		**$225,000**
COGS	20%	$45,000	45,000
Gross Profit	**80%**		**$180,000**
Other Variable Costs	12%	27,000	27,000
Total Variable Costs	32%	$72,000	
Contribution Margin	**68%**		**$153,000**
Fixed Costs	38%		85,000
Pre-Tax Profit	**30%**		**$68,000**
Taxes (20%)	6.0%		13,600
Net Profit	**24%**		**$54,400**

It is also a good idea to maintain a current ratio greater than 1. This indicates that, if you had to, you could sell some assets to pay off all your debts.

$$\text{Current Ratio} = \frac{\text{Current Assets}}{\text{Current Liabilities}}$$

Debt Ratios: Showing the Relationship between Debt and Equity

Most companies are financed by both debt and equity. The financial strategy of a company will be apparent from certain simple financial ratios. If

Step into the Shoes...
Estée Lauder Delivers Beauty

Estée Lauder (1906–2004, born Josephine Esther Mentzer) parlayed a skin-cream formula developed by her uncle into a company selling products in over 100 countries. Lauder started selling the cream in 1946, and introduced Youth Dew fragrance in 1953. The company that she built with her husband found a niche for women's beauty care and evolved from the single beauty cream into multiple complete lines of skin care, makeup, fragrances, and hair-care products. Today, the company bearing her name includes numerous brands, such as Clinique, Prescriptives, MAC Cosmetics, Coach, and Aveda.

The Lauder family continues to control 70 percent of the business.

Named one of *Time* magazine's 20 most influential business geniuses of the twentieth century, Estée Lauder's name is synonymous with beauty.

Estée Lauder.
(Time Life Pictures/DMI/
Time Life Pictures/Getty
Images)

debt-to-equity ratio the comparison of total debt to total equity.

a company has a **debt-to-equity ratio** of one-to-one (expressed as 1:1), for example, it means that for every one dollar of debt the company has one dollar of assets.

$$\text{Debt--to--Equity Ratio} = \frac{\text{Debt}}{\text{Equity}}$$

All the information you need to analyze a company's financing strategy is in its balance sheet, and can be used to create the following ratio.

$$\text{Debt Ratio} = \frac{\text{Total Debt}}{\text{Total Assests}}$$

debt ratio the comparison of total debt to total assets.

The **debt ratio** describes how many of the total dollars in the business have been provided by creditors. A debt ratio of 55 percent means you are in debt for 55 percent of your assets. You will not actually own those assets outright until you pay off the debt. On the other hand, if you need to go to a bank to borrow money, or to a supplier to establish credit, these creditors will want you to have a moderate debt ratio—so you will have to manage your debt based on your objectives, industry norms, and creditor requirements.

A debt-to-equity ratio of 100 percent would mean that for every dollar of debt the company has a dollar of equity. As noted previously, equity is ownership, which is either kept entirely by the entrepreneur or sold in pieces to investors. If the investors hold a significant enough portion of the equity in a business, they could take over control from the entrepreneur—and this sometimes happens.

Operating-Efficiency Ratios

Once the income statement and balance sheet have been prepared, you can analyze your business's operating efficiency by using the following ratios:

1. *Collection-period ratio.*

$$\frac{\text{Average Accounts Receivable (Balance Sheet)}}{\text{Average Daily Sales (Income Statement)}} = \text{\# of days}$$

This ratio measures the average number of days that sales are going uncollected. If you extend credit, it is critical to minimize this number to keep cash flowing. It can be compared to industry norms for additional information.

2. *Receivable turnover ratio.*

$$\frac{\text{Total Sales (Income Statement)}}{\text{Average Accounts Receivable (Balance Sheet)}} = \text{\# of times}$$

This also measures the efficiency of your company's efforts to collect receivables.

3. *Inventory turnover ratio.*

$$\frac{\text{Cost of Goods Sold (Income Statement)}}{\text{Average Inventory (Balance Sheet)}} = \text{\# of times}$$

Exercise

Using the balance sheet for the restaurant in Exhibit 8-7, calculate the quick, debt, and debt-to-equity ratios. Write your answers on a separate sheet of paper. What do the ratios tell you about how the restaurant is doing?

This is a measure of how quickly inventory is moving (is sold). The higher the turnover, the more effectively you are investing in inventory. Inventory that is held too long often becomes obsolete or, in the case of food and other perishable goods, literally spoils. Inventory that is not being turned over is tying up cash flow. At the same time, the amount of inventory in stock has to be balanced with customer needs and wants.

By using all of these ratios, you can create an internal scorecard for your business, perhaps on a consolidated key-performance-indicators report. You will be able to tell at a glance whether you are attaining your goals, where you stand from period to period, and how you compare with your industry. The Appendices in this book include a set of useful formulas and equations to use for such a scorecard.

Chapter Summary

Now that you have studied this chapter, you can do the following:

1. Understand an income statement.
   - An income statement shows whether the difference between revenue (sales) and expenses (costs) is a profit or a loss.
   - If sales are greater than costs, the income-statement balance will be positive, showing that the business earned a profit. If costs are greater than sales, the balance will be negative, showing a loss.
   - The elements of an income statement are:
     a. **Revenue.** Money a business makes for selling its products or services.
     b. **Cost of goods sold.** The cost of goods sold for one unit times the number of units sold. Never disclose your cost of goods sold. You want to keep your profit margin private.
     c. **Gross profit.** Revenue less the cost of the product or service.
     d. **Other variable costs.** Costs that vary with sales.
     e. **Contribution margin.** Sales minus variable costs (cost of goods sold + other variable costs).
     f. **Fixed operating costs.** Items that must be paid to operate a business. These items include utilities, salaries, advertising, insurance, interest, rent, and depreciation (referred to as USAIIRD).
     g. **Profit before taxes.** A business's profit after all costs have been deducted but before taxes have been paid.
     h. **Taxes.** A business must pay income tax on its profit. (Sales, property, and other taxes are business expenses and are not included on this line.)
     i. **Net profit/(loss).** A business's profit or loss after taxes.
2. Examine a balance sheet to determine a business's financing strategy.
   - A balance sheet is a financial statement showing the assets (items the business owns), liabilities (debts), and net worth of a business.
   - Every item a business owns was obtained through either debt (loans, bonds) or equity (selling ownership); therefore, the total of all assets must equal the total of all liabilities and owner's equity.

3. Use the balance sheet equation for analysis.

$$\text{Assets} - \text{Liabilities} = \text{Net Worth (or Owner's Equity or Capital)}$$

- The balance sheet shows the use of debt and equity to support the business.
- Comparing balance sheets from two points in time can provide insights into the business's operations and reveal opportunities for improvement.
- Depreciation affects the values of assets by reducing them to reflect wear and tear and obsolescence.

4. Perform the financial ratio analysis of an income statement.
- Expressing each item on the income statement as a percentage of sales makes it easy to see the relationship between items.
- Financial ratio analysis will also allow you to compare the income statements from different months or years more easily, even if the sales are for varying amounts.
- The percentages let you compare statements as if they were the same size. For this reason, financial ratio analysis is also sometimes called same-size, or common-sized, analysis.

5. **Return on sales (ROS)** is the percentage created when sales are divided into net income. This is an important measure of the profitability of a business.

$$\text{Return on Sales (ROS)} = \frac{\text{Net Income}}{\text{Sales}}$$

6. Calculate return on investment (ROI).
- ROI is the net profit of a business divided by the start-up costs, which are the original investment in the business.

$$\frac{\text{Net Profit}}{\text{Investment}} \times 100 = \text{Return on Investment (ROI \%)}$$

7. Perform same-size analysis of an income statement.
- Represent expenses as a percentage of sales or operating ratios.
- Compare with others in the industry.

8. Use quick, current, and debt ratios to analyze a balance sheet.

$$\text{Quick Ratio} = \frac{\text{Current Liabilities} - (\text{Inventory} + \text{Prepayments})}{\text{Current Liabilities}}$$

$$\text{Current Ratio} = \frac{\text{Current Assets}}{\text{Current Liabilities}}$$

$$\text{Debt Ratio} = \frac{\text{Total Debt}}{\text{Total Assets}}$$

$$\text{Debt-to-Equity Ratio} = \frac{\text{Total Debt}}{\text{Equity}}$$

Key Terms

current assets	debt-to-equity ratio
current liabilities	fiscal year
current ratio	investment
debt ratio	liquidity

long-term assets
long-term liabilities
marketable securities
net worth
operating ratio
owner's equity

profit margin
quick ratio
return on investment (ROI)
return on sales (ROS)
wealth

Entrepreneurship Portfolio

Critical Thinking Exercises

1. Repeat the exercise from Key Concept Questions using accounting software. Then run the following what-if scenarios and create graphs or other visuals showing how each would affect the business's monthly and yearly financial picture:

   - What if the restaurant finds a supplier that is willing to provide paper for only $8,000 in June and $96,000 for the year?
   - What if sales for June were $250,000 and sales for the year were $2,000,000? (Do not forget the taxes, assumed at 25 percent.)
   - What if the owner of this franchise faced start-up costs of $400,000 instead of $300,000? How would that affect the ROI?

2. If you were to open a clothing store, what do you think would be a reasonable operating ratio for the rent, and why?

3. Which items in your business would you depreciate, and why?

4. Using **Exhibit 8-12**, the balance sheet of Angelina's Jewelry Company at the end of July shown below, calculate all four financial ratios (quick, current, debt, and debt-to-equity) for the business.

5. Write a memo analyzing the financial strengths and weaknesses of Angelina's venture. Use the same-size analysis shown below. Would you invest in her business? Why or why not?

6. Using the restaurant balance sheet in Exhibits 8-7 and 8-8, answer the following:

   - What are the debt-to-equity ratios at the beginning and end of the 2011 fiscal (business) year? Has this ratio improved? If so, by how much?

Exhibit 8-12 *Balance Sheet for Angelina's Jewelry Company*

Angelina's Jewelry Company Balance Sheet as of July 30, 2009

Assets		Liabilities	
Current Assets		**Short-Term Liabilities**	
Cash	$ 1,000	Accounts Payable	$ 1,000
Inventory	1,000	Short-Term Loans	500
Securities	1,000	**Total Short-Term Liabilities**	**$ 1,500**
Total Current Assets	**$ 3,000**	Total Long-Term Liabilities	1,500
Long-Term Assets	7,000	Owner's Equity	$ 7,000
Total Assets	$10,000	Total Liabilities + Owner's Equity	$10,000

Exhibit 8-13 *Comparative Balance Sheet for Angelina's Jewelry Company*

Angelina's Jewelry Company Balance Sheet	As of July 30, 2009	As of Aug. 30, 2009	% Change
Assets			
Current Assets			
Cash	$ 1,000	$ 500	(50)%
Inventory	1,000	2,000	100%
Securities	1,000	1,500	50%
Total Current Assets	$ 3,000	$ 4,000	33%
Long-Term Assets	7,000	7,000	0%
Total Assets	$10,000	$11,000	10%
Liabilities			
Short-Term Liabilities			
Accounts Payable	$ 1,000	$ 1,500	50%
Short-Term Loans	500	0	(100)%
Total Short-Term Liabilities	$ 1,500	$ 1,500	0%
Total Long-Term Liabilities	1,500	500	(67)%
Owner's Equity	$ 7,000	$ 9,000	29%
Total Liabilities + Owners' Equity	$10,000	$11,000	10%

- The restaurant has less cash at the end of the year than it had at the beginning. Is this a bad thing or not? Explain.
- Do you think the restaurant has enough cash to pay its expenses going into 2012?
- The restaurant grew its owner's equity by 31 percent during the 2011 fiscal year. At that rate, how much will the business have in owner's equity after one more year (on December 31, 2012)?
- The restaurant added some capital equipment during the year. Do you think it took out another loan for that equipment or did it pay cash? Explain your thinking.

7. On a separate sheet of paper or using a spreadsheet, create a balance sheet for Tropical Aquaculture, a farm for shrimp, using the information below. Calculate and analyze the quick, debt, and debt-to-equity ratios.

Cash	$45,000
Accounts receivable	$12,000
Shrimp feed	$8,400
Accounts payable	$9,700
Equipment	$75,000
Bank loan	$20,000
Property and ponds	$124,000

8. Use the following balance sheet to answer the questions:

Jean M's Florida-Style Subs, Inc. Balance Sheet Ending December 31		
	2011	**2010**
ASSETS		
Current Assets		
Cash and cash equivalents	$10,000	$10,000
Accounts receivable	2,000	7,000
Inventory	20,000	25,000
Total Current Assets	**$32,000**	**$42,000**
Fixed Assets		
Plant and machinery	$5,000	$9,000
Land	9,000	8,000
TOTAL ASSETS	**$46,000**	**$59,000**
Liabilities		
Accounts payable	$10,000	$15,000
Taxes payable	6,000	5,000
Total Liabilities	**$16,000**	**$20,000**
OWNER'S EQUITY	**$30,000**	**$39,000**
LIABILITIES and OWNER'S EQUITY	**$46,000**	**$59,000**

As you can see, total liabilities and owner's equity equal the total assets.

a. What is the year-to-year percentage change in the value of the following:
   - inventory,
   - accounts payable,
   - land,
   - taxes payable, and
   - liabilities and owner's equity?

b. What are the ratios of the following:
   - Cash equivalent to inventory in 2011? How has it changed from 2010?
   - Owner's equity to total assets in 2011? How has it changed from 2010?

c. Investors and buyers like to put their money into companies that have a low ratio of liabilities to assets. Has that ratio become more or less appealing from 2010 to 2011?

9. Create a projected balance sheet for your business for one year.

a. Create a pie chart showing your current assets, long-term assets, current liabilities, and long-term liabilities.

b. What is your debt ratio?

c. What is your debt-to-equity ratio?

Key Concept Questions

1. Given the following data, on a separate sheet of paper create monthly and yearly income statements for this fast-food restaurant in New York City:

   a. Sales for the month of June were $300,000. Sales for the year were $2,600,000.

   b. The sum of $66,000 was spent on food in June (it was $792,000 for the year). The restaurant spent $9,000 on paper to wrap food items in June and $108,000 for the year.

   c. Taxes for June were $15,000. For the year, they were $233,000.

   d. Fixed operating costs for June were $175,000. For the year, they were $1,000,000.

   e. Use Excel or other software to create a graph showing the monthly and yearly income statements for this business.

2. If the owner of this fast-food restaurant invested $300,000 in start-up costs, what was his ROI for the year? (Assume June as average.)

3. Calculate the financial ratios (ROI and ROS) for the monthly and the yearly income statement. What do the financial ratios tell you about this business?

4. What would the profit before taxes be if the owner found a paper supplier that charged only $100,000 for the year?

5. What would the profit margin for the year be in that case?

6. Suppose you wanted to raise profits by $5,000 a month. What would you do, and why?

7. State the financial equation for the balance sheet in three different ways.

8. How is depreciation treated on the balance sheet and what is the logic behind this treatment?

Application Exercise

Below is a mogul's balance sheet (in millions) as of December 31, 1990. All the businesses in this real estate empire were separately incorporated for liability reasons, and many of them were heavily *leveraged*—debt-financed. Eventually, the mogul was unable to make certain loan payments, and the bank creditors took some of the properties. Through perseverance and determination, however, this particular mogul rebuilt her holdings and cleaned up her debt problems. Calculate the debt ratios for each of the mogul's properties, then answer the questions.

Asset	Estimated Worth	Debt	Net Worth	Debt Ratio*
The Pyramids of Gaza	$820	$820	$0	1.0
East Side Yards	450	175	30	
Phoenix Casino	640	275	345	
Mogul's Lair Casino	600	415	6	
Serena's Shuttle	400	400	0	
Serena's Tower	200	100	0	

Asset	Estimated Worth	Debt	Net Worth	Debt Ratio*
Cash	130	160	−30	
Iliana Condos	115	5	45	
Marketable Securities	90	75	15	
Serena's Palace	80	80	0	
Serena's Plaza	70	50	3	
Grand Brand Hotel (50%)	70	30	40	
Iliana Regency	65	85	−20	
Iliana Plaza Coops	45	0	25	
Mogul Air	40	0	30	
Personal Transportation	40	0	30	
Personal Housing	30	40	−9	
Total (in millions)	$___	$___	$___	

$$* \text{ Debt Ratio} = \frac{Debt}{Assets}$$

1. What was the mogul's highest-priced asset?
2. What was the mogul's net worth for Serena's Shuttle? Why?
3. On which asset was the mogul's net worth the greatest?
4. Which asset carried the most debt?
5. Which properties did the mogul own free of debt?
6. On which properties did the mogul owe one dollar of debt for each dollar of the asset?

Exploring Online

Use the Internet to find the balance sheets of two companies with which you are familiar. Use percentages to analyze these balance sheets, and compare how well each is doing against the restaurant example from this chapter. Then contrast them to each other. Consider choosing either two similar companies, such as Target and Wal-Mart, or two different industries, such as an airline and a car manufacturer.

1. How do the companies compare in growing owner's equity?
2. How do the companies compare in reducing debt?
3. Describe how you think market conditions (such as gas prices, for example) are affecting each company's growth.

BizBuilder Business Plan Questions

7.0 Financial Analysis and Projections

A. Describe your record-keeping system.
B. List the types of bank accounts you will open for your organization.

Note: Topics A & B are for your internal development. The final plan would include a summary of the financial information here.

7.3 Balance Sheet Projections

A. Create a projected balance sheet for your business for the first four quarters and the second and third years of operation.

B. Create a pie chart showing your current assets, long-term assets, current liabilities, and long-term liabilities.

7.4 Income Statement Projections

A. Create a projected income statement for your business for the first four quarters and the second and third years of operation.

B. Create a bar graph showing your gross revenues, gross profit, and net income.

7.5 Breakeven Analysis

A. Use Excel or another spreadsheet program to create a spreadsheet projecting the expenses for your business. Use this data to perform a breakeven analysis.

7.6 Ratio Analysis

A. Use your projected financial statements to calculate all of your key ratios.

B. Compare these ratios to your industry using publicly available data.

7.7 Risks and Assumptions

A. List the risks and assumptions that underlie your financial projections.

B. Identify any external factors that you feel should be disclosed as substantial risks.

Case Study | Cactus & Tropicals: Using Financials to Build Employee Performance

Case prepared by Hattie Bryant, creator of *Small Business School*, the television series made for PBS and Voice of America: http://SmallBusinessSchool.org. *Small Business School* video clips are available.

Lorraine Miller decided that she would rather be her own boss than work for someone who made her feel insignificant. That's why she started her own business in 1975. She had a secure job as a lab technician working in her field of study, but the owner of that company refused to answer her inquiries about how things worked, and made her feel undervalued and unrespected. She quit this disappointing but secure position and, with just $2,000 of her own money, she started selling plants.

Today, the company that Lorraine founded, Cactus & Tropicals, provides indoor and outdoor landscaping for over 500 customers, and its retail stores and greenhouses are full of exotic plants and gifts. Not only has Miller grown the business to one of the largest of its kind in Salt Lake City, she was named Utah's Small Business Person of the Year in 1994, and received a national award from the U.S. Small Business Administration. Lorraine was named by Ernst & Young as one of Salt Lake's outstanding entrepreneurs in 1997.

Lorraine has said, "I start from the premise that I can grow my business to a certain point, and then after that, I'm stuck, because I can only juggle so many bottles at once. If I don't teach employees everything I know, I simply cannot grow the company." This is the reason that teaching is Lorraine's top priority. She has to grow her own talent.

Lorraine's philosophy has always been that work should not be grueling; it should be pleasant—even fun. She believes in treating employees with great respect, as if the company were one big family. One of Lorraine's employees said, "I worked in the corporate world for about 11 years, and there you're just a number. And you come here, and each one of us is asked to express our opinion."

Part of being a member of a company of family members is that self-determination and

(Small Business School)

goal setting is expected from everyone, and at Cactus & Tropics employees set financial and performance goals for their own departments. This procedure involves reviewing the financial statements of the company. They are privy to the costs of doing business, in addition to knowing the revenue. It is fairly common for employees to know what the sales figures of the company they work for are, but rarely do they know what it costs to run the business.

As often happens when a company owner is brave enough to open its books to the employees, Lorraine's were surprised by the numbers, and had greater respect for her once they saw what the expenses really were. In fact, they encouraged her to take more personal salary and benefits from the business, once they learned to interpret the financial statements and reports. They realized that employees cost far more than their salaries or wages, because of the additional 25 to 30 percent (or even more), that employers pay for taxes and benefits. Employees are often shocked to see the cost of insurance, utilities, advertising, computer systems, telephones, a lease, and the like.

Lorraine argues against the notion that owners do not have time to teach employees to understand, or to share information with them. She says the benefits derived from sharing information far outweigh the cost of taking the time to do so. To learn how to run her company with open-book management techniques,

Lorraine took a course taught by Jack Stack, author of *The Great Game of Business*.

Lorraine's goal at Cactus & Tropicals has always been to deliver to customers more than they paid for, and to do that by finding people who want to work in a place where they are given guidelines—not rules. The staff at Cactus & Tropicals is expected to ask questions, create and improvise, and serve customers with little or no supervision. Lorraine cut her schedule by several days a week for a while and invested the time to teach everyone how to read a balance sheet, how to forecast sales, how to measure individual and team productivity, and how to earn performance-based bonuses. Lorraine learned to value her employees and give them the opportunity to succeed through their own knowledge, skills, and abilities.

Case Study Analysis

1. How can a person's life experience affect the way he or she manages people? Use Lorraine Miller's story to illustrate one example.

2. How did Lorraine finance the start-up of her business?

3. How do we know what others think of Lorraine and her business?

4. Why did Lorraine decide to involve her employees in the financial aspects of her business?

5. What is the risk in teaching employees how to read the company financial statements?

6. What do you think about the word *boss*? Would you rather be supervised by a person who is more of a teacher or mentor or coach than one who simply tells you what to do?

Portland Freelancers' Café: Amy and Steve's Business Idea*

In 2003, Amy Chan and Steve Lee formed a partnership to start an Internet café in Portland, Oregon. For many years, Amy and Steve had worked as freelance writers. They enjoyed bringing their laptops to local coffeehouses to complete their writing projects. Having an endless supply of good strong coffee at their disposal helped them to stay focused on their work.

Over time, they began to daydream about owning their own café. Although Portland already had many great coffee shops, Amy and Steve felt that none of them catered well to freelancers like themselves. More and more, people in Portland seemed to be doing their work in informal settings. Everywhere they turned, twenty- and thirty-somethings were sipping lattes while conducting business deals on cell phones. Amy and Steve sometimes wondered if anyone worked in a traditional office anymore.

We Can Do Better

As much as they enjoyed Portland's café culture, they felt that a fatal flaw compromised each of their favorite coffee spots. One was too loud. Another had uncomfortable chairs and tables that weren't well suited for laptop users. Their particular favorite, The Magic Bean, only had three electrical outlets, which meant that only that many laptops could be plugged in at one time. Just a handful of the coffee shops in downtown Portland offered high-speed Internet access at that time.

Amy and Steve felt that they could do a better job of running a café that catered to the needs of freelancers. They made a list of everything they would want in a café, and then asked their freelance friends for additional feedback. The two partners resolved that, in their café, customers would be able to enjoy high-speed Internet access; laser printers; a soundproof, quiet room; and comfortable, up-to-date work stations. To attract their target market, Amy and Steve decided to name their business the Portland Freelancers' Café.

Deluxe Purchases

They spent $10,000 up front installing superfast T1 Internet lines. They imported a $7,000,

(Ryan McVay/Photodisc)

top-of-the-line espresso machine from Italy. To make the café look sleek and modern, all of the furniture was custom-designed for the space, as were the curved metallic ceiling and wall panels. Installing the soundproof interior room was more costly than they had anticipated. Their equipment costs totaled $25,000. At $500 per month, they had negotiated a good deal on their rent, so they figured that they could afford to splurge on these other features.

Financing

The café's start-up investment totaled $100,000. This included a $10,000 cash reserve. Amy and Steve contributed a combined $20,000 from their personal savings. Steve's brother invested another $20,000, in exchange for a 20 percent equity stake. Amy's mother wrote a check for $10,000, which she gave to the partners as a gift. Also, Amy and Steve received a $50,000 loan from Amy's uncle. The partners agreed to pay back the loan with interest at an annual rate of 12 percent.

Funding Source	Equity	Debt	Gift
Personal Savings	$20,000 (80% equity)		
Steve's Brother	$20,000 (20% equity)		
Amy's Uncle		$50,000 (@12% interest)	
Amy's Mother			$10,000
Subtotal	$40,000	$50,000	$10,000
Total Start-Up Investment	$100,000		

*Note: This is a fictional case.

Computer Glitch

Because so much money was needed for start up, Amy and Steve tried to cut costs by hiring a local high school student, who agreed to work 100 hours per month for an hourly wage of $10. It soon became apparent to frustrated customers, however, that none of the staff, including Amy and Steve, knew how to solve the technical problems customers encountered with the computers and printers. Amy and Steve tried to find a permanent technical-support person, but computer experts were in high demand at the time, and the partners felt that they couldn't afford to pay a competitive salary.

Business Troubles Brew

Before starting their business, Amy and Steve assumed that revenue would come from two primary sources, food and beverage sales and computer/Internet services. Together they had calculated two economics-of-one-unit analyses, one for each of the two sources.

Amy and Steve's EOU

The partners originally assumed that the average customer would spend $6 at the café and that $2 of this revenue would be generated by food and beverage sales. The remaining $4 would come from the sale of computer and Internet services. They believed that the business could be very successful if they did well selling computer services. After all, they could charge customers $4 for an hour of service that would only cost them 45 cents to provide. In comparison, food and beverage sales would not be nearly as profitable. For every $2 of lattes and muffins sold, they would pay $1 in direct costs.

Amy and Steve built a 5 percent manager's commission into their EOU, even though they did not yet have the funds to hire a manager. They wanted to account for this cost because they did plan to hire a manager at some point in the future, and the commission would be a real cost of doing business. It was time for Amy and Steve to examine both revenue streams together.

In Hot Water

When the Portland Freelancers' Café first opened, Amy and Steve were encouraged by how busy things seemed. The café was buzzing with customers and they received some positive reviews in the local papers. They expected to lose money at first, but figured that, in a few months' time, the business would become profitable. After three months, they had a major shock when they realized that this was not happening. What went wrong?

EOU for Food and Beverage Sales	
Average Sale per Customer	
• Food/Beverage Sales	$2.00
Variable Costs per Unit	
COGS per Unit	
• Food/Beverage Costs	1.00
TOTAL COGS per Unit	$1.00

EOU for Food and Beverage Sales	
Other Variable Costs per Unit Manager's Commission @ 5%	0.10
Total Variable Cost per Unit	$1.10
Contribution Margin per Unit	$0.90

EOU for Computer/Internet Services	
Average Sale per Customer	
• Computer Services	$4.00
Variable Costs per Unit COGS per Unit	
• Paper, Toner	0.25
TOTAL COGS per Unit	$0.25
Other Variable Costs per Unit Manager's Commission @ 5%	0.20
Total Variable Cost per Unit	$0.45
Contribution Margin per Unit	$3.55

Changes in the Environment

Initially, Amy and Steve's customers willingly paid $4 an hour to use the computers and high-speed Internet connection. However, soon after the grand opening, wireless Internet service became available throughout the Portland area. Within two months, the café's customers no longer wanted to pay to go online. They put pressure on Amy and Steve to become a wireless hot spot. This meant that Amy and Steve would have to foot the bill of providing free Internet service.

The partners carried out some research and learned that it would cost $300 to purchase the basic equipment for wireless Internet connectivity, plus an additional $30 per month in service fees. They had counted on charging their customers for Internet access and now it looked like *they* would have to pick up the tab. They wondered how they could pay for this unexpected cost and also make up the lost revenue. On the other hand, they feared that the Portland Freelancers' Café would not be able to compete unless they adapted to changes in the market.

EOU: Average Sale per Customer	
Average Sale per Customer	
• Computer Services	$4.00
• Food and Beverage Sales	$2.00
Variable Costs per Unit	
COGS per Unit	
• Paper, Toner	$0.25
• Food/Beverage Costs	1.00
TOTAL COGS per Unit	$1.25
Other Variable Costs per Unit	
Manager's Commission—Computer Services @ 5%	$0.20
Manager's Commission—Food and Beverage @ 5%	0.10
TOTAL Commission Costs	$0.30
Total Variable Cost per Unit	$1.55
Contribution Margin per Unit	$3.20

Amy and Steve's EOU Revisited

Three months after they opened the café, Amy and Steve discovered that their monthly unit sales of computer services had been cut by more than half. In their first month, they had sold 1,500 units, but by month three they were only averaging 600. They worried that this number would only continue to decline.

The café was holding steady with its food and beverage sales—in fact, the monthly units sold had climbed steadily from 4,500 units in month one to 5,000 in month three. Customers were enjoying the café's free wireless service. This feature created a situation where people would stay longer and order more coffee. But even with increased sales of cappuccino, the overall finances of the operation were not improving. In looking at their economics-of-one-unit analysis of food and beverage sales, the partners could see that their gross profit per unit for food and beverage sales was only 90 cents. Even if they sold 5,000 food and beverage units per month, they would still only be earning $4,500 in gross profit. In the scheme of things, this was not very much money—not nearly enough to cover the monthly fixed costs of $8,332.

An Uncertain Future

One year into their venture, Amy and Steve began to seriously doubt their decision to start the Portland Freelancers' Café. In hindsight, they realized that they knew a lot about being customers but running a state-of-the-art coffee shop was a lot harder than they had imagined.

By the end of the year, the Portland Freelancers' Café was on the verge of going out of business. Take a look at the café's financial statements in **Exhibits 8-14** through **8-17** and then analyze why this happened.

Case Study Analysis

1. Evaluate the economics-of-one-unit analysis that Amy and Steve conducted and then answer the following:

   a. Amy and Steve assumed that, for every $6 in sales, $4 would come from selling computer-related services. Calculate what percentage of their total sales revenue per unit this $4 represents.

   b. For every $2 in food and beverage sales, Amy and Steve assumed that their COGS per unit would be $1. Calculate the markup percentage.

   c. For every $4 in computer services sales, Amy and Steve assumed that their COGS per unit would be 25 cents. Calculate the markup percentage.

2. List three things that Amy and Steve should have considered doing to adapt to the changes in the environment after their customers no longer wanted to pay for Internet services and expected the café to provide free wireless connection.

3. Evaluate Amy and Steve's income statement for their first month of operation:

   a. Is the café operating at a profit or a loss?

   b. How many units above or below break-even were sold?

4. Amy and Steve decided to take on a $50,000 loan to finance their start-up investment. Each month they are paying $1,469 in interest charges. Look at their total monthly fixed costs. What percentage of their total monthly fixed costs does this $1,469 represent?

5. What is the debt-to-equity ratio of the Portland Freelancers' Café?

6. Look at each section of the café's cash flow statement. Based on what you see, write a memo highlighting three reasons why this business is not succeeding.

7. Review the café's balance sheet. Explain why the net value of the café's property and equipment has decreased from $80,000 in month one to $64,000 by year's end.

Exhibit 8-14 *Start-Up Investment and Economics of One Unit*

Start-Up Investment	
Start-Up Costs	
Soundproof Room	$15,000
Espresso Machine	7,000
High-Speed Internet Access Setup	10,000
Workstations	20,000
Supplies/Equipment	25,000
Furniture	8,000
Fixtures	5,000
Cash Reserves	10,000
Total Start-Up Investments	**$100,000**

Economics of One Unit (EOU)
Unit of Sale: Computer/Internet Services (average per customer)

Average Sale Total (Revenue)			$4.00
Less COGS			
Computer time	–		
Printer materials	0.25		
Total COGS	0.25	0.25	0.25
Gross Profit			**$3.75**
Less Other Variable Costs			
Commission 5% to manager	0.20		
Total Other Variable Costs	0.20	0.20	0.20
Total Variable Costs (COGS + Other VC)		0.45	
Contribution Margin			**$3.55**

Economics of One Unit (EOU)
Unit of Sale: Food and Beverage Sales (average per customer)

Average Sale Total (Revenue)			$2.00
Less COGS			
Food	0.80		
Beverage	0.20		
Total COGS	1.00	1.00	1.00
Gross Profit			**$1.00**
Less Other Variable Costs			
Commission 5% to manager	0.10		
Total Other Variable Costs	0.10	0.10	0.10
Total Variable Costs (COGS + Other VC)		1.10	
Contribution Margin			**$0.90**

Exhibit 8-15 *Income Statement*

The Portland Freelancers Café
INCOME STATEMENT
for the Year Ending 12/31/2011

		Jan	Feb	Mar	Apr	May	Jun	Jul	Aug	Sep	Oct	Nov	Dec	Year
No. Units Sold—Computer Services		1,500	1,000	600	550	550	500	500	450	450	450	400	400	7,350
No. Units Sold—Food and Beverage		4,500	4,750	5,000	5,100	5,200	5,300	5,400	5,500	5,600	5,700	5,800	6,000	63,850
Revenue														
Computer Service Fees		$ 6,000	$ 4,000	$ 2,400	$ 2,200	$ 2,200	$ 2,000	$ 2,000	$ 1,800	$ 1,800	$ 1,800	$ 1,600	$ 1,600	$ 29,400
Food and Beverage Sales		9,000	9,500	10,000	10,200	10,400	10,600	10,800	11,000	11,200	11,400	11,600	12,000	127,700
Total Revenue		$15,000	$13,500	$12,400	$12,400	$12,600	$12,600	$12,800	$12,800	$13,000	$13,200	$13,200	$13,600	$157,100
Less COGS														
Printer Mat'ls (paper, ink)		375	250	150	138	138	125	125	113	113	113	100	100	1,838
Food		3,600	3,800	4,000	4,080	4,160	4,240	4,320	4,400	4,480	4,560	4,640	4,800	51,080
Beverages		900	950	1,000	1,020	1,040	1,060	1,080	1,100	1,120	1,140	1,160	1,200	12,770
Total COGS		$ 4,875	$ 5,000	$ 5,150	$ 5,238	$ 5,338	$ 5,425	$ 5,525	$ 5,613	$ 5,713	$ 5,813	$ 5,900	$ 6,100	$ 65,688
Gross Profit		$10,125	$ 8,500	$ 7,250	$ 7,163	$ 7,263	$ 7,175	$ 7,275	$ 7,188	$ 7,288	$ 7,388	$ 7,300	$ 7,500	$ 91,413
Less Other Variable Costs														
Commission, Computer	(5%)	300	200	120	110	110	100	100	90	90	90	80	80	1,470
Commission, Food/Bev.	(5%)	450	475	500	510	520	530	540	550	560	570	580	600	6,385
Total Other Variable Costs		$ 750	$ 675	$ 620	$ 620	$ 630	$ 630	$ 640	$ 640	$ 650	$ 660	$ 660	$ 680	$ 7,855
Total Var. Costs (COGS + Other VC)		5,625	5,675	5,770	5,858	5,968	6,055	6,165	6,253	6,363	6,473	6,560	6,780	73,543
Contribution Margin*		$ 9,375	$ 7,825	$ 6,630	$ 6,543	$ 6,633	$ 6,545	$ 6,635	$ 6,548	$ 6,638	$ 6,728	$ 6,640	$ 6,820	$ 83,558

* Remember: Revenue – COGS = Gross Profit – Other Variable Costs = Contribution Margin.

(continued)

Exhibit 8-15 (Continued)

The Portland Freelancers Café
INCOME STATEMENT
for the Year Ending 12/31/2011

	Jan	Feb	Mar	Apr	May	Jun	Jul	Aug	Sep	Oct	Nov	Dec	Year
Less Fixed Costs (USAIIRD)													
Utilities													
Electricity	150	150	150	150	150	150	150	150	150	150	150	150	1,800
Gas	250	250	250	250	250	250	250	250	250	250	250	250	3,000
Water	100	100	100	100	100	100	100	100	100	100	100	100	1,200
Telephone	75	75	75	75	75	75	75	75	75	75	75	75	900
High-Speed Internet	425	425	425	425	425	425	425	425	425	425	425	425	5,100
Wireless Internet Service	30	30	30	30	30	30	30	30	30	30	30	30	360
Total Utilities	$1,030	$1,030	$1,030	$1,030	$1,030	$1,030	$1,030	$1,030	$1,030	$1,030	$1,030	$1,030	$12,360
Salaries													
Amy & Steve Salary	1,000	1,000	1,000	1,000	1,000	1,000	1,000	1,000	1,000	1,000	1,000	1,000	12,000
Tech Support (Part time)	1,000	1,000	1,000	1,000	1,000	1,000	1,000	1,000	1,000	1,000	1,000	1,000	12,000
Total Salaries	$2,000	$2,000	$2,000	$2,000	$2,000	$2,000	$2,000	$2,000	$2,000	$2,000	$2,000	$2,000	$24,000
Advertising	1,000	1,000	1,000	1,000	1,000	1,000	1,000	1,000	1,000	1,000	1,000	1,000	12,000
Insurance	500	500	500	500	500	500	500	500	500	500	500	500	6,000
Interest	1,469	1,469	1,469	1,469	1,469	1,469	1,469	1,469	1,469	1,469	1,469	1,469	17,628
Rent	1,000	1,000	1,000	1,000	1,000	1,000	1,000	1,000	1,000	1,000	1,000	1,000	12,000
Depreciation	1,333	1,333	1,333	1,333	1,333	1,333	1,333	1,333	1,333	1,333	1,333	1,333	15,996
Total Fixed Costs	$8,332	$8,332	$8,332	$8,332	$8,332	$8,332	$8,332	$8,332	$8,332	$8,332	$8,332	$8,332	$99,984
Pre-Tax Profit	$1,043	($507)	($1,702)	($1,790)	($1,700)	($1,787)	($1,697)	($1,785)	($1,695)	($1,605)	($1,692)	($1,512)	($16,427)
Taxes (20%)	209	—	—	—	—	—	—	—	—	—	—	—	—
Net Profit	$ 834	($507)	($1,702)	($1,790)	($1,700)	($1,787)	($1,697)	($1,785)	($1,695)	($1,605)	($1,692)	($1,512)	($16,427)

Exhibit 8-16 *Cash Flow Statement*

The Portland Freelancers Café
CASH FLOW STATEMENT
for the Year Ending 12/31/2011

	Jan	Feb	Mar	Apr	May	Jun	Jul	Aug	Sep	Oct	Nov	Dec	Year
Number of Units—													
Computer Services	1,500	1,000	600	550	550	500	500	450	450	450	400	400	7,350
Number of Units—													
Food & Beverage Sales	4,500	4,750	5,000	5,100	5,200	5,300	5,400	5,500	5,600	5,700	5,800	6,000	63,850
Cash Flow from Operating:													
Cash Inflows:													
Computer Usage Fees	$ 6,000	$ 4,000	$ 2,400	$ 2,200	$ 2,200	$ 2,000	$ 2,000	$ 1,800	$ 1,800	$ 1,800	$ 1,600	$ 1,600	$ 29,400
Food and Beverage Sales	9,000	9,500	10,000	10,200	10,400	10,600	10,800	11,000	11,200	11,400	11,600	12,000	127,700
Total Cash Inflows	$15,000	$13,500	$12,400	$12,400	$12,600	$12,600	$12,800	$12,800	$13,000	$13,200	$13,200	$13,600	$157,100
Cash Outflows:													
Variable Costs													
COGS	$ 4,875	$ 5,000	$ 5,150	$ 5,238	$ 5,338	$ 5,425	$ 5,525	$ 5,613	$ 5,713	$ 5,813	$ 5,900	$ 6,100	$ 65,688
Other Variable Costs	$ 750	$ 675	$ 620	$ 620	$ 630	$ 630	$ 640	$ 640	$ 650	$ 660	$ 660	$ 680	$ 7,855
Utilities													
Electricity, Gas, Water, Telephone	$ 500	$ 500	$ 500	$ 500	$ 500	$ 500	$ 500	$ 500	$ 500	$ 500	$ 500	$ 500	$ 6,000
High-Speed Internet Access	425	425	425	425	425	425	425	425	425	425	425	425	5,100
Wireless Internet	30	30	30	30	30	30	30	30	30	30	30	30	360
Salaries													
Part-Time Tech Support Salary	$ 1,000	$ 1,000	$ 1,000	$ 1,000	$ 1,000	$ 1,000	$ 1,000	$ 1,000	$ 1,000	$ 1,000	$ 1,000	$ 1,000	$ 12,000
Amy and Steve's Salary	$ 1,000	$ 1,000	$ 1,000	$ 1,000	$ 1,000	$ 1,000	$ 1,000	$ 1,000	$ 1,000	$ 1,000	$ 1,000	$ 1,000	$ 12,000
Advertising	$ 1,000	$ 1,000	$ 1,000	$ 1,000	$ 1,000	$ 1,000	$ 1,000	$ 1,000	$ 1,000	$ 1,000	$ 1,000	$ 1,000	$ 12,000
Insurance	$ 500	$ 500	$ 500	$ 500	$ 500	$ 500	$ 500	$ 500	$ 500	$ 500	$ 500	$ 500	6,000
Interest Expense	$ 1,469	$ 1,469	$ 1,469	$ 1,469	$ 1,469	$ 1,469	$ 1,469	$ 1,469	$ 1,469	$ 1,469	$ 1,469	$ 1,469	17,623
Rent	$ 1,000	$ 1,001	$ 1,002	$ 1,003	$ 1,004	$ 1,005	$ 1,006	$ 1,007	$ 1,008	$ 1,009	$ 1,010	$ 1,011	$ 12,000
Total Cash Used in Operating Activities	$12,549	$12,600	$ 12,696	$12,784	$12,895	$12,983	$13,095	$13,183	$13,294	$13,405	$13,494	$13,715	$156,626
Net Cash Flow from Operating	$ 2,451	$ 900	($ 296)	($ 384)	($ 295)	($ 384)	($ 295)	($ 383)	($ 294)	($ 205)	($ 294)	($ 115)	($ 474)

(continued)

Exhibit 8-16 (Continued)

The Portland Freelancers Café
CASH FLOW STATEMENT
for the Year Ending 12/31/2011

	Jan	Feb	Mar	Apr	May	Jun	Jul	Aug	Sep	Oct	Nov	Dec	Year
Cash Flow Out from Investing:													
Soundproof Room	$ 15,000	$ 0	$ 0	$ 0	$ 0	$ 0	$ 0	$ 0	$ 0	$ 0	$ 0	$ 0	$ 15,000
Espresso Machine	7,000	0	0	0	0	0	0	0	0	0	0	0	7,000
High-Speed Internet Access													
Setup	10,000	0	0	0	0	0	0	0	0	0	0	0	10,000
Workstations	20,000	0	0	0	0	0	0	0	0	0	0	0	20,000
Supplies/Equipment	25,000	0	0	0	0	0	0	0	0	0	0	0	25,000
Furniture	8,000	0	0	0	0	0	0	0	0	0	0	0	8,000
Fixtures	5,000	0	0	0	0	0	0	0	0	0	0	0	5,000
Net Cash Flow Out from Investing	**$ 90,000**	**$ 0**	**$ 0**	**$ 0**	**$ 0**	**$ 0**	**$ 0**	**$ 0**	**$ 0**	**$ 0**	**$ 0**	**$ 0**	**$ 90,000**
Financing:													
Cash Received from Uncle (12% APR)	$ 50,000	$ 0	$ 0	$ 0	$ 0	$ 0	$ 0	$ 0	$ 0	$ 0	$ 0	$ 0	$ 50,000
Cash Received from Brother	20,000	0	0	0	0	0	0	0	0	0	0	0	20,000
Cash Received from Mother	10,000	0	0	0	0	0	0	0	0	0	0	0	10,000
Cash Received from Personal Savings	20,000	0	0	0	0	0	0	0	0	0	0	0	20,000
Net Cash Flow In from Financing	**$100,000**	**$ 0**	**$ 0**	**$ 0**	**$ 0**	**$ 0**	**$ 0**	**$ 0**	**$ 0**	**$ 0**	**$ 0**	**$ 0**	**$100,000**
Net Increase (Decrease) in Cash	$ 12,451	$ 900	($ 296)	($ 384)	($ 295)	($ 384)	($ 295)	($ 383)	($ 294)	($ 205)	($ 294)	($ 115)	$ 10,474
Cash, Beginning:	$ 10,000	$22,451	$23,351	$22,055	$22,671	$22,376	$21,992	$21,697	$20,314	$20,020	$20,815	$20,521	$ 10,000
Cash, End:	$ 22,451	$23,351	$22,055	$22,671	$22,376	$21,992	$21,697	$20,314	$20,020	$20,815	$20,521	$20,406	$ 20,474

Exhibit 8-17 *Balance Sheet*

Portland Freelancers Café
BALANCE SHEET
for the Year Ending 12/31/2003

	Opening	Closing
ASSETS		
Current Assets:		
Cash	$110,000	$20,474
Accounts Receivable	0	0
Total Current Assets	**$110,000**	**$20,474**
Fixed Assets (Property and Equipment):		
Soundproof Room	$ 15,000	$15,000
Espresso Machine	2,000	2,000
Workstations	30,000	30,000
Supplies/Equipment	25,000	25,000
Furniture	3,000	3,000
Fixtures	5,000	5,000
Total Property and Equipment	**$ 80,000**	**$80,000**
Less Accumulated Depreciation	**$ 0**	**$15,996**
Total Property and Equipment (Net)	**$ 80,000**	**$64,004**
Total Assets	**$190,000**	**$84,478**
LIABILITIES AND OWNER'S EQUITY		
Current Liabilities:		
Accounts Payable	$ 0	$ 0
Total Current Liabilities	**$ 0**	**$ 0**
Long-Term Liability (Uncle's Loan)	**$ 50,000**	**$32,377**
Total Liabilities	**$ 50,000**	**$32,377**
Owner's Equity	**$140,000**	**$52,101**
Amy	40%	40%
Steve	40%	40%
Steve's Brother	20%	20%
Total Liabilities and Owner's Equity	**$190,000**	**$84,478**

CASH FLOW AND TAXES

At age 28, David Kendricks started his own recording label, Kickin' Records. He began by searching for and producing the work of hip-hop artists from his hometown of Newark, New Jersey.

David invested $25,000 in his new business. He saved the money by working two jobs for five years. He set up a Web site to sell his CDs. He got a business telephone with voice messaging and created and printed his own stationery and business cards. He regularly invests time from eight in the evening until three in the morning at concerts and clubs, looking for groups to sign to his recording label.

David has been spending about $100 a night for tickets, drinks, and transportation. He has found, however, that the groups he sees are already signed and have producers. David has had no sales because he has not yet produced a CD. After six months, he is almost $20,000 in debt. David hasn't kept a close watch on his cash flow, and this has threatened the existence of his business.

Performance Objectives

1. Understand the importance of cash flow management.
2. Know the difference between cash and profits.
3. Read a cash flow statement.
4. Create a cash budget.
5. File appropriate tax returns for your business.

(UpperCut Images)

Cash Flow: The Lifeblood of a Business

Cash is the energy that keeps your business flowing, the way electricity powers a lamp. Run out of cash and your business will soon go out like a light. Without cash on hand, you will not be able to pay essentials, even while the income statement says you are earning a profit. If your phone is cut off, it will not matter what the income statement says. The success of your business will depend upon cash, from start-up through its entire existence. Cash is essential for the initial investment, ongoing operations, and growth. Managing cash is more critical than managing sales, because sales without cash receipts are a recipe for disaster. Cash truly is the lifeblood of a business.

The income statement shows you what the situation is with sales and profits over a period of time. It tells you how much revenue has come in and how it relates to the cost of goods sold and operating costs. The balance sheet is a snapshot of your business. It shows your assets and liabilities and net worth at a given moment. Each of these documents and the associated ratios are important, but without a firm handle on the cash situation, business success will be elusive.

The Income Statement Does Not Show Available Cash

Once you start a business and are using the accrual method of accounting, however, you will notice that, sometimes, even when the income statement says you are making a profit, you have no money. There is often a time lag between making a sale and getting paid. If you make a

BizFacts

You can calculate your ongoing cash balance by subtracting cash disbursements from cash receipts. You should never have a negative cash balance.

sale and the customer promises to pay you in a week, the sale is recognized on the income statement immediately, but you will not have the cash until the check is received, deposited, and the funds are available from the bank. Also, there may be a lag between paying for labor and/or materials and receiving payment for the finished goods. If a company is using the accrual method of accounting, it records sales when goods are shipped/delivered, even though payment has not been received. Thus, a company may show a profit and have a negative cash flow; cash and profit are not the same.

Performance Objective 1 ▶

Understand the importance of cash flow management.

cash flow statement
financial document that tracks the money coming into and going out of an organization.

For all the good information and guidance a monthly income statement can provide, you cannot base your business's daily operations on the income statement alone. You will also need a **cash flow statement** that summarizes the cash coming into and going out of the business in a specified time frame.

You can calculate your cash balance by subtracting cash disbursements from cash receipts, as you do when balancing your checkbook. Your goal is never to have a negative cash balance. A negative balance means that you are overdrawn on one or more of your bank accounts. This will damage your banking relationships and trigger the accumulation of fees and penalties. It may also result in bounced checks to critical suppliers, and the like. Basically, a negative cash balance means that there are problems with your cash flow.

Author William Stolze calls the cash flow statement, "By far the most important financial control in a start-up venture."[1] The cash flow statement records inflows and outflows of money as they occur. If a sale is made in June, but the customer does not pay until August, the cash flow statement will not show the revenue until August, when the cash "flows" into the business. If you are keeping your accounting records on a cash basis, you would not show the sale on the income statement until you received payment. If you use the accrual method, the sale will appear on the income statement in June, but not in the cash flow statement until August.

Step into the Shoes...
King C. Gillette Faces a Cash Crunch

(Keystone/Hulton Archive/Getty Images)

King Gillette was a traveling sales representative for 28 years. In his spare time, he tried to invent a successful consumer product. He invented all kinds of gadgets that did not pan out but, in 1885, when he cut himself shaving with his dull straight razor, inspiration hit. Gillette thought of a "safety" razor with disposable blades.

Gillette and a partner eventually got financing and launched their business. The future seemed bright, but soon the company was $12,500

in debt. By 1901, even though people were excited about the product, Gillette remembered, "We were backed up to the wall with our creditors lined up in front waiting for the signal to fire."[2]

Gillette convinced a Boston investor to put money in the company and, by the end of 1904, was producing a quarter million razor sets per year. This is an example of how crucial an infusion of money can be to a business. A temporary cash crunch nearly destroyed a company that is now more than a century old.

[1]William Stolze, *Start Up: An Entrepreneur's Guide to Launching and Managing a New Business* (Franklin Lakes, NJ: Career Press, 1994), p. 96.
[2]Russell B. Adams, *King C. Gillette: The Man and His Wonderful Shaving Device* (New York: Little, Brown, 1978).

Exercise

Name three kinds of businesses that bring in a lot of cash during part of the year and not much the rest of the time.

Rules to Keep Cash Flowing

Cash flow is primarily a factor of accounts receivable, accounts payable, and inventory. By controlling these factors, a company can control its cash flow. In order to avoid getting caught without enough cash to pay your bills, follow these rules:

1. **Collect cash as soon as possible.** When you make a sale, try to get paid immediately. If you must extend credit, make sure you collect the cash as scheduled.

2. **Pay your bills by the due date, not earlier.** You do not have to pay a bill the day it arrives in your mailbox. Look for the due date, and send your payment so it arrives by that day. This will conserve precious cash.

3. **Check on your available cash every day.** Always know how much cash you have on hand. Your cash flow will be reflected in your up-to-date accounting journal. Remember, your true balance takes into account any checks or bank debits outstanding.

4. **Lease or finance instead of buying equipment, where practical.** Leasing distributes costs over time. Better yet, if it makes sense, acquire functional used equipment rather than new equipment.

5. **Avoid buying inventory that you do not need.** Find the point where you stock the minimal inventory necessary to satisfy customer demand. Inventory ties up cash: the cash you use to purchase inventory and the cash you spend storing it.

Noncash Expenses Can Distort the Financial Picture

> **◀ Performance Objective 2**
> Know the difference between cash and profits.
>
> **noncash expenses** adjustments to asset values not involving cash, such as depreciation.

The income statement is not an accurate reflection of your cash position when it includes **noncash expenses** or expenses recorded as adjustments to asset values, such as depreciation. When you depreciate an asset, you are deducting a portion of its cost from your income statement. But you aren't actually spending that cash; you are reducing the value of the asset. You do not pay out actual money when you record a depreciation expense on your income statement.

Depreciation is a noncash expense because no money is disbursed. When depreciation is deducted from an income statement, therefore, the statement no longer accurately reflects how much cash the business is really holding. By the same token, the cash flow statement does not include depreciation, since no cash leaves the business.

The Working Capital Cycle

> **working capital** the value of current assets minus current liabilities.

Once a business is operational, an entrepreneur must keep an eye on the **working capital,** the formula for which is:

$$\text{Current Assets} - \text{Current Liabilities} = \text{Working Capital}$$

Working capital tells you how much cash the company would have if it paid all its short-term debt with the cash it had on hand. What was left over would be cash the company could use to build the business, fund its growth, and produce value for the shareholders.

All other things being equal, a company with positive working capital will always outperform a company with negative working capital. The latter cannot spend the money to bring a new product to market. If a company runs out of working capital, it will still have bills to pay and products to develop; it may not be able to stay afloat. When determining cash requirements for your business, remember working capital.

The Cyclical and Seasonal Nature of Cash Flows

The entrepreneur needs a cash flow statement to depict the cash position of the business at specified points in time. The cash flow statement records inflows and outflows when they occur. There are cash flow cycles that occur for every business that are important to understand because they can make the difference between success and failure. **Figures 9-1** and **9-2** show cash flow cycles for a manufacturer and a residential cleaning company, respectively.

The length of the cycle, amount of cash involved, and upfront cash outlays will differ substantially for these businesses. For example, a manufacturer may have to pay its suppliers and employees before getting paid by a customer. A residential cleaning service, on the other hand, may collect customer payments on the same day that the cleaning is provided, so wages can be paid soon after the cash for a job is received. Thus, their planning and budgeting will also differ significantly.

In addition to having cash flow cycles relative to specific transactions, cash flow can be seasonal for many businesses, meaning that the amount of cash flowing into a business may depend on where the business is in its fiscal year. A flower store will have a lot of cash coming in around Valentine's Day and Mother's Day, for example, but may have very little during the fall. A college campus bookstore will have to stock up on books before each semester starts, and will have a lot of cash coming in when students arrive to buy books for their classes.

This is why keeping an eye on cash flow at all times will be crucial to the survival of your business. Utility companies, vendors, and lenders will not care that you won't have money coming in over the next three months; they will want their regular monthly payments, unless you negotiate special payment schedules in advance. When you create your business plan, describe your expectations for seasonal changes in your cash flow, and how you will manage your cash to cope with this. Remember, you can ask lenders to create payment schedules based upon the seasonal nature of your business. It is often in their best interest to do so, and they may appreciate that you planned ahead.

Performance Objective 3 >

Read a cash flow statement.

Reading a Cash Flow Statement

Knowing how to read a cash flow statement is a valuable skill for any businessperson. Whereas income statements and balance sheets provide considerable insight into a company, the cash flow statement gives a clear picture of its cash position. A simple cash flow statement provides information about the cash that is coming into and going out of an organization. The first section records all sources of income. These are cash inflows, or *cash receipts* (not to be confused with receipts for purchases). The next section reports cash outflows, or necessary *disbursements* for the month: insurance and interest payments, cost of goods sold, salaries, and so forth. Some cash flow statements break

Figure 9-1 *Cash Flow Cycle for a Manufacturer*

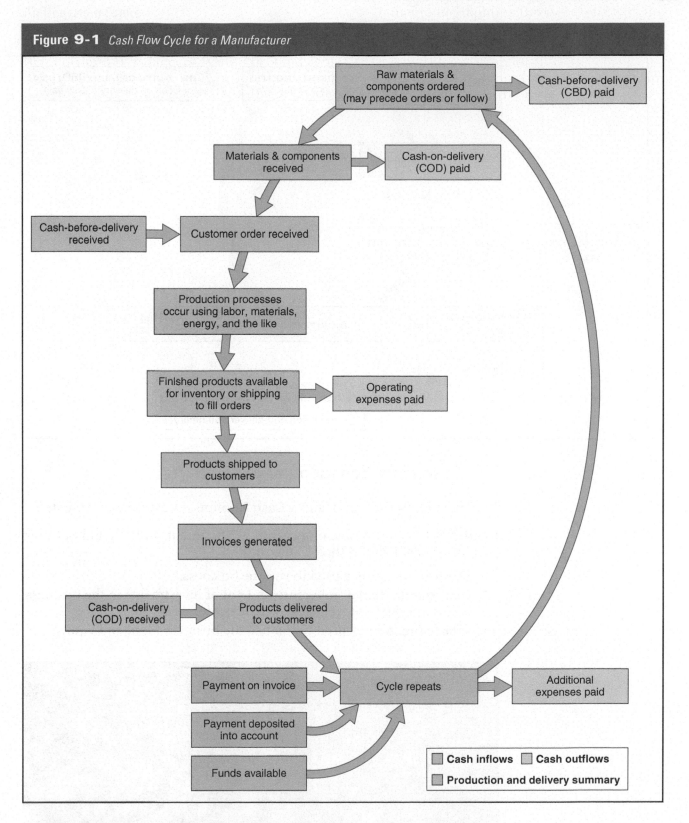

down inflows and outflows according to whether they are related to operations, investing, or financing (see below).

The last section shows the net change in cash flow. This tells the entrepreneur whether the business had a positive or negative cash flow that month. You can have all the sales in the world and still go out of business if you do not have enough cash flowing in to cover your monthly cash outflows.

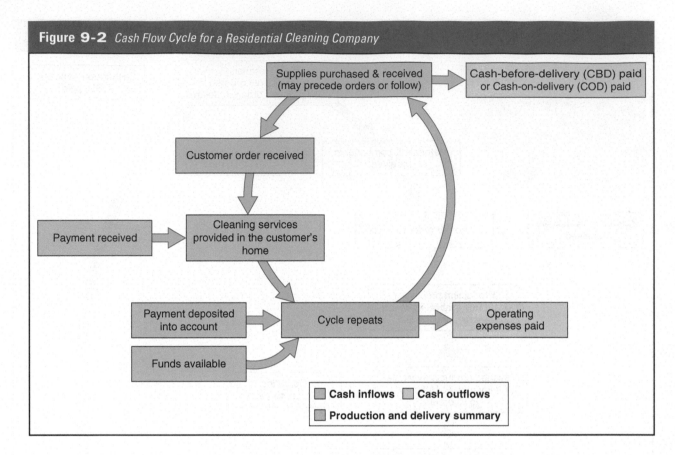

Figure 9-2 *Cash Flow Cycle for a Residential Cleaning Company*

(Diagram)

Supplies purchased & received
(may precede orders or follow) → Cash-before-delivery (CBD) paid
or Cash-on-delivery (COD) paid

Customer order received

Payment received → Cleaning services
provided in the customer's
home

Payment deposited
into account → Cycle repeats → Operating
expenses paid

Funds available

☐ Cash inflows ☐ Cash outflows
☐ Production and delivery summary

The Cash Flow Equation

Cash Flow = Cash on Hand + Cash Receipts – Cash Disbursements

Exhibit 9-1 is an example of a cash flow statement. Inflows and outflows of cash are divided into three categories:

1. *Operations.* Money used to run the business.
2. *Investment.* Money going into and out of investments in the business, such as equipment, vehicles, or real estate.
3. *Financing.* Money used to finance the business (debt and equity).

An employee in the receiving department of REI's Distribution Center in Sumner, Washington, sorts products during an October inventory.
(AP Photo)

Exhibit 9-1 *Sample Cash Flow Statement*

Cash Flow Statement for Lola's Custom Draperies, Inc., for the Month of March 2012

Cash Flow from Operations

Cash Inflows

Sales (net of returns)	$65,400	
Total Cash Inflows	**$65,400**	

Cash Outflows:

Variable Costs

COGS	$29,360	
Other Variable Costs (sales commissions)	6,540	

Fixed Costs

Factory Rent & Utilities	8,000	
Sales & Administrative	12,000	
Part-Time Tech-Support Salary	1,000	
Taxes	2,875	($11,500 × 0.25)
Total Cash Used in Operating Activities	**$59,775**	
Net Cash Flow from Operations	**$5,625**	$65,400 − $59,775)

Cash Outflow from Investing

Purchase of Building	0	
Purchase of Equipment	(6,000)	
Net Cash Flow from Investing	**($6,000)**	

Cash Flow from Financing:

Loans	$25,000	
Gifts	0	
Equity Investment	0	
Net Cash Flow from Financing	**$25,000**	
Net Increase/(Decrease) in Cash	**$24,625**	$5,625 − $6,000 + $25,0001)
Cash, Beginning	**$500**	
Cash, Ending	**$25,125**	($500 + $24,6251

Forecasting Cash Flow: The Cash Budget

> **Performance Objective 4**
> Create a cash budget.

As you get your business off the ground, and even after it has operated for many years, you should prepare cash flow projections to make sure there is enough money to pay the bills. In the beginning, monthly—or even weekly—cash flows are in order. There are two steps to forecasting cash flow receipts:

Step 1 Project cash receipts from all possible sources. Remember, orders are not cash receipts, because they may not become cash. Some may be cancelled and some customers may not pay. Cash receipts are checks that have cleared, or credit card payments, or cash itself. Plus, note the assumptions you are making to arrive at those figures, so that others can understand the logic behind the statements.

Step 2 Subtract expenditures that would need to be deducted to meet this level of cash receipts. Cash expenditures are only those expenses you will actually have to pay during the projected time period.

Exhibit 9-2 Cash Flow Budget for Three Months Ending June 30, 2011			
	April	**May**	**June**
Monthly Sales Net of Returns	$20,000	$22,000	$25,000
Inventory Purchased ($10,000 in March)	11,000	12,500	14,000
Cash Flow from Operations			
Cash Inflows			
In Month of Sales	$10,000	$11,000	$12,500
One Month Later	0	6,000	6,600
Two Months Later	0	0	4,000
Total Cash Receipts from Operations	$10,000	$17,000	$23,100
Cash Outflows			
Inventory Payments			
One Month after Purchase	$8,000	$8,800	$10,000
Two Months after Purchase	0	2,000	2,200
Total Cash for Inventory	$8,000	$10,800	$12,200
Payments for Other Operational Expenses	8,600	8,000	8,000
Interest on Loans	0	100	100
Taxes	0	0	0
Total Cash Payments for Operations	$16,600	$18,900	$20,300
Total Cash Flow from Operations	($6,600)	($1,900)	$2,800
Cash Flows from Investments			
Purchase of Equipment	($20,000)		
Cash Flows from Financing			
Commercial loan for Equipment	$20,000		
Line of Credit Draw			$10,000
Owner's Personal Investment	35,000		
Total Cash Flows from Financing	$55,000	$0	$10,000
Total Net Cash Flow	$28,400	($1,900)	$12,800
Beginning Cash Balance	$0	$28,400	$26,500
Ending Cash Balance	$28,400	$26,500	$39,300

Exhibit 9-2 is a sample company budget and **Exhibit 9-3** shows the assumptions underlying another sample budget.

You know that any projections will not be completely accurate, but you should create them to the best of your ability and review and update them routinely. They will be useful for anticipating any shortfalls, so that you can make adjustments to costs, push for increased sales, and/or arrange short-term financing as needed.

Exhibit 9-3 *Cash Flow Assumptions*	
Category	**Assumption**
Accounts Receivable	50% in month of sale
	30% one month later
	20% two months later
Inventory (Payable)	0% in month of purchase
	80% one month later
	20% two months later
Utilities	$500 per month
Salaries and Benefits	$6,000 per month
Advertising	$1,000 in April, and $600 per month thereafter
Insurance	$100 per month
Rent	2,000 square feet of space at $6 per square foot per year = $1,000 per month
Interest	Interest only on line of credit and commercial loan for three months
Depreciation	$0 (Depreciation is not a cash expenditure)
Taxes	Paid quarterly—none in this period
Commercial Loan 1	$20,000 for seven years at 6% for equipment purchase = $100 per month interest only for three months
Line of Credit	$50,000 revolving line of credit, interest only at 12% per year, and no funds drawn until June

Creating a Healthy Cash Flow

Healthy cash flow management means keeping sufficient cash on hand and available to pay your bills in a timely fashion, and in general to have financial resources available to you when you need them. Most entrepreneurs struggle at various times to have sufficient cash to pay for materials, rent, and other expenses. As a business becomes more stable and successful, deciding when and where to invest excess cash to maximize earnings at the appropriate risk level becomes an important part of managing the company.

Cash inflows and outflows can be managed to control overall cash flow. **Figure 9-3** shows categories of cash flows and the way they affect a company.

Global Impact...

Cash Flow Statements Are Not Required in Every Country

In the United States, public corporations are required by law to present cash flow statements as part of their compliance reporting. In some countries, however, businesses are not required to present either a statement of cash flow or statement of fund flow. This is the case in Germany, Italy, and Denmark. In Germany, many large companies voluntarily provide either a cash flow or fund flow statement. The United Kingdom does require cash flow statements but only for very large companies. The international trend, however, is moving toward the U.S. practice of requiring cash flow statements from public corporations as governments recognize that income statements do not reveal a company's true cash position and can be misleading to investors. In light of recent corporate scandals, the trend is toward greater transparency and more disclosure.

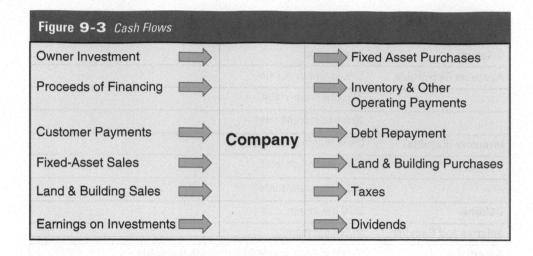

Figure 9-3 *Cash Flows*

Owner Investment ⟹ | **Company** | ⟹ Fixed Asset Purchases
Proceeds of Financing ⟹ | | ⟹ Inventory & Other Operating Payments
Customer Payments ⟹ | | ⟹ Debt Repayment
Fixed-Asset Sales ⟹ | | ⟹ Land & Building Purchases
Land & Building Sales ⟹ | | ⟹ Taxes
Earnings on Investments ⟹ | | ⟹ Dividends

Managing Inventory to Manage Cash

Inventory is often one of the largest components of a company's assets and controlling it is a critical step in managing company cash flow. An entrepreneur takes a risk every time he or she spends cash. If you buy inventory, for example, you run the risk that no one will buy it at a price that will give you a profit, or even buy it at all. When you invest in inventory, cash is tied up and cannot be used for other purposes, such as rent, payroll, and debt service. By managing the level of inventory on hand, you will be dealing with one of the three primary controllable factors in cash availability.

pilferage theft of inventory.

There are two other risks involved with inventory—storage costs and **pilferage,** which is theft of inventory. You will have to be sure you can sell the inventory at a price that will include the cost of storing it and cover pilfering. Barneys, the famous New York clothing store, eventually had a 7 percent pilferage rate, which helped drive the company out of business (although it made a comeback later). Remember to account for these inventory-related costs in your projections.

You should also be cautious about adding inventory based on the expectation of receiving cash from the customers who owe you money. Because a percentage of the receivables owed to you may never be collected, counting on getting all of the cash could cause liquidity problems. You must keep track of your cash flow, or you could get caught in a squeeze between your suppliers, who want you to pay for the inventory you have purchased, and customers who have not yet paid for what they bought. If you cannot pay your creditors, you could lose ownership of your business. That's what happened to Donald Trump and the Taj Mahal in Atlantic City some years ago. He couldn't pay his loans, so he had to turn over 80 percent ownership of the casino to the banks.

Freeing Up Cash by Reducing Inventory

Conceptually, it is clear that reducing inventory releases cash. However, reducing inventory once accumulated is generally easier said than done. If it is finished-goods inventory, it has to be liquidated—sold—if it is to be converted into cash. This often means discounting products in ways that are not in alignment with your overall pricing strategy. If inventory is in the form of work-in-process or semi-finished goods, additional materials and labor costs may have to be invested to make it ready to sell. Thus, freeing up cash by reducing inventory is a valid option that can work, but should be carefully considered and realistically projected.

Tracking Inventory

Keeping timely and accurate inventory records is vital to controlling inventory costs. Regardless of the methods you select to control your inventory levels and determine your order point(s), the process will only work effectively if you keep accurate records of what inventory you have on hand and on order. Depending on the type of business, you might use a computer-based tracking system, perhaps with bar codes or other automated techniques. More sophisticated methods can tell you where products are located at any given time and what quantity is available for sale. For a less complex business, you can keep a simple manual system or basic spreadsheet tabulation. You will also need to keep accurate track of the lead times on materials for production and inventory supplies, so that you can avoid stock outs and overages.

Controlling Inventory Levels

By using one of the many available inventory-control methods, you can minimize the amount of cash tied up in inventory. Tight inventory controls reduce waste, obsolescence, and spoilage. By managing inventory to control costs, you are also overseeing your cash flow.

Managing Receivables to Manage Cash

Managing your accounts receivable to generate prompt payment is another way to conserve cash. In retail trade, payments generally are made immediately (in cash) or with a slight delay (by debit or credit card or check). Once you are in a business that extends credit terms to its customers, you will need to manage the timing of payments. The sooner you collect on receivables the better, from a cash flow perspective.

The Cash Effects of Accounts Receivable

Receivables affect cash availability. If you are not actively billing and collecting the monies owed, you can rapidly find yourself with too little cash to operate your business. You will be, in effect, lending your precious cash to your customers while they have the use of your products and/or services.

The Life Cycle of Accounts Receivable

An accounts receivable has a life cycle and this cycle will vary according to your type of business. For most retail businesses, there is no extension of credit and receivables effectively do not exist. Wholesale and manufacturing companies routinely have receivables that depend upon their credit policies and collection efforts. One tool that companies employ to manage their receivables is an aging schedule for accounts receivable. **Exhibit 9-4** is an example of such a schedule.

By creating and updating an aging schedule on a routine basis, you can keep track of your collections and anticipate your cash flow. You can easily identify problem customers and attempt to work with them to improve payment promptness. Also, using aging information can help to establish a forecast of cash flow.

Of course, aging reports are only part of the cash-flow management process. Timely billing and effective collection are critical. If you are extending credit to your customers, a fundamental truth is: *if you don't ask, you won't get.* You have to invoice promptly and collect regularly.

Exhibit 9-4	Aging Schedule for Accounts Receivable, as of June 30, 2012						
Name	#	Not Due (in discount)	Not Due (no discount)	15 Days Past Due	30 Days Past Due	60 Days Past Due	90 Days Past Due	120 Days Past Due
Adams	0123	$120		$240				
Bourdon	0246						$190	$300
Chevaux	3579		$480	$960	$720			
Young	0579					$560	$240	
Zaninga	5811	$480	$1200					
Total		$600	$1,680	$1,200	$720	$560	$430	$300
%		10.9%	30.6%	21.9%	13.1%	10.2%	7.8%	5.5%

Whereas this may seem obvious, one of the most common cash-flow issues for companies is their failure to bill and collect effectively.

One challenge that entrepreneurs face is segregating the collection process from sales and customer relations. A legitimate concern is the potential for losing a customer by asking for—or demanding—payment for previous purchases. A failure to collect on a timely basis can lead to financial disaster for an entrepreneurial venture. Overly aggressive collection attempts can also lead to calamity, through the loss of key customers. However, there are a few guidelines to keep in mind that will help to keep a balance:

- establish clear credit arrangements with customers that reflect acceptable terms for both of you;
- create comprehensive written credit and collection policies, share them with your team, and implement them;
- use collection techniques appropriate to the level of delinquency;
- avoid using salespeople as collectors on their assigned accounts;
- comply with the Fair Debt Collection Practices Act and do not use intimidation or deception in collections;
- recognize that some clients are worth "firing" as credit customers.

The Financing of Accounts Receivable

factoring the act of a business selling its accounts receivables at a discount to a finance company (a "factor") in exchange for immediate cash.

Accounts receivable can provide a ready source of cash for your company if you are in a bind. Receivables financing, or **factoring,** provides cash to companies in exchange for the rights to the cash that will be collected from their customers. When you *factor* your receivables, you provide a list of the outstanding amounts and their status in an aging chart to the finance company, and they will offer you a percentage of each category of receivable in exchange for the right to those proceeds when collected. Fresh accounts are worth significantly more than aged ones. Sometimes, you can be charged for accounts that do not pay within a specified length of time. Factoring is common in some industries and highly unusual in others. You will need to understand your industry to determine the applicability. The key thing to remember is that you will forego the opportunity to control the collection process, and give up potential profits, in exchange for immediate cash. As a general rule, factoring is not the ideal option because it can become the proverbial slippery slope.

Step into the Shoes
Scott Gerber—Serial Entrepreneur

Scott Gerber earned tens of thousands of dollars a month by creating videos while a student at New York University's renowned film school. As he describes his experience, he "got really stupid" and decided that he wanted to be a "new media guru." Rather than continuing to accumulate cash from his thriving video-production business, Scott ended up bankrupt with $700 to his name. His mother, a teacher, told him to "get a real job."

However, Scott was not interested in ever getting a real job. He took the $700 and founded Sizzle It! This company creates Sizzle Reels, which are "3-to-5-minute videos made with fresh visuals, audio, and graphics served with a side of creativity and results."[3] These high-impact marketing tools have brought Scott more success. In addition, he authored the book

Never Get a Real Job and founded the Young Entrepreneur Council.

Scott claims that anyone can be an entrepreneur by focusing on simple services. He has learned that there is money to be made in those services. He also learned that it is critical to keep cash flowing so the business can thrive.

Sources
"The Future of Entrepreneurship Summit," Webcast from the University of South Florida, February 20, 2011.

Sizzle It!, http://www.sizzleit.com, March 15, 2011 "Future of Entrepreneurship Education Summit," Webcast from University of South Florida, February 20, 2011.

Never Get a Real Job, http://www.nevergetarealjob.com, March 16, 2011, and April 13, 2011.

Scott Gerber, serial entrepreneur. (Scott Gerber)

Managing Accounts Payable to Manage Cash

Credit is the ability to borrow money. It enables you to buy something without spending cash at the time of purchase. Once you have established a relationship with a supplier, he or she may be willing to extend credit. If you own a store, you might be able to buy Christmas ornaments from a supplier in October and pay for them in 60 days, after your Christmas sales.

If you aren't managing your cash carefully, however, you could get caught in the squeeze between your suppliers and your customers, described above. Your suppliers might not extend credit to you in the future. If you get into a position where you cannot pay your suppliers, you will have no additional inventory and, thus, no business.

credit the ability to borrow money.

Negotiating Payment

You will have multiple opportunities to negotiate vendor payments and you should be prepared to take advantage of them when they arise. When you establish a customer-vendor relationship, payment terms will be part of the price negotiation. The leverage that you have to negotiate will depend upon the balance of power in the relationship. Often, new accounts have less favorable terms with vendors until they establish a solid track record. Other times, a company may offer extended payment terms as part of a new-customer incentive or other promotional program. Once you have been a customer for a while, and have demonstrated that you are desirable in terms of purchase volume and timely payment, you can revisit your payment terms to secure additional time. As you become an increasingly significant customer for your vendor, you can renegotiate prices, including payment terms.

You also may be able to negotiate payment terms when you are experiencing difficulty with cash flow. This is not something that you should do routinely. However, if you can see that your cash flow will not permit you to pay part or all of the balance due on time, you should notify your supplier/vendor/creditor and negotiate realistic payment terms. This

[3]SizzleIt.com, March 15, 2011.

Exhibit 9-5 *Aging Schedule for Accounts Payable, as of June 30, 2012*

Name	Vendor Number	Not Due (in discount)	Not Due (no discount)	15 Days Past Due	30 Days Past Due	60 Days Past Due
Ace Supply	51-09238		$5,000			
Big Guys	62-78749				$1,000	
Champions	10-83297			$4,000		$2,000
Youth Style	23-83940	$7,500				
Zoo Pals	51-10239	$1,000			$2,000	
Total		$8,500	$5,000	$4,000	$3,000	$2,000
%		37.8%	22.2%	17.8%	13.3%	8.9%

should be handled deftly, so that they understand you genuinely need their cooperation, but they should not become alarmed and retrench on future supplies or credit terms. This can be a delicate transaction.

Timing Payables

Just as you should establish an accounts receivable aging schedule, you should also create an accounts *payable* aging schedule (see **Exhibit 9-5**). In addition to noting where you are in terms of days outstanding, be certain to indicate terms received and variances. Recognize that you may have to start out with prepayment, or payment upon delivery, which will be difficult for cash flow because you will have to disburse money before you sell anything. Depending upon the business you are in, this could be a long interval.

The aging schedule for accounts payable makes your cash requirements clear. You can see what is coming due, where you can benefit from discounts, and where there are problems. This simple approach can be invaluable to your cash management.

Capital Budgeting and Cash Flow

Cash management is not only for operating cash and financing. It also includes the planning for *capital assets* (fixed assets, or earning assets). The purchase of machinery, equipment and its installation, and the like, requires initial cash outflows for assets and incremental working capital for new projects, the inflow of cash from operations as a result of purchases, and terminal cash flows from liquidation of old, outdated, or replaced equipment.

Capital budgeting will help you understand the cash flow required for investments, and the expected impact on operating cash flows. Budgeting will lead you to calculate the depreciation associated with capital investment, so that you can anticipate the tax effects. (Remember, increased depreciation means decreased taxes.) Finally, as you budget for the terminal values, you will see cash flow effects from disposal of assets and the related tax consequences. Making a capital budget can shed considerable light on cash flow expectations. **Exhibit 9-6** shows a capital budget for NRG Savers, Inc., as it considers the purchase and installation of equipment for a new line of environmentally friendly products.

Exhibit **9-6** *NRG Savers, Inc., Capital Budget, 2012*					
	Year 1	**Year 2**	**Year 3**	**Year 4**	**Year 5**
Initial Investment					
Machinery and Equipment	$82,000				
Installation	18,000				
Working Capital	10,000				
Total Initial Investment	**$110,000**				
Operating Cash Flows					
Operating Cash Inflow	$200,000	$300,000	$400,000	$500,000	$550,000
Depreciation	20,000	32,000	19,000	12,000	12,000
Net Change in Income	$180,000	$268,000	$381,000	$488,000	$538,000
Tax Effect (@ 30%)	48,000	80,400	114,300	146,400	161,400
Net Operating Cash Flow	**$132,000**	**$187,600**	**$266,700**	**$341,600**	**$376,600**
Terminal Cash Flow					
Sale of Equipment					$40,000
Tax on Income (sale)					10,500
Net on Sale of Equipment					$29,500
Recover—Working Capital					10,000
Total Terminal Cash Flow					**$39,500**
Project Cash Flow	**$22,000**	**$187,600**	**$266,700**	**$341,600**	**$416,100**

We can see that the components of the capital budget fit into the full cash-flow budget of a company, once the project is accepted or rejected. By creating and analyzing each capital project separately, you can apply your decision criteria and determine which to accept and which to reject. You can plan for your financing needs well in advance and be prepared to justify your repayment plans.

The Burn Rate

When you start your business, it is normal to have a negative cash flow from operations for at least the first few months. You are likely to spend more than you earn in the beginning stages. Some businesses, such as biotechnology companies that spend a great deal on research and development (R&D), can have a negative cash flow of as much as $1 million per month. You will need to build these initial cash deficits into your business plan so that they can be covered in start-up costs.

Because a new company will probably spend more cash than it earns while it is getting off the ground, the question will be: How long can you afford to lose money? The answer will depend on the amount of capital invested and the amount of revenue being earned.

The pace at which your company will need to spend capital to cover overhead costs before generating a positive cash flow is called the **burn rate.** The burn rate is typically expressed in terms of cash spent per month.

burn rate the pace at which a company spends capital before generating positive cash flow.

A burn rate of $10,000 per month means that the company is spending that amount monthly to cover rent and other operating expenses. If the company has $20,000 in cash, and is bringing in $2,000 a month in sales, how long could it hold out?

$$\frac{\text{(Cash Available + Revenue)}}{\text{Negative Cash Outflow per Month}} = \begin{array}{l}\text{Number of Months}\\\text{before Cash Runs Out}\end{array}$$

The Value of Money Changes over Time

When considering cash and cash flow, it is also important to evaluate the changing value of money over time. A dollar today, available for investment, is worth more than a dollar tomorrow. Cash goes up or down in terms of buying power depending upon several factors. For example, the value of a dollar changes depending upon inflation rates and variations in exchange rate strength relative to foreign currencies. Finally, it can grow through the previously earned interest accumulating additional interest.

The Future Value of Money

Interest-earning funds grow fastest in investments that offer a *compound* rate of return, that is, those that are calculated on interest that has already accumulated. The younger you are when you start saving for a goal, such as retirement, the more compounding will help your money grow. Suppose you put $100 into an investment that pays 10 percent compounded annually. At the end of a year, you will have $110 ($100, plus $10 interest). At the end of the next year, you will have $121 ($110 plus $11 interest). Your money will grow faster each year because you are earning interest on the interest. The formula for this is

$$FV = PV(1 + i)^n$$

Where FV is the future value of the investment, PV is the present value, or amount invested today; i equals the interest rate per compounding period, and n equals the number of compounding periods. For example, $1,200 invested at 5% per year for 10 years will total

$$FV = \$1,200(1 + 0.05)^{10} = \$1,954.67$$

Figure 9-4 shows the effect of compounding $1,000 at 0%, 5%, 10%, and 20% for five years.

The **future value** of money is the amount it will *accrue* (gain) over time through investment. For a single investment at a constant interest rate, you can use the formula provided, or you can determine this easily using a future value chart, such as the one in **Exhibit 9-7**. Look up 10 periods at 10 percent on the chart, and you will find that $100 invested at 10 percent will grow to $259 over 10 years. Note that these values can also be figured on a financial calculator and via spreadsheet software, such as Excel. If there are multiple amounts, variable interest rates, and the like, you can consult a basic financial management book or the Internet for appropriate calculation methods. Remember, **compound interest**—money making money—is the essence of investment.

future value the amount an asset will gain over time.

compound interest the interest or rate of return accumulating on the interest or other returns in addition to earnings on the principal.

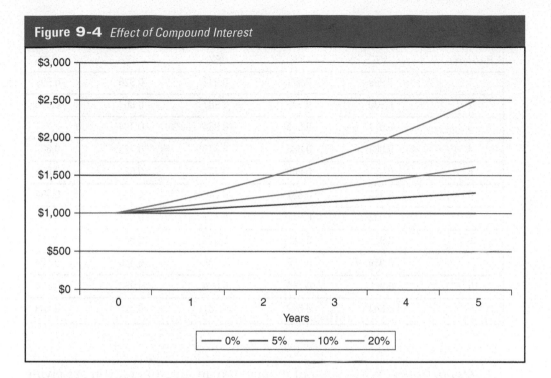

Figure 9-4 *Effect of Compound Interest*

Exhibit 9-7 *Future Value of $1 in n Periods*

Periods	1%	3%	5%	8%	10%
1	1.0100	1.0300	1.0500	1.0800	1.1000
2	1.0201	1.0609	1.1025	1.1664	1.2100
3	1.0303	1.0927	1.1576	1.2597	1.3310
4	1.0406	1.1255	1.2155	1.3605	1.4641
5	1.0510	1.1593	1.2763	1.4693	1.6105
6	1.0615	1.1941	1.3401	1.5869	1.7716
7	1.0721	1.2299	1.4071	1.7138	1.9487
8	1.0829	1.2668	1.4775	1.8509	2.1436
9	1.0937	1.3048	1.5513	1.9990	2.3580
10	1.1046	1.3439	1.6209	2.1589	2.5937
15	1.1610	1.5580	2.0789	3.1722	4.1773

The Present Value of Money

Another way to look at investing is summed up by the old saying, "A bird in the hand is worth two in the bush." You always prefer to have your money *now*. If you cannot have it immediately, you want to be compensated with a return. Your money is worth more to you when it is in your hand for three reasons:

1. *Inflation.* When prices rise, a dollar tomorrow will buy less than a dollar does today.
2. *Risk.* When you put money into an investment, there is always some risk of losing it.

Exhibit 9-8 *Present Value of $1 to be Received in n Periods in the Future*

Periods	1%	3%	5%	8%	10%
1	0.990	0.971	0.952	0.926	0.909
2	0.980	0.943	0.907	0.857	0.826
3	0.971	0.915	0.864	0.794	0.751
4	0.961	0.886	0.823	0.735	0.683
5	0.951	0.863	0.784	0.681	0.621
6	0.942	0.837	0.746	0.630	0.584
7	0.933	0.813	0.711	0.583	0.513
8	0.923	0.789	0.677	0.540	0.467
9	0.914	0.766	0.645	0.500	0.424
10	0.905	0.744	0.614	0.463	0.386
15	0.861	0.642	0.481	0.315	0.239

3. ***Opportunity.*** When you put money into an investment, you are giving up the opportunity to use it for what might be a better investment.

Say a customer promises to pay you $10,000 three years from now for designing a Web site. Your next-best opportunity for investment has an ROI of 10 percent.

present value the worth (face value) of a future asset or other investment discounted back to the present.

Present value is the amount an investment is worth discounted back to the present. Look at the present value chart (see **Exhibit 9-8**) under period three (for three years) and 10 percent. The present value of $1 at three years and 10 percent is $0.751. The present value of the promise of $10,000 in three years, therefore, is $7,510 ($10,000 × 0.751 = $7,510). Your client's promise is worth only $7,510 in the present. If you accept this arrangement, you should charge interest, because you are essentially providing a $10,000 loan for three years. Anytime you are asked to wait for payment, you should be compensated—because money in your hand now is worth significantly more than money promised for the future. If you want to calculate this using a mathematical formula, you can use the inverse of the future value procedure.

$$PV = FV \left(1/(1 + i)^n\right)$$

So, the prior example would be PV = $10,000 $(1/(1 + 0.10)^3)$ = $7,510.

Understanding the time value of money permits managers to compare investment options and other opportunities based upon their real values, so that they can better manage cash flows.

BizFacts

When you sell a business, the price reflects more than the nuts and bolts of the operation. You are also selling the future stream of income that the business will be expected to generate. This income will be reflected in the price of the business, which is its *present value*. This is why businesses typically sell for several times their annual net income.

Taxes

Another factor that affects cash flow for a business is taxes. Like other creditors, tax-levying bodies expect payment in a timely fashion. More importantly, tax payments must be kept current, because some delinquencies can result in business closure and substantial personal penalties.

Cash and Taxes

You will have to pay taxes on business profits whether or not you have a positive cash flow—which will also be affected by them. Self-employed people, such as consultants or sole proprietors, must pay their own **self-employment tax** on any wages paid to themselves. This is the Social Security tax obligation for the self-employed, and is the equivalent of the combination of the employee and employer taxes paid for employees. These taxes must be paid quarterly, so cash must be put aside in order to make the payments on the due dates.

As an employer, you will collect and pay all employment taxes to the appropriate government entities. These taxes are particularly important to report accurately and pay on time. Federal penalties for tax code violations with respect to wage taxes are especially harsh. The government may "sweep" your company bank accounts (take out any available funds), assess significant fines, and secure your personal assets. Using withheld wage taxes as a source of cash flow and/or failing to pay these taxes would be a disastrous decision.

The federal government is financed primarily by personal and corporate income taxes. States usually raise money from **sales taxes** on goods. Most states also levy an income tax. City and other local governments are supported primarily by taxes on property.

◀ **Performance Objective 5**
File appropriate tax returns for your business.

self-employment tax
federal tax that business owners pay on wages paid to themselves.

sales tax tax levied by governments on retail purchases and collected by merchants.

Filing Tax Returns

Corporate, partnership, and individual income tax and self-employment tax returns must be *filed* (mailed or submitted online) with the U.S. Internal Revenue Service (IRS) by specific dates each year. Corporate returns are due on a different schedule (earlier) from the traditional April 15 deadline for individual returns. If you file late, you may have to pay penalties and interest. You can check the IRS Web site at http://www.irs.gov for deadlines, instructions, and forms.

The tax code is very complex. Check the aforementioned IRS Web site for information, but if you are still not certain which tax forms to file and when to do so, the IRS also offers booklets and telephone services to help answer questions. Help with the 1040, the most common individual return form, is available at 1-800-424-1040. You can also go to your local IRS office and meet with an agent who will guide you through the forms for free. It can be worth investing the time and money to ensure your own correct tax filings (rates and forms can change from year to year). As soon as your business starts earning income, you will probably want to seek the services of a tax professional (an accountant or a CPA). Remember, in addition to federal taxes, businesses are subject to state and local taxes. Check with state and local revenue departments.

(moodboard/SuperStock)

Collecting Sales Tax

If you sell products or services to the public, you will have to charge sales tax in most states, and then turn over the collected money, monthly or quarterly, to the appropriate agency. Apply to your state's department of taxation for the necessary forms. In New York State, for example, entrepreneurs use the New York State and Local Sales and Use form to report quarterly sales taxes. Some states only charge tax on products; some charge tax on products and services. A very few do not have a sales tax at all.

Tax Issues for Different Legal Structures

The legal structure best suited to a business depends upon a number of variables, which will be discussed later in this text. Each legal structure has tax advantages and disadvantages.

- *Sole proprietorship.* All profit earned by a sole proprietorship belongs to the owner, and affects his or her tax liability. The business does not pay taxes on profits separately.
- *Partnership.* The tax issues are basically the same as for the sole proprietorship, except that profits and losses are shared among the partners, who report them on their respective personal income tax returns.
- *Limited partnership.* This is treated in the same way as a partnership, except that a limited partner can use losses as a tax shelter without being exposed to personal liability. This can be an incentive for potential investors.
- *Corporation (subchapter C).* A corporation's profits are taxed whether or not a portion of them is distributed to the owners. Owners must also pay personal income tax on any profit distribution they receive. This so-called double taxation is considered a disadvantage of C corporations.
- *S corporation.* Small companies can use this structure to avoid the double taxation mentioned above. The S corporation does not pay tax on profits. Profit is taxed only once, as owner/partner income on personal tax returns. This structure requires all partners to take profits and losses in proportion to their ownership (thus it does not offer the tax shelter advantages of the limited partnership).
- *Limited liability company (LLC).* This structure separates the owners/partners from personal liability and provides a more flexible allocation of profits and losses.

Finally, note that dividends paid by a business to stockholders are not tax deductible, but interest payments made to creditors are. This can be an incentive to raise capital via borrowing, depending on the tax issues your business faces.

Make Tax Time Easier by Keeping Good Records

You and your tax preparer will have an easier time if you have been keeping accurate records throughout the year. You will have to determine your net income. If you have kept accurate and timely accounting records, this should not be difficult.

Mistakes on your tax return, or just the luck of the draw, could cause the IRS to *audit* you. The IRS will send an agent (auditor) to your business to examine your ledgers and receipts and invoices to make sure your taxes were filed correctly. An audit can be a time-consuming and stressful process. This is another excellent reason to keep good records and file all invoices and receipts, whether or not you use an accountant for tax preparation.

Do not confuse accounting with taxation. Your accounting software generates financial records, but you will still need tax-preparation assistance, and/or tax software, to prepare your returns. Some accounting software will allow you to export your financial information into your tax program.

If you do prepare your own tax returns on a computer, it is still a good idea to have a tax professional review them. An accountant will be familiar with changes to the tax code and can offer valuable advice. An accountant often will not charge for questions asked throughout the year, if he or she has been hired to prepare your annual tax return.

One of the best business investments you can make is to hire a top-notch small-business tax accountant or attorney as a consultant. Maximize the amount of professional advice and you will minimize the chances of problems with the IRS.

Chapter Summary

Now that you have studied this chapter, you can do the following:

1. Understand the importance of cash flow management.
   - Cash flow is the difference between the money you take in and the money you disburse.
   - Without cash on hand, you can find yourself unable to pay crucial bills, even while the income statement says you are earning a profit.
2. Know the difference between cash and profits.
   - Profits are based upon accrued revenues and expenses for most businesses.
   - It is possible to be profitable and to be out of cash.
3. Read a cash flow statement.
   - The first section of the cash flow statement records all sources of cash income (inflows) that come into the business.
   - The next section reports cash outflows (disbursements) that must be made that month.
   - The last section shows the net change in cash flow.
4. Create a cash budget.
   - Project your cash receipts from all possible sources.
   - Subtract the expenses you expect to have from these projected cash receipts.
   - Understand the future value of money.
   - Calculate the present value of money.
5. File appropriate tax returns for your business.
   - Both income tax and self-employment tax returns must be filed by specific dates (corporate returns are due earlier than individual returns).
   - Tax returns must be filed on time and accurately.
   - Collect sales tax. If you sell products or services to the public, in most states, you will have to charge your customers applicable sales tax and periodically turn it in to the state.
   - Apply to your state's department of taxation for the necessary forms.

6. Calculate working capital.
   - The formula for working capital is: current assets minus current liabilities.
   - It tells you how much cash is left over after paying all your short-term debt.
   - Working capital should be considered when creating cash flow projections.

Key Terms

burn rate	noncash expenses
cash flow statement	pilferage
compound interest	present value
credit	sales tax
factoring	self-employment tax
future value	working capital

Entrepreneurship Portfolio

Critical Thinking Exercises

1. Describe what you think the seasonality scenario would be for one year for a business you can imagine starting. Explain how you think the cash flow would be affected over the course of the year.
2. Imagine you are the owner of an upscale clothing store, like Barneys in Manhattan, which was driven out of business by a 7 percent pilferage rate. What creative solutions could you identify to reduce pilferage?
3. Give three rules for managing your cash.
4. Calculate the projected burn rate for your planned business.
5. Figure out how much income tax each of the following individuals owes. The marginal tax rates are structured as follows:

   - income up to $42,350 is taxed at 15 percent;
   - income from $42,351 to $61,400 is taxed at 28 percent;
   - income between $61,401 to $128,100 is taxed at 31 percent.

The different rates apply to the different segments of one's income.

Taxable Income	Tax Due
Jim: $42,000	
Michael: $98,750	
Susan: $24,000	
Kate: $100,520	

Key Concept Questions

1. Create a cumulative cash flow graph for a business with the following monthly cash balances:

January	$40,000
February	$25,000
March	$13,000
April	$5,000
May	$12,000
June	$2,000
July	$0
August	$0
September	$1,500
October	$8,500
November	$12,000
December	$21,000

2. Fill in the following table, using the future value chart in this chapter, to show the amounts of one invested dollar's growth at the interest rates and time periods given.

Periods	Interest Rate (%)	Future Value of $10
2	5	$11.03
5	8	
10	10	
1	1	
7	3	

3. Fill in the following table, using the present value chart, to show the amounts of the net present value of $100 at the interest rates and time periods given.

Periods	Interest Rate (%)	Present Value of $100
2	5	$90.79
5	8	
10	10	
1	1	
7	3	

4. Calculate working capital for Angelina's company. Describe how her level of working capital might affect her business decisions.

Angelina's Jewelry Company 7/30/12		
ASSETS		
Current Assets		
Cash	$10,000	
Inventory	10,000	
Other Current Assets (Securities)	10,000	
Total Current Assets		$30,000
Long-Term Assets		70,000
TOTAL ASSETS		$100,000
LIABILITIES		
Short-Term Liabilities		
Accounts Payable	$10,000	
Short-Term Loans	5,000	
Total Short-Term Liabilities		$15,000
Total Long-Term Liabilities		15,000
OWNER'S EQUITY		70,000
TOTAL LIABILITIES & OWNER'S EQUITY		$100,000

Application Exercise

Create a projected cash flow statement for your business for one year.

Exploring Online

1. Print the tax documents list available at http://www.ideacafe.com/bizforms/tax.html and highlight the forms that a C corporation producing glass bottles would need.
2. Visit Business Owners Idea Café online and use the tool at http://www.businessownersideacafe.com/financing/index.htm to figure out how much capital you will need to get your business off the ground.

BizBuilder Business Plan Questions

7.2 Cash Flow Projections
A. List and describe your monthly fixed costs and add a cash reserve that covers three months of fixed costs.
B. Create a projected cash flow statement for your business for the first four quarters and the second and third years of operation.
C. Calculate the burn rate for your business.

Holterholm Farms—Radical Change for Maximum Impact

Ron Holter is a fifth-generation farmer in Jefferson, Maryland (in the Middletown Valley), who has learned to innovate in the management of his farm to create a desirable quality of life for his family while keeping profits and cash coming in. Holterholm Farms was purchased by William Holter, in 1889, and has been a dairy farm ever since.

Having grown up on this small family farm, Ron saw firsthand the challenges and opportunities inherent in managing it. After returning home to the farm to work full time in 1981, Ron realized that the prevalent industrial system of agriculture demanded an incredible amount of labor on his part for few tangible results. He was not going to be able to spend time with his children as they were growing up. He saw that the farm needed to make changes if it was going to remain viable in the 1990s. But small producers were barely able to eke out a living. He knew that there had to be a way to keep the farm successful and maintain a reliable cash flow.

In 1995, Ron planted the farm's 207 acres in permanent vegetative cover (grass) and put the entire herd of cows out to pasture the following year. This grazing system not only provided the animals with a grass-based diet, it also allowed Ron to work fewer hours at a lower intensity to take care of the same acreage, the same number of cows, and to improve his profitability. Because of the switch to a grazing system, Ron was able to realize a precipitous drop in expenses. Veterinary bills were almost nonexistent because the grazing animals were healthier on a grass diet than a confinement herd could ever be. Seed purchases ended, because the entire farm was planted in permanent grasses.

Due to the cows' all-grass diet, Holterholm produced nearly a third less milk. But because of the minimization of costs, it became one of the most profitable farms in Maryland, netting $1,199.90 per cow in 1996, in comparison to the state average of confinement farms of $471.00 per cow.

Ron took this low-input system of agriculture on Holterholm one step further by making the decision to operate as a seasonal enterprise. The switch to seasonal production meant a further loss in milk production. Despite that, Holterholm Farm's profitability stayed roughly the same, and the seasonal system meant less labor year-round to support new calves. All cows then born in a given year were roughly within two months' age of each other and thus could

The Holter Family at Holterholm Farms. (© 2011 David Nevala for Organic Valley)

be fed and cared for together; labor and feeding costs fell even lower.

Starting in 2000, Ron began to operate the farm organically. He did not use drugs or artificial hormones on the cows, nor did he treat the soil with artificial fertilizers or pesticides. When both Horizon and Organic Valley cooperatives moved into Maryland in 2005 looking for organic producers, Holterholm Farms was able to immediately certify its acreage as organic and it took only three months to certify the cows.

In the short term, securing a contract with Organic Valley meant that Ron was paid roughly twice for his milk than what he was getting previously. It also meant that Ron had to switch to feeding his cows organic grain, to supplement the grass cover. With organic grain prices as high as they were, he soon realized it was not profitable to feed the cows grain. His cash flow was being adversely impacted. He was losing money, despite producing more milk. So, in October 2007, Ron fed the last of the grain to his herd. Milk production dropped, as expected, but the financial results were astounding. In 2008, the farm made $858 per cow—this with no grain feed and less milk production. In 2009, the farm returned to the $1,000 mark, netting $1,004 per cow—again, with no grain-feed expenses.

Holterholm Farms began producing less milk than ever, over its days as a confinement operation. In 2009, two years into feeding no grain, the farm was producing only 22 pounds of milk per cow per day, yet earned as much as in 1996, and therefore significantly more than could ever have been earned prior to grazing.

Having adapted the dairy portion of Holterholm Farms to become more profitable with fewer inputs, Ron explored and adopted additional sources of revenue. He added beef, eggs, and produce to the mix. These were relatively small revenue generators, but required comparatively few cash outlays and generated reliably positive cash flows.

Ron's son, Adam, is adding his imprint on the farm's operations by creating a Community Supported Agriculture (CSA) venture that requires a front-end investment in used equipment and marketing that can be recouped quickly. The CSA has the particular benefit of collecting "shares" in advance, to the maximum available,

Adam and Ron Holter, Holterholm Farms.
(© 2011 David Nevala for Organic Valley)

while incurring only the costs of growing and distributing produce from the fertile Holterholm Farms' land. Customers buy shares of the season's produce based upon a weekly allocation of the total production, such that Adam may sell 50 shares in total to collect $25,000 at the beginning of the year and then provides each shareholder with 2 percent of the production each week. The payments are up front and the expenditures are at the back end.

The Holter family is managing the land to sustain it for generations to come.

Case Study Analysis

1. Why did switching to entirely grass-fed dairy cows improve Holterholm Farms' cash flow?

2. How can adding beef, eggs, and produce be beneficial from a cash flow perspective?

3. Search for Community Support Agriculture on the Internet. Why might it be good for Holterholm Farms to have a CSA? What are the risks involved? Why would consumers be willing to pay for their produce up front?

4. What would you ask the Holter family about the cash-managing aspect of Holterholm Farms?

Case Sources

Adam Holter, "A Study in Efficiency: Holterholm Farms," unpublished manuscript, Shepherd University, December 2010.

Case Study | Managing Cash: CakeLove and Love Café

How does a lawyer with a master's degree in public health from George Washington University become a cake magnate? Warren Brown was a 28-year-old Washington, D.C., attorney who, in 1999, made a New Year's resolution to learn how to bake. He practiced health care law in the Inspector General's Office for the U.S. Department of Health and Social Services from 1998 until he left to become a baker in 2000. Warren opened his first CakeLove bakery on U Street, N.W., in Washington in March 2002 and the Love Café 17 months later.

He became the owner of five more Cake-Love bakeries in the Washington, D.C., area and the Love Café, also in Washington. CakeLove pound cakes, brownies, scones, and cookies are available via the Internet for delivery nationwide (http://www.cakelove.com). Warren's first book, *CakeLove*, arrived on bookstore shelves in the spring of 2008, and his second, *United Cakes of America*, highlights his favorite recipes from each of the 50 states. To top it off, he hosted the Food Network's *Sugar Rush*. Warren was named the U.S. Small Business Administration's Entrepreneur of the Year in 2006, and CakeLove was selected top bakery in Washington in the *Washington Post Best Bets* readers' poll in 2005 and 2006, and by the *Washington Post Express* in 2009.

This meteoric rise in business required a number of essential ingredients. In addition to the all-natural components used in CakeLove products, the business aspects had to be properly balanced and mixed. Such rapid change demanded a lot of hard work, passion, determination—and cash flow. When Warren stepped from his full-time government job into full-time entrepreneurship, he began with $10,000 of personal resources, including his credit card. In order to open his first storefront, Warren needed $125,000. Fortunately, he was able to secure a commercial loan from his community bank, CityFirst Bank of DC. Commercial lenders at larger, mainstream financial institutions were not convinced that a self-taught baker who had abandoned a promising legal career was a particularly good credit risk. Warren still maintained 100 percent ownership of CakeLove after the

Warren Brown of CakeLove and Love Café.
(CakeLove)

acquisition of start-up capital, and he continues as the sole owner even after significant growth.

Within a couple of months of opening CakeLove, Warren decided to open Love Café—directly across the street from the bakery. The space popped up as an opportunity and he wanted to take advantage of it. This required an additional infusion of capital for leasehold improvements, equipment, furnishings, and other start-up costs. There were few expenses from CakeLove that Love Café could leverage for this start-up, to attain economies of scale. Aside from being able to sell bakery-direct to consumers, he had little obvious financial advantage. However, CakeLove is strictly a take-out facility, housing production and sales areas, whereas Love Café is a full-service establishment serving a menu of baked goods, sandwiches, and coffee in what Warren describes as a "laid back, relaxed atmosphere incorporating natural elements and including WiFi, sofas, large windows." Because CakeLove was new and had little positive cash flow, Warren could not finance the Café with the cash flow from the bakery. So, he turned again to CityFirst Bank.

(CakeLove)

Between September 2007 and July 2008, CakeLove opened three additional retail bakeries. Each successive expansion created a need for additional cash. Warren managed to avoid selling shares of the company by leveraging resources and partnering with a community lender. His banking partner, CityFirst, financed each location to supplement earnings generated from existing operations.

Growth in the number of retail bakery storefronts has carried the business to new heights. Warren continues to serve as the primary manager of cash flow and human resources for his organization. Inventory theft has not been a significant issue because of well-thought-out store layouts and careful procedures, and CakeLove has established cash-handling policies (cash-counting systems) to prevent pilferage from the cash drawers. Because CakeLove sells baked goods and other perishable items, spoilage and unsold product can become significant contributors to cash-flow problems. Warren and his team have instituted a waste-tracking system and have been able to keep a "pretty good eye on the way inventory is moving."

The growth of the organization has not been the greatest challenge to cash flow for CakeLove. Warren notes that diets have been more of a detriment to the business than expansion or an abysmal economy. CakeLove experienced its most significant cash tightness at the height of popularity for the Atkins Diet, when counting carbohydrates led dieters to cutting out sweets and bakery treats. During times of reduced cash inflow, Warren and his team have had to look to cut expenses, particularly by monitoring labor costs more closely than usual. When Warren opened his first CakeLove bakery, he had three employees, including himself. As of July 2008, he had 105. This meant meeting the cash-flow requirements of a payroll and associated expenses for the multiple locations, including supporting numerous families.

Warren Brown has the following advice for aspiring entrepreneurs, "Do the homework. Know the industry you want to enter cold, so that you absolutely know how to make or do whatever it is that you want to make or do. Don't rush in. See it well and don't be afraid to get messy and to keep an open mind. There is always a way to improve. Know the product very well and have good confidence in what you are selling. People will always have unsolicited advice for you. If you don't have that confidence, you will get little chinks in your armor that can make your business less enjoyable and even miserable. Confidence is critical." Warren's recipe for growth has produced sweet rewards.

Case Study Analysis

1. How has Warren Brown been able to finance the growth of his company?

2. What methods has CakeLove used to manage cash flow? What others might it adopt?

3. What types of cash flow management issues would you expect CakeLove to encounter if it continues to grow at a rate of three bakeries per year or more?

4. How do Warren Brown's recommendations to aspiring entrepreneurs pertain to cash flow?

Case Sources

CakeLove Web site at http://www.cakelove.com.

"Lawyer Turned Entrepreneur of the Year, Warren Brown of CakeLove," *The Africana Connect*, http://www.theculturalconnect.com/new/2007/11/23/warren-brown-africana, January 12, 2008).

Warren Brown, *CakeLove: How to Bake Cakes from Scratch* (New York: Stewart, Tabori and Chang, 2008).

Chapter 10

FINANCING STRATEGY

Exactostock/
SuperStock

Etsy, Inc., was founded in 2005 by Robert Kalin, Chris Maguire, and Haim Schoppik in an environment that Kalin describes as, "Early on it was a little bit like the Wild West where it starts with what you have on hand."[1] Frustrated by his inability to find online distribution for his handcrafted wood products, Kalin created a Web site that connected creators of handmade items and sellers of vintage goods and craft supplies with buyers through e-commerce.[2] With an estimated $314 million in Gross Merchandise Sales of goods and over 11 million registered users, it has grown from a bootstrap company to one that raised $20 million in its fifth round of seeking venture investment.

Kalin went to people he knew for his earliest financing. He had installed a bar for Spencer Ain and helped restaurateur Sean Meenan with a technology installation before they became his first (2005) and second (2006) round investors.[3] Next, working through his networks, Kalin got Caterina Fake and Stewart Butterfield, founders of Flickr, along with Delicious founder Joshua Schachter, Albert Wenger, and Union Square Ventures to invest $1 million—also in 2006.[4] Union Square Ventures invested again in Series B (January 2007) and C (July 2007) with $3.25 million each round.

The next financing round for Etsy raised $27 million, with the word on the street being that "Etsy was valued at $90 million pre money."[5] Accel Partners was a significant investor in the Series D financing. The fifth—$20 million (Series E)—round saw Index Ventures as a new lead investor, joined by Accel Partners and Burda Media.[6] The company's valuation rose to nearly $300 million.

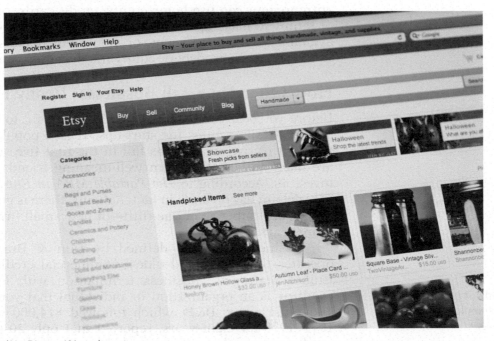

(NetPhotos/Alamy)

[1]Evelyn Rusli Visits Etsy in New York: Robert Kalin video interview, 2011, http://techcrunch.tv/interviews-and-profiles/watch?id=NubDNrMToBvPOXXVnACzktftfSHzFljz, April 21, 2011.
[2]"Etsy 2011 Sales Revenue Expected to Exceed $400 Million–Sales Grew 74.4% in 2010," *Quarterly Retail Review*, March 1, 2011.
[3]Op cit.
[4]PrivCo, "Etsy, Inc. Receives $1 million Series A Investment From Caterina Fake, Stewart Butterfield, Joshua Schachter, And Others," http://www.privo.com/private-company/etsy-inc/funding/etsy-inc-receives-venture-capital-investment-from-caterina-fake-stewart-butterfield-joshua-schachter-and-others-november-2006, April 21, 2011.
[5]Erick Schonfeld, "Etsy Raises $27 Million: Accel's Jim Breyer Joins Board," TechCrunch, January 30, 2008, http://techcrunch.com/2008/01/30/etsy-raises-27-million-accels-jim-breyer-joins-board/, April 21, 2011.
[6]Erick Schonfeld, "Index Ventures Buys Into Etsy, Triples Valuation To Nearly $300 Million," TechCrunch, August 26, 2010, http://techcrunch.com/2010/8/26/etsy-300-million-valuation, April 21 2011.

Performance Objectives

1. Explore your financing preferences.
2. Identify the types of business financing.
3. Compare the pros and cons of debt and equity financing.
4. Identify sources of capital for your business.
5. Understand stocks and bonds as investment alternatives.

Going It Alone versus Securing Financing

financing the act of providing or raising funds (capital) for a purpose.

To start or expand a business, you will need to have money, either on hand or through **financing**, which is the act of providing or raising funds (capital) for a purpose. For entrepreneurs, that means obtaining the money to start and operate a successful business.

There are three ways to finance a business venture, assuming you do not have enough funds in your savings:

1. obtain gifts and grants,
2. borrow money (debt), or
3. exchange a share of the business for money (equity).

Performance Objective 1 ▷

Explore your financing preferences.

For many (or even most) people who want to start a business, there is a need for financing. Whether that need is for $500 or $5 million, the entrepreneur will have to bridge the gap between what he or she has, and what the projected cash flows and prudent reserves require. Sometimes an entrepreneur can use home equity, credit cards, or funding from friends or family to make up this shortfall. In other cases, these resources are not available, are not sufficient, or would not make sense for the business. In those situations, debt or equity financing becomes a necessity.

How Often Do Small Businesses Really Fail?

Before you search for financing, you may want to know more about success and failure rates for start-ups. It is a popular misconception that four out of five small firms fail in the first five years of operation. You are likely to hear this from well-meaning friends, family, and potential investors. According to *The Portable MBA in Entrepreneurship*, however, "This claim has no basis in fact. Actually, there is good evidence that more than half—rather than one-fifth—of new small firms survive for eight or more years."[7]

creditor person or organization that is owed money.

Business failure is defined by Dun & Bradstreet (D&B)—which operates the largest and oldest commercial credit-rating service in the United States—as "business termination with losses to creditors." A **creditor** is an organization or individual that you have borrowed from and must repay. D&B, which followed 814,000 small firms formed in 1977–1978 for eight years, reported that only 20 to 25 percent of those small ventures that were recorded as terminated during their first eight years of operation actually closed because of bankruptcy. The other 75 to 80 percent were terminations, but they were:

- businesses that were sold to new owners;
- businesses that changed operations—for example, from a flower shop to a general nursery; or
- businesses that were closed when the owners retired or moved on to other businesses.

---

[7]William D. Bygrave and Andrew Zacharkis (eds.), *The Portable MBA in Entrepreneurship* (New York: John Wiley & Sons, 1997), p. 199.

The article concludes that the survival rate of the small firm, far from being one out of five, is closer to one out of two. More than half of all new small companies will survive for at least eight years.[8]

For many, a small business is considered a high-risk, high-return investment—although in truth entrepreneurs are generally calculated risk takers and only pursue opportunities after they have weighed the chances of success. For the investor willing to accept the risk, a small business can be a great opportunity. The return on investment (ROI) of a successful small business can be thousands of percent, but the possibility of business failure is also relatively high. If your business fails, you and your investors will lose money. Your task, when you write your business plan and do your research, will be to demonstrate to your investors how and why your venture will succeed, and that they can look forward to appropriate returns for the risk they are assuming.

What Is the Best Type of Financing for You and Your Business?

Financing is not a one-size-fits-all proposition. Each venture has unique requirements and circumstances, along with the structure and challenges of the selected industry. For some businesses, such as restaurants, standard commercial loans may not be an option because commercial lenders will not be willing to make them. For others, such as research-based technology firms, equity will probably be needed. Regardless of your preferences and the types of financing available, you will invariably have to be the first investor in your business. Lenders and investors alike will insist that entrepreneurs have their personal resources involved before they will put in additional funding. It is easier to persist and work hard when you have a personal financial stake in success. If putting your personal assets at risk is not something you (or your family) are willing to do, expect to be rejected by investors and lenders.

Your **risk tolerance**, meaning the amount of risk (threat of loss) that you are willing to sustain, will also help to define possible financing options. For example, if you own a home and are seeking a commercial loan, you will likely have to put it up as security, in case you cannot repay the debt. Or, if you are giving up ownership through equity, you may have to give up control of the company you founded to obtain needed financial resources. Be prepared to face these types of decisions, as you seek financing that works.

There are three ways for a business to raise the capital it needs to grow.

risk tolerance the amount of risk or threat of loss that an individual is willing to sustain.

◀ **Performance Objective 2**
Identify the types of business financing.

1. *Finance with earnings.* If a company is profitable and has positive cash flow, it can use some of its profits to finance expansion. This will help ensure that the company does not take on too much debt, or grow more quickly than its finances can handle.

2. *Finance with equity.* If a company is incorporated, it can sell stock privately, or publicly via the stock market, to raise capital. People who purchase shares of stock are getting *equity*. Other types of businesses may also have equity investors.

3. *Finance with debt.* Any type of business, depending upon its *creditworthiness*, and that of its owner(s), can borrow money. An incorporated company can also sell *bonds*, although it is difficult and cost-prohibitive for small businesses to do so. People who purchase bonds will receive interest on the loan they are making to the company, with the principal repaid in a lump sum at maturity (explained below).

Both stocks and bonds are heavily regulated by the federal government. Issuing either requires considerable technical guidance and monetary outlay.

[8]E. Lewis Bryan, "Financial Management and Capital Formation in Small Business," *Journal of Small Business Management*, July 1, 1984.

This is not a do-it-yourself procedure. Rather, the counsel of investment bankers, accountants, and attorneys is needed.

Gifts and Grants

The opportunities for gifts and grants to businesses do exist. However, these must be pursued with caution because gifts may come with strings attached and grants often have requirements. Informal gifts can include such categories as cash, free use of facilities and equipment, unpaid labor by friends and family, and forgiveness or deferral of debts. Official gifts—furnished primarily by the federal government—may be provided for certain types of investments to stimulate designated geographic areas or to support particular populations. These may be in the form of **tax abatements** (legal reductions of taxes) or **tax credits** (direct reduction of taxes). Business grants are primarily made for research and commercialization efforts and are difficult for start-up, low-technology companies to acquire. Because gifts and grants do not require repayment or incur financing costs, they are often at the top of the entrepreneur's list of desired resources. They are also among the hardest to obtain.

tax abatement legal reduction in taxes.

tax credit direct reduction of taxes.

Debt Financing

Many businesses have some combination of debt and equity financing. The variety of loans and investments is quite large and growing. One challenge that you may face is determining what type of debt financing to pursue, based upon your business type and life-cycle stage, your personal finances and preferences, and the options available to you. Before pursuing debt for your business, calculate your personal *net worth* by tallying your assets (i.e., cash, investment accounts, personal property, real estate, and intangibles) and subtracting your debts (i.e., credit card balances, vehicle loans, mortgages, and other loans). Your lenders will want to know what you own, what you owe, and what your business finances are. The percentage of small firms using credit by credit type is shown in **Exhibit 10-1**.

Debt financing comes in many forms, with widely varying repayment and qualification terms. Different types of lenders will have various rates and fees, so it is worthwhile to compare the costs of the total package. Some debt options are discussed below.

Debt Category	Description	Common Types	Terms
Commercial Loans	Business loans typically provided by a bank or other financial institution.	• Real estate • Equipment and improvements • Working capital • Asset based • Accounts receivable factoring	Up to 20 years Up to 7 years 1 year or less Depends on type of asset pledged. Often 30 days
Personal Loans	Loans taken out on your personal credit and used for the business. May have a fixed term (length) or a revolving one.	• Credit cards • Home equity loans • Title loan • Payday loan	Revolving Variable terms; some are lines of credit. Short-term fixed repayment Short-term fixed repayment
Leases	Debts incurred for the rights to use specific property, such as automobiles, trucks, or equipment.	• Vehicle lease • Equipment lease	Often for 2 or 3 years with a purchase option at the end of the term. Varies widely depending on the nature of equipment leased.
Bonds	Long-term debt instruments used by corporations to raise large sums of money.	See Bonds section later in the chapter.	

Exhibit 10-1 *Percentage of Small Firms Using Credit, by Credit Type*

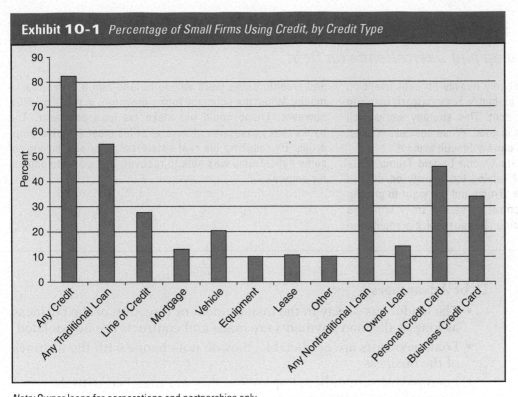

Note: Owner loans for corporations and partnerships only.
Source: U.S. Small Business Administration, Office of Advocacy, "Financing Patterns of Small Firms: Finding from the 1998 Survey of Small Business Finance," September 2003.

Debt Financing: Pros and Cons

To finance through debt, the entrepreneur applies to and contracts with a person or institution that has money and borrows it, signing a **promissory note**, a document that commits him or her to repaying a certain sum of money (with interest) by a specified date.

Interest is determined as a percentage (interest rate) of the loan principal. The **principal** is the amount of the loan or outstanding balance on the loan amount, not including interest. If $1,200 is borrowed at 10 percent to be paid back over one year, the interest on the loan is $120 ($1,200 × 0.10). Typically the borrower makes monthly payments until the loan is fully paid. The term, or length, of the loan generally depends on what is being financed, with working capital having the shortest term and real estate the longest.

The lender essentially has no say in the operation of the business as long as the loan payments are made on time and loan terms are met. The lender will have a say in how the funds are initially disbursed (according to a schedule that you provide) and may set restrictions (protective *covenants*). The payments are predictable, although they may vary with changes in key interest rate measures, if the interest rate is variable rather than fixed. If the loan payments are not made in a timely way, the lender can force the business into liquidation or bankruptcy, even if that loan balance is only a fraction of what the business is worth. Also, the lender may be able to take the home and personal possessions of the owner, depending on the agreement.

Debt should be carefully considered by the beginning entrepreneur because it often takes time for a new business to generate cash for repayment. One risk of debt is that failure to make loan payments can destroy the business before it can generate positive cash flow.

◀ **Performance Objective 3**
Compare the pros and cons of debt and equity financing.

promissory note a loan document that is a written promise to pay a specific sum of money on or before a particular date.

principal the amount of a loan before interest and fees are added.

Step into the Shoes...

Donald Trump and Overreliance on Debt

(AP Photo/Frank Franklin II)

Companies that rely heavily on debt financing are described as highly **leveraged**, meaning financed with debt. This strategy works well when business is good. When business is slow, debt payments can be difficult to meet.

Real estate tycoon Donald Trump made the mistake of relying too heavily on debt in the early 1980s. Trump did not want to give up managerial control by selling stock when he needed financing. Because of his reputation and wealth, banks were willing to lend him a great deal of money. When the economy took a downturn in the late 1980s, however, Trump could not make his loan payments. The banks took possession of several of his most valuable properties. By reducing his real estate holdings and paying off some debt, Trump was able to recover, and go on to expand his empire.

---

leveraged financed by debt, as opposed to equity.

Debt Advantages

- The lender has no say in the management or direction of the business, as long as the loan payments are made and contracts are not violated.
- Loan payments are predictable; they do not change with the fortunes of the business.
- Loan payments can be set up so that they are matched with the seasonal sales of the business.
- Lenders do not share in the business's profits.

Debt Disadvantages

- If loan payments are not made, the lender can force the business into bankruptcy.
- The lender may be able to take the home and possessions of the owner(s) to settle a debt in case of **default**—when the borrower fails to meet the repayment agreement.
- Debt payments increase a business's fixed costs, thereby lowering profits.
- Repayment reduces available cash.
- Lenders expect regular financial reporting and compliance with the loan contracts.

default the result of a borrower failing to meet the repayment agreement on a debt.

Equity Financing

Equity means that, in return for money, an investor will receive a percentage of ownership in a company. For the $1,200 investment discussed above, an equity investor might want 10 percent ownership of the company, which would mean 10 percent of the business's profits. (This would indicate that the business was valued at $12,000.) The investor is hoping that 10 percent of the profits will provide a high rate of return, over time, on the initial investment of $1,200.

Equity Financing: Pros and Cons

The equity investor assumes greater risk than the debt lender. If the business does not make a profit, neither does the investor. The equity investor cannot force the business into bankruptcy to get back the investment. If creditors force a business into bankruptcy, equity investors have a claim on whatever is left over after the debt lenders have been paid. The potential

BizFacts

Recently, a number of Internet sites have been created to link entrepreneurs in need of funds with investors. These are often called crowdfunding or person-to-person (P2P) lending sites. Businesses and investors can find sites tailored to their industries and funding requirements. Funds may be gifts or donations, investments or loans. The sites may screen potential participants and may only offer money to a company after its funding goal is reached. Others may issue partial funding. In some cases, rewards are used to attract repeat investor participation. Some popular crowdfunding sites are shown below.

Crowdfunder Web Sites

Kiva	Microenterprise	www.kiva.org
Profounder	Small business	www.profounder.com
Microfundo	Music	www.microfundo.org
Kickstarter	Creative projects	www.kickstarter.com
Rockethub	Creative arts	www.rockethub.com
Cat Walk Genius	Fashion	www.catwalkgenius.com
IndieGoGo	Creative art	www.indiegogo.com
Grow VC	Mobile & Web 2.0	www.growvc.com

for return is also higher. The equity investor should make an investment back many times over if the business prospers.

Money raised via equity does not have to be paid back unless the business is successful. Equity investors may offer helpful advice and provide valuable contacts. However, if the entrepreneur gives up more than 50 percent ownership, control of the business may be taken over by the equity holders. Even with less than half the ownership, investors may attempt to assert managerial influence.

Equity Advantages

- If the business does not make a profit, the investor does not get paid.
- There are no required regular payments in the form of principal or interest, and dividends for common stockholders are distributed at the discretion of the board of directors.

Step into the Shoes ...

Apple's Steve Jobs

Relying too heavily on equity can also be the downfall of a founding entrepreneur, as the story of Steve Jobs, co-founder of Apple Computer, illustrates. Because Jobs and his partner, Stephen Wozniak, were young men with very little money, debt financing was not an option. To raise money, they sold pieces of the company.

By the late 1980s, Apple had become so successful that Jobs hired a prominent PepsiCo executive, John Sculley, as Apple's chief executive officer. Sculley gradually convinced Apple's board of directors that Jobs was a disruptive influence on the company. Eventually a vote was taken of Apple shareholders, and Jobs did not own enough equity to fend off Sculley's effort to fire him. He was voted out of the highly successful company he started.

Jobs was invited back to lead Apple as interim CEO in 1997, however, and was elected permanent CEO by the shareholders in 2000.

(Tony Avelar/Bloomberg via Getty Images)

- The equity investor cannot force the business into bankruptcy in order to recoup the investment.
- The equity investor has an interest in seeing the business succeed and may, therefore, offer helpful advice and provide valuable contacts.

Equity Disadvantages

- Through giving up too much ownership, the entrepreneur could lose control of the business to the equity holders.
- Even with small amounts of equity, investors may interfere with the business via unsolicited advice and/or continuous inquiries.
- Equity financing is riskier for the investor, so he or she frequently wants both to receive a higher rate of return than a lender and to be able to influence how the company is run.
- The entrepreneur must share profits with the other equity investors.

Where and How to Find Capital That Works for You

Performance Objective 4 ▶

Identify sources of capital for your business.

The decision of where to seek capital is complex, and the options that are available will depend upon both personal and business factors. Your preferences should weigh heavily in the decision. However, it is a rare business owner that wants to pledge all family assets, pay high interest rates and fees, or give up majority ownership. Yet, many start-up and experienced entrepreneurs must do just that in order to secure the funds that they need. Identifying and securing financing often involves exploring multiple potential options, and creating a complex, multilayered financing mix. The optimal resources for a business may not be the obvious ones. Therefore, it is valuable to understand the range of sources.

There are many potential sources of capital, and it may take you numerous attempts to find what works. Some sources of capital are identified in **Exhibit 10-2**.

Having an Excellent Business Plan Goes a Long Way

When you seek financing for your business, the quality of your business plan could make the difference between success and failure. Lenders and investors alike will need to recover their principal plus interest, or investment plus a rate of return. If your business plan realistically, clearly, and convincingly demonstrates that you can and will achieve your goals, your chances of obtaining financing will greatly increase.

How Capital Sources Read Your Business Plan

People read business plans in different ways, but rarely are they read through from front to back as written. For example, a lender may look at the cash flow projections first. But one thing is for certain: You will need to capture the reader's attention in the executive summary or the plan is unlikely to be read at all.

Family and Friends

Family and friends are obvious sources for loans. But what about offering them equity instead? Explain that if they *loan* you money, they will only earn back the amount of the loan plus interest. If they invest capital in

Exhibit 10-2 Selected Sources of Business Financing

Financing Source	Category of Financing	Type(s) of Financing	Uses of Funds	Notes
Entrepreneur/Self	Debt or Equity	Loan or Owner's Equity	Any	Debt terms to be established at borrowing. Earnings through dividends and/or sale of company.
Friends or Family	Debt or Equity	Loan or Stock	Any	Negotiable on debt. Earnings through dividends and/or sale of stock.
Small Business Investment Companies (SBICs), Minority Enterprise SBICs (MESBICs), Rural Business Investment Companies (RBICs), New Markets Venture Capital funds (NMVC) http://www.sba.gov/inv/index.html	Debt or Equity	Loan or Stock	Varies according to licenses with the SBA and the types of entities served. Funds are to be used as requested by the businesses.	Generally installment loans for debt. Earnings through dividends and/or sale of stock.
Small Business Innovation Research (SBIR) or Small Business Technology Transfer (STTR) http://www.sba.gov/aboutsba/sbaprograms	Grant	Research Grant	Specific research as defined in grant application.	Must complete requirements of grant funding.
Community Development Corporations http://www.opportunityfinance.net	Linked Deposits and Savings	Gift	According to program guidelines.	Savings and financial literacy requirements.
Venture Capitalists	Equity	Stock	Start-up or growth	IPO, buy-out, dividends, royalties
Community Development Venture Capital Funds http://www.cdvca.org	Equity	Stock	Start-up or growth	IPO, buy-out, dividends, royalties
Angel Investors	Equity	Stock	Start-up or growth	IPO, buy-out, dividends, royalties
Investment Banks	Equity	Stock	Private or public placements (IPOs)	Paid in fee income.
Economic Development Agencies http://www.eda.gov	Debt	Varies	Varies	Varies broadly from state to state and other localities.
Leasing Companies	Debt	Vehicles or Equipment	To acquire use of vehicles and/or equipment.	Monthly payments of fees. Purchase option generally available at end of term.
Banks/Financial Institutions	Debt	Real Estate Loans	Real estate	Mortgage—long term with installment payments.

Exhibit 10-2 Continued

Financing Source	Category of Financing	Type(s) of Financing	Uses of Funds	Notes
Banks/Financial Institutions	Debt	Equipment, Vehicle, or Other	Equipment and other capital as specified in the loan request.	Promissory note—medium term with installment payments.
		Working Capital	Supplies, materials, cash flow.	Lines of credit usually with a maximum of 1-year term. Must be paid to $0 annually.
		Home Equity	Personal loan for any purpose secured against a home.	Many variations; often a monthly payment.
		Credit Card	Unsecured loan for business or consumer use.	Revolving credit with minimum monthly payments.
Mortgage Companies	Debt	Real Estate Loans	Real estate	Mortgage—long term with installment payments.
		Home Equity	Personal loan for any purpose secured against a home.	Many variations; often a monthly payment.
Insurance Companies	Debt	Policy Loan	Any	Reduces cash surrender value. Varies.
Community Development Banks http://www.opportunityfinance.net	Debt	Similar to Banks	Capital to rebuild communities through targeted lending.	Terms vary according to mission and community need.
Community Development Credit Unions http://www.natfed.org	Debt	Loans to Members	Per community ownership	Varies depending on type of loan.
Community Development Loan Funds http://www.opportunityfinance.net	Debt	Equipment, Leasehold, or Other Working Capital	Purchase of essential equipment and improvement for start-up and growth operation.	Primarily term loans. Some lines of credit. Typically for nontraditional credit. May include microloans, lending to not-for-profits, and to developers of affordable housing.
Microenterprise Development Loan Funds http://www.microenterpriseworks.org http://www.opportunityfinance.net	Debt	Primarily Working Capital and Start-Up	Relatively small loans ($35,000 maximum) for purpose detailed in applications and/or business plans.	Installment loans. Designed for nontraditional customers.
Receivable Factors	Debt	Accounts Receivable	Any	Factor is repaid by entrepreneur's customers. Receivables discounted and funds held back until they are paid.
Title Lenders	Debt	Title Loans	Any	Short terms with high interest rates.
Pay Day Lenders	Debt	Pay Day Loans	Any	Short terms with high interest rates.
Vendors	Debt	Trade Credit	Any	Entrepreneur delays payment of invoices.

exchange for equity, on the other hand, they could get back much more than the original amount. Acknowledge that equity is more risky than debt but explain that the potential for reward is much higher. Be careful not to take money from friends and family members who could not afford to lose it if the business failed.

Also, be sure that any financial agreements are properly documented and signed, so that there is no misunderstanding later. There are services such as VirginMoneyUS.com (formerly CircleLending.com) that create formal business agreements between family members. Nothing ruins a good relationship more quickly than a dispute over money. As Shakespeare's Polonius advises in *Hamlet*, "Neither a borrower nor a lender be; for loan oft loses itself and friends." Whereas borrowing may be unavoidable, the cautionary note on borrowing from friends is well directed.

Financial Institutions and Dimensions of Credit

It can be difficult for new entrepreneurs to get loans from banks and other financial institutions partially because bankers tend to be conservative lenders and start-ups are riskier than established businesses—performance is necessarily based upon projections rather than historical data. Banks are in the business of lending money they are confident will be repaid. Bankers operate on the principles of the Five C's of credit (see **Figure 10-1**):

1. *Collateral.* Property or other assets pledged against the loan that the lender can take and sell if the loan is not repaid. Examples of such assets are business real estate, equipment, inventory, an owner's home, certificates of deposit, money market accounts, stock certificates, and bonds. Commercial lenders never want to have to take such assets, but they need collateral so that they can be confident of some level of repayment.

2. *Character.* Typically analyzed in the form of the owner's *personal credit* (ability to borrow money) for a small business. Before a financial services company will lend you money, it will want to know your **credit history**, which is the record of how reliably and punctually you or your company has repaid past loans. The lender will obtain your credit report from a **credit reporting agency (CRA)**. These companies, primarily TransUnion, Equifax, and Experian, collect and analyze information supplied by financial institutions and others that extend credit.

credit history a record of credit extended and the repayment thereof.

credit reporting agency (CRA) an organization that collects and analyzes information supplied by financial institutions and others who extend credit, and then sells it.

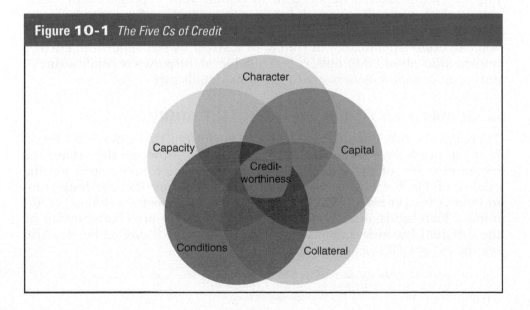

Figure 10-1 *The Five Cs of Credit*

Character

Capacity

Capital

Credit-worthiness

Conditions

Collateral

debt service the amount a borrower is obligated to pay in a given period until a loan is repaid.

3. *Capacity.* The business cash flow must be sufficient to cover the monthly loan payments and expenses. You will have to report your projected cash flow, so the lender can determine whether you will be able to repay the loan. Your **debt service** is the amount you will have to pay over a given period of time, until the loan is repaid.

4. *Capital.* How much of your own money have you invested in your business? Have you gotten friends or family to invest? As we have noted, a banker wants to see that you are risking your own resources before he or she risks the bank's.

5. *Conditions.* This is the state of the industry and economic climate at the time the loan is made and during its anticipated term. If inflation is on the rise, for example, the bank may be concerned that your earnings will not keep pace with it, thus reducing your capacity to repay the loan.

personal guarantee the promise to pay issued by an individual.

Lenders will expect you to sign a **personal guarantee**, which states that you will be responsible for paying off the loan in the event that the business cannot do so. In other words, in the case of default, the lender will have the right to take the business and personal assets.

charge account credit extended by a company allowing qualified customers to make purchases up to a specified limit, without paying cash at the time of purchase.

What constitutes good credit may not be objectively apparent. It is not merely the absence of bad credit. You may think that you have good credit because you have never borrowed money or used a credit card. What you have is *no* credit. To establish credit, you must prove that you are capable of making regular payments on debts. Typically, most banks will not lend to anyone without a credit history, but many stores will, through **revolving charge accounts**, which are credit accounts that have a single borrowing limit and may be used and repaid on a repeated cycle. One way to begin a good credit history is to open one of these store accounts, charge a few small purchases, and never miss a payment or pay later than the due date. This record of on-time payment will become a part of your credit report.

There have been efforts to encourage the acceptance of regular savings deposits and/or timely payments of rent and utilities in lieu of a traditional credit history.[9] However, when credit markets contract, these flexible credit options are easily discarded.

It will be wise to check your credit reports with the major credit reporting agencies at least once a year, to ensure accuracy. Under the Fair Credit Report Act, federal law gives you the right to see and challenge your credit reports from TransUnion, Equifax, and Experian. You can visit http://www.annualcreditreport.com to obtain your reports. Rather than getting the reports all at once, it is better to space them four months apart, so that you can better check for errors. For your business credit reports, you can establish a history at Dun & Bradstreet by self-reporting. Further information about this option is available at http://www.smallbusiness.dnb.com/manage-business-credit/get-duns-details.asp.

Community Development Financial Institutions

There are a number of alternate lending institutions that can serve a broad range of needs in emerging domestic markets.[10] Although they share the common vision of expanding economic opportunity, and improving the quality of life for low-income people and communities, the four community development financial institutions (CDFI) sectors—banks, credit unions, loan funds, and venture capital (VC) funds—are characterized by the different business models and legal structures discussed below. Also see the list of CDFI resources that follows.

---

[9]C. Glackin and E. Mahoney, "Savings and Credit for U.S. Microenterprises: Integrating Individual Development Accounts and Loans for Microenterprise," *Journal of Microfinance*, vol. 4, no. 2, 2002, pp. 93–125.

[10]Opportunity Finance Network Web site, http://www.opportunityfinance.net.

Community Development Banks

Community development banks (CDBs) provide capital to rebuild economically distressed communities through targeted lending and investing. They are for-profit corporations with community representation on their boards of directors. Depending on the individual charter, such banks are regulated by some combination of the Federal Deposit Insurance Corporation (FDIC), the Federal Reserve, the Office of the Comptroller of the Currency, the Office of Thrift Supervision, and state banking agencies. Their deposits are insured by the FDIC.

Community Development Credit Unions

Community development credit unions (CDCUs) promote ownership of assets and savings and provide affordable credit and retail financial services to low-income individuals, often with special outreach to minority communities. They are nonprofit financial cooperatives owned by their members. Credit unions are regulated by the National Credit Union Administration (NCUA)—an independent federal agency—or by state agencies, or both. In most institutions, deposits are also insured by the NCUA.

Community Development Loan Funds

Community development loan funds (CDLFs) provide financing and development services to businesses, organizations, and individuals in low-income communities. There are four main types of loan funds: microenterprise, small business, housing, and community service organization. Each is defined by the type of client served, although many loan funds serve more than one type of client in a single institution. CDLFs tend to be nonprofit and governed by boards of directors with community representation.

Community Development Venture Capital Funds

Community development venture capital funds (CDVCs) provide equity and debt-with-equity features for small- and medium-sized businesses in distressed communities. They can be either for-profit or nonprofit, and include community representation.

Community Development Financial Institution Resources

Opportunity Finance Network	http://www.opportunityfinance.net
Association for Enterprise Opportunity	http://www.microenterpriseworks.org
Aspen Institute	http://www.aspeninstitute.org
Calvert Foundation	http://www.calvertfoundation.org
Corporation for Enterprise Development	http://www.cfed.org
Coalition of Community Development Financial Institutions (CDFI Coalition)	http://www.cdfi.org
Community Development Venture Capital Alliance	http://www.cdvca.org
First Nations Oweesta Corporation	http://www.oweesta.org
National Community Investment Fund	http://www.ncif.org
National Federation of Community Development Credit Unions	http://www.natfed.org
Our Native Circle	http://www.ournativecircle.org

Venture Capitalists

venture capitalist an investor or investment company whose specialty is financing new, high-potential entrepreneurial companies and second-stage companies.

There are also investors and investment companies whose specialty is financing new, high-potential entrepreneurial companies and second-stage companies. Because they often provide the initial equity investment—venture capital—to start a business venture, they are called **venture capitalists**.

Venture capitalists seek high rates of return. They typically expect to earn six times their money back over a five-year period, or a 45 percent return on investment. Professional venture capitalists will not usually invest in a company unless its business plan shows it is likely to generate sales of at least $25 million within five years. The ideal candidates for venture capital are businesses with financial projections that support revenue expectations of over $50 million within five years, growing at 30 to 50 percent per year, with pre-tax profit margins over 20 percent.

If your business plan supports those kinds of numbers, you may be able to interest venture capitalists in your idea. Venture capitalists want equity in return for their capital. They are willing to take the higher risk for higher returns. Venture capitalists sometimes seek a majority interest in a business so that they will have the final word in management decisions. They can structure deals in a variety of ways.

To finance the Ford Motor Company, Henry Ford gave up 75 percent of the business for $28,000 in badly needed capital. It took Ford many years to regain control of his company. Still, many small business owners turn to venture capital when they want to grow the business and commercial banks are not a good fit.

Venture capitalists typically reap the return on their equity investments in one of two ways:

1. by selling their percentage share of the business to another investor through a private transaction, or
2. by waiting until the company goes public (starts selling stock on the open market) and trading their ownership shares for cash by selling them. The shares can now be traded in the stock market.

Angels

angel investor a wealthy individual who invests in businesses.

If your business does not meet the high-flying profit picture that would attract venture capitalists or does not require so much financing, it might still be of interest to **angel investors**—wealthy private individuals who are

Global Impact ...

Kiva—Person-to-Person Lending

A relatively new player in the field of socially responsible lending is Kiva. This not-for-profit company has served as a connector between businesses in need of small amounts of credit and individuals that want to support them. Kiva's mission is "to connect people through lending for the sake of alleviating poverty."[11]

The organization serves as an intermediary between individuals willing to invest at least $25 in a particular microbusiness and the microfinance institutions that will provide direct loans. What makes Kiva noteworthy is the ability to provide person-to-person lending and to have individuals make loans without expectation of financial return (no interest is paid to them).

Kiva's microlending partners made nearly $213 million in loans from October 12, 2005, through May 14, 2011, using the person-to-person lending model. The repayment rate was 98.74% percent. Until June 2009, all Kiva loans were made outside of the United States and, as of May 2011, loans had been made with partners in 60 countries.

---

[11]Kiva Web site, http://www.kiva.org, May 15, 2011.

interested in investing in entrepreneurial ventures for a variety of reasons, from personal friendship to a desire to support entrepreneurship in a given field. Bill Gates, for example, has invested in several biotechnology start-ups because of such an interest. Often, successful entrepreneurs want to invest some of their earnings in other ventures that interest them, and they become angel investors to do so. The University of New Hampshire Center for Venture Research reports that, in 2008, angel investors numbered 260,500, and funded 55,480 companies, for a total of $19.2 billion.[12]

If your business has good management in place and a solid business plan, you might be able to raise angel financing. This type of investment is typically in the $100,000 to $500,000 range. Angels tend to seek a return of 10 times their investment at the end of five years, but their requirements vary widely. Angels may ask for fees for applications and for presentations; their national association recommends that these be limited to several hundred dollars for applications and $500 for presentations.[13]

The idea is to get one angel in place and to recruit that individual to find co-investors. Angels can be hard to find. However, there are a number of national and regional venture capital networks that connect entrepreneurs with angels. The regional networks can be helpful because angels tend to invest in businesses they can visit frequently. The U.S. Small Business Administration developed ACE-Net (now Active Capital), which is a national network of angels. There is an annual fee and certain restrictions apply. However, the network provides investments of up to $5 million, with most being under $1 million. The Angel Capital Association (http://www.angelcapitalassociation.org) and *Inc.* (http://www.inc.com) compile directories of angel investors, with the association's list being global. If you search for angel investors, look for people who are interested in or familiar with your markets and field. Angels prefer manufacturing, energy, technology, and some service businesses. They tend to avoid retail ventures.

Insurance Companies

Business owners may obtain a **policy loan,** which is made to a business using a whole-life, variable-life, or universal-life insurance policy based on the policy's cash-surrender value. In essence, the owner is borrowing against personal savings.

policy loan a loan made against an insurance policy with cash value.

Vendor Financing

Entrepreneurs frequently benefit from the establishment of trade credit from vendors. By eliminating the need for cash in advance or at the time

---

Entrepreneurial Wisdom

Finding angel investors is a frequently cited funding option for entrepreneurs. Actually finding and attracting them requires focus and tenacity. Angelsoft is a company that was started in 2004 to "bring the power of collaboration technologies to the professional early-stage investment industry."[14] Entrepreneurs enter secure online deal rooms to connect with prospective investors. Some services, such as a basic investor search, are free for entrepreneurs. With more than 25,000 early-stage investors in over 530 angel groups and investor funds, connections are ready to be made.

---

[12]Jeffrey Sohl, "The Angel Investor Market in 2009: A Down Year in Investment Dollars but Not in Deals," Center for Venture Research, March 26, 2009.
[13]Angel Capital Association Web Site, http://www.angelcapitalassociation.org, October 31, 2009.
[14]About Angelsoft, 2011, http://angelsoft.net/a/about-us, May 9, 2011.

float the time between a payment transaction and when the cash is actually in the payee's account.

of purchase, businesses can hold onto the money for a longer period or will have more time to generate cash for payment. In essence, the vendor is providing financing for the business. A **float** is the term for the time between a payment transaction and when the cash is actually in the seller's account. If you receive your phone bill on March 1 and pay it on March 20, you have *floated* the bill for 19 days.

Accounts payable is money a business owes its suppliers. You should negotiate the best possible payment terms with your suppliers in advance, so that your business can use float to have as much cash on hand as possible. This is a form of short-term financing from your own company. As you grow and/or establish a record of timely payment, you can ask for better payment terms. If you are not able to pay on time, always call the creditor and discuss the late payment. Never just skip a payment.

Federally Supported Investment Companies

The U.S. government has supported the establishment of a number of privately owned and managed investment funds, primarily licensed and regulated by the SBA, that use their own capital, plus money borrowed with federal guarantees, to make equity and debt investments in qualifying small businesses.[15] They may provide debt or equity for early-stage companies that otherwise could not obtain financing.

The general name for these is Small Business Investment Companies (SBICs). If you are African American, Hispanic, Asian, or belong to another minority group, look into Minority Enterprise Small Business Investment Companies (MESBICs). Also, the SBA and the U.S Department of Agriculture (USDA) have partnered to create Rural Business Investment Companies (RBICs) to support profit-oriented rural enterprises. In addition, New Markets Venture Capital Companies (NMVCCs) serve smaller enterprises located in low-income geographic areas. All are described, and those in your locality can be found, on the SBA Web site at http://www.sba.gov.

Financing for Rural/Agricultural Businesses

Business owners often think of the SBA in terms of financial support and assistance, but the USDA also has a long tradition of providing financial and technical assistance to rural/agricultural businesses, through a variety of programs. In addition to the RBICs noted above, there are programs of grants, guarantees, and loans described on the USDA Web site at http://www.usda.gov. Some of these programs include the Farm Service Agency's farm ownership and operating loans, the Rural Development's Business and Industry (B&I) guaranteed loan program, and the Rural Energy for America Program (REAP) grants and loans. Each program has specific options and limits, and can prove invaluable if your business is located in an area served by these USDA grants or loans.

Youth Financing

If you are a young entrepreneur (generally defined as under age 25), you may qualify for grants, scholarships, or awards designed to promote youth entrepreneurship. Such sources of start-up capital and/or scholarships for young entrepreneurs are listed below.

---

[15]SBA Web site, http://www.sba.gov/aboutsba/sbaprograms/inv/esf/inv_sbic_financing.html.

Youth Entrepreneur Funding Sources

Name	Web Address
Ernst & Young Entrepreneur of the Year Award	http://www.ey.com/global/content.nsf
Guardian Life Insurance's Girls Going Places Entrepreneurship Award Program	http://www.guardianlife.com/womens. channel
National Association for the Self-Employed Scholarship Program	http://benefits.nase.org
NFTE Young Entrepreneur of the Year	http://www.nfte.com
SBA Young Entrepreneur of the Year Award	http://www.sba.gov

Self-Funding: Bootstrap Financing

Last but not least, there is always **bootstrap financing,** which is finding creative ways to stretch existing capital resources as far as they can go. If you cannot secure bank, venture, or angel funding, it does not mean that your business model or idea is not good. It may be that it simply does not fit conventional criteria. It is important to listen to constructive criticism and recommendations from the financing sources that do not fund you. They may provide you with valuable nuggets of information that will help you find ways to bootstrap more successfully. Many hugely successful businesses have been started for under $10,000 by entrepreneurs who used a variety of techniques to stay afloat, including:

bootstrap financing funding a business by creatively stretching existing capital as far as possible, including extensive use of the entrepreneur's time.

- hiring as few employees as possible by using temporary service agencies for staffing needs, to help cut down on insurance and tax expenditures;
- leasing rather than buying equipment;
- getting suppliers to extend your credit terms so you can take longer to pay bills;
- using personal savings, taking a second mortgage, arranging low-interest loans from friends and relatives;
- floating accounts payable;
- working from home, or borrowing office space, to save on fixed costs;
- starting on a smaller scale or with more used equipment to establish a track record for traditional financing in the future, and
- putting profits back into the business to keep it going.

Accessing Sources through Online Networking

The more people who are aware of your product or service and its benefits, the more likely they will be to buy it or refer it to someone who will do so. It is also true that the more you explore possibilities in financing options, the more likely you will be to find what you need. Networking is the exchange of valuable information and contacts among businesspeople. The Internet is an important extension to your options for networking. You can search for angels and connect with other entrepreneurs online. Use search engines such as Google, Bing, Excite, and Yahoo! to find Web sites such as the Entrepreneurs' Organization (http://www.eonetwork.org).

Useful Sites

Name	Web Address
ACCION USA	http://www.accionusa.org
Active Capital (formerly ACE-Net)	http://www.activecapital.org
Angel Capital Association	http://angelcapitalassociation.org
Association for Enterprise Opportunity	http://www.microenterpriseworks.org
ICR Angel Financing	http://www.icrnet.com
Opportunity Finance Network	http://www.opportunityfinance.net

Be wary of any service that requires upfront payment, will not provide complete references, or in any other way raises a red flag. If a financing source seems to be too good to be true, it probably is. That does not mean you should ignore or reject all online options. On the contrary, explore them—but use good judgment.

Investors Want Their Money to Grow: Can You Make It Happen?

When you ask a banker, or friend, for money for your business, you are asking for an investment. You should know, therefore, about some of the other options available to your potential investors. After all, they are only going to put money in your venture if you can convince them that it is a more attractive investment than their other options. As your company grows and prospers, you also may become more interested in financial investments. Or, you may already have one and need to decide whether your business idea is the best one.

There are three categories of financial investments:

1. *Stocks.* Shares of company ownership (equity).
2. *Bonds.* Loans (debt) made to companies or government entities for more than one year.
3. *Cash.* Savings accounts, Treasury bills, or other investments that can be *liquidated* (turned into cash) within 24 hours.

Global Impact...

The United States Encourages Other Nations to Become More Entrepreneurial

Entrepreneurship educators encourage you to think globally when it comes to finding customers, researching the competition, and looking for capital. If you live in the United States, you are probably in the best place to find capital for your business. According to a PricewaterhouseCoopers/National Venture Capital Association Money Tree report, venture capitalists made 3,980 deals totaling nearly $28 billion in the United States during 2008.[16] U.S. venture capital investment totaled $5.27 billion in 595 deals, whereas Europe had 272 deals worth $831 million of the $1.46 billion invested outside of the United States during the second quarter of 2009.[17] Europe's share of the venture capital market for that period was only 20 percent.

European countries are trying to change that, however. The members of the European Union have set forth an agenda for creating a dynamic, entrepreneurial, knowledge-based economy. Venture capital (called *risk capital* in Europe) was identified as a key factor in achieving this. Other countries and regions are undertaking similar efforts to become more entrepreneurial, which means more investors in these countries will be looking to finance small businesses.

---

[16]National Venture Capital Association Web site, http://www.NVCA.org, October 31, 2009.
[17]"International Venture Capital Investment Continues Decline, Down 63% in Q2," Dow Jones Venture Source, July 23, 2009 http://www.reuters.com, October 31, 2009.

Real estate, land, or buildings, is another kind of investment. All investments involve some risk, which is the possibility that the money could be lost. There is a definite relationship between risk and reward:

The greater the potential reward of an investment, the more risky it probably is.

High Risk = High Reward

And so, if an investment has little risk, the reward will probably not be great.

Low Risk = Low Reward

The following sections are a primer on securities investment.

How Stocks Work

A corporation, whether privately held or publicly traded, is owned by its stockholders. Each **share** of stock represents a percentage of ownership. A stock certificate indicates how many shares were purchased and therefore how big a piece of the company is owned.

If Street Scooters, Inc., has sold 10 shares of stock, each share to a different individual, it would mean there were 10 stockholders, each owning one-tenth of the company. If Street Scooters sold 100 shares of stock, each share to a different individual, there would be 100 stockholders, each owning one one-hundredth of the company.

The "stock market" is in more than one location. It is made up of a collection of *exchanges* around the world where stocks are traded. The New York Stock Exchange (http://www.nyse.com) is the most well known in the United States. In recent years it has expanded to become NYSE Euronext, having added a number of European exchanges and the American Stock Exchange (Amex). The electronic exchange that is home to many new and high-technology stocks is the NASDAQ (http://www.nasdaq.com); it is

◀ **Performance Objective 5**
Understand stocks and bonds as investment alternatives.

share a single unit of corporate stock.

A trader checks stock prices on his computer.
(John Stuart/Mira.com)

joined with regional exchanges. Overseas, the London, Tokyo, and Hong Kong exchanges are the most recognized. Stocks may be traded on multiple exchanges, but the companies must meet the criteria for each.

Public corporations sell their stock to the general public to raise *capital.* They use the capital to expand the company or pay off debts. Typically, a corporation sells its stock to an investment banker, who pays an agreed-upon price and then handles the marketing and sales to get the stock into the public market. A public corporation receives the proceeds from the sale before the offering. Once the stock is sold, however, the corporation no longer has control over it. It is traded in the secondary market; the stock can be bought and sold by anyone. Such trading activity occurs continually on the stock market between brokers. A *stockbroker* has a license that confers the right to make trades for customers.

Stocks may be either *preferred* or *common,* with preferred stock having aspects of debt and common stock being true equity. Preferred stock typically has a fixed dividend that is paid quarterly, and takes precedence over common stock in the case of liquidation. Many companies do not issue preferred stock. Common stock represents the true ownership of a company. It is the type of stock that is most often held, and can be made available in different classes that define whether it comes with voting rights or not. In case the business is liquidated, common stockholders get repaid after all debt holders and preferred stockholders.

The price of a stock at any given moment reflects investors' opinions about how well that business is going to perform. If the company does well, or its investors expect it to do well, the price of the stock is likely to rise. Investors make their returns by selling stock at a higher price than the one at which they bought it. They also may earn *dividends,* which are the portion of a corporation's earnings distributed to shareholders, typically on a quarterly basis. Dividends are paid at the discretion of a company's board of directors.

The daily record of trading activity appears in tables published in the *Wall Street Journal* and in the business sections of many other newspapers. They are also available online from numerous services. These tables allow investors to track the changing value of their investments. Information about stocks is available through brokerage firms and services, such as ValueLine and Morningstar.

Let's say you own 10 shares of a stock you bought at $10 per share (for a total of $100). You see in the stock table one day that the price per share has declined to $8.50. Your $100 investment is now worth only $85 (10 shares × $8.50/share = $85). You have three choices:

1. sell the shares before their value declines further;
2. keep them, hoping the decline is temporary and that the price will go back up; or
3. buy more shares at the lower price to increase your profit when the price does go back up.

How Bonds Work

Corporations may also use the financial markets to borrow money by issuing *bonds.* Bonds are interest-bearing certificates that corporations offer in order to raise capital. In addition, the federal government, state governments, and even city and town governments use bonds to finance roads, bridges, schools, and other public projects.

Bonds are loans; the original amount borrowed, plus interest, must be paid by the borrower. If you purchase a corporate or government bond, you are loaning your money to the company or government.

Owners of common stock cannot be certain that they will receive dividends or if the value of the stocks they own will increase. They may make or lose money on the investment. The risks, and therefore the rewards, can be high. Bondholders, on the other hand, are promised a specific return (the coupon interest rate on the bond) and will get the investment back after a given time period. Bonds are rated by several organizations to reflect the levels of respective risk. Bonds and stocks together are referred to as **securities.**

Bonds are different from other loans, because the corporation that issues a bond does not have to pay regular monthly payments on the principal (the amount of a debt before the interest is added). A bond usually pays its yearly interest rate semiannually to the bondholders until **maturity,** when it is *redeemed,* meaning that the investor gets the face value back on that date.

By financing with bonds instead of a bank loan, a company does not have to make payments on the principal, only on the interest. On the other hand, the company must manage its money carefully, so that it will have the cash available when the bond matures.

If a corporation stops paying interest on a bond, the bondholders can sue. A court may force the company to sell assets to pay not only the interest, but the full amount of the bond.

Until maturity, bonds may be traded publicly, with their price going above or below their **face value.** The face value of a single bond, also referred to as **par,** is usually $1,000 (with bonds being sold in lots of $10,000). This is the amount to be repaid by the corporation or government at the maturity date of the bond.

When the bond's market value rises above par, it means it is being traded for more than $1,000; perhaps it was purchased at $1,020. A bond trading above par is trading at a **premium;** in this case, the premium is $20. A bond trading below par is trading at a **discount.** If the above bond were trading at $940, the discount would be $60. Prices are quoted with the coupon rate (interest rate) and the price at maturity. For example, a five-year, 12 percent bond might be selling for $899.40 with a par value of $1,000. This means that coupon interest payments will be $120 per year and the investment will yield a 15 percent return based on annual interest payments. Another five-year, 12 percent bond might be selling for $1,116.70, for a yield of 9 percent. The price an investor is willing to pay will depend upon the return that he or she needs to earn on the investment.

When you are buying or selling a bond, the critical determinant of price is the combination of the coupon rate, maturity date, risk, and required return. As an issuer of bonds, you will need to obtain enough financing at a cost that works for you. As an investor, you will have to meet or exceed your required return at a risk level that you can tolerate and on a time horizon that suits your needs.

securities investment instruments representing ownership in an entity (stock) or debt (bond) held by an investor.

maturity the date at which a loan must be repaid, including when a bond must be redeemed by the issuer.

face value the amount of a bond, also known as par, to be repaid by a corporation or government at its maturity date.

par the face value of a bond (typically $1,000) and the stated value of a stock.

premium (regarding bonds) the amount above par for which a bond is trading in the market.

discount (regarding bonds) the difference between a bond's trading price and its par value when the trading price is below par.

Chapter Summary

Now that you have studied this chapter, you can do the following:

1. Explore your financing preferences.
   - Understand how much risk you are willing to take when financing your business.

- Know the success rate in your industry.
- Determine realistic financing options.

2. Identify the types of business financing.
   - *Gifts and grants.* Money or in-kind gifts obtained to support the business without a return required.
   - *Debt.* You borrow the money and promise to pay it back over a set period of time at a set rate of interest. Corporations sell debt in the form of bonds. You could borrow money from family or friends to finance your business.
   - *Equity.* You give up a percentage of ownership in your business for money. The investor receives a percentage of future profits from the business based on the percentage of ownership. Corporations sell equity in the form of stock. You cannot sell stock unless your business is incorporated, but you *can* sell equity. You could offer ownership and a share of your future profits in exchange for financing.

3. Compare the pros and cons of debt and equity financing.

Debt Advantages

- The lender has no say in the management or direction of the business as long as the loan payments are made.
- Loan payments are predictable; they do not change with the fortunes of the business.

Debt Disadvantages

- Debt can be an expensive way to finance a business if interest rates are high.
- If loan payments are not made, the lender can force the business into bankruptcy.
- The lender may be able to take the home and possessions of the owner of a sole proprietorship or of the partners in a partnership to settle a debt.
- Loan payments increase fixed costs and decrease profits.

Equity Advantages

- If the business does not make a profit, investors do not get paid. The equity investor cannot force the business into bankruptcy in order to retrieve the investment.
- The equity investor has an interest in seeing the business succeed, and may offer helpful advice and obtain valuable contacts.

Equity Disadvantages

- Through giving up ownership, the entrepreneur can lose control of the business to the equity holders.

- Equity financing is risky, so the investor frequently wants both to receive a higher rate of return than a lender, and to be able to influence how the company is operated.
- The entrepreneur will share profits with other equity investors.

4. Identify sources of capital for your business:
   - entrepreneurs, friends, family;
   - financial institutions;
   - community development financial institutions;
   - venture capitalists;
   - angels;
   - vendors;
   - federally supported investment companies.

5. Understand stocks and bonds as investing alternatives:
   - public corporations sell stock to the general public to raise capital;
   - bonds are interest-bearing certificates that corporations (and governments) issue to raise capital.

Key Terms

angel investor	par
bootstrap financing	personal guarantee
credit history	policy loan
credit reporting agency (CRA)	premium
creditor	principal
debt service	promissory note
default	revolving charge account
discount	risk tolerance
face value	securities
financing	share
float	tax abatement
leveraged	tax credit
maturity	venture capitalist

Entrepreneurship Portfolio

Critical Thinking Exercises

1. What type of financing will you seek as start-up capital, and why?
2. What steps could you take to improve your creditworthiness?
3. How would you counter the argument from a potential investor that most small businesses fail?
4. What challenges do start-up businesses face? Explain.

Key Concept Questions

1. Calculate the annual amount of interest (assuming no principal repayment) for each of the following:

   Term loan of $122,000 over 15 years at 6.5%.
   Line of credit for $50,000 drawn 50% in one year at 10%.
   Fifteen shares of stock purchased at $12.50 per share.
   Bonds trading at par for $2,000 with a 7% rate.

2. If the owner of Bright Rays Tanning Salon, Inc., invested $200,000 and found an investor to pay in $45,000 for 15% of the corporation, what is the valuation of the business?

Application Exercises

1. If you currently subscribe to or use an online service, BBS (bulletin board service), or ISP (Internet Service Provider), discuss what you like and dislike about the service and why you chose it.
2. How could accepting an equity investment change your business plans?

Exploring Online

1. Visit http://www.privacyrights.org/fs/fs6-crdt.htm to learn about your rights to financial privacy, and then answer the following:

   • Who has access to your credit reports?
   • What information cannot be legally included in your credit reports?
   • After how many years is unpaid debt erased from your credit reports?

2. Visit the SBA Web site at http://www.sba.gov. Find four possible funding sources for a computer rental and repair company. Describe the pros and cons of each and create a proposed financing mix, assuming a need for $58,000 in start-up funds divided as follows:

Equipment	$27,000
Software	$10,000
Supplies	$1,000
Marketing	$6,000
Utilities/services	$4,000
Working capital	$10,000

Exploring Your Community

1. Find and list three networking opportunities in your community. Describe how you could take advantage of them for your business.

2. Visit a local bank and ask about its commercial lines of credit. Have the banker explain the terms to you and what a small start-up venture would have to show to qualify for a line of credit. Report back to the class.

3. Are there any angel investors that might be interested in your business? Who are they and how did you find them?

BizBuilder Business Plan Questions

8.0 Funding Request and Exit Strategy

8.1 Amount and Type of Funds Requested

A. Clearly state how much money you are requesting in this plan and the terms under which you anticipate obtaining those funds.

B. Do you intend to use debt to finance your business? Explain.

C. Do you plan to issue bonds to finance your business at some point in the future?

| # Creative Financing for a Creative Business—Sandra Baquero Designs

Sandra Nieto always knew she wanted to be a fashion designer. In her native Colombia, "without a peso to invest," she started a successful business by building strong relationships and inspiring confidence in those who could invest. Sandra's business succeeded until the Colombian economy faltered.

While her business continued to struggle, Sandra's brother requested she turn in his application for a visa to visit the United States because she lived near the embassy. Sandra figured if she was going to wait in that long line, she might as well apply too. Her application was approved just before her business when bankrupt. "It was destiny."

Sandra decided to stay in New York after her visa expired. She, like many undocumented workers, took on whatever jobs she could get: babysitter, maid and assistant in a salon. "But in the back of my mind I knew I still wanted to be a designer." She continued to design clothes for herself and her daughter. "People would encourage me to start my own line. I was hesitant, because it's the type of industry that you have to fight hard in."

And fight she did. Sandra devoted seven days a week and many late nights to creating her clothes. She traveled with her handmade work to trade shows where she had some success. However, she did not have enough money to continue to design. "Everything I received, I needed for food." She investigated getting a bank loan, but no one would lend money to her without a credit history.

Sandra faced moments of little hope. "After investing so much...I would go to a show and think it is going to go really well. When it wouldn't, I would think, I don't want to do this anymore. It is too much money, time and stress for it to not work out... it was depressing to feel like I couldn't continue being a fashion designer."

One day, through Facebook, Sandra learned that a friend from Colombia was involved in microfinance. A little more research brought her to Accion, a lender that valued what others did not. "I applied and they gave it to me, surely because of my years of experience and momentum I already had going." Sandra put her $6,000 loan toward renting spaces in Madison Square Garden and Bryant Park and hosting two fashion shows. She was able to use revenues to continue to design and build her brand. The profits also came in handy when an unexpected household emergency occurred.

Sandra admits she still struggles. However, she plans to continue to go to shows and make sure the right people see her clothes. She has enough momentum with Sandra Baquero Designs

Sandra Nieto of Sandra Baquero.
(Courtesy of Accion USA)

and passion for her work to live out her dream. Sandra has already paid off half of her Accion loan and is confident she will be able to pay off the rest.

Because of her many experiences, Sandra has a lot of great advice for entrepreneurs, including the importance of pursuing what they are most passionate about. "If you have something you love and you are good at, then do it." Sandra describes how her love of fashion motivated her through hard times. "My head never stopped. I would see a tree or a piece of paper in the street and see something to design. This is what saved me." She also emphasizes the importance of bringing something unique in the world. "People like what I do because I do something different from everyone else. I don't make the same pants as everyone else. If you are going to start an empanada business, add a unique touch."

Thanks to Accion, a woman with a strong passion and great talent is able to continue building strong relationships, and a brand that will surely continue to grow.

Case Study Analysis

1. Why did Sandra Nieto turn to microlending as a source of capital for his business?
2. What factors made Sandra's company a business that did not qualify for mainstream financing (specifically discuss the C's of credit)?
3. When, if ever would you advise Sandra to approach mainstream lenders?
4. What challenges and set-backs has Sandra overcome?

Case Sources

Case information courtesy of ACCION USA.

Chilly Dilly's Ice Cream Company: Financing Growth

Case prepared by Dr. Jay Azriel and Dr. Andrew Sumutka of York College of Pennsylvania.

Dylan sat at his parents' kitchen table in York, Pennsylvania, going over the season's revenues. He smiled as he checked over his figures for a second time. He could hardly believe that his earnings had increased more than 250 percent over the previous year, despite the tough economic times. His hard work, careful planning, and creative ideas were responsible, at least in part, for a 105.7 percent increase in profits as well. His smile widened as he thought about the role that his entrepreneurship courses and professors at Temple University had played in his success. He had certainly come a long way from that night when he was stranded on the side of a highway with little cash, a dead cell-phone battery, and an ice cream truck that he had used all $5,000 of his savings to buy. However, his smile quickly faded as he got back to work on his strategic plan.

He looked up from the numbers and thought about what he should do next. He knew that growing his business by triple digits the next year would not be as easy as it was during the first two. He had maxed out his line of credit with the only bank in town that would loan his business money, so it would be a great risk to put even one additional truck on the road. He was glad that he resisted the temptation to pay back his loan early, and instead conserved his cash for investing in the growth of his business. However, his cash balance fell short of what was necessary to finance his business's growth plan. While Dylan had already booked several after-season sales at area companies, these would not generate enough profit to fund his expansion plan for the following year. He knew that putting three additional trucks on the road would extend his operations beyond the area of his hometown of York into some of Maryland's wealthier suburbs that had been overlooked by the few ice cream truck operators still in business. He hoped that he would not have to seriously consider his father's suggestion of inviting a partner into his business. He had heard too many stories of failed partnerships in his entrepreneurship classes. However, what choices did he really have?

(Dr. Jay Azriel & Dr. Andrew Sumutka/New York College of Pennsylvania)

Dylan thought hard about what his next steps should be. He knew that his business was at one of those important crossroads his professors mentioned. The business he was building was more than just a fleet of ice cream trucks. He wanted to bring back something essential that had been lost—the ubiquitous Good Humor man of the past. He just needed to figure out how to finance this growth. His family broke his concentration, as they piled into the kitchen to get ready for dinner. He put his paperwork aside and joined his family.

Dylan's Dream

Dylan had always been entrepreneurial. He got his first taste of the world of high finance at the age of nine, when he began operating a paper route he would continue for five years. While his $2,500 annual earnings were substantial for a kid of his age, Dylan always dreamed of something bigger. After his paper route, he started a lawn mowing business and, in high school, a concert promotion company. While Dylan learned a great deal from these ventures, "It was always a dream of mine to start an ice cream business." When he was a senior in high school, Dylan began plans to start his dream business to help pay for college. His first idea was to serve hand-scooped ice cream from a truck. However, this plan was short lived. "After researching this I realized that novelty ice cream is easier and more profitable."

Dylan kept thinking about his ice cream business while studying entrepreneurship at Temple University in Philadelphia. In fact, during his freshman year, Dylan investigated the ice cream industry for one of his courses and recognized an opportunity for starting such a venture in York. He learned that the ice cream vendor industry was fairly fragmented, mostly run by operators who owned one or two trucks. Thus, he would not have to contend with any large players in his market. During winter break in his freshman year, he began to seriously investigate purchasing his first ice cream truck. Dylan scoured a number of Web sites and found a truck on eBay that he thought might work. The vehicle he had set his sights on was a Good Humor truck from 1970. Dylan took the train to a small community on Long Island to examine the truck. Excited that he would actually be starting a business, he quickly handed over $5,000—almost all of his savings—without making more than a cursory inspection of the old GMC P30 Step Van.

On the long drive back to York, an excited Dylan made call after call on his mobile phone to tell people about his newly purchased truck. Then, right outside of Philadelphia, his truck just stopped running and coasted to a stop on the side of the interstate—more than two hours from home. Dylan called his local mechanic and had his crippled truck towed back to York. The mechanic's diagnosis was that only the freezer was worth saving. The rest of the truck went to the scrap yard. Dylan lost his truck and the $5,000.

However, he did not let this setback extinguish his dream of becoming York's ice cream king. Armed with more information, Dylan carefully checked out a 1971 Ford Good Humor truck. However, he did not have the $15,000 asking price. "After losing everything, I was forced to ask for money from the bank." Dylan secured a $20,000 loan, which was enough to pay for the truck with an additional $5,000 for start-up costs, including his initial inventory. The loan did not come easily, even with his carefully written business plan; the bank would not make the loan unless he had a qualified co-signer. His father co-signed his loan, and Dylan was in business. His business venture was finally on its way!

Revenue Streams

Food venders often seek out areas with high pedestrian traffic, such as parks and beaches.

Special permits may be needed to operate in these areas, which cuts down on competition. Dylan knew vendors who made a good living setting up near Temple and selling to the students. However, there were few areas in York that would lend themselves to a one-location setup.

Instead, like most ice cream truck operators, Dylan's Chilly Dilly trucks traveled from neighborhood to neighborhood to sell their products. Chilly Dilly drivers developed their own local routes, which they followed on a weekly cycle. The strategy behind weekly, instead of daily, visits was to create a loyal parental following by not overvisiting neighborhoods, while at the same time covering a broader geographic area with the same number of trucks. However, Chilly Dilly's trucks did visit parks and popular recreational areas on a daily basis, to serve the constantly changing clientele.

Dylan also recognized that greater-York-area companies were another outlet for his products and would provide revenues beyond September. Dylan offered these businesses two affordable but profitable group package rates:

Standard: $3.00 per person

Premium: $4.00 per person

Both packages had dozens of delicious choices, including sugar-free and all-natural items. A delivery charge was added to cover the cost of gas.

In his first year of operation, 20 companies hired Dylan to provide their employees with cold treats. This increased to 45 during his second year. In addition to these business outlets, Dylan adapted his package model to the catering of private parties, such as barbecues, church picnics, and weddings. Dylan added a third option for these customers: $2.00 per person for cones and slushies. He made sure he covered his costs by requiring a minimum order of 50.

Business Expansion

In May 2008, Dylan graduated with his degree in Entrepreneurship from Temple. He then was able to focus on his business full time. He purchased three used trucks at $6,500 each. He financed this expansion with a $25,000 loan from a local bank, at a rate of 6.5 percent (prime plus two). The season was profitable; however, the recession and fuel prices squeezed his margins.

In 2009, Chilly Dilly's had grown to eight additional employees. The company had six trucks on the road. Two of them sold soft-serve ice cream products, including coffee shakes, which were popular with adults. The first of these he had purchased for $36,500, fully outfitted. This truck was on the road seven days per week and was the most profitable of the six because soft-serve products have a higher profit margin. In addition, Dylan found that making his own high-profit ice cream novelties further boosted the company's bottom line.

Dylan's hard work on developing relationships with local companies had also met with success. Despite route sales being down, his overall sales were up, due to new and repeat business from corporate customers. "My Web site was paying off, as I was getting more leads from there than from the mailing lists," Dylan noted. However, the recession had put pressure on his business catering, as customers began cancelling bookings as a cost-saving measure: "A number of customers who gave me firm bookings cancelled at the last minute due to trying to cut costs. I was quite surprised by this, as we have a package to fit every budget and this just did not happen last year after someone made a commitment."

By the end of the 2009 season, Dylan had grown the business to the point where each truck averaged $30,000 in gross revenue. However, his trucks had been expensive to get into working order and could be expensive to keep on the road. Still, Dylan observed that, "We will be spending between $4,000 and $5,000 a year on each truck, since we are now keeping up rather than catching up with maintenance costs."

Dylan's business had started to take off. Grownups and kids alike were excited when one of his trucks rolled through the neighborhood. Parents liked to see the Chilly Dilly's trucks because they did not have to see them every day. The Chilly Dilly's driver offered a variety of products at different prices. The coffee-flavored drinks and soft-serve items also proved to be a hit with parents. Dylan's success was due in part to creating Chilly Dilly's as a local brand name, but he needed to figure out a way to expand the business beyond York County.

Funding Chilly Dilly's Growth

Dylan had grown his business from a single truck to eight in less than five years. However, his dream was to create a brand that spanned southcentral Pennsylvania and northern Maryland. Dylan also wanted to expand east into the wealthier areas of Lancaster, and establish a facility there so that his drivers could save 90 minutes a day in travel time. Dylan knew from his entrepreneurship courses that he would have to carefully plan this expansion. He could only manage so many employees on his own, and he was hesitant to increase his overhead and risk by hiring managers.

Thus, financing the company's growth was a critical issue for the young company. Dylan was able to finance his company's start-up through a local bank loan. However, this bank was not in a position to give him another. The economic conditions were such that banks in general were unwilling to extend loans to small businesses without significant collateral, even with an SBA loan guarantee. Dylan wanted to avoid asking his parents to co-sign another loan for him. Thus, he needed to look for other sources to fund Chilly Dilly's growth.

Organic Growth through Bootstrapping

The first option Dylan looked into was internally funding his business's expansion. He thought about new, higher-margin products that he could manufacture to provide some additional capital. He had found that his customers were willing to purchase high-margin soft-serve products. But outfitting another truck with this equipment required a greater investment. Then Dylan thought about new ways to increase revenues with the equipment he already owned or could purchase more cheaply. He also knew that he could grow the demand for his products through low-cost guerilla marketing techniques. He just needed to sit down and think of some new strategies.

Loans from Friends, Family, and Strangers

A second option for Dylan was to approach friends and family for some additional capital. The availability of such funding lay in the liquidity of the assets of his family and friends and the level of risk they would be willing to take. In addition, private investors were another potential group he might be able to tap for growth capital. However, the interest rate could well be higher, and an angel investor might be more interested in owning a piece of his business than lending money. An investor with some business savvy might be a smarter move, despite the potential cost. These "smart money" investors were often willing to mentor young entrepreneurs.

Dylan could have also applied for additional credit through a credit card company; however, the interest rate could have exceeded 20 percent. A fairly new option would have been to apply for a loan through a peer-to-peer lending Web site, which would have provided between $8,000 and $25,000. Peer-to-peer companies, such as Prosper and Lending Club, act as intermediaries, much like eBay, by matching potential investors with people who are seeking personal or business loans. Generally speaking, their borrowers have problems getting loans from traditional sources, like commercial banks, due to their credit history, debt-to-equity ratio, or a lack of collateral. The lenders seek a higher return than banks do, but interest rates can turn out to be lower than what an entrepreneur could obtain from a local bank because investors bid against one another and often a loan ends up with a dozen or more individuals each having a small part of it; thus, the risk is spread.

Equity Investors or Partners

Another option for financing Chilly Dilly's growth would have been to attract either equity investors or business partners. His dad, a chiropractor, was partnered with several other doctors in a professional corporation. This partnership not only allowed the doctors to see more patients and generate higher revenues, but also helped to spread fixed business expenses over a larger patient base. Dylan had given a great deal of thought to finding a partner. However, he did not know anyone with whom he would be willing to share his business. Dylan knew that entering into a partnership was like getting married. His professor, as well as several guest speakers in his entrepreneurship courses, had related stories of partnerships gone sour. Dylan was thus hesitant to take a partner.

Conclusion

Dylan spoke with his family about his growth plans over dinner. He explained the opportunity to rent space in the local indoor farmers market, which would "not only allow me to sell my products year round, but also give me manufacturing space to produce my novelties and lower my product costs and boost my profits." An earnest Dylan turned to his father and asked, "What should I do to make this happen?"

Case Questions:

1. What are the advantages and disadvantages for each of Dylan's funding options?
2. Are there options to fund Chilly Dilly's growth that Dylan has not considered?
3. Which option(s) do you suggest Dylan implement?

Table 10-1   Dylan's Time Line for Each Summer Season

2004	2005	2006	2007	2008	2009
Started Chilly Dilly's with the purchase of first truck.	First full season	Focused on business catering.	Hired first employee	Graduated from Temple University. Purchased three additional trucks and hired more employees.	Purchased two additional trucks. Started selling coffee drinks.

FASTSIGNS—Finding and Funding an Opportunity in Technology

Small Business School **video clips titles are in red**
Case prepared by Hattie Bryant, creator of Small Business School, *the television series made for PBS and Voice of America, http://SmallBusinessSchool.org.*

FASTSIGNS began on the back of a paper napkin at a breakfast discussion. Gary Salomon had seen the way a computer could make high-quality signs in hours instead of the days required for traditional production. He jumped at the opportunity to build a business offering this service internationally. Today, the company he founded in 1985 in Dallas, Texas, is America's leading sign company and has over 550 locations worldwide.

The typical FASTSIGNS is located in a strip shopping center, making it easily accessible to both businesses and individual consumers.

Gary Salomon, cofounder and Chairman of the Board. (FASTSIGNS)

MAKE THE OLD NEW

Salomon did his research and knew that the sign industry does $5.5 billion in U.S. sales annually. He also learned that the temporary sign business is a niche that big companies weren't interested in. The old-fashioned, hand-done methods were too expensive for people who just wanted to stick a sign in their yard announcing: Garage Sale Today.

Keep Your Eyes Open to Spot Opportunity

Salomon saw the technology he now uses while he was making a sales call for the first company he owned. He struck a deal with the inventor and, with vision and sweat equity, he now dominates the marketplace. There are two ways to look at the word "owns." You can own something in the legal sense, meaning you have the patent or copyright to a product or idea, which entitles you to use the courts to stop others from profiting from your property. In another sense, if the marketplace thinks of your company first when they think of a product or service, you *own* it.

Buy Someone Else's Idea

FASTSIGNS acquired the legal right to use the technology because the inventor only wanted to use it in his one location. Salomon wanted to take the idea international. He recognized that the technology was not being fully exploited by the inventor and negotiated a deal to get access. There were multiple ways for Salomon to do this. He could have paid a fee for usage, he could have made the inventor a part owner of the company, or he could have bought out the inventor.

Often inventors are reluctant to agree to any of these, because they think that the idea is everything. However, as veteran entrepreneur Bill Tobin told the *Small Business School*, the idea is only 2 percent of the success of a business. Certainly a business needs the right idea at the right time, but to exploit the idea, to deliver it to customers who are happy to pay for it, a business has to have what Salomon brought to FAST-SIGNS—vision, money, and the drive to develop sales and marketing.

Salomon not only owns the technology he uses, the growth and sales of FASTSIGNS tells us that he owns the mindshare of consumers. From the beginning, FASTSIGNS has been the leader in its niche, as measured by locations and sales. You have to own an idea legally to grow a business. It's even better if you also can own the business from the marketplace point of view, as does Salomon.

Put Skin in the Game

Salomon and his partners, Steve Mailman and Bob Schanbaum, put together about $40,000 by pooling their savings and then secured a small bank loan to open up the first FASTSIGNS store. They decided if this one location generated $15,000 per month in sales within the first year, they would go forward with a growth strategy using a franchise model. Starting a business is difficult, and money flows out before it flows in, so Salomon kept his job for ten months and used his paychecks plus some savings to take care of his personal bills.

CREATE A NEW BREED OF OWNERS

Salomon could see by operating the first FASTSIGNS himself exactly what needed to be done to make profits. He codified all of his activities and created systems so that he could then teach others to do exactly what he had done. This effort prepared him to grow the business by selling franchises. Each initial franchise fee fuels the home office with cash, and the monthly fees support all of the marketing and training provided by the home office to each owner in the field. These revenues reduce the need for external financing.

FASTSIGNS franchisee.
(FASTSIGNS)

Just as Salomon targeted his service to a small niche of the sign business, he targeted his franchise sales efforts. He never tried to find every single person who was thinking of owning a business. From the beginning, he reached out to sell franchises to engineers, CPAs, experienced managers, and even bankers—because people with these types of backgrounds thrive on systems. They find comfort in knowing precisely how someone else achieved success.

The general pool of people who want to own their own business is heavily weighted with the type of person who wants to act independently and create personal rules. These folks can be renegades and too creative to be happy following a system laid out by someone else. Salomon saved time and money by determining in advance who would make the best owner of a FASTSIGNS franchise.

Let Go to Grow

Small Business School taped a FASTSIGNS corporate meeting and found that Salomon focused on listening. He told me that when he was running the first store he could keep his finger on all the activities, and with just four or five employees he knew what every person on the payroll was accomplishing. Now he has to listen to and give authority to managers.

Salomon observed, "When you have a staff of 75 to 80 you've got to work through people, and you've got to make the shift from being an entrepreneur to being more of an organized business. That's a threshold that I had a great deal of difficulty with coming through many years ago. I finally decided to stop meddling with what they were doing.

"In the beginning I had to keep everything in my head and after a while it became evident that while that fed my ego it didn't allow the people that I had hired, put in place, and paid a decent wage to be able to be fulfilled by what they were doing. Because you put people in place you have to let them do their job properly. The more people we attracted over time the more I was looking for the areas that I was not really the best at. I'm great at ideas, I'm great at marketing, and I'm great at sales. But when it comes to the day-in-and-day-out activities of management, that's not my bailiwick."

Check Your Ego at the Door

By admitting to his weaknesses, Gary Salomon cleared a hurdle most owners either don't try to jump over, or they try and fail. He was able to stop doing and start leading. "I try to keep things as simple as possible. Basically, I try to have people get the feedback they need in order to be as productive as possible and I try to reward accordingly. I think the bottom line is I don't have much of an ego. I'm not really interested in as much being right as I am interested in having the best result or the best solution, and if it's not my idea, I really don't care. I'd rather it just be, you know, the best idea.

"When you have that attitude, people aren't afraid of giving you an opinion, because they know they're not going to be shot down. And as a matter of fact, you know, while I sometimes have some excellent ideas, I'm sometimes shown the door, in a manner of speaking, as to how unreasonable that idea might be. But what it does is, is it fosters the ongoing embracing of ideas coming from other people, because they know that it's going to be considered, and that we mean it.

"So, you know, does that necessarily mean that you always get the right solution to a problem? No. But at least people aren't afraid of offering it. And I think that, you know, compensation is a part of keeping good, quality folks, but it's not really the top item. It's creating an environment where people feel like they can make a difference, and that they're being listened to."

Salomon leads people by laying out the plans in writing, then giving them the freedom to succeed or fail. He doesn't depend upon a big personality to win people over to his side. Gary Salomon found a technology with promise and used his leadership skills and abilities to form a team that took advantage of the technology to develop a market.

Case Questions

1. How did Gary Salomon exploit an opportunity to start FASTSIGNS?
2. What are some of the keys to Salomon's success with FASTSIGNS?
3. How did the founders finance the start-up of FASTSIGNS?
4. How was FASTSIGNS's growth financed?
5. Why would an inventor sell the rights to an idea?
6. Why do you think people might enjoy working for Salomon in the corporate office?

OPERATING A SMALL BUSINESS EFFECTIVELY

Chapter 11
ADDRESSING LEGAL ISSUES AND MANAGING RISK

Chapter 12
OPERATING FOR SUCCESS

Chapter 13
MANAGEMENT, LEADERSHIP, & ETHICAL PRACTICES

Jupiter Images

ADDRESSING LEGAL ISSUES AND MANAGING RISK

On May 8, 1886, Dr. John Stith Pemberton, an Atlanta pharmacist, produced the syrup for Coca-Cola and brought a jug of it to Jacobs' Pharmacy, where it was mixed and sold as a soda fountain drink. The beverage was proclaimed to be "delicious and refreshing," a theme that Coca-Cola reinforces today.

Dr. Pemberton's partner and bookkeeper, Frank Robinson, thought that "two C's would look well in advertising," and recommended the name *Coca-Cola,* creating the famous trademark in his own script.

Over time, businessman Asa Candler bought into the company and eventually acquired complete control of it. According to the company's Web site, in May of 1889, Candler published a full-page advertisement in *The Atlanta Journal* that proclaimed his wholesale and retail drug business as "Sole proprietors of Coca-Cola.... Delicious. Refreshing. Exhilarating. Invigorating." By 1892, Candler's flair for merchandising had boosted sales of Coca-Cola syrup nearly tenfold. With his brother John, Frank Robinson, and two other associates, Candler formed the Coca-Cola Company as a corporation. The trademark *Coca-Cola,* which had been used since 1886, was registered in the United States Patent Office in 1893, and has been renewed periodically.[1]

Performance Objectives

1. Choose a legal structure for your business.
2. Understand the importance of contracts.
3. Recognize key components of commercial law.
4. Protect your intellectual property.
5. Protect your tangible assets and manage risk.

Dr. John Stith Pemberton.
(© Corbis)

Business Legal Structures

Performance Objective 1

Choose a legal structure for your business.

Most businesses, no matter how humble their beginnings, have the potential to grow into much larger ventures, so it is important that founders think through every step of the company's development. How the entrepreneur organizes the company, such as the legal structure chosen, the relationships developed with suppliers, and the managers hired, will all have vital impact on the ability to grow.

After you pick the kind of business and industry you want to be in, you will know where you fit in the production-distribution chain; you will be able to research markups, markdowns, and discounts in your industry in order to be competitive. You will also have to choose one of the three basic legal structures:

1. sole proprietorship,
2. partnership, or
3. corporation.

Sole Proprietorship

sole proprietorship
a business owned by one person, who has unlimited liability and unlimited rights to profits.

A **sole proprietorship** is a business owned by one individual, who often is the only employee. This owner receives all the profits from the business and is also responsible for all losses. Most U.S. businesses are sole proprietorships.

---

[1]Information from Coca-Cola Web site, http://www.Coke.com.

The sole proprietor is personally *liable*, or responsible, for any lawsuits that arise from accidents, faulty merchandise, unpaid bills, or other business problems. This means a sole proprietor could lose not only business assets in a lawsuit, but could be forced to sell private possessions, to satisfy a court judgment. He or she could lose a house or a car, for example.

Advantages of a Sole Proprietorship

- It is relatively easy to start. A person becomes a sole proprietor—albeit not a registered, legal one—simply by selling something to someone else.
- Proper registration does not require much paperwork, and registration is relatively inexpensive.
- There are fewer government regulations than for the other forms of business.
- Sole proprietors can make quick decisions and act without interference from others.
- A sole proprietor is entitled to all the profits from the business.

Disadvantages of a Sole Proprietorship

- It can be difficult to raise enough money by oneself to start or expand a business.
- A sole proprietor must often put in long hours, working six or even seven days a week, with no one to share the responsibilities.
- There is no way to limit personal legal liability from lawsuits related to the business.
- There is often no one to offer encouragement or feedback.
- All profits earned are taxed personally, whether or not the funds are withdrawn from the business or cash is left in it.

How to Register a Sole Proprietorship

In most states and localities, it is easy and relatively inexpensive to register a sole proprietorship. When you do, you will have a legal business.

- If you operate a business without registering it, you may be liable for civil or even criminal penalties.
- Registered sole proprietorships can use the court system and bring lawsuits.
- Banks like to see legal business ownership the way employers like to see that employees have had previous work experience. If your business is not registered, banks will not even *consider* loaning you money, although some alternative lenders might do so. The time that you operated without registration will be discounted. Lack of registration can be perceived as a lack of integrity.

Steps to Registering

The registration process varies from state to state and by municipality, but there will be a few common steps:

- Choose a name for your business.
- Fill out a registration form, which sometimes requires a *doing business as* (DBA) document that will show the name of the business and your name, so the state will know who will be responsible for tax payments.

- An official may then conduct a name search, to make sure the name you have chosen is not already being used in that jurisdiction. You may even be asked to help research the records yourself.

- Once your registration is completed satisfactorily, you will pay the required fee. This sum can range from under $100 to several hundred, depending upon the type of business and state and municipal laws and regulations. Professional firm registrations, in particular, can become quite expensive.

- You may be asked to take the form to a **notary**—an individual who has been given the authority by the state to witness the signing of documents—to have it *notarized* and then brought back to the registration office. You will have to show the notary valid identification to prove who is signing the form. There is usually a modest charge for this service.

notary a person who has been authorized by the state to witness the signing of documents.

Partnership

A **partnership** consists of two or more owners, who make the decisions for the business together and share the profits, losses, assets, and liabilities. As in a sole proprietorship, partners face unlimited liability in any lawsuits. This means that *each* partner can be held responsible for paying debts or judgments, even those incurred by other partners without their knowledge or agreement.

The exception to this is the **limited partnership**. The limited partners have no official say in the daily operation of the business and have, as a result, liability limited to the amount of their respective investments. One or more *general* partners manage the company and assume legal liability. There must be at least one general partner in a limited partnership, who will be liable for all partnership debts.

Ideally, partners bring different strengths and skills to a business. This can help the venture grow and succeed. In addition, partners can support and advise each other. On the other hand, disagreements can become intolerable and destroy the partnership, the friendship, and the business.

partnership a business with two or more owners that make decisions for the business together and share the profits, losses, assets, and liabilities.

limited partnership business partnership wherein there is a general partner with unlimited legal liability, and one or more limited partners who have no official input in daily operations, and limited liability.

(PhotoAlto/SuperStock)

Despite the advantages of partnerships, caution is the watchword. You should be extremely careful and thorough about entering into a partnership, particularly with a good friend or relative. A lawyer should be consulted, and a partnership agreement drawn up that carefully defines the roles and responsibilities of each partner. A partnership agreement is absolutely critical, regardless of how well or poorly the company ultimately performs.

Corporation

corporation a legal entity composed of stockholders under a common name.

There are several types of **corporations**, but each is considered a legal person, or *entity*, composed of stockholders under a common name. A corporation has rights and responsibilities under the law and it can buy and sell property, enter into leases and contracts, and be prosecuted. Corporations issue stock that is divided among the founders and sold to investors. These *shareholders* then elect a board of directors that is responsible for representing their interests in the management of the company. The shareholders who own the stock own the corporation, in proportion to the number of their shares.

The corporate legal structure offers three key advantages:

1. Corporations may issue stock to raise money. Essentially, the company sells pieces of itself in the form of equity to stockholders.
2. The corporation offers limited personal liability to its owners. Unlike sole proprietorships and partnerships, the owners of a corporation are protected from having their personal assets taken to pay business lawsuit settlements or debts. Only the assets of the corporation can be used to pay corporate debts. However, most lenders will not loan money to a small, closely held corporation unless the owners personally guarantee the debt, in which case the owners do become personally liable. In addition, it is possible to pierce the corporate veil if the business affairs of the corporation and its shareholders are tightly entwined, so that shareholders may be held personally liable in a lawsuit. This is a strong argument for keeping business and personal finances separate.
3. Corporations can exist indefinitely, so they do not close down when an owner dies or leaves the business.

As we have already noted, a disadvantage of corporations is that corporate income is "taxed twice." A corporation must pay corporate income tax on its earnings because it is a legal entity. Then, the corporation may distribute earnings as dividends to stockholders. The stockholders must include those dividends as personal income on their tax returns. For example, a corporation with taxable income of $100,000 that distributed $10,000 in dividends would have a tax bill of $34,000 (34 percent corporate tax rate), and its shareholders would owe $2,800 (28 percent personal tax rate) more, for a total tax of $36,800. The total tax on $100,000 for a sole proprietor could be $28,000 (28 percent personal tax rate), reflecting no dividends—for an $8,800 difference.

If corporate stock is privately held, the shares are typically owned by only a few investors and are not *traded* (bought and sold) publicly, such as on the New York Stock Exchange, or that of London or Tokyo. In a public corporation, such as Ford or IBM, the company's stock is offered for sale to the general public; anyone with sufficient resources may purchase it at the market price. Stockholders may be paid dividends when the company's management considers they are warranted, by profits or other considerations. Dividends are part of the stockholders' return on their investment in the company.

(Comstock)

There are several types of corporations:

- *C corporation.* Most large companies and many smaller ones are C corporations. They sell ownership as shares of stock. Stockholders have the right to vote on important company decisions at the annual meeting, or to vote by proxy. To raise capital, the C corporation can sell more stock, issue bonds, or secure other types of loans.

- *Subchapter S corporation.* This type of corporation has a limit of 75 stockholders. It offers most of the limited liability protection of the C corporation, but Subchapter S corporate income is only taxed once, as the personal income of the owners. It is a pass-through entity for tax purposes. Often, a company will start as an S corporation and change to a C type when it begins to earn profits, through a formal process with the Internal Revenue Service. The net profits

BizFacts

Advantages of Corporations

- Limited personal legal liability for shareholders.
- Funds can be raised through the issuance of stock.
- Ownership can be transferred easily.
- The legal entity survives beyond the life span or participation of individuals.

Disadvantages of Corporations

- Corporations are often more heavily taxed than sole proprietorships or partnerships. Their profits are taxed twice: first, as the income of the corporation (except S corporations), and again as personal income, when dividends are distributed to stockholders.

- The founder of a corporation may lose control to the stockholders if he or she no longer owns more than half the stock.

- It is more expensive to start a corporation than a sole proprietorship.

- Corporations are subject to many government regulations.

of an S corporation are taxed at the personal income tax rates of the individual shareholders, whether or not the profits are distributed.

- *Professional corporation (PC).* Medical practices, engineering firms, law firms, accounting firms, and certain other professions can form professional corporations. The initials PC after a doctor or lawyer's name means that that individual has incorporated the practice or belongs to a group of practitioners that has incorporated. Each state designates which professions can form such corporations. Professional corporations are subject to special rules, such as meeting the licensing requirements of bar associations or medical societies. Professional corporations cannot protect individual members from malpractice liability, but the other members of a PC are protected from liability arising from the negligence of one of the group.

- *Nonprofit corporation.* A nonprofit corporation is not set up for the purposes of shareholder financial gain, but rather with a specific mission to improve society. Churches, museums, charitable foundations, and trade associations are examples of nonprofit corporations (also called not-for-profits). Nonprofits are *tax-exempt*. Nonprofits may not sell stock or pay dividends. There are no individual shareholders for a not-for-profit corporation, and any net profits that are earned must go toward the advancement of the mission, so there are no dividends issued and income taxes are not paid. Not-for-profits may have members rather than shareholders. Such organizations must be careful to follow applicable laws, rules, and regulations in order to maintain their tax-exempt status.

- *Limited liability company (LLC).* The LLC combines the best features of partnerships and corporations, and can be an excellent choice for small businesses with a limited number of owners. In an LLC, profits are taxed only as the personal income of the members, whose personal assets are protected from lawsuits, as in a C corporation. In addition, many of the restrictions regarding the number and type of shareholders that apply to the Subchapter S corporation do not apply to LLCs, making them even more attractive. An LLC has a variety of options that make it a flexible type of legal entity. The advice of legal counsel is vital in establishing an LLC, because each state has different laws, and the creation and maintenance of LLC status requires continued compliance.

To compare these legal structures, see **Exhibit 11-1**.

Tips for Entrepreneurs Who Want to Start a Nonprofit Organization

There are huge needs in society for food, shelter, education, and more; there are many people who cannot access these fundamental conditions and requirements. In the United States, there is the 501(c)(3) nonprofit corporation to help address this situation. A 501(c)(3) is a tax-exempt legal structure (as discussed above) that can receive charitable donations from individuals, businesses, the government, and philanthropic foundations. Examples of well-known nonprofit corporations include the Boys and Girls Clubs, the YMCA, and the Sierra Club. People who donate money to not-for-profits benefit from their generosity by knowing that they are making a gift to a cause in which they believe. Also, they are able to deduct these contributions from their taxable income.

In the United States, close to 1 million organizations were registered with the IRS as public charities in 2007, compared with 600,000 in 1993.[2]

---

[2]The Urban Institute, National Center for Charitable Statistics, Business Master File 12/08, http://nccs.urban.org/statistics, November 12, 2009.

Exhibit 11-1 *Comparison of Legal Structures*

Comparison of Legal Structures

	Sole Proprietorship	General or Limited Partnership	C Corporation	Subchapter S Corporation	Nonprofit Corporation	Limited Liability Company
Ownership	The proprietor	The partners	The stockholders	The stockholders	No one	The members
Liability	Unlimited	Limited in most cases	Limited	Limited	Limited	Limited
Taxation issues	Individual* (lowest rate)	Individual* (lowest rate)	Corporate rate; "double taxation"	Individual* (lowest rate)	None	Individual* (lowest rate)
How profits are distributed	Proprietor receives all	Partners receive profits according to partnership agreement	Earnings paid to stockholders as dividends in proportion to the number of shares owned	Earnings distributed to stockholders in proportion to the number of shares owned	Surplus cannot be distributed	Same as partnership
Voting on policy	Not necessary	The partners	Common voting stockholders	Common voting stockholders	The board of directors/trustees	Per agreed-on operating procedure
Life of legal structure	Terminates on death of owner	Terminates on death of partner	Unlimited	Unlimited	Unlimited	Variable
Capitalization	Difficult	Easier than sole proprietorship	Excellent—ownership is sold as shares of stock	Good—same as partnership	Difficult because there is no ownership to sell as stock	Same as Partnership

* When the double taxation of corporations is taken into account.

Charitable donations rose from $148 billion to $308 billion in the same period, accounting for about 22 percent of total revenues in 2007.[3] Whereas competition for financial resources has increased, more technical and educational resources are now available to support the management and growth of organizations that choose to incorporate as not-for-profits.

Like any business, a not-for-profit will need to generate revenue to cover its expenses. Failure to meet cash requirements will mean a failure to survive. A not-for-profit needs to identify a target market (constituency) and determine how it will deliver its products and services. Some key differences and considerations exist, however, and you should be aware of them before you apply to the IRS for approval:

- *No individual can own a not-for-profit organization.* A nonprofit cannot be bought and sold like other businesses. You would not be able to dissolve and sell it for financial gain. Nor could you issue stock to raise money. These organizations are meant to improve society, not create wealth for the founder, shareholders, or employees.

- *Nonprofits are mission-driven.* Before you can operate as a nonprofit, you will need to be crystal clear about your organization's mission. What problem(s) are you trying to solve? The IRS will not grant tax-exempt status without such a stated mission and considerable additional information. Also, ask yourself if there is another organization that is working toward the same goal. Could you work together rather than creating a new entity and duplicating services and costs? Is there a large enough donor base and grant supply to combine with fee income for sustainability? Also, do you expect the organization to accomplish its mission and cease to need resources in the foreseeable future?

- *Define your unit of change.* In a for-profit business, the return on investment is calculated by looking at the corporation's financial records. Not-for-profit entrepreneurs need to think about their ROI a little differently. Not-for-profits do not exist to make money, so the ultimate measure of success will not be financial, although financial goals and measures are part of the equation. Your ROI will be based on how much it will cost you to provide your services as compared with the level of change that was brought about as a result of this investment.

- *Determine how you will evaluate your success.* As a not-for-profit entrepreneur, you will need to set goals regarding the changes you want to effect. How many homeless people will you feed? How many students will graduate as a result of your dropout-prevention program? What changes in knowledge, skills, or attitudes will result from the efforts of your organization? The output and outcome goals that you establish must tie back into your financial and human-resource inputs. How much does it cost to provide these services? Given the costs, how many units of change did your organization achieve? How can you document that your organization brought about these changes?

- *Analyze your financing strategy.* Nonprofit corporations can borrow money, as well as earn it. They also have access to a revenue stream that other business structures cannot tap. Not-for-profits generate revenue through grants and gifts (donations) from individuals and organizations, but they cannot sell stock to raise equity.

---

[3]The Urban Institute, National Center for Charitable Statistics, Business Master File 12/08, http://nccs.urban.org/statistics, November 12, 2009; and Jessica Stannard-Friel, *MBAs at the Crossroads of Corporate and Nonprofit America*, from On Philanthropy Web site, http://www.onphilanthropy.com, December 3, 2004.

Contracts: The Building Blocks of Business

Regardless of the type of legal entity you elect to establish, you will need to enter into a variety of legal contracts (*covenants*). A **contract** is a formal agreement between two or more parties to perform or refrain from performing particular actions. When you sign up for mobile telephone service with a provider, such as Verizon or AT&T, you are signing a contract. You agree to pay for the service at a specified price per month; in return, the company agrees to provide you with access to telephone service, voice mail, data services, text messaging, and the like. Remember that rental leases, any promissory notes or mortgages, and advertising or partnership agreements are all contracts. How they are written (their terms and conditions) can often make or break your business.

contract an agreement between two or more parties that is enforceable by law.

Contracts are the building blocks of business. The relationships between the links in a production-distribution chain are defined by contracts. For example, if a department store wants to sell your hammered-silver necklaces, you might create a six-month contract specifying how many necklaces you will supply at what price and how and when the store will pay you.

◀ **Performance Objective 2**
Understand the importance of contracts.

With that contract in hand, you can call your wholesaler. Because you have a large order, you will want to get your supplies in bulk. With the contract as written proof of your relationship with the store, wholesalers may give you credit. You can arrange to buy the silver you need now to fill the order, and pay for it after you sell the necklaces to the store. You can also plan ahead with your advertisers, or work out an advertising plan with the store as part of the contract. Or, you may be able to secure bank financing for the contract production.

The power of a contract is that, once the individuals or other entities involved have signed it, they are obligated to comply with its terms and conditions or risk being sued and penalized according to the contract terms in a court of law. If the store fails to buy your necklaces as agreed, you can go to court to force payment. Because of this contract, you will be able to honor the contract with your supplier. At the same time, the contract obligates you to produce what you have promised and deliver it when you said you would.

Working with an Attorney

There are certain times in the life of an organization when investing in the cost of professional services is essential, even though the out-of-pocket cost may seem high at the time. Contract drafting and review is one of them.

- Never sign a contract without having an attorney examine it for you.
- Never sign a contract that you have not read completely and carefully, even if your lawyer tells you it is all right. Ultimately, you are responsible for what you sign.

If you are ever taken to court and argue, "I didn't understand that part of the contract," it will not satisfy the judge. Your signature at the bottom tells the court that you read, understood, and agreed to every word.

Attorneys typically charge by the hour, so be as prepared and organized as possible before visiting one. Many issues can be resolved efficiently and effectively through e-mail and telephone calls, so that billable hours are minimized. Always read the contract ahead of time and make a copy of it. Mark sections that you do not understand or agree to, preferably using features of the word processing software. Indicate your suggestions for changes. This will help your attorney advise you effectively.

Drafting a Contract

Consult an attorney if you need to *draft*—write—a first version of a contract or agreement, with the understanding that it will need to be developed and rewritten. Be certain that you identify and make a list of the key points in advance. Attorneys often have standard formats for specific types of legal agreements, sometimes called **boilerplate language,** which can make the process quicker and less costly.

boilerplate language
a standard format for a specific type of legal agreement.

A Successful Contract Should Achieve the Four A's:
1. **Avoid** misunderstanding,
2. **Assure** work,
3. **Assure** payment,
4. **Avoid** liability.

Avoid Misunderstanding

When putting together a contract, clearly state everything that will be done by all parties, even what is obvious. Go into full detail (not just how many shirts you will supply to the store and when, but which types, colors, and sizes). If you do not cover all the details, the person with whom you are contracting may add provisions or find loopholes you will not like. At the same time, leave enough flexibility to accomplish what needs to be done successfully.

Assure Work

For a contract to be legally binding, all parties will be required to do one of the following:

- perform an action or exchange something of value, or
- agree *not* to do something the party was legally entitled to do.

Sometimes $1 is exchanged, as a token payment to legalize a contract. The contract should assure that each party fulfills some kind of obligation. The exact nature of the obligation, and the time frame for accomplishing it, should be specified in detail.

Assure Payment

A good contract specifies how payment will be made and when and for what. It should leave no room for misinterpretation.

Avoid Liability

Because this world is full of surprises, your contract should spell out **contingencies,** unpredictable events beyond your control that could cause delay or failure to fulfill contractual responsibilities. The contract should list contingencies for which you would not be liable. Common contingencies are "acts of God" (earthquake, hurricane, etc.) or illness.

contingency a condition that must be met in order for something else to occur.

When you share the draft or a list of key topics of your contract with an attorney, ask these two basic questions:

1. Will this agreement fully protect my interests?
2. What would you add, drop, or change?

Letter of Agreement

Sometimes you will not need a full, formal contract, because the relationship is going to be brief or the work and money involved are relatively minor. In such cases, a **letter of agreement** that puts an oral understanding in writing, in the form of a business letter, may be enough. The other party must respond to it in writing, either approving it or suggesting changes, until an agreement is reached. However, use this option with care and with legal advice.

letter of agreement a document that puts an oral understanding in writing, in the form of a business letter.

Breach of Contract

A contract is broken, or *breached*, when a **signatory**, an individual who signed the contract, fails to fulfill it. The person injured by the signatory's failure to comply with the contract may then sue for **breach of contract**.

For a contract to be breached, it must first be legally binding. Most states require that all signatories be at least 18 years of age and that the contract represent an exchange of value. If a contract is breached, legal action must be brought by the injured party within the state's **statute of limitations**, the time period within which legal action may be taken.

A lawsuit is an attempt to recover a right or claim through legal action. Because attorney's fees are expensive and court cases time-consuming, lawsuits should be avoided whenever possible. Other options are small claims court and arbitration.

signatory an individual who has signed a contract.

breach of contract the failure of a signatory to perform as agreed.

statute of limitations the time period in which legal action may be taken.

Small Claims Court

Conflicts involving less than a certain sum of money, which varies by state law, can usually be resolved in a **small claims court**. In Delaware, for example, claims for $15,000 or less can be settled through civil action in the Justice of the Peace court. In small claims court, each person is allowed to represent him- or herself before a court official. The official hears each side's arguments and makes a decision that is legally binding.

small claims court a legal option for solving conflicts involving less than a specified sum of money.

Arbitration

Sometimes contracts specify that conflicts may be settled through **arbitration** instead of in court. An *arbitrator*, someone both sides trust, is chosen to act as the decision maker to resolve the conflict. The parties agree in advance to abide by the arbitrator's decision.

arbitration a method of dispute resolution using an arbitrator to act as a decision maker rather than going to court.

A Contract Is No Substitute for Trust

A contract is not a substitute for understanding and communication. If you do not like or trust someone, having a contract will not improve the relationship, although it will address your concerns in writing. However, entering into a business contract with a party you do not trust could lead to a lawsuit. Avoid signing a contract with someone you do not trust.

Another important reason not to sign a contract with such a person is that you might need to renegotiate the terms at some point, and this could be unpleasant and difficult. Running a small business is challenging and unpredictable. In the jewelry example mentioned previously, how would you pay back the silver supplier if the store decided not to buy the necklaces after all? If you have a friendly relationship, you might be able to discuss your situation and renegotiate or cancel the contract.

The Uniform Commercial Code (UCC)

Performance Objective 3 ➤

Recognize key components of commercial law.

Contract law varies from state to state, with a common set of standardized practices. The Uniform Commercial Code (UCC) is a collection of business laws, adopted by most states, that directs a broad spectrum of transactions, such as loans, contracts, and the like. The UCC is a joint project of the American Law Institute and the National Conference of Commissioners on Uniform State Laws, and was first issued in 1952. It is not law; rather, it is made up of recommendations for laws that states can adopt as written or with modification or not at all. Because so many commercial transactions involve parties in more than one state, consistency becomes important. For example, if you buy a forklift that is manufactured in Michigan, warehoused in Georgia, sold to you by a company in New Jersey, and delivered to your warehouse in South Carolina, it is simpler to have uniform laws governing those transactions than four sets of statutes. Note that the UCC is focused on movable property rather than real (immovable) property.

The UCC consists of a series of articles that covers the range of commercial transactions:

ARTICLE	TITLE
1	General Provisions
2	Sales
2A	Leases
3	Negotiable Instruments
4	Bank Deposits
4A	Funds Transfers
5	Letters of Credit
6	Bulk Transfers and Bulk Sales
7	Warehouse Receipts, Bills of Lading and Other Documents of Title
8	Investment Securities
9	Secured Transactions

Source: Copyright © by the American Law Institute and the National Conference of Commissioners on Uniform State Laws. Reproduced with the permission of the Permanent Editorial Board for the Uniform Commercial Code. All rights reserved.

The Law of Agency

The subject of agency law (principal–agent) is a vital area of commercial contract law. An agent (third party) is authorized to act on behalf of a principal (primary party) to create a legal relationship with another individual or business. Common agency relationships include:

- employment (employer, employees);
- real estate (real estate agents);
- financial services (stock brokers, insurance agents);
- promotion (modeling, acting, music, publishing, and sports agents).

Agency law is the branch of legal activity that addresses relationships between each party in a situation where one individual or company is authorized to work on behalf of another.

Businesses commonly rely upon agents to conduct their affairs, although they are not always perceived as such. Employees are agents of their employers. All individuals carrying out the work of a corporation are agents, because a corporation is a legal entity (person). The principal in an agency relationship (company or person) is contractually bound by any agreement entered into by the agent, as long as the agent is operating within his or her authority.

This is particularly important for you to understand as an entrepreneur. When you authorize others to act for you, you can be legally bound by their actions—for better or worse. Authority can be granted, or perceived to have been granted, by several means:

- contractually, through a written contract;
- words or conduct, if the principals' actions or words would make it so that a reasonable person would assume authority (you say or do something that implies it);
- ostensible authority, if the principal makes it appear to the third party that the agent is authorized, such as putting the agent in a position of authority (think manager, supervisor, or sales representative);
- implied, the level of authority that is considered necessary to fulfill the agent's job, such as a partner or senior executive in a business (responsibility and authority are the norm in certain positions).

The area of agency law is quite complex and is significant to the entrepreneur. If you are in a partnership, any partner is presumed to have the authority to enter into agreements that bind the other partners (agency power). This could lead to financial disaster. Or, consider a salesperson attempting to close a sale. This individual could commit to giving discounts without your knowledge or approval. As far as the customer is concerned, your company has made the offer. If the offer is not satisfactory to you, as the owner, you are in the awkward position of either doing as promised to keep the customer happy, or attempting to renege and alienating the customer, with perhaps further consequences to follow. The law of agency sets parameters for the liability of each party.

Bankruptcy

Although entrepreneurs are an optimistic lot, business sometimes does not progress as planned, and **bankruptcy** becomes the best option. Bankruptcy is the legal process in which an individual or business declares the inability or impaired ability to pay debts as they come due. This may be a voluntary petition by the debtor or it may be forced by creditors (involuntary bankruptcy). Bankruptcy is often used as a way to reorganize finances and secure some breathing room for businesses that are insolvent. The process is meant to ensure fair treatment of creditors as well as the debtor.

bankruptcy the legal process in which an individual or business declares the inability or impaired ability to pay debts as they come due.

Many companies, large and small, have filed for and emerged from bankruptcy. For example, General Motors, Macy's, and Delta Airlines have all done it. **Figure 11-1** shows the number of business bankruptcy filings from 1985 through 2008. As a business owner, you will not want to file for bankruptcy unless it is your best remaining strategy. As a creditor, you do not want your customers to file for bankruptcy protection because you will have to wait for payment and may lose the money altogether.

The Bankruptcy Reform Acts of 1978 and 2005 govern the eight "chapters" under which bankruptcy may be filed. Chapters 7, 11, and 13 generally apply to small businesses, with Chapters 7 and 11 the most common. Entrepreneurs often have the choice of *liquidation* (conversion of assets to cash with business closure) or *reorganization* (creating a repayment plan and continuing operations).

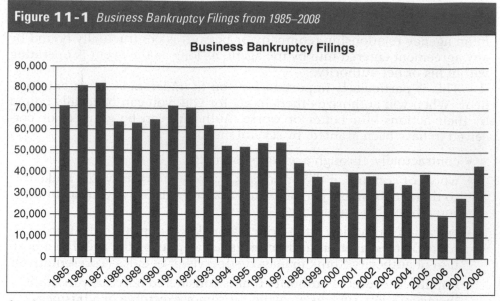

Figure 11-1 *Business Bankruptcy Filings from 1985–2008*

Courtesy of bankruptcydata.com, July 16, 2009.

Chapter 11: Reorganization

This is the form of bankruptcy that can prove to be a lifeline for a company. Businesses can pay off some or all of their debts under court supervision, while continuing to operate. Creditors cannot file legal claims against the company while it creates a reorganization plan and schedules debt repayment, or negotiates settlements on the amounts owed. The bankrupt party, known as the *debtor in possession*, gets 120 days to file a reorganization plan with the bankruptcy court. This plan must detail all debts, all categories or classes of creditors (i.e., secured, provisional, and unsecured), how much each will be paid, and the timing and method of compensation. If the debtor fails to file on time, creditors or any other parties involved may submit a plan. They then must approve or reject the plan.

Chapter 7: Liquidation

When this form of bankruptcy protection is sought by individuals or corporations, they must identify all assets and liabilities, turn the assets over to a trustee (court-appointed or elected by creditors), and allow them to be sold. Creditors receive funds from the proceeds ranging from 0 to 100 percent of their debt claims. Once the funds are paid out, any remaining debts are *discharged* (no longer owed), and the business, if a corporation, is officially dissolved.

It is important to note that debtors cannot avoid the liquidation of assets by transferring ownership to others just ahead of filing for protection. In fact, any transfers of property within the two years prior to filing may be ignored and the assets made a part of the bankruptcy case. Deliberate transfer of assets to avoid debt repayment is a form of fraud, and the entire Chapter 7 bankruptcy petition can be thrown out by the judge, if he or she feels that this has occurred.

On the other side, not all assets are subject to liquidation in a Chapter 7 proceeding. The items that are exempt vary by state. Regardless of the asset exemptions, a Chapter 7 bankruptcy filing is financially and emotionally painful, and has long-term impacts on credit.

Chapter 13: Individual Debt Reorganization

This is the consumer version of Chapter 11, which is available to individual debtors with secured debts less than $922,975 or unsecured debts below the sum of $307,675. Chapter 13 must be a voluntary filing and the repayment plan can only be filed by the debtor. The plan may include full or partial payment of debts through installments, taking into consideration the debtor's income expectations, and must be approved by a bankruptcy judge. Repayment typically occurs over a three-to-five-year period, and the filer can retain individual property. Because a sole proprietorship is essentially an individual, Chapter 13 is of significance to small business.

The bankruptcy of business partnerships, or of major stockholders for privately held corporations, can have other effects upon businesses and individuals that are beyond the scope of this text. For additional information, consult with appropriate advisory resources.

Protecting Intangible Assets: Intellectual Property

A critical practice for any entrepreneur is to protect his or her ideas, products, inventions, and designs. Federal and state laws are passed with the intention of helping individuals and organizations protect these kinds of assets from abuse, damage to reputation, or theft.

◀ **Performance Objective 4**
Protect your intellectual property.

Trademarks and Service Marks

Whether you are advertising your business with flyers at the local laundromat or through a storefront on the Internet, you will need an easily recognizable logo for your product or business (such as Apple's silhouette of an apple with a bite out of it). A logo should appear on the business's stationery, business cards, and flyers, and virtually any other company document or product.

As discussed previously, a trademark is any word, phrase, symbol, or design, or combination of words, phrases, symbols, or designs, that identifies and distinguishes the source of the goods (products) of one party from those of others.[4] A **service mark** is the equivalent of a trademark, except that it identifies and distinguishes the source of a service rather than a product.

A company uses a trademark so that people will recognize its product instantly, without having to read the company name or even having to think about it. NutraSweet's red swirl and the Nike "swoosh" are examples of trademarks most people recognize. Rights to a trademark are reserved exclusively for its owner. To infringe on a trademark is illegal.

service mark a design that identifies and distinguishes the source of a service rather than a product.

Exercise

Perform each of the tasks described below and record the information on a separate piece of paper.

Carry out a search online for the name you intend to use for your business. What did you find?

Will you still use this name? Why or why not?

How do you plan to protect the name of your business?

---

[4]U.S. Patent and Trademark Office, at http://www.uspto.gov/go/tac/doc/basic/trade_defin.htm.

Global Impact...

Intersections Matchmaking—Lawyer Turned Matchmaker

Finding a dating match for South Asians can prove culturally challenging. Jasbina Ahluwalia, a former practicing lawyer with a graduate degree in philosophy, recognized the demand for matchmaking services for people seeking culturally appropriate matches. Ahluwalia founded Intersections Matchmaking in Chicago in 2007.

Clients sign up for the service for free, but pay for consultations. Ahluwalia charges $375 for a one-and-a-half to two-hour consultation and up to $10,000 for a match.[5] Intersection Match operates through singles mixers, a radio program, and a network of scouts, which she has built up into a national network.[6]

The Web site of Intersections Match is copyrighted, reflecting that the company was founded by a lawyer. She establishes contracts with her clients and considers carefully what she promises. However, interestingly, the name itself is not trademarked or service marked, nor is the legal name of the company displayed. Contact information includes only an e-mail address and telephone number. Matches are not guaranteed and the initial $375 consultation fee is nonrefundable. Ahluwalia has built a company based upon cultural competency and awareness and has clearly considered the legal issues.

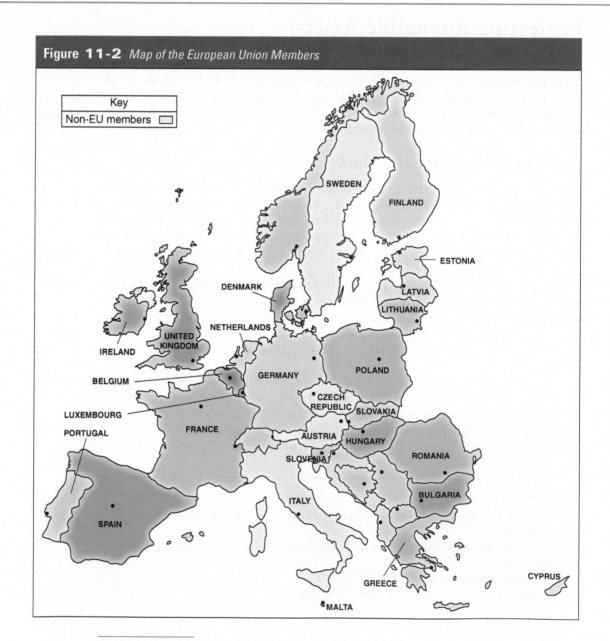

Figure 11-2 *Map of the European Union Members*

---

[5]Kavita Daswani, "Love Inc.," *Entrepreneur*, January 2011, p. 16.
[6]Intersections Matchmaking, http://intersectionsmatch.com, May 15, 2011.

A trademark or service mark does not have to appear on the U.S. Patent and Trademark Office's Principal Register to be legitimate, but there are advantages to being listed on it:

- a notice to the public of your ownership claim;
- legal presumption of your exclusive right to use the mark as registered;
- the ability to bring an action concerning the mark in federal court;
- the use of the U.S. registration to obtain registration of your mark in other countries;
- the ability to file this mark with the U.S. Customs Service, so that others cannot import foreign goods with your mark on them.[7]

You do not need to file an application with the Patent and Trademark Office to use ™ (trademark) or ˢᴹ (service mark). However, you cannot use the ® of a registered trademark until it has been officially approved, and then it can only be applied to what is listed in the federal registration. To obtain application information, go to http://www.uspto.gov.

Copyright

If you are a songwriter, author, or visual artist, you will be creating works that you might sell. If you do not protect your work, however, someone else can appropriate it. A copyright is the form of legal protection offered under U.S. law to the authors of "original works of authorship," including literary, dramatic, musical, and artistic works.[8] Copyright protection is offered for both unpublished and published works. The owner of a copyright has the sole right to print, reprint, sell and distribute, revise, record, and perform the work under copyright. The copyright protects a work for the life of the author/artist plus 70 years. Only the author or someone assigned rights by the author can claim a copyright.

When a work is created, its copyright is automatically secured. According to the U. S. Copyright Office, "A work is 'created' when it is fixed in a copy or phonorecord for the first time." The use of a notice of copyright is not required, but is recommended, and official registration of the copyright has certain advantages. The elements of notice for visually perceptible copies requires:

- the symbol © (the letter c in a circle) and/or the word "copyright," or the abbreviation "copr." and the current year, and
- the name of the owner of the copyright, or an abbreviation by which the name can be recognized, or a generally known alternative designation of the owner.[9]

An example is: *Copyright © 2008 by Janina Joyce.*

There are variations for sound recordings. Legal counsel should be sought for any issues that are unclear. To learn how to register a work, go to http://www.copyright.gov.

Electronic Rights

Now that writing, photographs, art, and music can be posted on the Web, entrepreneurs must protect their intellectual property online, as well. The right to reproduce someone's work online is called **electronic rights**.

Using artwork without permission, even if it is a song or photo or poem posted online, is Internet piracy. President Bill Clinton dealt a

electronic rights the entitlement to reproduce someone's work online.

[7]U.S. Patent and Trademark Office.
[8]U.S. Copyright Office, http://www.copyright.gov.
[9]U.S. Copyright Office.

blow to this kind of crime in 1998 when he signed the Digital Millennium Copyright Act into law. The act protects copyrighted software, music, and text on the Internet by outlawing the technology used to break copyright-protection devices.

There are certain steps that you should take to protect your electronic rights. Beware of contracts that include the following:

- **Work-made-for-hire.** This means you are giving up the rights to your work. Now the buyer can use it anywhere, without paying anything beyond the original negotiated fee.

- **All rights.** This means you are handing over all rights to your work to the buyer.

Some strategies for protecting your electronic rights include the following.[10]

- Get the buyer to define exactly what is included in the contract regarding electronic rights. Does it include online publication, CD-ROMs, or anything else?

- Put a limit on how long the buyer can have the electronic rights—one year, for instance.

- Ask for an additional fee for each additional set of rights. A good rule of thumb would be to request 15 percent of the original fee every time your work is used somewhere electronically. If you sell a drawing to a newspaper for $1,000, you could ask for $150 if the paper wants to use it on its Web site.

Patents

patent an exclusive right, granted by the government, to produce, use, and sell an invention or process.

If you have invented a product or process that you want to turn into a business or to license, you may want to obtain a patent from the U.S. Patent and Trademark Office. A **patent** is an exclusive right granted by the government to produce, use, and sell an invention or process. The term of

[10]Adapted from the *National Writers Union Guide to Negotiating Electronic Rights*. For more information, see http://www.nwu.org.

Step into the Shoes...

Louis Temple Invents the Toggle Harpoon and Dies Poor

(© Old Dartmouth Historical Society/ New Bedford Whaling Museum)

Obtaining a patent can mean the difference between earning millions and living in poverty, as the case of Louis Temple illustrates. Temple was an African American living in New Bedford, Massachusetts, in the first half of the nineteenth century. In those days, whales were hunted for the rich oil derived from their blubber (fat). The oil was used for lighting lamps and making candles. New Bedford was the capital of the whaling industry.

Whales were hunted with spears called *harpoons.* Temple, a blacksmith, invented a "toggle" harpoon, which had a moveable head that prevented the whale from slipping free. Temple gave prototypes of the harpoon to several New Bedford ship captains to try on their whale-hunting voyages.

Whaling voyages took about two years. By the time the ships returned and reported the harpoon's great success, Temple's invention had become "public domain" (see below). He had made no attempt to secure a patent during this time, and other black-smiths in the town were making their own versions of the harpoon. Although he made some money and opened a larger shop, it was nothing like the fortune he would have earned if he had patented his invention. Temple was injured in a fall at the age of 54 and died soon afterward. His family had to sell everything they owned to pay his debts. If his toggle harpoon had been patented, Temple and his family might have become extremely wealthy. How will you protect *your* intellectual property so you can profit from it?

a patent is generally 20 years from its date of filing. A patent grants "the right to exclude others from making, using, offering for sale or selling" the invention in the United States or bringing it into the country via import.[11] Patents come in three forms: *utility* (process or improvement), *design*, and *plant* (varieties of vegetation). A patent cannot be granted unless it is for something that is "useful, novel, and nonobvious."

A patent cannot be obtained for a mere idea or suggestion. An invention should be fully developed and actually viable before you seek patent protection. You will have to prepare detailed drawings showing exactly how it works. If an invention is put into use by the inventor or discussed publicly for more than one year without obtaining a patent, the invention is considered to be in the **public domain**, which means that a patent will no longer be granted; anyone may use or make it without payment. It is important that you not divulge a proprietary invention or concept in meetings or at events without seeking at least preliminary protection.

public domain property rights available to the public rather than held by an individual.

You do not need to obtain a patent unless you:

- have invented a product that you intend to market yourself or sell to a manufacturer, or
- believe that someone else could successfully sell your invention by copying it.

The average patent takes at least two years to obtain. A patent search has to be undertaken to ensure that the idea is new. Getting a patent is a complex legal process. Before starting it, consult with a registered patent agent or attorney.

The process of obtaining a patent is lengthy, time-consuming, and costly. There are many legitimate sources of assistance, including inventors' groups sponsored by state economic development offices, small business development centers, and community development venture capital groups. There are also unscrupulous companies and individuals that promise phenomenal success in commercializing ideas at prices that are inappropriate. Be careful to select reputable advisors, including patent attorneys. To learn more about patents, go to http://www.uspto.gov.

Protecting Tangible Assets: Risk Management

In addition to protecting your intellectual property, you should manage risk by protecting your physical property. Imagine if you lost your business to a fire or flood, and did not have the insurance to rebuild and restock. Or, think about an employee being injured and having no insurance for medical care. Risk management goes far beyond insurance. However, understanding business insurance is a good start.

Insurance Protects Your Business from Disaster

Insurance is a system of protection for payment provided by insurance companies to reimburse people or businesses whose property or wealth has been damaged or destroyed. There are many kinds of insurance and almost anything can be insured.

insurance a system of protection for payment provided by insurance companies to reimburse individuals and organizations for property or wealth that is damaged or destroyed.

If you owned a restaurant, for example, you would need fire insurance. Your insurance agent would help you calculate how much money it would take to rebuild and replace everything in it in case of fire. If you borrowed money from a bank to buy equipment for the restaurant, the bank would require you to carry insurance (with the bank as the named insured) to cover the loan in case the equipment was destroyed.

---

[11]U.S. Patent and Trademark Office, http://www.uspto.gov.

Assume that rebuilding your restaurant would cost $150,000. You would need an insurance policy that would guarantee $150,000 in case of fire. You might pay $100 per month for this insurance. The monthly cost of insurance coverage is called a **premium**.

As long as you pay the premiums on your fire insurance policy, you will not have to worry about losing your restaurant to a fire. If it does burn down, your insurance company will pay you to rebuild and restart the business. If you carry business interruption insurance (see below), you may get compensation for lost revenue. Insurance helps to prevent random events from destroying you financially.

Basic Coverage for Small Business

Performance Objective 5

Protect your tangible assets and manage risk.

You will not necessarily need insurance if you are selling ties on the street or candy at school, but the moment you move your business into a building or have concerns about people being injured while buying or using your product, you will need it.

deductible the amount of loss or damage a policyholder covers before the insurer pays on a claim.

A **deductible** is the amount of loss or damage you agree to cover before the insurance pays on a claim. In the restaurant example, the owner might feel confident that he or she could pay $5,000 for damages from a fire. The insurance company would then pay the remaining $145,000. With this higher deductible, the premium would be lower, perhaps $90 per month. The policyholder pays a lower premium in exchange for a higher deductible. When buying insurance, choose the policy with the highest deductible you can afford to cover. This will give you the lowest premium.

Lower deductible = Higher premium

Higher deductible = Lower premium

Although state laws vary, most require business owners who have people working for them to carry:

- *Workers' compensation insurance.* Compensates employees for loss of income and pays medical expenses in job-related injuries.
- *Disability insurance.* Compensates employees for loss of income due to a disabling injury or illness.

premium the monthly cost of insurance.

Insurance protects your business from disasters like this fire, being fought by firefighters in West Virginia. (Joe Sohm/Chromosohm, The Stock Connection)

If you have an automobile or truck that is owned or leased by the business, you must carry:

- **Commercial fleet insurance.** Covers your liability for personal injuries in an accident, damages to any vehicle involved, and injuries to others.

Other useful types of insurance are:

- **Property insurance.** Provides protection against risks to property, such as theft, fire, or weather damage, as specified in the policy. Certain types of disaster insurance, such as flood and earthquake insurance, also fall into this category.
- **Liability insurance.** Covers the cost of injuries to a customer or damage to property on a business's premises—for example, a customer slipping and falling in your store.
- **Product liability insurance.** Covers the risk of your product harming someone. It is a subset of liability insurance. For example, a caterer may need to be concerned about food-poisoning claims.
- **Business income insurance.** Also known as business interruption insurance, this is the equivalent of personal disability insurance for your business. It provides coverage if you have a temporary shutdown or a significant limitation on your business. Property insurance may replace your facilities and equipment, but it will not compensate for lost business revenue the way this form of insurance does.
- **Errors and omissions insurance.** Designed to cover you in the event that you have overlooked something and a customer is harmed. It is particularly valuable for service businesses.
- **Key person life insurance.** Covers the life of the owner(s) or other top employees, to assist in the transition and costs of recruitment in the case of death.

Still other types of insurance are available that can be tailored to the needs and resources of your business. When you are ready to take this step, ask other businesspeople to refer you to a good insurance agent. Be certain to shop for the best overall value.

How Insurance Companies Make Money

By now you may be wondering, "How can an insurance company afford to pay $150,000 to a restaurant owner whose business has burned down, if that individual has only been paying the insurance company $100 a month?"

Entrepreneurial Wisdom . . .
Lying about the Risks of Your Product Is Fraud

Failure to inform a customer of potential danger from your product or service, or misrepresenting it in any way for commercial benefit, is a type of fraud. If a customer proves that you knew your product or service was dangerous, but you sold it anyway, you could be directed by a court to pay damages. Your insurance company will not be expected to pay for costs in the case of fraud.

The entrepreneur has a moral duty to inform customers of possible danger. It is best not to sell a product or service that could cause harm when in normal use. Even if you are selling items supposedly as safe as neckties, make sure they are not made of highly flammable material!

Before you decide to sell a product or offer a service, try to imagine how it might possibly cause injury to someone. If you think it might harm a customer when used according to directions, do not sell it.

The answer is that insurance companies employ experts, known as actuaries, who calculate the odds of a particular event actually happening. A company that specializes in fire insurance will have information about fires in restaurants going back many years. Analysts at the company study this information and determine how often fires tend to occur and the value of what is destroyed. Even if some fires do take place, the cost of insurance paid out to one policyholder has been covered by the premiums paid by many others.

Protect Your Computer and Data

Data are critical to any business. Important business information on your computer might include mailing lists, invoices, letters, and financial records. The risk of the loss of this information is a very real one that you will need to address proactively. Because your computer is an electronic device, you should protect it from the three primary occurrences that can easily wipe out your data:

1. *Power surges* **or** *outages.* A power blackout can destroy data. You can purchase an uninterruptible power supply (UPS) that will keep your computer running for a certain amount of time after the power goes out. A power surge can damage your computer, as well as destroy the data stored on it. Plug all your computer equipment into a multi-outlet surge protector, which can be bought at any hardware store. Or, better yet, invest in a surge protector UPS unit for each computer.

2. *Computer viruses.* Viruses are malicious computer software that can attach to your software or files and ruin them. Protect your computer with virus-protection software such as Norton or McAfee. Remember to set the software to automatically scan your computer frequently.

3. *Disk failure.* Hard drives can crash (fail), destroying valuable data. To prevent this, save everything you do to back-up media, such as external drives, CDs, or jump drives. Periodically back up your entire drive and store it in another location.

Disaster Recovery Plans

What would you do in the case of fire or other catastrophe that would make carrying on your business difficult or impossible? Insurance policies may cover many things, but they do not ensure smooth business operations in times of disaster. Whether you operate a small, home-based business or a large, multinational enterprise, you should have a disaster-recovery plan appropriate to the scale and complexity of your organization. Be sure to write it down and share it with your employees. Practice it once or twice a year with the whole team; the investment of time and money is worthwhile. Include critical information that team members keep securely off-site. Some issues to address are:

- *Communications.* Who will contact each person in the company and critical vendors and customers? How will they reach them? Include names, titles, telephone numbers, e-mail addresses, and street addresses. Update the contact information regularly. Also, know what the message will be.

- *Base of operations.* Where will people go if the normal place of business is inaccessible? This could be someone's home, another company site, or another location entirely.

- *Priority activities.* Which business activities are most essential/time-sensitive? Which activities could be postponed? What is the time frame for reactivation?
- *Return to facility.* Define a process for regrouping and planning, and designate a leader.

The above is a partial and hypothetical list for a disaster recovery plan. Whereas it may seem to be more than is needed, a straightforward plan put in place before disaster strikes can make the difference between business failure and survival.

Licenses, Permits, and Certificates

There is more to creating a legal business than naming and registering it. Once registered, you will need to comply with any federal, state, and local regulations that apply to your business. You should research these regulations before starting your business because they may affect what you can do, how you can do it, where you can operate, and when. Such regulations can completely change your potential business operations.

Zoning regulations often prohibit certain types of businesses from operating in specified areas. There may be other regulations, too, such as restrictions on obtaining a liquor license for a bar or restaurant. If your business involves food, you will need to comply with safety and health regulations, conduct food-safety training, and obtain certain permissions and certificates.

Contact local, county, and state government offices, or your chamber of commerce, to find out which licenses and permits are necessary.

- *Permit.* A **permit** is an official document that gives you the right to engage in a specific activity, such as holding an outdoor concert.
- *License.* A **license** is an official document that gives you the right to engage in an activity for as long as the license is valid. A driver's license, until it expires, gives you the right to operate a motor vehicle. A child-care license permits you to operate a particular size and type of child-care facility.
- *Certificate.* A **certificate** is an official verifying document. A certificate of occupancy proves that a building is safe and ready for use.

If you hire people to work for you, there will be federal, state, and local regulations regarding employees that will come into effect.

permit an official document that gives a party the right to put on a specific event.

license an official document that grants the right to engage in an activity for a specified period of time.

certificate an official document that verifies an accomplishment or a level of expertise.

Chapter Summary

Now that you have studied this chapter, you can do the following:

1. Choose a legal structure for your business.
   - A sole proprietorship is owned by one person who also may be the sole employee.
   - A partnership consists of two or more owners who make the decisions for the business together and share the profits and losses.
   - A corporation is a legal entity composed of stockholders under a common name.
   - A Subchapter S corporation limits the number of stockholders to 75. It offers most of the limited liability protection of the C corporation, but Subchapter S corporate income is only taxed once—as the personal income of the owners.

- A nonprofit (or not-for-profit) corporation is set up with a specific mission to improve society. Churches, museums, charitable foundations, and trade associations are examples of nonprofit corporations. Nonprofit corporations are tax-exempt.
- A limited liability company (LLC) combines the best features of partnerships and corporations and is an excellent choice for many small businesses.

2. Understand the importance of contracts.
   - A contract is a formal agreement between two or more parties.
   - The relationships between the links in a production-distribution chain are defined by contracts.
   - Never sign a contract without having an attorney examine it.
   - Never sign a contract that you have not read yourself from top to bottom.
   - A successful contract should:
     - Avoid misunderstanding
     - Assure work
     - Assure payment
     - Avoid liability

3. Recognize key components of commercial law.
   - The Uniform Commercial Code (UCC) is a collection of business laws adopted by most states that covers a broad spectrum of transactions.
   - The law of agency addresses principal-agent relationships.
   - The bankruptcy code concerns the inability or impaired ability to pay debts as they come due.

4. Protect your intellectual property.
   - Your ideas and creations are your intellectual property.
   - Trademarks and service marks protect your brand identity.
   - Copyrights protect works of authorship.
   - Patents protect invented products and processes.

5. Protect your tangible assets and manage risk.
   - Insurance protects people and businesses from the risk of having property or wealth stolen, lost, or destroyed.
   - When buying insurance, choose the policy with the highest deductible you can afford. This will give you the lowest premium.
   - Consider the normal and customary types of business insurance:
     - workers' compensation,
     - disability,
     - commercial fleet,
     - property,
     - liability,
     - business income,
     - errors and omissions,
     - life.
   - Create and practice a disaster recovery plan.

Key Terms

arbitration
bankruptcy
boilerplate language
breach of contract
certificate
contingency
contract
corporation
deductible
electronic rights
insurance
letter of agreement
license

limited partnership
notary
partnership
patent
permit
premium
public domain
service mark
signatory
small claims court
sole proprietorship
statute of limitations

Entrepreneurship Portfolio

Critical Thinking Exercises

1. What can happen to an entrepreneur who is personally liable for the business? How can an entrepreneur protect him- or herself from personal liability? Say your friend wants to start a business making custom skateboards. Write a memo to your friend, explaining the risks involved and suggestions for limiting liability.

2. With a partner, make a list of the technological tools each of you could personally access. Brainstorm how you might combine your resources to create a successful business. Describe in detail how the partnership would work. For example, would the partner contributing more technology have a larger share of the business, or would profits and expenses be split equally? Draw up a partnership agreement that specifies each partner's duties and how much money and time each will invest.

3. Which legal structure will you choose for your business?
    Sole proprietorship_____
    Partnership_____
    Limited partnership_____
    C corporation_____
    Subchapter S corporation_____
    Limited liability company (LLC)_____
    Nonprofit corporation_____
    a. Why did you choose this structure?
    b. Who will the partners or stockholders for your company be?
    c. Describe the steps you will take to register your business.

4. If your business will be incorporated, what percentage of the company would be represented by one share of stock? Will your corporation's stock be publicly or privately held?

5. Use computer software to create a logo for your business. Do you intend to trademark your logo? Explain.

6. Describe any intellectual property you are developing (without improperly disclosing a potential patent).

7. How do you plan to protect your intellectual property? Explain why it would qualify for protection.
8. Give an example of a business in your community that you think may be infringing on someone else's intellectual property.
9. What types of insurance will your business need, and why? What is the highest deductible you feel you can afford? Pick one type of insurance you want to have for your business and find a company online that sells it. List the premium, deductible, and payout.

Key Concept Questions

1. What is the most important contract you will need to run your business? Describe any additional contracts you have or plan to secure.
2. Negotiate and write a letter of agreement between you and a fellow student. You could agree to become business partners, for example, or to supply a product or service for the other student's business.
3. Find a lawyer who might be willing to help you with your business. Ask your parents/guardians who are in business or store owners in your community for referrals. The Small Business Administration or Community Legal Aid Society sometimes offers free or low-cost legal services to entrepreneurs.
4. What is the purpose of having a form notarized?
5. What does your signature at the bottom of a contract mean in a court of law? Which two things should you do before signing a contract?
6. Suki is buying an old van from her brother to start her flower-basket delivery service. She planned to buy auto insurance that would pay all her expenses in case she ever got into an accident. She finds that such insurance would cost $3,000 per year, which, according to her business-plan projections, is more than she can afford. What do you think Suki should do?
7. Some businesses do sell products and services that can injure customers. List three examples and explain how these companies probably use insurance.

Application Exercise

Assume you and a friend have decided to produce and sell recordings of your original songs. Which legal structure do you think would work best? Explain. What type of intellectual property protection should you seek? What sort of contracts would you need? What types of insurance would be important?

Exploring Your Community

1. For the business you plan to start, research licensing regulations in your area and describe how they will affect your operation.
   a. Have you applied for a sales tax ID number?
   b. What are the zoning laws in your location? Does your business comply?
2. What nonprofit business could you start in your community? Answer the following questions to describe it:
   a. What is the name of your nonprofit?
   b. What societal problem(s) are you trying to solve?
   c. Describe the mission of your organization.
   d. Describe the programs and services you plan to create.

    e. How will your organization achieve the changes you intend to bring about?

    f. What is the unit of change (per person, animal, house, etc.)?

    g. How will you measure these changes?

    h. Who are your competitors?

    i. How much will it cost to deliver one unit of service?

    j. What sources of funding will you seek?

3. Interview an entrepreneur about insurance policies. Ask how he or she decided what kind of insurance to carry and whether to have high or low deductibles. Present a report on your entrepreneur's insurance plan to the class.

BizBuilder Business Plan Questions

1.0 Executive Summary

    A. What is the name of your organization?

    K. If there is more than one owner, describe how the ownership will be shared.

3.0 Company Description

    E. What is your organization's legal structure (sole proprietorship, partnership, LLC, C corporation, etc.)?

    F. Why did you choose this legal structure?

    G. In which state are you registered or do you intend to register?

    H. Where will you physically operate the organization?

    J. Who will be the owner(s), partners, or stockholders for your company?

    K. If your business is incorporated, describe what percentage of the company is owned by each shareholder.

6.0 Management and Operations

6.1 Management Team

6.2 Research and Development

    A. What type of research are you doing? What kind do you intend to do?

    B. What are others in the industry doing?

    C. How will you protect your intellectual property?

6.3 Physical Location

    A. Describe the actual physical place in greater detail than above.

    B. What are the zoning laws in your area? Does your business comply?

6.5 Inventory, Production, and Quality Assurance

    D. Have you developed and/or adopted any innovations in production, inventory management, or distribution that are significant? What are they and why are they meaningful?

    I. What types of insurance will your business need, and why?

    J. What methods will you use to ensure that you comply with federal, state, and local tax laws?

    K. Which laws—such as minimum wage and age requirements, health and safety regulations, or antidiscrimination laws—will affect your business?

Sam Jones, Mary Adams, and Larry Brown have been talking about starting their own business for several years. Sam is an electronics repairperson, Mary is a partner in a large law firm, and Larry is an excellent salesperson. It will cost $100,000 to start this business. Sam has no money, Mary has $60,000, and Larry has $40,000. Sam has contacts with three organizations that appear willing to buy services from the new company for a minimum of two years, each at about $50,000 annually. The service to be provided is new to the waste-disposal field and was developed by Larry and Sam over the previous three years. Mary has been their advisor on legal and design-protection issues, and she has so far not charged any fees with respect to the business. Because the service is new, there is some concern about the amount of liability insurance that would be necessary. One of the primary tasks of the new company will be to build a service center, which will require financing a building, probably through a bank loan. Sam and Mary have excellent credit ratings, but Larry has accumulated some credit problems relating to a failed housing-development venture four years earlier. Several of Sam and Larry's colleagues

(Jupiter images/Thinkstock)

have been following the plans for the new waste-disposal service and have expressed an interest in investing some money.

Case Study Analysis

1. What information about forms of organization does the group need?
2. What form of organization would you recommend to the group and why?

Magnetic Poetry

Dave Kapell's Magnetic Poetry, Inc., is a successful Minnesota-based business that designs and markets theme-based poetry kits, each containing 470 words on magnetic strips that people typically affix to their refrigerators and rearrange creatively, plus a multitude of related products. From 1993 through 2009, Magnetic Poetry sold over 3 million kits. But, almost 20 years ago, Kapell was a struggling songwriter who tried to overcome writer's block by cutting out words from newspapers and magazines and arranging them in random order for inspiration. Dave had allergies and would often sneeze, which sent the words of the lyrics flying. Then he had the idea of gluing the words on magnets and using a cookie sheet instead of paper.

When Dave's friends came over, they would play with the word magnets, which were on the refrigerator by this time. In 1993, a friend suggested that he try to sell his magnets as word sets at a local crafts fair. Kapell got to work and laboriously produced a hundred magnetic word kits, using a typewriter, a magnet sheet, laminate coating, and scissors. Much to his surprise, the kits sold within three hours. He knew that he was on to something.

Kapell realized that he couldn't tackle the manufacturing of the word kits on his own and decided to hire friends to help him. For $10 an hour, along with free pizza and beer, they created several hundred new kits. According to Kapell, "That was the start of about three years of absolute cranking, keeping up with demand."[12]

As word continued to spread about his product, he realized that he needed to upgrade his manufacturing process. He and his friends were losing sleep by staying up all night fulfilling orders. Kapell decided to invest $5,000 of sales revenue to hire a local graphic design firm to produce 1,000 prototype kits. He continued to use the same supplier, but became increasingly frustrated when his orders were placed at the end of the line whenever bigger clients needed their products made.

Dave Kapell, founder of Magnetic Poetry.
(Keith Philpott//Time Life Pictures/Getty Images)

Kapell realized that he had to have more control over his manufacturing. He decided to start a second business, separate from Magnetic Poetry, called U.S. Magnetix, which was solely dedicated to printing and producing flexible magnetic products. Kapell put up $100,000 from his cash flow to cover the basic equipment costs for launching U.S. Magnetix. This initial investment bought him a 40 percent stake in the business. He now had the means of production in place to turn around orders for magnetic word kits in three days. Magnetic Poetry was ready to go to the next level.

During the start-up phase of his business, Dave chose to operate Magnetic Poetry as a sole proprietorship. Initially, this structure worked well. All he had to do to make his business official was go down to the local county courthouse and file a DBA form and he was up and running. Yet, as his company grew, Dave's lawyer advised him to register his business as a Subchapter S corporation. Under this legal structure, Dave would not be personally liable in the event that Magnetic Poetry was sued or went bankrupt.

---

[12]Alyson Ward, "Still Drawn to the Tiles: Magnetic Poetry Strong after 10 Years on Market," *Contra Costa Times*, September 22, 2003.

The next problem Kapell needed to solve was how best to distribute his product. He had developed an ingenious, one-of-a-kind idea and had been successful in selling it locally. But how could he increase his distribution network? He began to investigate how he could sell Magnetic Poetry kits wholesale. Kapell approached Pam Jones, who managed a museum gift shop in Minneapolis. She liked Kapell's poetry kits but was unimpressed with his no-frills cardboard packaging. So Kapell got to work and repackaged the kits in clear-plastic boxes. Jones liked what she saw and bought several dozen kits at a wholesale price of $9.50 each. Within a day, she had sold a dozen kits at $20 retail.

In 1996, Magnetic Poetry took a major leap forward with its distribution when it made a deal with Barnes & Noble, the national book retailer. In celebration of National Poetry Month, Barnes & Noble announced that it would sell Magnetic Poetry kits at all of its retail outlets in the United States. Up until this point, Kapell had primarily been distributing his product to independent bookstores and specialty gift shops. The Barnes & Noble deal connected Kapell's company to a nationwide distribution channel. Soon customers in such locations as Texas and New Mexico were snapping up Magnetic Poetry kits. Then Kapell started producing kits in foreign languages. His distribution network now includes international retailers in France, Spain, Germany, and Italy.

Over the past 15 years, Magnetic Poetry has grown from a local business that was essentially started by accident into a multimillion-dollar enterprise with worldwide reach. Kapell's company has been credited with inspiring scores of people to find their inner poet or overcome writer's block.

In 2001, Kapell decided to sell the 40 percent stake in his second company, U.S. Magnetix, so that he could fully focus his energies on developing new products and marketing ideas for Magnetic Poetry. While he no longer owns the manufacturing arm of his business, he still serves as one of U.S. Magnetix's biggest customers, responsible for 15 percent of its annual revenue. Kapell believes that Magnetic Poetry is poised for further growth. Whereas his youthful dream was to become the next David Bowie, Dave Kapell found his niche as an entrepreneur.

Case Study Analysis

1. Magnetic Poetry kits are currently sold in bookstores, specialty gift shops, and online. Brainstorm three additional distribution outlets for this product.

2. Do you think it was a good idea for Kapell to sell his 40 percent ownership of U.S. Magnetix? What are some things he will need to consider now that he no longer has an ownership stake in the manufacturing aspect of his business?

3. As Magnetic Poetry evolved from a start-up into a thriving business, Dave made the decision to change his legal structure from a sole proprietorship to a Subchapter S corporation. What are the advantages and disadvantages of each of these forms? Why do you think that Dave's advisors encouraged him to change his legal structure?

4. Go online and visit Magnetic Poetry's Web site at http://www.magneticpoetry.com. What other products has the company developed? How do these products connect to Kapell's original concept?

5. Assume the following about Magnetic Poetry's cost structure: The wholesale price for one Original Magnetic Poetry Kit is $9.50. The retail price is $20. It costs the company as follows:

   $2.50 to manufacture one Original Magnetic Poetry Kit,

   $0.50 to package it,

   $0.50 for shipping and handling, and

   $1.00 of variable costs.

   a. Calculate the contribution margin.

   b. Assume that Magnetic Poetry has monthly fixed costs of $20,000. How many kits would the company need to sell in order to break even?

   c. Calculate the markup percentage for the following:
      • Manufacturer → Retailer
      • Retailer → Consumer

Case Sources

Magnetic Poetry Web site, http://www.magneticpoetry.com.

Paul Levy, "Magnetic Poetry Proves Attractive," *Minneapolis–St. Paul Star Tribune*, December 28, 2001.

Tim Gihring, "Poetry to the People: Mantra of Magnetic Poetry Kit Maker," *South Coast Today. com* (*The Standard Times*), http://www.south-coasttoday.com, May 20, 1996.

Monte Hanson, "A Magnetic Partnership," *Finance and Commerce*, http://www.finance-commerce.com/recent_articles/011229.htm, December 29, 2001.

Alyson Ward, "Still Drawn to the Tiles: Magnetic Poetry Strong after 10 Years on Market," http://www.contracostatimes.com/mld/cctimes/6831510.htm?1c, September 22, 2003.

Chapter 12

OPERATING FOR SUCCESS

Cramer Products, Inc. was founded in Kansas in 1918 by Charles Cramer, a pharmacist. Cramer had created a liniment to treat his own sprained ankle several years earlier. The company was the first devoted to helping athletes prevent injuries and return to action more quickly if hurt.[1] Cramer Products sold primarily to interscholastic sports teams and was an industry leader for over half a century. That changed in the early 1980s, when athletic programs were disappearing, new products appearing, and competition growing.

Cramer Products decided on a retail strategy to replace its lost revenues. In 1990, management signed super athlete Bo Jackson to a joint venture for a new brand, called Bo Med, and targeted it to people who engaged in recreational athletics. The line debuted in October. In January, after having been chosen for both the Major League Baseball All-Star Team and the National Football League's Pro Bowl, Jackson suffered an injury that ended his football career. Although he continued playing baseball, his star power suffered.

The Bo Med venture was a failure and Cramer Products was left deeply in debt, with a great deal of unsalable inventory. The company's position in its primary market was under assault, its viability as a retailer was damaged, and its management team was demoralized.

Cramer Products' president resigned and was replaced by Thomas Rogge. The new president introduced a style that encouraged a free exchange of ideas. He reorganized the management team and gave individual managers more authority. Cramer liquidated the Bo Med line, salvaging as much of the product as possible for repackaging under the Cramer label, and sold the rest to a distressed-inventory merchant.

To rebuild the core business, Rogge broadened the audience from coaches and trainers to include school nurses and physical therapists, and he set up a team to develop new products. He put out a new retail line, using the Cramer name. Packaging of both the retail and interscholastic products was consolidated into one format, creating a single inventory.

More than 60 new products were added. In 1994, new products accounted for 12 percent of sales. Rogge reexamined all operational departments; cut the workforce by 25 percent, to 65; and assigned tasks to underused employees, improving productivity.

After two years of decline, sales increased 8 percent in 1993 and 12 percent in 1994. Profits set records. Retail growth has improved steadily: four major sporting goods retailers with a combined 200 outlets were added the Cramer line in 1994 alone.[2] Cramer Products, like so many of the athletes it has helped, recovered from its injuries. Many years later, Cramer is still going strong.

(Sean Justice/Corbis)

Performance Objectives

1. Understand the significance of *operations* in a business.
2. Develop a production-distribution chain for your business.
3. Manage suppliers and inventory.
4. Know the key factors to consider in the location decision.

[1] Excerpted from Cramer Products: Treating an Injured Company. *Insights and Inspiration: How Businesses Succeed: the 1995 Blue Chip Enterprise Initiative.* Published by *Nation's Business* magazine on behalf of Connecticut Mutual Life Insurance Company and the U.S. Chamber of Commerce, in association with the Blue Chip Enterprise Initiative, 1995, p. 47.
[2] Available at http://www.cramersportsmed.com.

5. Explore the design of facilities and their layouts.
6. Ensure product quality.
7. Use technology to benefit your business.

Operations Permit Businesses to Deliver on Their Promises

Performance Objective 1 ▶

Understand the significance of *operations* in business.

operations a set of actions that produce goods and services.

In order for a company to be successful, it must deliver on its promises to customers. Marketing sets the expectations and makes the promises. Finance and accounting ensure that the financial resources are available to produce the promised products and services. Legal structures and staff are in place to support success. Ultimately, the company must deliver the product or service to the customer as expected, or better. **Operations** is the set of actions that produces goods and services, and operational efficiency is critical to business success.

What constitutes operations and the precise steps involved in carrying them out will depend on the nature of your industry and the specific business. As we have discussed, a manufacturing business is one that makes a tangible product and, generally, does not sell goods directly to consumers. It typically sells large quantities of product to wholesalers. A wholesale business sells smaller quantities to retailers, from warehouses. A retail business typically sells single items directly to consumers; they operate stores (physical and virtual) that are open to the public. The fourth type of business is service. A service business provides intangible benefits such as time, skills, or expertise in exchange for a fee. Your business may fit neatly into this construct or it may be a combination. For example, if you produce jewelry and sell it online and at fairs, you are both manufacturer and retailer. In any case, there is the process of converting inputs to outputs. See **Figure 12-1** for an illustration of this process.

Regardless of what route your business takes, it is important to understand the process of operations.

The Production-Distribution Chain

Performance Objective 2 ▶

Develop a production-distribution chain for your business.

The consumer is the final link in a chain that extends from the manufacturer through the wholesaler and retailer. When a consumer buys a pair of athletic shoes in a sporting goods store, for example, the chain would be:

1. the manufacturer produces a great quantity of a style of athletic shoe,
2. the wholesaler buys a large number of these shoes from the manufacturer,

Figure 12-1 *Converting Inputs to Outputs*

Input	Transformation/Conversion	Output
Materials Natural Resources Components Information Funds	Processes Labor Facilities Machinery Equipment	Products Services Ideas

Source: Adapted from Jae K. Shim and Joel G. Siegel, *Operations Management* (Hauppauge, NY: Barron's Educational Series, Inc., 1999), p. 2.

Figure 12-2 *Production-Distribution Chain Variations*

Traditional

Manufacturer ⟹ Wholesaler ⟹ Retailer ⟹ Consumer

Direct to Retailer

Manufacturer ⟹ Retailer ⟹ Consumer

Factory Direct

Manufacturer/Retailer ⟹ Consumer

3. the retailer buys a much smaller number of the shoes to stock a store, and

4. the consumer walks into the retailer's store and buys one pair of shoes.

At every link in the chain, there are suppliers and customers. For the manufacturer, the suppliers are those who sell the components and raw materials that are needed for production, and the customers are the wholesalers. For the wholesaler, the suppliers are the manufacturers and the customers are the retailers or, as in the case of a plumbing wholesaler, the contractors that provide a service using the wholesaler's goods. For the retailer, the suppliers are the wholesalers and the customers are the public—consumers. Consumers are the final customers. Some variations on this chain appear in **Figure 12-2**.

Supply Chain Management

The management of sourcing, procuring, production, and logistics to go from raw materials to end consumers across multiple intermediate steps constitutes **supply chain management (SCM).** In order to create and maintain efficient material (supply) flows between supply points, SCM addresses models and relations. Various partners must work together to use tools and techniques for increased efficiency and to apply their knowledge in making decisions. As you find a place for your company in a supply chain, or multiple chains, you can also develop relationships up and down the line to enhance your efficiency and that of your supply chain partners. Critical components of this process will be identifying and securing suppliers and managing inventory.

◀ **Performance Objective 3**
Manage suppliers and inventory.

supply chain management (SCM)
the supervision of sourcing, procuring, production, and logistics to go from raw materials to end customers across multiple intermediate steps.

Finding Suppliers

The world is literally your market for suppliers. Raw materials, component parts, subassemblies, and completed products may be available to you from around the world. You may be growing and packaging your own fruits and vegetables and have seed, fertilizer, packaging, and machinery and equipment suppliers. Or, you may be creating Web sites where your suppliers are software companies, hardware companies, and Internet service providers. Or, you may own a retail gift store with hundreds of suppliers who themselves each have dozens of suppliers. Regardless of the simplicity or complexity of your supply partners, you will have to find them and work together. Some places to look include:

- trade shows or conferences,
- trade catalogs or journals,
- the Yellow Pages,
- Internet search engines,
- wholesale supply houses and brokers,
- newspapers and magazines,
- competitors,
- firms like yours that are outside of your trading area,
- sales representatives, and
- customers.

Your suppliers will become partners in your business. Your success will depend upon their capacity to deliver what you need, when you need it, and at a price you are willing to pay. Their success depends on you delivering your product or service and getting paid for it, preferably on a repeat basis, so they can get paid and be successful, too.

Managing Inventory

Managing inventory is vital to marketing success and to cash flow and there will be an ongoing tension between them. If inventory is kept at a

Global Impact . . .

Paper Wealth

Zhang Yin (Cheung Yan) of Nine Dragons Paper (Holdings) Limited, in China, is the richest self-made woman in the world, with personal wealth estimated at $4.7 billion.[3] Her company recycles scrap paper, often from the United States, and produces cardboard. The cardboard is used to make boxes for Chinese goods, many of which find their way back to the United States.

Zhang Yin, originally an accountant from Guangdong Province, has moved between China and the United States, first opening a paper company in Hong Kong (1985) with $3,800 in cash, and then a paper-export company in the United States (1990). American Chung Namp, Inc., became the largest exporter of waste paper from U.S. sources. Working with her Taiwanese-born and Brazilian-raised husband and her brother, Zhang Yin, she co-founded Nine Dragons in Hong Kong in 1995. The company raised almost $500 million through its initial public offering on the Hong Kong Stock Exchange in 2006.

American Chung Namp and Nine Dragons are able to maintain low overhead by hauling away unwanted scrap and by creatively exploiting shipping opportunities.[4] Rates to China are particularly attractive because of the excess cargo capacity on ships returning to China from the United States.

As of 2007, Nine Dragons had 5,300 employees, 11 huge papermaking machines, and reported profits of $175 million on $1 billion in annual revenues.[5] It expanded into a third manufacturing plant located near Shanghai in August 2008, and a fourth facility opened in Tianjin in September 2009.[6] By using the latest in machinery and less costly labor and fuel, the company has significant production advantages. Nine Dragons met ISO quality and environmental standards and obtained Occupational Health and Safety management system certification to assist in continuous improvement. In addition to paper production, according to its Web site, the company has facilities to provide "...power, steam, water treatment and excellent logistical support. The integration of these facilities provides and increases the Group's operational flexibility and control, while enabling the Group to facilitate best practices in terms of environmental protection."

The Nine Dragons Web site clearly states the company's goal: "The Group aims to become the world's leading containerboard product manufacturer in capacity, profitability and efficiency."

[3]Allen Cheng, "Cardboard Puts Woman at Top of China's Rich List," *The Standard*, January 17, 2007, http://www.thestandard.com.hk/, November 14, 2009.
[4]Ibid.
[5]David Barboza, "Blazing a Paper Trail in China," *New York Times*, January 16, 2007, http://nytimes.com/2007/01/16/business/, November 13, 2009.
[6]Nine Dragons Paper (Holdings) Limited Web site, http://www.ndpaper.com, November 13, 2009.

maximum, customer satisfaction may be satisfied, but costs can become prohibitive. If inventory is maintained at very low levels, customers may become dissatisfied (even leaving entirely), but cash tied up in inventory is minimized. In order to balance service and cost management, factors such as demand, cost, sales price, carrying costs, order and setup costs, and lead times must be known values. In reality, demand projections, lead times, and other variables are generally estimated—with varying degrees of accuracy. Business owners can use the best information, as well as established techniques and tools, to make inventory management decisions.

Visual Control

A common approach to inventory management in small companies is **visual control,** which simply means that you look at the inventory on hand and when the stock level of an item appears to be low, you reorder. This decidedly unscientific method of choosing when to order will be dependent on you knowing the product-selling rate and delivery time. It is most effective when you sell relatively few items and are actively involved in the business.

visual control inventory-management method in which an individual assesses the stock level on hand by visual inspection and reorders when the supply appears low.

Safety Stock and Reorder Points

To avoid running out of materials, businesses frequently establish **safety stock** levels, which are the amounts of inventory or raw materials and work-in-progress that are kept to ensure satisfying customer demand. The inventory **reorder point (ROP)** is the level at which materials need to be ordered again. A challenge for any business is to find the optimal safety stock levels and reorder points for all items and supplies that are stocked. If too much inventory is on hand, the costs of storage and tying up money may be too great. If too little inventory is available, the costs associated with lost sales and loss of goodwill may be significant. In addition to the holding and stock-out costs, the expenses associated with last-minute (rush) ordering may be substantial.

There are a variety of methods for calculating safety stock and reorder points. The calculation of the ROP requires a knowledge or projection of demand, lead time, and safety stock level, and is calculated as

safety stock the amounts of inventory or raw materials or work-in-progress that are kept to guarantee service levels.

reorder point (ROP) the level at which materials need to be ordered again.

economic order quantity (EOQ) the amount of inventory to request that will equal the minimum total ordering and holding costs.

$$\text{ROP} = (\text{Average Demand per Unit of Lead Time} \times \text{Lead Time}) + \text{Safety Stock}$$

For example, if the lead time for showerheads is two weeks, and you sell 25 showerheads per week, so that you always want at least 10 showerheads in stock, the calculation is

$$\text{ROP} = (25 \times 2) + 10 = 60$$

So, whenever inventory falls to 60 showerheads, it is time to reorder. **Figure 12-3** shows this in graph form.

Economic Order Quantity

The **economic order quantity (EOQ)** is the amount of inventory that will equal the minimum total ordering and holding costs, and is calculated as

$$\text{EOQ} = \sqrt{\frac{2DO}{C}}$$

Figure 12-3 *Reorder Cycle*

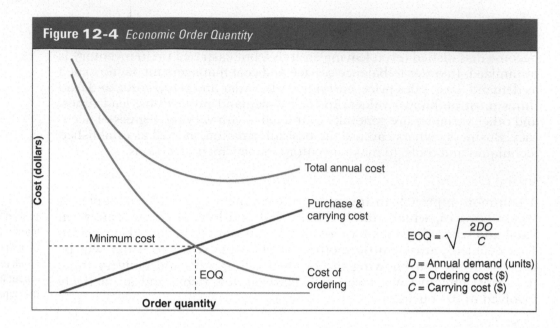

Figure 12-4 *Economic Order Quantity*

in which *D* equals annual demand for an item in units (not dollars), *O* equals ordering cost per order in dollars or other currency (not units), and *C* equals the carrying cost per unit in dollars or other currency. For example, Dominique's Bridal Shop buys bridal veils at $80 per unit from its supplier. Dominique's sells 640 veils annually, distributed evenly over the months. The holding cost (also known as *carrying cost*) is 5 percent of the total, or $4 per veil per year. The ordering cost is $20 per order. So,

$$\text{EOQ} = \sqrt{\frac{2(640)(\$20)}{\$4}} = \sqrt{6400} = \textbf{80 veils}$$

The total number of orders to place per year = D/EOQ = 640/80 = **8 orders**.

Total Inventory Costs = Carrying Cost + Ordering Cost
= (C 3 EOQ /2) + (O × D/EOQ)
= ($4) (80/2) + ($20) (500/80) = **$285 per year**

From this example, Dominique's Bridal Shop should have an inventory policy of ordering 80 veils at a time and should place eight orders per year. This inventory will cost the store $285 per year. **Figure 12-4** illustrates the calculation of economical order quantity in a graph.

If the company manufactured products and wanted to calculate the most economical size for a production run, it would use the same calculation methodology, but *O* = *setup costs* rather than *order costs*.

Facilities Location and Design

Performance Objective 4

Know the key factors to consider in the location decision.

The choice of location for your business can make the difference between success and failure. The oft-quoted business mantra, "location, location, location" is broadly accepted as critical for retail stores. However, the choice of site is a critical strategic decision for manufacturing, wholesale, and Web-based businesses as well, albeit for different reasons. The location decision may be a one-time process, although it may occur multiple times during the life of a business. Location strategy has critical impacts on revenues, customer satisfaction, fixed and variable costs, and the overall levels of risk and profitability.

Whether your business needs are to generate customer floor traffic; provide conveniently located services; have ready access to highways, a seaport, a railroad line, or an airport; or can operate virtually anywhere, the location decision will determine your access to markets and affect essential portions of your cost structure. For a traditional brick-and-mortar retailer, the amount of marketing expense required to generate floor traffic in a low-traffic location will probably be significantly higher than in an area where there is already high traffic. For businesses in which transportation costs are high, operating expenses can become prohibitive. On the other hand, distribution-cost efficiencies can save money and be a competitive advantage.

Key Factors in Deciding upon a Location

The key factors in deciding upon a location are dependent upon the nature of the business and its customers. Considerations include

- access for customers,
- access to suppliers,
- climate and geography,
- convenience,
- cost of facilities (rent, construction, and the like),
- demographics,
- economic conditions and business incentives,
- governmental regulations and laws, including environmental impact,
- labor pool,
- proximity to competitors, and
- visibility.

Figure 12-5 shows the factors affecting location decisions at the national, regional/community, and site levels.

Each business has a unique set of location criteria and priorities. Each industry and business type provides some insight into location issues through trade publications and industry information. What's important to a specialty retailer at a brick-and-mortar location might be meaningless for a

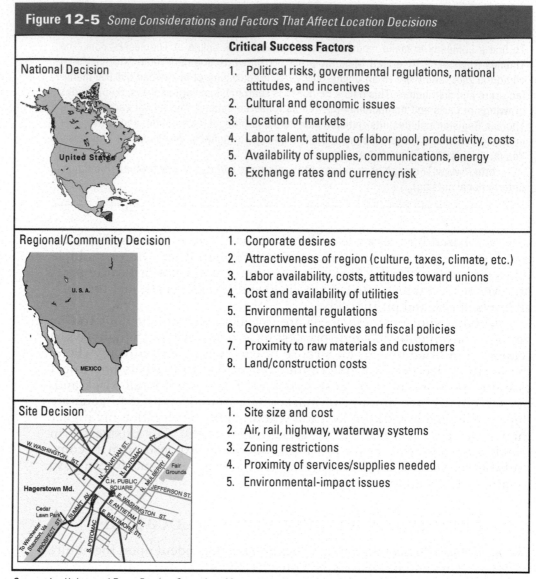

Figure 12-5 *Some Considerations and Factors That Affect Location Decisions*

	Critical Success Factors
National Decision	1. Political risks, governmental regulations, national attitudes, and incentives 2. Cultural and economic issues 3. Location of markets 4. Labor talent, attitude of labor pool, productivity, costs 5. Availability of supplies, communications, energy 6. Exchange rates and currency risk
Regional/Community Decision	1. Corporate desires 2. Attractiveness of region (culture, taxes, climate, etc.) 3. Labor availability, costs, attitudes toward unions 4. Cost and availability of utilities 5. Environmental regulations 6. Government incentives and fiscal policies 7. Proximity to raw materials and customers 8. Land/construction costs
Site Decision	1. Site size and cost 2. Air, rail, highway, waterway systems 3. Zoning restrictions 4. Proximity of services/supplies needed 5. Environmental-impact issues

Source: Jay Heizer and Barry Render, *Operations Management*, 8th ed. (Upper Saddle River, NJ: Pearson Prentice Hall, 2007), p. 249.

service business. The challenge is to identify the critical success factors for your business, tempered by the realities of budgetary and other constraints, to find your best available option.

The selection of a location is a critical business success factor, is often a one-time event, and is generally an expensive one to change; familiarizing yourself with some of the methods for evaluating location alternatives is good practice. These methods range from simple and inexpensive to highly sophisticated and costly; a few of the methods are detailed here. The expense of selecting a profit-maximizing location for your business can be an important investment in its future success.

The simplest way of selecting a location is that which is commonly employed by small business owners: Go with the location you know. Although this is a more intuitive method than the others, it can be effective. However, it is risky to assume that your perceptions are entirely correct. This method is best used as a preliminary filter, to be followed up with research.

Step into the Shoes...

Finding the Location That Fits

When José Echeverri left Merrill Lynch to start his own financial planning firm, he chose a location in a small city near his home on a well-traveled road and furnished it like an executive office at a major brokerage house. He invested precious start-up funds in leasehold improvements and in quality furniture and décor. A couple of years later, José determined that he could find opportunities in a small but rapidly growing community 20 miles away. He opened a second office in that town and hired a colleague to operate it.

After a year, José found that the majority of his business was coming from the second office, which had been chosen based on demographics rather than proximity. He moved his primary location to that town, expanded the office slightly, and closed

his initial location. As it turned out, he needed a modest office in a community with stronger demographics more than a fancy space in a less well-chosen location. José now says, "One of my biggest mistakes in starting this business was trying to create a mini-Merrill rather than finding my own niche from the beginning. Now that we are in the right place and doing the right things, the business is stronger than ever."

Courtesy of José Echeverri.

(José Echeverri)

Another common technique for location analysis is the **factor-rating method,** whereby decision criteria are prioritized and weighted to eliminate subjective factors. This method will incorporate quantitative and qualitative considerations into your decision. The factor-rating method can be employed for any type of business, and you can include as many or as few factors as you want to rate in its six basic steps:

1. develop a list of critical success factors,
2. determine the weight of each factor according to its relative importance,
3. create a measurement scale for the factors,
4. give each proposed location a score for each factor (best if done by a team) according to the scale,
5. multiply the factor weight times the factor score for each factor in each location, and
6. use the sum of these weighted factors for the locations, to compare them and make a location recommendation/decision.[7]

Exhibit 12-1 shows factor-rating for a proposed electric car manufacturing plant. In 2009, an innovative, federally funded and venture-backed company faced a location decision that literally included the entire United States (limited to a U.S. location because of the federal funding). After management decided to consider only locations where automotive plants had recently closed, the decision alternatives rapidly narrowed. Although the factor-rating decision is speculative, the firm did, in fact, make a commitment to a location in Delaware rather than in the heart of car country.

One tool that is available to entrepreneurs at all stages is geographic information systems (GIS). These structures include demographic data, extensive maps, topographic data, major transportation routes, health care facilities, and the like. When you identify the factors that are important to your business, you can use a GIS system to discover potential profit-maximizing locations. **Figure 12-6** shows a GIS map for Prince William County, Virginia.

> **factor-rating method**
> location-decision criteria that are prioritized and weighted to eliminate subjective considerations.

---

[7]Heizer and Render, p. 253.

Exhibit 12-1 *Factor-Ratings for a Hybrid Automobile Manufacturing Plant*

Critical Success Factors	Weight	Scores (out of 10)		Weighted Scores	
		Michigan	Delaware	Michigan	Delaware
Labor (United Auto Workers Union)/Management Relations	0.25	5	10	1.25	2.50
Readiness of Facility	0.20	7	9	1.40	1.80
Proximity to Customers	0.20	7	7	1.40	1.40
Tax and Financial Incentives	0.20	10	6	2.00	1.20
Proximity to an Atlantic Port	0.15	3	10	0.45	1.50
Total	1.00	xxx	xxx	6.50	**8.40**

A decidedly more low-tech approach to assessing location is to gather demographic, psychographic, and geographic data—and information on competitors—to create location options for consideration. The U.S. Census Bureau (http://www.census.gov) provides an abundance of data to inform your decision. Maps and traffic statistics can be added to the mix, as can information from trade associations. For example, if your trade association

Figure 12-6 *GIS Map for Commuter Lots in Prince William County, Virginia*

Source: © 2010 Prince William County; aerial imagery © 2009 Commonwealth of Virginia reports that customers will travel two miles to purchase jewelry, your target customer is a 45-to-55-year-old married woman who lives in a household that has a combined income of over $85,000, and you will need a population of 50,000 of these women within a two-mile radius, you can identify possible locations. Then, you can narrow your choice by assessing the competitive environment (both clustering in "jewelers' rows" and stand-alone should be considered), weighing personal preferences, site availability in the potential locations, traffic counts, and other success factors.

Facilities Design and Layout

Facilities are important for the geographic location and for suitability of use. You may have seen posted signs from real estate companies on vacant land stating: WILL BUILD TO SUITS. This means that they will build a facility appropriate for your business. A purpose-built structure will always be necessary for certain businesses, such as restaurants or hotels. Other buildings may be put up in a more generic manner and outfitted for a specific business through individualized modification. If a building is leased, these changes to adapt an existing structure for a particular business are called **leasehold improvements.**

The type and size of facility, as well as other physical requirements, depend upon the type of business you are operating. For manufacturing, warehousing, and distribution firms, key considerations will include:

- capacity for efficient movement of materials, equipment, and people (floor space and ceiling height will matter);
- flexibility to adapt to changing business requirements;
- loading docks and vehicle access for deliveries and outbound shipments;
- environment conducive to work requirements (natural light, appearance, and the like);
- ability to include requisite controls, such as regulation of temperature and humidity, and cleaning rooms;
- parking for commercial and employee vehicles, as well as spaces for visitors, including the handicapped;
- adequate utility services to the building, including power, water, and telecommunications;
- security and safety.

Retail facilities must meet such business requirements as:

- appropriate selling area and configuration of that space;
- permission to complete necessary leasehold improvements, or improvements to be made by landlord;
- space for offices, storage, restrooms, deliveries, and other special needs;
- signage for rules/regulations;
- parking that is adequate for the anticipated customer volume;
- lighting and security.

Service and professional businesses have unique facilities requirements. A plumbing service company may need space for basic parts storage and parking for service vehicles. A physician's office may need the same amount of floor space but require waiting areas, examination rooms, and safe, convenient patient parking.

> **◄ Performance Objective 5**
> Explore the design of facilities and their layouts.

> **leasehold improvements**
> changes made to adapt a rented property for a particular business.

Whatever business and facility you decide on, you will need to create a work space that is well suited to the business's operations. If you have a home-based venture, you will have to create an area in your living space for your business operations. With a retail store, floor design and storage will be critical to successful operation. For a factory, repair shop, or other production facility, the layout of the machinery, equipment, inventory, raw materials, and component areas will be of crucial importance. Another consideration is the access to loading and unloading areas. There are professionals who specialize in floor planning, space design, and work flow. Some of these may be employed by the equipment manufacturers and landlords who want you as a customer. Do not hesitate to ask for free services in these areas. **Figure 12-7** shows the layout of a mattress factory.

Store layout is a particularly important part of a retail business's marketing and revenue-generation operations. The exterior of the store, including window displays and signage, can attract customers or cause them to walk on by. Even the cleanliness of the windows themselves sends a message to the consumer.

Layout within the store should be designed to entice customers to purchase, preferably into buying more than they initially intended. Retail stores often place new items, or signature products, at the front of the store, and clearance or sale goods toward the rear, or against the walls, thereby compelling customers to pass by a variety of potentially enticing items. Endcaps and other prominent display areas throughout the store can be used to push certain items. Also, well-designed stores rarely place their check-out registers directly in front of the entrance doors, thereby avoiding reminders to the customers of the money they will be spending.

Special Considerations for Home-Based Businesses

Entrepreneurs starting home-based businesses face numerous special considerations, ranging from allocating work and family time to space and zoning. Certainly, starting a business at home reduces the overhead associated with leasing or purchasing a separate site and, with technological advances in communications and computing, many businesses can now be home-based. However, the decision to set up a business at home should be part of an overall strategy. The National Association of Home Based Businesses (NAHBB) provides links to numerous resources, and D&B Small Business Solutions (http://smallbusiness.dnb.com) has articles pertaining to home-based enterprises.

If you are considering starting a business venture in your home, thoroughly investigate zoning ordinances, deed restrictions, and civic association rules that will apply. You may have to check with several levels of government zoning offices for requirements—such as borough, city, township, or county. If you live in a deed-restricted community where there is a civic association or if you rent, you will need to check for restrictions on home-based businesses. Some places completely forbid the operation of home-based businesses; others may restrict the type of operation, number of cars, foot traffic, or commercial vehicles in the neighborhood. Sometimes hours of operation are limited and signage proscribed.

Often, you can operate a home-based business without a problem as long as your neighbors are not disturbed and do not report you. However, it is far better to be fully cognizant of zoning requirements before writing your business plan and investing funds. The last thing you need is to run afoul of zoning regulations and have to make costly changes, relocate, or close your business. Of course, if you are not happy with zoning ordinances, you can work to get them changed.

Figure 12-7 *Factory Layout, Mattress Factory*

Another issue to consider is the allocation of space within your home. A best practice is to clearly delineate your business/work area from your family's living area. This is a practical matter as well as one of professionalism, particularly if customers will be visiting your place of business. It will also be difficult to focus on your business in the midst of family activities. Crying children and barking dogs will detract from your customer interactions and make it appear that you are not seriously in business. Establish family ground rules with respect to the way you will interact while you are working, so that there aren't conflicts caused by differing expectations. Also, if you elect to have a home-based business, furnish it appropriately and get a separate telephone line. A separate entrance for customers is also desirable.

A home-based business may be viable from a zoning and space perspective but still not be the best choice. This is particularly true for businesses such as retail, service, and professional firms that have walk-in customers. Customers will need the location to be safe, convenient, and appealing. They may simply prefer to visit an office building or a store that is not in someone's house.

Special Considerations for Web-Based Businesses

Web-based businesses face many of the same location, facilities, and layout decisions as other types of enterprises but encounter unique opportunities and challenges, as well. Because they conduct business on the Internet, such companies can literally be located anyplace in the world, with staff that may work remotely from anywhere. The physical space needed for operations could be as small as a one-room office if you take orders only online and drop-ship directly from suppliers, provide online delivery of goods or services, or offer a service performed in the customer or client's home or office. For completely online businesses and those using drop shipments, location is more a function of personal preference, cost, or proximity of vendors.

Location, facility, and layout decisions for many Web-based businesses should minimize distribution costs (and time). Amazon.com can have its call centers, computer processing, and the like almost anywhere, but its distribution centers require considerable location analysis.

Defining Quality: It Is a Matter of Market Positioning

Performance Objective 6 ▶
Ensure product quality.

quality level or standard of excellence, especially as measured against similar things, or against itself over time.

The concept of **quality** is used broadly and has multiple definitions, including how to determine degrees of excellence and conformance to specifications or standards. As a business owner, quality products or services will be largely defined by your market-positioning strategy. For example, a meal at a five-star restaurant will be vastly different from one at a local diner. In either case, excellence is a matter of consistently performing (producing) to the standards that have been established to meet or exceed customer expectations. However you position your organization, the quality and the viability of the business will depend on the match between the expectations that you create through market positioning and the experience of your customers.

Profits Follow Quality

For many years, American companies had focused less on quality than on short-term profits. In the early 1950s, however, American economist W. Edwards Deming argued that business should focus on making quality

Step into the Shoes . . .

Positioning Stone Hill Winery through Quality

Jim and Betty Held took over the Stone Hill Winery in 1965, with four young children and a vision of restoring the historic Hermann, Missouri, property to its pre-Prohibition glory days.[8] They succeeded until the 1970s, when high interest rates combined with escalating costs. The winery grew slowly during the 1980s and into the 1990s, and then more rapidly from the later 1990s.

Sweet and semi-sweet wines have always been the most popular items that Stone Hill Winery produced. Jon Held states, "We have provided a wide spectrum of wine styles to satisfy all consumers rather than only the tastes of a select few wine elite. Most importantly, we have listened to our customers rather than to the wine pundits." The Helds analyzed consumer loyalty to wine brands, and discovered that one significant factor was first-time consumption of the product, specifically the atmosphere in which it was consumed. They changed their advertising message accordingly, inviting the public to, "Come out to the winery and have a great time."

The Helds knew that if they could invest in new vineyards and equipment they could attain economies of scale.[9] As recently as 2008, the winery expanded through the addition of new fermentation and storage capacity totaling 99,000 gallons. They needed

Stone Hill Winery.
(Courtesy of Lucinda Huskey)

to apply the latest grape- and wine-production technology so that the winery could consistently produce a range of wine styles of high quality and value. To raise money for this technology, they had to grow significantly. The marketing approach with the application of technology worked.

Stone Hill Winery is a three-location tourist destination. It now produces over 260,000 gallons of wine annually with gross revenues of over $9 million per year, while employing the Helds, two of their adult children, and more than 100 others. Stone Hill has 170 acres of vineyards under cultivation and uses grapes from other Missouri vineyards to supplement production.

Jim and Betty Held and their family combined market research, determination, state-of-the-art production equipment and techniques, and quality assurance to create an award-winning enterprise.

products instead of on maximizing profits and that profit would follow from that focus. His revolutionary concept was ignored by American corporations, so he went to Japan, which was rebuilding after the devastation of World War II.

In those days, Japan was notorious for the poor quality of its manufactured goods. The phrase "Made in Japan" was jokingly used to refer to anything poorly fabricated. Deming gave a series of lectures in Japan, though, that the Japanese took to heart. They began focusing on quality and soon proved that Deming's theory—profits follow quality—was correct. The subsequent quality of Japanese cars and stereos became famous and won customers worldwide.

American entrepreneurs and corporate executives traveled to Japan to study why the Japanese had become so successful. They brought Deming's ideas back home, where they finally began to be adopted.

As you develop your business, it will be the consistent quality of your product or service that will lead to profits. If you can develop a way to deliver quality consistently, you will have a business concept that can be profitable, with the potential for generating even greater revenues in the future.

Organization-Wide Quality Initiatives

It is clear that quality management and quality assurance is not solely the job of the production team. As organizations have evolved in our rapidly changing technology-and-service-driven environment, quality has

[8]Portions of this profile are available at http://www.stonehillwinery.com/ourWinery/, November 15, 2009.
[9]"Stone Hill Winery: New Tastes, New Approach," *Insights and Inspiration: How Businesses Succeed, The 1995 Blue Chip Enterprise Initiative®*. Published by *Nation's Business* on behalf of Connecticut Mutual Life Insurance Company and the U.S. Chamber of Commerce, in association with the Blue Chip Enterprise Initiative, 1995, p. 27. Courtesy of Stone Hill Winery.

come to mean the active involvement of the entire company. A number of initiatives and methods have been formed to help businesses ensure quality. Among these are lean manufacturing, benchmarking, ISO 9000, Six Sigma certifications, Total Quality Management (TQM), and the Malcolm Baldrige Award. Each of these can assist your company in providing the quality that your customers should expect.

Benchmarking

benchmarking the comparison of a company's performance against that of businesses in the same industry, or against best practices, standards, or certification criteria.

One the most basic organizationwide approaches that you can pursue is the use of **benchmarking,** which is the comparison of your company's performance against that of other companies in your industry, or against best practices, standards, or certification criteria. Benchmarking is what you are doing when you create a competitive comparison for marketing purposes, or when you compare your projected or actual financial ratios to industry levels. In addition to standard performance measures, such as return on investment, profitability, market share, and the like, individual industries have benchmarks. For example, retail stores measure sales per square foot and restaurants evaluate by customers per labor hour. By using benchmarking, you can identify opportunities for improvement.

A simple method of benchmarking is to create a list of measures that are important to your customers (using primary market research) or to customers in your industry (using secondary research, such as trade journal reports), and comparing outcomes. You can then compare other statistics, if it is helpful. **Exhibit 12-2** illustrates a portion of such a table for a restaurant.

ISO 9000

The family of standards for quality management systems established by the International Organization for Standardization (ISO) is ISO 9000. These standards are certified by independent companies to document that consistent business procedures are being used and that the organization has been independently audited for compliance. Initially, ISO standards were applied solely to manufacturing. However, service firms have become the predominant recipients of certificates. Organizations will sometimes market their ISO certification as a mark of excellence, although such qualification is, rather, a guarantee of compliance with standards.

process management the measurement, monitoring, and optimization of tasks.

There have been numerous standards employed under varying numbers. Beginning with the ISO 9001:2000 version, **process management**

Exhibit 12-2 *Quality Measures for a Country Diner*

Measure of Quality	Rating (1 is Poor, 5 is Excellent—Based on industry and customer data)				
Customers per labor hour	1	2	3	④	5
Average customer wait time for seating	1	2	3	4	⑤
Satisfactory inspection ratings	1	②	3	4	5
Number of meals returned to the kitchen	1	2	③	4	5
Customer satisfaction ratings	1	2	3	④	5
Amount of food wasted	①	2	3	4	5
Return on sales	1	2	3	④	5

(measuring, monitoring, and optimizing tasks), upper management involvement, continuous improvement, recording customer satisfaction, and utilizing numeric measures of effectiveness all became critical to the process. There are industry-specific variations that may apply to your business. There are eight quality-management principles for organizational improvement:

1. customer focus,
2. leadership,
3. involvement of people,
4. process approach,
5. system approach to management,
6. continual improvement,
7. factual approach to decision making, and
8. mutually beneficial supplier relationships.

Regardless of the size of your firm, you can find considerable information on the ISO standards and can build them into your organization from the start. Assistance is available through the American Society for Quality (ASQ) at http://www.asq.org, the American National Standards Institute at http://www.ansi.org, and ISO at http://www.iso.ch.

Six Sigma

Six Sigma is a measurement of quality that was originated in the 1980s by Motorola engineers. It is the use of statistical methods to eliminate defects to a failure rate of 3.4 defects per 1 million opportunities, or a 99.9997 percent success rate. This is a rigorous process-improvement program that aims to achieve near perfection. The two submethodologies employed are DMAIC and DMADV.[10] The DMAIC (define, measure, analyze, improve, and control) system is intended to enhance existing production. The DMADV (define, measure, analyze, design, and verify) process is meant to support new procedures and products.

For most enterprises, this is a very intense program, and maybe more so than is practical in the early stages of a business. However, it may be worthwhile to learn about it and consider whether you can include such methods to build in high standards from the start. Further information can be found at the sites listed below.

Six Sigma Information Sources

SSA & Company at http://ssaandco.com
The Quality Portal at http://www.thequalityportal.com
iSixSigma LLC at http://www.isixsigma.com
Motorola at http://www.motorola.com/motorolauniversity.jsp

Total Quality Management

The quality-assurance methodology of striving for strategic advantage through quality concepts inspired by Deming is called **total quality management (TQM).** Although developed in the 1950s, many of the principles of TQM are still valid and valued. The central notion of **continuous improvement,** or always identifying and implementing changes throughout the organization, to focus on requirements of internal and external

total quality management (TQM) the quality-assurance methodology of striving for strategic advantage through quality.

continuous improvement always identifying and implementing changes throughout an organization to focus on the requirements of internal and external customers.

---

[10]Available at http://www.isixsigma.com.

customers, is valid for any business. TQM involves constant improvement of processes, typically using specific measures of quality, such as compliance with product specifications and operating standards, volume of production, on-time delivery, and repeat rates.

TQM's success is dependent upon the commitment of all employees toward treating one another as customers, and working together to ensure that standards are met at all stages. Each employee accepts responsibility for a role in the production of the products and services.

Malcolm Baldrige Award

Whereas the previous concepts have focused on quality-management methodologies, the Malcolm Baldrige Award is a competitive process established by the United States Congress in 1987 that recognizes quality management. The Baldrige Award is given to businesses, educational, and nonprofit organizations by the president of the United States, and is administered by the National Institute of Standards and Technology (NIST).[11] Organizations apply for the award and are judged in the areas of

- leadership: organizational leadership and social responsibility;
- strategic planning: strategy development and deployment;
- customer and market focus: market and customer knowledge and customer relationships and satisfaction;
- measurement, analysis, knowledge management: measurement and analysis of organizational performance and management of information and knowledge;
- human resources focus: work systems, employee learning and motivation, and employee well-being and satisfaction;
- process management: value-creation and support processes; and
- business results, including customer focus, product and service, financial and market, human resources, organizational effectiveness, governance, and social responsibility.

Thousands of organizations use the Baldrige criteria for self-assessment, training, and the creation of business processes. You can obtain the Baldrige standards and incorporate them into your business at any time. They are more comprehensive than many of the specific production and process measures identified above.

Using Technology to Your Advantage

Performance Objective 7 ❯

Use technology to benefit your business.

Regardless of the size or nature of your business, technology can work to your advantage if you use it effectively. Even if your business is not technological, you can apply technology to make your operations more efficient and effective. The technology could be as simple and common as a telephone or as complex as a specialized piece of medical equipment. What *is* important is that you are aware of the technology available to you and how it might benefit your business. At the same time, you should be wary of adopting technology just for the "wow" factor. A cost/benefit analysis for technology implementation is as important as for any other substantial investment.

---

[11]Available at http://www.nist.gov/public_affairs/factsheet/.

Computer Access Is Essential

Advances in technology that ordinary people can use have been an important part of the entrepreneurial wave of at least the past decade. With this in mind,

- every entrepreneur should have access to a computer;
- every business should have a Web site and electronic mail access;
- every business should hire employees who are conversant and comfortable with technology, and
- every entrepreneur should be aware of the specialized computer software and equipment that is designed for his or her industry.

In 1989, an Englishman named Tim Berners-Lee invented **hyperlinks,** words that, when clicked on, transferred the reader to a new document page anywhere on the Internet. Today, pictures, or even video, can be links as well. Every Web page has an address, called a **URL (uniform resource locator),** and you can surf from one URL to another using hyperlinks. Web pages are **hypertext** documents, meaning they combine text with graphics, video, or sound.

One of the best early investments you can make for your business is a computer. You do not need to have the latest model or even a new one; refurbished computers can be purchased quite inexpensively. Even the most basic model can be used to

- access the Internet;
- create stationery and business cards (although professional designs are preferable);
- produce professional letters and check spelling, grammar, and syntax;
- keep financial records;
- maintain an updated mailing list of customers and printed mailing labels.

If you do not own a computer, consider making arrangements to borrow or use one part time until you can buy one. You can also rent computer time or get it for free at Internet cafés, or some office supply stores. Most public libraries and colleges offer free Internet access. However, it is best to have your own computer, so you can keep your company's books, records, and other proprietary information private.

hyperlink word(s) that, when clicked on, transfer the computer user to a new Web page.

uniform resource locator (URL) a Web page address.

hypertext Web-based documents that combine text and graphics.

Capture the Potential of the Telephone

Do not forget, however, that technology does not have to be new to be useful. The telephone is still one of the businessperson's most important technological tools. You can turn your phone into an answering service for your business by using a voice-mail system, or you can hire an answering service to provide a more personal touch. Either approach is acceptable until you have staff to answer customer inquiries, although today some companies use automated telephone-answering systems if they have hundreds, or even thousands, of employees.

Whether you use voice mail or an answering service, make sure the message that callers hear represents your desired business image and is clear and professional. Change your message periodically to advertise specials and sales and to keep customers listening. Use mobile phones to stay in touch with customers, employees, and suppliers.

A separate telephone line for your business will provide a number of advantages. Business telephones can be listed under your business name in the telephone book, and you will know to always answer with your business name when that phone rings. Also, if you have a home-based business and children, it will be easier to have them resist answering the phone when it is clearly the office line. With text messaging and e-mail sent over mobile phones, the versatility and importance of telephones to today's businesses cannot be overstated.

Identify Market-Specific Software and Technology

In order to increase efficiency and effectiveness in operations, businesses use software and technology designed for their industry or type of business. For example, retail stores often use point-of-sales (**POS**) systems that are tailored to their products and restaurants use ordering systems customized for their menus. Not-for-profits have specialized fund-raising and accounting software. Sports stadiums, concert venues, and movie theaters have ticketing systems. Manufacturing plants have materials-planning and inventory systems.

Typically, trade journals feature advertisements for software specific to an industry. The software companies commonly exhibit at trade shows and conferences. Evaluations and comparisons of hardware and software solutions are listed in trade publications and on the Internet.

The investment in industry-specific technology is often many times greater than in generic business equipment and software. However, the upfront investment may lead to both considerable efficiency and savings over the short and/or long term.

Electronic Storefront (Web Site)

electronic storefront an online site that customers can visit to view a company's catalog, price lists, and documentation.

No matter what type of business you have, opening an **electronic storefront** will make it more accessible to local customers and can introduce it to potential customers all over the world. An electronic storefront is an online site that customers can visit to view your catalog, price lists, and other information. It is relatively easy to add the option of purchasing your products online, either directly, through a credit card merchant account, or through a service such as PayPal.

You will need to decide if you want to put your store up with an online service or by yourself. An online service would typically build your storefront for you, and include promotion and advertisements as part of the deal to help make its subscribers aware of your store. On the other hand, if you put a site up yourself, you will have more control over what it looks like and where it is located, and your potential customers would not be limited to subscribers of a particular online service. One of the most cost-efficient ways to set up an electronic storefront is to hire a competent consultant to help you design it and choose which server to use.

Chapter Summary

Now that you have studied this chapter, you can do the following:

1. Understand the significance of operations in a business.
   - Operations is the delivery on promises.

- What is required depends on the specific industry and business.
- Inputs are transformed or converted into outputs through operations.

2. Develop a production-distribution chain for your business.
   - Manufacturers make products in large quantities.
   - Wholesalers buy smaller quantities in bulk from manufacturers.
   - Retailers buy from wholesalers (and sometimes manufacturers).
   - Consumers buy from retailers.

3. Manage suppliers and inventory.
   - Supply chain management is used to create and maintain efficient flow of materials between supply partners.
   - Suppliers may be found in a variety of ways and may be located worldwide.
   - Inventory can be managed to minimize cost and maximize customer satisfaction.

4. Know the key factors to consider in the location decision.
   - The most important factors will be governed by the nature of the business.
   - Key factors for most firms include:
     - access for customers and to suppliers,
     - climate and geography,
     - cost of facilities,
     - demographics,
     - economic conditions and business incentives,
     - laws and regulations,
     - workforce readiness,
     - competitive environment.

5. Explore the design of facilities and their layouts.
   - Manufacturing, warehousing, and distribution facilities must provide the space to operate cost effectively.
   - Retail facilities must draw maximum revenue from design and layout.

6. Ensure product quality.
   - Quality is determined by meeting and exceeding standards, including customer satisfaction.
   - Profits follow quality.
   - Organizationwide approaches to quality include:
     - benchmarking,
     - ISO 9000 certification,
     - Six Sigma certification,
     - total quality management (TQM),
     - Malcolm Baldrige Awards.

7. Use technology to benefit your business.
   - Technology can provide competitive advantage.
   - Computers are a necessity in today's business world.
   - The telephone continues to be a major asset.
   - Industry-specific software and equipment is frequently beneficial.
   - Electronic storefronts provide additional distribution opportunities.

Key Terms

benchmarking
clustering
continuous improvement
economic order
   quantity (EOQ)
electronic storefront
factor-rating method
hyperlink
hypertext
leasehold improvements

operations
process management
quality
reorder point (ROP)
safety stock
supply chain management (SCM)
total quality management (TQM)
traffic generators
uniform resource locator (URL)
visual control

Entrepreneurship Portfolio

Critical Thinking Exercises

1. Production-distribution chain
   a. How do you plan to distribute your product to your target market?
   b. What is the estimated delivery time between when you place an order with your supplier and when the product will be available for your customers?
2. Give an example of a business that is known internationally for the quality of its products; what defines quality for this company?
3. How does the design of a facility affect product quality and production efficiency?
4. Choose a partner in class and make a list of the technology each of you can personally access. Brainstorm how you might combine your technological resources to create a successful business. Describe in detail how the partnership would work. For example, would the person contributing more technology have a larger share of the business or would profits and expenses be split equally? Draw up a partnership agreement that specifies each partner's duties and how much money and time each will invest in the business.
5. Examine a readily accessible label on the shoes or clothing you are wearing today. Which items were made in foreign countries? How many dollars per hour do you think the people earned who made these items? Why do you think the company that manufactured these items had them made abroad?
6. Identify two sets of business clusters in your area. Explain why they may have formed.
7. Where would you locate your business, and why?
8. If you were to start a home-based business, what would it be? Why? What key factors would you consider before start up?
9. What is the role of demographic information in the selection of a retail location?

Key Concept Questions

1. Use your local telephone company's business-to-business directory or *The American Wholesalers and Distributors Directory* to locate wholesalers you could visit or from whom you could order products for resale.
2. Choose one of the quality-assurance methodologies described in this chapter and explain how it might apply to your educational institution.
3. What factors are most critical to the location decision for a manufacturer?
4. How can zoning affect location for a home-based business?

Application Exercises

1. What might the supply chain look like for one of the following:
   a. manufacturer of custom rims for automobiles
   b. car dealership
   c. building materials wholesaler
2. Suggest at least three quality-assurance measures for the following businesses:
   a. bank
   b. residential cleaning service
   c. commercial HVAC (heating, ventilation, and air conditioning) contractor
   d. computer manufacturer
3. Xavier Zumsteg is selecting a location for his upscale urban fashion boutique. He is considering three cities and needs to make a choice. Using the factor-rating method, identify the five key factors to consider and their weights. Then, rate each of the cities on a scale of 0 to 100. Calculate the most preferable option.

Factor	Factor Weight	Detroit Rating	Atlanta Rating	Boston Rating	Detroit Weight	Atlanta Weight	Boston Weight
Total	1.00	xxxxxx	xxxxxx	xxxxxx			

Exploring Your Community

1. Identify two businesses in your community with which you are familiar. Suggest four measures of quality for each. Rate each business on these quality dimensions. Then, answer the following questions by indicating the appropriate number.

Measure of Quality	Rating (1 is poor, 5 is excellent)				
Company Number 1					
Measure 1	1	2	3	4	5
Measure 2	1	2	3	4	5
Measure 3	1	2	3	4	5
Measure 4	1	2	3	4	5
Company Number 2					
Measure 1	1	2	3	4	5
Measure 2	1	2	3	4	5
Measure 3	1	2	3	4	5
Measure 4	1	2	3	4	5

  a. What do these measures tell you about the respective businesses?

  b. How might they improve on one of the indicators?

  c. Does each business have a customer feedback mechanism? If so, what is it? If not, what would you recommend?

2. Visit the Web site of a business that you know has at least three locations in your area (preferably not a franchise or chain).

  a. Obtain the addresses of the locations nearest to your home (up to 10).

  b. Map these locations on an ordinary street map.

  c. Map them on a census map.

  d. What geographic pattern, if any, emerges?

  e. Is there a common set of demographic data? If so, what is it?

  f. Name some competitors and map up to 10 of their locations.

  g. Does the pattern that emerges show clustering?

3. Visit the U.S. Census Bureau Web site at http://www.census.gov. Pull up the census tract data both for your home address and for your campus address. If the tracts are the same, pick another college or university. Compare and contrast the two locations as potential sites for each of the following. Use a street map, too, if it will help.

  a. A bookstore

  b. A store specializing in golfing-related goods

  c. A children's day care center

  d. A distribution center for cleaning supplies

BizBuilder Business Plan Questions

5.0 Marketing Strategy and Plan

5.4 Place

  A. Where do you intend to sell your product? Describe the advantages and disadvantages of your location(s).

  B. What are the surrounding businesses? Access routes?

  C. If vehicular traffic is important to your organization, what is the traffic count for this location?

6.0 Management and Operations

6.3 Physical Location

A. Describe the actual physical place in greater detail than above.

B. What are the zoning laws in your area? Does your business comply?

6.5 Inventory, Production, and Quality Assurance

A. Where are you purchasing the products you plan to sell, or the parts you will use to manufacture those products? Illustrate your supply chain.

B. Do you intend to manufacture your product? If so, describe the manufacturing processes you will use. If not, describe how your product is manufactured.

C. Are there any economies of scale to be attained for your business? At what point do you anticipate achieving them?

D. Have you developed and/or adopted any innovations in production, inventory management, or distribution that are significant? What are they and why are they meaningful?

E. How do you plan to distribute your product to your target market?

F. Show the production-distribution channel for your business, and the markups along the chain.

G. What is the estimated delivery time between when you place an order with your supplier and when you will have the product available for your customers?

H. What method(s) will you use to define and ensure the quality of your products/services?

Case Study | Virtual IT Training in a Classroom

ONLC Training Centers has used its many locations to drive significant sales growth and become one of the leaders in the IT training industry. In 2011, ONLC had over 250 locations from coast to coast but only seven years earlier they operated from only three offices. ONLC Training Centers was named the eighth-fastest-growing education company on *Inc.* magazine's list of fastest growing companies in 2009. It achieved remarkable growth in a declining industry during the worst economic downturn in 70 years.

ONLC was able to realize new revenue streams by rapidly expanding its geographic distribution of classroom training. In 2009, some 50 percent of ONLC's revenues came from sites that had not been open a year earlier. Key drivers to their success were the strategic use of locations and the redefinition of classroom training.

Andy Williamson and Jim Palic formed the company in 1983 and they were on the leading edge of the PC revolution when they began offering classroom training through personal computers to individuals in the workplace. Throughout the 1980s and 1990s, their facilities were IT classrooms designed for face-to-face instruction. As corporate training and travel budgets dried up after 2000, demand dropped precipitously and the industry consolidated rapidly.

Andy and Jim recognized that the demand for training had significantly declined but had not disappeared. To serve the remaining market for public IT training, they needed to transform their business model. They considered offering virtual training, where people would join classes from their homes or offices. However, years of experience had taught them that people preferred classroom training. A formal classroom provides an interruption-free environment in which to learn. There are also fewer technical issues. And going to an off-site location elevates the importance of the event and helps people focus on the job of learning.

Instead of abandoning bricks-and-mortar classroom-based training, they decided to go deeper into that strategy. They designed a virtual-training scenario that keeps the classroom as part of the solution—"remote classroom instruction" (RCI). This provides their clients with a higher-quality learning environment and gives ONLC a more defensible position in the market.

Jim Palic and Andy Williamson, ONLC.
(ONLC Training Centers)

RCI works like this: A single national training schedule is promoted on the ONLC Web site. For example, if a particular class is running on January 15, interested individuals can register for it in any one of the 250-plus locations. Each of these is a site for two to four people. The session might be taught in a traditional classroom in Philadelphia, for example, with an instructor teaching three students face-to-face. As many as nine other people could be joining the class from up to nine other physical locations around the country.

"It is our ability to easily aggregate low demand for public training that makes our model successful," says Andy. By combining the enrollments from hundreds of locations, they are able to have fewer classes cancelled because of low enrollments. Whereas competitors who needed a large number of students in a room with an instructor would have had to cancel the event, ONLC is able to run it with one attendee.

ONLC management has carefully studied potential opportunities and identified strategic roll-out priorities by examining U.S. Census data by Metropolitan Statistical Areas (MSAs). The new model relies on a network of executive-suite locations. The company can sign short-term leases for only the needed space. They can start by renting a single classroom in any city. If demand becomes strong enough, they can rent additional rooms; if demand is low, they can cancel the lease at the end of the term and redeploy their computer hardware in a new, more productive location.

By creating hundreds of very small but efficient training facilities, and aggregating the demand for training across the country through their RCI model, they are able to cost effectively capture the demand for public IT classes.

ONLC estimates that over 80 percent of the U.S. population is within an hour's drive from one of their training sites. Andy explains how ONLC has overcome the tyranny of geography that author Chris Anderson defines as an audience being spread so thinly that it is the same as no audience at all.[12] Andy observes, "People wanting training in remote locations have been suffering from the tyranny of geography where no classroom training is available to them because demand is so low. When demand for a particular class drops below a certain point,

a traditional face-to-face class is taken off the schedule of the local training company. When demand for IT training in general drops below a certain point, the traditional training company closes its doors."

By attaining nationwide coverage and redefining classroom training, ONLC can economically deliver classroom training where its competitors cannot. As Andy says, "Lowering the cost of delivery has radically changed the economics of providing training, and has democratized distribution. It has also positioned ONLC for a successful future delivering virtual training in a classroom."

Case Study Analysis

1. What does ONLC do to determine where to offer training? What are the critical location factors?

2. How does this business model democratize distribution?

3. How can ONLC have over 200 locations and maintain an efficient cost structure at low volumes in each?

4. What is the level of importance of the location of the ONLC headquarters? Why?

5. What were the main differentiating characteristics of ONLC's remote classroom instruction offering, compared to the competitors who were also offering virtual training?

---

[12]Chris Anderson, The Long Tail: Why the Future of Business is Selling Less of More (New York: Hyperion, 2006).

Case Study | Sewing Up Business in New Ways—Sew What? Inc.

Question: What do Maroon 5, Slip Knot, Green Day, Rod Stewart, Elton John, Madonna, and schools near you have in common?

Answer: They are customers of Sew What? Inc., a manufacturer of custom draperies and curtains for theaters, concert tours, exhibitions, and special events.

Sew What? founder Megan Duckett has been passionate about theater and concert production since high school. She started her career as a part-time employee at the Arts Centre in Melbourne, Australia, before she graduated from a Church of England girls' grammar school (high school). The Arts Centre, the heart of theater in Melbourne, provided an opportunity to apprentice as a lighting technician with master theater electrician Jim Paine. There, Megan was exposed to the businesses that serve the theater industry and she discovered that working in this field was what she was born to do.

Not long after that, 18-year-old Megan moved into the rock-and-roll marketplace and continued to work as a lighting technician and on other backstage aspects of the business. A critical turning point in her life came unexpectedly one year later. She was assigned to driving Billy Joel's band around while they were in Melbourne. They had an instant rapport and the crew invited her to visit the United States. Much to their surprise, Megan showed up on their doorstep shortly thereafter and soon got a job at a staging company for rock concerts. Megan knew that she needed to find her niche and stand out from everyone else. As she has noted, "I needed to be invaluable and irreplaceable." Little did she know that sewing would be her ticket to success.

The opportunity to make her mark through sewing essentially came out of nowhere. However, Megan quickly realized that it was the opportunity she sought. Her first sewing job was to reupholster 10 coffins for a Halloween show. She had neither the equipment nor the materials to do the job when she accepted it. Undeterred, Megan rented a sewing machine and went to a local fabric store, where she bought the necessary supplies (at full retail price) and did the work at her kitchen table. The customer could see that it was wonderfully done and called two

Megan Duckett.
(Sew What? Inc.)

weeks later with more work. That customer referred others and the business took off. That was in 1992. For five years, Megan says, "The phone kept ringing with orders."

As Megan was preparing her taxes in 1997, she realized that her earnings from the custom projects sewn at her kitchen table matched the pay from her 40-hour-a-week job. She and her husband, Adam, had just purchased a home and had transformed the garage into a sewing room. After considerable discussion, Megan left her steady full-time employment, incorporated Sew What? a few weeks later, and rented an 800-square-foot space a few miles from her house. She had no formal advisors and no written plan, but she did have a strong customer base, determination, and an understanding of the business. Just six weeks later, Megan landed a contract big enough so that she had to hire her first employee—a stitcher named Maria—who continues as part of the Sew What? family to this day. In 2002, Adam quit his own job and joined Sew What?

Megan relates, "The soft-goods industry is traditionally very much a cottage industry and is not known for embracing technology. We didn't like the way that felt." From the beginning, the Ducketts incorporated technology into the business. The company team recognized that, as the quality of the clientele and the size of the contracts increased, customers would expect excellence. Sew What? began deliberately streamlining and fine-tuning both the product and service aspects of the business.

Advances in technology were instituted throughout the operation. The office equipment was upgraded to include a network setup, faster computers, and multiple servers to increase speed in order to function in real time with customers. Sew What? is currently on its third inventory-management system. The first was an Excel-based configuration that they developed themselves. The second method was part of the automated accounting program. The most recent arrangement is a sophisticated manufacturing system called VISTA, from Epicor. Sew What? has moved into lean manufacturing procedures and every function is timed, scanned, and measured to reduce waste and maximize use of resources. In addition, some patterns are cut using computer-guided tools, although many are still cut by hand because runs of fabric can be so long

and the tolerances so tight that hand cutting makes the most sense.

The company's Web site is a particularly important sales tool. Megan lost a substantial job early on because, without one, her business lacked credibility with that prospective customer. Megan resisted the idea of putting up a Web site, but she came to realize that she needed it, and built one over a weekend using clip art, a far cry from the professional site Sew What? has today. Megan notes, "Generation Y will be the purchasing agents of the future. They expect a Web site. They need the visual communication." A Web site is particularly helpful for Sew What?, which has clients across the country and around the world (the company is headquartered in Rancho Dominguez, California). The site includes e-swatches, so that visitors can look at fabric samples online.

The sales force and production team also benefit from the use of technology, through a custom software program. By means of a series of drop-down menus, they can select such variables as fabric, color, and production method. To that they add dimensions and other specifications. The system calculates a "bid window" of the high and low price that can be offered. It determines the minutes of labor and the yards of materials. Once the job is sold and a contract secured, the file is digitally

The Sew What! team.
(Sew What? Inc.)

editable and the Sew What? team can make final adjustments. It is then sent to a report generator (Crystal Reports) and automatically translated into Spanish for the team of stitchers. This system permits Sew What? to sell more effectively, quote more accurately, replicate the work more easily, and make fewer mistakes. Sew What? has used its technological infrastructure to maximize productivity.

The company won the Dell/NFIB (National Federation of Independent Business) 2006 Small Business Excellence Award, and was featured on the Dell Web site for the integration of technology into a business. With a 15,000-square-foot building and a staff of more than 30, finding ways to maximize technology was essential.

The sales and order cycles for Sew What? are largely dependent on the type of customer. For example, rock-and-roll touring curtains might take anywhere from three days to four weeks from inquiry to order fulfillment. These customers may also recycle or replace their curtains after a tour. They may even donate them to charity. Often, quick delivery is important for the touring customers, and because Sew What? generally uses only U.S.-milled products, the production cycle can be relatively quick after the order is placed.

For a school or church group buying or replacing stage curtains, the cycle is often three to six months. The process generally includes multiple steps, such as when a group realizes the drapes don't open/close properly or it needs new ones. A student or PTA parent researches available vendors and calls Sew What? The sales team helps by focusing first on making sure the individual knows what is needed and what will be provided. The customer is directed to samples and possible solutions, often through the Web site. Sew What? submits a price, the gatherer compares prices, and the school or church group raises funds. With money in hand, the order is finalized and Megan's team speaks with the person who will install the drapes. Sew What? makes and ships the drapes, the customer receives and installs them, and Megan reaches out to see that they are satisfied.

In July 2008, Megan Duckett launched a second company, Rent What? Inc. with partner Marce Forrester. Offering rental stage curtains (manufactured by Sew What?) and theatrical equipment to the concert and special event market, Rent What? gives customers the means to rent the same high-quality products as are available through Sew What? Rent What? has provided rental drapery and equipment to diverse clients that include Journey, Lady Antebellum, and the television show *Glee*. In Summer 2010, Rent What? began its third year of operation with the launch of a new customer-focused redesign of its Web site (http://www.rentwhatinc.com).

Megan was thrilled to have her products on the cover of the thousandth issue of *Rolling Stone*. She won a 2007 Stevie Award for Most Innovative Company of the Year (up to 100 employees), was a finalist for the 2008 Enterprising Woman of the Year, and Sew What? was named to DiversityBusiness.com's 2008 list of the top 500 small businesses in the United States. In her feature as a young millionaire in *Entrepreneur* magazine, Megan stated, "The secret [to success] is hard work, dedication, and being able to take a blow and get up and move forward again. Be willing to accept criticism and comments, find mentors and learn from others. Try to be inspired by other people's success." With sales of about $5 million annually, the answer to Sew What? is "sewing up business." Or, as the company's Web site declares: *Sew What? Inc. It's not a question, it's the answer.*

Case Study Analysis

1. How does technology sustain Megan Duckett's business?

2. Why does Megan credit computer technology and the Web for a significant portion of her company's growth?

3. What have been some critical steps in the growth of the company?

4. What is (are) the sales cycle(s) for Sew What?

5. What channels of distribution would you expect the company to use?

Case Sources

Dell Case Studies at http://www.dell.com/html/us/segments/bsd/case_studies/sew/index.html.

Sew What? Inc. Web site, http://www.sewwhatinc.com, November 15, 2009. Courtesy of Sew What? Inc.

"Young Millionaires Say More," http://www.entrepreneur.com/slideshow/184476.html.

Chapter **13**

MANAGEMENT, LEADERSHIP, & ETHICAL PRACTICES

> "Give a man a fish and you feed him for a day. Teach a man to fish and you feed him for a lifetime."
>
> —Lao Tzu, founder of Taoism

Madam C. J. Walker was born Sarah Breedlove to a poor couple in Louisiana in 1867. Her parents died when Sarah was a child, and she was reared in poverty by her married sister. After having overcome incredible difficulties, in her 40s she became the first self-made American female millionaire and one of the first African American millionaires.

Breedlove worked for many years in the cotton fields and as a laundress, moving to St. Louis, Denver, and Indianapolis, before inventing and marketing hair-care products for African American women. Madam Walker (her married name) quickly became successful enough to build a factory to manufacture her line of products. At first she had sold her shampoos and hair-growth merchandise door to door, but soon organized and trained a group of agent-operators.

At the peak of her career, Walker employed 2,000 agents. One of her successful marketing strategies was to organize the agents into clubs that promoted social and charitable causes in their respective African American communities. She offered cash prizes to the clubs that accomplished the most. She also encouraged her agents to open beauty salons and other corollary businesses. Not only did Madam Walker's methods foreshadow the emphasis we see on socially responsible entrepreneurship, she also created a rich legacy of black female entrepreneurial leadership.

Performance Objectives

1. Identify leadership styles.
2. Describe the 10 basic tasks handled by managers.
3. Develop your organizational culture.
4. Determine your organizational structure.
5. Understand the functions of human resources management.
6. Pursue ethical leadership to build an ethical organization.
7. Incorporate social responsibility into your company.

Madam C. J. Walker.
(Library of Congress)

The Entrepreneur as Leader

Performance Objective 1
Identify leadership styles.

No matter who you hire to manage your company, *you* will set the tone for how the business operates. Are you disorganized and chaotic? Chances are your company will be, too. Are you honest and straightforward? Your managers and employees are likely to behave similarly.

leader a person who gets things done through influence, by guiding or inspiring others to voluntarily participate in a cause or project.

A **leader** is someone who gets things done through influence, by guiding or inspiring others to voluntarily participate in a cause or project. *Leadership* comes from self-esteem applied to knowledge, skills, and abilities. If you believe in yourself and know what you are doing, you can accomplish things confidently and inspire others. Develop a positive attitude and you can become a leader. Great leaders are optimists; they have trained themselves to think positively. Running a successful business requires leadership.

Leadership Styles That Work

As your business grows, the type of leader that you are will be reflected throughout your company. Some leadership styles are more conducive to internal competition, whereas others foster teamwork and a collaborative environment. You may find that you have to blend leadership styles, or shift from one to another to some extent, as circumstances change.

Companies like Wal-Mart and Home Depot invest significant sums to create a work environment that inspires and motivates their employees. You may not have the sort of funds that they do, but you can model a positive leadership style. How you or your managers treat one another, and the employees, will determine the company culture. Adopt the best leadership style for your company, maintain it consistently, and learn to adapt it as needed. The principal styles and their advantages and drawbacks as identified by researcher Daniel Goleman are noted below.[1]

- *Coercive.* To *coerce* means to pressure someone into doing what you want. This commanding approach can be effective in a disaster scenario or with problem employees who need a forceful manager. In most situations, however, a coercive leadership style damages employee morale and diminishes the flexibility and effectiveness of the company. Employees stop thinking and acting for themselves.

- *Authoritative.* An authoritative leader takes a "come with me" approach, stating the overall goals but giving employees freedom to figure out how best to achieve them. This can work well if the leader is an expert, but may not be so effective if the scenario is one of a nominal leader heading up a group of individuals who have more expertise in the field than he or she does (a team of scientists, for example).

- *Affiliative.* This is a "people come first" method that is effective when the business is in the team-building stage. It can fail when employees are lost and need direction.

- *Democratic.* This style gives employees a strong voice in how the company is run. It can build morale and work if employees are prepared to handle responsibility, but it could result in endless meetings and a sense of leaderlessness and drifting.

- *Pacesetting.* This type of leader sets very high personal performance standards and challenges employees to meet them, too. This can be very good when employees are also self-motivated and highly devoted, but can overwhelm those who are not so committed.

- *Coaching.* This style focuses on helping each employee to grow, through training and support. This can be a good approach for starting and growing a business but may not work with employees who have been with the company for a while and may be resistant to change.

How Entrepreneurs Pay Themselves

Before you hire employees, figure out how to pay yourself. Tax and legal rules that govern different type of ownership forms affect what you call and how you account for owner's compensation. Once you decide on the type of business you are creating, check with an attorney and accountant regarding the appropriate business form and record keeping requirements. Your options depend upon your legal entity, so it is best to

---

[1] Daniel Goleman, "Leadership That Gets Results," *Harvard Business Review*, March–April 2000.

confirm what you intend to do with your accountant before doing it. But remember, you can change what you do among your available options to fit evolving circumstances. The main choices are:

- **Commission.** A set percentage of every sale. It is treated as a variable operating cost because it fluctuates with sales.
- **Salary.** A fixed amount of money paid at set intervals. You could choose to receive your salary once a week or once a month, if you are not a sole proprietor or partner. A salary is a fixed operating cost for corporations.
- **Wages.** If you have a service or manufacturing business, you could pay yourself an hourly wage. Wages are considered a cost of goods sold for a corporation, because they are factored into the cost of the product or service.
- **Dividend.** Usually a share of a company's profits issued to shareholders, based upon what remains after investments; but you, as a sole owner of a corporate entity, could use this method to pay yourself—your compensation would depend on how the business was doing. If there are other shareholders, they will have to receive dividends proportionate to their ownership stake with limited exceptions.

Entrepreneurs who do not pay themselves regularly overstate their return on investment; they have not taken their effort as a cost of business. Recognize that you can only pay yourself (or anyone else) when you have sufficient cash to do so.

Another reason to pay yourself is that it enables you to be honest about whether or not the business is really worth your time. Could you be making more money in a different business or working for someone else? What are your opportunity costs? Is the best choice to keep working for yourself? Thinking entrepreneurially includes a realistic consideration of whether you would be happier *not* running a business, at least for a time.

Manage Your Time Wisely

Leaders learn how to manage their time so that they can accomplish more with less. One of the most important things you can do is to learn how to manage your time efficiently. Getting more done in less time can contribute to success.

Even if you do not have employees to manage, you could probably use your own time better. **Exhibit 13-1** is an example of a valuable tool called a PERT chart (Program Evaluation and Review Technique) that you can use to organize the many things you need to do. This one is related to business start-up tasks. As your venture grows, you can use the PERT concept to manage more complex operations. You can also create charts using software, such as Microsoft Project, and share them among team members. The best method to select is the one that you will actually use.

Leaders perpetually have more tasks to complete than there is time to complete them, even when project-management tools are in active use. It is easy to get sucked into unexpected meetings and conversations. For founders, this issue is compounded by the fact that they are often the locus of more company and product expertise than others, because of being a "one-person band"—or at least a large percentage of a small founding team. This means being called in as the "firefighter" or problem solver. The balancing act between being accessible and creating a positive environment, and being inaccessible, is a difficult situation that each entrepreneur addresses individually. Time-management issues are also more difficult for leaders who cannot let go of decision making and involvement in every aspect of the company, when in fact they need to delegate some of the responsibilities.

Exhibit **13-1** *Sample PERT Chart*						
Task	**Week 1**	**Week 2**	**Week 3**	**Week 4**	**Week 5**	**Week 6**
Befriend banker	✓	✓	✓	✓	✓	✓
Order letterhead		✓				
Select location	✓					
Register business	✓					
Obtain bulk mail permit			✓			
Select ad agency	✓					
Meet with lawyer				✓		
Meet with accountant				✓		
Create vendor statement					✓	
Pay utility deposits					✓	
Order marketing material					✓	
Install phone system			✓	✓	✓	
Have Web site designed						✓
Set up database						✓
Network computers						✓

There is a seemingly endless variety of books and articles on time management, as well as managerial and organizational effectiveness. Some tips that can assist in increasing such effectiveness include:

- Prioritize. Know what is important.
- Set realistic daily goals, allowing for customer contact, meetings, and some flexibility for surprises.
- Don't spend too much time on e-mail. It is easy to become distracted by nonessential correspondence. If you check at the beginning, middle, and end of the day, you will be able to focus better on other tasks that need to be done.
- Avoid letting your attention get caught up in portable electronic devices, such as Blackberries and iPhones. Whereas multitasking and constant availability may seem to increase efficiency, each interruption is a diversion from the work in progress and may cause you to lose your train of thought. These disruptions may also distract your co-workers, decreasing productivity even more. If you are using your mobile phone as your customer-contact number, this suggestion will need to be adapted.
- Schedule sit-down meetings only when they will be more efficient than other, less time-consuming, methods of communication. Try stand-up meetings. Also, consider going to staff members' offices so that you can end the meetings more easily.
- Only accept meeting invitations where your presence is required in order for progress to occur. As the firm grows, many of the operational meetings should disappear from your schedule. If you don't know why you have been invited to a meeting, don't attend it (but first try to find out why you should).
- Delegate responsibility and authority, and trust your team to do the right things and do them correctly. Hire the best people for the job and support them in their success. There is little that is more wasteful

and counterproductive than a manager who does not delegate, or who nominally delegates and then undermines the team's work.

- Remember to allow yourself downtime, play time, and creative-thinking time. One of the reasons people become entrepreneurs is to gain control over their time. One of the positive characteristics of entrepreneurs is their creativity. By allowing time to think and relax, your company will benefit.

Business Management: Building a Team

As a small business grows, it will reach a point where the entrepreneur and only a few employees cannot handle operations efficiently. At that stage, the company will probably need professional management to meet its goals efficiently.

Many successful entrepreneurs are creative individuals who tend to get bored with the everyday details of running a business, until suddenly there is a crisis in management. Or, they simply dislike managing employees or recognize that their own strengths lie elsewhere. Wise entrepreneurs acknowledge these characteristics if they have them and hire managers to run the business.

An entrepreneur with a growing corporation can raise capital by selling stock. Some of this capital can be used to hire managers to organize the business. This will free the entrepreneur to spend less time managing and more time thinking up new ideas, pitching product, or doing whatever he or she does best.

What Do Managers Do?

There are numerous descriptions, conceptions, and misconceptions about what managers do and do not do with their time. Nathan Himmelstein, of Rutgers University, breaks management into 10 functions, using the acronym POLDSCCRIM.

◀ **Performance Objective 2**
Describe the 10 basic tasks handled by managers.

1. *Planning.* Managers perform three types of planning: strategic, tactical, and operational.
   - *Strategic plans* are typically three-to-five-year overall strategies for achieving a business's long-term growth, sales, and positioning goals.
   - *Tactical plans* provide the short-term implementation to accomplish strategic goals. Tactical plans are made for one year or less and have limited, specific objectives.
   - *Operational plans* are short-term procedures for achieving tactical goals. These include budgets, regulations, and schedules for day-to-day operation of the business.
2. *Organizing.* This function includes everything from finding resources to hiring employees to buying/leasing equipment. It includes setting up an organizational chart and defining each employee's responsibilities.
3. *Leading.* This function is about the style in which you and your managers direct the company. Achievement-oriented managers encourage employee input, share authority and responsibility, and focus on achieving long-term goals. This style is usually the most appropriate for a small business, although sometimes managers will have to temporarily adopt another style to deal with a crisis or to stabilize operations.

4. *Directing.* After you and your managers have made your plans and organized your employees and resources, it is time to direct and motivate employees to perform the work that will move the company toward its strategic goals.

5. *Staffing.* This function involves managing the people in the company by making sure they are in the positions that best use their respective skills and experience. It includes screening, recruiting, and hiring employees, training and developing them, and setting up pay and benefits packages.

6. *Controlling.* This step involves measuring the business's performance and determining how to improve it. Is the business adhering to its budget? Are products achieving the level of sales and quality goals that were set? How about customer service? If there are variances between what was planned and what the company actually achieved, controlling will require corrective action to align plans and actions.

7. *Coordinating.* This is the task of combining all management efforts into a unified system. Coordinating includes creating in-house communications and teaching everyone to use them, scheduling regular meetings and updates, and generally making sure all managers are using appropriate styles and are working toward the same goals.

8. *Representing.* Managers represent a company to its people and its people to the company; they also represent the company to the outside world. Managers need to appear and behave in a way that accurately reflects the company culture.

9. *Innovating.* Managers should always be developing new ways to meet strategic, tactical, and operational goals. The entrepreneur may be the guiding creative force behind the company, but managers should also be innovative problem solvers.

10. *Motivating.* Managers need to understand their employees' skills, knowledge, and work styles to be effective. It is important that managers understand that employees are not all the same and will need to be handled individually. Effective managers can adapt to the employee or situation. Decisions managers make may affect employee motivation and morale—positively or negatively. A manager's assumptions about the employees may have an effect. If a manager assumes that people need to be pushed in order to work, for example, and treats them that way, he or she may incur resentment. A manager who assumes that employees want to do their best and embrace responsibility will likely be more successful. Some ways managers can motivate include involving employees in decisions, providing meaningful work, recognizing contributions, giving consistent, honest feedback, regularly evaluating performance, and rewarding achievement.[2]

Adding Employees to Your Business

One of the most important things you can do as a business owner is to bring in capable, motivated people. It is a major decision to become responsible for the wages and salaries of others. For many entrepreneurs, the decision to hire is an agonizing one because they fear having to let the individual go at a later date or may not want to give up some control of the business. Businesses may bring in employees too soon and not be able to afford them, or too late and face overwhelming challenges. If you have a carefully developed operational plan for your business, and keep

---

[2]Kathleen R. Allen and Earl C. Meyer, *Entrepreneurship and Small Business Management*, 3rd ed. (Blacklick, Ohio: Glencoe/McGraw-Hill, 2005).

it updated, you should know when to add employees to the mix. The process of finding and hiring employees is often called **recruitment**.

recruitment the process of finding and hiring employees.

In *Good to Great*, management expert Jim Collins says that great leaders "get the right people on the bus—sometimes even before a company decides exactly what business it will be in."[3] Louise Hay, founder of Hay House, Inc., a publisher, once said, "In the early days, I didn't have the money to pay decent salaries, so I didn't get good people. I got nice people, but I didn't get good employees." Be certain to get the best employees you can!

Some possible ways to bring good employees into your business are:

- ***Bring them in as partners.*** Partners share the risks and rewards of the venture and will co-own the business with you. They will have the incentive to work diligently for the company's success.

- ***Hire experts to accomplish specific tasks on a contractual or hourly basis.*** You may not need full-time, or even part-time, employees for professional staff positions, but some expertise will be needed on a limited basis. For example, you might hire a professional accountant to work one day per month to review your record keeping.

- ***Hire someone as a part-time or full-time regular employee.*** Be prepared to invest the time and money required to recruit and hire the best-qualified person you can afford. Remember that taxes and benefits add to employee costs, beyond basic salaries or wages.

There are specific steps in the recruiting process:

1. ***Defining the job.*** First, think about what you need this employee to do and what kinds of skills are needed. Create a job profile and then develop a position description. A **job profile** identifies the knowledge, skills, and abilities required to perform the specific tasks of a position. A **position description** includes the knowledge, skills, and abilities from the job profile, as well as the required reporting and working relationships, and what the position's goals and objectives will be. It should also contain a description of the physical requirements and special working conditions of the job (for example, lifting, bending, walking, etc.). Prioritize the list of key requirements that you will develop with those who will work with the new hire. Be certain to designate the experience, qualifications, characteristics, and traits that will be expected. Also, decide on the wage or salary range that fits your budget before beginning to recruit.

job profile the identification of the knowledge, skills, and abilities required to perform the specific tasks of an employment p osition.

position description an exposition of needed knowledge, skills, and abilities as taken from a job profile, as well as the requisite reporting and working relationships in the company, plus the proposed goals and objectives.

2. ***Posting and advertising the job.*** Determine how people will find out about the position. Are there potential internal candidates? Will you place an ad in a newspaper, run online ads, or solicit employee referrals? Finding good employees has become much easier with the advent of online job-listing services such as Career Builder (http://www.careerbuilder.com) and Monster.com (http://www.monster.com), as well as industry-specific sites, which are often managed by trade and professional associations.

3. ***Screening resumes and/or applications.*** A resume is a concise summary of an individual's education and work experience. When you post the opportunity, ask interested parties to send their resumes. Some online services permit you to screen resumes using keywords that will be important to your search. Other times, you might have an individual, team, or committee review all applicants against basic requirements. You then may want to have a secondary review to

---

[3]Jim Collins, *Good to Great: Why Some Companies Make the Leap...and Some Don't* (New York: HarperCollins Publishers, 2001), p. 13.

narrow the selection to the top three to five candidates, whom you will then interview.

4. *Assessing skills.* Identify pertinent skills and determine ways to assess them. For example, if a new employee is supposed to write grants, ask for the creation of a short document according to your specifications. For an administrative staff member, typing skills, as well as written communications and editing skills, may be required and can be tested using well-developed instruments. If a job requires measurement and math skills, both can be evaluated easily. It is far better to eliminate unqualified applicants early in the process rather than waste their time and yours. The time to find out if a candidate is capable is before the hiring rather than after.

It is critical to use the same process (such as a typing test) at the same stage in the interview for all applicants, to guard against the appearance of discrimination, especially vis-à-vis "protected classes." For example, if a typing test is given to administrative job applicants, it should be given to all applicants at the same stage (usually prior to the interview itself). It is also important to ensure that the assessment-instrument design could not be perceived as discriminatory. It is best to use instruments that have already been validated. Instruments that are not scientifically validated are potentially dangerous, because a protected-class applicant who is not hired because of a test score might have a valid case for legal action.

5. *Interviewing candidates.* Based on the resumes you receive, select several individuals to interview. Before any hiring, prepare an **interview guide**, a document to assist you or your interviewer in developing questions regarding an applicant's knowledge, skills, abilities, and interests. You will need to determine who will interview the candidates and whether the interviews will be performed one-on-one or by a panel of several interviewers together. There are many books, articles, and online resources that can guide you in creating a **behavioral interview**, which is designed to determine the fit of a prospective employee with the requirements of the position, using prior-experience examples. Remember, the candidate should be provided with the interview schedule in advance. **Exhibit 13-2** suggests the topics to cover in an interview. **Exhibit 13-3** provides some sample interview questions.

6. *Checking references.* Ask the candidates that interest you to provide at least three references from previous employers or others who could tell you about their character and work performance. Check them. Create a few questions that are pertinent to the job being filled and the related career paths. Include questions about how the candidate

interview guide a document to assist in question development regarding an individual's knowledge, skills, abilities, and interests.

behavioral interview a dialogue designed to determine the fit of a prospective employee with the requirements of a position, using prior-experience examples.

Exhibit 13-2 *Examples of Competencies That May Be Included in Job Interviews*

- General questions on skills and interests
- Teamwork
- Problem solving
- Communications
- Productivity/time management
- Customer service (internal or external customers)
- Interpersonal

Exhibit 13-3 *Sample Interview Questions*

General

- Could you share with us a recent accomplishment of which you are proud?
- What are your qualifications in this area of expertise; that is, what skills do you have that make you the best candidate for this position? Discuss any special training you have had (on-the-job, at college, continuing education, seminars, reading, etc.) and related work experience.
- Tell us about a personal or career goal that you have accomplished and why it was important to you.
- Why should we hire *you*?
- If you were offered this position, when would you be available to start?
- Tell us anything else you would like us to know about you that will help us make our decision.
- What questions would you like to ask us?

Teamwork

- How do you think the people you work with would describe you?
- Tell us about the most effective contribution you have made as part of a task group or special-project team.
- When groups work together, conflicts often emerge. Tell us about a time that conflict occurred in one of your work groups and what you did about it.

Problem Solving

- What was one of the toughest problems you ever solved? What steps did you take to solve it?
- How do you analyze the different options to determine which is the best alternative? Give an example of when you have done this.

Communications

- Describe a time when you were able to overcome a communication barrier.
- Give an example of how you consider your audience prior to communicating. What factors have influenced your communication style?

Productivity/Time Management

- When you have a lot of work to do, how do you get it all done? Give us an example.
- Describe a time you identified a barrier to your (and/or others') productivity and what you did about it.
- How do you determine the amount of time that is reasonable to complete a task? Please give an example.

Customer Service

- Who were your clients and how did you identify them?
- Tell us about a time when you went out of your way to give great service to a customer.
- Tell us about a time when you had trouble dealing with a difficult or demanding customer. How did you handle this?

Interpersonal

- Describe what you see as your strengths related to this job/position. Describe what you see as your weaknesses related to this job/position.
- Describe how you prefer to be managed, and the best relationship you've had with a previous boss/supervisor.
- What kind of people do you find most difficult to work with? Give an example of a situation where you had difficulties dealing with someone different from yourself. How did you handle it?
- What do you do when you know you are right and your manager disagrees with you? Give an example of this happening in your career.
- Describe a difficult time you have had dealing with an employee, customer, client, or co-worker. Why was it difficult? How did you handle it? What was the outcome?
- Describe a situation you wish that you had handled differently, based on the outcome. What would you change if faced with a similar situation?

Adapted from the Society for Human Resource Management, http://www.shrm.org, January 2, 2010.

and his or her reference know each other. One question that often provides critical insight (used only with former co-workers, managers/supervisors, and others with direct experience) is, "Would you rehire this individual?" Remember, some employers will only provide confirmation of former employees' dates of employment, so you might need to request additional references. Reference-check forms should be consistent, and ask the same questions for each candidate being considered for a particular position.

Some search firms and other potential employers will request an extensive list of references. For example, Diversified Search, a top headhunting firm in Philadelphia, routinely requests 10 references and completes 30-minute or longer interviews with each of them. By the time the recruiter has completed the reference-checking process, a comprehensive picture of the candidate will have emerged. Such an extensive process is reserved for the finalists in executive-level searches, but could be applied at whatever level you might deem helpful. The exercise of requesting so many references offers information in and of itself. Some candidates can send the complete list almost immediately, whereas others will have good reasons for not complying and simply vanish. One human resources professional tells the story of calling several references provided by a candidate—who looked excellent on paper and interviewed like a dream. Each and every reference told her to avoid hiring him at all costs. This story reinforces the grounds for checking references.

You also may want to call previous employers and see if you can interview each supervisor (be sure to get a release signed by the applicant). This vetting process is time-consuming, but it can prevent considerable trouble down the line. Consider the case of a small business that had found what seemed to be an ideal marketing manager, until it made reference checks and was repeatedly told to stay away from that individual for both legal and ethical reasons.

Whether you request a few or many references, be sure to contact them and ask sound, well-thought-out questions.

7. ***Negotiating compensation.*** You and the candidate you choose will have to negotiate how much you will pay, as well as any benefits the job includes, such as paid vacation, sick leave, and health insurance. You should have a clearly defined pay range for each position, and stay within it. Don't fall in love with a candidate you simply cannot afford. However, you also should be realistic about the compensation package you are offering. Benchmark your total package against that of other potential employers.

Recently, one top manager found himself in an untenable position. He had begun a search to fill a critical leadership slot, formed a search committee, advertised in professional journals and at conferences, had extensive two-day interview schedules for five finalists, received two recommendations from the committee, and threw out the search. He decided he needed a more experienced candidate and insisted on a second search. Committee members were outraged. They had found two fully qualified candidates based upon the position description and the charge given to them and the salary available. Some of the committee members participated in a second-round search, eventually making an offer to a candidate satisfactory to their manager. The candidate declined the offer. Again, the committee members conducted a search, with particular weight placed on meeting individuals at an annual professional conference. Round three also fell flat, because the salary to be offered was $25,000 to $35,000 too low to attract ideal candidates. The position has remained unfilled for almost two years while the search has dragged on; the compensation issue stands in the way, not to mention the frustration level of the search committee and the unfilled responsibilities of the job.

8. *Hiring.* After negotiating compensation, you will have additional work to complete before the new employee's start date. Some of these tasks include background checks, drug testing, offer letters, and physicals. The **job offer letter** is a formal, written invitation extended by an employer to a candidate selected for hiring that states basic employment terms such as the start date, the position being offered, the salary, the benefits start date, and other pertinent information. Employers typically have the candidate sign and return the letter to indicate acceptance and an understanding of what is being offered. A physical examination may be required, depending upon the physical demands of the job, and it must be performed after the offer has been accepted but prior to the start date.

job offer letter a formal, written invitation extended by an employer to a candidate selected for hiring that states basic employment terms, such as the starting date, the position offered, the salary, and so forth.

The nature and extent of a background check (including reference checking) will depend upon the specific position. It is good practice to do a basic background check, a criminal background check, and drug testing. The $50 or so investment in a criminal background check could save literally thousands of dollars. You do not want to be guilty of negligent hiring because you have ignored this precaution. A small, rural taxi service recently closed after the bad publicity generated by the arrest of one of its drivers on charges of assaulting an elderly passenger. The driver had a history of assaulting older women, and the company was held liable for putting him in a position in which he had the opportunity to commit another crime. In addition to criminal background checks, you may also want to examine official copies of college transcripts or high school diplomas and check previous employment history, such as positions held and dates of employment. If the job requires driving, a check with the state's department of motor vehicles is also appropriate.

Be certain to comply with all employment laws in carrying out these checks and investigations, and that you get signed release forms as required. Drug-test authorization and background-check release forms are typically provided as part of the employment application package, and should be completed prior to interviewing the candidate. Once you decide to hire someone, you will also have to complete tax and payroll forms and an I-9. The I-9 form must be completed on the first day of hire, to ensure that the employee is legally authorized to work in the United States.

9. *Orientation.* This is the process of introducing the employee to the company, including its mission and culture, and teaching him or her about the position. It can save you a great deal of money to have a printed employee manual that has passed legal review before you begin hiring. Orientation should be more than a brief talk about employee benefits and how to complete necessary forms, and more than reviewing the employee handbook. Ideally, orientation is an extensive process of helping a new employee understand the structure of the organization and its mission, facilitating meeting the other employees, and taking him or her through the various departments. Some companies, such as the innovative online financial institution ING Direct, require all new hires, regardless of position, to work in

customer service as part of orientation. Retail organizations may have all employees work on the floor or as a cashier or point-of-sales employee, to experience customer contact. What would you do to orient your employees?

Growing Your Team

Once you decide to add employees to your company, it could take considerable time and effort to identify and hire the right talent (as indicated by the section above). Even in times when the economy is weak and unemployment is high, qualified candidate pools may be thin. You might have to go out and find individuals to bring into your organization, rather than waiting for them to come to you. The less known your company is, or the more remote its location, the more likely it is that you will have to actively recruit candidates.

Companies plan and hire according to staffing requirements and budgets, and typically use a combination of internal recruiters (employees), outside recruiters (retained search firms or contingency search firms), and Internet job-board postings. Certainly, advertising and online postings may uncover strong candidates and eliminate the need for internal or external recruiters. However, from time to time, you may need to use either or both of them. If you are growing rapidly and are looking for a skilled, educated work force, or are hiring executives, recruitment may well be the key to successful hiring. Some ways to find the employees that fit your company include:

- *Campus recruiting.* Established companies from all industries visit college campuses every year to meet and scout students who are about to graduate. Firms in banking, consulting, accounting, consumer products, technology, health care, and other segments of the economy are all major recruiters on college campuses. Smaller employers also may attend job fairs and other recruitment events. Contact the career service offices of the colleges and universities of interest to find out about recruitment and internship possibilities.

- *Executive or retained searches.* When companies need to hire a senior executive, they may engage in an executive, or *retained*, search. These top job openings often are not advertised, and the process is frequently managed by a retained search firm. Executive search companies perform a full range of recruitment, screening, interviewing, and reference services. They will work with you to develop a detailed job profile and position description, and create a profile of the ideal candidate. In the end, though, you will decide which candidate to hire. Retained search firms are paid for searches regardless of whether they fill the position or not. Contingency searches are much like retained searches, but compensation is based upon finding a successful applicant.

Creating and Managing Organizational Culture

Performance Objective 3
Develop your organizational culture.

A primary role of the founding entrepreneur is to carry and convey the vision for the company and to foster its culture. The *culture* of an organization is the shared beliefs, values, and attitudes among employees—also referred to as "how things are done around here." The culture of an entrepreneurial firm can be its competitive advantage. As a company grows and adds employees, one challenge for an entrepreneur is to maintain the culture or to guide its evolution strategically. When culture is explicit and strategic, it is more readily conveyed through orientation and storytelling. Hewlett-Packard was famously recognized for stories told about its founder that conveyed and reinforced "the Hewlett-Packard way."

The culture that you create for your business should be a strategically developed translation of your vision and mission into norms, values, and behaviors. It should combine the best practices in business with the type of work environment you want the company to have. Your business will reflect the messages you send. Consciously or not, employees take their cues from their managers. For better or worse, what you say and do (or don't do) telegraphs messages to your team.

Culture is not an isolated aspect of your business, rather a combination of its parts. Company culture incorporates qualities of integrity; diversity; concern for society, community, employees, and customers; quality of products and/or services; and mission. For many companies today, this includes a focus on the balance between work and family life and the need for a positive, enjoyable environment.

Determining Organizational Structure

As you create and grow your company, you will change its organizational structure to meet your evolving requirements. Initially, you may be handling all the responsibilities yourself. Or, you may start out with a founding team that serves as a centralized locus of control, with team members serving in multiple roles. With growth comes a need for specialization, delegation, supervision, and management. Whereas a relatively "flat" organization may work with a small staff and ready communications, as the number of employees increases, so must the organizational structure. Often, the most difficult transition for a founding entrepreneur is the one from entrepreneur to entrepreneurial manager—but making it will be a critical success factor for growth.

A number of organizational structures may be viable for emerging companies. The evolutionary process for a business involves moving from one stage of maturity and structure to another. This process is not defined by time. A five-year-old company could be a nascent business. It is not strictly defined by the number of employees, either, but communications, control, and coordination are primary drivers. With emerging structural changes, companies often evolve from simple **line organizations**, in which each person reports to one supervisor, to **line and staff organizations** that also include specialists, such as attorneys, who assist in the management. Managerial **spans of control**, or the number of direct reports, become more defined, and the **chain of command**, or hierarchy of reporting and communications, is more distinct. A management organizational chart for a typical small business might look like **Figure 13-1**.

◀ **Performance Objective 4**
Determine your organizational structure.

line organization a structure where each person reports to a single supervisor.

line and staff organization a structure that includes the line organization, plus staff specialists (such as lawyers) who assist management.

span of control the number of direct reports to a manager or supervisor.

chain of command hierarchy of communication and authority.

Figure 13-1 *Management Organizational Chart*

FRED-CITY RECORDS, INC.

PRESIDENT
Fred Xavier

| **PRODUCTION** Vice President Gina Arnold | **MARKETING** Vice President Chris Morales | **SERVICE** Vice President Tony Arsenio | **FINANCE** Vice President Jorge Esteban |

Whatever organizational structure you choose for your company at each stage of its growth, it should be a strategic design based upon the needs of the business. Be careful not to create a hodgepodge of positions in a convoluted structure in order to keep people who do not fit.

Getting the Best Out of Your Employees

When you do hire people, treat them fairly and with appropriate regard. As noted in a previous section, a culture of respect for individuals, diversity, and a balance of work and family will create an environment that affirms the value of employees. People who feel valued are likely to go the extra mile for their employers. In addition to creating a strong, positive culture, many companies give their employees ownership through shares of corporate stock, thereby entitling them to participate in the company's success, or they offer various incentives to reward positive performance.

Follow these basic guidelines to be a good employer:

- Get the right people. Taking the time and effort to get the right people in the right jobs is at least half the battle. This means getting to understand each employee's knowledge, skills, abilities, interests, and character traits.
- Provide a competitive salary and superior working conditions.
- Share your vision for the company and create an environment that encourages buy-in.
- Give employees incentives to work effectively. Ensure that the incentives match the company's goals and objectives and do not skew results.
- Empower employees by giving them control over their work.
- Provide career opportunities and training and development.
- Communicate expectations and goals clearly and provide ongoing feedback and recognition.

Human Resources Fundamentals

Performance Objective 5
Understand the functions of human resources management.

human resources the segment of a business that hires, trains, and develops a company's employees.

Human resources is the department of a company that is responsible for staffing, training and development, compensation and benefits, employee relations, and organizational development. Human resources is commonly referred to as HR, human capital, casting (Disney's term), or personnel.

For a business just starting out, it may not be practical to have a director of human resources, as the entrepreneur will handle these tasks. A business will probably not need a full-time human resources professional until it has 20 or more employees.

Regardless of how many, once you have employees, there will be human resources functions to be managed. For companies of sufficient size, each of the following areas might represent one or more full-time jobs in the HR department:

- *Compensation and payroll.* This addresses such issues as the level of wages and base salary, bonuses, sales commissions, stock grants, stock options, other forms of compensation, and the issuance of payroll and associated taxes (although the payroll is often a finance function).
- *Benefits.* Full-time employees expect to be provided an array of paid benefits—and opportunities to purchase discounted benefits—as part of their compensation package. Basics may include health insurance

Step into the Shoes...

Malden Mills—Leadership and Ethics

In 1906, a Hungarian immigrant named Henry Feuerstein built a textile mill, Malden Mills Industries, Inc., outside of Boston. The business was passed down to Henry's grandson, Aaron. Malden Mills invented and marketed a unique fabric, called Polartec; it was a lightweight, warm, and durable fleece made from recycled plastics. Malden Mills used Polartec to manufacture jackets, vests, and other outerwear garments. In 1999, *Time* recognized Polartec as one of the top inventions of the century.

In the meantime, many manufacturing businesses had relocated overseas or to Mexico, where labor and production costs were lower. But Malden Mills kept its operations firmly planted in Massachusetts. Aaron Feuerstein had been raised by his father and grandfather to value his workers and to treat them with respect. As Feuerstein explained, "We have a mission of responsibility to both shareholders and our top asset: our employees. We're not prepared to skip town for cost savings."

Late in 1995, a devastating fire broke out at the Malden Mills plant and most of the factory burned to the ground. The 3,000 employees feared that their jobs had been destroyed. Instead, Feuerstein announced that he would rebuild the factory buildings and vowed to use the insurance money to continue paying his employees with full benefits until the plant was back in business.

It took Feuerstein months to rebuild, and it cost millions of dollars to fulfill the promise he had made to his employees. "I consider our workers an asset, not an expense," he explained. "I have a responsibility to the workers, both blue-collar and white-collar. I have an equal responsibility to the community. It would have been unconscionable to put 3,000 people on the streets and deliver a deathblow to the cities of Lawrence and Methuen. Maybe on paper our company is worth less to Wall Street, but I can tell you it is worth more."[4]

(including the employee's family), life and AD&D (accidental death & dismemberment) insurance, paid holidays, vacation and sick time, and retirement savings plans. Other options may include tuition reimbursement, disability, and insurance discounts (such as automobile), long-term care, and pet health insurance. HR usually leads the process of selecting the benefits programs that the company makes available.

- *Organizational development.* The HR team plays a pivotal role in organizational development, particularly with respect to organizational structure, employee retention, and succession planning.

- *Education and development.* Even senior executives require professional-development education from time to time. Human resources managers develop employee training in-house, and may also use outside training providers for specific situations.

- *Labor law and HR compliance.* The United States has well-developed laws to protect the rights of employees. Everyone involved in hiring, firing, and managing people needs to be aware of both the letter and the spirit of these laws, which are typically translated into policies by the HR and legal teams at a company. As the business grows and you hire employees, you will have to become familiar with the laws and tax issues affecting employment. Some of the laws and tax issues of concern include:

  - **Payroll tax,** a series of wage taxes based on earnings that will be deducted from your employees' pay.

  - The **Equal Pay Act of 1963** requires employers to pay men and women the same amount for substantially equal work.

payroll tax a given percentage of money that employers deduct from their employees' pay and forward to the designated governmental entity.

BizFact

Many companies staff their human resources units using a ratio of one human resources executive per 50 to 200 employees.

---

[4]Articles and press releases featured on the former Malden Mills Web site. See http://www.polartec.com/about/corporate.php.

- The **Fair Labor Standards Act** was passed in 1938 and requires that employees receive at least the federally mandated minimum wage. It also prohibits hiring anyone under the age of 16 full time. Minimum-wage information must be posted where it is visible.

- **Title VII of the Civil Rights Act of 1964** prohibits discrimination against applicants and employees on the basis of race or color, religion, sex, pregnancy, or national origin, including membership in a Native American tribe. It also prohibits harassment based on any protected characteristics, such as those listed here, and prohibits employer retaliation against those who assert their rights under the Act.

- The **Age Discrimination in Employment Act (ADEA)** prohibits discrimination against and harassment of employees aged 40 or older. Employers may not retaliate against those who assert their rights under the act.

- The **Americans with Disabilities Act (ADA)** prohibits employers from discriminating against a person who has a disability, or who is perceived to have a disability, in any aspect of employment. It also prohibits discrimination against or refusal to hire someone related to or an associate of someone with a disability. ADA prohibits harassment and retaliation in the cases above.

- The **Immigration Reform and Control Act (IRCA) of 1986** prohibits employers from discriminating against applicants or employees on the basis of their citizenship or national origin. In addition, it affirms that it is illegal for employers to knowingly hire or retain in employment individuals who are not authorized to work in the United States.

Performance Management

performance appraisal
the formal process used to evaluate and support employee performance.

Just as you want to take the time to develop job specifications and position descriptions and follow best practices in hiring, you can maintain and build your team through appraisal and thorough follow-up. Although it has a tradition of being dreaded, a **performance appraisal**, the formal process used to evaluate and support employee performance, is valuable for both employees and employers when done well. It is an opportunity to set goals, assess progress, identify opportunities for improvement, plan for individual growth and development, and provide performance feedback. Done poorly, the process is a waste of time and energy at best and counterproductive at worst.

The key to valuable performance appraisal is planning and consistency. Be clear about the purpose of the evaluation and create a system for it. Clearly, nothing in an appraisal process should come as a surprise for anyone involved if performance feedback is discussed routinely and course corrections are made throughout the year. Good channels of communication will make a performance-appraisal procedure work more fluidly.

Performance appraisal is an opportunity to communicate goals, establish training and development needs, and provide feedback to increase productivity and employee retention. An effective process will also link performance to pay, which will help create a high-accomplishment culture in which superior performers earn higher pay increases than lower ones. It also can help to protect a company against lawsuits by employees that have been fired, demoted, or not given a pay raise. Appraisals provide formal documentation for specific discussions on performance that can be used for any of these purposes.

There are multiple methods of implementing performance appraisal, and these often vary according to the size and culture of an organization. A condensed version of the supervisor/manager portion of a performance review form appears in **Exhibit 13-4**. There are numerous variations on the forms used and the style of presentation. Consulting any of the many books on human resources, or visiting the Society for Human Resource Management (http://www.shrm.org), should provide ample information.

Exhibit 13-4 *Sample Performance Review Form—Supervisor/Manager Portion*

Name: _____   Date of Review: _____

Period Under Review: _____   Department: _____

Part A. Success Factors

Factors	Rating					Comments
I. KEY RESPONSIBILITIES FOR THIS POSITION						
Performs key responsibilities as articulated in the job description *(insert each essential function from the position description).*	1	2	3	4	5	
II. CORE COMPETENCIES						
1. Inclusiveness (defined in greater detail)	1	2	3	4	5	
2. Problem solving / decision making	1	2	3	4	5	
3. Planning and organizing	1	2	3	4	5	
4. Communication	1	2	3	4	5	
5. Quality focus	1	2	3	4	5	
6. Leadership	1	2	3	4	5	
7. Teamwork	1	2	3	4	5	
8. Department-specific competency	1	2	3	4	5	

Part B. Last Period's Goals

Rate the progress made on each of the goals established at the beginning of the period and new goals. Note any modifications to the original goals.

Goal	Rating					Comments
1. (specify as many goals as are appropriate for the employee)	1	2	3	4	5	
2.	1	2	3	4	5	
3.	1	2	3	4	5	

	Rating					Comments
OVERALL RATING (based on Parts A and B)	1	2	3	4	5	

Part C. Next Period's Goals

Enter the performance goals for the next period to be evaluated.

1. Measure of success:
2. Measure of success:
3. Measure of success:

Progress toward meeting these goals will be reviewed at the time of the next evaluation.

(continued)

Exhibit 13-4 *(Continued)*

Part D. Professional Development Plan

Signatures:

Employee: Date: _____

My signature indicates that I have received a copy of this evaluation.

_____ I would like to include comments from my self-assessment.

Manager/Supervisor Name: _____

Signature: _____   Date: _____

Department Manager Name: _____

Signature: _____   Date: _____

Firing and Laying Off Employees

Sometimes you hire someone and it just does not work out, even after repeated attempts to fix the problems. If you have to let someone go, you should document the reasons as they occur. You can be sued for wrongful termination or breach of contract, if an employee believes he or she was fired for no good reason. The rules for termination vary from state to state, so it is essential to know your state's law.

- Protect your company from wrongful-termination claims by conducting regular employee-performance reviews. Use performance-improvement or development plans to give the employee an opportunity to fix those aspects of performance that are subpar.

- If an employee is violating rules, give notification in writing (and keep a copy for your records) and work on corrections as the problems arise, rather than waiting for a performance review. If performance continues to be unsatisfactory and you have to let the employee go, you will have documentation that there were problems with his or her performance. Be very careful to keep a written record of the problem as it develops, not to editorialize or speculate about the employee.

Sometimes you might have to *lay off* employees. They may have performed their jobs well, but you either no longer need their skills or cannot

---

Global Impact...

Human Resources Service Firms

Many companies, large and small, are dedicated to providing human resources services to corporate clients around the globe. Here is how some leading firms got started: Adecco was founded in 1957, when Henri-Ferdinand Lavanchy, an accountant at the time, was asked by a client to help him fill a position. Today, Adecco provides staffing services to 250,000 clients around the world. In 1969, Lester Korn and Richard Ferry started a recruitment firm with a $10,000 investment. Having grown to over $650 million in revenue, Korn/Ferry International specializes in helping clients hire top executives, including CEOs. When companies have thousands of employees, the task of getting paychecks out twice a month can be daunting. Payroll provider Automatic Data Processing Inc. (ADP) cuts checks for over 50 million people on behalf of its clients. ADP was started by Henry Taub in 1949, when he was 22. The company had eight clients and $2,000 in revenue in its first year.

afford to continue paying them. To minimize complications, if you can do so, offer employees **severance**, pay that is continued for a limited time as compensation for being let go, and make serious efforts to help them find new employment.

Ethical Leadership and Ethical Organizations

True leadership is more than the components described previously. It is all of the actions and attributes that have been noted, plus the personal values underlying them. **Ethics** are a system of principles that define a code of behavior to distinguish between good and bad or right and wrong. The Golden Rule, "Do unto others as you would have others do unto you," is a well-known and widely accepted ethic. A behavior may be legal and still not be ethical.

Ethical business behavior is not only moral, but it also makes good business sense. Have you ever bought something from a store and felt as if you were cheated? How did you react? Did you want to go back? Probably not. You may have even told your friends about the experience. The store lost more than just one customer.

An Ethical Perspective

For a business, ethics are individual and organizational moral principles applied to actions and issues within the business context. In order to create an organization that is ethical, the values and standards of conduct must be clearly and broadly understood and accepted. Each substantive decision made has an ethical component, although sometimes the right thing to do is so evident to everyone that many choices are virtually automatic.

However, the right thing to do is not always easy to determine. Often the choice is not between right and wrong, but rather between partially right and partially wrong, so that making a choice is difficult at best. There is sometimes a gray area between right and wrong that cannot be clarified by relying on individuals to simply "know what's right."

Establishing Ethical Standards

One of the best ways to create an ethical business is to codify the fundamental rules of the game. Whereas the underlying values provide a basis for ethical behavior, clear, written guidelines can create a firmer foundation and more consistent implementation. Many companies create a code of ethics, a code of conduct, or a code of ethics and business conduct. A **code of ethics** is the statement of the values of a company. A **code of conduct** is a set of official standards of employee behavior. A **code of ethics and business conduct** combines the written statement of values with the official standards of employee behavior. By creating, disseminating, and establishing employee buy-in, a business will have empowered employees, meaning they can make decisions and take action on their own, with a core set of ethical norms and rules for action.

A code of conduct can help to eliminate the problem of **ethical relativism**, which arises when ethical standards are believed to be subject to interpretation. It can also help to prevent or resolve **ethical dilemmas**, which are situations in which employees do not have a clear choice. By clarifying which actions should and should not be taken, many of the gray areas that invite confusion are eliminated. One general recommendation is that organizations need to put into place a documented procedure

severance pay that is continued for a limited time upon separation from a company.

◀ **Performance Objective 6**
Pursue ethical leadership to build an ethical organization.

ethics a system of moral conduct and judgment that helps determine right and wrong.

code of ethics a statement of the values of a company.

code of conduct a set of official standards of employee behavior for a company.

code of ethics and business conduct a combination of a written statement of values with official standards of employee behavior.

ethical relativism the belief that ethical standards are open to interpretation.

ethical dilemma a circumstance in which there is a conflict of ethical values, which thus muddies decision making.

Exhibit 13-5 *Six Pillars of Character: Ethical Values*

Value	Actualized Form
Trustworthiness	Honesty, integrity, reliability (promise-keeping), loyalty
Respect	Civility, courtesy, decency, dignity, autonomy, tolerance, acceptance
Responsibility	Accountability, pursuit of excellence, self-restraint
Caring	Concern for others, compassion, benevolence, altruism
Fairness	Process (open and impartial), impartiality, equity
Citizenship	Law abiding, volunteerism, environmental awareness, action

Six Pillars of Character® adapted from the Josephson Institute of Ethics, http://josephsoninstitute.org, January 25, 2010. Six Pillars of Character is a registered trademark of the Josephson Institute. Used by permission.

for dealing with ethical challenges. This document will contain a basic method, with a multistep process of asking key questions, to get at the best answer with regard to ethical considerations. It should be customized for your company and the real scenarios that have arisen or that could be expected to occur.

A comprehensive list of all potential ethical values would be quite long, but they are neatly summarized in the Six Pillars of Character, as described in **Exhibit 13-5**.

By selecting six to ten of these actualized concepts, you can develop a core value set and create a code of conduct that specifies the actions that are in alignment with the values. For example, if impartiality is critical, the code of ethics might require that employees refrain from accepting personal gifts from stakeholders, such as vendors.

As with any standards, a code of ethics and business conduct is only as good as its practice. There have to be appropriate rewards for compliance, and consequences for breaches of ethics, in order to have a viable code of ethics. What happens to an employee who takes company funds? What if an employee consistently takes extra-long lunches, comes in later than scheduled, or leaves early? What if he takes home pens and paper? What if she goes on Facebook or eHarmony during working hours?

Corporate Ethical Scandals

The issue of business ethics exploded in 2002 when several large corporations were found to have published inaccurate financial statements. The false numbers had made the companies look so good that they were some of the most highly recommended stock picks on Wall Street.

Top executives at Enron, WorldCom-MCI, Tyco, Global Crossing, and other well-known firms had inflated corporate earnings so that they would receive huge bonuses, while misleading shareholders and employees. When the truth came out, public confidence in the stock market plummeted along with stock prices. Investors lost millions.

One of the companies, the energy giant Enron, had strongly encouraged its own employees to invest their retirement funds in company stock, even while top executives knew the worth of that stock was based on false numbers. These employees had their life savings wiped out by the unethical behavior of the executives.

Enron collapsed, and thousands of employees lost their jobs and saw their pensions reduced to nothing. Tyco was split into four different companies. Its CEO was forced to resign when it was learned that he had used company money to buy an $18 million apartment in Manhattan and furnish it with expensive artwork, among other egregious abuses.

The scandals of 2002 were a failure of **corporate governance**, meaning that these companies did not have rules and safeguards in place to ensure that executives behaved legally and ethically. Even at an early stage in developing your business, you must think about how you will guarantee that your company remains both ethical and legal as it grows. Some basics of corporate governance include:

- ***Do not treat company profits as personal funds.*** Haphazardly taking business profits for your own use is a bad habit. Decide on a wage or salary you will pay yourself and always document this, as well as your business expenses. You should enjoy the rewards of a successful venture, but you need to be careful to do it ethically and legally. In particular, **tax evasion**, which is trying to avoid paying taxes through illegal or deceptive means, is to be avoided.

- ***Keep accurate records.*** Have your business records checked once a year by a professional accountant. By the time your company becomes a multimillion-dollar corporation, you will have established a reputation for honest financial reporting.

- ***Use financial controls.*** This will help to eliminate the potential for embezzlement, which is the crime of stealing money from a company. Once you have employees, use such simple financial controls as:

  - Always have two people open the mail, so no one is tempted to take company checks.

  - Arrange for yourself and one other person to be required to sign all checks sent out by the business. Using a double signature will ensure that no one can use the company money for personal expenses.

  - Implement a cash-counting and control system, if employees will be handling cash.

- ***Create an advisory board.*** Ask businesspeople and other community leaders you respect to be on your **advisory board** or **advisory council**. This group of people will provide you with sound, ethical business advice without having the responsibilities of a board of directors. Choose the members carefully, and listen to what they have to say.

corporate governance
rules and safeguards to ensure that executives behave legally and ethically.

tax evasion the deliberate avoidance of an obligation to pay taxes; may lead to penalties or imprisonment.

advisory board or **council** a group that provides advice and counsel, but does not have the responsibilities of a board of directors.

Doing the Right Thing in Addition to Doing Things Right

As a business, ethical practices involve doing the right things and doing them ethically. There is a potential conflict between strategic priorities and ethical behavior. Profit maximization is one of the most common challenges to ethical behavior. By harming the environment, using substandard components, or cutting corners, a company can maximize its short-term profitability. A clearly defined and commonly shared code of ethics and business conduct can go a long way toward incorporating ethical decision making into strategic priorities. This will facilitate incorporating the right thing into company strategy from the start, thereby avoiding ethical conflicts.

Balancing the Needs of Owners, Customers, and Employees

Although it may seem simple and straightforward to retain your integrity, it can become more complex as you add partners, customers, and employees to the equation. People's moral compasses do not always point in the same direction. What seems just, right, and fair to one person may seem unjust, unfair, and wrong to another. Often, this is caused by the conflicting needs of owners, customers, and employees.

Owners face multiple pressures, such as the need to have their businesses survive, the repayment of debts, and the welfare of employees. Customers need products and services that meet expectations. Employees need to earn a living wage and experience job satisfaction. On the surface, this should not pose ethical challenges.

However, as each constituency strives to meet its needs, ethical dilemmas may arise. As a business owner, for example, you may have to make a choice between paying a vendor in accordance with the credit terms or as otherwise promised, and having sufficient cash to cover the employee payroll. Or, you might have to choose between paying a vendor for critical production materials or paying withholding taxes to the federal government. Making a choice between the two would certainly be an ethical dilemma. Who would you make wait for the money? Or, imagine yourself as an employee that has to make a choice between reporting illegal pollution by your employer, which could close down the company and result in your unemployment, or turning a blind eye to the situation to keep your family housed and fed. The short-term interest of both the company and the employee in the above examples would be to act unethically.

Or, envision the customer that benefits from a company's mistake and has to decide what to do. Have you ever been given too much change for a purchase or had an item left off a bill? You benefit and the company loses. On the flip side, a company may overcharge, double-bill, or somehow provide less than promised. Then you lose and the company benefits. The relationship between a company and its customers is fraught with potential ethical challenges.

Social Responsibility and Ethics

Performance Objective 7 ▶

Incorporate social responsibility into your company.

corporate social responsibility the ethical obligation of a company to its community.

social entrepreneurship the sale of products or services on a for-profit basis to benefit a social purpose.

in-kind donation a contribution of products or services that may include time, rather than cash.

Ethics, corporate social responsibility, and social entrepreneurship are three related topics that are often conflated. **Corporate social responsibility** is the ethical obligation of a company to its community. **Social entrepreneurship** is the sale of products and/or services on a for-profit basis to benefit a societal mission. Both have ethical components and can be of value to entrepreneurial firms.

Companies exhibit their commitment to the communities they serve through a variety of means and with varying motivations. Some examples of this are financial contributions to not-for-profit community organizations, supporting volunteerism, and in-kind donations. An **in-kind donation** is a contribution of products or services, including employee time, rather than cash. Companies can also show this commitment through the payment of livable wages and the provision of safe and sanitary working conditions. Another aspect of corporate social responsibility is to be sure to make any financial investment in only ethical and legal ventures in countries with human rights values in alignment with the company's ethics. Environmental friendliness is another way of demonstrating community care. For example, Peninsula Regional Medical

Center, on the Eastern Shore of Maryland, is working toward becoming eco-friendly and energy efficient.

Leading with Integrity and Examples

Leading by example is the best way to command the attention and respect of others. If you refuse to accept inferior goods, your employees will, too. If you give voice and form to company values and demonstrate integrity, the workplace will become and remain a community of stakeholders that values integrity, honesty, and open communication. Modeling the behavior you desire is an excellent route to attaining the desired results.

Encourage Your Employees to Be Socially Responsible

Early in the twentieth century, Madam C. J. Walker motivated her employees by encouraging them to get involved in helping their communities; in the process, she became the first African American millionaire. There are many ways that entrepreneurs can use their businesses to contribute to society. By being an entrepreneur, you have already made an important contribution by providing goods or services to consumers in your area who need them. You can also use your business to support social issues that are important to you. By running your company in a way that is consistent with your ethics and core values, you will develop a socially responsible business.

Ways to make your business socially responsible include:

- recycling paper, glass, and plastic;
- donating a portion of your profits to a charity;
- refusing to use animal testing on products;
- offering employees incentives to volunteer in the community;
- establishing a safe and healthy workplace.

sustainable scenario in which current needs are met while preserving future resources.

You can also emphasize being a **sustainable** business, as you ensure meeting the Earth's current needs while preserving resources for future generations.

Global Impact . . .

Mohammad Yunus and Grameen Bank: Banker to the Poor

Mohammad Yunus, Nobel Peace Prize winner, social entrepreneur, and "banker to the poor," has used his enterprising spirit to foster entrepreneurship and lift literally millions of people out of poverty. As he describes his activities: "I did something that challenged the banking world. Conventional banks look for the rich; we look for the absolutely poor. All people are entrepreneurs, but many don't have the opportunity to find out."

Grameen Bank, founded in Bangladesh in 1976, became an official bank in 1983, and is largely owned by its borrowers. As of November 2009, Grameen Bank had disbursed $8.65 billion and had $7.95 million in loans outstanding, from a population distributed across 83,453 villages, served by 2,562 branches, with a staff of 23,311. Fully 97 percent of the borrowers are women. The stated mission of Grameen Bank is to assist borrowers' families in rising above the poverty line, and Grameen reports that 68 percent of them have done so.

The basis of Grameen Bank's relationship with its borrowers is a core set of values explicitly stated in its Sixteen Decisions. Grameen has found a way to flip conventional banking knowledge on its head. For Grameen Bank, credit is perceived as a human right, not a benefit for the wealthy. Its branches are distributed across rural areas, bringing the bank to the people.

In 2002, Grameen created its Struggling Members Programme, targeted at beggars. This initiative has encouraged people to give up begging and make a living as door-to-door salespeople. As of November 2009, nearly 20,000 of the 112,000 who joined the program had left begging. About 10 percent of the program members became members of mainstream Grameen groups, and 76 percent of the funds disbursed have been repaid.

Source: Grameen Bank Web site, http://www.grameen-info.org/, January 10, 2010.

Chapter Summary

Now that you have studied this chapter, you can do the following:

1. Identify leadership styles.
   - A leader is someone who has the confidence and energy to do things on his or her own.
   - Leadership comes from self-esteem. If you believe in yourself, you can do things with confidence and you will inspire confidence in others.
   - Leaders learn how to manage their time so they can get more done.
2. Describe the 10 basic tasks handled by managers.
   - Planning: strategic, tactical, and operational
   - Organizing
   - Leading
   - Directing
   - Staffing
   - Controlling
   - Coordinating
   - Representing
   - Innovating
   - Motivating
3. Recruit your employees.
   - Define the job.
   - Post the job.
   - Screen resumes and/or applications.
   - Assess required skills.
   - Interview candidates.
   - Check references and other background information.
   - Negotiate compensation.
   - Hire a candidate.
   - Orient the new employee.
4. Develop your organizational culture.
   - The culture of a company is the shared beliefs, values, and attitudes among employees.
   - The entrepreneur can strategically determine the culture.
   - Cultures vary, from entrepreneurial to administrative.
   - There are a multitude of cultural components that are conveyed through words, actions, and structures.
5. Determine your organizational structure.
   - Structure evolves as the company grows and changes.
   - The transition from entrepreneur to entrepreneurial manager is often difficult.
   - There are different organizational stages related to the maturation of the company.
6. Understand the functions of human resources management.
   - Compensation and payroll
   - Benefits administration

- Organizational development
- Education and development
- Labor law and HR compliance
- Performance of appraisal and review
- Human resources strategy
- Firing and laying off employees

7. Pursue ethical leadership to build an ethical organization.
   - View decisions through an ethical lens.
   - Establish ethical standards.
   - Build ethical employer/employee relationships.

8. Incorporate social responsibility into your company.
   - Encourage environmentalism.
   - Support charitable efforts.
   - Maintain a safe and healthy workplace.
   - Consider sustainability throughout the organization.

Key Terms

advisory board or council	job offer letter
behavioral interview	job profile
chain of command	leader
code of conduct	line organization
code of ethics	line and staff organization
code of ethics and business conduct	payroll tax
corporate governance	performance appraisal
corporate social responsibility	position description
ethical dilemma	recruitment
ethical relativism	severance
ethics	social entrepreneurship
human resources	span of control
in-kind donation	sustainable
interview guide	tax evasion

Entrepreneurship Portfolio

Critical Thinking Exercises

1. Will you be hiring employees during your first year of operations? If so, name their positions and describe the required qualifications, anticipated compensation, and how they will help your business.
2. How can managers make a business a positive and rewarding place to work?
3. Why is establishing job profiles and position descriptions before recruiting important?
4. What are the benefits of a well-executed performance-appraisal process?
5. Describe the components of an organizational culture that you would find appealing.

6. What are the characteristics of an organizational culture that you would find unappealing?

7. Describe three leaders you admire. What characteristics do you most admire about them and why?

8. Consider ways that you might find 10 additional hours in your weekly schedule to manage your business. Create a weekly time-management schedule for yourself reflecting this activity.

9. Fill out a PERT chart for your business or one that you can imagine, or use Microsoft Project or other software package to do the same thing.

10. Thinnow Corporation, an entrepreneurial venture, has developed a weight-loss drug, Fatgo. After an intense FDA review and approval process, Thinnow has received permission to market Fatgo. Testing had shown that there may be serious (even deadly) side effects to consumers of Fatgo. A warning label is being provided. Identify the legal and ethical issues in this case.

Key Concept Questions

1. How old does someone have to be before he or she can work full time in the United States?

2. What is one kind of tax employers have to pay for employees?

3. Can you legally fire an employee if you have an argument about religion?

4. What is an interview guide? What are the critical components of an interview guide?

5. What are the 10 functions of management? Why are they important?

6. What are antidiscrimination laws? What protections do they include?

7. Compare and contrast two leadership styles as identified in this chapter.

8. What is a code of conduct? What are its potential benefits?

9. What is the relationship between social responsibility and ethics?

Application Exercises

1. What qualities and qualifications would you look for in employees for your business? List five and explain why they are the most important to you.

2. What would push you to fire an employee? List five reasons that you believe would justify termination. Describe how you would handle the firing.

3. Visit a local brick-and-mortar business (not a Web site) where you buy products or services. Go through your shopping experience as you normally would. Once you have left the premises, describe its culture.

4. Identify a business leader, preferably an entrepreneur. Describe his or her leadership style based upon at least two public sources (excluding any wikis, such as Wikipedia) and give examples to support your conclusion.

5. Keep track of the direct opportunities to decide whether to act ethically/unethically and/or legally/illegally that arise during a 48-hour period. What, if anything, surprises you about the list?

6. Choose three things you would plan to do to run a socially responsible business. Explain why you made the selections you did.

Exploring Online

1. Visit the Web site for a U.S. state, or use another reliable source, to identify the antidiscrimination laws in that state. What form(s) of discrimination do they prohibit? When were they enacted? To which organizations (type and size) do they apply?

2. Search the Internet for two position descriptions from different businesses. Make a chart identifying which of the following are included: job title, job summary, duties to be performed, nature of supervision, and the job's relation to others in the company. How might each description be improved?

3. Using an online search engine, find a company that practices corporate social responsibility and answer the following:

   - Which values are important?
   - How are these values translated into action?
   - Are the values shared broadly within the company, or are they primarily those of the president/CEO?

In Your Opinion

Discuss with a group: Should an employer be able to fire an employee if the latter is often ill? Before the discussion, prepare by searching the Internet to determine the legal issues that may be involved.

BizBuilder Business Plan Questions

6.0 Management and Operations

6.1 Management Team

A. Create an organizational chart for your business.

B. Will you be hiring employees? If so, describe what their qualifications should be, what you intend to pay them, and how they will help your business.

C. Do you intend to pay yourself a salary, wage, dividend, or commission? Explain.

D. What will your policies toward employees be? How will you make your organization a positive and rewarding place to work?

E. Describe the corporate governance plan for your organization. It should include five policies (rules) that will be the backbone of your organization's ethics.

F. Provide information for each of your mentors or advisors. If there is a board of advisors, list each member and describe his/her commitment to the board.

Appendices

Resumes and Position Descriptions

A. Include a resume for each key team member.

B. Add position descriptions for any vital start-up positions that are not yet filled.

If At First You Don't Succeed—Enablemart Learns a Valuable Lesson

Nick Tostenrude and Dennis Mouton founded Enablemart when they were freshmen at the University of Portland to bring rehabilitation software—developed by Dennis's father—to market. Founded in 1999 as Mindnautilus.com, and incorporated in 2000, Nick and Dennis soon discovered that their original business concept was not viable, and switched to making computers that were accessible to people with disabilities. This became a niche market to be served by Enablemart, which began marketing assistive technologies in 2001. Enablemart (enablemart.com) grew to become the world leader in assistive technology, with 14 employees and $9 million in annual sales in the United States, and a subsidiary in the United Kingdom (TechReady.co.uk), at the time of its acquisition by Manufacturers Resource Network in 2007.

The path from the dorm room to the boardroom was not always smooth. Creating an advisory board with numerous industry pioneers went relatively well. However, Enablemart needed someone with credibility and access to capital. For Nick and Dennis, local entrepreneurial events provided networking opportunities and led to finding a candidate. Nick said, "We couldn't have asked for a better person to have in our corner." They found an individual who was older, appeared to have experienced success as an entrepreneur, and had a passion for the work.

The next step was to secure an employment contract. The founders were pleased that the candidate offered to provide a contract that he had used previously. The contract was daunting, but Nick and Dennis trusted their new colleague. Nick later wrote, "We were a bit thrown back, but this individual seemed trustworthy because, after all, he believed in our idea. So we signed the contract and celebrated hiring our new chairperson."

This new chairperson was active for a couple of months, helping to find an excellent CFO, and then he gradually stopped working and communicating with Nick and Dennis. Lawyers reviewed the employment contract and, after they stopped laughing at how ludicrous it was, explained that the best thing to do was to avoid accomplishing the things that would trigger payouts to this individual. The contract

(Meeyoung Son/Alamy)

included giving him a portion of stock with a nondilution clause, and an option that permitted him to sell it to anyone he wanted at any time. Whenever they raised capital, he would receive substantial compensation. There was no way to hold him accountable for poor performance because his job duties were so unclear. On top of all of these issues, rather than signing the agreement on behalf of the corporation, the founders had signed it personally.

Instead of continuing to pursue the high-growth strategy and raising significant capital as they had planned, Nick and Dennis again revised their game plan. They knew that investors would avoid them as long as the chairperson's contract hung over them. After two years of a slow-growth strategy, fueled primarily with funds from friends and family, Enablemart bought out the contract for $20,000 and terminated the contract, ending the protracted agony of their first executive hiring experience.

Case Study Analysis

1. Enablemart's founders created a board of advisors early in the life of the company. How might they have taken advantage of the advisors' counsel when hiring their chairperson?

2. Name at least three steps that Nick and Dennis could have taken to avoid the dreadful experience they had with their first executive hire.

3. What are the implications of signing an employment contract personally, rather than as a representative of a corporation?

4. Nick and Dennis sought legal counsel when their chairperson simply stopped working and they had to slow down their growth plans. Comment on how you think this affected them and the company.

Case Sources

Nick Tostenrude, "Turning 25¢ into $1: The Unique Advantages and Disadvantages of Being Young Entrepreneurs," in *Student Entrepreneurs: 14 Undergraduate All-Stars Tell Their Stories*, compiled by Michael McMyne and edited by Nicole Amare (Nashville: Premium Press America, 2003).

Profile of Nick Tostenrude on http://www.LinkedIn.com, January 4, 2010.

Agritechno geneticist Dr. Lev Andropov is working in his laboratory with his colleague, geneticist Dr. Tamika Brown, and two lab assistants, André and Bonita. As the four are conducting their work, Donna Holbrook from marketing, Stefan Girard from accounting, and Jaylen Castillo from product development enter the lab with some discouraging news. They have been getting early reports from growers in the South that some of the caterpillar-resistant transgenic corn developed by Agritechno and planted this year is failing in areas that are having higher than normal rainfall. The group must decide what and how, if at all, they should report the information to growers and investors.

Andropov led the team that developed the caterpillar-resistant transgenic corn, in addition to having come up with numerous other strains of insect- and disease-resistant hybrids and varieties of the plant. Brown has worked alongside Andropov for many years, and is hoping to be promoted to heading up her own lab for the development of transgenic fruits. The success of the caterpillar-resistant corn would be essential to her being promoted this year. Andropov and Brown are disappointed to hear of the crop failures and would like to investigate the cause. They do not want to commit to time lines or solutions without proper scientific inquiry.

Girard is focused on shareholder value, and the potential damage to stock prices if these problems leak out to investors. He wants to send a letter to shareholders immediately, stating that the few incidents of crop failure are flukes. At the same time, Holbrook insists on sending a letter to the growers, alerting them to an overwatering problem. Girard, Holbrook, and Castillo all agree that the letters have to be sent right away because heavy rains are expected in Nebraska, where 40 percent of the seeds have been sold.

Andropov is frustrated and nearing anger at these suggestions. He asks, "How can we do this? We don't even know that our product is flawed. We cannot send out conflicting messages." Also, he asked what they should tell people who are both growers *and* investors. Brown adds that they do not know that the problem is in the seeds, and they cannot say with certainty when an analysis will be completed and a solution found. She does not want to promise what the company cannot deliver.

Castillo is more anxious about getting a letter out to investors immediately. She suggests

(Mira/Alamy)

telling them that Agritechno's scientists have figured out the problem and found a solution. The scientists bristle at the suggestion.

Holbrook then attempts to find a satisfactory approach for all participants by reframing the situation to focus on yields for the coming year. Andropov is not satisfied with this option, noting that Agritechno won't know how many bushels of the transgenic corn have been produced for another four or five months, and they won't be able to fully identify the problem until then. He suggests sending out a letter stating that a few crops have failed and Agritechno is investigating.

Girard grumbles that he hates to report problems to investors because it scares them away.

Case Study Analysis

1. Why are Andropov and Brown frustrated and angry about the suggestions from Holbrook, Girard, and Castillo?
2. What are the arguments for and against notifying Agritechno's investors? What is the basis for each argument?
3. What are the arguments for and against notifying Agritechno's growers? What is the basis for each argument?
4. What method of communication, if any, would you recommend for investors? Growers?
5. What should Agritechno tell its investors and growers, if anything, about the crop failures and solutions?

Case adapted from Craig C. Lundberg and Cheri A. Young, *The Hospitality Case Manual: Developing Competencies in Critical Thinking and Practical Action* (Upper Saddle River, NJ: Pearson Education, Inc., 2009).

In the early afternoon of June 20, 1992, as Roger Parks, the reservations manager of Casino Grande was packing his briefcase to go out of town to a hospitality association conference, Randolph Jackson, the general manager, called him into his office and the following conversation ensued.

Jackson: Damn it, Roger, didn't I tell you to talk to those two girls about getting to work on time? All they do around here is drink coffee. I guess I'm going to have to install martial law around here. They both recently got raises, too; who do they think they are, anyhow? You tell them in no uncertain terms that if they don't shape up, we'll give them the sack. We can still hire people who follow the rules.

Parks: Whoa, back! What's going on? What in the heck are you talking about?

Jackson: Don't pretend with me. You know just what I'm talking about. It's those two girls, Kane and Palumbo. I saw them come into the employee cafeteria this morning at 8:00 and they were still there when I left at 8:20 to come upstairs. They couldn't have gotten to their desks until 8:30 or later! Then, at 10:30 they were back down there for coffee; I saw them with my own eyes! They're just going to have to shape up. Other people have noticed as well. Why, Cooperider (housekeeping assistant manager) mentioned it just the other day. Why on earth didn't you talk with them like I told you to do?

Parks: Cool it, Randy. I did talk the whole thing over with Marshall, and she talked with the two women. She told me later that she had, and said the women had agreed to do better from then on.

Jackson: Posh, they aren't doing it! We just gave them salary increases, too. We gave them increases, and that's how they're showing their appreciation. I say, if they don't shape up we fire their butts. That Kane's a pain. She says she wants more responsibility, we give it to her, and a raise; and then she comes in late every morning and drinks coffee all day long.

Parks: Simmer down, Randy. You'll have to admit we don't set much of an example. It seems there is always a gang of supervisors in the coffee line at all times, and your secretary and her friend stand around the cigarette machine way after 8:00 a.m.

Jackson: That's not relevant. You can't get cigarettes unless you stand in that line. Cripes, we can't go clear out to the lobby stand, can we? Oh, it's all right to grab a cup of coffee on occasion, but those two girls are always out together. They're abusing the privileges. They drive to work together every day; I've seen them, and then they go into the cafeteria at 8:00 and have breakfast. It's got to end.

Parks: Okay, okay. We'll have another chat with them. The offices and the whole back-of-the-house are pretty lax in regard to timeliness. I agree we don't want reservations standing out as the worst offenders. Part of it is that they go out together, and that makes it conspicuous alright. I'm leaving town this afternoon, but I'll talk with them personally today and let you know before I take off.

Jackson: Okay. Just make it good. We've got to stop abuses, or we'll just have to crack down on everyone. It's always a few who make it hard on everyone.

On the way back to his own office, Mr. Parks detoured into reservations and found Ms. Jean Marshall, talking on the telephone. When she hung up, Mr. Parks related his conversations with Mr. Jackson. This was the second time in two months that Mr. Jackson had called the behavior of Kane and Palumbo to his attention. After a brief discussion, they decided that the proper thing to do was to call the two women into the departmental conference room and talk with them. When Mr. Parks, Ms. Marshall, Mrs. Kane, and Mrs. Palumbo had assembled, the following conversation took place.

Parks: While I sure don't like to bring up a complaint a few hours before I go out of town, I've just come from Mr. Jackson's office. He has complained again about you two getting to work late and about you taking so much time away from your desks for coffee. He rather emphatically stated that he has seen you in the cafeteria after 8:00 several times and that you both seem to be there having coffee together every time he stops by. I believe Jean spoke with you about this several weeks ago. What do you think we ought to do about it?

Kane: Yes, Ms. Marshall talked to us before about it. We've been trying to watch it since then. I believe we've been doing a lot better. You know how hard it is to get to work winter mornings, and we do go down once in a while for a cup of coffee. The new cafeteria is so nice now. Everybody is using it more. Why shouldn't we?

Parks: Yes, you're right, of course. More people are using the cafeteria. You'll agree with me, I'm sure, that this property has a pretty relaxed attitude about getting to work on time occasionally and about getting out of the office for coffee or Coke or a smoke. But let's face it. Mr. Jackson is riled. If we abuse the privileges we have, it will be necessary for Jackson to create some rules that constrict us. We'll all suffer then. There must be some way you can work it out so you'll not be so conspicuous when you take a break once in a while? Isn't it possible for you two to get to work on time so when you take a break it won't be so objectionable?

Kane: All the other reservations women do it. All the office force does it. The smokers go out all the time. Most use the lavs, but it's always so crowded there we prefer to go down to the cafeteria.

Parks: Part of the problem, of course, is that you two are always seen together. That makes you stand out. Why can't you split up, or go some other place?

Mrs. Kane, you've indicated more than once that you want more responsibility in reservations. Let's face it; we can't get it for you if the GM thinks you're abusing the situation.

Kane: Of course that makes sense. What do you want us to do? Stop taking breaks altogether?

Parks: Mrs. Palumbo, what do you think you should do?

Palumbo: Gee, I don't know. We don't do anything that the others don't do. But we don't want to get into trouble. The Casino has been generous enough.

Parks: The way things stand now, well, you can see how things are. Both Mr. Jackson and Cooperider have commented on you. Jackson's the GM, remember, he approves all job changes and all recommendations for raises. It's just not smart to have him on your case.

Kane: We want to do what's right, of course. I sure wouldn't want to do anything that would hinder my next promotion. I suppose we could go somewhere else and maybe not take so many breaks—at least not together. Suppose we lay low for a while until the top brass forgets about it?

Parks: And, get to work a little more promptly in the morning. Sure, all of us are a touch lax sometimes about getting in on time, but the finger is pointing at you, so how about doing a bit better than you've been doing of late?

Kane: Okay, but as you know, I've three kids to get off to school every day. What with car problems, the storms tying traffic up, it's awfully hard to get here on time.

Parks: I'll leave it up to you. I know you're both good workers, and I know you're both trying to get ahead here. You must realize that if old Jackson doesn't see an immediate turnaround, well, I'm not sure what he'll do. You've been talked to twice now. We wouldn't want our GM to do something that would hurt all of the staff, now, would we? (Pause) Jean, what do you think is the best thing to do?

Marshall: You've outlined the situation very well, Mr. Parks. I think these women are attracting undue attention by going out together all the time. The whole staff has been lax about starting promptly. I'll certainly work with reservations to see that we put a drive on to get us to work on time. I think they shouldn't take quite so many breaks, and not together. That way they won't cause so many negative comments.

Parks: Well, it's up to these women. I'm about to leave for a conference, tonight, in fact. I'll be away, so I won't hear anything. If Jackson gets in a twit, he'll no doubt call you down, Jean, and I know you'll do whatever he says. See if you two ladies can't stay out of trouble, please. I'll be back in five days. Good luck.

Roger Parks returned to his own office and telephoned Mr. Jackson. He told Jackson that he and Ms. Marshall had talked to Kane and Palumbo and that he believed that Jackson would see an immediate improvement. Parks asked Jackson to call Ms. Marshall if there were any further complaints. Jackson replied, "You're darn right I will."

About Casino Grande

Casino Grande was an older, mid-sized casino hotel, employing approximately 2,000 people, on the boardwalk section of a mid-Atlantic city. Mr. Randolph Jackson was the general manager of Casino Grande and, as such, had the ultimate authority over all departments and functions at the property. He took unusual interest in the human resource activities of the casino/hotel, establishing both personnel policies and office procedure personally. The ordinary interpretation of these policies and procedures, however, was handled by the department managers and section supervisors with consultation available from the employee relations department.

Roger Parks was the manager of Casino Grande's reservations department. He had begun his employment with the casino in 1982 as a night programmer in the accounting department, while he was finishing his B.S. in hotel administration from a prominent Eastern university. After graduation, Roger continued to work in accounting for two years, then he requested a transfer to the newly established computer system group, where he worked for another two years before he replaced a section head and, thus, acquired his first truly supervisory experience. In late 1987, Roger obtained an interview for a section manager's position in the front desk department, and for which he was hired.

In 1990, Casino Grande significantly upgraded its computer facilities, including a sophisticated reservations system. Roger was transferred to the reservations unit to take charge of it. When he began to organize this function, he hired Ms. Marshall and two clerks. About a year later, when an opening occurred, Mrs. Kane was hired. In Mr. Parks's opinion, Ms. Marshall was a technical whiz who got along fairly well with her people. She had a reputation within the reservations group of sometimes being impatient; she kidded her workers a lot and usually got a lot of high-quality work from them, but was considered somewhat lax in enforcing discipline.

Mrs. Kane, about 39 years old, had three children of ages 11, 8, and 6. Her husband was a sales trainer with a major manufacturing company and was away from home for extended periods. Mrs. Kane's mother lived with them, taking care of the children so that Mrs. Kane could work. She was made senior reservations clerk on January 1, 1992, receiving a substantial raise. At that time, Mrs. Kane was told she was doing excellent work but had a quick temper that sometimes disturbed her fellow employees. She was also told that she often disrupted the office by talking too loudly and too often. The position of senior reservationist provided a wage differential over the others and required her co-workers to bring their questions about procedures and assignments to her. All other matters, such as salary and training questions as well as performance appraisals, were handled by Ms. Marshall. Mrs. Kane took her work seriously and expressed resentment toward the indifferent attitude of the younger reservation clerks. She was trying to get ahead financially. She did not like housekeeping or child care and planned to continue working as long as her mother could look after her children.

Mrs. Palumbo was about 28 years old and a college graduate. Her husband was in the Army and had been in the Middle East for two tours after Operation Desert Storm. Mrs. Palumbo lived alone in a small apartment and planned on working only until her husband was posted in the United States. Mrs. Palumbo did a good job as a reservation clerk and got along well with everyone in the department. She also got a raise on January 1, 1992.

The office rules at Casino Grande did not permit smoking on the job but allowed personnel to leave the office to do so, although there were no designated smoking spaces.

On Monday, August 15, 1992, the following notice was posted on the bulletin board just inside the employees' entrance to the property:

TO: All Casino Grande Office Personnel

Some employees have been taking advantage of our company's coffee break privilege. In order to be fair to those who are being reasonable about going to the cafeteria for coffee, we do not wish to rescind this privilege altogether. We do expect all office employees to start work at 8:00 in the morning, meaning come ready to work, already having had breakfast. There is no excuse for having coffee, therefore, after 8:00 a.m.

From now on the following rules will apply to coffee breaks:

1. No one should visit the cafeteria for coffee before 9:30 a.m.
2. Groups from the same department should not take breaks together, since this would disrupt the service provided.
3. No one should stay away from his/her workstation for longer than 15 minutes.
4. It is unnecessary to leave one's office for coffee or any other beverage more than once a day.

These simple rules should be clear to everyone. If, in the future, these rules are ignored, the coffee break privilege will be canceled altogether. Your wholehearted cooperation is expected.

R. L. Jackson
General Manager

Case Study Analysis

1. List the pros and cons of Mr. Jackson's decision to post the coffee break notice. Was it a good management decision? Why or why not?
2. Imagine a scenario where you are Mr. Parks. What do you think you would have done after the conversation with Mr. Jackson? Write a paragraph describing your action plan.
3. Write a paragraph describing Mr. Jackson's philosophy of human resources management.
4. List some examples of why the women might see the reprimands as unfair or unjust.
5. What is Jackson's leadership style?

Mo's Chowder: Sharpening the Pencil to Operate Effectively

Small Business School **video clips titles are in red**
Case prepared by Hattie Bryant, creator of Small Business School, *the television series made for PBS and Voice of America, http://SmallBusiness School.org.*

BE THE AFFORDABLE HANGOUT

Cindy McEntee is owner of Mo's Restaurants, a place famous for serving hot clam chowder since 1951. There are three locations on the Oregon coast, and a chowder-base factory. The home office is in Newport, and the operation employs up to 200 people during peak season, generating $3.5 million in annual sales. Cindy owns an additional three locations with a group of partners. We [Cindy and Hattie Bryant] met in the White House in June 2001, when Cindy was named Oregon's Small Business Person of the Year and first runner-up for the National Small Business Person of the Year award.

Cindy states, "Mo's is just a plain and simple restaurant with simple seafood dishes that aren't complex—it's for the everyday person. A Seattle food critic called us a dive and that's okay. I'm laughing all the way to the bank."

When her grandmother—Mo—opened for business, the town of Newport had a lively fishing industry, with hundreds of fisherman and a fish-processing plant across the street. Back then, Mo's was a fisherman's hangout, but today it is the foundation for Newport's tourism. This transition had to happen in order for Mo's to survive. In this case, the evolution demonstrates both the need to adapt to a changing market and the business acumen of its owner.

IMPLEMENT COST ACCOUNTING

Mo's is a landmark institution. Some would call it a national treasure, like a park or a historic site. People come from miles away to eat there. People have even told us they had *flown* in to eat at Mo's. Of course, it's the food. Every restaurant owner will tell you that their staying power rests on the quality of the food. Good service cannot make up for poor ingredients, stale bread, or wilted lettuce.

But, it is more than chowder.

Mo's has a story to tell. Cindy loved her grandmother and what she stood for and considers herself to be the caretaker of a legacy. Cindy herself has been part of this story for 40 of the 50 years. And she knows that these stories about her grandmother capture a larger truth.

TURN A HOBBY INTO A BUSINESS

When Cindy was 21 years old and working at Mo's, she asked her grandmother whether she knew how much they were paying for clams. Mo said she didn't know. This did not seem to be good operating practice, so Cindy began installing cost accounting and food preparation systems.

Mo's never made much profit before Cindy started her sharp-pencil techniques. At the same time Cindy was working to improve the internal processes, she was also telling stories, creating legends about how Mo gave plenty of fishermen food even when they couldn't pay and about the lady who drove her car right into the restaurant, then stayed to eat.

On the walls in the original location there are photos, drawings, and framed write-ups about what has happened at Mo's through the years. The storytelling builds the legacy. Storytelling makes Mo's bigger than life. But, without systems that produce a quality product day in and day out and that nurture employees, the legends are of no value.

Mo was happy operating one restaurant, but Cindy was hungry for more. When there were frequent lines of customers waiting outside the door, Cindy knew she could add locations to serve more customers. She realized that she had to put infrastructure in place. She attended seminars and classes to learn more about expanding a business. As a leader in her local chamber of commerce, she knew many business owners to whom she could turn for advice.

PASS OWNERSHIP FORMALLY

Mo was inspired and impressed by her granddaughter and decided to give Cindy the opportunity to become the owner, through the purchase of stock over time. To do that, Mo changed her legal form of business from a sole proprietorship to a corporation and, in 1975, Cindy started buying stock in the company through payroll deductions.

CHANGE WHEN THE MARKET CHANGES

Newport is still a working port, with all the sights and smells that come with hauling in fish from the sea. However, as the fishing industry has changed, there is less processing taking place. At the same time, the city leaders (and that includes Cindy) have been working on making the waterfront attractive, so tourists will come and watch the fishermen and spend money in the town. Knowing that their waterfront has maintained its turn-of-the-twentieth-century charm, they pooled resources to make Newport an important West Coast tourist destination. Cindy has not only worked hard to promote tourism in Newport, she has completely reinvented Mo's image to fit the tourism trade. Plenty of fisherman still stop in for chowder and beer, but the Mo's Chowder restaurants today are light, bright, family-friendly places where children are treated with great respect. Cindy says, "We eat where our children want to eat."

One very visible result of Cindy's tireless efforts to promote her hometown is the art that tourists and locals enjoy. She recruited well-known artists to paint murals on Newport's waterfront buildings. Cindy has also commissioned an artist to make a bronze statue of her grandmother, Mo, and other business owners who are doing their part to make their storefronts attractive, and at the same time keep the spirit of the working port.

HELP EMPLOYEES ACCUMULATE WEALTH

Cindy has built a business based upon tried-and-true recipes, but she had to learn through experience to operate an expanding company. In addition to monitoring every detail of the business by the numbers, to keep the company financially healthy, Cindy is committed to making employment at Mo's good enough work so that morale remains high. Employees at Mo's have excellent medical benefits and a 401(k) plan. Helping employees feel safe and secure maintains morale and keeps turnover, always costly to any business, low. Cindy uses both fixed compensation plans and variable rewards to maintain a strong team of valued employees. All employees can count on fixed compensation, fair salaries, and medical plans, but what's really special about Cindy's are the occasional rewards.

For example, in a year when breakage was low and there were no accidents, Cindy demonstrated the direct connection between these statistics and cost savings by taking 47 employees on a vacation to Hawaii. By doing this, she acknowledged the fact that both the low breakage and excellent safety record were a result of the employees' efforts and that they deserved a share of the benefits.

ENGAGE THE TEAM

At monthly meetings, everyone is encouraged to comment on how they think the business is going. Often, there are 15-minute training sessions to improve service. Customer comment cards, which are time- and date-stamped, are discussed. When specific employees are praised by customers, they are recognized at the meeting. When customer comments are negative—for example, "The food was cold," "My fish was undercooked," or "The chowder wasn't hot"—the team works together to figure out what happened so the problem will not recur.

Key numbers from Mo's financial statements are shared, so that employees understand how their performance affects the bottom line. Because of this training, when a tray of dishes is dropped, or a meal is returned to the kitchen, everyone knows how much money the restaurant just lost.

START CHILDREN AT THE BOTTOM

The third generation has joined the business and has brought fresh energy and technological know-how to the operation. Cindy's son Dylan started by peeling potatoes, and her daughter Gabrielle began as a dishwasher. By doing every job in the business, these two are becoming better and more compassionate managers, fully aware of the challenges faced by the employees. They will find ways of improving the business at each level of operations as they fully participate in it. And perhaps most importantly, the other employees will know that the next generation is qualified to lead, that they have served the apprenticeship, and will be well positioned to strengthen the organization.

Gabrielle has a B.A. in sociology and Dylan has a B.A. in hospitality management with a minor in business, then another degree in finance. Dylan says that, when he finished earning the second degree, "I got a job at GE and after about a year I realized—there is a lot of corporate bureaucracy." There was no guarantee that Mo's would have a place for Cindy's children, but about one month after Dylan decided he wanted to leave GE, the manager of Mo's chowder factory left. This provided an opening for Dylan, so he accepted his mother's offer of a job in the family business.

Gabrielle and Dylan have helped grow the business, and the family knows that their college degrees and big-business experience will continue to be beneficial for Mo's. Cindy is optimistic: "My children have joined this company and they are determined to make lots of changes. I mean, I took my grandmother to the calculator and they are taking me to the Web. We are doing it right."

Case Analysis

1. How did Cindy McEntee turn a hobby into a business?
2. How has Cindy operated the business to incorporate change over time?
3. What methods does Mo's Chowder use to retain and recruit employees?
4. Do you think Mo's will be in business 20 years from now?

CASHING IN THE BRAND

Chapter 14
FRANCHISING, LICENSING, & HARVESTING:
CASHING IN YOUR BRAND

Comstock Images

FRANCHISING, LICENSING, & HARVESTING: CASHING IN YOUR BRAND

Comstock

Some entrepreneurs have experienced more than one way to exit from a business. Paula Jagemann is a serial entrepreneur who has taken one company public, sold another one, and then retired. Paula was the Vice President of Investor and Public Relations at UUNET Technologies, Inc., which was the largest Internet Service Provider in the world when it went public on the NASDAQ in 1995. She was there when it was acquired by Metropolitan Fiber Systems (MFS) for $2 billion in 1996, and when WorldCom acquired MFS for $12.4 billion later that year, and stayed on through the merger of MCI and WorldCom.

In her early 30s and not ready to retire, Paula formed OnLineOfficeSupplies.com as the first online office-supply retail company, reaching $18 million in sales in 18 months. She and her co-founders sold it in 2001 to First Call Office Products. She also co-founded eCommerce Industries, Inc. (ECI²) to support the business systems needed for OnLineOfficeSupplies, and recognized that the greater potential was in ECI². The company was awarded Microsoft's Ecommerce Solution of the Year in 2000, and continues to thrive. Paula sold the company for $95 million in 2005 and retired from that company in 2005, vowing to avoid start-ups.

In 2010, Paula was serving on the Board of Trustees of her local hospital when she discovered a need for convenient, accessible, and reliable sources for products that served people who had breast cancer. She quickly learned that there also was a need for a funding mechanism to support the high cost of products that were required and valued, but not covered by private health insurance or Medicare. So, Paula was lured out of retirement to create Someone With, LLC, which was launched in 2011. Whether Someone With will eventually be acquired or go public, it is not likely that Paula will exit via retirement any time soon.

(Courtesy of Paula Jagemann)

Performance Objectives

1. Determine how you want to grow your business and eventually exit from it.
2. Describe how businesses use licensing to profit from their brands.
3. Explain how a business can be franchised.
4. Learn methods of valuing a business.
5. Discuss five ways to harvest a business.

What Do You Want from Your Business?

Performance Objective 1

Determine how you want to grow your business and eventually exit from it.

Just as people start businesses for a variety of reasons and have different goals and objectives, they have different reasons for leaving them—and different ways of doing so. Some entrepreneurs enjoy the stability and earnings associated with carrying on a successful business they have established. Others want to "grow and go." Still others are serial entrepreneurs, who create new ventures repeatedly. What do you want? **Exhibit 14-1** identifies some of the options available.

Regardless of which route you choose, your business plan should clearly state your intentions. If you are asking people to invest in your enterprise, you should tell them how they will realize the return on their investment. If it will take several years to grow the business, that should also be spelled out.

Exhibit 14-1 *Growth, Harvesting, and Exit Strategies*

SELL (Sell to others) (Merge)	Continue for a predetermined or indefinite period
	Exit and start a new venture
	Exit and secure employment
	Exit and retire
MAINTAIN	Remain as a manager
	Hire others to become managers and exit day-to-day operations
GROW (Generate internally) (Acquire others) (License your brand) (Franchise the business)	Lead through the growth
	Step aside for a more suitable manager and remain active
	Hire others to become managers and exit the day-to-day operations
CLOSE (Cease operations) (Bankruptcy)	Exit and seek alternate employment
	Exit and start a new venture
	Exit and retire

Continuing the Business for the Family

The multigenerational family-owned-and-operated business best exemplifies the company that provides continued employment and wealth to an entrepreneur and his or her relatives. Malden Mills in Chapter 13 is an example of a firm that was operated as a closely held private company for three generations and had a clear interest in maintaining employment in its community. For this type of business, sufficient cash flow for wages and continued operations is primary. If this kind of venture is your goal, create a growth plan that permits you to buy back investments from outsiders, so that the business will be truly family-owned.

Growth through Diversification

diversification the addition of product or service offerings beyond a business's core product or service.

One way to grow your business is to use **diversification**, which is the addition of offerings beyond your core product or service. By diversifying your business, you are increasing the potential for sales. To a budding entrepreneur or a seasoned executive, diversification can appear to be the way to get more market share. On the flip side, author and marketing expert Al Ries argues that diversification comes at a price: "It unfocuses the company and leads to loss of power."[1] Focusing, in contrast, attracts exactly the right employees to a company and reinforces its strength in the marketplace.

---

[1] Al Ries, *Focus: The Future of Your Company Depends on It* (New York: Harper Business, 1996), p. 273.

Growth through Licensing and Franchising

One way to grow without direct investment in considerable physical and human capital is through **licensing,** or renting your brand or other intellectual property to sell products. Another way to replicate a business formula is through franchising.

It is important that you are aware of the possibilities offered by licensing and franchising from the moment you start your business. Stay motivated to keep your business organized and to try to develop a foolproof operational system. After all, someday hundreds, or even thousands, of entrepreneurs might be eager to buy or rent that system from you.

Licensing and franchising are called **replication strategies** because they are ways to obtain money from a business you created by letting others copy, or *replicate*, it.

licensing renting your brand or other intellectual property to increase sales.

replication strategy a way to obtain money from a business by letting others copy it for a fee.

Focus Your Brand

As noted in Unit 3, a *brand* identifies the products or services of a company and differentiates them from those of competitors—representing the company's promise to consistently deliver a specific set of benefits to its clientele. Customers who buy Liz Claiborne clothes, for example, expect classic styling suitable for the workplace. They have come to trust that brand to meet their needs.

Businesses do better when customers know what to expect from their brands, according to Ries.[2] He argues that, in industry after industry, the narrowly focused companies are the big winners. He contends that too many managers are hooked on growth for its own sake, and develop misguided expansion that dilutes the strength of a company's brand.

Many companies known for one type of merchandise, such as Adidas with its athletic shoes, have applied their brand with disastrous results—such as Adidas cologne. Sneakers and cologne were not a good association! BIC, known for its pens, branched into panty hose and had a similar failure.

Using an established brand to promote different kinds of products is called **line extension**. It can work if the brand is strong and the new product is not completely dissimilar to the original. For example, the Jell-O brand name was successfully applied to a line of puddings, after it had been established as the preeminent gelatin dessert.

line extension the use of an established brand to promote different kinds of products.

◀ **Performance Objective 2**
Describe how businesses use licensing to profit from their brands.

When Licensing Can Be Effective

A company can profitably license its brand when it has a core group of loyal customers. Licensing is effective when the licensor is confident that the company name will be enhanced by the licensee's use of it. If Coca-Cola licensed its name to a T-shirt manufacturer that wanted to print its logo on T-shirts, Coca-Cola would get free advertising as well as royalties.

However, licensing, if not handled carefully, can damage your brand. For example, if the T-shirt maker used the Coca-Cola logo on T-shirts that contained obscene messages, the company's reputation would be tarnished. Coca-Cola would not license its name to a soft-drink manufacturer, because a licensing agreement would not necessarily ensure standards or quality and, in any case,

The Hard Rock Hotel and Casino, Las Vegas: A clearly focused brand can go a long way.
(Wesley R. Hitt/Mira.com)

---

[2]Ries, *Focus.*

would become a direct competitor. Licensing your brand is one potential way to increase brand recognition and extend your product line, without investing in the costs of entry into additional markets, or investing in the expense of producing new product lines.

Franchising Revisited from the Franchisor Perspective

As discussed, a franchise is a business that markets a product or service in the exact manner prescribed by the founder or successors of the parent business. Whereas one way for you to start a business would be to secure a franchise, you also could develop a concept and a business operation that would be reproduced and licensed to other entrepreneurs. They would buy the right to run the business in the way you prescribed, and pay you a franchise fee and a royalty. There are both benefits and drawbacks to being a franchisor.

The benefits include:

- growth with minimal capital investment,
- lower marketing and promotional costs, and
- royalties.

The drawbacks of franchising to the franchisor include:

- the franchisee may disregard the training and fail to operate the business properly, tarnishing the reputation of the entire franchise;
- it can be difficult to find qualified or trustworthy franchisees;
- franchisees that do not experience success may withhold payment and/or sue the franchisor;
- there are many federal and state regulations regarding franchising, making it difficult and costly in some circumstances.

How a McDonald's Franchise Works

Let's look at how franchising can grow a business. McDonald's is a classic example of a franchise operation. McDonald's was developed by Ray Kroc, who, in 1955, persuaded the McDonald brothers to let him become the franchising agent for their highly successful hamburger restaurant in San Bernardino, California. Kroc's great insight was to realize that the people who bought McDonald's franchises would need extensive training and support in order to make the food taste like that of the original restaurant. Kroc timed and measured everything exactly. McDonald's franchisees are taught precisely how many minutes to fry potatoes and when to turn a burger, among a host of other details. They are even taught how to greet customers.

A McDonald's franchisee owns the restaurant, but agrees to market the food under the McDonald's name and trademark in the exact fashion developed by Kroc. This is spelled out in the franchise agreement. In return, the franchisee knows that he or she is investing in a proven, successful business concept. The franchisee also benefits from use of the McDonald's trademark, and from the management training, marketing, national advertising, and promotional assistance provided by the parent company. McDonald's, as franchisor, receives a franchise fee and royalties.

Although franchising has been around in the United States since the Singer Sewing Machine Company first developed it in the 1850s, its popularity has exploded over the past several decades. The number of individual franchises has grown to approximately 750,000, with literally thousands of franchisors in the market space.

Do Your Research before You Franchise

Before you get involved in franchising your business, consult with a franchise attorney and carry out extensive research. The International Franchise Association (http://www.franchise.org) provides considerable information for current and potential franchisors, including a prospective franchise forum. Use the resources available to you to understand what is expected of a franchisor and how the relationship works, before speaking with an entrepreneur who is interested in a franchise. Recognize that your franchisees will expect significant support and attention for the fees that they pay you. To better understand the franchisee perspective, you can visit the American Association of Franchisees and Dealers at http://www.aafd.org. You must offer products or services that are sufficiently original, and create unique marketing strategies, to justify the cost of the franchise.

Part of the process of franchising a business is to create a franchise agreement, which is the contract between the franchisor and franchisee. This contract establishes the standards that assure uniformity of product (or service) throughout the franchise chain.

 Performance Objective 3
Explain how a business can be franchised.

Harvesting and Exiting Options

Licensing and franchising provide possible growth strategies for entrepreneurs who want to stay in one business. For those who do not want to continue their businesses in perpetuity, harvesting and exiting are options.

When to Harvest Your Business

There will probably be times in the life of your business when you may want to close or leave it. **Harvesting** your business means you sell it, take it public, or merge with another company. This differs from replication in that the entrepreneur is usually no longer involved once the business is harvested; he or she walks away with a portion of the business's value as cash, stock, or a combination of the two. In the case of a merger, the founding entrepreneur may also work in the new organization for a specified time period.

In William Petty's article on harvesting,[3] he quotes Steven Covey, author of *The Seven Habits of Highly Effective People*, who says that a key to being effective in life is "beginning with the end in mind." To that, Petty adds, "If the entrepreneur's goal with the venture is only to provide a living, then the exit or harvest strategy is of no concern. But if the goal is to create value for the owners and the other stakeholders in the company, a harvest strategy is absolutely mandatory."

Although you want to be aware of all harvesting opportunities, it usually requires at least 10 years to build a company of sufficient value to harvest. You can make the timing of harvesting part of the plans for your business. The harvest strategy is important not only to the entrepreneur, but also to investors, because it lets them know up front how their investment should eventually be turned into cash or stock.

Not every business can be harvested. Some are loaded with debt or have not created a product or service of lasting value. The entrepreneur

harvesting the act of selling, taking public, or merging a company to yield proceeds for the owner(s).

---

[3]William Petty, "Harvesting," in *The Portable MBA in Entrepreneurship*, 2nd ed., William D. Bygrave, ed. (New York: Wiley, 1997).

Global Impact . . .

VISTA Staffing Solutions: Global Physician Staffing Founders Acquired

VISTA Staffing Solutions is a leading provider of permanent-physician search services and *locum tenens*, or temporary physician staffing. The business was founded in 1990 as an employee-owned company with medical practices, hospitals, and governments as its primary clients. VISTA provides short- and long-term placements in the United States and internationally in Australia and New Zealand. VISTA founders Mark Brouse, Katie Abby, and Clarke Shaw combined their industry and professional expertise to form the company.

On January 3, 2007, VISTA Staffing Solutions was acquired by On Assignment, Inc., a NASDAQ-traded leader in the professional staffing industry. The VISTA sale included $41 million in cash and an earn-out provision. VISTA shareholders and option holders could receive an additional $8 million, depending upon its performance for the first two years after the sale. At the time of its acquisition by On Assignment, VISTA had a pool of more than 1,300 physicians and had anticipated revenues in excess of $60 million.

Mark Brouse stated, "We are excited for our well-established physician staffing business to join an organization that shares our focus on providing highly skilled health care professionals. The two companies have remarkably similar cultures, putting people first and providing the best professional for each assignment. With the VISTA management team staying in place following the completion of the transaction, we believe the combined organization will be well positioned to maximize growth opportunities and achieve operating efficiencies." Two years after the acquisition, all three founders continued to manage VISTA Staffing Solutions.

Sources: On Assignment, Inc. Web site, http://www.onassignment.com, press release, December 21, 2006, and VISTA Staffing Solutions Web site, http://www.vistastaff.com, January 13, 2009.

---

liquidation the sale of all assets of a business concurrent with its being closed.

Performance Objective 4 ▶

Learn methods of valuing a business.

can only leave such a business via **liquidation** (selling all the assets), closure, or bankruptcy.

How to Value a Business

Business valuation is both an art and a science. A business that is profitable and likely to be so in the future can be sold for a sum that represents its *net present value* today. This is net present value in action. (Most wealth is created by buying and selling assets that will have a future value.) Ultimately, a business is worth what others are willing to pay and what the owner will accept for it.

There are many ways to estimate the net present value of a business. Value, after all, is *subjective*, meaning it is conditional on individual opinion or preference. One person might be willing to pay a higher price for a particular business than another would. The first buyer feels more optimistic about the business's future (and may have some personal insight in that regard) or may simply want it more than another potential buyer does.

Here are some methods entrepreneurs use to estimate the value of a business:

- Compare it with similar businesses. If you are looking to sell your dry-cleaning company, check out, if possible, how much other dry-cleaning stores in your area are bringing in when they are sold.

- In most industries, there are one or two key benchmarks that help to value a business. For gas stations, it might be barrels of gasoline sold per week; for a dry cleaner, it might be the number of shirts laundered per week.

- Look at a multiple of net earnings. One rule of thumb says a business can sell for around three to five times its annual net earnings. If the business earns $100,000 net profit per year, for example, it could be expected to sell for at least $300,000.

The ultimate goal of company valuation is to arrive at a **fair market value,** which, according to the IRS, is "The price at which property would change hands between a willing buyer and willing seller, neither under any compulsion to buy or sell and both having reasonable knowledge of the relevant facts."[4]

fair market value the price at which a property or business is valued by the marketplace; the price it would fetch on the open market.

The Science of Valuation

There are three primary methods that buyers and sellers use: book value, future earnings, and market-based value. In practice, these three methods are often used concurrently, and all provide helpful perspectives on a company's value. Furthermore, there are many variations on each method. The SBA Web site provides assistance in valuation, and accountants and other professional business advisors can provide assistance as well.[5] Below is a more in-depth description of each.

- *Book value (net worth = assets – liabilities).* One of the most common methods for computing a company's valuation, the **book value** technique, looks at a company as assets minus liabilities. This way is the most common one used for valuing companies, and also the simplest.

book value valuation of a company as assets minus liabilities.

- *Future earnings.* This method uses a company's estimated future earnings as the main determinant of its value. It is most useful for companies that are growing quickly. In these cases, past earnings are not accurate reflections of future performance. This method of valuation must take into account the time value of money, as well as the rate of return.

- *Market based (value = P/E ratio × estimated future net earnings).* In the market-based approach, the value of the company is compiled from the price/earnings (P/E) ratio of comparable public companies. The P/E ratio is determined by dividing a company's stock price by its earnings per share. This method is effective because of its simplicity, but may be lacking when there are no similar public companies with which to compare the business.

Despite the sophistication of these three techniques, all of them are ultimately only estimates. Each business will have particular characteristics and special circumstances. In the end, it will be the entrepreneur's job to use negotiation to get the highest price possible.

Once you do decide to sell your business or pursue some other exit strategy, use the Internet to maximize your prospects. If you decide to sell, you can list your business with databases such as http://www.BizBuySell.com or http://www.BizQuest.com, which send registered users who might want to buy your business e-mails alerting them to your offer.

Creating Wealth By Selling a Profitable Business

As noted above, a successful small business can usually be sold for between three and five times its yearly net profit, because the buyer expects the business to continue to keep generating income. If your net profit for one year is $10,000, you should be able to get at least $30,000 (3 × $10,000).

---

[4]Available at http://www.irs.gov.
[5]One source of information is SBA's Small Business Planner section, at http://www.sba.gov/smallbusinessplanner/exit/sellyourbusiness/index.htm.

From the buyer's perspective, this represents a 33 1/3 percent annual return on the investment required to buy the business ($10,000/$30,000 = 33 1/3%), which is a very attractive return.

If you are in business for three years, however, and increase your net profit each year, your business will be worth even more. If your company earns $10,000 in year one, $25,000 in year two, and $60,000 in year three, it could be valued at $180,000 by applying the three-times rule of thumb. How a business grows will affect its value. A business with increasing yearly net profit will be considered more valuable than a business with static earnings.

Entrepreneurs establish successful businesses, sell them, and use the resulting wealth to create new enterprises and more wealth. Entrepreneurs also use their wealth to support political, environmental, and social causes. What will you do with *your* wealth?

Harvesting Options

> **Performance Objective 5**
>
> Discuss five ways to harvest a business.

An overview of harvesting strategies should help you plan the final stage of your relationship with the company you are starting to create now. Harvesting options for exiting a business fall into five categories:

1. ***Increase the free cash flow.*** For the first 7 to 10 years of the business, you will want to reinvest as much profit as possible into the company in order for it to grow. Once you are ready to exit, however, you can begin reducing investment and taking cash out. This strategy will require investing only the amount of cash needed to keep the business effective in its current target markets, without attempting to move into new ones.

   Advantages
   - You can retain ownership of the firm with this strategy.
   - You do not have to seek a buyer.

Step into the Shoes . . .

Flickr Turns Online Photo Sharing into Opportunities for Its Founders

(Gary Lucken/Alamy)

Stewart Butterfield and Caterina Fake launched Flickr in early 2004 and sold it just over one year later to Yahoo!. The sale price was $35 million in cash. It would appear that the couple harvested their company very quickly, but the story begins several years earlier.

Flickr is an online site that hosts images and videos, is an online community, and provides Web services. It is most widely known and used for its photo-sharing capacity. However, Flickr was actually created by Vancouver-based Ludicorp (founded in 2002 by Butterfield and Fake) using tools for an online game, Game Neverending, that was never launched. Fake recognized that the photo-sharing technology was more marketable than the game, and Ludicorp pursued Flickr.

The couple remained at Yahoo! for the requisite three years after the sale but departed soon afterward. Fake left Yahoo! in June 2008, and her husband announced his resignation in the same month. Then Fake, a 1991 graduate of Vassar College, founded and became chief product officer at Hunch, an Internet start-up that provided recommendations on a multitude of user-generated topics. She is a board member and investor in Etsy, has written a book about start-ups, and continues blogging on Caterina.net. In addition, Fake has invested in 20 × 200, Small Batch, Flowgram, Maya's Mom, and DailyBooth. Butterfield, a graduate of the University of Victoria and the University of Cambridge, has co-founded Tiny Speck and invested in Flowgram, Etsy, and Rouxbe.

This couple found a way to translate a business idea into wealth, and to use that wealth to found and invest in other start-up companies.

Sources: Jefferson Graham, "Flickr of Idea on a Gaming Project Led to Photo Website," *USA Today*, February 27, 2007, http://www.usatoday.com. Crunchbase at http://www.crunchbase.com. Ludicorp Web site, http://www.ludicorp.com, January 13, 2010.

Disadvantages
- You will need a good accountant to help avoid major taxes.
- It can take a long time to execute this exit strategy.

2. *Management buyout (MBO).* In this strategy, the entrepreneur sells the firm to its managers, who raise the money to buy it via personal savings and debt.

Advantages
- If the business has value, the managers often do want to buy it.
- The entrepreneur has the emotional satisfaction of selling to people he knows and has trained.

Disadvantages
- If the managers use primarily debt to buy the company, they may not be able to finish paying off the arrangement.
- If the final payment to the entrepreneur depends on the company's earnings during the past few quarters, the managers may have an incentive to attempt to lower the profits.

3. *Employee stock ownership plan (ESOP).* This strategy both provides an employee retirement plan and allows the entrepreneur and partners to sell their stock and exit the company. The firm establishes a plan that allows employees to buy company stock as part of their retirement; when the owners are ready to exit, the ESOP borrows money and uses the cash to buy their stock. As the loan is paid off, the stock is added to the employee benefit fund.

Advantages
- The ESOP has some special tax advantages; among them are that the company can deduct both the principal and interest payments on the loan and that the dividends paid on any stock held in the ESOP are considered a tax-deductible expense.

Disadvantages
- This is not a good strategy if the entrepreneur does not want the employees to have control of the company. The ESOP must extend to all employees and requires the entrepreneur to open up the company's books.

4. *Merging or being acquired.* Selling the company to another company can be an exciting exit strategy for an entrepreneur who would like to see his or her creation have an opportunity to grow significantly by using another company's funds.

Advantages
- This strategy can finance growth that the company could not achieve on its own; the entrepreneur can either exit the company at the time of the **merger** or acquisition, or be part of the growth and exit later.

merger the joining of two companies to share their respective strengths.

Disadvantages
- This can be an emotionally draining strategy, with a lot of ups and downs during negotiations; a sale can take over a year to finalize.

5. *Initial public offering (IPO).* An initial public offering (IPO), or "going public," will mean selling shares of your company in the stock market. It requires choosing an investment banker to develop the

IPO, making sales presentations ("the road show") to brokers and institutional investors nationally (and perhaps internationally) and, finally, offering your stock on the market and holding your breath as you watch its price go up—or not.

Advantages

- If your business is hot, this can be a very profitable way to harvest it. The market may place a sizeable premium on your company's value.

Disadvantages

- An IPO is a very exciting, but stressful, all-consuming, and very expensive way to harvest a company, and it requires a lot of work from the entrepreneur—and ultimately it is the market that will determine the outcome. Very few entrepreneurial firms ever complete an IPO but, for many of them, it brings significant financial rewards.

Exit Strategy Options

Simply claiming that your business will go public one day will probably get a skeptical reaction from potential investors. They understand that you cannot *guarantee* either how they will recoup their investment or your exact exit strategy, but you can show you are aware that, for the vast majority of small businesses, going public is a fantasy. Demonstrate your understanding of exit strategies by thinking through the four basic possibilities below. Which one do you think best describes what you intend to make happen for your business?

1. *Acquisition.* Do you believe you could create a business that someone would want to buy (*acquire*) one day? Your exit strategy could be creating a business that would be valuable for one of your suppliers or a major competitor. The plan would be that the purchase price will pay you and your equity investors more money than you put into the business. A fair sale price, based on the business's annual net profit, should allow the original investors to realize a good return on their investment. As we have said, a common rule of thumb says that a small business is worth at least three times its annual net profit.

2. *Earn-out.* To use an earn-out strategy, you will need projected cash flow statements that show the business eventually generating a strong positive cash flow. At that point, you can start offering to buy out your investors' shares at a price greater than they paid for them. The purchase price usually rises over time.

3. *Debt/equity exchange.* If your investors will be lending you money, eventually you can offer to trade equity for portions of the debt. This will slowly reduce the interest due over time (as the face value of the loan decreases). In this way, you can decide at what pace and at what price to reduce your debt.

4. *Merge.* This strategy is similar to that of acquisition but, with a merger, two companies join together to share their strengths. One company might have an extensive customer base; the other might possess a distribution channel the first company needs. Or perhaps each company is doing well in different geographical areas, and a

CHAPTER 14: Franchising, Licensing, & Harvesting: Cashing in Your Brand **475**

merger would open up these respective markets to the other's products/services. Regardless, cash will change hands and the original investors can make their shares available for sale to complete the merger.

Investors Will Care about Your Exit Strategy, Too

Your exit strategy will be important to your investors. Your business plan should spell out in how many years you expect them to be able to cash out, and you will need to include financial data in your plan to forecast specifics. Again, it will not be enough to mention that someday the company will go public and their share of the business will be worth "a lot" of money. Of the thousands of new ventures launched every year in the United States, only a small percentage will ever go public. Yet, according to David Newton, on Entrepreneur.com (January 15, 2001), over 70 percent of formal business plans presented to angel investors and venture capitalists cite going public as the primary exit strategy. Most estimate that going public will happen within just four years from the launch date. You will need to be more realistic.

Chapter Summary

Now that you have studied this chapter, you can do the following:

1. Determine how you want to grow your business and then exit from it.
   - Decide what your ultimate goals and objectives are.
   - Consider creating a business that will provide employment and wealth for your family.
   - Identify options to broaden product and service offerings through diversification.
   - Evaluate replication strategies.
2. Describe how businesses use licensing to profit from their brands.
   - A brand is a name, term, sign, logo, design, or combination of these that identifies the products or services of a company and differentiates them from those of competitors.
   - The licensee pays a fee for the license and may also pay a royalty (share of the profits) on sales to the licensor.
   - Licensing is only effective when the licensor is confident that his or her company name will not be tarnished by how the licensee uses it.
3. Explain how a business can be franchised.
   - A franchise is a business that markets a product or service in the exact manner prescribed by the founder or successors of the parent company.
   - As an entrepreneur, you could develop a concept and business operation that can be reproduced and sold to other entrepreneurs. They would pay you a fee for the right to run the business exactly the way that you direct, and pay you a royalty as well.
4. Learn methods of valuing a business.
   - Book value (net worth = assets − liabilities)
   - Future earnings
   - Market based (value = P/E × estimated future net earnings)

5. Discuss five ways to harvest a business.
   - Increase the free cash flows. Once you are ready to exit, you can begin reducing reinvestment and collecting revenue as cash.
   - Management buyout (MBO). The entrepreneur sells the firm to the managers, who raise the money to buy it via personal savings and debt.
   - Employee stock ownership plan (ESOP). This provides an employee retirement plan and allows the entrepreneur and partners to sell their stock to the employees as they exit the company.
   - Merging or being acquired. Joining together with another company or being bought by one.
   - Initial public offering (IPO). Going public is getting your company listed on the stock exchange to be traded on the open market.

Key Terms

book value	line extension
diversification	liquidation
fair market value	merger
harvesting	replication strategy
licensing	

Entrepreneurship Portfolio

Critical Thinking Exercises

1. Describe the differences between a licensing and a franchising agreement.
2. Give an example of a business that could lead to licensing agreements and a business that could be franchised.
3. Do you plan to franchise your business or license any of your products? Explain.
4. Describe the exit strategy you plan to use to harvest your business. Why do you think this exit strategy will be attractive to potential investors?

Key Concept Questions

1. Identify two companies that merged during the past three years. Describe the structure of the merger and what has happened to the resulting organization since then.
2. Choose one of the harvesting strategies described in the chapter and research it in depth. Write a one-page report to present to the class.

Application Exercise

1. Look around your local community and select a popular business that is an independent company—not a franchise or part of a major corporation. Identify the possible harvesting strategies that the owners(s) could employ. What would you recommend and why?

2. Select five companies that are profiled in this text from the Step into the Shoes and Global Impact features. Indicate whether each has been harvested (you may need to do an Internet search). If so, what strategy did the owner(s) employ? If not, what would you recommend?

Exploring Online

The American Association of Franchisees and Dealers (AAFD) is a national trade association that represents the rights and interests of franchisees and independent dealers across the country. Visit this association online at http://www.aafd.org to learn more about franchises and the resources available. As a potential franchisor, you should know what your prospective customers are reading.

1. Search the site for the article, "AAFD Road Map to Selecting a Franchise." Read the section called "Eight Things to Look for in a Franchise." For each of the eight tips in the article, write a one-sentence summary and note how it might apply to your business as a franchisor.
2. Find a franchise online like the one you might want to create. Answer the following:
   a. What is the franchise? What does it sell?
   b. Why are you interested in it?
   c. What is the franchise fee?
   d. What are the start-up costs?
   e. What is the royalty fee?
   f. Describe the training the franchisor offers to franchisees.
   g. Describe the marketing the franchisor provides for franchisees.
3. Find a company online that is similar to the type of business you would like to launch. Assume you would want to sell it. Describe how much you would expect from a buyer and explain your valuation method.

BizBuilder Business Plan Questions

8.0 Funding Request and Exit Strategy

8.2 Exit Plan

A. How will investors get paid back/out? Public offering? Employee buyout? Merger or acquisition? Liquidation? Stock buyback?
B. When will this happen?
C. Do you plan to franchise your business, or license any of your products? Explain.

8.3 Milestones

A. Create a PERT chart for your organization to make your plans clear to potential investors.

Case Study | Wahoo's Fish Taco® Franchises for Growth

Before it became a successful franchise chain, Wahoo's Fish Taco, LLC, was a small California restaurant born from the craving of three brothers for fish tacos. Growing up in Brazil and California, Wing Lam, Ed Lee, and Mingo Lee learned a lot about running a business by helping out in their family's Chinese restaurants in Sao Paulo and Orange County. After discovering fish tacos while surfing in Mexico, the three brothers combined their knowledge of and passions for the surfing culture and the restaurant industry into an entrepreneurial venture of their own.

When they opened the first Wahoo's Fish Taco in 1988 in Costa Mesa, California, the brothers decorated the restaurant with donated products from local surf businesses. The food was a combination of the Brazilian, Mexican, and Asian flavors, and featured ingredients that the brothers loved. The restaurant quickly became popular because of its unique, fresh, and healthy food. In 1990, the brothers brought in Steve Karfardis who headed up their expansion through company stores and some franchising.

Franchise Expansion Strategy

Wahoo's took a gradual approach to franchising, waiting until they had established a number of company-owned stores before moving into franchising at all, and then shifting to an aggressive strategy after 20 years in business. Wing Lam describes the decision to begin franchising, "We waited until, I think, about four or five years that we were into business then we chose to start our first franchise to go out-of-state in Colorado, just in case it didn't work."[6] The initial choice of locations had to do with similar market demographics and the market opportunities in Denver. From there, Wahoo's followed a targeted approach to franchise selection and growth.

In August 2009, the brothers appointed Tom Orbe as a vice president with responsibility for the Wahoo's franchise program. Orbe owned and operated the Wahoo's franchise in Temecula, California, and was previously vice president of sales, product development, and marketing

A Wahoo's franchise.
(Wahoo's Fish Taco)

for Kawasaki Motors Corporation U.S.A.[7] He had successfully established numerous new franchisees while a vice president at Nissan Motor Corporation, U.S.A. At the time of Orbe's hiring, Wahoo's announced plans to add a minimum of 100 new franchise locations within five years, with 19 of them being selected in the same year.

When Wahoo's management appointed Orbe, they had over 30 company-owned stores and 18 franchise locations, of which 13 were operated by one franchisee.[8] At the time, an additional company location was slated to open the following year, but the strategy was to shift to franchising. Demand was sufficiently strong, despite the recession, so that Wahoo's was using a lottery system to select some franchises. In September 2010, franchisee Michael Duplantis opened the first of his eleven planned units in the Houston area, demonstrating significant growth in short order.[9] As of 2011, there were more than 50 Wahoo's franchise locations in California, Colorado, Texas, and Hawaii.

The Franchise Experience

The Wahoo's franchise chain targets a particular customer mindset. This customer focus includes individuals who participate in extreme sports such as surfing, skateboarding, and snowboarding.

[6]"Deciding to Franchise: Video Interview with Wing Lam, "Wahoo's Fish Taco, Perfect Business," nondated, www.perfectbusiness.com/video/ViewVideo.cfm?vid=87, May 18, 2011.

[7]"Wahoo's Fish Taco Names Tom Orbe as Vice President to Lead New Franchise Expansion Projects," Wahoo's Fish Taco LLC press release, August 24, 2009, www.businesswire.com/news/home/20090824005100/en/Wahoo's-Fish-Taco-Names-Tom-Orbe-Vice-President, May 18, 2011.
[8]Lisa Jennings, "Wahoo's Fish Taco Ramps Up Franchising Push," Nation's Restaurant News, August 25, 2009, www.nrn.com/article/wahoo's-fish-taco-ramps-franchising-push, May 18, 2011.
[9]John Hampton, "Wahoo's Fish Taco Launches First Store in Houston Area as Part of Franchise Expansion," PRWeb, September 14, 2010, www.prweb.com/releases/2010/09/prweb4511534.htm, May 18, 2011.

However, a much larger market segment is made up of those who simply want to live vicariously through others who are living a sports lifestyle. Wahoo's encourages their franchisees to use regional sports and charity events, as well as other types of local grassroots opportunities, to help market their businesses.

Wahoo's Fish Taco seeks franchise candidates who have restaurant experience (in particular, multi-unit restaurant experience). However, applicants with other types of business backgrounds may be considered.

Wahoo's also prefers applicants with the financial means to own and operate at least three restaurants in a certain geographical area. More than one restaurant provides the franchisee with a greater economy of scale and Wahoo's with a stronger franchisee base. The initial franchise fee is $30,000 for the first restaurant and $25,000 for each additional one. The ongoing royalty fee is 5% of gross sales, paid weekly. Also, each franchisee must allocate 2% of gross sales for marketing and advertising. Wahoo's estimates that the cost of building a brand new restaurant will range between $540,000 and $715,000, depending on store location and size, materials used, and other local factors.

The recommendation from Wahoo's is that a franchisee should provide his or her own start-up money, rather than borrow it. In the restaurant business there are seasonal ups and downs that affect cash flow, so it is always best to have some available working capital to help avoid getting caught in a financial crunch. Wing Lam believes that store sales of about $60,000 per month are sufficient to break even, while $100,000 per month will yield a comfortable living and $120,000 per month is sufficient to live well.[10]

---

[10]"Deciding to Franchise" video interview.

Case Study Analysis

1. What benefits does Wahoo's gain from franchising?
2. What benefits do franchisees get from the Wahoo's name?
3. Given the franchise fee structure, what initial payments would Wahoo's have received with the Houston franchisee's commitment to 11 outlets? If he generates $110,000 per month per restaurant, what would the *annual* royalties to Wahoo's be?
4. What challenges might Wahoo's face as it grows rapidly through franchising?

Case Sources

Wahoo's Fish Taco, LLC, corporate Web site at www.wahoos.com.

Deciding to Franchise: Video Interview with Wing Lam, "Wahoo's Fish Taco, Perfect Business," nondated, www.perfectbusiness.com/video/ViewVideo.cfm?vid=87, May 18, 2011.

"Wahoo's Fish Taco Names Tom Orbe as Vice President to Lead New Franchise Expansion Projects," Wahoo's Fish Taco LLC press release, August 24, 2009, www.businesswire.com/news/home/20090824005100/en/Wahoo's-Fish-Taco-Names-Tom-Orbe-Vice-President, May 18, 2011.

Lisa Jennings, "Wahoo's Fish Taco Ramps Up Franchising Push," *Nation's Restaurant News*, August 25, 2009, www.nrn.com/article/wahoo's-fish-taco-ramps-franchising-push, May 18, 2011.

John Hampton, "Wahoo's Fish Taco Launches First Store in Houston Area as Part of Franchise Expansion," PRWeb, September 14, 2010, www.prweb.com/releases/2010/09/prweb4511534.htm, May 18, 2011.

Honest Tea—From Start-Up to Harvest

Mission Statement:

> *Honest Tea creates and promotes delicious, truly healthy, organic beverages. We strive to grow with the same honesty we use to craft our products, with sustainability and great taste for all.*

Seth Goldman likes to say that Honest Tea got started because he was thirsty. Apparently, so were a lot of other people! Honest Tea grew from an operation with three employees and revenues of $250,000 in 1998 to one with 98 employees and $47 million in sales in 2009. Along the way, exit strategies described in the 1999 Honest Tea Business Plan have been executed. Seth and his co-founder, Barry Nalebuff, identified "investment by a strategic partner" and "complete acquisition" as potential exit strategies for investors. Honest Tea honestly followed these strategies in 2008 and 2011, respectively, when the company concluded an installment sale to the Coca-Cola Company. This is a clear case of entrepreneurs planning for the harvest from the start, and doing what they set out to do.

The Honest Tea Story

During one of Seth's classes at the Yale School of Management, he and his professor, Barry Nalebuff, found they shared a passion for a less sweet but flavorful beverage while discussing a Coke versus Pepsi case study. While he liked the idea of creating the perfect beverage, Seth de-

(Courtesy of Seth Goldman and Honest Tea)

cided to follow his passion for social change and work for the Calvert Group, managing marketing and sales for this socially responsible investment firm. While doing so, he expanded his already keen interest in social enterprise.

The entrepreneurial drive that began early in Seth's life became even stronger after a long run in Central Park, when he couldn't find any drinks to quench his thirst. Thinking back to the Coke versus Pepsi case study discussion, Seth e-mailed Barry, who had just returned from India where he had been studying the tea industry. Barry had learned that most U.S. beverage companies do not use whole tea leaves to make their bottled tea. Instead, they take whatever is left after the quality leaves have been packaged for products such as tea bags, leftover bits of tea described as "dust" or "fannings." Seth and Barry had a sense that they were homing in on an opportunity. Even better, Barry had already come up with a name for a company that would make beverages using top-of-the-line tea leaves. The company would be called Honest Tea.

Seth decided to leave the Calvert Group to pursue the idea, brewed batches of tea in his kitchen, and launched Honest Tea in February of 1998. During their first meeting with the Whole Foods Regional Office, the buyer sampled teas that Seth brought with him in borrowed thermoses and placed an order for 15,000 bottles. Honest Tea made its first deliveries in June 1998, offering five varieties of tea. Today, the product lines have expanded into Honest Tea (22 varieties in glass or PETE-1 [plastic] bottles,

Seth Goldman, Co-Founder and TeaEO, Honest Tea.
(Courtesy of Seth Goldman and Honest Tea)

Honest Ade [5 varieties], Honest Kids [5 varieties in pouches], Honest CocoaNova [3 varieties in glass bottles], and a zero-calorie line made with organic Stevia [2 varieties]. For most of the company's history, its products were distributed through independent beverage distributors with the greatest success in natural foods outlets.

Exhibit 14-2 shows the growth of Honest Tea's revenues from 1998 through 2009. The remarkable upswing in revenues between 2004 and 2005 is due in part to the company's teas becoming USDA certified organic. These remarkable revenue increases did not initially translate into profitability, according to Seth's blog. This is where financing options became critical.

(Courtesy of Seth Goldman and Honest Tea)

Honest Tea's Competitive Advantages

The team at Honest Tea worked hard to define the brand around the features that make Honest Tea stand out from the competition. In Seth's own words, "Given that this is a highly competitive market, the most important factor in our favor is that we offer a differentiated product. What we are offering is a very strong brand that is consistent with what is in the package and very meaningful to customers."

For example, Honest Tea was the first brand to make a certified-organic bottled tea. What does this mean and why does it matter? When an item is labeled USDA certified organic, it confirms that chemical pesticides and fertilizers have not been used in growing or producing the ingredients. Increasingly, consumers, particularly the health-conscious, are seeking out organic goods in the marketplace.

Honest Tea also uses up to two-thirds less sugar in its teas compared with competitors, such as Snapple and Arizona. Most varieties include

the phrase, "Just A Tad Sweet" on the label. This feature appeals to consumers who care about their health and diet.

Socially Responsible Business

Honest Tea's mission extends beyond using organic ingredients, whole tea leaves, and less sugar than most other beverages. The company goes to great lengths to educate customers about its ethical and socially responsible business practices. It wants them to know that when they buy Honest Tea, they are also doing something good for the community. As Seth puts it, "A commitment to social responsibility is central to Honest Tea's identity and purpose. The company strives for authenticity, integrity, and purity in our products and in the way we do business."

Staying in the Game

The beverage market is highly competitive, but Honest Tea appears to be thriving because it is delivering a differentiated product that customers

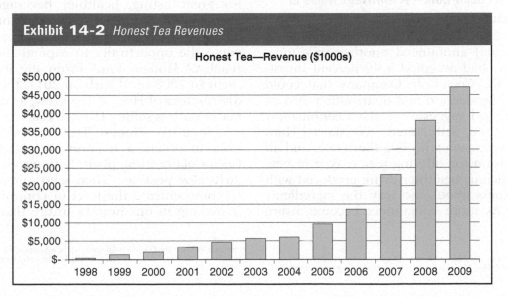

Exhibit 14-2 *Honest Tea Revenues*

feel good about buying, and it uses organic ingredients. However, this does not happen magically. The Honest Tea team has had to expend considerable efforts to secure the financial resources needed to fulfill their dream.

Initially, Seth and Barry invested their own funds and those of friends and family to seed the company. This initial round of investors put in approximately $500,000 to get the business started. The money was primarily used to pay for the first production run. It was rapidly apparent that additional funding would be necessary to pay for more production and a sales staff was needed to support additional growth. Barry created an innovative financing structure, using warrants to protect the interests of the founders.

The 1999 Business Plan that appears in this text is the one that was developed to secure additional funding. By the end of 1999, Honest Tea had raised in excess of $1.2 million in capital investment, primarily from small, private investors. Rather than going out to the venture capital community, as they expected to do, Seth was able to secure commitments from a number of consumers who had expressed an interest in investing in the company.[11] He writes, "The hardest money to raise was the $1.2 million in 1999, when we took in money from people we didn't know."[12] In the same year, Honest Tea jointly purchased ownership of Three Rivers Bottling, LLC, to have greater control over production and to eliminate potential problems of production shortfalls. The following year, the company secured additional funding from earlier investors. Over the following years the enterprise continued to grow, fueled in part by sales growth and additional equity raises.

Honest Tea and Coca-Cola—A Marriage Made in Beverage Heaven?

In February 2008, Honest Tea celebrated its tenth anniversary and announced another milestone. The company had accepted a 40 percent investment from the Coca-Cola Company that could help expand production and distribution, just as the founders had suggested in the 1999 business plan. At the time, Seth stated, "We started Honest Tea ten years ago with five thermoses and an ambitious vision for offering a new type of beverage—a delicious healthier drink produced with a consciousness about the way the ingredients are grown. As more consumers become aware

of how their decisions impact the health of the planet and themselves, we are thrilled to receive this investment from the world's largest beverage company to help take our brand and our mission to a larger scale and wider audience."[13] As part of the investment, Coca-Cola North America's Venturing and Emerging Brands (VEB) Business Unit retained an option to purchase the remaining ownership in 2011.

There was considerable concern among loyal Honest Tea customers as they became aware of the investment by Coca-Cola. Many were unhappy that this mission-driven company with a focus on health and organics would be subsumed by a large, multinational corporation with a different agenda. At the time, Gary Hirshberg, president and "CE-Yo" of Stonyfield Farm, and mentor and advisor to Seth, responded with the following: "The knowledge and access that Coca-Cola North America and its distribution system can provide comes at a perfect time as Honest Tea is at an exciting inflection point. I look forward to helping Seth and the team continue to build the business the right way in the years ahead."[14] Barry added, "This is our chance to bring organic beverages to the mainstream."[15]

In his February 5, 2008 blog, Seth addressed the customer questions head on: "So how do we move from the ideal to the real without screwing up what we've created? The world of mission-driven business is littered with entrepreneurs whose companies lost their soul or at least lost their leadership....I am determined to make sure that never happens with Honest Tea. Our challenge is to find a partner who wants to 'buy in' to our mission, rather than one who wants us to 'sell out.' Any partner that we consider must understand that the 'Honest' brand stands for great-tasting, healthier beverages that are produced in a more sustainable manner. As long as that partner buys into our approach, we welcome the opportunity to expand the scale and reach of Honest Tea." From the initial investment in 2008 until early in 2011, the number of distributors of Honest Tea grew, as did the number of outlets selling Honest Tea.

In 2010, Honest Tea worked with Coca-Cola to create a tea-brewing system inside a Coca-Cola bottling plant. Seth wrote, in an April 2010 blog posting, "There's no more visible way to communicate the level of commitment Coke is making in our brand's future than to show a

[11]Paul Gompers, "Honest Tea," Harvard Business School case study, 2001.
[12]Seth Goldman, "Seth's Blog," Honest Tea Web site, http://www.honesttea.com, April 28, 2009, April 20, 2011.
[13]Samme Menke, "The Coca-Cola Company Signs Agreement for 40% Stake in Honest Tea," Honest Tea press release, Bethesda, Maryland, February 5, 2008.
[14]Ibid.
[15]Op cit.

picture... of the Big Brewer—not only because it is a financially significant investment (more than $1 million) but because it takes up such a large piece of real estate in the middle of a production plant where space is limited and quite expensive.... The payback on such an expensive system is at least three years, far beyond the investment timeframe that Honest Tea could make on its own—we're rarely in a position to make capital investments beyond the next two months."

The company had been growing, but still had not become profitable. It needed to expand distribution and reach more people to fulfill its mission. As Seth noted in his blog posting on March 1, 2011: "...but even with our aggressive pace of growth, we kept losing money. Our margins were thin because our buying power was weak compared to the big brands, and we needed to hire more people to keep building the brand up and down the street. In order to stretch our limited funds, we've always been very frugal..."

In the same blog entry, he added, "More importantly, we were fortunate to develop a group of angel investors who helped us stay in business by continuing to support us financially with equity and debt investments." Honest Tea needed to give back to its patient investors. Seth suggested, "The only way we were able to stay in business was because our investors believed they would gain a return for the investments. Given our margins, dividends weren't going to be an option, so an exit would have to come either via acquisition or IPO." Although the team at Honest Tea briefly thought that an IPO would be an option, it reconsidered in 2007. Recognizing that "distribution is the key to winning in the beverage industry," and that the current network of independent distributors could not yield the necessary reach, it was determined that discussions with Coca-Cola made sense.

Honest Tea continues to operate as a separate division within Coca-Cola. Seth elected to reinvest the majority of his proceeds from the sale back into Honest Tea. The company has the opportunity to help fulfill the dream of bringing organics into the mainstream marketplace. In fact, in one of Seth's most recent blog posts, he wrote: "I can't imagine walking away from the business now that we finally have a national

(Courtesy of Seth Goldman and Honest Tea)

footprint in place and the chance to democratize organics in a way that's never been done. This tea party is just getting started."

Case Study Analysis

1. What are Honest Tea's competitive advantages?

2. Look at the list you generated. Which is most important to you as a consumer and why?

3. Given what you already know about Honest Tea's business philosophy and practices, if you were Seth's business advisor, what additional competitive advantages would you encourage him to develop?

4. What does it mean for a company to engage in "socially responsible business practices"?

5. What methods of capital acquisition did Honest Tea employ? Why?

6. How did the sale to Coca-Cola impact Honest Tea's investors?

7. What are the arguments for and against selling equity to Coca-Cola?

Case Sources

Honest Tea, http://www.honesttea.com, April 18, 2011.

Seth Goldman, "Seth's Blog," http://www.honesttea.com, April 18, 2011.

Paul Gompers, *Honest Tea*, Harvard Business School case study, 2001.

Samme Menke, "The Coca-Cola Company Signs Agreement for 40% Stake in Honest Tea," Honest Tea press release, Bethesda, Maryland, February 5, 2008.

Avocent Corporation

Small Business School video clips titles are in red
Prepared by Hattie Bryant, creator of Small Business School, *the television series made for PBS and Voice of America, http://SmallBusinessSchool.org.*

FIND A BIG PROBLEM TO SOLVE— SOLVE IT AND GROW

Avocent Corporation provides IT operations and infrastructure management solutions, including software and hardware. Its KVM equipment remotely controls personal computers and servers from 25 feet to 25,000 miles away. In December 2009, Avocent (based in Huntsville, Alabama) was acquired by Emerson Electronics, the St. Louis–based Fortune 100 company.

Avocent's story illustrates what can happen when an entrepreneur starts a business to solve a huge problem for customers that can afford to pay for the solution. In 1981, when he was 33 years old, Remigius Shatas started out with a big idea, and then incubated, nurtured, and grew it, and ultimately sold his company for a profit of millions. His path to financial success, however, was full of twists and turns.

While working in a grommet factory on the night shift, Remigius observed that there was not enough room on the desks for all the requisite equipment—computers, keyboards, a mouse, and a printer. That got him thinking, and he came up with an inspired concept. But before he was able to build and sell that product, he experienced many false starts and delays. The company he launched with his co-founders was called Cybex Computer Product Corporation—Cybex being an acronym for "cybernetic excellence"—and they originally intended to build robots. Remigius did consulting work to support himself while he developed his ideas and, in 1981, he recognized that the IBM Personal Computer (PC) would change the world of business.

Initially, Cybex generated sales by building mainframe-quality software for the PC, focusing on vertical markets, including retail pharmacy, veterinary, and modular business systems. The business was able to survive with these, but it was the company's eighth product that changed everything. That product today is called KVM.

Remigius invented KVM (keyboard, video, mouse) technology. According to Avocent's Web site, analog and digital KVM appliances, "consolidate access at the desk, at the rack or across the entire data center. Avocent has been at the forefront of KVM development from the start, saving space and improving staff efficiency in leading companies across the globe."[16] KVM not only keeps the desktop free of computers, it also keeps company-owned data safe in remote locations, rather than on multiple desks.

Company president Steve Thornton said, in his *Small Business School* interview, "The bottom line is we make a very large problem manageable. Without our product, if you had 1,000 computers you would need 1,000 separate keyboards, monitors, and mice." The problem was so big that,

---

[16]Avocent Web site, http://www.avocent.com, May 3, 2010.

when we met Remigius and Steve, they were up to $228 million in annual sales. Cybex had gone public, with a $32.6 million IPO, in 1995. It merged with Apex, Inc., in 2000, its largest KVM competitor, to form Avocent Corporation. Avocent then made a series of acquisitions—prior to being bought by Emerson Electric—as noted in the table below.

Avocent Acquisitions	
Company Acquired	**Year**
Equinox Systems	2001
2CComputing	2002
Soronti, Inc.	2003
Crystal Link Technologies	2004
OSA Technologies, Inc.	2004
Sonic Mobility, Inc.	2004
Cyclades Corporation	2006
LANDesk Corporation	2006

PREPARE TO SUCCEED

Remigius explains in the interview why he was able to build a company that won the attention of the world. "I got the bug—I call it the bug of ambition—and I found out the bug of ambition is fatal. Once you've caught it, there's no cure except success. And it just drives your life. I didn't know at the time—in my early 30s—that what you have to do is look at markets. I was still looking at products. And the difference between a small company and a large company is the transition between the product mentality and the market mentality."

Going back to the origin of Cybex, we learned that Remigius liked his work at the grommet factory, but he was troubled by the work environment. He did not like the way people were treated, and he also did not like driving the 100-mile-round-trip commute.

Remigius was thinking about others, not only himself. Imagine being exhausted from working nearly 24 hours and then facing a 50-mile drive so you could see your family and sleep in your own bed. One cold December morning, after spending the night at the office because he could not work on the computer systems during the day (employees needed them for their production work), Remigius decided to pursue his ideas and start a business in which people could actually enjoy their jobs. Dissatisfaction with an existing situation was a critical factor in Remigius's decision to start a business, as it often is for entrepreneurs.

He did not say to himself that he wanted to make a lot of money, or be a boss, or change the world. Remigius was thinking about what work *could* be like. He had a vision of the type of business he could create, and whereas he wanted to have financial security, it was the business culture and concepts that drove him. He wanted to solve a business problem, and help others become financially secure while doing so.

In addition, Remigius reported that he had to stop thinking about what product to make and start thinking about what problem to solve. And of course he knew that, the bigger the problem he could solve, the more he could grow his business. An owner cannot expand a business in the long term or sell it at a significant profit, if it is solely built on personality or an insubstantial product that few people would need. Remigius Shatas prepared to succeed, and that preparation included understanding his deep motivation, and the market he wanted to enter.

HIRE YOUR OWN BOSS

In order to grow his firm, Remigius did what relatively few founders do voluntarily: He hired his own boss. He did this when it became clear that the product he invented had huge market potential and that he was not equipped to manage the firm as it was going to grow. He learned from his early experience at Cybex, with co-founders who quit within the first year after start up, that managing an entrepreneurial enterprise is neither easy nor natural. As he began to experience success, Remigius acted on his own insight that he needed to hire a CEO for the company. This was a brilliant decision. Making such a choice exemplified a stereotypical founder that had to reflect on his or her knowledge, skills, abilities, and interests honestly enough to recognize that someone else might be more capable of actually *managing* a growing company. Remigius had never been the CEO of anything; he had always been the "computer guy," focused on how to make things work. Making computers operate correctly is a very different task from making an organization work well and become successful.

Remigius did not have sufficient funds to hire the experienced leader he wanted. However, he figured out how to value the company and its potential, and then asked Steve Thornton and Bob Asprey, managers he knew and respected, to bet on the company's future revenues. Rather than pay them the salaries they deserved, he offered them stock in the company. Remigius had to sell them on the bright future for KVM technology in general, and his business in particular. Both accepted the challenge and, because they did, became extremely wealthy when Cybex went public.

When Remigius finally landed on the right product at the right time, he had to stop accomplishing things on a small scale and look for ways to manage fast growth. While he worked on the markets, Asprey worked on the product and Thornton worked on the processes.

There were continuous cash flow problems in the early days, because it turned out they had the wrong business model. In many of the lean years, and when Steve, Bob, and Remigius could see that they would realize a profit, they did not write themselves paychecks; rather, they took a year-end bonus.

As they grew, their bankers determined that the Shatas/Thornton formula was not quite right, and initially turned them down for a working line of credit. The company had to stop building its new products in-house. This caused great disappointment among the team that had worked so hard over the years to get the products built, but the leadership realized that their personnel did not have the expertise to build the new products. They had to find a factory to take over the work.

Remigius said, "Bob would keep me in check. I always had ideas, but it was Bob who could figure out if the idea could be manufactured and if it would make us money. He forced us to measure the cost of my wild ideas before we spent too much cash." Getting the balance right requires the business owner to continuously decide if conceptions are worth investing

CHAPTER 14: Franchising, Licensing, and Harvesting: Cashing in Your Brand

time, money, and attention to develop. The downside of having many inspired ideas is that they can take a business "off track" so that it never completes or succeeds at anything. Fortunately for Remigius, with help from people like Bob, the business stuck to its core, winning products. Remigius Shatas's ownership was bought out in 2000 and, since then, he has spent his time and energy investing in the ideas of other promising entrepreneurs.

Case Analysis

1. What are some of the key decisions Remigius made that positioned his company for success?
2. Why was Remigius Shatas able to go public and then to leave the business with millions in his pocket?
3. Did Remigius launch the company with a winning product?
4. How did Avocent grow?

Appendix 1

The Daily Perc

Attractive visual.

Prepared by:

Bartholomew & Teresa Fisher
The Daily Perc, Inc.
P.O. Box 888
Coffee City, WA 99999-0888
777-777-7777

Fisher@TheDailyPerc.com

Contact information.

Nondisclosure.

The information provided in this business plan is confidential; therefore, the reader agrees not to disclose it without express written permission. By accepting this document, the reader acknowledges that information furnished in this business plan is in all respects confidential in nature, other than information that is in the public domain through other means, and that any disclosure or use of same by reader may cause serious harm or damage to The Daily Perc. Upon request, this document is to be immediately returned. This business plan does not imply an offering of securities.

Table of Contents

Well-organized, neatly
presented Table of
Contents.

Page numbers
included.

Appendices

1. Executive Summary

The Daily Perc, Inc. (TDP) is a specialty beverage retailer. TDP uses a system that is new to the beverage and food service industry to provide hot and cold beverages in a convenient and time-efficient way. TDP provides its customers the ability to drive up and order (from a trained barista) their choice of a custom-blended espresso drink, freshly brewed coffee, or other beverage. TDP is offering a high-quality option to the fast-food, gas station, or institutional coffee.

The Daily Perc offers its patrons the finest hot and cold beverages, specializing in specialty coffees, blended teas, and other custom drinks. In addition, TDP will offer soft drinks, fresh-baked pastries, and other confections. Seasonally, TDP will add beverages such as hot apple cider, hot chocolate, frozen coffees, and more.

The Daily Perc will focus on two markets:

The Daily Commuter—someone traveling to/from work, out shopping, delivering goods or services, or just out for a drive.

The Captive Consumer—someone who is in a restricted environment that does not allow convenient departure and return while searching for refreshments, or where refreshments stands are an integral part of the environment.

The Daily Perc will penetrate the commuter and captive consumer markets by deploying Drive-thru facilities and Mobile Cafés in the most logical and accessible locations. The Drive-thru facilities are designed to handle two-sided traffic and dispense customer-designed, specially ordered cups of premium coffees in less time than required for a visit to the locally owned café or one of the national chains.

In addition to providing a quality product and an extensive menu of delicious items, to ensure customer awareness and loyalty, as well as good publicity coverage and media support, we will be donating up to 7.5% of revenue to local charities based upon customer choices.

The Daily Perc's financial picture is quite promising. Since TDP is operating a cash business, the initial cost is significantly less than many start-ups these days. The process is labor intensive and TDP recognizes that a higher level of talent is required. The financial investment in its employees will be one of the greatest differentiators between it and TDP's competition. For the purpose of this pro forma plan, the capital expenditures of facilities and equipment are financed. There will be minimum inventory on hand so as to keep the product fresh and to take advantage of price drops, when and if they should occur.

The Daily Perc anticipates the initial combination of investments and long-term financing of $515,000 to carry it without the need for any additional equity or debt investment, beyond the purchase of equipment or facilities. This will mean growing a bit more slowly than might be otherwise possible, but it will be a solid, financially sound growth based on customer request and product demand.

The Daily Perc chooses to become the Drive-thru version of Starbucks between the mountains, obtaining several million dollars through an initial public or private offering that would allow the company to open 20 to 30 facilities per year in all metropolitan communities in the North, Midwest, and South with a population of over 150,000.

Margin annotations (left column):

- Introduced with a positive opening statement.
- Industry definition.
- Use of innovative equipment to increase efficiency.
- Innovation in product and service delivery. Use of trained staff to ensure product quality. Capacity to produce coffee on a custom basis.
- The offer: the bundle of products and services to be provided.
- Setting quality by comparison with other suppliers of coffee.
- Quality statement.
- More about offer.
- Target markets that TDP will serve.
- Logic for selecting locations.
- Facilities designed for the purpose of TDP. Design contributes to competitive advantage.
- Production and delivery capability.
- The offer: adding philanthropy to the mix.
- Staffing as a component of quality.
- Employees as a competitive advantage is using operations as an advantage.
- Critical financial and operational assumptions.
- Inventory management plan.
- Definition of financing need.
- Growth strategy defined.
- Proposing an IPO or private offering to generate cash.

This is the preferred Exit Strategy of the Management Team. The danger in this is that competitors would rise up and establish a foothold on a community before—or in the midst of—the arrival of The Daily Perc, causing a potential for a drain on revenues and a dramatic increase in advertising expenditures to maintain market share. Knowing these risks—and planning for them—gives TDP the edge needed to make this scenario work.

The balance sheet estimates a Net Worth of $1,724,505 for the third year, cash balances of $1,097,010, and earnings of $1,294,371, based on thirteen Drive-thrus and four Mobile Cafés, it is not unrealistic to put a market value of between $4 million and $9 million on the company. At present, such companies are trading in multiples of 4 to 10 times earnings, and it is simple mathematics to multiply the success of TDP by the number of major and smaller metropolitan areas between the mountain ranges of the United States.

Highlights

1.1. Objectives

The Daily Perc has established three firm objectives it wishes to achieve in the next three years:

1. Thirteen Drive-thru locations and four fully booked Mobile Cafés by the end of the third year.

2. Gross Margin of 45% or more.

3. Net After-tax Profit above 15% of Sales.

1.2. Keys to Success

There are four keys to success in this business, three of which are virtually the same as any food service business. It is our fourth key—the Community Mission—that will give us that extra measure of respect in the public eye.

1. The greatest locations—visibility, high traffic pattern, convenient access.

2. The best products—freshest coffee beans, cleanest equipment, premium serving containers, consistent flavor.

3. The friendliest servers—cheerful, skilled, professional, articulate.

4. The finest reputation—word-of-mouth advertising, promotion of our community mission of charitable giving.

Offering is not only for growth, but also the exit option the managers prefer.

Showing net worth, cash, and earnings to value the company.

Providing current valuation standard. A citation for the source of this information would make it more credible.

Clear visual representation.

Statement of performance objectives over three years.

Physical location as a key to achieving objectives. Three factors identified. Need to attach clear measures.

Competitive advantage.

Location and delivery advantage.

Product quality, as defined along four dimensions, to assist in achieving objectives. Need to attach clear measures.

Quality advantage.

Employees as a critical factor in achieving objectives. The four factors need clear measures.

Service advantage.

Customer perception as defined by two measures. Clear measures needed.

2. Mission, Vision, and Culture

The mission, vision, and culture of The Daily Perc are aligned for success. This is an organization that understands doing well by doing good and is designed to be profitable and an asset to the communities it serves.

2.1. Mission

The Daily Perc Mission is threefold, with each being as integral to our success as the next.

Product Mission—Provide customers the finest-quality beverage in the most efficient time.

Community Mission—Provide community support through customer involvement.

Economic Mission—Operate and grow at a profitable rate through sound economic decisions.

2.2. Vision

The Daily Perc will be the purveyor of the finest-quality beverages and baked goods in the most efficient time while sustaining our uncompromising principles and contributing to our communities.

2.3. Culture

The Daily Perc values teamwork; family and social responsibility; diversity; customer satisfaction; and a fun, healthy work environment. This creates a culture of collaboration and of high performance in small units.

3. Company Summary

The Daily Perc is a specialty beverage retailer. TDP uses a system that is new to the beverage and food service industry to provide hot and cold beverages in a convenient and time-efficient way. TDP provides its customers the ability to drive up and order from a trained barista their choice of a custom blended espresso drink, freshly brewed coffee, or other beverage. TDP is offering a high-quality option to the fast-food, gas station, and institutional coffee.

3.1. Company Ownership

The Daily Perc is a Limited Liability Corporation. All membership shares are currently owned by Bart and Teresa Fisher, with the intent of using a portion of the shares to raise capital.

The plan calls for the sale of 100 membership units in the company to family members, friends, and Angel Investors. Each membership unit in the company is priced at $4,250, with a minimum of five units per membership certificate, or a minimum investment of $21,250 per investor.

If all funds are raised, based on the pricing established in the financial section of this plan, Bart and Terri Fisher will maintain ownership of no less than 51% of the company.

3.2. Start-Up Summary

The Daily Perc's start-up expenses total just $365,670. The majority of these funds—roughly $300,000—will be used to build the first facility, pay deposits, and provide capital for six months of operating expenses. Another

The following margin notes appear alongside the page:

- Product quality.
- Service quality.
- Focus on growth.
- Clear, concise, compelling.
- Operational goal.
- TDP vision is future-oriented, compelling, built upon core values, and energizes employees.
- Summary of quality and operational goals along with ethics.
- Orientation toward people.
- Concern about the customer.
- Concerns about people.
- Focus on teams and outcomes.
- TDP culture conveys core values.
- Culture defined and underlying factors identified.
- Concise restatement of the Business Definition from the Executive Summary.
- Tells the reader the type of organization and ownership.
- Legal structure defined.
- Owners and their ownership intentions.
- Funding proposal that will need to be reflected in financials.
- Statement shows that owners intend to keep majority interest.
- Uses of start-up funds summarized.

The Daily Perc Business Plan provided by Business Plan Pro® and used by permission of Palo Alto Software.

$35,000 will be used for the initial inventory and other one-time expenses. The Daily Perc anticipates the need for roughly $25,500 in operating capital for the first few months of operation.

4. Market Analysis Summary

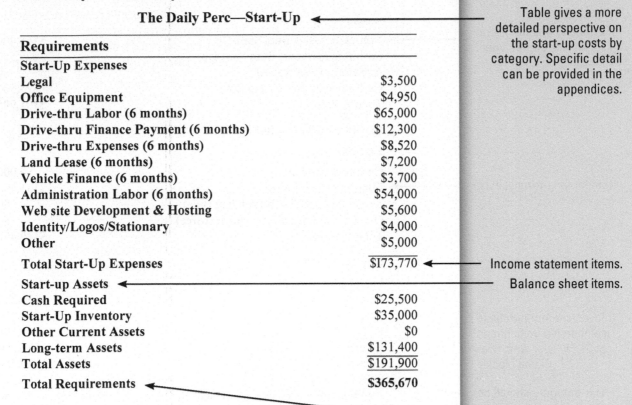

The Daily Perc—Start-Up ◄———— Table gives a more detailed perspective on the start-up costs by category. Specific detail can be provided in the appendices.

Requirements

Start-Up Expenses	
Legal	$3,500
Office Equipment	$4,950
Drive-thru Labor (6 months)	$65,000
Drive-thru Finance Payment (6 months)	$12,300
Drive-thru Expenses (6 months)	$8,520
Land Lease (6 months)	$7,200
Vehicle Finance (6 months)	$3,700
Administration Labor (6 months)	$54,000
Web site Development & Hosting	$5,600
Identity/Logos/Stationary	$4,000
Other	$5,000
Total Start-Up Expenses	**$173,770**

Total Start-Up Expenses ◄———— Income statement items.

Start-up Assets ◄———— Balance sheet items.

Start-up Assets	
Cash Required	$25,500
Start-Up Inventory	$35,000
Other Current Assets	$0
Long-term Assets	$131,400
Total Assets	**$191,900**

Total Requirements ◄———— **$365,670**

Total amount of funding needed is clearly stated.

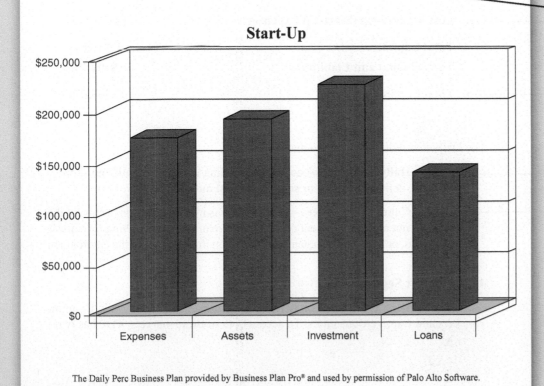

Start-Up

(Bar chart with vertical axis labeled from $0 to $250,000 in $50,000 increments. Categories: Expenses, Assets, Investment, Loans.)

The Daily Perc Business Plan provided by Business Plan Pro® and used by permission of Palo Alto Software.

The Daily Perc—Start-Up Funding

Start-Up Expenses to Fund	$173,770
Start-Up Assets to Fund	$191,900
Total Funding Required	**$365,670**
Assets	
Non-cash Assets from Start-Up	$166,400
Cash Requirements from Start-Up	$25,500
Additional Cash Raised	$0
Cash Balance on Starting Date	$25,500
Total Assets	**$191,900**
Liabilities and Capital	
Liabilities	
Current Borrowing	$9,000
Long-term Liabilities	$131,400
Accounts Payable (Outstanding Bills)	$0
Other Current Liabilities (Interest-free)	$0
Total Liabilities	**$140,400**
Capital	
Planned Investment	
Partner 1	$21,250
Partner 2	$21,250
Partner 3	$42,500
Partner 4	$25,500
Partner 5	$29,750
Other	$85,020
Additional Investment Requirement	$0
Total Planned Investment	**$225,270**
Loss at Start-Up (Start-Up Expenses)	($173,770)
Total Capital	$51,500
Total Capital and Liabilities	$191,900
Total Funding	$365,670

Carried over from previous table.

Inventory and long-term assets are included.

Debt for long-term assets.

Investors that purchase membership units priced at $4,250 in at least five-unit blocks.

This category should be explained.

Start-up loss is set to equal start-up expenses.

This total matches the total start-up requirements.

The Daily Perc will focus on two markets:

Target market # 1.

1. **The Daily Commuter**—someone traveling to or from work, out shopping, delivering goods or services, or just out for a drive.

Target market # 2.

2. **The Captive Consumer**—someone who is in a restricted environment that does not allow convenient departure and return while searching for refreshments, or where refreshments stands are an integral part of the environment.

4.1. Market Segmentation

The Daily Perc will focus on two different market segments: Daily Commuters and Captive Consumers. To access both of these markets, TDP has two

The Daily Perc Business Plan provided by Business Plan Pro® and used by permission of Palo Alto Software.

different delivery systems. For the commuters, TDP has the Drive-thru cof-feehouse. For the captive consumer, TDP has the Mobile Café.

Distinctive differen-tiation in approach to the segments.

Commuters are defined as any one or more individuals in a motorized vehicle traveling from point "A" to point "B." The Daily Perc's greatest concentra-tion will be on commuters heading to or from work, or those out on their lunch break.

Definition of target market #1—no limit of distance or time stated.

Captive Consumers would include those who are tethered to a campus environment, or in a restricted entry environment that does not allow free movement to and from. Examples would include high school and college campuses, where there is limited time between classes, and corporate cam-puses where the same time constraints are involved, but regarding meetings and project deadlines, and special events—such as carnivals, fairs, or festi-vals—where there is an admission price to enter the gate, but exiting would mean another admission fee, or where refreshments are an integral part of the festivities.

Definition of target market #2—easily understood.

Good examples to clarify the definition.

The following chart and table reflect the potential numbers of venues avail-able for the Mobile Cafés and what growth could be expected in those markets over the next five years. For a conservative estimate of the number of Captive Consumers this represents—multiply the total number of venues in the year by 1,000. As an example, in the first year, The Daily Perc is show-ing that there are a total of 2,582 venues at which we might position a Mobile Café. That would equate to a Captive Consumer potential of 2,582,000.

Explanation of a key assumption for volume.

Total market size clearly stated.

Similarly, there are well over 2,500,000 commuters in the metropolitan area, as well as visitors, vacationers, and others. It can also be assumed that these commuters do not make only one purchase in a day, but in many cases, two and even three beverage purchases.

Identification of another target.

Frequency of purchase es-timate—critical for sales projections.

The chart reflects college and high school campuses, special events, hos-pital campuses, and various charitable organizations. A segment that is not reflected in the chart (since it would skew the chart so greatly) is the number of corporate campuses in the metropolitan area. There are over 1,700 corpo-rate facilities that house more than 500 employees, giving us an additional 1,700,000 prospective customers, or total of 2,582 locations at which we could place a Mobile Café.

Explanation of another market opportunity and why it is not included in the chart.

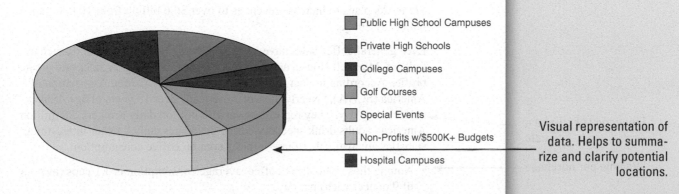

- Public High School Campuses
- Private High Schools
- College Campuses
- Golf Courses
- Special Events
- Non-Profits w/$500K+ Budgets
- Hospital Campuses

Visual representation of data. Helps to summa-rize and clarify potential locations.

The Daily Perc Business Plan provided by Business Plan Pro® and used by permission of Palo Alto Software.

Market Analysis

Potential Customers	Growth	YR1	YR2	YR3	YR4	YR5	CAGR
Public High School Campuses	1%	80	81	82	83	84	1.23%
Private High Schools	0%	88	88	88	88	88	0.00%
College Campuses	0%	77	77	77	77	77	0.00%
Golf Courses	0%	99	99	99	99	99	0.00%
Special Events	3%	43	44	45	46	47	2.25%
Non-Profits w/$500K+ Budgets	2%	362	369	376	384	392	2.01%
Hospital Campuses	0%	100	100	100	100	100	0.00%
Total	1.10%	849	858	867	877	887	1.10%

4.2. Target Market Segment Strategy

TDP's target market is the mobile individual who has more money than time, and excellent taste in a choice of beverage, but no time to linger in a café. By locating the Drive-thrus in high traffic/high visibility areas, this unique—and abundant—consumer will seek The Daily Perc out and become a regular guest.

To penetrate the target market for the Mobile Cafés, these units will do what they were designed to do. The Daily Perc will take the café to the customer! By using the community support program TDP is instituting, arrangements will be made to visit a high school, college campus, or a corporate campus once or twice a month (even visit these facilities for special games, tournaments, recruiting events, or corporate open houses). And, for every cup or baked good sold, a portion is returned to the high school or college. It becomes a tremendous, painless way for the institution to gain a financial reward while providing a pleasant and fulfilling benefit to their students or employees.

4.3. Industry Analysis

The coffee industry has grown by tremendous amounts in the United States over the past five years. According to e-imports.com, "Specialty coffee sales are increasing by 20% per year and account for nearly 8% of the 18 billion dollar U.S. coffee market." Starbucks, the national leader, had revenues in fiscal 2000 of $2.2 billion. That is an increase of 32% over fiscal 1999. Starbucks plans to increase revenues to over $6.6 billion from 10,000 retail outlets by 2005.

Even general coffee sales have increased, with international brands such as Folgers, Maxwell House, and Safari coffee reporting higher sales and greater profits. According to data gathered by the Specialty Coffee Association of America (SCAA), "Nearly 52% of Americans over 18 years of age drink coffee every day. They represent over 100 million daily drinkers. 30 million American adults drink specialty coffee beverages daily." Other interesting statistics are available from e-imports.com on coffee consumption:

- Among those who drink coffee, average consumption is 3.1 cups (average of 9 ounces each) per day.

- The price is $2.45 on average for an espresso-based drink.

The Daily Perc Business Plan provided by Business Plan Pro® and used by permission of Palo Alto Software.

498

- Brewed coffee averages $1.38 each.

- Coffee is primarily consumed during breakfast hours (65%), with 35% consumed between meals and the balance with other meals.

- Black coffee is preferred by 35% of coffee drinkers.

- The average number of cups of espresso and coffee drinks sold per day at an espresso Drive-thru business with a great visible location is 250, with 500 cups being extraordinary.

- 69% of the coffee sold by independent coffee shops is brewed coffee and 31% is espresso-based.

America is definitely a coffee country and the coffee industry is reaping the rewards.

4.3.1 Competition and Buying Patterns

There are four general competitors in The Daily Perc's Drive-thru market. They are the national specialty beverage chains, such as Starbucks and Panera, local coffeehouses—or cafés—with an established clientele and a quality product, fast-food restaurants, and convenience stores. There is a dramatic distinction among the patrons of each of these outlets.

Patrons to a Starbucks, or to one of the local cafés, are looking for the "experience" of the coffeehouse. They want the ability to "design" their coffee, smell the fresh pastry, listen to the soothing Italian music, and read the local paper or visit with an acquaintance. It is a relaxing, slow-paced environment.

Patrons of the fast-food restaurants or the convenience stores are just the opposite. They have no time for idle chatter and are willing to overpay for whatever beverage the machine can spit out, as long as it's quick. They pay for their gas and they are back on the road to work. Although they have the desire and good taste to know good from bad, time is more valuable to them.

Competitors to the Mobile Cafés on campuses would include fast-food restaurants—assuming they are close enough to the consumer that they can get there and back in the minimal allotted time—vending machines, and company or school cafeterias. The consumers in this environment are looking for quick, convenient, fairly priced, quality refreshment that will allow them to purchase the product and return to work, class, or other activity.

Competitors to the Mobile Cafés at events such as festivals and fairs would include all the other vendors who are licensed to sell refreshments. Attendees to such events expect to pay a premium price for a quality product.

5. Strategy and Implementation Summary

The Daily Perc will penetrate the commuter and captive consumer markets by deploying Drive-thru facilities and Mobile Cafés in the most logical and accessible locations. The Drive-thrus are designed to handle two-sided traffic and dispense customer-designed, specially ordered cups of specialty beverages in less time than required for a visit to the locally owned café or one of the national chains.

Timing of consumption.

Product preference measure.

Volume of sales by a particular business type.

Data that can be used in TDP sales and financial projections.

Unique Selling Proposition.

Market positioning determined through the totality of experience. Quality factors described in subsequent sentences.

Emphasis on the difference in what defines a quality experience for a different customer segment.

Unique Selling Proposition for these patrons is speedy service, and concern for quality is not significant.

Important factors are speed of delivery and convenience.

Excellent example of defining competitors. Important factors are speed of delivery, convenience, fair pricing, and quality of products.

Limited competition based upon geography. Less of a clear distinction.

Place defined.

Product defined.

The Daily Perc Business Plan provided by Business Plan Pro® and used by permission of Palo Alto Software.

The Daily Perc has identified its market as busy, mobile people whose time is already at a premium, but desire a refreshing, high-quality beverage or baked item while commuting to or from work or school.

In addition to providing a quality product and an extensive menu of delicious items, to ensure customer awareness and loyalty, as well as positive public and media support, The Daily Perc could be donating up to 7.5% of revenue from each cup sold in individual Drive-thrus to the charities of the customers' choice.

5.1. Products

The Daily Perc provides its patrons the finest hot and cold beverages, specializing in specialty coffees and custom blended teas. In addition, TDP will offer select domestic soft drinks, Italian sodas, fresh-baked pastries, and other confections. Seasonally, TDP will add beverages such as hot apple cider, hot chocolate, frozen coffees, and more. The beverages come with a social mission, as up to 7.5% of revenues go to local charities selected by the customers. The precise list of products will be specific to the Drive-thru location selected.

5.2. Competitive Edge

The Daily Perc's competitive edge is simple. TDP provides a high-quality product at a competitive price in a Drive-thru environment that saves time.

5.3. Marketing Strategy

First and foremost, The Daily Perc will be placing its Drive-thru facilities in locations of very high visibility and great ease of access. They will be located on high traffic commuter routes and close to shopping facilities in order to catch customers going to or from work, or while they are out for lunch, or on a shopping expedition. The Drive-thrus are very unique and eye-catching, which will be a branding feature of its own.

The Daily Perc will be implementing a low-cost advertising/promotion campaign, which could involve drive-time radio, but not much more.

The Daily Perc will rely on building relationships with schools, charities, and corporations to provide significant free publicity because of its community support program. By giving charitable contributions to these institutions, they will get the word out to their students/ faculty/employees/partners about TDP. Word of mouth (or viral marketing) has always proven to be the greatest advertising program a company can instill. In addition, the media will be more than willing to promote the charitable aspects of TDP and provide the opportunity for more exposure every time TDP writes a check to another organization.

5.4. Sales Strategy

There will be several sales strategies put into place, including posting specials on high-profit items at the Drive-thru window. The baristas will also hand out free drink coupons to those who have purchased a certain number of cups or something similar. TDP will also develop window sales techniques such as the baristas asking if the customer would like a fresh-baked item with their coffee.

5.4.1. Sales Forecast

In the first year, The Daily Perc anticipates having two Drive-thru locations in operation. The first location will open in the third month of this plan and be fully operational beginning on the 1st day of September. The second Drive-thru will open six months later. TDP is building in a

The Daily Perc Business Plan provided by Business Plan Pro® and used by permission of Palo Alto Software.

Philanthropy defined for TDP.

Product quality as a positioning strategy. Some definition noted. Could enhance the description by identifying particular suppliers of high-end products. This is explained at the end of the section by the need to customize the product selection by location.

Clear description of the competitive edge.

Competitive advantage based upon quality, value, and timeliness.

Description of the selection of locations and their design. Relationship between the location and the market.

Advertising plan limited to potential drive-time radio. This section could be expanded to include more information about the advertisements and the placement and costs.

Public relations strategy of providing community support.

Viral marketing as a marketing strategy.

Using price reductions to generate sales.

Sales techniques with the baristas to encourage add-on sales.

Using design of the facilities to enhance sales.

Detailed sales projections translate concepts into product sales.

Using technology to support the business.

certain amount of ramp-up for each facility while commuters become familiar with its presence. The Drive-thrus will generate 288,000 tickets in the first year of operation, or approximately $558,000 in revenue. A detailed sales forecast for the first year appears in Appendix 1-A.

In the second year, The Daily Perc will add two more Drive-thrus and, in the third year, TDP will add an additional nine Drive-thru facilities. The addition of these facilities will increase the revenue from Drive-thrus to a total of over 1,000,000 tickets or $2.35 million in the second year and 2,675,000 tickets or just over $6 million in the third.

In addition to the Drive-thrus, The Daily Perc will deploy one mobile unit in the fourth quarter of the first fiscal year. TDP expects this mobile unit to generate 10,000 tickets each, at an average ticket price of $2.45, which will generate gross revenues of approximately $24,500.

In the second quarter of the second fiscal year, The Daily Perc will deploy a second and third mobile unit. TDP expects all three mobile units to generate 150,000 tickets, or gross revenue of $375,00 in the second year. In the third fiscal year, with an additional fourth mobile unit deployed, TDP expects to see 264,000 mobile unit tickets, or $673,200 in gross revenue.

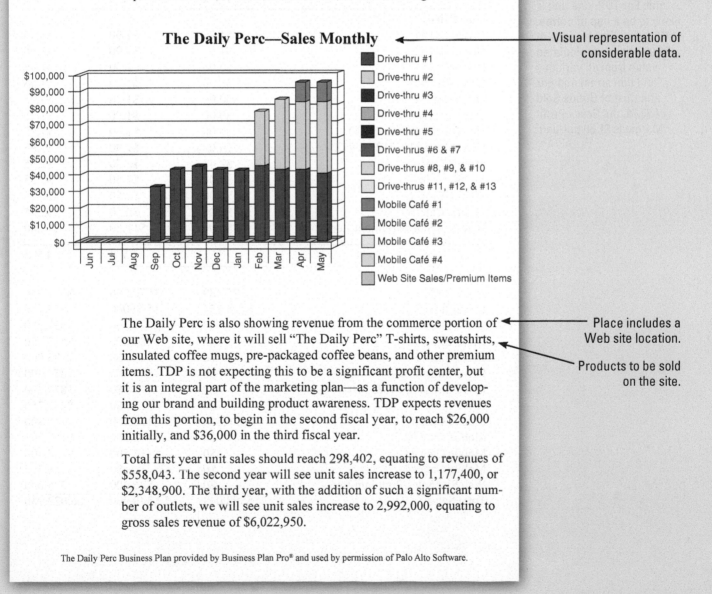

The Daily Perc—Sales Monthly ◄———————— Visual representation of considerable data.

Legend:
- Drive-thru #1
- Drive-thru #2
- Drive-thru #3
- Drive-thru #4
- Drive-thru #5
- Drive-thrus #6 & #7
- Drive-thrus #8, #9, & #10
- Drive-thrus #11, #12, & #13
- Mobile Café #1
- Mobile Café #2
- Mobile Café #3
- Mobile Café #4
- Web Site Sales/Premium Items

The Daily Perc is also showing revenue from the commerce portion of ◄——— Place includes a Web site location.
our Web site, where it will sell "The Daily Perc" T-shirts, sweatshirts, ◄——— Products to be sold on the site.
insulated coffee mugs, pre-packaged coffee beans, and other premium items. TDP is not expecting this to be a significant profit center, but it is an integral part of the marketing plan—as a function of developing our brand and building product awareness. TDP expects revenues from this portion, to begin in the second fiscal year, to reach $26,000 initially, and $36,000 in the third fiscal year.

Total first year unit sales should reach 298,402, equating to revenues of $558,043. The second year will see unit sales increase to 1,177,400, or $2,348,900. The third year, with the addition of such a significant number of outlets, we will see unit sales increase to 2,992,000, equating to gross sales revenue of $6,022,950.

The Daily Perc Business Plan provided by Business Plan Pro® and used by permission of Palo Alto Software.

Detailed visual representation of the expected sales.

Note: The Daily Perc does not include a calculation of the economics of one unit. For TDP, one unit is likely to be a cup of coffee. With an average price of $2.00 per cup (calculated value from all varieties and cup sizes) and per unit Cost of Goods Sold of $0.70, the Gross Profit Margin is $1.30 per unit.

The Daily Perc—Sales Forecast

	FY 1	FY 2	FY 3
Unit Sales			
Drive-thru #1	202,913	300,000	325,000
Drive-thru #2	85,489	300,000	325,000
Drive-thru #3	0	275,000	325,000
Drive-thru #4	0	150,000	325,000
Drive-thru #5	0	0	300,000
Drive-thrus #6 & #7	0	0	450,000
Drive-thrus #8, #9, & #10	0	0	450,000
Drive-thrus #11, #12, & #13	0	0	225,000
Mobile Café #1	10,000	60,000	66,000
Mobile Café #2	0	45,000	66,000
Mobile Café #3	0	45,000	66,000
Mobile Café #4	0	0	66,000
Web Site Sales/Premium Items	0	2,400	3,000
Total Unit Sales	298,402	1,177,400	2,992,000

	FY 1	FY 2	FY 3
Unit Prices			
Drive-thru #1	$1.85	$1.90	$1.95
Drive-thru #2	$1.85	$1.90	$1.95
Drive-thru #3	$0.00	$1.90	$1.95
Drive-thru #4	$0.00	$1.90	$1.95
Drive-thru #5	$0.00	$1.90	$1.95
Drive-thrus #6 & #7	$0.00	$1.90	$1.95
Drive-thrus #8, #9, & #10	$0.00	$1.90	$1.95
Drive-thrus #11, #12, & #13	$0.00	$1.90	$1.95
Mobile Café #1	$2.45	$2.50	$2.55
Mobile Café #2	$0.00	$2.50	$2.55
Mobile Café #3	$0.00	$2.50	$2.55
Mobile Café #4	$0.00	$2.50	$2.55
Web Site Sales/Premium Items	$0.00	$11.00	$12.00

	FY 1	FY 2	FY 3
Sales			
Drive-thru #1	$375,389	$570,000	$633,750
Drive-thru #2	$158,154	$570,000	$633,750
Drive-thru #3	$0	$522,500	$633,750
Drive-thru #4	$0	$285,000	$633,750
Drive-thru #5	$0	$0	$585,000
Drive-thrus #6 & #7	$0	$0	$877,500
Drive-thrus #8, #9, & #10	$0	$0	$877,500
Drive-thrus #11, #12, & #13	$0	$0	$438,750
Mobile Café #1	$24,500	$150,000	$168,300
Mobile Café #2	$0	$112,500	$168,300
Mobile Café #3	$0	$112,500	$168,300
Mobile Café #4	$0	$0	$168,300
Web Site Sales/Premium Items	$0	$26,400	$36,000
Total Sales	$558,043	$2,348,900	$6,022,950

The Daily Perc Business Plan provided by Business Plan Pro® and used by permission of Palo Alto Software.

	FY 1	FY 2	FY 3
Direct Unit Costs			
Drive-thru #1	$0.64	$0.61	$0.59
Drive-thru #2	$0.64	$0.61	$0.59
Drive-thru #3	$0.00	$0.61	$0.59
Drive-thru #4	$0.00	$0.61	$0.59
Drive-thru #5	$0.00	$0.61	$0.59
Drive-thrus #6 & #7	$0.00	$0.61	$0.59
Drive-thrus #8, #9, & #10	$0.00	$0.61	$0.59
Drive-thrus #11, #12, & #13	$0.00	$0.61	$0.59
Mobile Café #1	$0.64	$0.61	$0.59
Mobile Café #2	$0.00	$0.61	$0.59
Mobile Café #3	$0.00	$0.61	$0.59
Mobile Café #4	$0.00	$0.61	$0.59
Web Site Sales/Premium Items	$0.00	$6.50	$6.50
Direct Cost of Sales			
Drive-thru #1	$129,864	$183,000	$191,750
Drive-thru #2	$54,713	$183,000	$191,750
Drive-thru #3	$0	$167,750	$191,750
Drive-thru #4	$0	$91,500	$191,750
Drive-thru #5	$0	$0	$177,000
Drive-thrus #6 & #7	$0	$0	$265,500
Drive-thrus #8, #9, & #10	$0	$0	$265,500
Drive-thrus #11, #12, & #13	$0	$0	$132,750
Mobile Café #1	$6,400	$36,600	$38,940
Mobile Café #2	$0	$27,450	$38,940
Mobile Café #3	$0	$27,450	$38,940
Mobile Café #4	$0	$0	$38,940
Web Site Sales/Premium Items	$0	$15,600	$19,500
Subtotal Direct Cost of Sales	**$190,977**	**$732,350**	**$1,783,010**

6. Management and Operations Summary

The Daily Perc is a relatively flat organization. Overhead for management will be kept to a minimum and all senior managers will be "hands-on" workers. There is no intention of having a top-heavy organization that drains profits and complicates decisions.

Owners Bart and Teresa Fisher will be actively involved in the management and operations of the sites. The founders of TDP bring a strong management and technical foundation to TDP. Terri Fisher has approximately 15 years of progressive experience at Starbucks Coffee Company, starting out as a barista and moving through the ranks to senior financial management (see Appendix 1-G for her resume). Bart Fisher brings talents and experience in retail sales and marketing, having owned and operated an advertising agency and several Krispy Kreme franchises (see Appendix 1-G for his resume). They will initially divide the overall management responsibilities, with Terri

Management designed to create a culture of equality.

Presumption that decisions will be simplified and profitability enhanced.

Role of founders matched to the culture.

Background of founders identified. Pertinent details noted and readers referred to the appendices for resumes.

Division of responsibilities.

The Daily Perc Business Plan provided by Business Plan Pro® and used by permission of Palo Alto Software.

503

emphasizing accounting and finance and Bart leading marketing and sales. They also will be part of the staff at the Drive-thru sites.

Identification of executive positions.

At the zenith of this three-year plan, there will be four "Executive" positions: chief operating officer, chief financial officer, chief information officer, and director of marketing. There will be other mid-management positions, such as district managers for every four Drive-thrus, and a facilities manager to oversee the maintenance and stocking of the Mobile Cafés, as well as overseeing the maintenance and replacement of equipment in the Drive-thru facilities.

Identification of mid-management roles and ratio of district managers to Drive-thrus.

6.1. Personnel Plan

First-year plan, scaled to the startup with details included in the appendices.

The Daily Perc expects the first year to be rather lean, since there will only be two locations and one mobile unit—none of which will be deployed for the entire year. The total headcount for the first year, including management, administrative support, and customer service (production), will be 15, with a total payroll of $242,374, a payroll burden of $36,356, and a total expenditure of $278,730. The detailed first year personnel plan is in Appendix 1-B.

Plan for growth in the second year with specific positions, including initial mid-management, and payroll information.

The second year, with the addition of two Drive-thrus and two mobile units, The Daily Perc will add customer service personnel, as well as a district manager and some additional support staff at headquarters, including an inventory clerk, equipment technician, and administrative support.

The headcount will increase by nearly 100% in the second year to 29, with a payroll of $846,050 and a payroll burden of $126,908.

Creation of senior management team and significant growth in year 3.

The third year will see the most dramatic growth in headcount, due to the addition of nine Drive-thrus and another mobile unit. In the third year, there will also be an increase of 180% over the previous year. Total payroll for the third year will be $2,024,250, with a payroll burden of $303,638. There will be a significant increase in the senior management team, with the addition of a chief financial officer, a chief information officer, and a director of marketing. There will also be a second and third district manager, and a corporate events sales executive. Total personnel will reach 81.

Descriptions of the roles of the senior managers. Proposed position descriptions could be included in the appendices.

The chief financial officer will be brought on to oversee the increase in numbers of retail outlets and to manage a dramatically more detailed P&L statement and to manage the Balance Sheet. The chief information officer will be brought in to help us with the deployment of a point-of-sale computerized cash register system that will make tracking and managing receipts and charitable contributions more robust. Ideally, this individual will have a large amount of point-of-sale and Internet experience. Specifically, how to tie in POS systems to the Internet and inventory controls. Also, knowledge in establishing technology guidelines for the company and franchisees in the future. This individual will also be added in fiscal year three.

The director of marketing will be charged with managing the relationships with advertising agencies, public relations firms, the media, and our Web site.

The Daily Perc—Personnel Plan

	FY 1	FY 2	FY 3
Drive-thru Team	$135,474	$439,250	$1,098,650
Mobile Café Team	$9,400	$172,800	$225,600
Equipment Care Specialist (Headquarters)	$0	$22,000	$77,000
Other	$0	$12,000	$24,000
District Manager (Four Drive-thrus)	$0	$22,000	$77,000
Corporate Events Sales Exec	$0	$0	$36,000
Director of Marketing	$0	$0	$72,000
Other	$0	$0	$0
Bookkeeper/Office Administrator	$24,500	$46,000	$54,000
Warehouse/Site Manager	$7,000	$42,000	$48,000
Inventory Clerk	$0	$12,000	$42,000
Other	$0	$6,000	$12,000
Chief Operating Officer	$66,000	$72,000	$78,000
Chief Financial Officer	$0	$0	$96,000
Chief Information Officer	$0	$0	$84,000
Other	$0	$0	$0
Total People	15	29	81
Total Payroll	**$242,374**	**$846,050**	**$2,024,250**

6.2. Physical Locations/Facilities

One of the most exciting aspects of The Daily Perc is the flexibility in selecting locations. The Drive-thrus are relatively small and the Mobile Cafés are just that. Site selection is based upon population demographics and traffic patterns. With a focus on the Daily Commuter and the Captive Customers, locations are well-defined. Drive-thru espresso shops will be opened in metropolitan communities with a population greater than 150,000. These facilities will be located on accessible sites with high visibility, on high-traffic commuter routes and close to shopping facilities. Each Drive-thru will be double-sided and attractively decorated. According to the previously compiled market segmentation information, TDP has calculated 2,582 venues where Mobile Cafés might be positioned.

6.3. Inventory, Production, and Quality Assurance

The Daily Perc uses innovative coffee brewing technology and tight inventory controls with excellence in quality assurance. TDP has adopted a new type of coffee equipment that produces espresso drinks very rapidly with consistently excellent flavor. By having trained baristas personally take customer orders and produce hot and cold beverages, quality is increased and production errors are decreased. Because of this delivery system, customers can buy high-quality, freshly prepared beverages in less time than is required for a visit to a locally owned café or chain.

Because of the technology used and the delivery system, inventory can be controlled through economic order quantities with a computer-based reorder system. The product line is sufficiently broad to satisfy customer requests, but sufficiently narrow as to yield relatively straightforward inventory control.

The Daily Perc Business Plan provided by Business Plan Pro® and used by permission of Palo Alto Software.

Coffees and teas served are all Fair Trade goods and the coffee beans are roasted locally. Bart Fisher manages the quality assurance with respect to the roasted beans. Each manager has a quality assurance manual and a test system for beverage production. Terri Fisher manages the quality assurance process for baked goods.

7. Financial Plan

The Daily Perc's financial picture is quite promising. Since TDP is operating a cash business, the initial cost is significantly less than many start-ups these days. The process is labor intensive and TDP recognizes that a higher level of talent is required. The financial investment in its employees will be one of the greatest differentiators between it and TDP's competition. For the purpose of this pro forma plan, the facilities and equipment are financed. These items are capital expenditures and will be available for financing. There will be a minimum of inventory on hand so as to keep the product fresh and to take advantage of price drops, when and if they should occur.

The Daily Perc anticipates the initial combination of investments and long-term financing of $515,000 to carry it without the need for any additional equity or debt investment, beyond the purchase of equipment or facilities. This will mean growing a bit more slowly than might be otherwise possible, but it will be a solid, financially sound growth based on customer request and product demand.

7.1. Important Assumptions

The financial plan depends on important assumptions, most of which are shown in the following table. The key underlying assumptions are:

- The Daily Perc assumes a slow-growth economy, without major recession.

- The Daily Perc assumes, of course, that there are no unforeseen changes in public health perceptions of its general products.

- The Daily Perc assumes access to equity capital and financing sufficient to maintain its financial plan as shown in the tables.

- Assumptions for the first year appear in Appendix 1-C.

The Daily Perc—General Assumptions

	FY 1	FY 2	FY 3
Plan Month	1	2	3
Current Interest Rate	10.00%	10.00%	10.00%
Long-term Interest Rate	9.00%	9.00%	9.00%
Tax Rate	0.00%	0.00%	0.00%
Other	0	0	0

7.2 Break-even Analysis

To arrive at the average monthly fixed costs, The Daily Perc calculated the fixed costs for the Drive-thru to be $28,294. Using the average price per unit, less the average cost per unit, divided into the fixed costs of operation, TDP concludes that we will need at least 23,001 units per month to reach break-even at $43,016 per month.

The Daily Perc Business Plan provided by Business Plan Pro® and used by permission of Palo Alto Software.

Product line considers customer satisfaction and inventory control.

Should reduce lead times, increase product freshness, and permit lower inventory levels.

Specific, written quality criteria and testing methodologies used to ensure customer expectations are met or exceeded.

Best to articulate more detailed financial assumptions in an appendix.

Showing fundamental financial assumptions in a table.

Tax rate of 0% assumed because TDP is an LLC and taxes fall to the members.

Break-even equals the fixed cost of operations divided by the difference between the average price per unit and the average cost per unit.

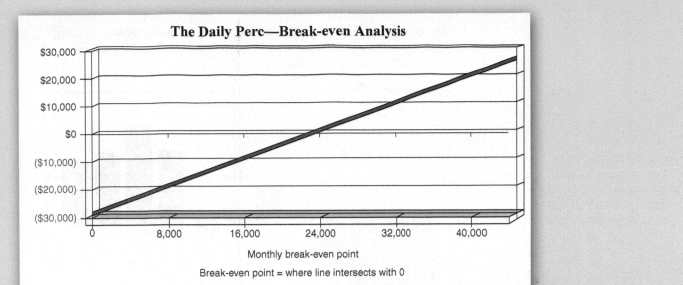

The Daily Perc—Break-even Analysis

$30,000
$20,000
$10,000
$0
($10,000)
($20,000)
($30,000)

0   8,000   16,000   24,000   32,000   40,000

Monthly break-even point

Break-even point = where line intersects with 0

The Daily Perc—Break-even Analysis

Simple chart that shows break-even information.

Monthly Units Break-even	23,001
Monthly Revenue Break-even	$43,014
Assumptions:	
Average Per-Unit Revenue	$1.87
Average Per-Unit Variable Cost	$0.64
Estimated Monthly Fixed Cost	$28,294

7.3. Projected Profit and Loss

The Daily Perc is expecting some dramatic growth in the next three years, reaching $558,043 in sales and a 65.5% Gross Profit Margin by the end of the first year. Expenses during the first year leave a Net After-tax profit of $9,960, or 1.8%. Detailed profit and loss information is included in Appendix 1-D.

Starting with a statement to generate interest and enthusiasm.

Describes the information contained in the income statement.

Summary data is clear and matches the figure that follows.

Refers to an appendix for in-depth data. Shortens the body of the plan and reduces confusion.

Aside from production costs of 34.4%, which include actual production of product and commissions for sales efforts, the single largest expenditures in the first year are in the general and administrative (G&A) area, totaling 54.7% of sales. G&A includes expenses for rents, equipment leases, utilities, and the payroll burden for all employees.

Explanation of the cost structure.

Sales increase by nearly 400% in the second year, due to the addition of two more Drive-thrus and two more Mobile Cafés, reaching a total of $2,348,900. Although operating expenses double in the second year, The Daily Perc will be able to realize a Net After-tax profit of $368,675 or 15.7% of sales. In that same year, TDP will make charitable contributions of $70,000.

Steps to profitability.

Fulfilling the social promise (the fifth "P" of philanthropy).

The third year is when The Daily Perc has the opportunity to break into markets outside the metropolitan area. TDP will see nine additional Drive-thru facilities open in the third year, which will drive sales to $6,022,950 and, even with a 200% increase in production costs, help reach a Gross Profit Margin of 68.9%. Several expenses take substantial jumps this year—advertising increasing from $36,000 to $72,000 and donations increasing from $72,000 to $180,000—and TDP will be adding several key management team members.

Expansion plans. How TDP will grow significantly.

Increased expenses explained and positive impact still shown.

The Daily Perc Business Plan provided by Business Plan Pro® and used by permission of Palo Alto Software.

These increases, as well as those for increased equipment leases and rents, raise our operating expenses to $2,772,993, leaving a Net After-tax profit of $1,294,371, or 21.5% of sales.

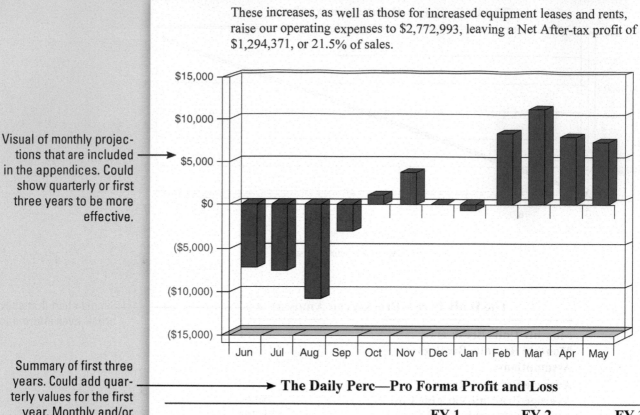

Visual of monthly projections that are included in the appendices. Could show quarterly or first three years to be more effective.

Summary of first three years. Could add quarterly values for the first year. Monthly and/or quarterly values can be in the appendices. Also called "Projected Income Statement."

Clear statement of gross margin in the financial statement is helpful in the business plan.

TDP should show advertising and other marketing expenses explicitly. Charitable contributions also should be shown.

TDP is showing a small net profit in the first year. This is unusual among start-up businesses. Do not be alarmed if you suffer a loss in year 1.

The Daily Perc—Pro Forma Profit and Loss

	FY 1	FY 2	FY 3
Sales	$558,043	$2,348,900	$6,022,950
Direct Costs of Goods	$190,977	$732,350	$1,783,010
Sales Commissions	$1,416	$35,234	$90,344
Cost of Goods Sold	$192,393	$767,584	$1,873,354
Gross Margin	$365,650	$1,581,317	$4,149,596
Gross Margin %	65.52%	67.32%	68.90%
Expenses			
Payroll	$242,374	$846,050	$2,024,250
Sales and Marketing and Other Expenses	$0	$0	$0
Depreciation	$21,785	$92,910	$196,095
Leased Offices and Equipment	$0	$6,000	$18,000
Utilities	$9,640	$19,800	$41,100
Insurance	$12,570	$32,620	$63,910
Rent	$16,800	$50,400	$126,000
Payroll Taxes	$36,356	$126,908	$303,638
Other General and Administrative Expenses	$0	$0	$0
Total Operating Expenses	$339,525	$1,174,688	$2,772,993
Profit before Interest and Taxes	$26,125	$406,629	$1,376,603
EBITDA	$47,910	$499,539	$1,572,698
Interest Expense	$16,165	$37,954	$82,232
Taxes Incurred	$0	$0	$0
Net Profit	$9,960	$368,675	$1,294,371
Net Profit/Sales	1.78%	15.70%	21.49%

The Daily Perc Business Plan provided by Business Plan Pro® and used by permission of Palo Alto Software.

7.4. Projected Cash Flow

Cash flow will have to be carefully monitored, as in any business, but The Daily Perc is also the beneficiary of operating a cash business. After the initial investment and start-up costs are covered, the business will become relatively self-sustaining, with the exception of seasonal dips, which TDP has attempted to account for through changes in the menu items.

Assuming an initial investment and financing of $515,000, which would include $25,500 of operating capital, The Daily Perc anticipates no cash flow shortfalls for the first year or beyond. March and May are the greatest cash drains, since TDP will be experiencing the cost of a second Drive-thru and mobile unit start-up. Again, TDP sees heavier than normal drains of cash in December and January, as there will be certain accounts payable coming due. A detailed pro forma cash flow for the first year of operations is included in Appendix 1-E.

The Daily Perc—Pro Forma Cash Flow

	FY 1	FY 2	FY 3
Cash Received			
Cash from Operations			
Cash Sales	$558,043	$2,348,900	$6,022,950
Subtotal Cash from Operations	$558,043	$2,348,900	$6,022,950
Additional Cash Received			
Sales Tax, VAT, HST/GST Received	$0	$0	$0
New Current Borrowing	$0	$0	$0
New Other Liabilities (Interest-free)	$0	$0	$0
New Long-term Liabilities	$181,463	$253,970	$729,992
Sales of Other Current Assets	$0	$0	$0
Sales of Long-term Assets	$0	$0	$0
New Investment Received	$0	$0	$0
Subtotal Cash Received	$739,506	$2,602,870	$6,752,942

(Continued)

Need for monitoring cash flow mentioned and that TDP is a "cash business" is highlighted. Unlike many companies, TDP does not offer credit to its customers.

A business should not project cash shortfalls in the business plan. Debt or equity should be sufficient to compensate for any operating deficits.

Explanation of anticipated variances due to startup.

Visual representation shows that cash flow is negative in certain months, but that the cash balance is always positive and on an upward trend after just a couple of months.

Cash from operations and cash sales are the same for this particular business.

TDP is anticipating that no taxes are collected on food or other sales. Some states and certain businesses will have to collect these taxes and reflect them in the cash flow.

Expansion plans include no short-term borrowing.

Borrowing for expansion.

Assuming all investment occurs before the operations begin.

The Daily Perc—Pro Forma Cash Flow   Continued

	FY 1	FY 2	FY 3
Expenditures			
Expenditures from Operations			
Cash Spending	$242,374	$846,050	$2,024,250
Bill Payments	$240,175	$1,091,066	$2,573,382
Subtotal Spent on Operations	$482,549	$1,937,116	$4,597,632
Additional Cash Spent			
Sales Tax, VAT, HST/GST Paid Out	$0	$0	$0
Principal Repayment of Current Borrowing	$1,500	$0	$0
Other Liabilities Principal Repayment	$0	$0	$0
Long-term Liabilities Principal Repayment	$26,469	$0	$0
Purchase Other Current Assets	$0	$0	$0
Purchase Long-term Assets	$191,850	$429,700	$1,356,993
Dividends	$0	$0	$0
Subtotal Cash Spent	$702,368	$2,366,816	$5,954,625
Net Cash Flow	$37,139	$236,054	$798,317
Cash Balance	$62,639	$298,693	$1,097,010

7.5. Projected Balance Sheet

The Daily Perc's projected balance sheet shows an increase in net worth to just over $1 million in FY 3, at which point it also expects to be making 21.5% after-tax profit on sales of $6.02 million. With the present financial projections, TDP expects to build a company with strong profit potential, and a solid balance sheet that will be asset heavy and flush with cash at the end of the third year. The Daily Perc has no intention of paying out dividends before the end of the third year, using the excess cash for continued growth. The first year projected balance sheet for TDP appears in Appendix 1-F.

The Daily Perc—Pro Forma Balance Sheet

	FY 1	FY 2	FY 3
Assets			
Current Assets			
Cash	$62,639	$298,693	$1,097,010
Inventory	$35,159	$134,826	$328,252
Other Current Assets	$0	$0	$0
Total Current Assets	$97,798	$433,519	$1,425,263
Long-term Assets			
Long-term Assets	$323,250	$752,950	$2,109,943
Accumulated Depreciation	$21,785	$114,695	$310,790
Total Long-term Assets	$301,465	$638,255	$1,799,153
Total Assets	$399,263	$1,071,774	$3,224,416

The margin notes (left side):

- Since no taxes are collected, none are paid out.
- Indicates the repayment of principal on current debt. Typically, there will be some each year if there is new debt.
- No principal repayment reflected in this cash flow. Normally, a portion of the long-term debt is repaid annually, so that there would be a value in each year.
- This number is higher than the new long-term debt and investment total, indicating that a significant portion of the expansion will be paid through operations.
- Shows a strong positive cash balance, such that TDP might even be able to reduce debt significantly if desired.
- Clear statement of goal.
- Investors know not to expect any dividends during this period, because TDP makes it explicit.
- Shows a snapshot of the assets and liabilities at the end of each year.
- Matches cash flow statement.
- If TDP extended credit to its customers so that there were Accounts Receivable, it would be reflected here.
- Assets at their initial value.
- Depreciation accumulated over the life of the assets.
- Typically, a business has a chart to record depreciation for each long-term asset.
- Net value of assets after depreciation is subtracted.

	FY 1	FY 2	FY 3
Liabilities and Capital			
Current Liabilities			
Accounts Payable	$43,909	$93,775	$222,054
Current Borrowing	$7,500	$7,500	$7,500
Other Current Liabilities	$0	$0	$0
Subtotal Current Liabilities	$51,409	$101,275	$229,554
Long-term Liabilities	$286,394	$540,364	$1,270,356
Total Liabilities	$337,803	$641,639	$1,499,910
Paid-in Capital	$225,270	$225,270	$225,270
Retained Earnings	($173,770)	($163,810)	$204,865
Earnings	$9,960	$368,675	$1,294,371
Total Capital	$61,460	$430,135	$1,724,505
Total Liabilities and Capital	$399,263	$1,071,774	$3,224,416
Net Worth	$61,460	$430,135	$1,724,505

Reflects trade credit that TDP receives from its suppliers.

Total long-term portion of debt remaining. Remember, each year the part of long-term debt that is due within 12 months becomes current debt.

Equity from investors.

Initial profit or loss (likely a loss due to start-up costs) plus each year's earnings.

Equals Paid-in Capital plus Retained Earnings plus Earnings (Net Profit).

7.6 Business Ratios

Standard business ratios are included in the following table. The ratios show a plan for balanced, healthy growth. The Daily Perc's position within the industry is typical for a heavy-growth start-up company. Industry profile ratios based on the Standard Industrial Classification (SIC) code 5812, Eating Places, are shown for comparison.

Comparing the ratios in the third year with the industry, this pro forma plan appears to be within an acceptable difference margin.

TDP's return on net worth and net worth number differ from the Industry Profile due to the lack of overhead when compared to a typical walk-in café. The Drive-thru and Mobile business model is lean, thus allowing for an increased return ratio and providing a lower Net Worth.

Ratios match up with the path set out in the business plan.

Comparing TDP to an industry profile. Indicate which SIC or NAICS code you are comparing it to, with the source of the industry data.

Explanation of TDP's variance industry data.

The Daily Perc—Ratio Analysis

	FY 1	FY 2	FY 3	Industry Profile
Sales Growth	0.00%	320.92%	156.42%	7.60%
Percent of Total Assets				
Inventory	8.81%	12.58%	10.18%	3.60%
Other Current Assets	0.00%	0.00%	0.00%	35.60%
Total Current Assets	24.49%	40.45%	44.20%	43.70%
Long-term Assets	75.51%	59.55%	55.80%	56.30%
Total Assets	100.00%	100.00%	100.00%	100.00%
Current Liabilities	12.88%	9.45%	7.12%	32.70%
Long-term Liabilities	71.73%	50.42%	39.40%	28.50%
Total Liabilities	84.61%	59.87%	46.52%	61.20%
Net Worth	15.39%	40.13%	53.48%	38.80%
Percent of Sales				
Sales	100.00%	100.00%	100.00%	100.00%
Gross Margin	65.52%	67.32%	68.90%	60.50%

(Continued)

High growth. TDP is starting at a low base and adding locations.

Higher than industry norms, probably because the low base requires further discussion.

This significant variance should be described in the text.

TDP is carrying a lower trade debt and current portion of long-term debt.

Described in the business plan text.

Matches the income statement.

Not detailed in the income statement.

Radical difference from the industry warrants an explanation.

Quick ratio is also radically different.

Explained in the text.

	FY 1	FY 2	FY 3	Industry Profile
Selling, General & Administrative Expenses	44.74%	30.63%	29.15%	39.80%
Advertising Expenses	3.23%	1.53%	1.20%	3.20%
Profit before Interest and Taxes	4.68%	17.31%	22.86%	0.70%
Main Ratios				
Current	1.90	4.28	6.21	0.98
Quick	1.22	2.95	4.78	0.65
Total Debt to Total Assets	84.61%	59.87%	46.52%	61.20%
Pre-tax Return on Net Worth	16.21%	85.71%	75.06%	1.70%
Pre-tax Return on Assets	2.49%	34.40%	40.14%	4.30%

	FY 1	FY 2	FY 3	
Additional Ratios				
Net Profit Margin	1.78%	15.70%	21.49%	n.a
Return on Equity	16.21%	85.71%	75.06%	n.a
Activity Ratios				
Inventory Turnover	7.02	8.62	7.70	n.a
Accounts Payable Turnover	6.47	12.17	12.17	n.a
Payment Days	27	22	21	n.a
Total Asset Turnover	1.40	2.19	1.87	n.a
Debt Ratios				
Debt to Net Worth	5.50	1.49	0.87	n.a
Current Liabilities to Liabilities	0.15	0.16	0.15	n.a
Liquidity Ratios				
Net Working Capital	$46,389	$332,244	$1,195,708	n.a
Interest Coverage	1.62	10.71	16.74	n.a
Additional Ratios				
Assets to Sales	0.72	0.46	0.54	n.a
Current Debt/Total Assets	13%	9%	7%	n.a
Acid Test	1.22	2.95	4.78	n.a
Sales/Net Worth	9.08	5.46	3.49	n.a
Dividend Payout	0.00	0.00	0.00	n.a

Explained in the text.

Description of the total need.

Uses the precise wording of previous sections. Reiterates the structure of the equity offering. Does not tell the sources of these in significant detail nor is there information regarding the intended or secured sources of debt financing.

8. Funding Request and Exit Strategy

8.1 Funding Request

The Daily Perc, LLC requires initial financing of $515,000 for its start-up phase without any anticipated need for additional equity or debt except for as needed to complete the purchase of additional facilities and/or equipment.

The plan calls for the sale of 100 membership units in the company to family members, friends, and Angel Investors. Each membership unit in the company is priced at $4,250, with a minimum of five units per membership certificate, or a minimum investment of $21,250 per investor.

The Daily Perc Business Plan provided by Business Plan Pro® and used by permission of Palo Alto Software.

If all funds are raised, based on the pricing established in the financial section of this plan, Bart and Terri Fisher will maintain ownership of no less than 51% of the company.

8.2. Exit Strategy

There are three scenarios for the investors and management to recover their investment—two with significant returns on each dollar invested.

TDP offering multiple exit strategies.

Exit options that make investment more attractive. This should strengthen the business plan.

Scenario One:

The Daily Perc becomes extremely successful and has requests from other communities for Daily Perc operations to be opened there. This opens the door for franchising opportunity. When one looks at the wealth that has been created by the likes of McDonald's, Wendy's, Kentucky Fried Chicken, Burger King, and Taco Bell, the value of franchising a great idea cannot be dismissed. However, developing a franchise can be extremely costly, take years to develop, and be destroyed by one or two franchisees who fail to deliver the consistency or value on which the founding company had built its reputation.

Franchising strategy as a form of replication.

Scenario Two:

The Daily Perc chooses to become the Drive-thru version of Starbucks, obtaining several million dollars through an initial public or private offering that would allow the company to open 20 to 30 facilities per year in the region of the country between the mountain ranges, in both major and small metropolitan communities. This is the preferred Exit Strategy of the Management Team. The danger in this is that competitors would rise up and establish a foothold on a community before—or in the midst of—the arrival of The Daily Perc, causing a potential for a drain on revenues and a dramatic increase in advertising expenditures to maintain market share. Knowing these risks—and planning for them—gives TDP the edge needed to make this scenario work.

Expansion strategy fueled by an IPO or private offering.

Scenario Three:

By the third year, the growth and community support for The Daily Perc will have made the news in more than just the metropolitan area. It can be assumed that competitors, such as Starbucks or Quikava, will have seen the press and realized the value proposition in The Daily Perc's business plan. This will make TDP an attractive target for buyout. The company could be purchased by a much larger competitive concern by the end of the third year.

Three years is relatively quick for such a scenario.

Exit through buyout by a competitor.

Taking a conservative approach to valuation and estimating that The Daily Perc would be valued at $7.5 million, and assuming that all 250 units of ownership in TDP are distributed to investors, a cash purchase of TDP would net each unit $30,000. With each unit selling at $4,250, that constitutes a Return on Investment of 705% over the three years. However, any buyout will most likely involve a cash/stock combination. A cash/stock buyout would be favorable, since the buying company would pay a higher price and the transaction would not have such severe tax consequences to the sellers.

This falls within the $4 million to $9 million estimate provided earlier.

Calculation of the purchase price per unit permits the calculation of return on investment.

ROI calculation.

Why a cash/stock combination is preferable.

Conclusion:

Of the three scenarios, the management team prefers Scenario #2. The same numbers would relate to a public or private offering as are used in Scenario #3, but to make an offering available, there would be a dilution of shares that would provide additional shares for sale to the new investors.

The Daily Perc Business Plan provided by Business Plan Pro® and used by permission of Palo Alto Software.

Assuming the capital acquisition described in this plan is completed, there will be 250 units of the company in the hands of investors, constituting 100% of the authorized and issued units. For purposes of future fund-raising, it will be necessary to authorize a stock split of perhaps 5,000 to one, turning the current 250 units into 1,250,000 units.

Using the balance sheet for the third year, which estimates a Net Worth of just over $1.7 million, cash balances of $1.1 million, and earnings of $1.3 million, based on thirteen Drive-thrus and four Mobile Cafés, it is not unrealistic to put a market value of $15 million to $25 million on the company. At present, such companies are trading in multiples of 20 to 30 times earnings, and it is simple mathematics to multiply the success of TDP by the number of commuter-heavy metropolitan areas in the United States.

With a corporate valuation of $7,500,000, each of the new units would have a market value of $6/unit. By authorizing an additional 750,000 units, there would be a total of 2,000,000 units with a market value of $3.75 per share. By offering the 750,000 shares at the price of $3.75 per unit, TDP would raise an additional $2,812,500 in expansion capital, which would be sufficient to open locations in an additional three to five cities.

8.3. Milestones

The Milestone table reflects critical dates for occupying headquarters, launching the first Drive-thru and subsequent Drive-thrus, as well as deployment of the mobile units. The Daily Perc also defines our break-even month, our Web site launch and subsequent visitor interaction function, and other key markers that will help us measure our success in time and accomplishment.

The Daily Perc—Milestones

Milestone	Start Date	End Date	Budget	Manager	Department
Light Web Site	6/1/YR1	8/15/YR1	$5,600	COO	Mktg.
Open First Drive-thru	7/15/YR1	8/31/YRl	$105,400	COO	Admin.
First Break-even Month	12/1/YR1	12/31/YR1	$0	COO	Finance
Open Second Drive-thru	12/15/YR1	2/1/YR1	$105,400	COO	Admin.
Receive First Mobile Unit	3/1/YR1	3/30/YRl	$86,450	COO	Admin.
Launch Web Site Voting	5/1/YR1	6/1/YR1	$12,500	COO	Mktg.
Open Third Drive-thru	4/15/YR1	6/1/YR1	$105,400	COO	Admin.
Receive Second and Third Mobile Units	7/15/YR2	9/1/YR2	$172,900	COO	Admin.
Open Fourth Drive-thru	12/15/YR2	2/1/YR2	$105,400	COO	Admin.
Install Point-of-Sale System	12/1/YR2	2/1/YR2	$21,000	CIO	MIS
Occupy Headquarters	4/1/YR2	5/15/YR2	$45,000	COO	Admin.
Open Fifth Drive-thru	4/15/YR2	6/1/YR3	$105,400	COO	Admin.

The following margin notes appear to the left of the main text:

Returned to the $7.5 million valuation from above.

Specific number of additional shares. The value ($7.5 million) divided by the total number of shares (2 million) yields the market value of $3.75 per share.

By multiplying the number of new shares (750,000) by the price per share ($3.75), TDP calculates the infusion of capital.

Using milestones to ensure measurement.

The Daily Perc Business Plan provided by Business Plan Pro® and used by permission of Palo Alto Software.

Milestone	Start Date	End Date	Budget	Manager	Department
Receive Fourth Mobile Unit	4/15/YR2	6/1/YR3	$86,450	Equip.	Admin.
Open Drive-thrus 6 and 7	7/15/YR3	9/15/YR3	$210,800	COO/Dir.	Mgmt.
Open Drive-thrus 8, 9, and 10	10/15/YR3	12/15/YR3	$316,200	COO/Dir.	Mgmt.
Open Drive-thrus 11, 12, and 13	1/15/YR3	3/1/YR3	$316,200	COO	Admin.
Expand to Kansas City	1/15/YR3	6/1/YR3	$176,943	COO	Mgmt.
Open First Franchise	10/31/YR3	9/1/YR4	$45,000	CFO	Finance
Initiate Exit Strategy	10/1/YR4	1/1/YR4	$100,000	CFO	Mgmt.

Appendices

The appendices for The Daily Perc business plan appear follow.

The Daily Perc
Appendix 1-A

The Daily Perc—Sales Forecast

Unit Sales		Jun	Jul	Aug	Sep	Oct	Nov	dec	Jan	Feb	Mar	Apr	May
Drive-thru #1	0%	0	0	0	17,500	23,047	24,199	22,989	23,047	24,199	22,989	23,047	21,895
Drive-thru #2	0%	0	0	0	0	0	0	0	0	17,500	23,047	21,895	23,047
Drive-thru #3	0%	0	0	0	0	0	0	0	0	0	0	0	0
Drive-thru #4	0%	0	0	0	0	0	0	0	0	0	0	0	0
Drive-thru #5	0%	0	0	0	0	0	0	0	0	0	0	0	0
Drive-thrus #6 & #7	0%	0	0	0	0	0	0	0	0	0	0	0	0
Drive-thrus #8, #9, & #10	0%	0	0	0	0	0	0	0	0	0	0	0	0
Drive-thrus #11, #12, & #13	0%	0	0	0	0	0	0	0	0	0	0	0	0
Mobile Café #1	0%	0	0	0	0	0	0	0	0	0	0	5,000	5,000
Mobile Café #2	0%	0	0	0	0	0	0	0	0	0	0	0	0
Mobile Café #3	0%	0	0	0	0	0	0	0	0	0	0	0	0
Mobile Café #4	0%	0	0	0	0	0	0	0	0	0	0	0	0
Website Sales/Premium Items	0%	0	0	0	0	0	0	0	0	0	0	0	0
Total Unit Sales		0	0	0	17,500	23,047	24,199	22,989	23,047	41,699	46,036	49,942	49,942

Unit Prices	Jun	Jul	Aug	Sep	Oct	Nov	Dec	Jan	Feb	Mar	Apr	May
Drive-thru #1	$1.85	$1.85	$1.85	$1.85	$1.85	$1.85	$1.85	$1.85	$1.85	$1.85	$1.85	$1.85
Drive-thru #2	$1.85	$1.85	$1.85	$1.85	$1.85	$1.85	$1.85	$1.85	$1.85	$1.85	$1.85	$1.85
Drive-thru #3	$1.85	$1.85	$1.85	$1.85	$1.85	$1.85	$1.85	$1.85	$1.85	$1.85	$1.85	$1.85
Drive-thru #4	$1.85	$1.85	$1.85	$1.85	$1.85	$1.85	$1.85	$1.85	$1.85	$1.85	$1.85	$1.85
Drive-thru #5	$1.85	$1.85	$1.85	$1.85	$1.85	$1.85	$1.85	$1.85	$1.85	$1.85	$1.85	$1.85
Drive-thrus #6 & #7	$1.85	$1.85	$1.85	$1.85	$1.85	$1.85	$1.85	$1.85	$1.85	$1.85	$1.85	$1.85
Drive-thrus #8, #9, & #10	$1.85	$1.85	$1.85	$1.85	$1.85	$1.85	$1.85	$1.85	$1.85	$1.85	$1.85	$1.85
Drive-thrus #11, #12, & #13	$1.85	$1.85	$1.85	$1.85	$1.85	$1.85	$1.85	$1.85	$1.85	$1.85	$1.85	$1.85
Mobile Café #1	$2.45	$2.45	$2.45	$2.45	$2.45	$2.45	$2.45	$2.45	$2.45	$2.45	$2.45	$2.45
Mobile Café #2	$2.45	$2.45	$2.45	$2.45	$2.45	$2.45	$2.45	$2.45	$2.45	$2.45	$2.45	$2.45
Mobile Café #3	$2.45	$2.45	$2.45	$2.45	$2.45	$2.45	$2.45	$2.45	$2.45	$2.45	$2.45	$2.45
Mobile Café #4	$2.45	$2.45	$2.45	$2.45	$2.45	$2.45	$2.45	$2.45	$2.45	$2.45	$2.45	$2.45
Website Sales/Premium Items	$10.00	$10.00	$10.00	$10.00	$10.00	$10.00	$10.00	$10.00	$10.00	$10.00	$10.00	$10.00

Sales	Jun	Jul	Aug	Sep	Oct	Nov	Dec	Jan	Feb	Mar	Apr	May
Drive-thru #1	$0	$0	$0	$32,375	$42,637	$44,769	$42,530	$42,637	$44,769	$42,530	$42,637	$40,505
Drive-thru #2	$0	$0	$0	$0	$0	$0	$0	$0	$32,375	$42,637	$40,505	$42,637
Drive-thru #3	$0	$0	$0	$0	$0	$0	$0	$0	$0	$0	$0	$0
Drive-thru #4	$0	$0	$0	$0	$0	$0	$0	$0	$0	$0	$0	$0
Drive-thru #5	$0	$0	$0	$0	$0	$0	$0	$0	$0	$0	$0	$0
Drive-thrus #6 & #7	$0	$0	$0	$0	$0	$0	$0	$0	$0	$0	$0	$0
Drive-thrus #8, #9, & #10	$0	$0	$0	$0	$0	$0	$0	$0	$0	$0	$0	$0
Drive-thrus #11, #12, & #13	$0	$0	$0	$0	$0	$0	$0	$0	$0	$0	$0	$0

The Daily Perc

	Jun	Jul	Aug	Sep	Oct	Nov	Dec	Jan	Feb	Mar	Apr	May
Mobile Café #1	$0	$0	$0	$0	$0	$0	$0	$0	$0	$0	$0	$0
Mobile Café #2	$0	$0	$0	$0	$0	$0	$0	$0	$0	$0	$0	$0
Mobile Café #3	$0	$0	$0	$0	$0	$0	$0	$0	$0	$0	$0	$0
Mobile Café #4	$0	$0	$0	$0	$0	$0	$0	$0	$0	$0	$0	$0
Website Sales/Premium Items	$0	$0	$0	$0	$0	$0	$0	$0	$0	$0	$0	$0
Total Sales	$0	$0	$0	$32,375	$42,637	$44,769	$42,530	$42,637	$77,144	$85,167	$95,392	$95,392

Direct Unit Costs		Jun	Jul	Aug	Sep	Oct	Nov	Dec	Jan	Feb	Mar	Apr	May
Drive-thru #1	0.00%	$0.64	$0.64	$0.64	$0.64	$0.64	$0.64	$0.64	$0.64	$0.64	$0.64	$0.64	$0.64
Drive-thru #2	0.00%	$0.64	$0.64	$0.64	$0.64	$0.64	$0.64	$0.64	$0.64	$0.64	$0.64	$0.64	$0.64
Drive-thru #3	0.00%	$0.64	$0.64	$0.64	$0.64	$0.64	$0.64	$0.64	$0.64	$0.64	$0.64	$0.64	$0.64
Drive-thru #4	0.00%	$0.64	$0.64	$0.64	$0.64	$0.64	$0.64	$0.64	$0.64	$0.64	$0.64	$0.64	$0.64
Drive-thru #5	0.00%	$0.64	$0.64	$0.64	$0.64	$0.64	$0.64	$0.64	$0.64	$0.64	$0.64	$0.64	$0.64
Drive-thru #6 & #7	0.00%	$0.64	$0.64	$0.64	$0.64	$0.64	$0.64	$0.64	$0.64	$0.64	$0.64	$0.64	$0.64
Drive-thrus #8, #9, & #10	0.00%	$0.64	$0.64	$0.64	$0.64	$0.64	$0.64	$0.64	$0.64	$0.64	$0.64	$0.64	$0.64
Drive-thrus #11, #12, & #13	0.00%	$0.64	$0.64	$0.64	$0.64	$0.64	$0.64	$0.64	$0.64	$0.64	$0.64	$0.64	$0.64
Mobile Café #1	0.00%	$0.64	$0.64	$0.64	$0.64	$0.64	$0.64	$0.64	$0.64	$0.64	$0.64	$0.64	$0.64
Mobile Café #2	0.00%	$0.64	$0.64	$0.64	$0.64	$0.64	$0.64	$0.64	$0.64	$0.64	$0.64	$0.64	$0.64
Mobile Café #3	0.00%	$0.64	$0.64	$0.64	$0.64	$0.64	$0.64	$0.64	$0.64	$0.64	$0.64	$0.64	$0.64
Mobile Café #4	0.00%	$0.64	$0.64	$0.64	$0.64	$0.64	$0.64	$0.64	$0.64	$0.64	$0.64	$0.64	$0.64
Website Sales/Premium Items	0.00%	$6.50	$6.50	$6.50	$6.50	$6.50	$6.50	$6.50	$6.50	$6.50	$6.50	$6.50	$6.50

Direct Cost of Sales	Jun	Jul	Aug	Sep	Oct	Nov	Dec	Jan	Feb	Mar	Apr	May
Drive-thru #1	$0	$0	$0	$11,200	$14,750	$15,488	$14,713	$14,750	$15,488	$14,713	$14,750	$14,013
Drive-thru #2	$0	$0	$0	$0	$0	$0	$0	$0	$11,200	$14,750	$14,013	$14,750
Drive-thru #3	$0	$0	$0	$0	$0	$0	$0	$0	$0	$0	$0	$0
Drive-thru #4	$0	$0	$0	$0	$0	$0	$0	$0	$0	$0	$0	$0
Drive-thru #5	$0	$0	$0	$0	$0	$0	$0	$0	$0	$0	$0	$0
Drive-thru #6 & #7	$0	$0	$0	$0	$0	$0	$0	$0	$0	$0	$0	$0
Drive-thrus #8, #9, & #10	$0	$0	$0	$0	$0	$0	$0	$0	$0	$0	$0	$0
Drive-thrus #11, #12, & #13	$0	$0	$0	$0	$0	$0	$0	$0	$0	$0	$0	$0
Mobile Café #1	$0	$0	$0	$0	$0	$0	$0	$0	$0	$0	$0	$0
Mobile Café #2	$0	$0	$0	$0	$0	$0	$0	$0	$0	$0	$0	$0
Mobile Café #3	$0	$0	$0	$0	$0	$0	$0	$0	$0	$0	$3,200	$3,200
Mobile Café #4	$0	$0	$0	$0	$0	$0	$0	$0	$0	$0	$0	$0
Website Sales/Premium Items	$0	$0	$0	$0	$0	$0	$0	$0	$0	$0	$0	$0
Subtotal Direct Cost of Sales	$0	$0	$0	$11,200	$14,750	$15,488	$14,713	$14,750	$26,688	$29,463	$31,963	$31,963

517

The Daily Perc
Appendix 1-B

The Daily Perc—Personnel Plan

		Jun	Jul	Aug	Sep	Oct	Nov	Dec	Jan	Feb	Mar	Apr	May
Drive-thru Team	0%	$0	$0	$0	$10,500	$10,850	$9,800	$9,800	$10,500	$19,624	$21,700	$21,000	$21,700
Mobile Café Team	0%	$0	$0	$0	$0	$0	$0	$0	$0	$0	$0	$4,700	$4,700
Equipment Care Specialist (Headquarters)	0%	$0	$0	$0	$0	$0	$0	$0	$0	$0	$0	$0	$0
Other	0%	$0	$0	$0	$0	$0	$0	$0	$0	$0	$0	$0	$0
District Manager (Four Drive-thrus)	0%	$0	$0	$0	$0	$0	$0	$0	$0	$0	$0	$0	$0
Corporate Events Sales Exec	0%	$0	$0	$0	$0	$0	$0	$0	$0	$0	$0	$0	$0
Director of Marketing	0%	$0	$0	$0	$0	$0	$0	$0	$0	$0	$0	$0	$0
Other	0%	$0	$0	$0	$0	$0	$0	$0	$0	$0	$0	$0	$0
Bookkeeper/Office Administrator	0%	$0	$0	$0	$0	$1,750	$1,750	$3,500	$3,500	$3,500	$3,500	$3,500	$3,500
Warehouse/Site Manager	0%	$0	$0	$0	$0	$0	$0	$0	$0	$0	$0	$3,500	$3,500
Inventory Clerk	0%	$0	$0	$0	$0	$0	$0	$0	$0	$0	$0	$0	$0
Other	0%	$0	$0	$0	$0	$0	$0	$0	$0	$0	$0	$0	$0
Chief Operating Officer	0%	$5,500	$5,500	$5,500	$5,500	$5,500	$5,500	$5,500	$5,500	$5,500	$5,500	$5,500	$5,500
Chief Financial Officer	0%	$0	$0	$0	$0	$0	$0	$0	$0	$0	$0	$0	$0
Chief Information Officer	0%	$0	$0	$0	$0	$0	$0	$0	$0	$0	$0	$0	$0
Other	0%	$0	$0	$0	$0	$0	$0	$0	$0	$0	$0	$0	$0
Total Staff		1	1	1	5	6	6	6	6	11	11	15	15
Total Payroll		$5,500	$5,500	$5,500	$16,000	$18,100	$17,050	$18,800	$19,500	$28,624	$30,700	$38,200	$38,900

The Daily Perc
Appendix 1-C

The Daily Perc—General Assumptions

	Jun	Jul	Aug	Sep	Oct	Nov	Dec	Jan	Feb	Mar	Apr	May
Plan Month	1	2	3	4	5	6	7	8	9	10	11	12
Current Interest Rate	10.00%	10.00%	10.00%	10.00%	10.00%	10.00%	10.00%	10.00%	10.00%	10.00%	10.00%	10.00%
Long-term Interest Rate	9.00%	9.00%	9.00%	9.00%	9.00%	9.00%	9.00%	9.00%	9.00%	9.00%	9.00%	9.00%
Tax Rate	0.00%	0.00%	0.00%	0.00%	0.00%	0.00%	0.00%	0.00%	0.00%	0.00%	0.00%	0.00%
Other	0	0	0	0	0	0	0	0	0	0	0	0

The Daily Perc
Appendix 1-D

The Daily Perc-Pro Forma Profit and Loss (Income Statement)

		Jun	Jul	Aug	Sep	Oct	Nov	Dec	Jan	Feb	Mar	Apr	May
Sales		$0	$0	$0	$32,375	$42,637	$44,769	$42,530	$42,637	$77,144	$85,167	$95,392	$95,392
Direct Costs of Goods		$0	$0	$0	$11,200	$14,750	$15,488	$14,713	$14,750	$26,688	$29,463	$31,963	$31,963
Sales Commissions		$0	$0	$0	$0	$0	$0	$0	$0	$0	$0	$708	$708
Cost of Goods Sold		$0	$0	$0	$11,200	$14,750	$15,488	$14,713	$14,750	$26,688	$29,463	$32,671	$32,671
Gross Margin		$0	$0	$0	$21,175	$27,887	$29,281	$27,817	$27,887	$50,456	$55,704	$62,721	$62,721
Gross Margin		0.00%	0.00%	0.00%	65.41%	65.41%	65.41%	65.41%	65.41%	65.41%	65.41%	65.75%	65.75%
Expenses													
Payroll		$5,500	$5,500	$5,500	$16,000	$18,100	$17,050	$18,800	$19,500	$28,624	$30,700	$38,200	$38,900
Sales and Marketing and Other Expenses		$0	$0	$0	$0	$0	$0	$0	$0	$0	$0	$0	$0
Depreciation		$0	$310	$310	$1,565	$1,565	$1,565	$1,565	$1,565	$2,820	$2,820	$3,850	$3,850
Leased Offices and Equipment		$0	$0	$0	$0	$0	$0	$0	$0	$0	$0	$0	$0
Utilities		$0	$0	$700	$800	$920	$920	$1,050	$1,050	$1,050	$1,050	$1,050	$1,050
Insurance		$0	$1,257	$1,257	$1,257	$1,257	$1,257	$1,257	$1,257	$1,257	$1,257	$1,257	$1,257
Rent		$0	$1,200	$1,200	$1,200	$1,200	$1,200	$1,200	$1,200	$2,400	$2,400	$2,400	$2,400
Payroll Taxes	15%	$825	$825	$825	$2,400	$2,715	$2,558	$2,820	$2,925	$4,294	$4,605	$5,730	$5,835
Other General and Administrative Expenses		$0	$0	$0	$0	$0	$0	$0	$0	$0	$0	$0	$0
Total Operating Expenses		$6,325	$6,635	$9,792	$23,222	$25,757	$24,550	$26,692	$27,497	$40,445	$42,832	$52,487	$53,292
Profit Before Interest and Taxes		($6,325)	($6,635)	($9,792)	($2,047)	$2,130	$4,732	$1,125	$390	$10,012	$12,872	$10,234	$9,429
EBITDA		($6,325)	($6,325)	($9,482)	($482)	$3,695	$6,297	$2,690	$1,955	$12,832	$15,692	$14,084	$13,279
Interest Expense		$1,042	$1,018	$1,058	$1,019	$1,019	$1,019	$1,019	$1,019	$1,756	$1,702	$2,282	$2,210
Taxes Incurred		$0	$0	$0	$0	$0	$0	$0	$0	$0	$0	$0	$0
Net Profit		($7,367)	($7,653)	($10,850)	($3,066)	$1,110	$3,712	$106	($630)	$8,256	$11,170	$7,952	$7,219
Net Profit/Sales		0.00%	0.00%	0.00%	-9.47%	2.60%	8.29%	0.25%	-1.48%	10.70%	13.12%	8.34%	7.57%

The Daily Perc
Appendix 1-E

The Daily Perc—Pro Forma Cash Flow

Cash Received	Jun	Jul	Aug	Sep	Oct	Nov	Dec	Jan	Feb	Mar	Apr	May
Cash from Operations												
Cash Sales	$0	$0	$0	$32,375	$42,637	$44,769	$42,530	$42,637	$77,144	$85,167	$95,392	$95,392
Subtotal Cash from Operations	$0	$0	$0	$32,375	$42,637	$44,769	$42,530	$42,637	$77,144	$85,167	$95,392	$95,392
Additional Cash Received												
Sales Tax, VAT, HST/GST Received 0.00%	$0	$0	$0	$0	$0	$0	$0	$0	$0	$0	$0	$0
New Current Borrowing	$0	$0	$0	$0	$0	$0	$0	$0	$0	$0	$0	$0
New Other Liabilities (Interest-free)	$0	$0	$0	$0	$0	$0	$0	$0	$0	$0	$0	$0
New Long-term Liabilities	$0	$0	$5,300	$0	$0	$0	$0	$0	$98,184	$0	$77,979	$0
Sales of Other Current Assets	$0	$0	$0	$0	$0	$0	$0	$0	$0	$0	$0	$0
Sales of Long-term Assets	$0	$0	$0	$0	$0	$0	$0	$0	$0	$0	$0	$0
New Investment Received	$0	$0	$0	$0	$0	$0	$0	$0	$0	$0	$0	$0
Subtotal Cash Received	$0	$0	$5,300	$32,375	$42,637	$44,769	$42,530	$42,637	$175,328	$85,167	$173,371	$95,392

Expenditures	Jun	Jul	Aug	Sep	Oct	Nov	Dec	Jan	Feb	Mar	Apr	May
Expenditures from Operations												
Cash Spending	$5,500	$5,500	$5,500	$16,000	$18,100	$17,050	$18,800	$19,500	$28,624	$30,700	$38,200	$38,900
Bill Payments	$62	$1,866	$1,950	$5,095	$6,930	$14,585	$23,185	$21,242	$23,186	$50,340	$43,684	$48,049
Subtotal Spent on Operations	$5,562	$7,366	$7,450	$21,095	$25,030	$31,635	$41,985	$40,742	$51,810	$81,040	$81,884	$86,949
Additional Cash Spent												
Sales Tax, VAT, HST/GST Paid Out	$0	$0	$0	$0	$0	$0	$0	$0	$0	$0	$0	$0
Principal Repayment of Current Borrowing	$0	$0	$0	$0	$0	$0	$0	$0	$0	$0	$500	$1,000
Other Liabilities Principal Repayment	$0	$0	$0	$0	$0	$0	$0	$0	$0	$0	$0	$0
Long-term Liabilities Principal Repayment		$3,116	$0	$5,166	$0	$0	$0	$0	$0	$7,216	$0	$8,471
Purchase Other Current Assets	$2,500	$0	$0	$0	$0	$0	$0	$0	$105,400	$0	$0	$0
Purchase Long-term Assets	$0	$0	$0	$0	$0	$0	$0	$0	$0	$0	$86,450	$0
Dividends	$0	$0	$0	$0	$0	$0	$0	$0	$0	$0	$0	$0
Subtotal Cash Spent	$8,062	$10,482	$7,450	$26,261	$25,030	$31,635	$41,985	$40,742	$157,210	$88,256	$168,834	$96,420
Net Cash Flow	($8,062)	($10,482)	($2,150)	$6,114	$17,607	$13,133	$546	$1,895	$18,117	($3,089)	$4,537	($1,028)
Cash Balance	$17,438	$6,956	$4,806	$10,920	$28,527	$41,660	$42,206	$44,101	$62,218	$59,129	$63,666	$62,639

The Daily Perc

Appendix 1-F

The Daily Perc—Pro Forma Balance Sheet

Assets	Starting Balances	Jun	Jul	Aug	Sep	Oct	Nov	Dec	Jan	Feb	Mar	Apr	May
Current Assets													
Cash	$25,500	$17,438	$6,956	$4,806	$10,920	$28,527	$41,660	$42,206	$44,101	$62,218	$59,129	$63,666	$62,639
Inventory	$35,000	$35,000	$35,000	$35,000	$23,800	$16,225	$17,036	$16,185	$16,225	$29,356	$32,410	$35,159	$35,159
Other Current Assets	$0	$0	$0	$0	$0	$0	$0	$0	$0	$0	$0	$0	$0
Total Current Assets	$60,500	$52,438	$41,956	$39,806	$34,720	$44,752	$58,697	$58,391	$60,326	$91,575	$91,539	$98,825	$97,798
Long-term Assets													
Long-term Assets	$131,400	$131,400	$131,400	$131,400	$131,400	$131,400	$131,400	$131,400	$131,400	$236,800	$236,800	$323,250	$323,250
Accumulated Depreciation	$0	$0	$310	$620	$2,185	$3,750	$5,315	$6,880	$8,445	$11,265	$14,085	$17,935	$21,785
Total Long-term Assets	$131,400	$131,400	$131,090	$130,780	$129,215	$127,650	$126,085	$124,520	$122,955	$225,535	$222,715	$305,315	$301,465
Total Assets	$191,900	$183,838	$173,046	$170,586	$163,935	$172,402	$184,782	$182,911	$183,281	$317,110	$314,254	$404,140	$399,263

Liabilities and Capital	Starting Balances	Jun	Jul	Aug	Sep	Oct	Nov	Dec	Jan	Feb	Mar	Apr	May
Current Liabilities													
Accounts Payable	$0	$1,805	$1,782	$4,872	$6,454	$13,810	$22,478	$20,501	$21,501	$48,889	$42,079	$46,535	$43,909
Current Borrowing	$9,000	$9,000	$9,000	$9,000	$9,000	$9,000	$9,000	$9,000	$9,000	$9,000	$9,000	$8,500	$7,500
Other Current Liabilities	$0	$0	$0	$0	$0	$0	$0	$0	$0	$0	$0	$0	$0
Subtotal Current Liabilities	$9,000	$10,805	$10,782	$13,872	$15,454	$22,810	$31,478	$29,501	$30,501	$57,889	$51,079	$55,035	$51,409
Long-term Liabilities	$131,400	$128,900	$125,784	$131,084	$125,918	$125,918	$125,918	$125,918	$125,918	$224,102	$216,886	$294,865	$286,394
Total Liabilities	$140,400	$139,705	$136,566	$144,956	$141,372	$148,728	$157,396	$155,419	$156,419	$281,991	$267,965	$349,900	$337,803
Paid-in Capital	$225,270	$225,270	$225,270	$225,270	$225,270	$225,270	$225,270	$225,270	$225,270	$225,270	$225,270	$225,270	$225,270
Retained Earnings	($173,770)	($173,770)	($173,770)	($173,770)	($173,770)	($173,770)	($173,770)	($173,770)	($173,770)	($173,770)	($173,770)	($173,770)	($173,770)
Earnings	$0	($7,367)	($15,020)	($25,870)	($28,937)	($27,826)	($24,114)	($24,008)	($24,638)	($16,382)	($5,211)	$2,741	$9,960
Total Capital	$51,500	$44,133	$36,480	$25,630	$22,563	$23,674	$27,386	$27,492	$26,862	$35,118	$46,289	$54,241	$61,460
Total Liabilities and Capital	$191,900	$183,838	$173,046	$170,586	$163,935	$172,402	$184,782	$182,911	$183,281	$317,110	$314,254	$404,140	$399,263
Net Worth	$51,500	$44,133	$36,480	$25,630	$22,563	$23,674	$27,386	$27,492	$26,862	$35,118	$46,289	$54,241	$61,460

BARTHOLOMEW J. FISHER III
123 Money Lane
Seattle, Washington
bjfisheriii@dailyperc.com
(999) 999-9999

PROFILE

An experienced professional with strong interpersonal, managerial, and problem-solving skills. Resourceful, organized, analytical, and versatile.

EDUCATION

STANFORD UNIVERSITY   Master of Business Administration, 1988
Entrepreneurial Management major. Strategic Planning and Marketing concentrations.

UNIVERSITY OF SEATTLE   Bachelor of Science, 1983
Economics major. Marketing minor. Varsity lacrosse player.

PROFESSIONAL EXPERIENCE

WASHINGTON CENTER FOR ENTERPRISE DEVELOPMENT
Seattle, Washington

Director   2000–Present

Direct this Small Business Development Center program that develops human capital among current and prospective entrepreneurs and enterprise managers for the support and growth of sustainable enterprises and wealth in the state of Washington.

FISHER INDUSTRIES, INC.   Seattle, Washington

General Manager   1993–2000

Managed the Sales, Marketing, and Operations of this Krispy Kreme Doughnuts franchise.

FISHER, BAKER AND SCHNIDER   Berkeley, California

President   1988–1993

Operated this advertising and marketing firm, which specialized in the design and implementation of marketing programs. Performed services including strategic and market analyses and advertising campaign creation. Conducted workshops, focus groups, and facilitation services. Wrote articles and press releases for client firms. Marketed FBS services to corporations and organizations.

STARBUCKS CORPORATION

Seattle, Washington

Marketing Manager

1983–1986

Trainee in the Marketing Department. Performed strategic and tactical planning, forecasting, budgeting, financial analysis and modeling, and media and publicity planning.

AWARDS, AFFILIATIONS, & ACTIVITIES

Minority Business Advocate of the Year—Washington Office—U.S. Small Business Administration

Social Venture Partners Seattle—Partner

Urban League of Metropolitan Seattle—Economic Development Advisory Council Member

Rotary Club of Seattle—Member and member of scholarship committee

American Marketing Association—Puget Sound Chapter—Board of Directors

Greenpeace—Member

TERESA ANNE FISHER
123 Money Lane
Seattle, Washington
tafisher@dailyperc.com
(999) 888-8888

WORK EXPERIENCE

STARBUCKS CORPORATION

Senior Financial Analyst   1996–Present

- Lead the development of the business unit's annual operating budget and quarterly forecasts.
- Support the development of strategic and operating plans. Identify and communicate plans' risks and opportunities.
- Conduct decision analyses and communicate results. Build and maintain financial models.
- Perform due diligence for new initiatives.
- Build financial models and provide analytical support for business initiatives and contract negotiations. Identify, analyze, and communicate trends and issues affecting the business.
- Provide analysis and feedback on financial performance and key performance measures.
- Provide financial information and guidance to all levels of management. Ensure financial statements are complete, accurate, and timely.

Financial Analyst   1992–1996

- Supported the development of strategic and operating plans.
- Built financial models and provided analytical support for business initiatives and contract negotiations. Identified, analyzed, and communicated trends and issues affecting the business.
- Ensured financial statements were complete, accurate, and timely. Facilitated process development and improvement initiatives.

Store Manager	1990–1992
Assistant Store Manager	1988–1990
Barista	1986–1988

EDUCATION

UNIVERSITY OF SEATTLE   BS, Accounting, 1988

ACTIVITIES

Seattle Area Chamber of Commerce—Retail Alliance member
Cascadia Loan Fund—Loan Review Committee
Rotary Club of Seattle—Member and Chair of Finance Committee
Junior League of Seattle—Life member
Northwest Sierra Club—Treasurer
Social Venture Partners Seattle—Partner

Appendix 2

Sample Student Business Plan

University Parent, Inc.

Fesehaye Abrhaley
Michelle Dorenkamp
Kara Grinnell
Ryan Roth
Sarah Schupp

Table of Contents

Appendix

Executive Summary

University Parent, Inc.
University Parent (UPI) produces institution-specific guides and comprehensive websites for parents of college students. Revenues are generated through the sale of advertising in the local guides and on the websites.

Today, there are 32 million parents of college students
According to surveys and interviews conducted by UPI, parents do not receive the information they need from colleges. They want to know where to have a nice dinner in their student's college town, where to stay, and fun activities to do while visiting. They also want to know how to parent their college student and need to understand the issues their child is facing such as managing money, avoiding credit card debt, and balancing school, a part-time job, and extra-curricular activities.

UPI can help
UPI will produce three free guides per year for each college that will be distributed during summer orientation and August move-in, Fall Parent's Weekend, and in the Spring to prospective parents through the Admissions Office and Campus Tour Office. At the University of Colorado, over 25,000 prospective parents tour the campus. The magazines will be distributed through the university, hotels, and restaurants. The magazine content will include: restaurant reviews, a lodging directory, a shopping guide, calendar of events, graduation requirement Information, map of the city, and a Q&A section.

Proven track record
The first issue of the *Parent's Guide to Boulder* was published in October 2003 and immediately profited from advertising sales. The second edition will be published June 2004, and due to advance advertising sales, will also be profitable. Demand for these first guides have proved that advertisers are committed to purchasing space in the guide and that parents are interested in reading the guide.

Experienced, enthusiastic management team
Sarah Schupp is the founder, CEO, and Chairman of the UPI Board of Directors. She published the initial *Parent's Guide to Boulder* in 2003. A graduate of the University of Colorado with degrees in Business Administration and English Literature, Sarah is capable of expanding the vision of UPI to Colorado and Texas. In Year 3, UPI plans to hire a CEO with national rollout experience.

Other UPI employees include VP Marketing Michelle Dorenkamp, CFO Kara Grinnell, and CTO Ryan Roth. In addition to an excellent management team,

UPI is in the process of developing a board of twelve directors that bring experience in advertising, magazine writing, start-ups, and venture capital.

Plan for expansion
Because of the initial success of the *Parent's Guide to Boulder*, UPI is currently expanding its marketing base to Colorado State University and the University of Denver. A regional office in Boulder will handle advertising sales for the three guides. UPI plans to broaden its base beginning in Year 2, with a goal of being in 44 schools by Year 5.

The offering
UPI is offering 35% of the company for $500,000. This will provide investors with a 60% rate of return, translating to $4.3 million in Year 5 when UPI plans to sell to Hearst Publishing or Conde Nast Publishing. UPI breaks-even in Year 2, generating revenues of $1.8 million. In Year 5, UPI will have revenues of $12 million and a net profit of $4.1 million.

Company Overview

With two successful publications for the University of Colorado and established relationships with over 35 advertisers, UPI is positioned for nation-wide expansion. In October of 2004, UPI plans to produce a total of 9 publications and 3 websites for the University of Colorado, the University of Denver, and Colorado State University. We project UPI will produce 132 publications and high-traffic websites for 44 colleges and universities by Year 5. This will result in net revenues of $12.3 million, net profits of $4.1 million, and a valuation of $70 million. Also in Year 5, UPI plans to market the company to suitable buyers such as Hearst Publishing or Conde Nast Publishing.

Product/Service Description

Introduction

You arrive on campus to drop off your freshman student. This is always one of the hardest times of the year for you. Leaving your child miles from home, millions of questions are running through your head. How do they register for classes? How many credits will they need to graduate? What issues will they face being away from home? As you are signing in for orientation, you receive a magazine that specifically answers these questions. Not only does it answer campus life questions, it also offers restaurant reviews, lodging suggestions, and a detailed map of the city. The magazine directs you to a website where you can talk to other parents who have your same concerns. Suddenly you have a sense of relief. Now you have a source of information at your fingertips.

As a Boulder business, you have always wondered how you can directly advertise to CU parents who visit often and spend thousands of dollars while visiting. One day a packet arrives at your business with the first *Parent's Guide to Boulder* from the 2003 Parent's Weekend and a rate card. You are excited that there is now a reasonably priced and direct way to contact CU parents and inform them of your business. You know that purchasing advertising will be well worth every dollar. (Boulder, Colorado served as UPI's test market.)

Description

University Parent produces a comprehensive local guide as well as a website for parents of college students. Through its compilation of articles, pictures, maps, current events, and advertisements, it provides a convenient, thorough source of information for CU parents.

Parent

Guide Feature	Benefit
Distribution through the university, hotels, and restaurants	Convenience
Provides useful information about their student's environment and community	Comfort, Sense of Security
Makes navigating Boulder easier and allows for advance planning	Saves Time
Free! Gives information and coupons for good values in: lodging, eating, shopping, and having a good time	Saves Money

2890 Shadow Creek – Boulder, Colorado – 303.579.9871 – info@upi.com

University Parent, Inc.

Advertiser

Guide Feature	Benefit
Targets specific niche	Targeted ROI
Mid-ranged priced advertising	Saves Money
Effective distribution channels	Reaches Target Market, Generates Revenue

Market Comparison

Unlike other publications in college towns, UPI offers its readers focused, relevant information that is unavailable through local newspapers and magazines. It also offers advertisers a targeted, identifiable market.

Stage of Development

UPI produced its first guide in Boulder for Parent's Weekend '03. The profitability of the first guide demonstrated UPI's ability to sell advertising and to produce a useful product. UPI is currently marketing and creating articles for its Summer '04 publication. Our CTO, Ryan Roth, launched the Guide to Boulder's website in April of '04, http://www.guidetoboulder.com. Advertising sales for the website are scheduled to begin in May '04.

Client Base

UPI currently has over 35 clients for the *Parent's Guide to Boulder*. These advertisers include: Wells Fargo, Walnut Realty, McGuckin Hardware, the CU Book Store, the CU Foundation, Greenbriar Inn, Boulder Broker Inn, Boulder Outlook Hotel & Suites, Boulder Express Shuttle, and many more. Of the initial advertisers in the Fall '03 guide, 100% of advertisers solicited purchased advertising for the Summer '04 guide.

Potential Readership Base

Demographic

> 32 million U.S. parents of college students, growing at an annual rate of 6%
>
> We expect 20% of each college's parent population to read our magazines

Family Income

> Most families sending children to college have a combined household income ranging from $80,000 to $150,000

Cost of Education

> A college education is likely the biggest investment they will make in their student
>
> A college education costs anywhere from $30,000 to $200,000
>
> Parents typically provide for their children while in college, paying for expenses such as transportation (car, bike), car insurance, textbooks, clothing, computers and software, food, rent, etc.

6

These expenses average between $800–$1,500 per month.

Potential Advertisers

Independent marketing firms that handle national accounts
Local business owners and/or Marketing Managers representing hotels, restaurants, retail stores, travel agencies that must make buying decisions based on distribution and cost.

Industry and Marketplace Analysis

The publication industry has over 17,000 magazines that gross $24 billion in revenue each year. Historically, this industry has grown at a rate of 7 percent, and is expected to grow 6 percent in the future. There is little demand for new titles with the exception of demand for specialty, niche magazines that enable advertisers to reach a well-defined market. Our primary, unexplored niche consists of parents of college students. According to surveys, virtually all CU parents (95%) are uninformed about campus activities, news, and pertinent issues. Currently no other publications are addressing these needs and concerns of CU parents.

In recent years, there has been an increase in online magazines and online versions of print magazines. Major threats in the periodical industry include other advertising mediums such as television, radio, and print. The most competition for publications is in print advertising, which ranges from daily newspapers to monthly magazines. Another threat to the publication industry is the rising cost of paper, which is driving down profits. Some of the internal market changes revolve around a concern over rising paper costs because of deforestation.

Leading advertisers in the magazine industry include: automobile manufacturers, consumer goods companies, entertainment conglomerates, and tobacco firms. Some of the internal market changes revolve around a concern over rising paper costs because of deforestation.

Leading advertisers in the magazine industry include: automobile manufacturers, consumer goods companies, entertainment conglomerates, and tobacco firms. The publication industry is affected by changes in economic conditions since revenue is advertising-dependant.

7

Marketing Strategy

Introduction

UPI's target readership market will include students, parents of present and future students, university faculty and staff, and high school counselors. Aggressive distribution will insure that all sectors of our target market will receive our free guide as well as website information. Our target market for advertising is businesses that want to make parents of college students aware of their products and/or services. We provide these businesses an opportunity to reach a specific, identifiable market at a reasonable cost.

Target Market Advertising Strategy

We will position ourselves as the only publication offering information specifically for parents of CU students and as the only publication offering businesses the opportunity to advertise to these parents.

In Boulder, the primary advertising media are the *Colorado Daily*, *Daily Camera*, *The Onion*, and *Boulder Magazine*. UPI's targeted, niche market strategy offers businesses a superior, more cost-effective media product at a lower cost than these publications. UPI will produce a quarterly mailing to businesses in Boulder that offer a product/service that CU parents may be interested in purchasing. The mailing will be directed to the "businesses' owners" and will include a previous *Parent's Guide to Boulder*, a cover letter specifying why advertising with UPI is effective, testimonials from current advertisers, and a rate card.

As UPI moves into additional markets, this strategy will be replicated and customized as needed.

Pricing Strategy

University Parent will generate revenue from two sources: print advertising in our guides and online advertising on our website.

Print advertising prices (per guide):

Size	Full Color
Eighth Page	$250
Quarter Page	$400
Half Page	$600
Full Page	$800
Back Cover, Inside Cover, Back Inside	$1000

University Parent, Inc.

Website advertising prices (per month):

Size	Full Color
2" x 1"	$400
2" x 2"	$500
Banner, 1"x 7"	$700
Pop Up	$1000
Ad in email newsletter	$500

Businesses can purchase yearlong magazine and website advertising at a 10% discount. The website advertising prices are likely to change based on our website's traffic. The higher the traffic, the higher the price we can charge.

Distribution Strategy

UPI will distribute guides to parents through the university admissions office, parent relations office, and campus tour office. The guide will also be distributed in hotels, restaurants, businesses, and through the Chamber of Commerce. There will be an option on the website to download the guide or have it mailed for a small fee (postage).

Advertising, Sales & Promotion Strategy

UPI will be promoted to advertisers through local networking at Boulder Chamber of Commerce events, press releases in local papers, direct mailings, and referral incentives for current clients. In addition, the website will serve as an effective tool to inform both businesses and parents of our services.

Marketing & Sales Forecasts

UPI's revenue is generated through print and website advertising sales. We project revenues from print advertising at 54% and website advertising sales at 46% of total revenues.

Advertising revenues are calculated by using the print advertising rates multiplied by expected sales for three guides. UPI projects sales of 25 print advertisements per issue at an average cost of $1,000 and 72 website sales per year per institution at an average cost of $750.

Revenue (In thousands $)

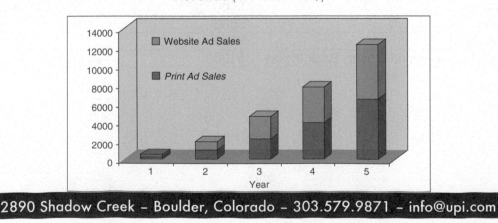

University Parent, Inc.

Revenue Projections

	Year 1	Year 2	Year 3	Year 4	Year 5
Product A—Magazine					
Number of Schools	3	9	22	32	44
Total Issues/Year	9	36	66	96	132
Magazines Printed/Year	90,000	360,000	660,000	960,000	1,320,000
Printing Cost/Per Magazine	0.25	0.23	0.21	0.19	0.17
Number of Units/Ad	225	900	1,800	2,925	4,425
Avg. Price/Ad Page	$1,000	$1,100	$1,210	$1,331	$1,464
Print Adv Total	$225,000	$990,000	$2,178,000	$3,893,175	$6,478,643
Product B—Website					
Advertisements Sold/Yr	360	1,080	2,640	3,840	5,280
Price per unit	$750	$825	$908	$998	$1,098
Web Adv Total	$270,000	$891,000	$2,395,800	$3,833,280	$5,797,836
Net Revenue	$495,000	$1,881,000	$4,573,800	$7,726,455	$12,276,479

Operations Plan

Operations Strategy

Our strategy is to establish a reputation with readers and advertisers that UPI consistently delivers well-received, well-designed, informative magazines and websites. We will develop this reputation by providing products that are professionally designed, error-free, and exceed the expectations of both our readers and our advertisers. We will measure our success through in-person as well as online surveys of our customers.

Our goal is to have highly satisfied customers—our parent readers and our advertisers. To that end, UPI will provide training for all employees that stresses the necessity of exceeding the expectations of our customers in ways such as delivering advertising proofs early or following up with a parent's question promptly and thoroughly.

Scope of Operations

At UPI headquarters, there will be 15 full-time employees. In Year 1, this office will handle advertising sales for the CU, DU, and CSU guides, as well as negotiate next year's Texas expansion.

10

Ongoing Operations

UPI headquarters will coordinate with the regional offices to produce a website and three magazines annually for each college. Issues will be published every summer, fall, and spring. The website will be updated as needed, daily if necessary. Advertising sales as well as contact with parents and university faculty and staff will be continuous throughout the year

Operating Expenses

	Year 1	Year 2	Year 3	Year 4	Year 5
Total Operating Expenses	$854,967	$1,547,676	$2,588,328	$3,611,938	$5,083,166
% of Revenue	172.7%	82.3%	56.6%	46.7%	41.4%

11

Development Plan

Development Strategy

The first priority for UPI is to establish a strong brand and reputation within each new market. UPI will publish a guide approximately every four months. Our relationship with advertisers will become much stronger with each issue as they realize the value from advertising in our magazine. After three issues (one year), we believe our relationships with advertisers will significantly increase revenues. In year two, returning clients will purchase more advertisements and clients who watched their competitors gain revenue from advertising with us. For the second issue of the *Parent's Guide to Boulder,* advertising sales doubled and every client who purchased an advertisement in the Fall guide purchased an advertisement in the Summer guide.

During the publication cycle for each issue, the first order of business is to brainstorm new ideas and themes. Once the themes are decided, we make those themes available to the advertisers. We then give advertisers a three-month window to purchase advertising space. Contact is made with potential advertiser through "cold-selling," a variant of cold calling.

The "cold-selling" begins with a mass mailing, which is followed up with an e-mail. One week after the e-mailing, our staff follows up with a telephone call. The next seven weeks in the ad purchasing "window" are reserved for meetings with potential advertisers. Through our past experience, we have found that such meetings are vital for closing most deals.

The artwork acceptance window is open from the moment an advertising contract is signed until the artwork acceptance deadline, one week after the close of advertising sales. The first payment for the advertisement is due on the last day of advertisement sales. The second payment is due one week before we send the magazine to the printer.

While ad sales are in full swing, the design of the magazine is developed. Concurrently, article research and story writing for the magazine are performed. Immediately after the design and story writing are finalized, we finalize the layout and update the website; both of these occur over a two-week period.

As soon as the layout is finished, the final copy is sent to the printer. Within 5 days, the printer overnights a digital proof for UPI's approval. Once approved, printing takes approximately one week. Once the copies are received, the magazine is ready for distribution. Distribution takes place over a two-week period. Most magazines are mailed directly from the printer to the distribution point. These distribution points include: the university, hotels, restaurants, and other local businesses.

12

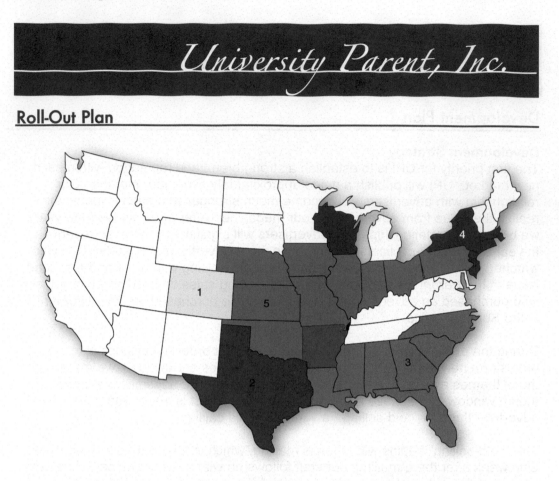

Roll-Out Plan

Year 1: Colorado
3 Schools: CU, University of Denver, and Colorado State University

Year 2: Colorado and Texas
9 Schools: *New Regional Office opens in <u>Dallas</u>: Southern Methodist University, University of Texas at Austin, A&M, Trinity University, Baylor University, Rice University

Year 3: Colorado, Texas, South
22 Schools: *New Regional Office opens in <u>Atlanta</u>: University of Georgia, University of the South, University of North Carolina, University of South Carolina, Duke University, University of Florida, Rollins College, University of Virginia, University of Richmond, University of Louisiana, Louisiana State University

13

University Parent, Inc.

Year 4: Colorado, Texas, South, Northeast
32 Schools: *New Regional Office opens in **Boston**: Harvard, MIT, Tufts, Boston University, Boston College, Princeton, New York University, Columbia University, Barnard College, Villanova University, University of Connecticut

Year 5: Colorado, Texas, South, Northeast, Midwest
44 Schools: *New Regional Office opens in **Kansas City**: University of Kansas, Kansas State University, University of Oklahoma, Oklahoma State University, University of Missouri, Missouri State University, University of Ohio, Ohio State University, Purdue University, University of Michigan, University of Wisconsin, University of Illinois

Year 6: *Continued Expansion*: Northeast, Midwest, West

2890 Shadow Creek – Boulder, Colorado – 303.579.9871 – info@upi.com

University Parent, Inc.

Management

Sarah Schupp, Chief Executive Officer

Sarah founded *The Parent's Guide to Boulder* in June of 2003. A graduate of the University of Colorado with degrees in Business Administration and English Literature, Sarah is capable of expanding the vision of UPI across the U.S. In addition, she has developed relationships with the University of Colorado through her 2004 position as the Senior Class President and member of the President's Leadership Class.

Ryan Roth, Chief Technology Officer

Ryan comes to UPI with an extensive background in high-level web technology and information system deployment strategies. As team leader of numerous successful system development projects, Ryan is a valuable addition to UPI as Chief Technology Officer. He joined our team in early 2004 to provide in-depth, focused research on technology issues and solutions to provide University Parent with customized solutions unmatched by any other magazine publisher today. Ryan graduated from the Leeds School of Business at the University of Colorado with a B.S. in Business Administration and an emphasis in Information Systems.

Kara Grinnell, Chief Financial Officer

Kara is equipped with the financial knowledge needed to accomplish all the tasks included in the job of Chief Financial Officer. With a degree in Finance from the University of Colorado, Kara has the appropriate background to help UPI meet its financial goals. Kara has firsthand field experience with financial measurements and is prepared to help UPI become a $100 million venture.

Michelle Dorenkamp, VP Marketing

Michelle will graduate with a Bachelor of Science Degree in Business from the University of Colorado in May 2004. For the past three summers, she has worked in marketing and advertising for a real estate company. She has successfully worked with companies doing a direct mail campaign similar to the one that will be used to attract advertisers for the local guides.

2890 Shadow Creek – Boulder, Colorado – 303.579.9871 – info@upi.com

University Parent, Inc.

Business Risks

Another company will copy our idea.
Because of a magazine's low start-up costs, it is likely that people will copy our concept. However, we can mitigate this risk by negotiating with national advertisers for annual contracts and with universities for distribution rights. Another way we can mitigate this risk is through strategic growth. By identifying the best regions for expansion, we will capture a new region each year. We are targeting geographically central locations with a high concentration of colleges and universities.

Universities will not cooperate to help us distribute the guide.
When selling advertisements to businesses, our greatest strength is that universities allow us to distribute the guide on campus. This distribution point makes advertisers believe their ROI will be greater because parents pay close attention to materials given to them by the university. However, our guide is an effective public relations tool for universities to give to parents and by maintaining appropriate content, we eliminate this obstacle.

Businesses will not buy advertising.
Our revenue projections are based on selling 25 or more print advertisements per issue and 10 Web ads per month per location. If businesses do not believe that our magazine will serve as an effective marketing tool, they will not purchase advertising. We must prove to advertisers that parents do and will read our magazine and will make buying decisions based on our information.

Each university has a different environment with different demographics.
Because we are producing guides with location-specific information, we must insure that the information we publish is accurate and appropriate for the area. If we miss the target demographic or culture of the area, parents will not read the guide and advertisers will not purchase advertising. To make sure we understand the area, representatives from our regional office will be familiar with every location in their region and will have student interns at each school that will help UPI understand the area and its parent population. In addition, we will use our website to collect marketing data. Weblogs, an online parent chat room, will allow us to track parents' comments and their geographic location, which will enable us to understand the issues at each university.

2890 Shadow Creek – Boulder, Colorado – 303.579.9871 – info@upi.com

Financial Plan

Financial Summary

Revenue for UPI is derived from magazine and website advertising sales. UPI plans to sell advertising to both national and local advertisers. As more people read our magazine and visit our website, the prices we can charge advertisers will increase.

The following table summarizes five years of pro forma financial statements. Assumptions for the financial statements are located in Section G of the Appendix.

	Year 1	Year 2	Year 3	Year 4	Year 5
Operating Revenue	$495,000	$1,881,000	$4,573,800	$7,726,455	$12,276,479
Operating Expenses					
Salaries, Wages, & Benefits	$323,000	$692,230	$1,152,524	$1,526,238	$1,907,539
Depreciation	$6,667	$20,000	$40,000	$60,000	$80,000
Rent & Utilities	$40,000	$85,600	$131,592	$180,803	$233,460
Total Operating Expenses	**$854,967**	**$1,547,676**	**$2,588,328**	**$3,611,938**	**$5,083,166**
Income Taxes	$0	$0	−$550,989	−$1,542,198	−$2,749,048
Net Income (Loss)	**($401,329)**	**$197,583**	**$1,227,012**	**$2,313,297**	**$4,123,572**

2890 Shadow Creek – Boulder, Colorado – 303.579.9871 – info@upi.com

Balance Sheet
Years 0–5 ($)

	Begin	Year 1	Year 2	Year 3	Year 4	Year 5
ASSETS						
CURRENT ASSETS						
Cash	530,000	117,763	281,640	1,616,578	4,006,443	8,252,410
Accounts Receivable		0	0	0	0	0
Inventories		0	0	0	0	0
Other Current Assets		113	3,947	50,228	63,484	75,729
Total Current Assets	530,000	117,875	285,588	1,666,806	4,069,927	8,328,139
PROPERTY & EQUIPMENT	0	16,533	50,133	81,733	109,333	136,133
TOTAL ASSETS	530,000	134,409	335,721	1,748,539	4,179,261	8,464,272
LIABILITIES & SHAREHOLDERS' EQUITY						
CURRENT LIABILITIES						
Short-Term Debt	0	0	0	0	0	0
Accounts Payable & Accrued Expen		5,625	9,281	191,445	306,567	464,840
Other Current Liabilities		113	186	3,829	6,131	9,297
Current Portion of Long-term Debt	0	0	0	0	0	0
Total Current Liabilities	0	5,738	9,467	195,274	312,698	474,137
LONG-TERM DEBT (less current portion)	0	0	0	0	0	0
STOCKHOLDERS' EQUITY						
Common Stock	30,000	30,000	30,000	30,000	30,000	30,000
Preferred Stock	500,000	500,000	500,000	500,000	500,000	500,000
Retained Earnings		(401,329)	(203,746)	1,023,266	3,336,563	7,460,135
Total Equity	530,000	128,671	326,254	1,553,266	3,866,563	7,990,135
TOTAL LIABILITIES & EQUITY	530,000	134,409	335,721	1,748,539	4,179,261	8,464,272

18

University Parent, Inc.

Offering

Investment Requirements
UPI initially requires $500,000 in seed funding for the first year of operations. This amount will fund the expansion to the University of Denver and Colorado State University as well as funding new employee salaries and the opening of a Colorado regional office in Boulder. Investors will own 35% of the venture.

Valuation
Using the venture capital method, in Year 5, assuming net earnings of $4.1 million, and an industry P/E ratio of 17.3, UPI will have a market value of $70 million.

Financing
UPI seeks $500,000 in seed funding in Year 0. This round will provide the investor with a 35% stake in the venture at a 60% annual rate of return.

Exit Strategy
In Year 5, UPI we be marketed to Hearst Publishing and Condé Nast Publishing. These are logical acquirers because both companies own over 30 niche magazines.

2890 Shadow Creek – Boulder, Colorado – 303.579.9871 – info@upi.com

Appendices

2890 Shadow Creek – Boulder, Colorado – 303.579.9871 – info@upi.com

University Parent, Inc.

Appendix A, Income Statement, Years 1–5 ($)

	Year 1	Year 2	Year 3	Year 4	Year 5
NET REVENUES	495,000	1,881,000	4,573,800	7,726,455	12,276,479
COST OF REVENUE	26,362	90,741	152,471	204,023	255,692
% of Revenues	5.3%	4.8%	3.3%	2.6%	2.1%
GROSS PROFIT	468,638	1,790,259	4,421,329	7,522,432	12,020,787
% of Revenues	94.7%	95.2%	96.7%	97.4%	97.9%
OPERATING EXPENSES					
Sales & Marketing	240,750	364,610	674,953	1,023,764	1,734,098
Research & Development	219,800	291,186	360,569	434,809	514,245
General and Administration	394,417	891,880	1,552,806	2,153,364	2,834,823
Total Operating Expenses	854,967	1,547,676	2,588,328	3,611,938	5,083,166
% of Revenues	173%	82%	57%	47%	41%
EARNINGS FROM OPERATIONS	(386,329)	242,583	1,833,001	3,910,495	6,937,620
EXTRAORDINARY INCOME / (EXPENSE)	(15,000)	(45,000)	(55,000)	(55,000)	(65,000)
EARNINGS BEFORE INTEREST & TAXES	(401,329)	197,583	1,778,001	3,855,495	6,872,620
INTEREST INCOME / (EXPENSE)	0	0	0	0	0
NET EARNINGS BEFORE TAXES	(401,329)	197,583	1,778,001	3,855,495	6,872,620
TAXES	0	0	(550,989)	(1,542,198)	(2,749,048)
NET EARNINGS	(401,329)	197,583	1,227,012	2,313,297	4,123,572
% of Revenues	−81.1%	10.5%	26.8%	29.9%	33.6%

21

Appendix B, Balance Sheet, Years 0–5 ($)

	Begin	Year 1	Year 2	Year 3	Year 4	Year 5
ASSETS						
CURRENT ASSETS						
Cash	530,000	117,763	281,640	1,616,578	4,006,443	8,252,410
Accounts Receivable		0	0	0	0	0
Inventories		0	0	0	0	0
Other Current Assets		113	3,947	50,228	63,484	75,729
Total Current Assets	530,000	117,875	285,588	1,666,806	4,069,927	8,328,139
PROPERTY & EQUIPMENT	0	16,533	50,133	81,733	109,333	136,133
TOTAL ASSETS	530,000	134,409	335,721	1,748,539	4,179,261	8,464,272
LIABILITIES & SHAREHOLDERS' EQUITY						
CURRENT LIABILITIES						
Short-Term Debt	0	0	0	0	0	0
Accounts Payable & Accrued Expen		5,625	9,281	191,445	306,567	464,840
Other Current Liabilities		113	186	3,829	6,131	9,297
Current Portion of Long-Term Debt	0	0	0	0	0	0
Total Current Liabilities	0	5,738	9,467	195,274	312,698	474,137
LONG-TERM DEBT (less current portion)	0	0	0	0	0	0
STOCKHOLDERS' EQUITY						
Common Stock	30,000	30,000	30,000	30,000	30,000	30,000
Preferred Stock	500,000	500,000	500,000	500,000	500,000	500,000
Retained Earnings		(401,329)	(203,746)	1,023,266	3,336,563	7,460,135
Total Equity	530,000	128,671	326,254	1,553,266	3,866,563	7,990,135
TOTAL LIABILITIES & EQUITY	530,000	134,409	335,721	1,748,539	4,179,261	8,464,272

2890 Shadow Creek – Boulder, Colorado – 303.579.9871 – info@upi.com

Appendix C, Cash Flow Statement, Years 1–5 ($)

	Year 1	Year 2	Year 3	Year 4	Year 5
OPERATING ACTIVITIES					
Net Earnings	(401,329)	197,583	1,227,012	2,313,297	4,123,572
Depreciation	7,467	24,400	48,400	72,400	97,200
Working Capital Changes					
(Inc.)/Dec. Accts. Rec.	0	0	0	0	0
(Inc.)/Dec. Inventories	0	0	0	0	0
(Inc.)/Dec. Other CA	(113)	(3,835)	(46,281)	(13,256)	(12,245)
(Inc.)/Dec. Accts Pay Expenses	5,625	3,656	182,163	115,122	158,274
(Inc.)/Dec. Other CL	113	73	3,643	2,302	3,165
Net Cash Provided/(Used) Operating Activities	(388,237)	221,878	1,414,937	2,489,865	4,369,967
INVESTING ACTIVITIES					
Property & Equipment	(24,000)	(58,000)	(80,000)	(100,000)	(124,000)
Other					
Net Cash Used in Investing	(24,000)	(58,000)	(80,000)	(100,000)	(124,000)
FINANCING ACTIVITIES					
(Inc.)/Dec. Short-Term Debt	0	0	0	0	0
(Inc.)/Dec. Curr. Portion LTD	0	0	0	0	0
(Inc.)/Dec. Long-Term Debt	0	0	0	0	0
(Inc.)/Dec. Common Stock	0	0	0	0	0
(Inc.)/Dec. Preferred Stock	0	0	0	0	0
Dividends Declared	0	0	0	0	0
Net Cash Provided/ (Used) by Financing	0	0	0	0	0
INCREASE/(DECREASE) IN CASH	(412,237)	163,878	1,334,937	2,389,865	4,245,967
CASH AT BEGINNING OF YEAR	530,000	117,763	281,640	1,616,578	4,006,443
CASH AT END OF YEAR 530,000	117,763	281,640	1,616,578	4,006,443	8,252,410

23

Appendix D, Monthly and Quarterly Cash Flow Statements, Years 1–5 ($)

	Year 1	Year 2	Year 3	Year 4	Year 5
OPERATING ACTIVITIES					
Net Earnings	(401,329)	197,583	1,227,012	2,313,297	4,123,572
Depreciation	7,467	24,400	48,400	72,400	97,200
Working Capital Changes					
(Inc.)/Dec. Accts. Rec.	0	0	0	0	0
(Inc.)/Dec. Inventories	0	0	0	0	0
(Inc.)/Dec. Other CA	(113)	(3,835)	(46,281)	(13,256)	(12,245)
(Inc.)/Dec. Accts Pay Expenses	5,625	3,656	182,163	115,122	158,274
(Inc.)/Dec. Other CL	113	73	3,643	2,302	3,165
Net Cash Provided/(Used) Operating Activities	(388,237)	221,878	1,414,937	2,489,865	4,369,967
INVESTING ACTIVITIES					
Property & Equipment	(24,000)	(58,000)	(80,000)	(100,000)	(124,000)
Other					
Net Cash Used in Investing	(24,000)	(58,000)	(80,000)	(100,000)	(124,000)
FINANCING ACTIVITIES					
(Inc.)/Dec. Short-Term Debt	0	0	0	0	0
(Inc.)/Dec. Curr. Portion LTD	0	0	0	0	0
(Inc.)/Dec. Long-Term Debt	0	0	0	0	0
(Inc.)/Dec. Common Stock	0	0	0	0	0
(Inc.)/Dec. Preferred Stock	0	0	0	0	0
Dividends Declared	0	0	0	0	0
Net Cash Provided/(Used) by Financing	0	0	0	0	0
INCREASE/(DECREASE) IN CASH	(412,237)	163,878	1,334,937	2,389,865	4,245,967
CASH AT BEGINNING OF YEAR	530,000	117,763	281,640	1,616,578	4,006,443
CASH AT END OF YEAR 530,000	117,763	281,640	1,616,578	4,006,443	8,252,410

24

2890 Shadow Creek – Boulder, Colorado – 303.579.9871 – info@upi.com

Appendix E, Break-Even Analysis, Years 1–5 ($)

	Year 1	Year 2	Year 3	Year 4	Year 5
Revenue	495,000	1,881,000	4,573,800	7,726,455	12,276,479
Cost of Revenue					
Variable	24,562	85,341	141,671	186,023	228,692
Fixed	1,800	5,400	10,800	18,000	27,000
Total	26,362	90,741	152,471	204,023	255,692
Operating Expenses					
Variable	49,500	188,100	457,380	772,646	1,227,648
Fixed	805,467	1,359,576	2,130,948	2,839,292	3,855,519
Total	854,967	1,547,676	2,588,328	3,611,938	5,083,166
Total Costs & Expenses					
Variable	74,062	273,441	599,051	958,668	1,456,340
Fixed	807,267	1,364,976	2,141,748	2,857,292	3,882,519
Total	881,329	1,638,417	2,740,799	3,815,960	5,338,858
Variable Costs/Revenue Ratio	0.15	0.15	0.13	0.12	0.12
Break-Even Point Revenues	949,301	1,597,154	2,464,540	3,262,032	4,405,087

Appendix F, Capital Expenditure Detail

	Year 1	Year 2	Year 3	Year 4	Year 5
Net Revenues	495,000	1,881,000	4,573,800	7,726,455	12,276,479
Capital Expenditures					
Computers, Software, & Office Equipment	20,000	40,000	60,000	80,000	100,000
Plant & Equipment	0	0	0	0	0
Other	4,000	18,000	20,000	20,000	24,000
Total Capital Expenditures	24,000	58,000	80,000	100,000	124,000

2890 Shadow Creek – Boulder, Colorado – 303.579.9871 – info@upi.com

Appendix G, Financial Assumptions

General Assumptions

First Month of Operations	June 2004
Estimated Inflation	2.5%
Corporate Tax Rate	38%

Annual Projections

	Year 1	Year 2	Year 3	Year 4	Year 5
Product A—Magazine					
Number of Schools	3	9	22	32	44
Total Issues/Year	9	36	66	96	132
Number of Units/Ad	225	900	1,800	2,925	4,425
Avg. Price/Ad Page	$1,000	$1,100	$1,210	$1,331	$1,464
Print Advertising Sales	$225,000	$990,000	$2,178,000	$3,893,175	$6,478,643
Product B—Website					
Advertisements Sold/Year	360	1,080	2,640	3,840	5,280
Price per Unit	$750	$825	$908	$998	$1,098
Web Advertising Sales	$270,000	$891,000	$2,395,800	$3,833,280	$5,797,836

Printing Costs

	Year 1	Year 2	Year 3	Year 4	Year 5
Magazines Printed/Year	90,000	360,000	660,000	960,000	1,320,000
Printing Cost/Magazine	0.25	0.23	0.21	0.19	0.17
Total Costs	22,500	82,800	138,600	182,400	224,400

Funding

Total Shares Outstanding	2,000,000
Preferred Shares (Investors)	700,000 (35%)
Common Shares (Founders/Employees)	130,000 (65%)
Expected Investor IRR	60%
Total Funding Required	$500,000
Founders' Contribution	$30,000

2890 Shadow Creek – Boulder, Colorado – 303.579.9871 – info@upi.com

Appendix H, Development Timeline, Year 1

Market Development Timeline: University Parent, Inc.																							
Activities / **Months**	1	2	3	4	5	6	7	8	9	10	11	12	13	14	15	16	17	18	19	20	21	22	23	24
Enter New Market																								
Hire Employees																								
Develop Partnerships																								
Magazine #1																								
Initial Selling																								
Customers Return																								
Magazine #2																								
Initial Selling																								
Customers Return																								
Magazine #3																								
Initial Selling																								
Customers Return																								

Performed by Staff
Min Return Customers
Med Return Customers
Max Return Customers

Development Timeline: University Parent Inc.																															
Activity / **Weeks**	1	2	3	4	5	6	7	8	9	10	11	12	13	14	15	16	17	18	19	20	21	22	23	24	25	26	27	28	29	30	31	32
Brain Storm Ideas																																
Advertisements on Sale																																
Mass Mailing																																
Follow Up Email																																
Follow Up Call																																
Meetings																																
Ad Artwork Accepted(Y) Due(R)																																
1st 1/2 Payment due																																
2nd 1/2 Payment due																																
Design Layout																																
Story Writing																																
Layout																																
Web Updates																																
Printing																																
Distribution																																

Performed by Staff
Waiting Period
Outsource
Deadline

University Parent, Inc.

Appendix I, Customer Survey Results

40 Parents were interviewed about the UPI concept.

- Parents currently purchase:
  - ✓ Newsweek, Time, Weekly Standard, Economist, Forbes, Money, Sports Illustrated, AAE Journal, Martha Stewart Living, Real Simple, Family Circle, People, Young Riders, Redbook, Budget Traveler, Business Week, Kiplingers, Smithsonian, Business World, Outside, New Yorker, More, Good Housekeeping, In Style, Cosmopolitan, Allure, Fast Company, Inc, Prevention, Readers Digest, Sunset, Tennis, Golf, Consumer Reports, Veranda, Scientific American

- Currently purchase magazines:
  - ✓ Subscription, Airport, Grocery Store

- 90% percent of parents surveyed would purchase the magazine

- Parents want information about:
  - ✓ Grades, Scholarships, Travel Opportunities, Housing Expenses, Activities in College Town, Time Management, Social Life, Programs, Internships, Job Placements, Curriculum, Student Safety, Speakers, Career Guidance, Graduation Requirements, Student Groups, Transportation

- Currently receive information:
  - ✓ From the student, from the college, media

- Would like to purchase UP:
  - ✓ Subscription

- Would be willing to pay:
  - ✓ $1–$5

- 60% of parents would like a website

- 70% of parents would like to receive a monthly newsletter

2890 Shadow Creek – Boulder, Colorado – 303.579.9871 – info@upi.com

Appendix 3

BizBuilder Business Plan

Congratulations! If you've made it this far, you have given yourself a comprehensive, basic education in entrepreneurship and you will have made progress toward writing a business plan that will work for your operations and impress potential investors and lenders.

At this point, you will probably want to expand and enhance your business plan to reflect all that you have learned. Worksheets to complete for the following questions are in the MyBizSkills Kit for this text. Use them to create a more professional-looking business plan. Follow the guidelines in Chapter 2 to ensure the quality of the business plan. These features will make your plan a better road map for running your organization and will make it more attractive to investors.

The MyBizSkills Kit also includes a PowerPoint template you can use to create a Business Plan Presentation. With a PowerPoint Business Plan Presentation, you can quickly show potential employees, partners, and investors the highlights of your plan.

The BizBuilder Business Plan includes an additional section for students wishing to start a not-for-profit organization. If you are starting a nonprofit, please fill out this section and adjust your business plan accordingly.

Business Plan Pro software in the MyBizSkills Kit gives you another option for preparing your plan. Explore Business Plan Pro to see if it's a better fit for your business plan. Both the BizBuilder components and Business Plan Pro can help you write a professional business plan.

BizBuilder Business Plan Worksheet Questions/Notes

Cover Page

A. What is the full name of your organization?
B. Provide contact information for the organization including the names of majority owners.
C. What confidentiality/nondisclosure language will you include?
D. Provide the date of the plan.

Table of Contents (Can Be Placed Before or After the Executive Summary)

A. List the key sections of the plan and the page numbers.

1.0 Executive Summary

A. What is the name of your organization?
B. Describe your business idea and the nature of the target market.
C. What type of organization are you starting?

D. What products and/or services will you offer?

E. What is your marketing and sales strategy? Explain how your business idea will satisfy a customer need.

F. Describe the key success factors for the organization.

G. Calculate the "economics of one unit" for your organization.

H. What are your short-term business goals (less than one year)?

I. What are your long-term business goals (from one to five years)?

J. What resources and skills do you (and the other owners and managers) have that will help make your organization successful? What other skills are needed and how will they be obtained?

K. If there is more than one owner, describe how the ownership will be shared.

L. What are the sources and uses of funds?

M. Include a summary of the financial projections.

N. What is the growth and exit strategy?

2.0 Mission, Vision, and Culture

A. Write a mission statement for your organization in 21 words or fewer that clearly states your competitive advantage, strategy, and tactics.

B. Create a vision statement for your organization.

C. Describe the core beliefs you will use to run your organization and how they will be reflected in its culture.

D. Identify the ways you plan to run a socially responsible organization.

3.0 Company Description

A. What industry are you in?

B. What type of organization is it (manufacturing, wholesale, service)?

C. What needs will this business satisfy?

D. What is your strategic advantage?

E. What is your organization's legal structure (sole proprietorship, partnership, LLC, C corporation, etc.)?

F. Why did you choose this legal structure?

G. In what state are you registered or do you intend to register?

H. Where will you physically operate the organization?

I. What is the geographic reach of the organization?

J. Who will be the owner(s), partners, or stockholders for your company?

K. If your business is incorporated, describe what percentage of the company is owned by each shareholder.

4.0 Opportunity Analysis and Research

A. Describe your research methods (surveys, focus groups, general research, and statistical research).

B. Describe your target customer along as many dimensions as you have defined (demographic, geographic, needs, trends, and decision-making process).

4.1 Industry Analysis

A. What is the industry or set of industries in which your organization operates (include the NAICS codes)?
B. What factors influence the demand for your product or service?
C. What factors influence the supply for your product or service?
D. How large is your industry (historic, current, projected size)?
E. What are the current and anticipated characteristics and trends in the industry?
F. What are the major customer groups for the industry (consumers, governments, businesses)?
G. How large is your target market (number of customers, size of purchases, frequency of purchases, trends)?

4.2 Environmental Analysis

A. Perform a SWOT analysis of your organization.
B. What external/environmental factors are likely to impact your business?
C. Are there customers for your business in other countries? How do you plan to reach them?

4.3 Competitive Analysis

A. How do you define/describe your competition, both direct and indirect?
B. Describe your competitive advantage.
C. Find three competitors and describe them.
D. Describe any international competitors you have found who may be able to access your customers. How do you intend to compete?
E. Describe your strategy for outperforming the competition.
F. What tactics will you use to carry out this strategy?
G. What barriers to entry can you create to block out competitors?

5.0 Marketing Strategy and Plan

A. Explain how your marketing plan targets your market segment.
B. What percentage of the market do you feel you need to capture for your business to be profitable?
C. Write a positioning statement for your business.
D. How do you plan to grow the organization (self-generated, franchising, acquisition)?

5.1 Products/Services

A. What products/services do you intend to sell?
B. Explain how your product will meet a customer need.
C. Where is your product/service in the product life cycle?
D. Describe the features and benefits of the product/service your business will focus on selling.
E. What existing copyrights or patents do you own or expect to own?

F. How will your organization help others? List all the organizations to which you plan to contribute. (Your contribution may be time, money, your product, or something else.)

G. Do you intend to publicize your philanthropy? Why, or why not? If you do, explain how you will work your philanthropy into your marketing.

5.2 Pricing

A. Describe your pricing strategy and structure, and the gross margins you expect to generate.

B. What will your discount structure, if any, be?

C. Will you accept personal checks from customers? Credit cards? Will you offer charge accounts or customer credit?

5.3 Promotion

A. Identify the ways you plan to promote your product or service, including the message, the media, and the distribution channels. Describe why you have chosen these methods and why you think they will work.

B. Show examples of marketing materials you intend to use to sell.

C. What is your business slogan?

D. Do you have a logo for your business? How do you intend to protect it?

E. Where do you intend to advertise (be specific, including identifying reach and frequency)?

F. How do you plan to get publicity for your organization?

G. List ways you intend to provide superior customer service.

H. Write a one-minute sales pitch for your product/service and describe five sales prospects you intend to pitch.

I. How will you keep your customer database? What essential questions will you ask every customer for your database?

5.4 Place

A. Where do you intend to sell your product? Describe the advantages and disadvantages of your location(s).

B. What are the surrounding businesses? Access routes?

C. If vehicular traffic is important to your organization, what is the traffic count for this location?

D. What is the workforce availability in the area as it pertains to your needs?

6.0 Management and Operations

6.1 Management Team

A. Create an organizational chart for your business.

B. Will you be hiring employees? If so, describe what their qualifications should be, what you intend to pay them, and how they will help your business.

C. How do you plan to compensate yourself: a salary, wage, dividend, or commission? Explain.

D. What will your policies toward employees be? How will you make your organization a positive and rewarding place to work?

E. Describe the corporate governance plan for your organization. It should include five policies (rules) that will be the backbone of your organization's ethics.

F. Provide information for each of your mentors or advisors. If there is a board of advisors, list each member and describe his/her commitment to the board.

G. Provide contact information for your accountant, attorney, banker, and insurance agent.

6.2 Research and Development

A. What type of research are you doing? What do you intend to do?

B. What are others in the industry doing?

C. How will you protect your intellectual property?

6.3 Physical Location

A. Describe the actual physical place in greater detail than above.

B. What are the zoning laws in your area? Does your business comply?

6.4 Facilities

A. What type of building and equipment will you have?

B. Identify which technological tools you plan to use for your organization, and explain why.

C. How do you plan to get access to the technology you need?

6.5 Inventory, Production, and Quality Assurance

A. Where are you purchasing the products you plan to sell, or the parts you will use to manufacture those products? Illustrate your supply chain.

B. Do you intend to manufacture your product? If so, describe the manufacturing processes you will use. If not, describe how your product is manufactured.

C. Are there any economies of scale to be attained for your business? At what point do you anticipate attaining them?

D. Have you developed and/or adopted any innovations in production, inventory management, or distribution that are significant? What are they and why are they meaningful?

E. How do you plan to distribute your product to your target market?

F. Show the production-distribution channel for your business, and the markups along the chain.

G. What is the estimated delivery time between when you place an order with your supplier and when you will have the product available for your customers?

H. What method(s) will you use to define and ensure the quality of your products/services?

I. What types of insurance will your business need, and why?

J. What methods will you use to ensure that you comply with federal, state, and local tax laws?

K. What laws—such as minimum wage and age requirements, health and safety regulations, or antidiscrimination laws—will affect your business?

7.0 Financial Analysis and Projections

A. Describe your recordkeeping system.

B. List the types of bank accounts you will open for your organization.

7.1 Sources and Uses of Capital

A. How much capital do you need? When? What type and on what terms?

B. How will you use the money that you raise? Be specific.

C. List the items you will need to buy to start your business and add up the items to get your total start-up capital. Then, add a cash reserve of one-half your total start-up capital.

D. List the sources of financing for your start-up capital. Identify each source as equity, debt, or gift. Indicate the amount and type for each source.

E. What is your payback period? In other words, how long will it take you to earn enough profit to cover start-up capital?

F. Describe financing sources that might be willing to invest in your business in exchange for equity.

G. Describe any debt financing you intend to pursue. What is your debt ratio? What is your debt-to-equity ratio? Add a cash reserve of one-half your total start-up capital.

H. Do you plan to use bootstrap financing? Explain.

I. Do you plan to pursue venture capital? Why, or why not? List potential sources of venture capital.

7.2 Cash Flow Projections

A. List and describe your monthly fixed costs and add a cash reserve that covers three months of fixed costs.

B. Create a projected cash flow statement for your business for the first four quarters and the second and third years of operation.

C. Calculate the burn rate for your business.

7.3 Balance Sheet Projections

A. Create a projected balance sheet for your business for the first four quarters and the second and third years of operation.

B. Create a pie chart showing your current assets, long-term assets, current liabilities, and long-term liabilities.

7.4 Income Statement Projections

A. Create a projected income statement for your business for the first four quarters and the second and third years of operation.

B. Create a bar chart showing your gross revenues, gross profit, and net income.

7.5 Breakeven Analysis

A. Use Excel or another spreadsheet program to create a spreadsheet projecting the expenses for your business. Use this data to perform a breakeven analysis.

7.6 Ratio Analysis

A. Use your projected financial statements to calculate all of your key ratios.
B. Compare these ratios to your industry using publicly available data.

7.7 Risks and Assumptions

A. List the risks and assumptions that underlie your financial projections.
B. Identify any external factors that you feel should be disclosed as substantial risks.

8.0 Funding Request and Exit Strategy

8.1 Amount and Type of Funds Requested

A. Clearly state how much money you are requesting in this plan and the terms under which you anticipate obtaining the funds.
B. Do you intend to use debt to finance your business? Explain.
C. Do you plan to issue bonds to finance your business at some point in the future?

8.2 Exit Plan

A. How will investors get paid back/out? Public offering? Employee buy-out? Merger or acquisition? Liquidation? Stock buyback?
B. When will this happen?
C. Do you plan to franchise your business, or license any of your products? Explain.

8.3 Milestones

A. Create a **PERT** chart for your organization to make your plans clear to potential investors.

Appendices

Resumes and Position Descriptions

A. Include a resume for each key team member.
B. Add position descriptions for any vital start-up positions that are not yet filled.

Sample Promotional Materials

A. Include any sample logos, letterhead, advertisements, brochures, or other items that can be inserted into the plan.
B. Add photos of any promotional items, signage, or larger materials to provide examples.

Product Illustrations/Diagrams

A. If you have nonproprietary drawings or properly authorized proprietary drawings, illustrations, or diagrams of your product or service concept, insert them here.
B. Any floor plans, assembly layouts, or the like should be included.

Detailed Financial Projections

A. Monthly financials and other financial projections that are in too great of detail for inclusion in the main document go here.

B. Include detailed assumptions and notes underlying the projections.

C. Significant contracts.

If You Are Starting a Not-for-Profit Organization, Also Consider

1. What is the name of your nonprofit?

2. What problem(s) are you trying to reduce or eliminate?

3. Describe the mission of your organization.

4. Describe the programs and services you plan to create.

5. How will your organization achieve the changes you intend to bring about?

6. What is the unit of change (per person, animal, house, etc.)?

7. How will you measure these changes?

8. Who are your competitors?

9. How much will it cost you to deliver a unit of service?

10. What are your sources of funding?

Index